Reading Publics

Reading Publics

New York City's Public Libraries, 1754–1911

Tom Glynn

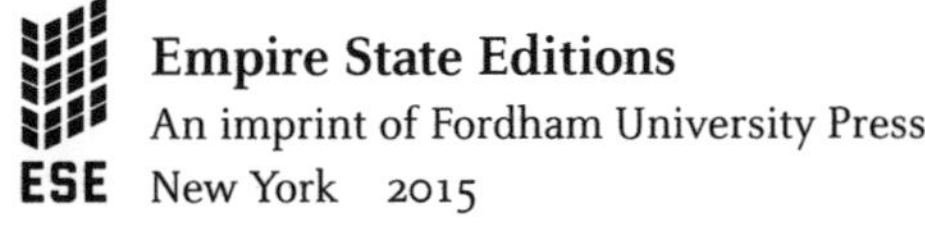

Empire State Editions
An imprint of Fordham University Press
New York 2015

Fordham University Press also publishes its books in a variety of electronic formats. Some content that appears in print may not be available in electronic books.

Visit us online at www.fordhampress.com.

Library of Congress Cataloging-in-Publication Data is available from the publisher.

Printed in the United States of America
17 16 15 5 4 3 2 1
First edition

To my grandmothers, Peggy Chapin and Vicki Glynn

Contents

Acknowledgments

A number of people have generously offered valuable advice and criticism over the years. I am especially grateful to Alisa Harrison, Ellen Gilbert, Andrew Urban, Paul Clemens, Peter Wosh, Thomas Frusciano, Benjamin Justice, Peter Mickulas, Susan Schepfer, Virginia Yans, Christine Pawley, Wayne Wiegand, and, above all, Ruth Crocker and Anthony Carey. I also wish to express my appreciation to my friends and colleagues at Alexander Library, Rutgers University Libraries, for "closing ranks" during my sabbatical and a number of short research leaves. Thanks also to the staff in our Interlibrary Loan Department, especially Rebecca Luo and Glenn Sandberg. They never let me down. Finally, and appropriately for a book on the history of libraries, I thank all of the librarians and archivists who helped with my research, including, but not limited to Robert Sink and James Moske at the New York Public Library; Maurita Baldock at the New-York Historical Society; Mary Collins at the Mercantile Library Association; Janet Greene and Angelo Vigorito at the General Society of Mechanics and Tradesmen; Mark Bartlett, Erin Schreiner, and Edmee Reit at the New York Society Library; Maria Deptula and Mary Cordato at the American Bible Society; Carol Salomon at the Cooper Union; Sydney Van Nort at City College of New York; Karen Murphy at New York University; Jennifer Ulrich and Jocelyn Wilk at Columbia University; Bruce Abrams at the New York County Clerk's Office, Division of Old Records; Thomas Knoles at the American Antiquarian Society; and Ryan Bean at the University of Minnesota. I sincerely appreciate their invaluable assistance. Without the help and guidance of these dedicated professionals, this book would never have come to fruition.

Early versions of Chapters 1 and 2 appeared as articles in *Libraries & Culture* in fall 2005 and fall 1999, respectively, and are used here with the permission of the University of Texas Press.

Publication of this book was made possible in part by a grant from the Rutgers University Research Council.

Introduction

Readers, Libraries, and New York City Before 1911

On May 23, 1911, with nearly six hundred dignitaries crowded into the ornate entrance hall, and as less privileged citizens thronged the steps and streets outside, the New York Public Library officially opened its grand new Central Building on Fifth Avenue and Forty-Second Street.[1] The event, in the words of the guest of honor, President William Howard Taft, inaugurated "a work of National importance."[2] Accounts in the national press echoed his sentiments. The *Independent*, an influential journal of politics and opinion, described the opulent structure as "a symbol of the modern idea of what an American library should be," and *Harper's* predicted "a new era of American life, an ultimate and Olympian generation directly shaped by" the books collected there. The *Dial*, a literary periodical published in Chicago, noted enthusiastically that it was "the greatest library event in library history," while the correspondent for a children's magazine, *St. Nicholas*, reported that the building was "as satisfactory as it is beautiful."[3] During the week that followed, the harried staff devoted much of their time to crowd control, as a steady stream of approximately 250,000 members of the reading public inspected the "marble palace for booklovers."[4]

The opening of the marble palace on Forty-Second Street was the culmination of more than a century and a half of public library development on the island of Manhattan.[5] The New York Public Library Astor, Lenox and Tilden Foundations was created in 1895, when the libraries bequeathed to the city by John Jacob Astor and James Lenox merged with a public trust established by Samuel J. Tilden. Before that time New Yorkers had access to a range of collections for shared reading—in some cases for free, more often for an annual subscription or a membership fee. This book is a history of those early public libraries. Some of them, such as the Astor, were major local institutions. Others—the Biblical Library of the American Bible Society, for example—were highly specialized and consulted mostly by scholars. All of them, however, were public libraries as the term was defined when the first such collections were founded in the eighteenth century; they were accessible, at least ostensibly, to the general public, and they were established for the public good. The chapters that follow explore the various ends, both public and private, that these institutions served in the city of New York before the creation of the New York Public Library. While most other histories focus solely on the "modern" public library around or after the founding of the American Library Association in 1876, this book begins in the eighteenth century and traces changes in the public's understanding of the term over time.[6] These shifts in meaning are an important part of the history of public libraries and public institutions and of readers and reading in the United States.

In 1796, when the state legislature passed the new nation's first law governing the establishment of public libraries, New York City was a fairly small seaport town. Most of its thirty-three thousand inhabitants lived and worked near the waterfront at the tip of Manhattan. The land north of what is now Canal Street was still mostly undeveloped.[7] Compared to later decades, New York's population was relatively homogeneous, primarily of English and Dutch descent. Social, political, and economic leadership remained in the hands of a few patrician families from the colonial period, often related by marriage. Although New York was the most populous city in the new republic, it was not much larger than its nearest rival, Philadelphia. Moreover, Philadelphia and, to a lesser extent, Boston were the nation's cultural centers.[8] Manhattan was considered too preoccupied with commerce to appreciate culture. When John Sharpe, a local Anglican minister, tried and failed to found a public library earlier in the century, he complained that "the Genius of the people [is] so inclined to merchandise that . . . letters must be in a manner forced upon them not only without their seeking, but against their consent."[9]

The 1796 "Act to incorporate such individuals as may associate for the purpose of . . . erecting public libraries" simply permitted private citizens to form associations—"societies"—to purchase and share collections of books. They were considered public because they promoted the public good, because "it is of the utmost importance to the public that sources of information should be multiplied and institutions for that purpose encouraged."[10] As late as 1850, when the Smithsonian Institution conducted a national survey of public libraries, its librarian Charles Coffin Jewett included all "libraries which are accessible—either without restriction or upon conditions with which all can easily comply—to every person who wishes to use them" and added that "in this sense I believe it may be said that all libraries in this country which are not private property . . . are public libraries."[11] In the eighteenth century and for much of the nineteenth century, the Crown and, later, state legislatures and other bodies commonly empowered associations of private individuals to undertake what today are considered public functions. For example, in 1805 the state legislature incorporated the Public School Society to operate free schools in the city of New York. It was not until 1853 that a local Board of Education assumed control and the schools became public in the modern sense of the term: free to all, tax-supported, and managed by elected or appointed public officials.[12]

A number of important public libraries in the city were part of larger organizations and reflected the particular public purposes for which they were founded. For example, the collection of the American Bible Society aided the propagation of evangelical Protestantism, and the library of the New-York Historical Society provided material for histories of the new nation. More often, the libraries developed wide-ranging collections to encourage good reading and thereby promote the public good. The first public library, the New York Society Library, was established in 1754 and granted a royal charter incorporating "sundry persons conceiving [that] a public library would be useful . . . to our said city."[13] Its earliest surviving catalog, published in 1758, offered an extensive selection of titles in the sciences, theology, law, history, art, music, belles-lettres, and especially the classics. There was only one novel, an English translation of *Don Quixote*.[14] Taken as a whole, the Society Library's collection represented the broad range of knowledge with which a well-informed, enlightened gentleman was expected to be conversant in the colonial period and in the early republic. Such self-improving reading, in turn, improved society. An article from 1792 in the *New-York Magazine or Literary Repository*, "On the Utility of Public Libraries," noted that "the advantages resulting to a community at large in consequence of a general attention to education [are] too apparent . . . to need any comment." It emphasized in particular that "of all forms of civil government the republican depends most on an enlightened state of society, [that] . . . its very existence is intimately connected with the mental improvements of its citizens."[15]

New York's public libraries during the colonial period and the early republic were imbued with the civic values of republicanism. An enlightened, well-informed electorate was essential to republican government, but just as important was the intimate connection between mental and moral improvement. The security of the republic rested upon the morality of the people, and good reading instilled good morals. A supporter of the Mercantile Library Association, founded by merchants' clerks in 1820, expressed "the greatest satisfaction" with its growing collection since "in proportion as you enlighten your mind, you awaken it to the perception of moral beauty and the practice of virtue."[16] Above all, republicanism exalted the commonweal, the common good of a presumably homogeneous public. New York's earliest public libraries were intended in large part to uphold the republic, to promote the public weal. A member of the Society Library in 1754, for example, urged his fellow citizens to "let the general good take the place of a contracted selfishness." He rallied them to "invite the arts and science to reside among us" so that with "a united harmony of public spirit" they might "make war upon ignorance and barbarity of manners."[17] The collections of the city's earliest public libraries were founded as a means of self-improvement, but the improvement of the private citizen was intimately connected with the good of the republic.

In 1822, a new constitution granted the franchise to all adult white males in the state of New York.[18] The rise of Jacksonian democracy challenged elite New Yorkers' leadership in cultural affairs as well as in politics, and in the decades that followed the cultural institutions they patronized become more and more exclusive. In 1825, with the opening of the Erie Canal, Manhattan became the gateway to the West, and its markets expanded at an unprecedented rate. By 1850, with a population of more than a half million, it was a major industrial city and the commercial emporium of a growing nation. The burgeoning economy created new opportunities but also increased economic disparities and engendered class conflict. At midcentury nearly half of the city's residents were foreign-born, newcomers whose language, customs, and religion often seemed alien, even threatening, to native New Yorkers.[19] In just a half-century after the state passed its first law governing public libraries, the city of New York was a radically different place from the relatively small republican town in which the New York Society Library had been founded. It epitomized the values that historians have associated with modern liberalism; it was expansive, commercial, democratic, individualistic.

One of the most important emerging industries in the city in the early nineteenth century was publishing. When the Society Library established its collection in 1754, all of the books were imported from London. With the introduction of stereotyped printing plates (1811), steam power (1836), and the cylinder press (1847), book production in the United States became faster and cheaper, and by midcentury Manhattan was the center of the national book trade.[20] In an article on the Mercantile Library Association in 1841, the *New York Evangelist* noted approvingly that "the present age, however else it may be characterized, is one of reading. . . . Books have been multiplied at a rate, and produced at a cost, that renders them as well the source of instruction and pleasure to [even] the poorest." What the author did not approve of, however, and what increasingly drove the publishing industry, was the production of fiction. Novels, "designed for amusement rather than profit," were, for most of the nineteenth century, considered frivolous at best and therefore inimical to the public good that public libraries were intended to promote.[21]

In fact, a range of negative connotations was associated popular fiction, especially earlier in the century. The crux of the opposition to novels in libraries, however, was the conviction that works of the imagination appealed to the emotions rather than the intellect. In 1840, for example, the New York Lyceum circulated a pamphlet as part of an unsuccessful attempt to establish a public library. It charged that "nearly . . . all the public libraries [in the city] are composed . . . of works of a character unfitted" to develop "stronger minds, more enlightened reasoners, and better citizens." They circulated instead "that light and trifling kind of reading" which appealed to "the feeling and not the intellect—the excitable, or spontaneously active powers of the mind." Citing "reports of some of the French hospitals for lunatics," the pamphlet concluded that "the reading of [novels] is . . . one of the standing causes of insanity." The Lyceum proposed to build a collection that excluded all "works of fiction (except those of a religious or moral character)."[22]

Women were considered especially excitable, ruled by their emotions, and thus inordinately susceptible to the allure of the popular novel. They were assumed to be the mainstay of the many private, for-profit circulating libraries in the city that rented books to readers and in which, according to the Lyceum's pamphlet, "twenty-five to one [was] the proportion of fictitious to solid reading." An article in the *New York Advocate*, for example, referred disparagingly to the thousands of "young lady customers who devour the contents of every new novel that appears."[23] This presumed nexus between gender and popular fiction is one key to understanding how reading was idealized in early public libraries in New York and elsewhere.

Reading "solid" literature—science, philosophy, history, classical works—was rational and masculine. Reading imaginative works was frivolous and feminine. Nonfiction was self-improving and therefore promoted the public good. Fiction was self-indulgent, demoralizing, and private. The idealized public library reader reflected gendered values that distinguished the public from the private in antebellum American culture.[24]

In fact, by midcentury practically all of the public libraries in New York offered a generous selection of recreational reading, and it was avidly devoured by men as well as women. For example, in 1850 more than 25 percent of the volumes added to Mercantile Library were novels. At the Society Library, from 1854 to 1856, fiction accounted for nearly half of the books borrowed by both male and female readers.[25] Because both libraries relied, in part, upon annual subscriptions to build their collections, they were, as the New York Lyceum pamphlet noted, "to a considerable extent obliged to comply with the general requirements of their frequenters." Yet even public libraries that were free, such as the Apprentices' Library, established in 1820 by the General Society of Mechanics and Tradesmen, needed to lure readers with works of fancy, if only so that they could then be encouraged to read more substantial, self-improving literature. Just as important, in the age of the penny press, as newspapers, magazines, and paperback books became cheaper and more widely available, New Yorkers, even those of relatively modest means, could afford to purchase their own reading material.[26] Like the commercial circulating libraries, New York's public libraries were obliged to compete for consumers of print in a dynamic, expanding market. As they provided more and more popular fiction to meet a growing popular demand, there was increasing tension between self-culture and commerce, between promoting the commonweal and catering to customers.

In 1849, the City of New York revoked the New York Society Library's tax exemption on the grounds that it was "not in the strictest sense of the term a Public Library."[27] The library sued the city and lost. To make their case before the Superior Court, the city's attorneys argued, in effect, that the Society Library was, like New York's commercial libraries, a private, for-profit enterprise. They held that, because space in its building was rented out to various businesses, the library was "used for the purpose of gain or traffic" and therefore not a public institution. Significantly, however, the city's attorneys concluded their argument with a fundamentally new definition of public libraries. The Society Library's collection was "not open to the free use and enjoyment of the public and . . . is not a public library."[28] This obscure legal dispute over taxable property reflects the beginning of a gradual shift in the popular conception of the term. Although the New York Society Library continued to refer to itself as a public library, in the decades that followed this seemed increasingly anachronistic. Certainly by the end of the nineteenth century, a public library was one that was free to everyone in the community.

One reason for the changing definition of the term was the establishment of the Astor Library. Incorporated in January 1849, shortly after the death of John Jacob Astor, and opened to the public five years later, it was, according to the terms of Astor's will, "free of expense to all persons resorting thereto." With approximately eighty thousand volumes, the Astor was at that time the largest library in the city and the second largest in the nation. Only Harvard College's collection, developed over the course of two centuries, was more extensive.[29] Astor's bequest to the city foreshadowed what Sydney Ditzion termed the "big philanthropy" of the Gilded Age. Earlier free libraries, such as the General Society's Apprentices' Library, were established and supported by the aggregation of relatively modest, individual contributions from well-off, civic-minded citizens. In the case of the Astor Library and, for example, the Cooper Union Library, founded by Peter Cooper in 1859, one man's private fortune was devoted to the creation and maintenance of a major public institution.[30] Private funding, however, also meant private governance. The trustees of the Astor, chosen by John Jacob Astor and appointed in his will, made this abundantly clear even before the library opened. In their annual report for 1853, they declared that, although the extensive collection would be accessible to all, "they only are the constituted judges of the proper mode of" managing it.[31]

From the beginning, the management of Astor's bequest was the subject of frequent criticism in the local press. In particular, New Yorkers were disappointed to learn that the library would not circulate any of the books for home use and that it would not be open in the evening, the only time when working people might make use of it. More generally, there was a sense that the library was not intended for the average reader, that there was a "stifling air of reserve and repulsion" that discouraged the reading public from frequenting it. One critic went so far as to charge that the Astor was "not, strictly speaking, a public library at all" but rather "a private library to which outsiders are occasionally admitted."[32] In response, Joseph Cogswell, the Astor's first superintendent, dismissed such criticism as "silly clamor." He explained that John Jacob Astor's intention was not to create a "popular library" for "the mere momentary gratification of the community" but rather to serve a "small class of the population," the "men of leisure and the men of letters." Cogswell justified this exclusivity on the grounds that the scholarly tomes in the Astor would be used to write popular books for the masses. The library would serve the public good as a "fountainhead . . . feeding the streams, which diffuse the blessings of knowledge through every dwelling, as well the humblest as the proudest."[33]

The persistent complaints that the Astor Library was not a truly public institution were, in part, a reflection of rising class tensions in a much larger, more diverse, and more economically stratified city. By 1876, New York was home to more than a million inhabitants, half of them crowded into tenements in poor neighborhoods.[34] In the decades that followed, new immigrants from central and southern Europe seemed alien, inassimilable to native-born New Yorkers. During the same period, immense fortunes were made, and the city became the capital of a national elite. The word *society* acquired a new, exclusive meaning, denoting the families listed in the *Social Register* and chronicled in the society columns. New York society, reigned over by Caroline Astor, the wife of John Jacob Astor's grandson William, increasingly looked for ways to set themselves apart from the lower classes and the nouveau riche. One way to do so was to document one's family history. Older libraries, such as the New York Society Library and the New-York Historical Society, and new ones like the New York Genealogical and Biographical Society, developed collections that allowed the elite to "establish that they are the descendants of the . . . founders of civilized life upon this continent, not the hordes of foreigners."[35]

Another means by which the city's elite defined and distinguished itself from other classes was culture. Like the term *society*, this took on a more restrictive meaning later in the nineteenth century. Earlier, *culture* or *cultivation* was used more broadly to denote a general process of growth and self-improvement—practical, moral, and intellectual. For Caroline Astor and her circle it meant "high culture," the ability to appreciate the beautiful in art, music, or literature. Assumed the exclusive province of the true elite, it was perhaps the primary means by which the Gilded Age upper class distanced itself from parvenus and the masses.[36] Around the same time, the wide-ranging, self-improving kind of culture that the New York Society Library had sought to foster in its earliest years became segmented and professionalized within the modern research university. At Columbia, New York University, and other institutions of higher education across the country, modern scholarly disciplines emerged, and extensive library collections were developed to meet the needs of specialized scholars. The Astor Library remained a valuable local resource, but it became less important as "men of leisure and men of letters" became professional academics.[37]

Not everyone, of course, agreed that the upper class had a monopoly on the appreciation of beauty. A series of articles on "The Poor Taste of the Rich" in early issues of *House Beautiful*, for example, ridiculed the "vulgar," "ostentatious" homes of wealthy New Yorkers, including society leader Bradley Martin's mansion on West Twentieth Street. Lavishly illustrated, it described in scathing detail interior decorating that was a "monument to ugliness," including "libraries that are museums of costly furniture and . . . priceless volumes in gold and fine leather," but "never book rooms."[38] More important, many civic-minded New Yorkers questioned whether, amidst the growing disparities of the Gilded Age, it was just or prudent to deny the working class access to the civilizing influence of culture. In 1886, with the advice and support of Melvil Dewey, then chief librarian at Columbia College, and several of the city's most prominent citizens, the state legislature passed "An Act to Encourage the Growth of Free Public Libraries." Unlike the Astor, the "free circulating libraries" that were established under the terms of the act loaned books for home use, were open in the evening, and welcomed New Yorkers from all walks of life. They were also publicly funded. The key provision of the law permitted the New York City Board of Estimate to make appropriations to each free library based upon the number of volumes circulated annually.[39] As a result, by the turn of the twentieth century there were twenty-seven small libraries, managed by fourteen library organizations, spread across Manhattan. These free circulating libraries later became the nucleus of the New York Public Library's Circulation Department. They resembled the Astor Library, however, in one critical respect: Each was managed by a private board. The trustees of the free libraries expended public funds with no oversight from elected public officials. They were immune from what they considered the contagion of local politics, "the Tammany bacillus."[40]

Dewey and his fellow supporters of the free circulating libraries were inspired by the ideals of the "public library idea." This meant not simply a collection of good books loaned for free to the public, but circulating the books from branches located in working-class neighborhoods.[41] In these small local libraries the librarian was presumably better able to foster personal relations with readers, thereby guiding their reading and cultivating the masses. The buildings themselves, well lit and adorned with flowers and tasteful works of art, were designed to evoke the typical middle-class home and thus inculcate uplifting middle-class values among the city's tenement dwellers. The role of the female librarian in the branch library was therefore essential. Women founded the largest and most influential of the city's free libraries, the New York Free Circulating Library, and were the mainstay of the public library idea across the United States. Public librarianship was regarded as a natural extension of a woman's nurturing, maternal role from the domestic to the public sphere. As such, like other "helping professions" that emerged about the same time, such as nursing and social work, it was considered a respectable alternative to marriage for an educated middle-class female. Similarly, women were seen as particularly well suited to librarianship because their innate feminine appreciation of beauty made them, to use historian Dee Garrison's phrase, the ideal "apostles of culture."[42] The stereotypical image of the refined lady librarian thus contrasted sharply with an older, yet still prevalent stereotype of women as frivolous devourers of cheap novels.

The publication of novels increased dramatically throughout the nineteenth century. From 1825 to 1850, American presses published approximately sixteen hundred titles in adult fiction. During the last quarter of the century, that number had increased to nearly seven thousand.[43] Although the free circulating libraries collected far fewer novels than subscription libraries such as the Society Library and the Mercantile Library Association, they were by far the most popular titles, usually accounting for 50 percent or more of a branch's total circulation.[44] Throughout the century the argument that librarians used most frequently to justify the provision of fiction was that it would attract readers to the library, where they would be exposed to good books and naturally develop a preference for more substantial works. In one of the earliest annual reports of the Mercantile Library, for example, the directors explained that a "few of the best imaginative works are permitted, and these are at first oftenest called for; but the voice of wisdom has made itself heard, and many who were wont to devour the pages of romance alone have become readers of history and lovers of science." The free circulating libraries also collected fiction as a stepping-stone to better books, but by 1886 there was a fundamental shift in what was considered good reading. When the Mercantile Library was founded, *literature* (like *culture*) was a broad, inclusive term. It encompassed all learning or knowledge made available in print, including, for example, history and science, as well as belles-lettres. The librarians at the free circulating libraries defined literature as fiction of the highest moral and artistic caliber.[45] Their aim was to lure working-class readers to the branches with second-rate novels so that that they might develop a taste for literature. They hoped to cultivate the masses by fostering an appreciation of beauty, of literary excellence, in works of fiction.[46]

This was the essential public purpose of the public library in New York City in the later nineteenth century. The librarians of the free circulating libraries, the "missionaries of literature," sought to use culture, not, like some members of the elite, to affirm class boundaries, but rather to uplift the working class to "their" cultural level and thereby create a more harmonious, unified community. In a period of rising class conflict and sometimes violent labor unrest, there was certainly an element of self-interest in this. For example, Ellen Coe, the head librarian of the New York Free Circulating Library, at an early conference of the American Library Association warned her colleagues that "in these troublous times popular ignorance is invested with terrors unknown before."[47] At the same time, however, the supporters of the public library idea were genuinely concerned about the plight of the poor in a modern, industrialized economy and hoped to promote good reading to mitigate class divisions and mend a fractured public. In this sense, the free circulating libraries can be seen as a Gilded Age effort to restore republican harmony and promote the public weal. At a meeting in 1882 to raise funds for the New York Free Circulating Library, one of the speakers called upon "rich men [to] aid this work by bridging over the chasm between themselves and the less fortunate or wealthy classes."[48]

In promoting the public good, the proponents of the public library idea assumed an irreconcilable conflict between commerce and culture, between marketing and the mission of literature. To employ crass "business methods," such as advertising and catering to popular demand, was considered "fatal to the elemental principle of the public library" and "the cause of higher culture." For example, the two largest free libraries, the Aguilar and the New York Free Circulating Library, both stressed in their first annual reports that they never advertised to attract readers to their branches.[49] By the end of the century, however, there was a dramatic shift in attitudes regarding the promotion of public libraries that was embodied in the "modern library idea." As the trustees of the New York Free Circulating Library explained in their final report, the modern library idea embraced the tenets of the public library idea—the free circulation of uplifting literature from neighborhood branches—yet added a wide range of new and innovative services to the public, such as interlibrary loans and story hours for children.[50] It also included various methods of "pushing" the library. Arthur Bostwick, the first chief of the New York Public Library's Circulation Department, was the nationally recognized exponent of the modern library idea. He argued that extensive advertising and other business methods were essential to the modern library because, like "the successful distributor through trade," the librarian must "obey the laws that all distributors obey" and "not sit down and wait for customers." By 1900, in the words of another enthusiast of the modern library idea, the public library had "come out of the cloister and gone into the market place."[51]

In 1892, the State of New York passed legislation that codified the procedures by which municipalities could establish public libraries. Whereas the statute of 1796 simply encouraged individuals to "associate to procure and erect . . . public libraries," the new law a century later defined the term in the sense that we understand it today. It required that "every library established . . . shall be forever free to the inhabitants of the locality" and that they were to be funded by "appropriations . . . levied and collected yearly . . . as are other general taxes."[52] In New York City, however, the free circulating libraries still had no guaranteed source of income. The Library Law of 1886 permitted but did not require annual funding from the Board of Estimate. This changed in 1901 when Andrew Carnegie gave $5.2 million to build fifty branch libraries in the boroughs of Manhattan, Staten Island, and the Bronx. Under the terms of his gift, the City of New York was required to appropriate annually at least 10 percent of that sum to support the newly created Circulation Department of the New York Public Library. As a result, practically all of the free circulating libraries were soon incorporated into the new public library.[53] If the Astor and Lenox libraries were examples of "big philanthropy," then Andrew Carnegie's private benefactions for public libraries were huge philanthropy. They were of a magnitude that could actually influence or even create public policy.

By the time the Central Building on Forty-Second Street opened in 1911, the New York Public Library had completed thirty-two of the fifty Carnegie branches. That same year, the Circulation Department loaned approximately 7,725,000 volumes, more than double the total for all of the city's free circulating libraries in 1900.[54] That it was now explicitly a tax-supported institution, that, in the words of Andrew Carnegie, "every citizen . . . now walks into this, his own library," effected a dramatic change in both how the public perceived the library and how the library promoted, "pushed" itself to the public.[55] Shortly before the grand opening of the Central Building, the City published *Results Not Shown by Statistics in the Work of the Public Libraries of Greater New York.* Consisting mostly of quotes from satisfied, supportive readers, the pamphlet highlighted the public's sense of ownership. One "old resident, a property owner" was pleased that "[I am] now at last getting something in return for money paid in taxes, . . . something worthwhile." Another user reported that she had stolen a book that someone left unattended in a local market, but immediately returned it when she discovered that it belonged to the public library.[56]

Whereas the missionaries of literature who founded the free circulating libraries were concerned primarily with the moral uplift of the masses, *Results Not Shown by Statistics* emphasized the practical advantages that the New York Public Library afforded New Yorkers from all walks of life. It included enthusiastic testimonials from, for example, a gardener and a mechanic, but also a minister, a lawyer, and a physician.[57] Readers frequently referred to the economic advantages of a library membership, and some even calculated how much money they had saved by borrowing rather than buying their books. A drayman described how his reading had enabled him "to qualify as a [driver], thus saving his position and increasing his salary when his firm changed from horse to motor delivery." A man who had once worked as a lowly clerk in a shoe store studied at his branch library and started his own electrical shop. He could "not say enough good words for the public library which has made my life happy which otherwise would have been drudgery." Instead of moral uplift, the library stressed economic mobility.[58]

References in *Results Not Shown by Statistics* to recreational reading also made it clear that the New York Public Library could be used for pleasure as well as profit.[59] Arthur Bostwick discussed this at some length in a talk before the American Library Association in 1903 on "The Purchase of Current Fiction." Implicitly criticizing the lofty aims of his predecessor at the New York Free Circulating Library, Ellen Coe, he held that "the recreative function of the public library has not been sufficiently emphasized of late." He even advised that in smaller branches with limited budgets, librarians should "in some cases leave out a somewhat dull book of high literary merit and buy an entertaining story of little purely literary interest." Reading simply for pleasure was, in his view, "a proper object for the expenditure of a considerable portion of such public money as may be received by the library." This more liberal attitude toward the provision of fiction reflected more extensive expectations of the municipal government on the part of the taxpaying public. In fact, Bostwick explicitly linked popular novels in the branch libraries to other new public services such as playgrounds in the public schools and "recreation piers" along the city's waterfront.[60]

The New York Public Library, however, was not a public institution in the same sense as the public schools or the public parks. It was not paid for entirely by tax monies. The city government supposed the Circulation Department, while the Reference Department was funded from the income of the Astor, Lenox, and Tilden endowments.[61] Nor was it publicly governed. Its board of twenty-five trustees served for life and elected its new members, except for three municipal officials serving ex officio: the mayor, the comptroller, and the president of the Board of Aldermen.[62] John Shaw Billings, the library's first director, described this mix of public and private funding and governance as a "partnership arrangement between the city and the New York Public Library."[63] This was and is fairly common for large public library systems. A survey from 1935 found that libraries in one of six large cities in the United States were not part of the municipal government.[64] Moreover, quasi-private entities performing public functions are a pervasive and distinctly modern phenomenon. The New York Power Authority and the Metropolitan Transportation Authority (MTA), for example, are both "public corporations" that serve millions of New Yorkers each day. The founding of the New York Public Library is an example not only of government taking on new, more expansive roles, but also its doing so in complex ways that confounded the distinction between public and private.

Public libraries are institutions that connect and mediate between readers and books. Yet, the definition, the common understanding, of the term *public library* has shifted significantly over time. One way to make sense of their history in New York City before 1911 is to trace which readers they included in or excluded from the reading public and what kinds of books public libraries collected to serve the public good. In the eighteenth century and roughly the first half of the nineteenth century, the most common type of public library was a subscription library. Ideally, such libraries were public institutions because they provided "solid literature"—science, history, the classics—that cultivated public virtue and thereby fortified the republic. Readers who were not included in these reading publics were, most obviously, the poor, those who were unable to afford an annual subscription. Yet, women too, again ideally, were excluded to the extent that they were dismissed as mere devourers of popular novels. In practice, however, most of these public libraries even early in the nineteenth century collected and a circulated a relatively wide selection of fiction in order to meet the demands of their subscribers.

Increasingly after 1850, and certainly by 1886, readers expected a public library to be free. In New York City, the free libraries that were founded under the terms of the library law passed in the latter year loaned books without charge to any member of the reading public. The libraries were clearly intended for the working class, however, and by this period the emphasis had shifted from providing solid literature to providing fine literature. New York's free circulating libraries sought to inculcate among the city's tenement dwellers an appreciation of "high culture," of "literary and moral excellence."[65] By civilizing the masses—uplifting them to "their" cultural level—the elites who founded and managed the city's public libraries in the later nineteenth century hoped to ensure public order and morality and restore a fractured republic by bridging the chasm between the rich and the poor. Women now played a critical role in the mission of the library because their presumably innate sensitivity and appreciation of the beautiful made them the ideal keepers of culture. Like the subscription libraries, the free libraries were obliged to collect and circulate popular novels in order in order to attract the reading public. They were regarded, however, as simply a means to an end, a stepping-stone to more substantial literature.

The New York Public Library in 1911 was a modern public library. Not only was it free to all residents, but it also had ongoing public funding and at least a degree of (all-male) public governance. Rather than the unlettered, uncultivated masses, the library's reading public was now constructed as the middle-class, tax-paying public. Instead of self-improvement through an appreciation of high culture, there was a new emphasis placed upon the practical benefits to be derived from a library membership. Books could be used as a vehicle for upward mobility as well as a means of moral and cultural uplift. At the same time, there was a greater tolerance for, a degree of acceptance of, popular fiction. This was in part simply because the library was funded by the reading public and therefore obligated to at least accommodate popular demand. The New York Public Library was not only a new kind of public library; it was also a new kind of public institution.

It reflected an expanded role for and the public's rising expectations of government.

The chapters that follow are in part local history. Although there are significant similarities, public libraries developed in different ways in different places. The differences between urban and rural communities, for example, are particularly pronounced.[66] The history of New York's public libraries reflects and was influenced by, among other local circumstances, the city's size, diversity, and especially its political and social reform movements. At the same time, however, their use and perceptions of their use over time shed light on the public and private values that Americans associated with reading, on shifting views of literature and popular fiction, and on how constructions of readers mirrored constructions of class and gender. *Reading Publics* places the development of the idea of the public library within a local and a national context and examines the various motives and values that influenced both those who founded and managed shared collections of books and those who read them. The history of these libraries is an important part of the social and cultural history of New York City and the United States.

1 The New York Society Library

Books, Authority, and Publics in Colonial and Early Republican New York

In 1754, a group of earnest young men founded the New York Society Library to advance the cause of learning and refinement in a small seaport town on the fringe of the British Empire. It was the first successful public library in the colony and one of the first in North America. As a public institution, its history from the colonial era through the early republican period mirrors changes in the ways that the public, and public and private activity, were conceived during these years. As a public collection, its development and use traces shifts in attitudes toward the kinds of knowledge that were regarded as socially useful and the bases of authority for disseminating such knowledge. The history of the New York Society Library through the 1840s thus sheds light on issues that were critical to the development of the United States as a modern, liberal society. Generally, it reflects a trend toward a broader, more inclusive conception of the public and a more democratic conception of public authority. Just as important, the history of the Society Library shows the ambiguities and tensions that arose as elite New Yorkers struggled to come to grips with these new ideas.

The Society Library's founding and early years were imbued with the ideals of republicanism. *Republicanism* was and is a term that defies any precise definition.[1] It is best understood not as a formally articulated political philosophy but rather as a constellation of mutually reinforcing values.[2] The republican founders of the Library believed in the division of civil and religious authority, in the separation of church and state, and in the power of rationalism to dispel myth and dogma. They sought, to varying degrees, to break the bonds of hierarchy that tied individuals in a monarchical society so that they were judged on personal merit rather than the accident of birth. Above all, the founders sought to promote and safeguard the commonweal. They valued a public good that transcended selfish, private interests and believed that the Society Library served the public good by educating and refining a republican citizenry.

Although they were closely related in certain respects, republicanism and democracy, particularly for the founders of the Library, were not the same. Democracy was linked to liberalism, which celebrated equality rather than independence, individualism rather than the commonweal. During the complex process by which the country shifted from a republican to a liberal society, the character of the New York Society Library transformed as well. After the Revolution, as republican enthusiasm waned, it became progressively more exclusive. Although it had never been quite as inclusive as the founders' republican ideals and rhetoric had suggested, in the nineteenth century the Library was increasingly at odds with and less relevant to the liberal, democratic society around it. Its largely patrician membership steadily withdrew from the active role it had played in the cultural and intellectual life of the city.

The idea of a public library as it is currently understood—a tax-supported, circulating collection, managed by public officials and freely available to everyone in a community—is a relatively recent development. It was not until the 1840s that states began to pass laws permitting municipalities to levy taxes to fund libraries, and many towns and cities, including New York, did not establish a public library system until much later in the century.[3] In the eighteenth century, a public library was public in the same sense that a public house or public conveyance was public. The term meant not that the collection was free but simply that it was available ostensibly to any member of the public, as opposed to one belonging to an individual or a closed, private organization such as a school.[4] Moreover, in this monarchical society, as Gordon Wood has made clear, the "modern distinctions between state and society, public and private, were just emerging." Aside from the military and the courts, government in North America and in the mother country largely acted passively, granting private individuals or organizations the authority to pursue public ends.[5] This was in fact how all the American colonies were settled. In the eighteenth-century sense of the term, the first person to attempt to found a public library in the city of New York was Thomas Bray, a minister and missionary of the Church of England. A brief history of Bray's library suggests by contrast the degree to which the New York Society Library represented a break from this premodern, monarchical world.

Thomas Bray was born in Shropshire in 1656 and graduated from Oxford's All Souls College in 1678. He was ordained an Anglican minister in

1681 and appointed the Bishop of London's commissary, or agent, to the colony of Maryland in 1695. Bray's influence, however, extended to all of the colonies in North America. In 1699, he founded the Society for Promoting Christian Knowledge and in 1701 the Society for the Propagation of the Gospel in Foreign Parts. The aim of these complementary organizations was to foster piety and learning and thereby reassert the authority of the Church of England overseas.[6] New York in particular was considered rife with ignorance and dissent. Although the Anglican Church was legally established, it was far outnumbered by the Presbyterian and Dutch Reformed churches.[7]

At the heart of Bray's mission to bring Christian enlightenment to the overseas plantations was an ambitious plan to establish a system of public libraries in every colony. Each was to be provided with three kinds of collections, organized by the Society for the Propagation of the Gospel and financed by pious and public-spirited clergy, gentry, and merchants. First, Bray promoted the founding of parochial libraries, comprising mostly theological works and intended for the private use of the minister in each parish. He considered these an essential means of encouraging poor clergymen to serve in the American wilderness.[8] Next there were to be "layman's libraries" located in towns throughout the provinces, circulating collections of books designed to promote morality and piety, entrusted to the care of the local minister.[9] Finally, in its capital each colony was to have a noncirculating "Library of more Universal Learning, for the Service and Encouragement of those who shall launch out farther in the pursuit of Useful Knowledge, as well Natural as Divine."[10] The first consignment of 220 volumes for New York arrived in 1698 and was kept in the vestry of Trinity Church, the first Anglican church in the city.[11]

Bray's extensive writings to promote his library plan, in particular his enthusiasm for collections of "universal learning," at times seem to mirror the expansive, critical spirit of eighteenth-century thought. In an unpublished manuscript entitled "*Bibliothecae Americanae*, or Catalogues of the Libraries sent into the Severall Provinces," he explained that the purpose of the collections was to "give Requisite Helps to Considerable Attainments in all the parts of necessary and usefull knowledge . . . that great Perfection of the Rational Nature." Prefaced to the catalogs is an extensive outline of all knowledge, divine and humane, and brief descriptions of the types of books to be found in each type of library, including the *bibliothecae provincialis*. The collections in New York and the other provincial capitals were to be "more than ordinarily furnished with books" on all of the most useful of the humane sciences.[12] In reality, all of the Bray libraries were predominantly theological. In New York, of the 156 titles in the original consignment, 117, or 75 percent, were works of theology. The proportions were similar in the four other provincial libraries.[13]

There are also suggestions in Bray's writings of a more modern, inclusive notion of the public that his libraries would serve and a more modern, meritocratic conception of authority over books and knowledge. In "*Bibliothecae Americanae*," he explained that the libraries of universal learning in the provincial capitals were intended for "the use and Improvement . . . of the whole Country." In an essay titled "Promoting all Necessary and Useful Knowledge," he held that learning "does more distinguish the Possessors of it, than Titles, Riches, or great Places," that "the Man of Understanding is . . . [more] inwardly and truly respected" than he who "may command the Cap and the Knee."[14] In practice, however, Bray's libraries served an exclusive public and were part of a hierarchy in which authority was legitimated by titles. Bray stated repeatedly in his writings that the books sent to North America were necessary to enable the church's ministers to instruct the people, and this paternalistic relation is graphically illustrated in the bookplate of the Society for the Propagation of the Gospel that was affixed to them. It depicts a larger-than-life missionary on a ship preaching down to a horde of tiny but grateful colonists on the shore of the American wilderness.[15] Moreover, the hierarchy of the Church was legally and theologically connected with the hierarchy of the Crown. In addition to the Society for the Propagation of the Gospel's bookplate, each of the books was also labeled on its cover, in capitals, "*sub auspiciis Wilhelmi III*."[16] Further, the public that had access to the collections was by no means "the whole country." In New York, when the titles of the first consignment of books were entered into the vestry minutes of Trinity Church, as prescribed in Bray's instructions, it was stipulated that they were "for the use Of the Ministers." There is no evidence that any layperson ever used the collection, and it appears likely that the books were kept under lock and key. Most of the other provincial libraries were also used only by the clergy.[17]

Bray's New York library was augmented occasionally by local ministers and crown officials and remained in the vestry of Trinity Church until the Revolution.[18] In September 1776, when the British occupied the city, fire destroyed the library. It was not public in any sense of the term, and the knowledge that it disseminated and the authority to control that knowledge emanated from and were circumscribed by the Crown and the

Bookplate of the Society for the Propagation of the Gospel

Church. The early history of the New York Society Library shows the ways in which these accepted notions of knowledge, authority, and the public were contested in the city in the decades before the Revolution.

Bernard Bailyn and others have noted that "there was no sharp break between a placid pre-Revolutionary era and the turmoil of the 1760s and 1770s." The conflict between the Tories, who supported the Crown, and the Whigs, who sought to place limits on the royal prerogative, increased sharply throughout the first half of the eighteenth century, and the arguments employed by each party were honed in innumerable attacks in pamphlets, newspapers, legal actions, and personal correspondence.[19] The context of this conflict was distinctly local. Within each colony, political divisions arose from a unique and complex combination of personal, familial, religious, and economic motives. The founding of the New York Society Library reflected and was part of prerevolutionary colonial politics.

The conflict between Whigs and Tories in New York escalated sharply in the 1730s. John Peter Zenger, a printer and the editor of the *Weekly Journal*, in the midst of the heated municipal elections of 1734, launched a spirited attack on Governor William Cosby, Chief Justice James De Lancey, and other members of the provincial government. Purposefully echoing the arguments and rhetoric used a decade earlier by John Trenchard and Thomas Gordon in the mother country in their savaging of the Walpole administration in the *Independent Whig*, Zenger accused the royal officials of corruption, incompetence, and "tyrannically flouting the laws of England and New York." Governor Cosby promptly ordered the most offensive issues of the *Journal* burned in public and had Zenger jailed for seditious libel. When the case came to trial, he was ably defended by James Alexander and William Smith, who successfully argued that Zenger was guilty of nothing more than printing the truth.[20]

In the ensuing decades, political conflict in the colony most often revolved around a bitter contest between the De Lanceys, representing the Crown, and the Livingstons, who led the "popular party." To an extent, their rivalry reflected conflicting economic interests. The De Lanceys were backed by wealthy merchants who wanted to shift the tax burden as much as possible to New York's landowners. The Livingstons represented families with landed estates that wanted increased revenue from import and export duties, in part to finance a stronger military that could protect their isolated holdings in the North. The animosity between the two factions was also founded to an extent upon religious differences. The Church of England, nominally the established church, was the smallest but also the wealthiest and most powerful denomination in the colony, and De Lancey and most crown officials belonged to it. The Livingstons led the dissenting congregations, including the Presbyterian and Dutch Reformed churches, the two largest in New York City.[21]

Beginning in the early 1750s, the popular party's most effective polemicists were three young lawyers: William Livingston, John Morin Scott, and William Smith Jr. All three were Presbyterians, and all three had studied for the bar in the office of William Smith Sr. Known throughout the colonies as the "New York triumvirate," or to their enemies as the "wicked triumvirate" or the "vile and despicable Triumvirate," they led the attack in the local press on the De Lancey faction and on the royal prerogative generally.[22] Even one of their most implacable opponents, the Reverend Samuel

Johnson of Trinity Church, grudgingly admitted that it was "indeed fencing against a flail to hold any dispute with them."[23] The triumvirate also promoted a variety of public enterprises designed to refine the cultural and moral climate of their city. In 1748, they organized an informal club called the Society for the Promotion of Useful Knowledge, which, unlike Bray's Society for Promoting Christian Knowledge, welcomed members from every Protestant denomination.[24] In 1754, the triumvirate founded the New York Society Library.

The founding of the Society Library was a controversy within a controversy. In 1746, the provincial assembly had authorized a lottery to help establish a publicly supported college.[25] In 1754, Trinity Church donated fifty acres of land in New York City on the conditions that the presidents of the school be communicants of the Anglican faith and that Anglican prayers be used in the daily services.[26] William Livingston was one of only three non-Anglicans appointed to the school's ten-member board, and, like any good republican, he detected a conspiracy. He, Scott, and Smith were convinced that the establishment of King's College (later Columbia University) was an Anglican plot to subvert the city's intellectual as well as its religious liberty. In the words of its founding articles, the Society Library was established in part to be "advantageous to our intended College." For the triumvirate, this meant not simply that the students would have access to the books but also that the collection would help counteract the Anglican influence. The controversy attending the founding of the Library was thus a skirmish in the war of words over the founding of King's College.[27]

In 1752 and 1753, Livingston, Scott, and Smith published a weekly journal to disseminate their views on the college and other local issues. The *Independent Reflector* was consciously modeled on Gordon and Trenchard's *Independent Whig*.[28] Each issue was a single essay in which the public-spirited Reflector dared "to attempt the Reforming of the *Abuses of my Country*, and to point out whatever may tend to its Prosperity and Emolument."[29] Although the library for the college was mentioned only briefly, the *Independent Reflector* set forth the triumvirate's republican conception of legitimate authority and the proper use of knowledge in an enlightened society, ideals that were central to the founding of the Society Library.[30]

Primarily, Livingston, Scott, and Smith were adamantly opposed to the Anglican domination of King's College or any other civil institution. Before they were forced to cease publication, they had planned a separate essay attacking the Society for the Propagation of the Gospel for "the settlement of their missionaries *amongst Christians* in the American plantations."[31]

Remarkably latitudinarian for their time, they held that "our Faith like our stomachs may be overcharged, especially if we are prohibited to chew what we are commanded to swallow."[32] They considered authority in civil matters to be justly derived only from the public, "for great is the Authority, exalted the Dignity, and powerful the Majesty of the People." While the members of the triumvirate were certainly no rank democrats, they railed passionately against the "vanity of birth and titles" and the "absurdity of respect without merit."[33] Unlike Bray's gentry, who were simply born into their station, a gentleman in their view earned that status through character, virtue, and learning.[34] Further, they argued that the "Advantages flowing from the Rise and Improvement of Literature are not to be confined to a Set of Men: They are to extend their chearful Influence thro' Society in general." Finally, the triumvirate stressed that the knowledge to be imparted at the new college must be of practical use to the community. Dismissing the "learned lumber of gloomy pendants, which hath so long infested and corrupted the World," they insisted that "whatever literary Acquirement cannot be reduced to Practice, or exerted to the Benefit of Mankind, . . . is in Reality no more than a specious Kind of ignorance."[35]

According to Smith's *History of the Province of New York*, in March 1754, as the controversy over King's College intensified, the triumvirate and "a few private friends" met "to carry about a subscription towards raising a publick library." Within a month they had collected nearly £600 and written a constitution, the "Articles of the Subscription Roll of the New York Library."[36] Modeled after the Library Company of Philadelphia, which Benjamin Franklin in his autobiography called "the mother of all subscription libraries," the New York Society Library was set up as a private corporation in which members of the public could purchase shares or "rights."[37] Shareholders paid five pounds initially for a share and an annual "subscription" of ten shillings to maintain their borrowing privileges. The subscribers or shareholders elected a twelve-member Board of Trustees annually that was empowered to hire a librarian, buy books, secure a room in which to house them, and draw up regulations for the use of the collection. Members could repeal decisions of the board by a majority vote at the annual meeting.[38]

In the words of William Smith Jr., the founders encountered "some obstacles at first from . . . the narrow views and jealousies of sectarian zeal."[39] The election of trustees immediately became embroiled in the controversy over King's College, as each side sought to gain control of the books intended to serve as its library. In a contribution to the *New-York Mercury* in May 1755, William Livingston warned that "a Bigot, now heightened into madness by the late frequent controversial Defeats of High-Church on the Subject of the College," had devised a "dirty scheme . . . for excluding as many *English* Presbyterians, as possible from the Trusteeship." He went on to assure the public, however, that the "Subscribers were so obstinately impartial, as to chuse Persons who, from their Acquaintance with Literature . . . were able to make a proper Collection of Books."[40]

These rancorous annual elections continued until 1758, when King's College established its own library. Thereafter, most board members tended to be reelected year after year apparently without opposition. Of the thirty-five trustees who served during the colonial period, about half were Tories and half were Whigs.[41] This does not mean, however, that all of them contributed equally to the administration of the library. William Livingston, for example, was particularly active in selecting books for the collection during its earliest years and designed the library's first bookplate.[42] John Morin Scott served as the first librarian, and both Livingston and William Smith Jr. served on the board almost continually until the Revolution. By contrast, James De Lancey, by this time the colony's acting governor, apparently made no effort to secure a royal charter for the Society while he served on its board.[43]

At the first meeting of the board on May 7, 1754, each subscriber was requested to "prepare . . . a catalogue of books as he may judge most proper to be first purchased."[44] The trustees made selections from these lists, and the initial collection arrived from a London bookseller on October 14. One week later, the Society published its first catalog of approximately 250 titles in 650 volumes. The second and earliest surviving catalog was published four years later and lists 335 titles in 859 volumes.[45] The library reflected to a great extent the enlightened ideals the triumvirate had propounded five years earlier in the *Independent Reflector*. There was a reasonably wide selection of theology, more than 30 titles in total. In addition to the usual tracts and sermons, however, the catalog offered such heretical works as the Koran and *Lives of the Popes*. Considering that lawyers were often a majority on the board during this period, the number of legal works was surprisingly small.[46] There were only six, including *Corpus Juris Civilis* and *Select Tryals at the Old Baily*. The 1758 catalog proffered useful knowledge to Society members engaged in other vocations as well. A merchant might borrow an atlas, a treatise on insurance, or the *Dictionary of*

William Livingston

Trade and Commerce. For gentlemen farmers there were titles such as *The Modern Husbandman* and *Scotch Improvements in Husbandry*.

While Austin Baxter Keep's official *History of the New York Society Library* somewhat overstates the case when it refers to "the utter absence of light reading," the collection certainly reflected the broadly edifying intentions of its founders.[47] There was, for example, a wide range of titles in "natural philosophy" and "natural history." Society members inclined to explore the emerging modern sciences could choose among such seminal authors as Isaac Newton, Robert Boyle, and Benjamin Franklin or browse among the *Philosophical Transactions* of the Royal Society in London. In 1758, an enlightened gentleman was expected to be conversant in the scientific advances of an enlightened age.

Beyond the collected works of Shakespeare, there was very little fiction, and the only novel was an English translation of *Don Quixote*.[48] There was, however, an extensive selection of poetry and other literature, broadly speaking, of an improving nature. Subscribers could borrow such titles as *Musical Expression, The Art of Painting, The Art of Speaking in Public,* and *Manners*. This impulse toward refinement should not be interpreted simply as an attempt to affirm one's gentility, or even as a desire for upward mobility, a striving to join the ranks of the gentry. Rather it reflects what Gordon Wood has called "new republican standards of gentility," new ideals in which one's own refinement was intimately connected with and promoted the moral and material progress of the community.[49] As the *Independent Reflector* had urged just a few years earlier, many founding members of the New York Society Library firmly believed that New Yorkers, "just emerged from the rude unpolished condition of an infant Colony," should, with "a united Harmony of public Spirit," . . . "make War upon Ignorance and Barbarity of Manners." This new urbanity and fashionable gentility were perhaps best exemplified by Joseph Addison and Richard Steele's *The Spectator*, which the *Independent Reflector* praised for having "embellished the gravest Precepts with the Decorations of Gaiety."[50] The Society Library held a complete run of the journal, as well as issues of its many successors and imitators, including the *Guardian* and the *Rambler*.[51]

The *Independent Reflector* of course also had the highest praise for Trenchard and Gordon's *Independent Whig*, which "sham[ed] Tyranny and Priestcraft" and "struck Terror into a whole Hierarchy."[52] Although the triumvirate's own journal was apparently too controversial, the 1758 catalog did include the *Independent Whig* and other periodicals in a similar vein, such as Henry St. John, Viscount Bolingbroke's the *Craftsman*. These titles exhibited the same wit and polish as the *Spectator*, but were more overtly political.[53] They were critical components of what Bernard Bailyn has termed the "sources and traditions" of the "literature of revolution," the war of words carried on in newspapers and pamphlets during the imperial crisis of the 1760s and early 1770s.[54] In 1758, Society subscribers could borrow a wide range of works that Bailyn identifies as part of the intellectual foundation of the American Revolution. The classics, particularly histories of republican Rome, were well represented, including, for example, Thomas Gordon's translation of Tacitus.[55] There was as well a wide selection of Enlightenment authors, such as John Locke and Voltaire; and polemicists from the period of the English Commonwealth and the early eighteenth century, such as James Harrington and Algernon Sydney.[56] Just as much as poetry and works on painting and music, all of these writers were considered essential to the instruction of a gentleman. Taken as a whole, the Society Library in 1758 was representative of the ideal of enlightened education in the mid–eighteenth century. It was wide-ranging, eclectic, and intended to refine society as a whole as well as the individual.

Appended to the catalog of 1758 was a list of the 118 original subscribers.[57] For this early period it is difficult to gauge the degree of exclusivity that prevailed in the Society Library, to measure how broadly inclusive this society of readers was. According to the Articles of the Subscription Roll, each of the shareholders should have been formally approved by a vote of the trustees. There is no record of such a vote in their minutes, and it appears unlikely that they actually voted in prospective members during these years. The membership list in 1758 certainly included many of the oldest and most prominent families in the city, names such as Alexander, Livingston, Van Cordlandt, and Stuyvesant. Moreover, the price of five pounds for a share in the Society and the annual subscription of ten shillings were beyond the means of many New Yorkers. Nonetheless, the Society Library was less expensive than certain other public libraries of the period (the Charleston Library Society, for example, charged an initial fee of fifty pounds) and membership was not confined exclusively to the local patriciate.[58] When the Society finally received a royal charter in 1772 to "erect within our said city of New York a *public library*," the document included the occupations of all of the current shareholders. Of seventy-one members, only five were listed simply as "gentlemen," and there were five prosperous artisans or tradesmen.[59] Within the context of mid-eighteenth-century monarchical society, the New York Society Library seems to have been relatively inclusive. While a degree of wealth and a certain social position were undoubtedly expected of the subscribers, in their pursuit of refinement they did reach beyond the boundaries of the traditional gentry to include New Yorkers of more humble origins.

The Society's original collection did not survive long after it was incorporated by royal charter. British troops looted the library when they occupied Manhattan in September 1776. The Revolution scattered the membership as well, as subscribers were forced to choose sides in the conflict. Of the founding triumvirate, for example, William Livingston and John Morin Scott both served in the Continental Congress, while William Smith Jr., after a period of neutrality and indecision, sided with the Crown.[60] Declaring himself "a Whigg of the old Stamp, . . . one of King William's Whiggs, for Liberty & the Constitution," he eventually moved to Quebec and became chief justice of the province.[61] The library these three friends founded in the comparatively tranquil years before the imperial crisis reflects the pervasive yet divisive nature of republican thought in colonial New York. That its founders in the end divided over the issue of independence suggests the complexities and ambiguities of republicanism as the coming of the Revolution forced New Yorkers to choose between the Crown and the new republic.

The New York Society Library did not reopen until more than five years after the British evacuated the city. In December 1788, subscribers met to elect a new Board of Trustees, and the following February the state legislature passed an act validating under state law the royal charter issued in 1772.[62] The late 1780s and early 1790s were years of energy, optimism, and prosperity. In 1789, there were 239 members, and the Society published a catalog of nearly 3,100 volumes. Just four years later, a new catalog of more than 5,000 volumes listed 892 subscribers.[63] This interest and activity clearly reflects the city's postrevolutionary republican enthusiasm for the diffusion of knowledge. An article in the *New-York Magazine or Literary Repository* in 1791, "On the Utility of Public Libraries" lauded the Society Library as an edifying example of "the spring . . . given the human mind, by means of the American revolution." Urging his fellow citizens to join, the author reminded them that "of all forms of civil government, the republican depends most on an enlightened state of Society" and enlarged upon the "advantages resulting to a community" from a collection "for universal and critical research."[64]

This period of prosperity was relatively short-lived. In his official history of the Library, Austin Baxter Keep characterized the first three decades of the nineteenth century as "years of public indifference and private embarrassment."[65] The private embarrassment was due in large part to financial difficulties that ensued after the Society constructed its first building on Nassau Street in 1795. It borrowed $3,750 to pay construction costs and sundry expenses and for more than forty years continued to pay interest annually on this debt. Indeed, throughout this period, although the collection grew steadily, expenditures frequently exceeded income, while at the same time the membership declined. In 1838, for example, there were only 420 subscribers, less than half the number in 1793.[66] What Keep termed public indifference refers only in part to this decline in subscriptions. More significantly, he was bemoaning the public's changing attitude toward municipal support for the city's first public library.

Before it moved into that first building on Nassau Street, the Society Library had received limited assistance from the City of New York. From 1754 to 1776 and from 1789 to 1795, the collection was housed for free in a room in City Hall. In May 1814, an ambitious project was undertaken to secure municipal patronage on a wider scale. Officers of the New York Society Library, the New-York Historical Society, the Literary and Philosophical Society, and other cultural organizations petitioned the Common Council for the use of Brideswell, the recently vacated almshouse located behind City Hall. In June of the following year, the aldermen readily agreed, praising New York for its "distinguished munificence to private institutions" and expressing confidence that the confederation of learned societies would become "justly famous as an Institute of the elegant fine & liberal Arts" and "a garden spot in which the young plants of science would be cultivated."[67] What became known as the New York Institution eventually comprised ten different organizations, including the Historical Society, a chemical laboratory, and the Academy of Fine Arts. Thomas Bender has described the Institution as a critical development in the cultural history of New York, a sustained effort on the part of the city's elite and municipal authorities to "consolidate and concentrate the existing elements of the city's intellectual culture in the interest of invigorating it and giving it more social force."[68] The New York Society Library, however, did not participate. In November 1816, the Board of Trustees, unable to find a suitable buyer for its own building, voted to reject the offer of free accommodation at Brideswell.[69] As a result, the Society was relatively marginalized during this critical period.

In the late 1820s, the board petitioned the Council on three separate occasions for real estate or space in a municipal building so that they could sell the property on Nassau Street and pay off their debts.[70] By this time, however, the public's attitude toward municipal patronage of elite organizations had changed markedly. After 1827, for example, the Council would grant the New York Institution only short-term leases and in 1831 evicted it from Brideswell altogether.[71] Councilman James Roosevelt certainly spoke for many New Yorkers when he explained that "the great length of time during which so large an amount of public property has been suffered to be applied . . . almost exclusively to private uses, has been a subject of frequent and . . . just animadversion."[72] Twenty years earlier, it had been widely accepted that the city's elite should direct its cultural organizations. With the demise of the New York Institution, it became clear that in the aggressively egalitarian public sphere of Jacksonian New York, their leadership was no longer taken for granted. What Keep termed public indifference was in large measure public resentment of municipal support for upper-class cultural institutions.

Public indifference was certainly manifested in a steady decline in the Society's membership. Faced with shrinking revenues from subscriptions and a rising debt, the trustees might have alleviated their financial distress by taking steps to make the library more attractive to the burgeoning reading public. Instead, they raised both the cost of the shares and the annual fee in a vain attempt to achieve solvency. During a period without significant, sustained inflation, the price of a "right" increased on five occasions, from $12.50 in 1788 to $40.00 in 1841, while the yearly subscription rose four times, from $1.25 in 1788 to $6.00 in 1842.[73] Alternatively, the trustees might have generated significant income by allowing nonmembers to use the library for a fee. The Apprentices' Library and the Mercantile Library Association, two of the most popular public libraries of the period, both employed this strategy, the latter with considerable success. Members of the public were permitted to borrow books for a modest annual sum but were not entitled to hold office or to vote in the annual elections. Money from "pay readers" increased revenues, which enabled these libraries to buy more books, which, in turn, attracted more outside readers.[74] Essentially, they were able to expand by adapting a business model to a nonprofit enterprise.

The steady rise in the price of a share and in the annual subscription was not just a reflection of the Society's increasing elitism. Certainly, making the library more expensive also made it less inclusive, but this does not mean the board was purposefully exclusive. In fact, although the Articles of the Subscription Roll, the charter, and the by-laws all required the trustees to vote on admitting new subscribers, there is no evidence in the minutes or elsewhere that they ever bothered to exclude anyone. In raising the subscription and the cost of a share, the board simply adopted the easiest and most obvious solution to their financial problems. The first three decades of the century were years of somnolence and inertia. The Society's patrician leadership was mired in complacency and lacked the energy and imagination to make fundamental changes.[75] Trustees served long terms, an average of approximately fifteen years during this period, and, as was the practice during the colonial era, they were essentially self-selected; at each annual meeting the board drew up a slate of candidates, which a handful of subscribers then perfunctorily voted in.[76] The only occasion on which the Society roused briefly from its somnolence was during a contested election in 1825.[77]

In April of that year, instead of the usual ten or twelve voters, sixty subscribers cast ballots at the annual meeting. They re-elected only three of the twelve incumbent trustees. One of the newly elected board members received only twenty-eight votes, three short of a majority. At a special meeting the following day, a group of shareholders contested the results on the grounds that many of those voting had never been formally approved as members. The board then engaged James Kent, chancellor of the State of New York and a former trustee, to arbitrate the dispute. Three days later Kent ruled that the election was void and that the old board should remain in office for another year. He rejected the opposition candidate who had not received a majority of the ballots cast and found that another was ineligible because the board had never approved his membership. Since "the Charter discovers a solicitude to preserve a full constitutional board of trustees," the entire election was invalid and "the former Trustees are entitled to hold over." The old board happily concurred and passed a resolution to that effect the same day.[78] Perhaps the most significant practical effect of the dispute was that thereafter the trustees always voted on prospective subscribers and were careful to include the names of the newly admitted members in their minutes.[79]

It is not clear what the new members hoped to accomplish by gaining control of the board. Years later some trustees claimed they intended to use the corporate powers conferred in the charter to turn the library into a bank.[80] However implausible that explanation may seem, it does reveal much about the larger society in which the Society functioned. Particularly after the opening of the Erie Canal in 1825, New York was an intensely commercial city expanding at a feverish pace, and it is perhaps not remarkable that some members of the board would ascribe sinister economic motives to their opponents. Moreover, banking was an explosive political issue throughout the early nineteenth century. For many people, any group viewed as manipulative and conspiratorial could easily be connected with a bank. The election dispute of 1825 also mirrored the often tumultuous politics of the period. The state constitutional convention of

1821 significantly expanded the franchise, and New York would soon become notorious for fractious, intensely partisan electioneering.[81] The contested election of 1825 thus sheds light on two seminal forces that by the 1820s were beginning to transform the United States and New York City in particular, rapid economic expansion and Jacksonian democracy. It also foreshadowed the more intense and protracted conflicts within the Society during the following decade.

The 1820s and 1830s were years of change, experimentation, and adjustment for New York's public libraries and other cultural institutions. In 1831, a special report of the General Society of Mechanics and Tradesmen proposed to concentrate the Society's efforts on developing its Apprentices' Library and to devote fewer resources to its traditional role of providing charity to indigent members.[82] That same year the American Bible Society resolved to refocus its distribution of the Scriptures on Christian missions overseas rather than the United States, and thereafter its library developed into a highly specialized resource for biblical translation.[83] Similarly dramatic changes occurred at other libraries about this time, including the New-York Historical Society and the Mercantile Library Association.[84] This is not to argue that all of these organizations pursued similar aims or evolved in similar directions. Rather, all of them in various ways were striving to remain relevant in a rapidly changing commercial, democratic society.

As a result of these new cultural initiatives, the means for pursuing knowledge and self-improvement were more widely and readily available than ever before. Richard D. Brown has described this as part of "an underlying shift from a society of scarcity, where public information and learning generally flowed from the upper reaches of the social order downward to common people . . . to a society of information abundance . . . a diffusion marketplace animated by multiple preferences and constituencies."[85] In this new environment, cultural organizations might actually compete for consumers of culture. Since its founding with the Society Library in 1754, Kings College, now Columbia College, had remained steeped in the classics, a bastion of conservatism, elitism, and Anglicanism. In December 1829, plans were laid for a University of the City of New York, later New York University, which would be nondenominational, would provide free tuition for promising young men from humble backgrounds, and would stress modern, useful subjects such as English, science, and mathematics.[86] In response, Columbia circulated a pamphlet assuring New Yorkers that there were "no reasonable data which warrant the conclusion" that a "rivalship between the two institutions will promote the interests of education and science" and promised scholarships and a revised curriculum to include courses in "all the various branches of science and literature."[87] About the same time, a similar rivalry developed between the New York Society Library and the New York Athenaeum. Founded in 1824, the Athenaeum aspired to provide the city a library "in which the curious student can find all the works necessary to the thorough investigation of any branch" of knowledge.[88] That same year the trustees of the Society Library took the unprecedented step of lowering the price of a share from forty dollars to twenty-five.[89]

Even though it abandoned its ambitious plan to establish a comprehensive research collection, the New York Athenaeum provided the stimulus that in the 1830s roused the Society from its complacency. Instead of its library, the Athenaeum directed its efforts primarily toward providing New Yorkers with "oral instruction in the form of popular lectures."[90] It had a complex organizational structure with different levels of membership, each of which were accorded different privileges and responsibilities. One hundred "patrons," for example, contributed two hundred dollars to join and were allowed four votes at the annual meetings and substantial control over the treasury. One of the classes of "subscribers" paid a ten-dollar annual subscription and had only one vote. Each year the membership elected up to one hundred "associates" who planned and in most cases delivered the lectures. These regular addresses covered a wide and eclectic range of topics. During the first year, there were a total of sixteen, ranging from elementary chemistry to poetry to phrenology.[91] They were designed to appeal not to the scholar, but to the general public, "that immense multitude who are at once invested with the privileges of Freedom and the prerogatives of Power."[92]

Many members of the New York Society Library were also ardent supporters of the New York Athenaeum. This became the source of bitter and prolonged conflict within the library during the 1830s, as pro- and anti-Athenaeum factions fought for control of the board. In all, fourteen Society Library trustees also served as directors of the Athenaeum.[93] Perhaps the most active and influential Athenaeum supporter was Gulian Crommelin Verplanck, a founder and associate of and lecturer for the Athenaeum; he also served on the Society's board nearly continually from 1810 until his death in 1870, longer than any other trustee. Almost forgotten today, he was one of the most prominent and influential New Yorkers of his time. He graduated from Columbia at the age of fourteen, the school's youngest graduate ever, studied but never practiced law, and served in a number of elective offices, including a term in the U.S. House of Representatives. He wrote prolifically and eclectically on subjects ranging from literature to economics to religion and was also a much sought after public speaker.[94] Although none of his Athenaeum lectures have survived, several others delivered about the same time were published. One in particular is significant in the way that it reflects continuities and changes in Americans' views on books, knowledge, and authority since the triumvirate founded the New York Society Library in the years leading up to the Revolution.[95]

In 1831, Verplanck gave a "Lecture Introductory to the Several Courses Delivered before the Mercantile Association of New York." The Mercantile Library Association, in addition to its library, had begun an annual series of popular (and profitable) addresses on the arts and sciences that catered to the same broad, self-improving audience for which the Athenaeum competed.[96] Verplanck explained that his aim was to show "the true advantages of general knowledge to men engaged in active business." Much of his lecture echoed views on the utility of knowledge expounded by the *Independent Reflector* in the years in which the Society Library was founded. He began by lauding the public spirit of the gentlemen who had volunteered to deliver the courses, "an animating example of . . . unflagging devotion to the common good . . . worthy of republican antiquity."[97] He then went on to describe the benefits of a broad, albeit informal education both to the individual and to society. On a personal level, "general knowledge makes a man more respectable, more useful, and more happy," and "fill[s] the soul with kindling and ennobling thoughts."[98] More important, Verplanck stressed repeatedly that, "in proportion as knowledge is widely diffused, morals are secured and liberty protected," that "only in an enlightened republic [do] the people know all their rights, and feel all their duties."[99]

Verplanck's conception of the utility of knowledge, however, differed from the New York triumvirate's in critical respects. He did begin with a classical hero, describing at length Cicero's selfless efforts "to apply his powerful intellect to such studies only as had a direct bearing on the uses of society." Yet he went on to assure his audience that they were better able to pursue knowledge than even the Roman republic's most revered citizen, since they all had access to libraries "far superior in amount, in variety, and . . . in excellence to the treasured volumes of Cicero's much loved collection!"[100] Many of Verplanck's exemplary heroes were Enlightenment figures, men like Joseph Priestley and Benjamin Franklin, part-time scholars whose "studies [were] snatched . . . amidst the calls of business."[101] He reserved his highest praise, however, for an amateur scholar whose career spanned the eighteenth and nineteenth centuries, the English author and reformer William Roscoe. Roscoe is perhaps best known as the founder of the Liverpool Athenaeum, which influenced the establishment of both the New York Athenaeum and the Mercantile Library, but Verplanck was most impressed by the ways in which he applied his talents to "all the best and most practical uses of society," in particular to "the machinery of social government, to the statistics of vice, the police of prisons, and the prevention and punishment of crime." In fact, Verplanck argued that, although "guarding our civil liberties" remained a critical duty, the most "constant and useful" service a patriot could render his country was to become familiar with "the management of the ordinary machinery of society." In 1831 true patriotism required that every citizen become "well fitted to comprehend and judge" such subjects as banking, taxation, criminal justice, and education.[102]

Verplanck's references to the "machinery of society" point toward the beginnings of an entirely new body of knowledge, the social sciences. In this address to a popular audience, however, he was more concerned with the benefits of a broad, liberal education to the average, self-improving citizen of the early republic. It was not simply that new kinds of knowledge were developing in a new kind of society. The public role of knowledge itself was changing in revolutionary ways. Whereas the republican founders of the Society Library railed against the threat posed to the community by the machinations of selfish factions, Verplanck, a Jacksonian Democrat, assured his listeners that in an "enlightened republic," the "rage of faction" would always be "mitigated into the fair contest of parties."[103] He acknowledged that with the "division of labor" in an industrializing economy there was a "danger that . . . each individual may be narrowed to the limits of his personal occupation," becoming a mere "cog in a huge and complicated machine." Yet, he contended that such economic specialization, which ensured the nation's progress and prosperity, "carried with it its own corrective, . . . the opportunity of liberal inquiry, and that variety of contemplation which exercises and disciplines the whole intellectual man."[104] Verplanck thus argued that a liberal education was more than simply the hallmark of a republican gentleman. It would act as an antidote to the negative effects of industrialization and the tumult of Jacksonian democracy.

In 1828, shortly after the Mercantile Library Association began sponsoring its own courses, the New York Athenaeum discontinued its lecture series.[105] Although the Athenaeum had earlier abandoned its plan to develop an extensive research library, it still maintained the city's most comprehensive collection of foreign and domestic newspapers and periodicals. In 1831, Verplanck and two other Society Library trustees were appointed to a joint committee to confer regarding a union of the two institutions. Although they reported favorably, the Society board rejected the proposal by a slim majority.[106] Thus began a series of protracted and sporadic negotiations over the terms under which the collections might be merged. For seven years the Society Library trustees remained divided over the question, and at each annual election tensions escalated between the Athenaeum supporters and its opponents. The gentlemen of the pro-Athenaeum and the anti-Athenaeum factions attacked each other, often in decidedly ungentlemanly terms, at special meetings, in the local newspapers, and in a series of pamphlets circulated to the subscribers. Ostensibly at issue were such mundane matters as the value of local real estate and the transfer or purchase of library shares. In fact, in the 1830s the Society Library entered a critical period of self-definition in which it struggled to determine the purpose of its collection and the public it intended to serve.

The trustees who opposed the merger with the Athenaeum made little effort to win over their opponents on the board or to win favor among the shareholders. Rather in defiance of the facts, they declared that by their "untiring industry" and "good management," without assistance from the State or municipal authorities, "the Library [had] attained a state of prosperity that could never have been expected."[107] Their claim to authority and right to continue in office were founded upon their long association with the institution and their intimate knowledge of its history. In fact, the first pamphlet they circulated began with a brief history of the Society since its founding. The anti-Athenaeum trustees repeatedly dismissed their opponents as mere "recent members" who knew nothing of the past struggles of the institution they hoped to govern, upstarts whose criticism of the current board's policies, "so authoritatively put," were highly impudent. They referred to the Athenaeum supporters not as "gentlemen," but as "persons," a not-so-thinly veiled insult that suggests how nasty the dispute had become.[108] The anti-Athenaeum party even went so far as to ascribe pecuniary motives to the movement to combine the two institutions, intimating that it was "a case of [Athenaeum members] wanting to speculate in the shares of another society."[109] That is, they charged that the Athenaeum members anticipated an increase in the price of a Society Library share once the merger was accomplished and intended to sell their newly acquired shares at a profit.

The trustees of the pro-Athenaeum party "cheerfully concede[d] that the present list of [anti-Athenaeum] trustees is composed of the names of highly respectable citizens," although they added, somewhat defensively, that "on the score of respectability . . . the ticket [we] offer for your support will bear comparison with that of any preceding year's." They went on to argue, however, that "a reputable standing is [not] the sole requisite for a trustee," that their right to office, their authority, should also be based upon "the requisite amount of knowledge in forming a suitable collection."[110] They also insisted that the board's powers be legitimately conferred by the democratically expressed will of the shareholders. Dismissing "the monstrous farce of annual elections," the Athenaeum supporters compared the management of the Library to a "closed borough" in which "the trustees nominated themselves and their friends from year to year."[111] They contrasted the "snug and private manner" in which the Society Library conducted its affairs with "associations of a similar nature," such as the Mercantile Library Association, that were "organized more in accordance with our free institutions." The anti-Athenaeum members deserved to be ousted for arrogantly disregarding the views "of the very members to whom they owe their existence."[112]

The pro-Athenaeum faction heatedly denied any personal interest in the negotiations over the merger. They "boldly avow[ed] that [their] only object [was] to increase the usefulness and respectability of the library." Their sense of public duty demanded that they expand the public's access to the collection. Disavowing the "churlish or monopolizing spirit" that had made the Society Library "the resort and solace of a few hundred persons," the pro-Athenaeum trustees promised to "spread its benefits to a constantly increasing circle."[113] At the same time, however, they were careful to distinguish the kinds of books they intended to make available to this expansive public. They roundly criticized the current management for developing a collection that "scarcely offers more attraction than . . . an ordinary circulating library," a disparaging reference to the commercial libraries, often parts of bookshops or general stores, that rented out works of popular fiction.[114] Members of the Athenaeum and other deserving members of the reading public were invited "to become citizens of our literary community," and with their help the Society Library would take its rightful place as "the chief literary establishment of our beloved city."[115] The self-styled reformers argued for a popular readership, but not a popular collection, and they saw no contradiction between these two goals.

Aside from specific grievances concerning the development of the collection and the exclusivity of the membership, the pro-Athenaeum trustees took issue with the entire tone of the Library's management. They complained that the board was simply behind the times, mired in the past in an era that looked eagerly toward the future. The pamphlets circulated by the opposition were replete with references to "the torpid and monastic state" of the leadership, to "an institution that has been peacefully slumbering for nearly a century."[116] They argued that change would only be effected by "selecting a new set of trustees from among the younger and more active of our members," forward-looking men who would bring about a "new era of prosperity . . . [and] commence a splendid and progressive march of improvement."[117] This sentiment was frequently echoed in letters to the local newspapers, in which Athenaeum supporters proudly designated themselves the "movement party" and dismissed their opponents as the "sedentaries."[118] There was a pervasive sense that the Library's management was out of touch with the commercial, democratic city that had long since emerged from its staid colonial past. In fact, the movement party seemed at times to conflate democracy and commerce, as when they discussed the value of the shares. When the anti-Athenaeum faction accused them of hoping to "speculate in shares," they responded that the fact that members often sold their memberships for considerably less than the price of twenty-five dollars set by the board showed the true "estimation of the public, who are the proper judges."[119] In the new marketplace of culture, cultural consumers comprised an electorate who voted with their pocketbooks.

Throughout most of the 1830s, the pro-Athenaeum faction steadily gained support. In the hotly contested election of 1833, they fell short of gaining a majority on the board by only a handful of votes.[120] By 1836, the trustees were evenly split on the question of the merger and a deadlock ensued.[121] Finally, in 1838, a pro-Athenaeum ticket, led by Verplanck, swept the annual election. By the terms of an agreement finalized in July of that year, the New York Athenaeum used its remaining funds to purchase for its members 316 Society Library shares and transferred to the Society all of its books, periodicals, and real estate.[122] The movement party was now in a position to effect the changes it had been advocating since the beginning of the controversy.

In the 1840s and 1850s, the new trustees instituted a number of the broader reforms that had been promised in the course of the electoral campaigns of the 1830s. In 1840, for example, the hours of the reading room were extended to ten o'clock in the evening, and in 1856 the Society began printing and circulating for the first time annual reports of the condition of the library.[123] The complexion of the board itself, however, changed little during this period. For the most part, it remained a "closed borough" in which men from the city's wealthiest and most prominent families, usually in their forties or fifties, were nominated and elected without opposition.[124] Terms of service, however, tended to be shorter. In the first three decades of the century, for example, only three of thirty-five trustees served for five years or less. Between 1840 and 1870, approximately half of the sixty-seven board members served five years or less. With the increased pace of economic activity, it was increasingly common for the city's elite, in the words of Verplanck's address to the Mercantile Library Association in 1831, and echoed in one of the pro-Athenaeum pamphlets a few years later, to pursue their social and cultural interests "in intervals snatched from business."[125]

The trustees after 1838 achieved a measure of success in expanding the Society's membership. Before the election, the Library had just 420 subscribers. Just four years later that number had risen to 1,120, including approximately 165 members of the Athenaeum who joined under the terms of the merger.[126] In context, however, this increase appears less impressive. For example, in 1794, at the height of the Society's prosperity in the eighteenth century, when the city's population was approximately thirty-two thousand, there had been 965 shareholders. This was only 155 less than the number of subscribers in 1842, by which time the city's population had increased almost tenfold.[127] Moreover, other libraries were growing at a much faster rate. That same year, for example, the Apprentices' Library had 1,830 members, and the Mercantile Library Association had 3,372.[128] One reason the Society Library was less attractive than it might have been is that the trustees consistently refused to lower the cost of a share. In fact, for a brief period in 1841 and 1842 they actually raised the price from twenty-five to forty dollars.[129] Despite all the rhetoric during the campaigns of the 1830s calling for inclusivity and public spirit, the new leaders were quite as exclusive, as "snug and private," as their predecessors. In

1839, the year after it assumed control, the new board deemed "inexpedient" a request to grant access to the collection to the teachers of the Public School Society.[130]

Another of the pro-Athenaeum faction's campaign promises had been to provide adequate cataloging of the Library's holdings. The Society published a new catalog in 1838, the first since 1813 and another twelve years later. During that period, the collection grew from approximately twenty-five to thirty-five thousand volumes.[131] By 1850, it was the largest library in the city, although the Astor Library, which opened to the public in 1854, soon surpassed it.[132] The catalogs in 1838 and 1850 were the first to provide a subject arrangement of the collection, and the most striking difference between the two, aside from the increase of about ten thousand volumes, was a marked decrease in the titles classed as fiction. In 1838, there were 726 entries under novels, about 8.4 percent of the collection, and in 1850 that number had declined to 389, or 3.3 percent of the collection.[133] The Society's new leadership purposefully removed fictional works from the shelves in fulfillment of its campaign promise to develop a collection that was more substantial, more improving than a popular circulating library. This was a remarkable policy that was directly contrary to the trend in public libraries during this period. Fiction in public collections continued to be a controversial issue throughout the nineteenth century, but at the same time that they decried the public's appetite for popular novels, librarians and library managers begrudgingly purchased them in increasing numbers. In the Apprentices' Library, for example, the proportion of "novels, tales, and romances" quadrupled during roughly the same period, from just four percent in 1833 to sixteen percent in 1855.[134]

The rate at which the collection grew after 1838 shows the extent to which the new trustees were able to reinvigorate the Society Library. The relatively modest rise in the membership, however, and especially the decrease in works of fiction, suggest the ambiguity of their success. They sought to develop the Library within the context of an increasingly obsolete and discredited model of cultural leadership. By the 1840s, the era had passed in which New Yorkers assumed that elites, by virtue of their superior breeding and refinement, should lead the city's cultural institutions. The spirit of Jacksonian democracy, as well as competitive pressures within the cultural marketplace, demanded that readers' tastes should help guide the development of a public library.[135] However distasteful it seemed to the Society Library board, the public wanted fiction, and the decline in fiction was a symptom of their inability to recognize that the Library was operating in a radically changed environment. This is not to argue that the rhetoric of the pro-Athenaeum trustees in the campaigns of the 1830s was insincere. Rather, they were inspired by the spirit of the times, but were unable to come fully to terms with its realities.

Bray's library and the early history of the New York Society Library reveal critical shifts in the ways that authority, knowledge, and the public were conceived as New York grew from a colonial seaport town to a commercial city in a democratizing nation. Bray's library was founded in a monarchical, hierarchical world in which authority emanated from the Crown and the Church, in which knowledge was constrained by theology, and in which a public sphere was only just emerging. The Society Library in the eighteenth century represented a republican challenge to that world. Its founders sought to loosen the bonds of hierarchy, pursue enlightened knowledge, and broaden the public it served beyond the traditional gentry. By the 1830s, however, the Library was overtaken by the logic of that republican impulse. It seemed elitist and anachronistic in a commercial, democratic, liberal society that defined itself in opposition to stasis and hierarchy. In the decades that followed, New York's first public library was overshadowed by institutions that increasingly appealed not to readers' public spirit, but to their tastes as consumers.

2

Books for a Reformed Republic

The Apprentices' Library in Antebellum New York

In 1785, a group of upstanding master craftsmen founded the General Society of Mechanics and Tradesmen. The Society began as a fraternal organization whose primary purpose was to aid members who had fallen on hard times. In 1820, it started a library for the use of the city's apprentices. By 1865, the library had become its most important function.

The early development of the Apprentices' Library of New York City occurred during a period of unprecedented political, economic, and social change. The franchise was rapidly expanded until all adult white males, including the foreign-born, had the vote. Methods of craft production gradually gave way to a factory system based, in part, on the unskilled labor of women, children, and immigrants. The traditional republicanism embodied in the craft system competed with the values associated with modern liberalism. In response to these and other changes, a wide-ranging reform movement undertook a myriad of efforts aimed at educating and guiding what appeared to be an unreliable, even threatening work force and electorate. The development of the Apprentices' Library before 1865 reflects many facets of this reform movement.

The history of the library during this period also illustrates trends and practices in antebellum public libraries and librarianship. Its readership expanded rapidly and eventually comprised not only young apprentices but also any member of the reading public who paid a small annual subscription. The librarian, who was initially little more than a clerk, became more of a professional whose task it was to manage and facilitate access to the collection. Use of the books was enhanced by the publication of classed catalogs. The library's holdings grew substantially and gradually included a significant amount of fiction. Moreover, the collection sheds light on the educational aims of antebellum reform movements. The early history of the Apprentices' Library therefore illustrates important aspects of reform in industrializing America and the evolution of public libraries before the rise of modern, tax-supported institutions.

The General Society of Mechanics and Tradesmen was founded on November 17, 1785, and was incorporated by the State of New York on March 14, 1792.[1] Membership was limited to craftsmen who were at least twenty-one years of age. The by-laws also required that a candidate be proposed by two members who could attest to his "industry, honesty, and sobriety," and be approved by two-thirds of the membership. There was an initiation fee of five dollars, and monthly dues were twelve and a half cents.[2] The address used at the initiation ceremony urged that new members "let sobriety, industry, integrity, and uprightness of heart continue to be the ornaments of your name."[3]

The original aims of the General Society were typical of the craft benefit societies that flourished during this period. These groups combined the functions of a private charity with the camaraderie of a fraternal lodge. Normally craftsmen in a particular trade would band together and pay dues into a common fund. Members or their dependents would then be entitled to assistance in times of economic distress. Before the days of insurance companies, pensions, and government relief, craft benefit societies were an important source of aid during the recurring depressions of the early nineteenth century. Although the Society was permitted to lend money to members and nonmembers, its "leading motive" was to "relieve the distressed of its members that may fall in want by sickness, or other misfortunes." Four "overseers of the indigent" were elected annually to appropriate aid to destitute members or the widows and orphans of deceased members.[4] In an apparent reference to these appropriations, the initiation address enjoined members of the Society "on its private transactions [to] be as silent as the grave."[5]

The General Society celebrated and idealized the centrality of labor and the craft community. Besides their charitable activities, the brothers played a prominent part in the festivities that marked patriotic holidays in the city, carrying banners emblazoned with their motto "By Hammer and Hand All Arts Do Stand."[6] The Society's motto embodied the essence of what classical economists such as David Ricardo termed the labor theory of value. The theory held simply that labor produces all wealth, that all material value in the world is solely the product of the producer's toil. It was widely popular throughout the nineteenth century, in part because it was so expansive and ambiguous; almost anyone except a banker, a speculator, or a landlord could claim to belong to the producing classes.[7] Its

Seal of the General Society of Mechanics and Tradesmen

corollary, at least for the members of the General Society of Mechanics and Tradesmen, was that, in the words of President Edwin Dobbs in 1878, "all the progress made in the world was made by mechanics."[8] Whereas the merchants and professionals in the Society Library tended to look down upon those associated with manual labor, the brothers in the General Society considered it a badge of honor. Self-improvement, self-culture for the upright mechanic as well as his apprentices, always meant rising within, not out of, the mechanic class.

Members of the Society at least early in its history considered the craft system of production the bulwark of sturdy republicanism, the embodiment of moderation, simplicity, reciprocity, and civic virtue. The virtuous craftsman and citizen conducted his affairs with due regard for the public weal and guarded the republic against the corrupting influences of the greed and luxury associated with unbridled commercialism.[9] The craftsman's workshop, in which the master was a fellow worker as well as an employer and was bound to his employees by reciprocal obligations, was a microcosm of the ideal polity. Members of the Society during these early years so conflated the values of the craft community and the virtues of the republic that, in the words of Sean Wilentz, "as far as they were concerned, republicanism and the system of 'the Trade' were so analogous as to be indistinguishable from each other."[10] Long after craft production had waned, particularly in times of economic distress, the General Society continued to extol the republican virtues of the artisan. President Ira Hutchinson, in his inaugural address in 1858, blamed the severe depression in 1857 on "the banker, the merchant, and the speculator," and lamented that "the simple fact that labor is disreputable" had engendered an aristocratic "system that has destroyed every spark of humanity in the Old World, and . . . is wide-spreading and deep-rooting in this new republic!"[11]

By the time the Apprentices' Library was founded in 1820, however, changes were already occurring that would eventually render this artisanal ideology obsolete. Industrialization was already transforming many of the trades. The workshop in which the master worked side by side with his journeymen and apprentices was being eclipsed by a factory system in which unskilled laborers, often women, children, and immigrants, fashioned goods through a division of labor. Skilled artisans became production workers who performed repetitive tasks for wages and thereby lost their economic independence. Master craftsmen became capitalists who took no part in the production process and concerned themselves solely with the tasks of management and distribution.[12] Instead of celebrating the centrality and mutuality of the trades, many employers placed a greater emphasis upon wealth and personal advancement. An emerging liberal ideology held that competition between conflicting interests ultimately redounded to the public good. It celebrated honest ambition, equality of opportunity, and the autonomy of the individual.[13]

This effected profound changes in the lives of working men and women in New York City and across the nation. The presumed republican harmony of the traditional system of apprenticeship slowly gave way to new economic relationships in which the interests of labor and capital were inherently at odds. During the same period, electoral laws were rapidly liberalized until all white males, including the foreign-born, were allowed to vote. New York State, for example, had, with minor exceptions, universal white male suffrage by 1822.[14] To many the political destiny of the new nation seemed to be in the hands of an uneducated and potentially disaffected laboring class. By 1820, these developments had begun to produce tensions and fears that sharply contradicted the idealized view of the artisanal republic.

In response to these perceived threats, voluntary associations of substantial, public-spirited citizens undertook a variety of reform efforts. Although most reformers were evangelical Protestants, it is difficult to generalize about the antebellum reform movement, since it encompassed reactions to so many social, political, and economic conditions.[15] Many historians, however, have noted two fairly distinct strains within antebellum reform. One element, which was most prevalent before the 1830s, sought to impose external controls upon the behavior of the working class.[16] These reformers hoped to forcibly remake industrializing America into their own vision of a productive, moral, pious, and orderly society. Certainly the most significant example of this coercive aspect of reform is the campaign to abolish the sale and consumption of alcohol. Before the rise of the factory system, social drinking was commonplace in the typical artisan's workshop. The master often imbibed with his journeymen and apprentices, and the practice was normally not frowned upon, provided it was done in moderation. As master craftsmen became industrial employers, they became increasingly concerned about the effects of alcohol in the workplace. The first temperance society was organized in Moreau, New York, in 1808, and by 1833 there were approximately four thousand such organizations with more than a half million members nationwide. Their aim was not simply to curb the use of alcohol but to prohibit it altogether.[17]

A more dramatic example of coercive reform involves the treatment of criminals and the administration of penitentiaries. Antebellum prison reformers sought to rehabilitate lawbreakers through extraordinarily harsh discipline. In the state prison in Auburn, New York, for example, prisoners were kept in solitary confinement at night and forced to work in complete silence all day. Any infraction of the rules was punishable by flogging. Radical proponents of this system proposed that it be applied to factories, orphanages, schools, and even private homes. Louis Dwight, the founder of the Boston Prison Discipline Society, predicted its adoption would help ensure "order, seriousness, and purity."[18] Although this is an extreme example, it aptly illustrates the repressive character of certain antebellum reforms.

There was, however, another side of the reform movement that was less coercive and more progressive. This humanitarian aspect of reform was most prominent in the three decades before the Civil War. Although issues such as temperance continued to enjoy widespread support, other concerns began to occupy antebellum reformers. The two major reform movements of the period, the campaigns to abolish slavery and to extend political and other rights to women, reveal a more optimistic and democratic approach to effecting change. In a sense, the goals of these later reformers were not radically different from those of men such as Louis Dwight. They, too, yearned for order, seriousness, and purity, but the means they employed were less coercive, and they looked to the future with more hope than fear. Whereas the earlier generation of reformers intended to force others to help themselves, those who followed them were more inclined to help them help themselves. The General Society's Apprentices' Library was part of this more humanitarian element within antebellum reform.[19]

Education was the most important means of self-help that reformers sought to make available to the less fortunate. Throughout the first half of the nineteenth century, they organized free school societies in many cities to educate the children of the urban poor. They also lobbied state and local governments to establish tax-supported school systems.[20] Moreover, these efforts were by no means directed solely at the young and the indigent. Throughout the antebellum period there was an unprecedented movement to educate all ages and classes within society. Museums, libraries, and lyceums, which sponsored lectures and debates, were established in villages, towns, and cities throughout the country to provide universally accessible means of self-improvement.[21]

Reformers established these educational institutions for a variety of reasons. They saw education as a bulwark of democracy. Without it, an illiterate electorate would fall prey to demagogues, and elected officials would be unable to carry out their public duties wisely and effectively. Related to this was a more general focus on mental improvement. The ideal citizen was not simply literate, but well-informed and well-rounded culturally as well; he was familiar with current events, fine literature, and the principles of modern science. Antebellum educational reform was also concerned, indeed preoccupied with moral improvement. Civic and religious education would help combat the crime and vice that reformers came to fear in industrializing urban areas. Education would provide an alternative to drinking, gambling, and other dangerous and immoral pursuits. Finally, on a more practical level, vocational instruction was a means of economic advancement. With an education in mechanical principles, for example, a young apprentice or journeyman could learn to compete successfully in the marketplace and thus contribute to the general prosperity. The founders of the Apprentices' Library had all of these educational purposes in mind in 1820.

As the various antebellum reform campaigns began to gain momentum, interest in the more traditional activities of the General Society began to wane. For most of 1819, so few members attended the monthly meetings that there was never a quorum to conduct business. In March of that year, a special committee was appointed to "inquire whether any, and if any, what arrangements can be made for the education of the children of indigent members." Reporting nearly a year later, the committee strongly recommended founding a school, and a second committee was then charged with hiring a teacher and renting rooms. The original committee also urged another course of action, "from which, if properly conducted, results equally beneficial will doubtlessly follow, to wit, the establishment of a Library for the use of the apprentices of mechanics generally." Its purpose would be to provide for "the gratuitous reading of elementary, moral, religious, and miscellaneous books, and others as may have a tendency to promote them in their several vocations." A library committee of nine members was appointed to make the necessary arrangements.[22] The founding of the school and library signaled the beginning of a new and more active role for the General Society. It also began a debate within the Society over its primary purpose. In the decades before the Civil War, less attention was accorded its original goal of "reliev[ing] the distressed of its members that may fall in want by sickness, or other misfortunes," as the Society concentrated its efforts more upon maintaining and improving the library. By 1865, the General Society was similar in many respects to the myriad of other reform organizations devoted to education.

In March 1820, Thomas Mercein, a master baker and the chairman of the Library Committee, wrote a letter to William Wood requesting his advice. Wood, a prosperous merchant and philanthropist from Canandaigua, New York, played a leading role in establishing apprentices' libraries in Boston, New Orleans, and Montreal. He subsequently traveled to New York and helped solicit financial support and donations of books from the city's employers. The library officially opened on November 25, Evacuation Day, an important patriotic holiday that celebrated the British withdrawal from the city during the Revolution. A large audience attended the ceremony, including the mayor and members of the Common Council and state legislature. Apprentices later in the day borrowed nearly three hundred books from a collection of approximately four thousand donated volumes.[23]

Mercein delivered the keynote address. Parts of his speech reflect the civic-minded, craft-conscious character of the General Society. He celebrated patriotism, craft pride, and artisanal republicanism. Mercein stressed, for example, the "importance and respectability" of the city's artisans and referred to the library as one of "the securities which we are planting around the fortress of Liberty, erected in the glorious and triumphant struggle of the Revolution." There were also allusions to the traditional paternal role of a master toward his apprentices. The library would be a place where young men could acquire "those sound and commendable habits that will mold the character, and elevate it to a standing equally congenial to individual and general happiness." Yet, he also emphasized other values more closely associated with modern liberalism. Mercein assured the apprentices in the audience that their "opportunities [were] great and liberal"; that "industry, ardour, sobriety, and perseverance will lead to successful competition . . . [and] prosperity."[24] The founding of the library suggests the beginning of a subtle shift in the values espoused by the General Society.

The various purposes of the library, as explained by Mercein, closely reflect the aims of antebellum educational reform organizations generally. First, it would strengthen American democracy by enabling young men to fulfill "the representative and official capacities, which they may find it necessary to assume, in a government like ours." "Ignorance and despotism have shown their kindred qualities." The library would also be culturally enriching, producing well-rounded, self-cultured readers, as they joined "the march of education, literature, and science." In addition, the books would provide moral guidance. Mercein urged the apprentices to be sober and industrious and "avoid the alluring but fatal paths of vice and dissipation." Finally, he implied a practical, vocational purpose for the library, calling it a "source of rational and useful information," and praising "new combinations and new discoveries . . . constantly developed in the useful arts."[25] Mercein's address reflects the confidence of the antebellum reform movement that educational opportunity improved both the individual and society.

Some of the rules and regulations adopted for the Apprentices' Library in 1820 would seem rather onerous to modern public library readers. Borrowing privileges were available at no cost to any apprentice who was able to "produce from some responsible person, a certificate that they are worthy of confidence, and guarantying the safe return, in good order of all books." Loans circulated for two weeks and could be renewed. Two volumes of duodecimos or one volume of octavos, quartos, or folios could be checked out at one time. Overdue fines were assessed at three to twelve-and-a-half cents a week, depending on the size of the book. The borrower or his guarantor was liable for the entire value of a book not returned within a month. The library was opened from six until nine in the evening, but closed on Sundays. A separate reading room was provided for newspapers and magazines, and the rules for this room were particularly strict. "No conversation [was] allowed . . . under any pretense whatever." Smoking and spitting on the floor were prohibited, and "all boys admitted . . . must have clean hands, face, and shoes, and sit with their hats off."[26] New regulations published in 1833 required apprentices to check out and return books only one evening a week; each was assigned a day according to the first letter of his last name. The regulations also stated that the "librarian is particularly directed to withhold books from any coming to the library with dirty hands."[27] The General Society was eager to help young apprentices help themselves, but only under the strict supervision of their betters.

The library grew steadily in the 1820s, both in terms of the number of readers and the size of its collection. As it developed, the membership debated the manner in which it would be funded and the role it would play relative to the original purpose of aiding members of the Society who had fallen upon hard times. A special committee was appointed in 1830 to inquire into "extending the usefulness of the Mechanics' Society . . . so far as it relates to education generally, and the application of the Sciences to the Mechanic Arts."[28] The committee recommended erecting a new building in order to enlarge the school and the library. It also suggested instituting a series of free lectures on science and establishing a vocational school for apprentices to teach mathematics, drawing and design, architecture, and engineering. Its report urged that "every dictate of duty and of patriotism, every impulse of Mechanic pride" required the Society to adopt this more expansive role. The committee estimated that $20,000 to $25,000 would be required and proposed that it be raised by subscription from the city's craftsmen. Their report emphasized that "they do not contemplate in any manner to impair the general funds," which were "pledged to the sacred cause of charity."[29] The Society adopted most of these changes. In 1832, it purchased a building on Crosby Street and expanded the school and the library. In 1833, it began an annual series of free lectures.[30]

The expansion certainly increased the library's usefulness, but it did not involve substantial alterations in the way the library was administered or the role it played within the General Society. The report of the Library Committee for 1830 however, which was appended to the special committee's report, urged more fundamental changes. In effect, it recommended that the school and library become the Society's primary functions. Without them, the General Society would be nothing "more than a mere common *benefit society* . . . an old, venerable matron, sore beset to find means

Membership certificate of the General Society of Mechanics and Tradesmen, probably from the 1840s, illustrating the Society's dual mission. A brother on the left offers a widow support and sympathy, while another on the right introduces a boy to the Society's "twin daughters," the free school and the library. (Courtesy of the General Society of Mechanics and Tradesmen)

to satisfy its widowed dependents, and its host of juvenile starvelings." Its "twin daughters," the school and the library, had "increased in splendour, they yearly renew their age and add to their lustre, until in their brightness and beauty the matron is almost eclipsed."[31] The Library Committee proposed that the Society expand dramatically and focus its efforts on educating the city's apprentices.

In order to "lay a sure foundation for the preservation of the library and its gradual increase," the committee identified three potential sources of income. It recommended that apprentices be charged an initiation fee of twenty-five cents, that journeymen who had been readers when they were apprentices be admitted for a modest annual subscription of one dollar, and that members of the Society also pay a dollar annually to use the library.[32] Only the last of these proposals was adopted. For a time after

1830, there was a separate fund that consisted of the members' annual fees, the interest on which was included in the library's appropriation.[33] The response to the Library Committee's report in 1830 suggests tensions within the General Society over the future role of the library. Members disagreed over the manner in which it should be funded and whether it should become the Society's primary function.

Over time, a majority came to adopt the committee's view that education should be the General Society's most important purpose. This is clearly indicated in a comparison of the annual appropriations for charitable pensions and the library. In 1847, the first year for which figures are available, $2,900 was spent on pensions, while the library received only $1,000. In 1854, $3,100 was allocated for pensions, and $2,300 was set aside for the library. Finally, in 1865, the library's appropriation was $8,000, and $5,075 was paid out in pensions.[34] Thus, while the members spent progressively more for both education and fraternal charity during this eighteen-year period, the proportions changed significantly, until considerably more money was appropriated for the former than for the latter. By the Civil War, the library was clearly, in the words of President Noah Worral, "the most notable feature of our Society."[35]

The Library Committee's report for 1830 is also significant in that it proposed that certain journeymen be allowed the use of the library for an annual fee. This was the first time the Society considered charging a subscription and admitting anyone other than members and apprentices. Although this proposal was initially rejected, it was later adopted, apparently for financial reasons. The library was evidently affected by the Panic of 1837, a severe depression that lasted through 1843. The numbers of readers rose from 1,643 in 1837 to 1,844 in 1843, while, at same time, appropriations for new books were limited by the increased demand for charity for the Society's indigent members. Under these conditions, the library, according to the committee report for 1842, "was not and could not be self-sustaining."[36] A new source of income was needed to help maintain the collection.

On February 7, 1842, the state legislature passed an act authorizing a change in the General Society's charter. It permitted the Society to admit persons other than members or apprentices to use the library for an annual subscription.[37] Initially, subscribers were charged just one dollar annually. The regulations in 1855 required that employers pay two dollars, but by 1865 all subscribers paid that amount.[38] They did not need to be artisans; any "suitable person" was allowed access. Although the number of "pay readers" increased steadily over the years, before the Civil War they were always far outnumbered by the free readers. In 1851, the first year in which these statistics were included in the annual reports, there were just eighteen subscribers, and by 1854 that number had risen to only thirty-nine. In 1860, there were 199 pay readers, and in 1865 there were 829. At no time during this period, however, were subscribers more than one quarter of the total readership.[39] Nonetheless, the admission of men and women who were not artisans was a significant departure for the General Society. It indicates the Society had lost some of its craft-conscious character and that the library itself was no longer solely a charitable institution. It was, in addition, source of income and potentially a means of self-improvement for members of the reading public outside of the craft community.

In part with the additional funds from the annual subscriptions, the Society was able to expand its educational efforts in the 1840s and 1850s. In 1845, it inherited the personal collection of Benjamin Demilt, a member of the special committee in 1830. According to the terms of Demilt's will, it was to be maintained separately, "to be used and improved as a pay library."[40] In 1854, the Demilt collection became a noncirculating "reference" collection.[41] Members and subscribers were allowed to use it at no cost, but free readers, apprentices had to be at least sixteen years of age and were required to pay an annual subscription of fifty cents.[42] In his inaugural address in 1857 President Thomas Earle advised that the collection be more effectively advertised, since it had "not been as productive as the donors anticipated." The Demilt Library seems to have been intended solely for the cultural improvement of the Society's readers. The collection contained, in Earle's words, "little of light literature."[43] Of 895 titles in an 1855 catalog, none were classified as "novels, tales, romances, etc.," although there were fifteen works of "prose fiction" and seventy-six works of poetry. A little more than a third of the collection was classed as "history and geography," while somewhat more than a quarter of it comprised "mental and moral science," a very broad class that included philosophy, music, literature, and fine arts.[44] Earle suggested that it would have been more popular if Demilt had not required in his will that it be maintained by subscriptions.[45]

In 1850, both libraries moved into new rooms after the construction of an addition to the north wing of the building on Crosby Street. Extensive improvements were financed, in part, by a donation of $7,000 from Benjamin Demilt's sisters, Sara and Elizabeth.[46] This expansion was the most important event in the library's early history. The reopening was marked by a dedication ceremony on September 23, at which journalist and editor Mordecai Noah delivered the keynote address.[47]

In explaining the public purposes of the library, Noah touched upon many of the same themes and values in Thomas Mercein's speech at its opening thirty years earlier. He stressed, for example, the importance and respectability of the craft community and advised parents that "a knowledge of the mechanical arts, steadily and industriously carried out, must . . . be forever . . . the true road to independence."[48] Further, the founding of the library was an act of patriotism as well as charity. The "rapid progress of our country in arts, civilization, literature, commerce, and science" was due, "above all, [to] that free education which visits all alike . . . and places mankind on an equality in all that relates to genius and intellect." Moreover, the nation's apprentices in particular needed the means for self-improvement in order to carry out their civic duties as citizens in a democracy. Noah maintained that "it has become apparent that the destinies of our country are finally to be placed under the control of the mechanics and laboring men of the Union," and looked forward to the day when "well-educated mechanics will . . . command the highest stations in the Government." Like Mercein, he also placed considerable emphasis upon the benefits of competition, for both the individual and the nation. He held that "the great secret of [America's] success" was the fact that "each man is for himself, and the energy of each combined constitutes the wealth and power, the genius, resources, and permanency of the republic."[49]

In some respects, however, Noah's address was perhaps less optimistic than Mercein's. There was in it an element, an undertone of anxiety and a desire in part to use the library to control as well as to empower, to educate young workers. In 1820, Thomas Mercein simply advised young men to "abjure the path of vice." Thirty years later, Mordecai Noah warned that, without an institution such as the library to provide constructive recreation, they would be "scouring the streets, visiting barrooms or theaters, mingling with idle, vicious companions."[50] An uneducated workforce could in fact threaten the very foundations of a democratic society. The Apprentices' Library would help protect American democracy from an ignorant, disaffected working class. After referring to the dominant role that workingmen were destined to assume in the governance of the republic, Noah asked, "in what will be our guarantee for the safety of the country? I answer, in the education and intelligence of this class of our citizens."[51] Parts of Noah's address, like Mercein's, expressed unbounded confidence in the country's ability to progress indefinitely, but there an undercurrent, a suggestion of pessimism in his optimistic vision of the future. In the decades to come, as class tensions increased, this mingling of fear and hope was typical of American reform movements.

In the 1850s and 1860s the Society changed how it defined gratuitous readers in ways that reflected critical shifts in economic and social relationships. Before this time, free readers were always referred to simply as "apprentices." In a new set of by-laws adopted in June 1855, they were redefined as "Apprentices of Mechanics and Tradesmen, and Youths employed as Apprentices of Mechanics and Tradesmen."[52] The new and seemly redundant definition apparently was intended to include employees who were simply wageworkers in factories, as well as those serving formal apprenticeships. Any young man employed in industry could use the library. In his inaugural address two years later, President Thomas Earle proposed another significant change. He recommended granting free access to "a class of operatives for whom no provision of this kind has ever been made . . . the large number of females engaged in the various employments connected with the mechanic and manufacturing interests."[53] This change was eventually adopted in 1861. The Library Committee's report for that year stated that the "usefulness of the library has been considerably extended" by the new rule and that "little, if any, inconvenience has arisen from admitting the females at the same time with the males."[54] Women were by far the fastest growing class of readers during this period. There were 200 in 1862, 606 in 1863, and 1703 in 1864. By 1865, there were 2,599 female readers, compared with 3,663 male readers.[55]

By the time of the Civil War, the General Society had altered its definition of free readers in its library in a manner that reflects a new, expanded role in antebellum reform. These changes tacitly acknowledged the precipitous decline of the traditional system of apprenticeships and the rise of modern forms of industrial production. The ideal of the harmonious artisan's workshop in which the master worked side by side with his apprentices had waned as more and more goods were fashioned in factories through mechanization and the division of labor. By the 1860s, brothers of the Society still firmly believed that "by hammer and hand all arts do stand," but they were much more likely to be charitable industrialists than benevolent master craftsmen. According to Thomas Earle in 1857, "the mission of the General Society of Mechanics and Tradesmen is to all the working classes."[56] Although it was still ostensibly a common benefit society, it had been completely transformed from its original character in the eighteenth century, when its primary purpose was to aid indigent members and their dependents. By 1865, it was similar to other liberal reform organizations that provided the means for self-help and self-improvement to the urban poor.

The 1860s were prosperous years for the library. The combined funding for the Demilt and Apprentices' Libraries increased from $2,898 in 1860 to $8,000 in 1865. The total number of volumes in both collections grew from 22,469 to 33,700. In 1860, there were 2,359 readers, and 47,756 volumes circulated. In 1865 there were 7,282 readers, and 135,840 volumes circulated.[57] The library was one of the most substantial in New York City during this period. In 1859, in his *Manual of Public Libraries, Institutions, and Societies in the United States,* William J. Rhees, the chief clerk of the Smithsonian Institution, listed only nineteen libraries in Manhattan with collections of more than ten thousand volumes. The Apprentices' Library ranked sixth with 19,026. The list also included two collections maintained by theological seminaries, one for a private college, Columbia, and another for the Free Academy, a new, publicly supported college. By far the largest library in New York was the Astor, established in 1848 with a bequest in the will of John Jacob Astor. Its collection totaled more than 80,000 volumes in 1859, but they were for reference only and did not circulate. The second and third largest, the New York Society Library with 35,000 volumes and the Mercantile Library Association with 31,647, were both subscription libraries. The Apprentices' Library was the only extensive circulating collection in the city that was free to working-class youths.[58]

At this time, most public libraries were still not free. In 1849, Charles Jewett, the librarian of the Smithsonian Institute, listed twenty-nine libraries supported by state governments in his *Notices of Public Libraries in the United States of America.* Of these, only thirteen were open to the public, and all of them loaned books only to members of the government or officers of the courts. Ten years later, Rhees reported 153 "state and city libraries." Many of these were public libraries in the modern sense of the term, free, tax-supported, circulating collections. Most were in New England, where state legislatures had passed laws in the late 1840s permitting municipalities to levy taxes to support them.[59] Rhees also reported at least twenty-three apprentices' libraries and thirty-four collections belonging to mechanics' institutes. The latter were educational institutions for urban workers that sponsored lectures, classes, and debates. Most also supported a library that was often free to apprentices.[60] After 1850, the popular conception of the term began to shift slowly, but free, circulating collections such as the General Society's were still relatively rare when the Smithsonian published Rhees's *Manual of Public Libraries.*

As libraries of all types multiplied and their collections grew, librarianship began to evolve into a profession. Early in the nineteenth century, the job was considered essentially clerical, requiring no special training or qualifications. In most colleges and universities, for example, it was usually assigned to a junior member of the faculty.[61] When the first tax-supported public library was established in Peterborough, New Hampshire, in 1833, the town's postmaster was its first librarian. However, as libraries attracted more readers and developed more extensive collections, librarians assumed more complex responsibilities and began to develop a sense of professionalism. The annual report of the Mercantile Library Association for 1851 stated that "'a librarian requires a distinct education upon the prominent parts of his profession—an education that can only be acquired by years of preparation and study.'"[62] Two years later, the world's first library convention was held in New York City to bring together "those believing that the knowledge of Books, and the foundation and management of them for public use, may be promoted by consultation and concert among librarians."[63] In 1859, in his *Memoirs of Libraries,* Edward Edwards listed eighteen "routine duties" of a librarian in order of their importance, including collection development, cataloging of books, and the preparation of catalogs.[64] Although the American Library Association was not founded until 1876, by the 1850s there was clearly a growing sense among librarians, if not the general reading public, that librarianship was a distinct and valuable profession.

This trend toward professionalization is evident in the history of the Apprentices' Library. The special committee in 1820 that first proposed establishing a library recommended that the teacher in the Society's school be given charge of the collection, in order to "save the expense of a librarian."[65] A librarian was in fact hired, but his duties appear to have been mainly clerical. According to the by-laws adopted in December 1823, a six-member Library Committee, elected annually by the members of the Society, was directed to "take charge of and generally superintend the concerns of the library [and] to employ and discharge librarians."[66] By 1855, new regulations stipulated that "the Libraries and Reading Rooms shall be under the care and administration of the Librarian." He was required to submit detailed monthly and annual reports enumerating, among other things, the total number of volumes in both libraries, the number of pay and free readers, and the number of overdue and damaged books. More menial tasks, such as lighting fires and shelving books, were delegated to an assistant librarian.[67]

A librarian's most important professional responsibility during this period was the preparation of a catalog. Because they were expensive to produce, printed catalogs were relatively rare in the antebellum period and were published mostly by larger institutions. They were frequently used by public libraries in part as a promotional tool, to solicit donations of books and recruit readers.[68] More important, they became a necessary means of navigating increasingly larger, more varied collections. In an editorial in 1855, the year in which the Apprentices' Library produced its first subject catalog, *American Publishers' Circular* proclaimed that during the previous half-century "almost every variety of literature found in the United States a reading public" and that "more books have been printed, sold and read here than in any other nation, of equal population, on the face of the inhabitable Globe!"[69] In order to properly, professionally serve these reading publics, a public librarian had to provide intellectual access to the library through a well-constructed catalog.

With very few exceptions, catalogs in the colonial period were simply alphabetic lists, usually with the author as the main entry. In 1807, the Library Company of Philadelphia produced a catalog with both an alphabetic listing by author and a classified index arranged under thirty broad subject headings. This classification was widely used by other libraries, although some adopted the arrangement employed in the catalog of the Mercantile Library Association of New York in 1844. Instead of broad subjects, its classed index consisted of a longer list of specific subject headings arranged alphabetically.[70] Regardless of the relative merits of the various classification schemes, their development helped to democratize public libraries by making their collections more accessible to the public. Readers could browse for books by topic and were no longer required to know the exact title or author of a work in order to find it. Cataloging was also becoming a distinct body of knowledge unique to librarians. As such, it was an important element in the professionalization of librarianship.[71]

The General Society's library printed six catalogs between 1820 and 1865. The first and third, published in 1820 and 1839, were arranged by title in roughly alphabetical order. For example, the first section listed all works beginning with the letter *A*, but not alphabetically. The second catalog, produced in 1833, was arranged in much the same manner, but was

Table 2.1: Total numbers of volumes, free and pay readers, and annual appropriations, 1820–1865

	Total Volumes	*Total Readers*	*Annual Appropriation*
1820	4-5,000	800	*
1830	7,697	1,576	*
1839	11,161	*	$1,200
1850	14,940	1,533	$1,250
1860	22,469	2,359	$2,899
1865	33,700	7,282	$8,000

Sources: Annual Reports of the Library Committee for 1839, 1850, 1860, and 1865. Report of the Special Committee, 1830.

Total volumes include the Demilt Library for 1850 through 1865. Annual appropriations do not include additional sources of income, such as the annual subscription fees.
* = Figures not available.

first divided into four parts by size: duodecimo, octavo, quarto, and folio. In all three, the title sometimes included the author's name. In 1820, for instance, two copies of the same work appear as *Guthrie's Geography* and *Geography by Guthrie.* Some titles were listed with a subject word first, as in *Geography (Introduction to).* An apprentice might have to know the title, the author, or the subject of a book, and even then he would have to browse under the first letter in order to find it.

The catalogs published in 1855, 1860, and 1865 were "classed" catalogs. The first two were divided into five parts. The first and second parts listed all works in the Apprentices' Library, except "novels, tales, romances"; and all the works in the Demilt Library, alphabetically by author and by title. The third and fourth parts were all the fiction in the Apprentices' Library arranged alphabetically by author and by title. The fifth part was a classed subject index of all the nonfiction works in both libraries. It consisted of nine major classes: theology, mental and moral science, political science, geography and history, mathematics, natural sciences, medical science, technology, and encyclopedias. Each major class was further divided into several subclasses. Geography and history, for example, had more than fifty subclasses, including the United States, all the countries of Europe, ethnology, Indians, and female biography. The major classes, the subclasses, and the titles within each subclass were not arranged in alphabetical order. The 1865 catalog added a sixth part that listed the books under the approximately five hundred subclasses found in the fifth part. In this part, the subclasses were arranged alphabetically.

Although these later catalogs, particularly their nonalphabetical, classed indexes, may have been somewhat difficult to use, they were vast improvements over their predecessors. They were designed, in the words of the preface to the 1855 catalog, to "furnish, to some extent, at least, the necessary guidance in selecting books, and also afford greater facility in finding a book, not only on any subject, but on any branch of a subject that one may desire to peruse."[72] For the first time, readers could select a book by topic, and they no longer needed to browse haphazardly through a roughly alphabetical list of titles to find a known item. The catalogs therefore offered greatly improved access at a time when the number of readers and the size of the collection were expanding rapidly. At the same time, they indicate that the General Society's librarians were employing skills unique to their profession.

The Apprentices' Library contained between four and five thousand volumes in 1820 and approximately eight thousand in 1833. The Apprentices' and Demilt libraries together totaled 17,931 volumes in 1855 and 33,700 in 1865.[73] It is difficult to compare the proportions of different subjects in the catalogs for these years, because the first two were simply roughly alphabetic lists of titles, and the second two included classed indexes. For the 1855 and 1865 catalogs, I simply counted the number of titles under each major class and selected subclasses, and the number of titles under "novels, tales, and romances," and calculated the percentage each represented of the total of both collections. For 1820 and 1833, I first selected a random sample of one hundred works from each catalog. I then assigned each title one of the nine major classes from the 1855 and 1865 indexes or classed them as fiction. In a sample of one hundred, the number in each of these ten categories is an estimate of the percentage of that major class within of the whole collection. If an item in the 1820 or 1833 sample was also in the Apprentices' or Demilt Library in 1855 or 1865, I used the major class heading from the later catalog. If it did not, I had only a brief title from which to infer the subject matter of a work, so that assigning a major class was in some cases problematic. Nonetheless, my sampling suggests some broad generalizations regarding the varying proportions of different subjects in the Apprentices' and Demilt Libraries during the period from 1820 to 1865.

Generally, the percentages of different classes changed relatively little in the four catalogs. By far the two largest major classes in all of them were geography and history and mental and moral science. Together they comprised at least half of the collection in each year. Theology was a some-

Table 2.2: Percentage by class of the total number of titles in the Apprentices' Library for 1820 and 1833, and combined totals of the Apprentices' Library and the Demilt Library for 1855 and 1865

CLASS	*1820*	*1833*	*1855*	*1865*
Geography and history	30	40	36	32
Mental and moral science	42	34	19	19
Theology	16	10	10	9
Political science	5	2	5	6
Natural science	1	6	5	5
Technology	1	4	5	6
Medical science	—	—	2	2
Mathematics	1	—	.59	.44
Encyclopedias	—	—	.36	.28
Novels, tales, and romances	4	4	16	20

what distant third, and proportionally it actually decreased slightly, from 16 and 10 percent of the 1820 and 1833 samples to 10 and 9 percent of the catalogs from 1855 and 1865. The remaining classes were very small. Political science, natural science, and technology each were never more than 6 percent of the collection for any year.[74] Medical science, mathematics, and encyclopedias were 2 percent or less of the total in all four years.

On the whole, therefore, political science, natural science, technology, medical science, mathematics, and encyclopedias constituted a very small proportion of the library. However, this generalization needs to be qualified in two important respects. First, the library in 1820 consisted entirely of donations, so the initial collection of books was determined solely by what members were willing to donate. More important, there were significant external constraints upon the areas in which the collection might have developed. It is not surprising that certain major classes were proportionally smaller, since publishers issued relatively few titles for those subjects during this period. For example, American publishers between 1819 and 1849 printed 636 works in history, but only thirty in mathematics and geometry.[75] However, it is still safe to generalize, for example, that the collection included few titles that, in the words of the 1820 report that recommended establishing a library, would "have a tendency to promote [apprentices] in their several vocations."

In his address at the dedication ceremony in 1850, Mordecai Noah provided an interesting, detailed exposition of the uses that the various classes of books in the library would serve. He suggested a course of reading for "a poor, little ragged apprentice boy" who wanted to take full advantage of the "rich repast spread before him." It begins with "fiction, wit and humor, always the first to whet the appetite for reading."[76] Popular fiction, that is, the titles listed separately under "novels, tales, and romances" in the 1855 and 1865 catalogs, made up a relatively small proportion of the collection, but increased significantly more than any of the major classes in the classed indexes. Fiction was only 4 percent of the samples for 1820 and 1833, but 16 and 20 percent of the combined libraries in 1855 and 1865. During this period there was also a dramatic increase in the works of fiction available for purchase. American publishers issued 128 such titles between 1820 and 1829, 290 between 1830 and 1839, 765 between 1840 and 1849, and 90 in 1850 alone.[77]

As Noah implied, novels, tales, and romances were intended to lure young readers into the library, "to whet the appetite for reading," but members of the Society never wholly approved of recreational reading for apprentices, especially earlier in the century. In 1828, for example, the Library Committee considered "the expediency of discontinuing hereafter the issuing of Plays, Novels and Romances; and report[ed] what proportion of such books compose the present library."[78] The librarian in 1857, W. Van Norden, reported that the free readers borrowed "a large proportion" of fiction, but he anticipated that that this would "in many cases, gradually change for the better." Moreover, he argued that such works nonetheless served a salutary purpose "by withdrawing them from idle and vicious associations, and cultivating a habit of spending their leisure" time in reading.[79]

Moreover, the distinction between fiction and "literature" was somewhat ambiguous. Several titles in the 1855 and 1865 catalogs, including *Robinson Crusoe*, *Don Quixote*, and *Ivanhoe*, that were listed under the subclass of prose fiction within the major class of mental and moral science also appear in the lists of novels, tales, and romances. More important, much popular fiction during this period served an explicitly moralizing purpose. Various antebellum reform movements used novels and short stories to dramatize their causes. The 1865 catalog, for example, included *Temperance Tales* by Lucius Manley Sargent, one of the leading temperance propagandists of his day.[80] Many other works, such as *Rising in the World* by T. S. Arthur or *The Mechanic's Bride* by William G. Cambridge, were also intended to guide and reform Noah's ragged apprentice boy.

Still, despite its popularity and its increase proportionally in the later catalogs, fiction was considered inferior to more substantial, self-improving reading.

The next step in Mordecai Noah's suggested course of reading was history. The major class of history and geography comprised 30 and 40 percent of the 1820 and 1833 samples, and 36 and 32 percent of the Apprentices' and Demilt Libraries in 1855 and 1865. It was the largest class in every year except 1820. Only seventy-five of a total of 2,795 titles within this major class in 1865 fell under the subclasses of geography or physical geography. There were also small subclasses for ethnography; correspondence; and antiquities, manners, and customs. Most of the others were for particular countries or regions, including Africa, Asia, China, and the Pacific, all of which contained both historical works and travel literature. By far the largest subclass was individual biography, with 371 titles listed. There were also subclasses for collective biography, with 125 titles, and female biography, with forty-eight. Ten separate subclasses dealt with the United States or North America. American history and travels alone had 203 titles. Noah explained that works in history were to be the "foundation" upon which the poor apprentice "builds his superstructure," after he had progressed beyond popular fiction.[81]

The end of Noah's course of reading was achieved when the apprentice "slides insensibly into a course of *belles-lettres* and polite literature . . . [and] becomes familiar with the fine arts." The major class that most closely approximates these subjects was mental and moral science, constituting 42 and 34 percent of the samples of the 1820 and 1833 catalogs and 19 percent of both libraries in 1855 and 1865. Mental and moral science was the most broad and eclectic of all the major classes. It included such subclasses as temperance, slavery, elocution, anecdotes, and games and sports. Most of them, however, dealt with some aspect of literature or philosophy. Miscellaneous literature was the largest subclass, with 149 titles, and practical ethics or morals was second with 119. Once he was thoroughly versed in the mental and moral sciences, Noah's "poor, little ragged apprentice boy . . . steps forward as accomplished a gentleman as many who have taken their degrees at Oxford and at Eton."[82]

For Mordecai Noah and for the members of the General Society, mental and moral science was the most important part of the library. Although it decreased at approximately the same rate that novels, tales, and romances increased, it was nonetheless the key major class in the collection. Its decline proportionally relative to fiction is explained by the need to attract young working men and women to the library, to draw them from, in Noah's words, "the streets, . . . mingling with idle, vicious companions." The General Society felt it necessary to lure morally susceptible youths from less constructive pastimes and also, after 1842, to compete with subscription libraries for readers who paid an annual fee. At the same time, mental and moral science was the essential major class in achieving the broad purposes of the General Society's public library.

The way in which the classed catalogs were organized sheds light on the self-image of the brothers of the General Society of Mechanics and Tradesmen and the role they envisioned for their library. Mental and moral science brought together a great variety of subclasses that, to a modern reader, would seem quite disparate. For Mordecai Noah and his audience in 1850, however, they were all essentially related in that they included the books a "ragged apprentice" would be expected to read in order to become "an accomplished gentleman." This was the fundamental aim in establishing the Apprentices' Library. For members of the Society, a gentleman was not a mere aristocrat. He was moral, productive, self-cultured, and fully prepared to carry out his civic duties in a democracy. Mental and moral science thus comprehended all of the qualities outlined, for example, in Thomas Mercein's address at the opening of the library in 1820, as well Noah's address thirty years later. What the Society members hoped to accomplish was to mold young workers in their own image, or at least in the image that they preferred to have of themselves. This goal was a hallmark of moral reform movements throughout the nineteenth century.

3

The Past in Print

History and the Market at the New-York Historical Society Library

On February 12, 1805, an address "To the Public" appeared in the *New-York Herald* and other local newspapers announcing the formation of "an association for the purpose of discovering, procuring, and preserving whatever may relate to the natural, civil, literary, and ecclesiastical history of our country and particularly of the State of New-York." The founders intended to build a library and thus solicited from the "liberal, patriotic, and learned" citizens of the city donations of books, magazines, newspapers, manuscripts, and other material relating to "History of any State, City, Town, or District."[1] In the decades before the Civil War, the New-York Historical Society discovered, procured, and preserved one of the finest collections of American history in the nation. The library of the Society sheds lights on both the public and private uses of history in the new republic and the ways in which the historical enterprise was sustained during this critical period.

The address also informed the public that "it will be our business to diffuse the information we may collect . . . by means of the press."[2] Like most historical societies, the New-York Historical Society periodically published primary documents from its library, as well as other material it deemed conducive to the public weal. Thus, it not only collected print but also played an active role in the print market. More so than any other public library in the city, the Society's collection must be considered in the context of the development of a broad and diverse print culture in the early republic. Its early history provides perspective on the public and private functions and effects of the printed word.

The Historical Society was founded by John Pintard, a trustee of the New York Society Library active in an array of local scholarly and civic organizations.[3] On November 20, 1804, Pintard called a meeting in City Hall attended by eleven "men of taste and refinement" who, according to the first minutes of the Society, agreed that its "principle design [would] be to collect and preserve whatever may relate to the . . . History of the United States in general and of this State in particular." The founding members then appointed a committee to draft a constitution and adjourned until December 10. Adopted at the following meeting, the constitution stipulated that new members would by admitted by a ballot vote of the membership at the quarterly meetings and pay an initiation fee of ten dollars and annual dues of two dollars. Officers—a president, two vice presidents, treasurer, and corresponding and recording secretaries—were elected annually. A seven-member standing committee, also elected annually, was responsible for soliciting donations to the library and for the overall direction of the Society. According to the by-laws adopted in April of the following year, guests were allowed to borrow from the collection if a member applied to the librarian and provided a receipt for the book or manuscript.[4]

Unlike other public libraries in the city, the Historical Society's librarian was also an annually elected, unpaid position. According to R. W. G. Vail, the Society's most recent official historian, he "had oversight of the day-to-day executive functions" until the office of director was created in an amendment to the by-laws in 1937.[5] In the very early years, however, the librarian had little to oversee. No books were purchased before 1809, and, despite the request for donations in the address "To the Public," very few were donated. The library really began in September of that year when John Pintard sold his extensive and valuable collection of primary and secondary material in American history to the Society at cost. The Historical Society's modest library during this period was shelved in space granted by the New York Society Library.[6] Before 1810, when Pintard was elected to the office, both associations in effect shared a librarian. John Forbes served as the paid librarian of the Society Library from 1794 to 1824 and the elected librarian of the Historical Society from 1805 to 1809. One month after purchasing Pintard's collection, the Society moved its library to the second floor of Government House, a municipal building at the tip of Manhattan, the first floor of which served as the city's customhouse.[7]

The New-York Historical Society was the second state historical society established in the United States. The address "To the Public" states that the founders were "encouraged to follow in this path by the honourable example of the Massachusetts Historical Society," which was organized by John Pintard's friend Jeremy Belknap in 1791.[8] The Massachusetts and New York associations, in turn, became models for what David Van Tassel termed a "national pastime." By 1860, there were sixty-five historical societies in the United States. In addition to numerous local societies, there was a state institution established in every state east of Texas except Delaware.[9] Typically, one founder, like Belknap or Pintard, provided the organizational talents and enthusiasm necessary to bring together a group of interested individuals. Their constitutions often mirrored the New-York Historical Society's and included provisions for an executive board to direct the society's activities, a corresponding secretary, and a librarian to develop a collection of books and manuscripts. Members tended to be affluent and well educated. Clergymen, physicians, merchants, and especially lawyers usually predominated.[10] According to George H. Callcott, in these state and local historical societies, "more than in the colleges, was the origin of historical association and professionalism."[11]

The eleven men who met in City Hall in 1804 to organize the New-York Historical Society were typical of the local elites who founded historical societies in other states and, to a great extent, those who joined the Society in its early years. Except for John Pintard, who lost his entire fortune in the Panic of 1792, all of them were wealthy.[12] All were college educated, most of them graduates of either Princeton or Columbia. Again with the exception of Pintard, all of them were highly successful professionals: Five were ministers, four were lawyers, and one, David Hosack, was on the faculty at Columbia. The founders were gentlemen scholars, men who were, in the words of librarian George Folsom in an early history of the Society, "esteemed in their day for professional skill, literary taste, and classical or scientific attainments."[13] Moreover, a number of them, namely, Pintard, Hosack, Samuel Miller, and DeWitt Clinton, were very active in a number of the city's learned or cultural institutions. Clinton, for example, helped found or support the Historical Society, the Society Library, the Literary and Philosophical Society, the American Academy of Fine Arts, the Lyceum of Natural History, and the Society for the Promotion of Useful Arts. Leadership in these kinds of organizations in New York City during this period tended to be shared among relatively few members of the local elite, in what Thomas Bender has termed "interlocking directorates at the top."[14]

Members joined the New-York Historical Society for a variety of related personal reasons.[15] Certainly one of the most important was simply sociability. The Society functioned in part as a social club in which the city's elite could gather and discuss topics of common interest. Moreover, being admitted as a member of a relatively exclusive organization served as recognition that one was in fact a member of an exclusive class. "Throughout the years," according to R. W. G. Vail, "membership carr[ied] with it a certain distinction."[16] Similarly, taking part in the Society's activities could serve as a means of affirming ones scholarly as well as social standing, of confirming ones status as a gentleman scholar. In a review of the second volume of its *Collections* in 1814, the *Analectic Magazine* poked fun at the Society's scholarly pretensions, suggesting that the list of the names of all 140 members was included only because they hoped to emulate, to "shine in the dignity of the F. R. S. [Fellows of the Royal Society]."[17] Last, and perhaps most important in terms of personal motivations, New Yorkers joined the New-York Historical Society simply because they enjoyed history. Discovering and procuring material that shed light on the past was an amusing avocation. But for a gentleman scholar, history had a distinct advantage over other forms of personal entertainment. It was self-improving as well as fun; it was "rational amusement." In an address before the Society in 1810, "The Benefits of Civil History," Hugh Williamson was merely stating a truism when he said that "history may be read with pleasure and advantage. It is not only the most amusing, but the most instructive part of human literature."[18]

Members also joined the New-York Historical Society as a matter of civic duty, in order to sustain an institution that promoted the common weal. It was for them self-evident that, aside from the personal pleasure it afforded, history served a valuable public function. President Gouverneur Morris, for example, in his inaugural discourse in 1816, observed that "we live in a period so enlightened, that to display the use of History would be a superfluous labour." Nonetheless, he and fellow members of the Society frequently labored to do just that. They believed generally that all forms of rational amusement inculcated public morality. In that same address, Morris held that "the influence of learning . . . and taste over the hearts and minds" of the people "promote[d] virtue and multipl[ied] the sources of social bliss." History, however, by its very nature was especially conducive to moral instruction. Gulian Verplanck, in his own presidential discourse in 1818, explained that by "looking to our own annals for examples of life, . . . in paying the tribute of . . . gratitude to virtue, we ourselves become wiser and better." James Kent, ten years later, reflected that "historical reviews have a salutary influence on the manners and morals of the times; for they help us . . . to rebuke selfish ambition, check false patriotism, and humble arrogant pretension."[19] History, particularly American history, fostered public morality by providing personal models for the citizen to emulate.

Because they were regarded as agencies for promoting the public good, even during this period of limited government, many historical societies receive some kind of government support.[20] The City of New York, for example, granted the Historical Society rent-free rooms for its meetings and its library, first in City Hall and later in Government House. However, the assistance the Society received was also due at least in part to the fact that, in the words of John Francis at the semi-centennial celebration of the founding, "though few in number, our founders included a rare amount of influence."[21] Certainly the most influential of them all was DeWitt Clinton. By the time he left the U.S. Senate in 1803, Clinton had become the most powerful politician in the state. Among other offices, he was mayor of New York City from 1803 to 1815, while simultaneously serving first as a state senator, then as lieutenant governor. Later he was governor from 1817 until his death in 1828. Aside from his role in the creation of the spoils system in American politics, he is best remembered for the Erie Canal, "Clinton's ditch," which was critical to the economic expansion of New York in the early nineteenth century.

Although it was John Pintard who first proposed consolidating the city's scientific and cultural organizations in the New York Institution, it was Clinton's political skill and influence that secured municipal patronage in 1815. The Historical Society moved there from Government House the following year. In 1814, Clinton obtained from the State a grant of $12,000 to be paid from a projected lottery for the support of literature and education. The Society's petition to the legislature for the grant, composed by the mayor, perhaps best expresses Clinton's and his friend Pintard's ambition to combine government support with the energy and enthusiasm of civic-minded individuals cooperating in voluntary associations. He wrote that if the Society, "comprehending a mass of information and talent . . . without any other excitement than a desire to be useful," had accomplished so much on its own, "what might we not effect if public bounty should be united with individual contribution."[22] This active support from the state's most powerful politician was a distinct advantage in the earliest years of the Society. In the words of George Folsom in his "Historical Sketch" in 1841, "the library still remains as . . . a monument of the earnestness with which Clinton furthered" the aims of the New-York Historical Society.[23]

The DeWitt Clinton Monument in Greenwood Cemetery (Courtesy of the photographer, Jonathan Wolfson)

The address "To the Public" in 1805 emphasized the Society's obligation to procure primary sources, that, "not aspiring to the higher walks of general science, we shall confine the range of our exertions to the humble task of collecting and preserving whatever may be useful to others."[24] Similarly, the preface to the first volume of the *Collections* (1811) stated that, "conformably to the professed objects of their institution," the editors had compiled "*materials* for historical composition," and the preface to the second (1814) lauded "the efforts of the Society in rescuing from oblivion documents which must constitute the materials for the use of the future historian."[25] In this sense, the public served by the New-York Historical Society was the reading publics of coming generations. Thus, President Luther Bradish, in his address at the dedication of a new building for the library in 1857, explained to the members and guests that "here will each succeeding age, for the instruction of those to come after it, bring its record of the current events of the time, [so that] the Genius of History from these accumulated treasures [may] construct its variegated but harmonious narrative."[26]

What the Society's collection offered to the reading publics of future generations was truth. Members often criticized historians of other nations, particularly classical authors, for recording myth instead of writing true history. Bradish, for example, in remarks at a meeting in 1849, warned that unless steps were taken to preserve the proceedings of the Common Council, local history "would become, if not utterly blank, at least as fabulous as the legendary history of infant Rome." In his discourse on "The Benefits of Civil History," Hugh Williamson held that "Herodotus himself, who is called the father of history, was a dealer in romance [who] sought to please rather than instruct."[27] The Historical Society, by contrast, dealt only in facts. John Francis, at the semicentennial celebration, praised the founders for appreciating that "the preservation of contemporary records was the data from which future history was to receive its true impress," while George Folsom, in his preface to the *Collections* in 1841, stressed that "we give [here] only the *materials* of history, the original documents to which historians must resort . . . and therefore naked facts . . . are all that can be expected in the volume." Only history based upon such data, upon primary sources, provided rationale amusement. In his address in 1816, Gouverneur Morris warned that without such material, it was, like the history of ancient Greece and Rome, "at best an entertaining novel, with the ornament of real names."[28]

The address "To the Public" stressed the difficulty of procuring and the consequent danger of losing forever documents relating to the early history of the state and the nation. The term used most often by the New-York Historical Society and other historical societies was *oblivion.* Clinton's petition to the State in 1814, for example, referred to "the destructive hand of time [that was] rapidly sweeping into oblivion many important objects of inquiry."[29] Such dramatic language was obviously crafted in part to win the sympathy and support of the legislature, but it is nonetheless remarkable what little was known about the early settlement of the state when the Society was founded. The address in 1805 posed to the public a long list of "queries . . . points on which the Society requests particular information." These included not simply minutiae of local history, such as the establishment of a town's first printing press and public libraries, but also more substantial and fundamental facts, including the date of the founding of New Netherlands and the years in which the first forts were built in Albany and New York.[30] However, unlike the states of Europe, whose early histories were forever shrouded in myth and romance, materials documenting the exploration and settlement of New York did in fact exist.[31] The Historical Society had to act quickly in order to "rescue from the dust and obscurity of private archives" the "fast perishing memorials of the earliest history of the commonwealth."[32] "Scattered among individuals," these sources were "for the most part inaccessible," so that "the proper depositories for those of value are the archives of public institutions."[33]

During its earliest years, the Society at times found it difficult to balance its dual responsibilities for providing access and ensuring preservation. For a time, the library was not accessible at all. During the War of 1812, the collection was packed in boxes and stored in a warehouse in anticipation of a British bombardment. When the books and manuscripts were finally unpacked and moved into the Society's rooms in the New York Institution in 1816, John Pintard reported that they were "very damp and molded after being cased up for two years."[34] In 1818, the by-laws were amended to prohibit the lending of any of the material under any circumstances. About the same time, the Society also hired its first assistant librarian, the first salaried employee of any historical society in the United States. Stephen B. Hutchins, "a young man of probity and well-known to some members," received one hundred dollars per year to assist in managing the collection and to open the library to the members on Wednesday and Saturday afternoons.[35]

Although he only served as librarian from 1810 to 1811, John Pintard was the person most responsible for the early development of the collection. Aside from his personal library that was purchased in 1809, he donated many very rare and valuable items to the Society, including one of only three known copies of the first map of the city, printed by William Bradford in 1731. Pintard also did most of the work involved in unpacking and arranging the books and manuscripts in the New York Institution. In a letter to his daughter about this time, he wrote that "it is our object to make our Library one of research for all that is curious and valuable, . . . like the extensive Libraries of the Old World, inestimably valuable to the erudite Scholar."[36] The first catalog, published in 1813, consists almost entirely of donations and lists approximately 4,265 books, 130 newspapers and periodicals, 134 maps, and a number of valuable manuscript collections, including the papers of William Alexander and Horatio Gates.[37] Pintard's friend John Francis, who was elected librarian from 1812 to 1818, later observed that it was "swelled in amount at least by . . . spelling books, . . .

sermons, . . . hymn books [and] lectures on rhetoric." He explained however, that the Society's intention was to preserve the intellectual production of the young republic, to do "service to the mental progress of the country in bringing together . . . the offspring of its authors, however widely scattered."[38] An article in the *Analectic* in 1819 "On the Means of Education and the Scientific Institutions of New York" regretted that the city "cannot boast of its public libraries," including the New York Society Library, but did concede that "the Historical Society has a most valuable, but not extensive collection."[39]

In fulfillment of its pledge "To the Public" in 1805 to "diffuse the information we may collect," the Society issued the first volume of its *Collections* in 1811. Its entry into the print market was just one small part of what historian David Van Tassel described as "a national obsession—documania." Before the Civil War, historical societies in the United States produced nearly two hundred volumes of primary documents. The New-York Historical Society during this period published two series, the first in five volumes between 1811 and 1829, and the second in four volumes between 1841 and 1859.[40] One object of this national effort of course was dissemination, to make the facts of the early history of the republic available to the people. Just as important, however, the historical societies generally regarded the print market as a means of preservation. At a time when rare books and manuscripts could be swept into oblivion by fire and other disasters, "the surest way," according to the editors of the Historical Society's first volume, "to preserve a record is to multiply the copies."[41] However, the Society could not diffuse everything in its library, and selection inevitably involves interpretation. The material collected in the *Collections* sheds light on how the members constructed history and on the broader purposes it served beyond simply instilling patriotism and inculcating public virtue.

The Society published a total of thirty-nine primary documents in the first two series. More than half, twenty-two of them, were sources from the Dutch colonial period. In part this was because the earliest years of European settlement were most in need of rescue from oblivion, "the dark period," according to John Romeyn Brodhead, the Society member who edited *Documents Relative to the Colonial History of New York*.[42] Just as important, however, was state pride. Throughout the antebellum period, states and regions competed for national leadership in a variety of ways, and one important means by which a state asserted its preeminence in the present was to chronicle its glory in the past. Thus, as the Empire State's merchants and early industrialists contended for economic supremacy within the Union, its historians and antiquarians sought to lay claim to the nation's republican legacy. New York enjoyed a distinct advantage in this respect. It was founded not by the monarchical British, but by sturdy settlers from the Dutch Republic.[43] This was stressed repeatedly in the *Collections* and in other publications of the Society, perhaps even more than the Massachusetts Historical Society, for example, eulogized the Pilgrims and Plymouth Rock. In his annual discourse in 1828, James Kent held that "an appeal to the simple and severe records of truth" would show that the state was settled by "grave, temperate, firm, persevering men, who brought with them the industry, the economy, the simplicity, the integrity, and the bravery of their Belgic sires." Three decades later, at the dedication of the new library, George Bancroft intoned that "the glory of the Dutch republic, . . . the republican liberty of the Netherlands . . . is ours, all ours."[44]

More than 40 percent of the titles published in the first two series of the *Collections* were, in fact, not primary documents. There were in total twenty-eight secondary works, almost all of them addresses delivered at the Society's annual meetings. A number of reasons explain why an organization ostensibly devoted to "the humble task of collecting and preserving" historical sources published so many historical essays. The "original contributions" in the *Collections* were in part an expression of cultural nationalism. In the early nineteenth century, much of what the American reading public read were either imported or reprinted titles by British writers. In fact, according to James Green, until at least the 1820s an American book was understood to mean not necessarily a book written by an American author, but one printed by an American press.[45] As late as 1845, Evert Duyckinck, editor, publisher and a member of the Historical Society's Committee on Print Publications, complained that "native authors were mutilated, despised, insulted" and "vampers up of English matter have got all the money."[46] Cultural nationalists, sensitive to the "taunts of transatlantic rivals," demanded that "the American mind must be up and doing."[47] John Francis, in his address at the dedication of the new library in 1857, boasted that New York "had furnished noble intellect and strong muscle in the work of colonial disfranchisement" and that the Society had effectively countered the efforts of British writers who had "nullified facts" of American history.[48]

Yet, the public purpose of publishing the annual discourses and other secondary works went beyond merely correcting the historical record for future generations. Although they rarely acknowledged it, members clearly understood that the facts did not speak for themselves.[49] Their addresses interpreted American history for the American reading public. In part, that interpretation, like the documents printed in the *Collections*, highlighted the role played by the state of New York. In the first volume of the second series, George Folsom lamented that "American historians have written with English prejudices, expiating with ardour upon the heroic enterprise and religious zeal that led to the colonization of Virginia and New England, while they have almost forgotten to record . . . the persevering efforts of the Dutch" in settling the New World.[50] Yet, ultimately the history of New York State was simply one part, however preeminent, of the history of the nation that the members interpreted in the Society's publications. Thus, Thomas DeWitt, in his address at a meeting in April 1848, spoke of "the lessons which our history unfolds," stressing that "no section of the country may make exclusive or towering claims over others," because they all exhibited "the spirit of liberty in its lofty aspirations." Similarly, in the preface to the fourth volume of the first series of the *Collections*, the editors expressed their hope that New York's "example [may] shed a salutary influence over her sister states," but emphasized nonetheless that "we are a united people . . . under the benign influences of republican institutions."[51]

The interpretation of American history offered to the American reading public in the Society's "original works" was by no means original. During the antebellum period, the nation produced and consumed a grand narrative that had as much to do with the future as the past and comprehended not just the United States but also the world.[52] One way of interpreting this interpretation is that it started with the present, with the republic civilizing the North American continent, and moved both back and forward in time and in and outward in space. The hardy, liberty-loving Dutch, in isolated settlements on the shores of the Hudson (along with, for instance, the Pilgrims on Plymouth Rock), had planted the seed of American republicanism. Yet, the American republic was not the end of American history, but future of the world. In his inaugural address in 1820, David Hosack stressed the importance of collecting in the library "every work connected with [our] history and literature," because "our political institutions [are] a source of remark and speculation in every civilized nation of the globe," while seven years later, Joseph Blunt spoke of "the glorious promise" that the United States "held out to mankind by her past history and present institutions."[53]

The grand narrative, however, was about more than simply the past, present, and future of republican government. Republicanism was just one part, one subplot, albeit the most important one, in the story of the progress of Western civilization. The grand narrative comprehended a constellation of presumably mutually reinforcing institutions or developments that included the printing press, commerce, science, and the Protestant religion. The New-York Historical Society's publications held, for example, that its library was "of an age . . . which witnessed the . . . progress of intellectual, moral, and religious liberty;" that the "whole tendency" of the republic's history was "to perpetuate the sway of reason, [and] to establish political, religious and commercial freedom;" that "the sceptres and crowns and regalia of kings" paled in importance to "the great discoveries of science, the great achievements of liberty, and the general progress of the human race."[54] Although the grand narrative linked the past with the future, it was essentially ahistorical. There was no causation in history, but rather Divine Providence. Alexander Bradford, in his annual discourse before the Society in 1845, offered a sweeping view of "the great movements of humanity," the "great current ever flowing onward," and demonstrated that its "Laws are divinely instituted, [and therefore] History is not only orderly and methodical, but full of wisdom." Charles King, president of Columbia College, in his address at the dedication of the library in 1857, was more succinct. The Society's collections "teach . . . that God, and therefore Truth, is in History."[55]

Aside from the public purpose that these "original contributions" fulfilled in interpreting history for the reading public, they served personal and institutional ends as well. The secondary works published by the New-York Historical Society provided both the Society itself and the aspiring gentlemen scholars who led it with the opportunity to "shine in the dignity of the F.R.S.," to demonstrate their supposed erudition in print. In a particularly caustic entry in his diary, member George Templeton Strong wrote that the "lectures and 'papers' it generates" were nothing more than "gaseous secretions of vanity and dilettantism."[56] Certainly many of the addresses before the Society would strike modern readers as insubstantial or even comical. For example, in his "Discourse on the Benefits of Civil History," which appeared in the *Collections* in 1814, Hugh Williamson pointed out that, although the earliest periods of Chinese history were lost in oblivion, it was "nearly certain" that Noah was the first emperor of China.[57] Even at the time, the reading public must have regarded some of the Society's publications as rather gaseous at best. The *Proceedings* for

1845, for instance, included a long "Report of the Committee on a National Name." It argued that *United States of America* was an insufficiently "distinctive appellation," that the country sorely needed a more elegant, sonorous name that would "prove efficient in History, Poetry, and Art." Despite its best efforts, the Society was unable to convince their fellow citizens to rename the republic the United States of Alleghania.[58]

Strong expressed his disdain for the Historical Society's "'scholars' . . . laboriously writing dissertations . . . on the First Settlement of the Township of Squankum" in the privacy of his diary.[59] On rare occasions, divisions within the Society appeared in public, in print as well. Certainly the most widely read work by any member was a good-natured, very funny burlesque of the Society's favorite subject, the sturdy, liberty-loving Dutch who founded New Netherlands. Washington Irving's *History of New York*, ostensibly written by Diedrich Knickerbocker, gave a nickname to the descendants of the original settlers, the first families of the city, that has stuck for over two centuries.[60] Dedicated to the Historical Society and published in 1809, the same year that Irving became a member, it sought "to rescue from oblivion . . . and to render a just tribute . . . to the many great and wonderful transactions of our Dutch progenitors." Knickerbocker was a voluble, eccentric antiquarian, "one of the *literati*" (which his landlord thought was a new political party), who, when he was not compiling his history, spent his time arguing with his friend, the librarian of the Society Library. He wrote that colony's early Dutch governors were "tranquil and inert," except of course for Peter the Headstrong (Peter Stuyvesant), "who defended the city by dint of his head." When Richard Nicolls demanded the surrender of Manhattan in 1664, the valiant burghers had "a most singular aversion to engage in a contest where they could gain little more than honour and broken heads" and immediately submitted to the British. However, the town's leading citizens later met in private and all vowed never to invite them to dinner.[61]

The Historical Society's *Collections* were, in a sense, in but not of the print market. The volumes were offered for sale, hopefully to cover the expense of publication and ideally to generate income to build the library. Yet, the primary purpose was not to realize a profit, but to diffuse and preserve historical sources and to make public the erudition of the Society's gentlemen scholars. Washington Irving's *History of New York*, by contrast, was a purely commercial endeavor and a highly successful one. Its success in the market explains why, even after Irving became one of the country's most beloved authors and the Society's most famous member, he

Diedrich Knickerbocker, illustration from the second edition of Irving's *History of New York* (1812) (Miriam and Ira D. Wallach Division of Art, Prints and Photographs, The New York Public Library, Astor, Lenox and Tilden Foundations)

was never quite forgiven for his early satire of the Dutch colonists. Knickerbocker's history was so popular with the reading public that the names of "the fathers of the New York colony . . . could scarcely be mentioned without creating a smile."[62] Members of the Society and the Knickerbocker elite resented not simply that Irving had cast the Dutch progenitors in a ridiculous light, but that he had done so in such a public fashion, in work circulated so widely in the print market.

Another form of publication in which divisions within the Society were made public were "privately printed" works. These were ostensibly private, circulated among the author's acquaintances and therefore divorced entirely from the market for print.[63] For example, *Procès Verbal of the Ceremony of Installation of President of the New York Historical Society*, published anonymously by Gulian Verplanck in 1820, also parodied the scholarly pretensions of the gentlemen scholars, but with perhaps less good humor than his friend Irving's best seller. The process included, for example, discourses by the members in Dutch, French, Greek, Hebrew, Russian, Swedish, Irish and Chinese, as well as one by the president-elect, David Hosack, "on the comparative merits of the two patron saints of the Institution, Santa Claus . . . and DeWitt Clinton." Replete with pseudo-Latin, the ceremony concluded with the members, in "clean linen, and well shaved; coats, hats, and shoes brushed," surrounding a bust of Clinton and chanting "Never mortal shone as you do/Tune, grant to us a FUNDUM."[64]

Although Verplanck's burlesque of the Society was privately printed, the term itself is something of a contradiction. Once a text is in print, in circulation, the author has no assurance that it will remain entirely private. *Procès Verbal of the Installation*, for example, was even reviewed (and sharply criticized) in the *Analectic*.[65] That the private would become public was certainly more likely in the realm of politics, and DeWitt Clinton and Gulian Verplanck were bitter political enemies. In 1815, Clinton, a Democratic-Republican, circulated *An Account of Abimelech Coody and the Celebrated Writers of New York*, a satirical (although not particularly funny) attack on Verplanck, a Federalist. What is most interesting in his account, however, is not their political rivalry, but what it reveals about generational conflict within the New-York Historical Society and conflicting views of the gentleman scholar. Written by "A Traveller" describing his visit to New York City to meet her "wits and literary worthies," it dismisses Verplanck and young writers of his circle as "puppies" who had "disregard[ed] the truth" and "dash[ed] venom in the faces of their superiors" by ridiculing the founders of the Historical Society and the Literary and Philosophical Society.[66] Not only were men like Coody (Verplanck) and Knickerbocker (Irving) "literary striplings," they were not even true gentlemen. They came from plebian families (the Traveller refers sneeringly to the fact that Irving's family ran a hardware store) and could not even read Latin and were thus "prevented by the defect of education from drinking the Pierian springs of classic lore." Yet perhaps the most pointed criticism of Coody and his friends was that they wrote for money, that, while "almost in every other place men write for amusement, or for fame, . . . here there are authors who make it a business and a living." Knickerbocker in particular was disparaged for abandoning a gentlemanly profession, the law, and "becom[ing] the salaried editor of a magazine."[67] According to the Traveller, a writer forfeited his status as gentleman scholar once his words became a commodity in the print market.

The Historical Society was particularly diligent in its efforts to discover, procure, and preserve magazines and newspapers. David Hosack, in his inaugural discourse in 1820, stressed the importance of acquiring "such productions," which, although "fugitive and comparatively insignificant, still, collectively . . . show the 'the form and pressure of the times.'" At the dedication of the new library building in 1857, John Francis, alluding to the same line from Shakespeare, assured the members that they "may well boast of the vast accumulation of that species of recorded knowledge within your walls."[68] During the period between these two addresses, there were fundamental and far-reaching changes in the newspaper and periodical market in the United States. More than any other public library in the city, the New-York Historical Society reflected those changes. While it collected newspapers and periodicals for the use of future generations, accounts of the Society in the contemporary press show the benefits and occasionally the pitfalls of such publicity for a public institution.

The first issue of the *New York Magazine and General Repository of Useful Knowledge*, published in May 1814, included "A Brief Sketch of These Periodical Works Commonly Called Magazines." It reported with pride that they had "now become extensive and of popular import," a "means of diffusing a general habit of reading [and] both moral and literary knowledge throughout all ranks of this widely extended country."[69] This enthusiasm and optimism was somewhat premature. Early in the nineteenth century, magazines were comparatively expensive and attracted a relatively small, elite reading public. They did begin to create, however, for the first time extended communities of readers, particularly for more specialized periodicals such as the *Herald of Gospel Liberty*, the *Literary Magazine and American Register*, the *Medical Repository*, and the *Agricultural Museum.* Unfortunately, as the article in May 1814 noted, most of them did not survive. In fact, the *New York Magazine* itself ceased publication after only two more monthly issues. Nonetheless, they did provide a venue for the new republic's aspiring authors, and many of the Historical Society's most prominent and gifted members, including Samuel Mitchell, Samuel Miller, William Dunlap, and James Kent were frequent contributors. However, despite Clinton's claim in *Abimelech Coody* that New York's literary worthies were writers for hire, most of the magazines did not pay.[70] As John Francis recalled in his address in 1857, in the early decades of the century "authorship . . . [was] a very good walking stick, but very bad crutches."[71] Writing for periodicals was not a means of support, but rather, with few exceptions, an accoutrement, an avocation for a gentleman of leisure.

Newspapers during this early period were in many respects similar to magazines. They were sold only by subscription, expensive (usually ten dollars a year), and read by a select community of readers, mostly merchants and professionals. Many of them were party organs, subsidized by first by the Democratic-Republicans or the Federalists, then by the Democrats or Whigs.[72] William Beach Lawrence, in an address on the "Purposes and Attainments of the Society," remarked upon the "revolutions [which had] occurred since Newton and Boyle looked to the transactions of the Royal Society as the medium of their communications with the learned world." He observed that "newspapers and . . . periodicals . . . furnish to all who have occasion to present to the public either their discoveries or reflections more ready facilities than the tardy proceedings of learned bodies can afford." The first issue of the *New York Magazine*, for example, included the Historical Society's petition to the legislature for funding in 1814 and an article extolling the "praise-worthy designs . . . of [that] learned and respectable institution" in rescuing from "mystery and obscurity" the early history of the state.[73] One practical reason for providing extensive publicity to the scholarly societies of the young republic, for reprinting verbatim their proceedings and addresses, for example, was simply that the press needed copy. During this period, even the daily and weekly newspapers published relatively little news, mostly political intelligence and commercial information, such as commodity prices and ship sailings.[74]

More important, both the magazines and newspapers recognized a duty to serve the nation by promoting cultural nationalism. The *Analectic,* for instance, in its review of *Procès Verbal of the Ceremony of Installation,* while "conced[ing] . . . hypothetically" that there was "among the most prominent members of the Historical Society . . . a portion of ostentation and even *charlatanery,*" criticized the "fashion . . . of turning into ridicule and burlesque both persons and things connected . . . with the best interests of literature." Such "shafts of satire" were ill advised when "our national literature is at present struggling with many difficulties" and promoted "learning and philosophy imported from abroad."[75] Most magazines and newspapers in the early nineteenth century, however, enlisted enthusiastically in the crusade for cultural independence. They reported effusively on the activities and publications of learned societies and commended, often in the most extravagant terms, any work by an American author. Such exaggerated praise was known as "puffing" and was, according to Evert Duyckinck, "a besetting sin of our literature." In his review of the "Literary Prospects of 1845" in the *American Review,* he held that these "nauseous puffs," the "paroxysms of admiration" were inspired by "the strong feeling of nationality in the Press" and resulted in a "genius epidemic."[76]

According to contemporaries, America in the middle of the nineteenth century was in the throes of a "magazine mania." Historian Frank Luther Mott estimated that 2,500 periodicals were published between 1850 and 1865 alone. As in earlier decades, many of them survived only a short time, but some, such as *Harper's* and *Graham's American Monthly* were widely read, highly profitable and, for the first time, compensated their most prominent authors handsomely. Literary reputations became a valuable commodity that editors employed to attract consumers of print. The *Knickerbocker,* for example, from 1839 to 1841, paid Washington Irving $2,000 annually to "chat sociably with the public."[77] In addition to these general-interest magazines, there were many others that sought to exploit new niche markets, new communities of readers, especially women and children.[78] The magazine mania was also induced in part by a range of new technologies, including the railroad, the steam press, and processes for manufacturing wood-pulp paper and printing illustrations, all of which enabled publishers to produce print more quickly and cheaply and distribute it more widely.[79]

The revolution in newspaper publishing was more dramatic and occurred somewhat earlier. In September 1833, Benjamin Day founded the

New York Sun. Unlike the *Commercial Advertiser* and other subscription dailies, the *Sun* featured entertaining human-interest stories and a wealth of local news, especially lurid reports from the police court of robbery, prostitution, street brawls, and murder. The articles were usually very brief, and the prose was always brisk and engaging. Within one year, Day had purchased a steam press and claimed a circulation of eight thousand, the highest in the city. His most radical innovation, however, and what sparked the newspaper revolution, was that the *Sun* could be purchased on the street from legions of newsboys for just a one cent, "a price," as Day pointed out on the first page of his first issue, "within the means of everyone."[80] Philip Hone, former mayor and vice president of the Historical Society, complained in his diary that "everyone wonders how people can buy and read those receptacles of scandal, the penny papers, and yet everybody does encourage them."[81] That the *Sun* appealed in particular to working-class readers, who enjoyed the sensationalistic stories and could afford a penny to buy a newspaper, did not mean of course that Benjamin Day was class conscious. Rather, Day had a consciousness, a keen appreciation of the market for print. He calculated that he could realize a steady profit by lowering the price, increasing advertisements, and selling to a much wider reading public.[82]

James Gordon Bennett employed the same market strategy, with even greater success, when he founded the *New York Herald* in 1835. His newspaper was similar in style and content to Day's and was also hawked by "newsies" on the street. But Bennett charged two cents instead of one and thus targeted somewhat more prosperous readers, those who would emerge over the course of ensuing decades as the great middle-class reading public.[83] At times, the *Herald* covered the New-York Historical Society no differently than the subscription newspapers. It reported regularly on the Society's meetings, sometimes even printing the members' discourses verbatim, although it did note that they were "more interesting to the historian than to the readers of a newspaper."[84] Perhaps more often, however, the *Herald* made fun, not just of the "solons," the "savants" who collected and preserved the state's history, but also of the "newspaper toadies" who "impaired" their usefulness with "ridiculous puffery."[85] It of course had a field day with the silly plan to change the name of the country. The *Herald* did "not agree . . . that the present unfortunate appellation . . . presents an insurmountable obstacle to its poetic immortality." After all, what true patriot did not fondly recall "that beautiful ode, commencing,"

If I was President of these United States
I'd lick 'lasses candy and swing on the gates[86]

Bennett did not feel obliged to puff the Historical Society like the subscription papers did in part because he did not share the sense of cultural inferiority that prompted their efforts to promote cultural nationalism. He was proudly indifferent to European culture. The headline of an editorial from April 1836 succinctly summed up his attitude: "We Have No News from Europe. Who Cares?"[87]

The New-York Historical Society was lampooned in the periodical press as well. The magazine mania of the mid–nineteenth century included numerous reform journals dedicated to uplifting the public mind and morals, but also many publications conducted solely for profit. *John Donkey*, a weekly humor magazine that made money by making the reading public laugh, seemed to take particular delight in deflating the pretensions of the gentlemen scholars of the Historical Society. It solemnly described, for example, a meeting at which a special committee supposedly presented a report on "the consumption of peanuts in the city of New York and its effects on the moral character . . . of the population," after which the members discussed the advisability of establishing a peanut bank.[88] It also reported extensively, and of course satirically, on a letter written by George Washington that was presented to the Society in October 1847. In it, the founding father asked a friend in New York to recommend a competent tailor to sew him a new pair of breeches, stressing that unless they were made "roomy in the seat," he would find it difficult to fit into them.[89] *John Donkey* published a series of articles on the capacious breeches, which the civic-minded editors subsequently discovered, procured, and donated to the Society. At one meeting, for example, the entire membership, in a "scientific manner . . . gradually inserted themselves, one after another, into the breeches," and at another the chairman intoned that "in an age which witnessed . . . the progress of intellectual, moral and religious liberty," it was the Society's solemn duty to "preserve inviolable these breeches . . . where future generations might find them unpatched and unharmed." The latter article also displayed a new coat of arms for the Historical Society in which the roomy-seated breeches were prominently featured and a new motto in pseudo-Latin: *Sopht Ass Mushe.*[90] *John Donkey* survived less than one year, but its demise probably had nothing to do its profitability or its popularity with the reading public. By the time its final issue was

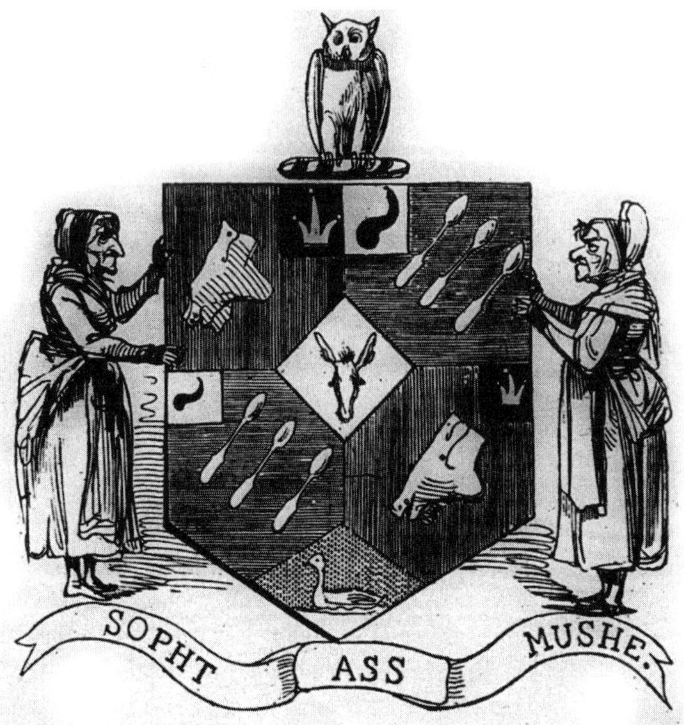

New-York Historical Society motto and coat of arms, featuring George Washington's roomy breeches (*John Donkey,* March 11, 1848)

published in October 1848, there were seven libel suits pending against the editors.[91]

That the *New York Herald* would publicize the New-York Historical Society in one article and ridicule it in another was not, from a market perspective, inconsistent. James Gordon Bennett frequently boasted that his newspaper was based upon "the cash principle." By this he meant that, because it was sold for cash on the street, the *Herald* was independent of the "scoundrels and cheats" in the political parties and banks that controlled "the Wall Street press." Yet the phrase also reflects the new commercial orientation of the penny papers and the periodical press in general. Despite Bennett's lofty rhetoric about "the revolution that has taken place in a great portion of the public mind," the *Herald* was in the business of selling print that appealed to a broad reading public.[92] This increased market consciousness (along with a decline in cultural nationalism and a rise in class tensions) changed the way that public libraries and other public institutions appeared in print. They were no longer guaranteed favorable, deferential coverage in "puffs." They could get good press, bad press or no press, depending in part upon what made good copy.

At the same meeting in 1814 at which President Egbert Benson reported on the State's grant for the library of $12,000 from a prospective lottery, the members voted to borrow $1,500 from the Washington Mutual Insurance Company, using the anticipated monies from the lottery as collateral.[93] The Society apparently spent most of the loan in purchasing a collection of rare books from Timothy Alden, the librarian of the Massachusetts Historical Society, "under the idea that if the present opportunity was lost, the like might not again ever occur, of securing to this institution, and to the public, so desirable and important an acquisition."[94] Year after year the running of the lottery was delayed, and the Society continued to borrow money against it to further build the collection and, in 1818, to hire the "sub-librarian" so that the library could be opened to the members on Wednesday and Saturday afternoons.[95] By 1824, when the annual income was less than $500, the debt had reached $13,000, more than the amount of the lottery grant itself. A special committee appointed that year to examine the Society's financial condition "confess[ed] their entire inability to devise any means to liquidate a debt of this magnitude."[96]

In an address to the members in 1827, President David Hosack claimed that "we fell into embarrassments" by "a combination of circumstances, which no human sagacity could foresee."[97] In fact, it is remarkable that the leaders of the Historical Society seemed not to understand, or perhaps refused to recognize, the unreliability of public monies raised by a state lottery or the specific terms of the legislature's grant in 1814. In the eighteenth century, lotteries were a popular means of reducing taxes and funding public improvements, especially those related to education. Columbia College, for example, was founded in part with the profits from a provincial lottery in 1747, and in 1790 the municipal corporation held a lottery to build City Hall, where the Historical Society held its first meeting. By the early nineteenth century, however, public lotteries were increasingly viewed as an incitement to gambling and rapidly fell into disrepute. Just five years after the legislature's grant to the library, a special committee of the assembly reported that "the foundation of the system . . . is so radically vicious that . . . no system of regulation [could] divest it of all the evils of which it has hitherto proved so baneful a cause." The new state constitution approved in 1822 prohibited lotteries altogether, both public and private.[98]

The terms of "An Act Instituting a Lottery for the Promotion of Literature" made it clear that there would almost certainly be a delay in the appropriation for the library of the Historical Society. It granted an unprecedented sum, in total $352,000, mostly to institutions of higher learning across the state, including Columbia College, but the bulk of the profits from the lottery, $200,000, were to go Union College in Schenectady, whose shrewd and politically connected president, Eliphalet Nott, had first proposed and lobbied for the legislation.[99] The law required that all of the outstanding state lotteries be concluded before the lottery for the colleges was held and, to compensate them for the anticipated delay, the schools were to receive annually, for up to six years, interest on their grants. However, the appropriation for the Historical Society's library was not part of the lottery act itself, was added later in the session as part of an omnibus appropriations bill, and did not include six years of interest. Because of complications and controversies connected with the earlier lotteries, the 1814 lottery was essentially in limbo for several years.

Finally, in April 1822 the legislature passed, again at Eliphalet Nott's urging, "An Act to Limit the Continuation of Lotteries." With it, the State divested itself of the "Lottery for the Promotion of Literature" and permitted the grantees to conduct it jointly on their own or to appoint an agent to do so.[100] Nott then hired a firm of professional lottery managers, John Yates and Archibald McIntyre, and convinced each of the colleges to sell its interest in the new lottery at a substantially reduced cost. The institutions were thereby "relieved from the hazard of future losses," and Nott in effect gambled that Yates and McIntyre would be able to turn a profit running a private lottery solely for Union College. In August 1823, the Historical Society accepted $8,000 in lieu of the $12,000 appropriated for its library almost a decade earlier. Nott and his partners went on to manage the lottery so successfully that Union College eventually doubled its money. By 1827, it had made more than $400,000, compared to the $200,000 originally granted by the State in 1814.[101]

With $8,000 from Eliphalet Nott the Society was able to pay off some of its creditors, but was still heavily in debt. In early 1824, the sublibrarian was dismissed and the library was closed.[102] Later that year and early in 1825 members briefly considered a proposal to cooperate with the New York Athenaeum, the Society Library, and Columbia College to "form a great public library," but apparently there was limited interest in this ambitious plan, and it never came to fruition.[103] In April, a special committee was appointed "to endeavor to extricate this Society from its present embarrassments." Empowered to "use any means they may deem proper for obtaining that object," on May 24, in the *Commercial Advertiser*, the committee announced the sale of the library by auction in July.[104] This decision evoked a storm of protest within the Society and in the local press. However, at a sparsely attended meeting the following month, the membership, certainly after contentious debate, voted to sell the collection, but only on the condition that it was purchased in its entirety by or for an institution in the city of New York. President David Hosack, Vice President John Trumbull, and two members of the standing committee then resigned in protest and left the meeting.[105]

The Historical Society did not meet again for nearly a year. In the meantime, no local institution or public-spirited citizen offered either to purchase the collection or help to pay the Society's debts. Finally, with interest continuing to accumulate and the creditors threatening legal action, the members resolved once more to petition the State for assistance. In March 1827, upon the advice of Governor DeWitt Clinton, and the senate's Committee on Literature, whose report on the bill warned that if the library were sold the books would "probably be scattered over Europe," the legislature agreed to provide $5,000, roughly the amount the Society would have received if, like the colleges, it had been appropriated interest for six years on its grant of $12,000 under the Lottery Act of 1814. There were, however, strings attached. Before receiving the money, officers of the Society were required to provide evidence to the state comptroller that the Society would thereafter be solvent, that its total debt had been reduced to no more than $5,000.[106]

The Society complied with the terms of the grant, in the words another special committee appointed in 1828, only "by many and great difficulties." In part, the reduction of the debt was made possible by the generosity of John Francis, who agreed to accept just $3,000 for the $5,000 owed to him.[107] The founder of the New-York Historical Society, however, received nothing. John Pintard was unable to provide receipts for over $3,000 worth books he claimed to have purchased for the library, and the committee, "though painful the task, . . . reject[ed] all claims not fully evidenced and founded on proper authority." The Society did offer him $600 worth of stock in a local bank and claimed that Pintard signed a receipt accepting it, as required by the act of the legislature.[108] Yet he later "declared that he never received a cent," that he had refused to sign a release because of the "injustice of the settlement."[109]

The State's grant in 1827 did nothing more than save the Historical Society from dissolution. In the late 1820s and for much of the 1830s it had at best a marginal existence. When the Common Council evicted the New York Institution from Brideswell in 1831, the Society was forced to relocate. With many of the members in arrears in the payment of dues and an exorbitant rent of $500 a year for its new quarters in the Remsen Building on Broadway and Chambers, it once again fell into debt. The membership met infrequently and for nearly three years, between June 1833 and January 1836, did not meet at all.[110] All of the founders and most of the early supporters were gone. DeWitt Clinton died in 1828, shortly before the State rescued the Society. John Pintard, no doubt angry and disillusioned when the institution he had founded refused to reimburse him for the books he purchased for its library, cut all ties. Not long after leaving the Society, he wrote to his friend John Francis that he had "retired into the vale of obscurity."[111] For most of this period the library was closed. Officers had keys to the rooms and would occasionally provide access to members or their friends. The New-York Historical Society's valuable collection was, in the words of Philip Hone, "a closed book" to the reading public.[112]

What ultimately revived the New-York Historical Society was not support from the State, but a dramatic rise in the popularity of history. Beginning in the 1820s and especially from the 1830s through the Civil War, there was an intense and pervasive interest in America's past. Certainly, the passing of the revolutionary generation raised historical consciousness and concerns that the record of the settlement of the colonies and the founding of the republic might pass into oblivion. William Campbell, in an address before the Society in 1850 on "Historical Inquiry in the Last Twenty-Five Years," held that "with wealth and general comfort come desire to know the events of the past and our connection to it." He also pointed to the new public schools, which, of course, taught history, and their libraries, which "form[ed] a great reading public, anxious to know all that can be learned of the history of the land of their birth."[113] Whatever the reasons, the popular interest in history was manifested in, among many other developments, the founding of historical societies. Beginning with Massachusetts in 1791 through 1829, only twenty-four state and local organizations were founded. Between 1830 and 1860 there were eighty-three.[114]

The popularity of historical fiction was both a sign of and a reason for the popular interest in history. An historical setting, in a sense, lent respectability to a novel, made it a more rational amusement, and at the same time heightened its drama and verisimilitude.[115] According to Frank Luther Mott, in the 1820s fully 75 percent of the titles he identified as best sellers were historical romances, although most of these were written by just two authors, James Fenimore Cooper and Sir Walter Scott.[116] In the following decades, American publishing, spurred by many of the same technological advances that made possible the magazine mania, expanded at an unprecedented rate. The total value of books printed and sold in the United States rose from $2.5 million in 1820 to $12.5 million in 1850.[117] Despite the disapproval of conservatives like John Pintard, who complained that "truth requires no fiction to emblazon the almost romantic scenes" of the nation's past, popular authors capitalized upon the success of Scott and Cooper to appeal to a rapidly expanding reading public. From 1830 to 1859, historical fiction accounted for approximately 30 percent of the best-selling novels in the United States and nearly 20 percent of best sellers overall.[118] In fact, the past was so lucrative in the fiction market that publishers sometimes added *History of* to the title of a novel that was in no way historical simply to increase sales.[119]

History was nearly as popular as historical fiction. Between 1830 and 1859, there were twenty-two best sellers, compared to just seven for the remainder of the century.[120] Writers of historical romances, especially Sir Walter Scott, had a profound influence on the writing of history. Washington Irving, who published the first of his seven historical works, *History of the Life and Voyages of Christopher Columbus*, in 1828, claimed it was Scott who made him a historian. Many others, including George Bancroft, the preeminent American historian of the period (and a member of the Historical Society's Executive Committee), also acknowledged their debt to the most popular novelist of the day.[121] Authors such as Irving and Bancroft helped fulfill the cultural nationalists' ambition of producing an American literature, and the history they wrote was crafted as romantic art. They emulated, for example, Scott's forceful, dauntless heroes and the beauty, the elegance of his prose. Moreover, as Gregory Pfitzer and others have argued, history as it was conceived by Americans in the decades before the Civil War was ideally suited to the conventions of romantic fiction. The struggle to preserve the people's liberty, for example, pitted good against evil and thereby lent drama and pathos to historical works. The grand narrative of history, the story of freedom, Protestantism, commerce, science, of progress and civilization, provided organic unity, an essential quality of romantic art.[122] For example, the first chapter of the first volume of Bancroft's immensely popular *History of the United States* begins: "The United States constitute an essential portion of a great political system embracing all the civilized nations," then goes on to enumerate the republic's distinctive institutions and values, "call[ed] . . . into being" by "a favoring Providence," including the Constitution, unrestricted markets, a prolific press, religious liberty, and "the force of moral opinion."[123]

Of course, not all of the history published in the United States in the decades before the Civil War was literary art. Some of what the reading public so avidly consumed was essentially the historical equivalent of cheap fiction, marketed to those who, in the words of John Warner Barber, author of *Incidents in American History* (1847), "cannot spare the time or expense of reading or procuring a full and complete history."[124] Nor was history during these decades necessarily strictly accurate. Thomas Ward's poem "The Romance of American History," read at the annual meeting of the Historical Society in 1845, praised "our own faultless Irving," whose *Life of Columbus* was "a sketch so wondrous, yet so surely true." Actually Irving's history includes a number of dramatic scenes, in particular the description of Columbus's first landfall in the Americas and his triumphant reception in Barcelona after his first voyage, that are largely a product of the author's imagination.[125] Readers and critics did not object when Irving embellished his facts with "romantic colouring," because it enhanced the "intrinsic truth" of the narrative. Like much antebellum popular fiction, popular history was intended to be didactic, to convey transcendent, moral truths beyond mere facts.[126] A review of *The Life of Columbus* in the *Critic*, for example, praised Irving for "combining the thrilling interest of romance with the moral impressiveness of truth." One reviewer did object that he was too willing to excuse his subject's moral failures, in particular his role in introducing slavery into the New World. Irving, however, dismissed the "meddlesome spirit" that "goes prying about the traces of history, casting down its monuments." He held that such "pernicious erudition" defeated "one of [its] most salutary purposes, . . . that of furnishing examples of what human genius and laudable enterprise may accomplish."[127]

Another reason to embellish historical facts with "romantic coloring" was that it sold well in the market. At a special meeting of the Historical Society in 1860 to commemorate the death of Washington Irving, his friend William Cullen Bryant praised *A Chronicle of the Conquest of Granada* (1829), which was "wrought up with such picturesque effect" that "a young lady might read it by mistake for a romance."[128] Irving purposefully and skillfully crafted not only how he wrote but also what he wrote to appeal to his reading public. For example, *Astoria, or Anecdotes of an Enterprize over the Rocky Mountains* (1836), a history of John Jacob Astor's fur-trading venture in the Pacific Northwest, was published after Irving had lived for many years abroad and was intended at least in part to meet the public's demand for books on the Far West and to counter the criticism that he had neglected American for European themes in his writing.[129] In a magazine article in 1807, Irving said of his literary circle that "we write for no other earthly purpose but to please ourselves."[130] However true that may have been when Irving was a young man, certainly by the 1830s the day of the gentleman scholar and the gentleman *littérateur*, of the man of leisure who scribbled for a small literary journal or pronounced a discourse at a meeting of the Historical Society, had waned. Despite his carefully cultivated literary persona as America's genial man of letters, Washington Irving and, for example, George Bancroft, were professional writers. They wrote for the reading public, and their reputation and influence were measured by their success in the market for print.[131]

The three decades before the Civil War also saw the publication of more volumes of historical documents than any time in American history. Many of the original thirteen states, for example, printed extensive compilations of primary sources from the colonial period in an effort to "bring the sacred truths of our history to each man's own door and fireside."[132] In New York, the Historical Society petitioned the legislature in 1841 to send a member, John Romeyn Brodhead, to Holland, France, and England to transcribe and translate public records. Brodhead urged the Society "not [to] rest . . . until every repository has been ransacked" and spent three years in European capitals collecting the sources that later comprised the fifteen volumes of *Documents Relative to the Colonial History of the State of New York*.[133] During this period, the State also published the *Journal of the Legislative Council of the Colony of New York* (1861); the *Journals of the Provincial Congress, Provincial Convention . . . and Council of Safety* (1842), and a four-volume *Documentary History of the State of New York* (1849–51).[134] At the national level, between 1830 and 1860 Congress produced twelve extensive collections of primary documents, including *Diplomatic Correspondence of the American Revolution* (1829–30); *Debates on the Adoption of . . . the Federal Constitution* (1827–30); and the works of George Washington (1834–37), John Adams (1850–56), Thomas Jefferson (1853–54), and James Madison (1840). It "appeared," according to John

Washington Irving (*Harper's New Monthly Magazine*, April 1851)

Francis in 1857, that "the Republic at large [was] determined to secure her history from doubt and uncertainty."[135]

Some of the documentary collections published by the states and the Congress—Jared Sparks's twelve-volume *Writings of George Washington*, for example—were certainly popular with the reading public, but since they were subsidized, they circulated in a sense outside of the market for print.[136] *Collections of the New-York Historical Society*, however, were subject to the market and, in the words of a review in 1842 of the first volume of the second series, "engage[d] little attention in the busy haunts of commerce." Despite the fact that its publications seem to have consistently lost money, the Historical Society continued to publish.[137] In fact, in a report to the legislature shortly after the State's grant in 1827, a special committee optimistically reported that they hoped to begin issuing a volume of the *Collections* "annually or oftener."[138] This eagerness to disseminate what, according to the preface of the *Collections* in 1849, was "long regarded as obscure, dry, and uninteresting," can be explained in part simply by a desire to rescue from oblivion evidence of the early history of the state. Yet there was also a kind of elitism implied in selling at a loss "works [that] must rely upon a small class of readers for their support." Publishing documents and discourses that the common reader deemed unappealing, but which the membership purportedly found "most interesting and instructive" proved that the members were true scholars.[139] For the gentlemen of the New-York Historical Society, failure in the market for print could be read as a sign of success.

It was not until the late 1830s that the Historical Society finally began to recover from its brush with insolvency in the 1820s. In February 1838, the *American Monthly Magazine* reported that "this institution, after a long sleep like Rip Van Winkle's, . . . has of late been raised by the exertions of few individuals to a palmier state than ever."[140] A new generation of leaders, including Luther Bradish, Frederic De Peyster, George Folsom, and George Henry Moore, was able to take advantage of the "popular gale" in favor of American history and revive "the interest excited in the days of Clinton."[141] In 1841, the books and manuscripts were moved to the library of New York University on Washington Square, where, for the next sixteen years, the two institutions shared their collections and expenses.[142] Eight years later, the membership had reached approximately five hundred, more than double the number in 1827, when the State rescued the Society from bankruptcy. An annual report from this period declared that "the simple announcement of subjects interesting to the lovers of history for discussion [was] sufficient to fill the rooms" at every monthly meeting.[143]

The new leadership changed how the Society's meetings were conducted in ways that certainly attracted new members. Beginning in 1842, for example, nonmembers were invited to attend, and light refreshments were served afterward.[144] More generally, the monthly meetings became less formal and more fun. In December 1843, Charles Hoffman, before his "remarks" to the membership on the colonial history of the state, observed that a "formal . . . essay" would be "better suited to the lecture-room . . . than to social gatherings like this." Similarly, the annual report for 1847 noted that the "meetings continue to be well attended, and are a popular . . . medium of intercourse among members, affording opportunity for social intercourse [and] kindly exchange of friendship," as well as "agreeable toil in the search for historic truth."[145] This new emphasis on fun and sociability seems to have coincided with the attendance of women (as guests) for the first time in considerable numbers at the monthly meetings. Reports in the local newspapers frequently described an "an array of female beauty and fashion" or an "audience embracing [not only] intelligence, talent, eminence of character and personal worth, [but] female loveliness as well." Women were clearly considered not toilers, but ornaments to the social functions of the Society. Samuel Osgood, for example, at a meeting in 1857, "expected that . . . the feminine elements in the audience would act favorably upon the manner and matter of the speaking and reading, . . . driv[ing] all dullness from the rostrum, as sunshine drives away the cloud."[146]

In addition to what Charles Hoffman termed the "brief and informal paper" delivered at each monthly meeting, the new leadership also instituted public lectures as a means of raising revenue. The first series, offered in 1838, was so successful that the Historical Society was able to pay all of its outstanding debts. Lectures were a popular form of entertainment during this period, but the Society had to compete other local organizations, including the Mercantile Library Association and the Lyceum of Natural History, which offered their own series.[147] One way to ensure success in marketing the lectures was to engage a speaker who already had a firmly established reputation in print. In 1841, for example, the course on the American Revolution delivered by Jared Sparks, best-selling author of *The Life of George Washington*, was so popular that the Society's room in the University was too small, and it was held instead in the Broadway Tabernacle, the largest venue in the city.[148] As a public institution, the Society's lectures were of course expected to provide rational amusement. Nonetheless, in order to succeed the subjects had to appeal to the public, not just the gentlemen of the Society. Lectures in 1838 and 1839 on witchcraft and Pocahontas, for instance, attracted an audience and made money. The following year, in which Orville Dewey delivered a lecture on "The Philosophy of History," the course was cancelled in midseason.[149]

With a larger and more active membership, the Historical Society was able to expand the library substantially for the first time since the State's "grant" in 1814. Shortly after moving to New York University, the Executive Committee announced its intention to "possess every known work of authority on American history."[150] Although the collection continued to grow largely through donations, a portion of the members' dues, from one hundred to two hundred dollars annually, was appropriated for books. In addition, income from the course of lectures in 1839 and proceeds from a successful fundraising campaign in 1847 were devoted exclusively to the library.[151] Wealthy supporters, such as James Lenox, who later founded the Lenox Library, donated many valuable books and manuscripts, as did the corresponding members, a new class of membership created in 1844 primarily as a means of soliciting contributions.[152] The Society's collection grew from approximately 10,000 volumes in 1843 to 25,000 in 1859.[153] In his paper on the "Purposes and Attainments of the New-York Historical Society," William Lawrence "express[ed] the gratification every member must experience on the rapid increase of our library, not in works that add merely to the number of its volumes, but in those which extend its real utility."[154]

For the first time since the early 1820s, the collection became a valuable and comparatively accessible resource for scholars. Beginning in 1843, the library was open to members and their guests for six hours daily, except Sundays, including two hours in the evening.[155] In 1841, George Henry Moore, then a sophomore at New York University, was appointed assistant librarian and eight years later became the Society's first full-time, paid librarian, although he was still elected to the position annually, as required by the constitution. He served until 1876, when he became the first superintendent of the Lenox Library.[156] Moore made the resources of the Society much more useful to researchers in a number of ways. In the late 1840s, for example, he organized the library's large and wide-ranging collections of pamphlets and newspapers and began work on a catalog of the books that was finally published in 1859.[157] The annual report for 1846 claimed that the Society was "free to every historical investigation, [that even] mere curiosity is not debarred from gratification in searching its records and examining its accumulations." By 1849, Moore estimated that five hundred researchers accessed the library annually.[158]

As the collection became more extensive and valuable, members became increasingly concerned for its preservation, particularly because of the danger posed by fire. At the annual meeting in 1843, the Executive Committee referred for the first time to the urgent need for a fireproof building for the library. Later George Henry Moore reported on the "black catalogue" of library fires in the United States, "statistics of conflagration, which bear directly on our case," as well as on a small fire which broke out in the New York University chapel, directly above the room the Society shared with the university library.[159] In 1847, the membership approved a resolution, introduced by Moore, to solicit donations to erect a fireproof building. It directed a committee of nine members to raise $50,000, select a site, and supervise the construction. The Building Fund Committee was instructed not to incur any debt and to appropriate any additional money raised to buy material for the library.[160]

At a meeting the following year, the committee was also authorized to petition the state legislature for funds. The memorial they presented in January 1850 was similar in many respects to the one that DeWitt Clinton wrote in 1814 to request monies to purchase books for the library. It stressed, for example, that "the objects in which this society is engaged are strictly of a general or public character," and "the inappreciable value of [the collection] in which the public has so deep an interest." The committee also emphasized, as did Clinton, that their memorial proposed what today would be termed a public–private partnership, that rather than relying exclusively on support from the legislature, "before making its present appeal to the munificence of the State, the society has already put forth its own efforts." Despite favorable reports from both the assembly and senate committees to which the petition was referred, the bills they presented failed in both houses.[161] In 1850, in spite of the widespread popularity of American history, the Historical Society no longer exercised the influence in Albany that it took for granted in the days of Clinton.

When the Building Fund Committee was appointed in 1847, it was authorized to publish an address to the public in local newspapers, just as the founders had done in 1805. The committee, however, declined to do so. Instead, it wrote an appeal that was printed and circulated privately, and each of the members "personally commenced the obtaining of subscriptions to the building fund." That is, rather than soliciting support from the general public, the committee chose to address it efforts to an exclusive public, to, in the words of their appeal, "the wealthy and patriotic citizens of this great metropolis."[162] By 1847, a public library required large sums of money for a building (the Historical Society's library eventually cost $85,000) and an extensive collection of books. In the absence of government funding, New York's public libraries required the active support of the city's elite. That four other libraries—the Astor, the Mercantile, the Society Library, and the Cooper Union Library—all opened buildings in the 1850s near the Historical Society's new home on Second Avenue and Eleventh Street indicates the increasing popularity of public libraries. It also shows the growing affluence of the city's wealthy and patriotic citizens and their support for those libraries.

The wealthiest and most influential public benefactors were the leaders of New York's mercantile community. Men like William B. Astor and Benjamin Field, both of whom served on the Building Fund Committee, were the mainstay of public libraries and other public institutions during this period.[163] A number of the speakers stressed this point at the dedication of the library in November 1857. Frederic De Peyster, Chairman of the Trustees of the Building Fund, for example, praised "the liberal hearts of the liberal men of this great commercial city," while John Francis said that the building was "erected by the liberality of our citizens, and in an especial manner by that class so often found generous in good works, the mercantile community."[164] Moreover, by 1857, the gentlemen who erected and directed the library were no longer assumed to be scholars. There were now distinct roles for those who provided the material for history and those who produced history. George Bancroft, the republic's most respected professional historian, expressed this best when he urged at the dedication that "the comprehensive and liberal spirit of our merchants and the vivifying intelligence of our scholars join together to promote . . . every capacity for good."[165]

Although the New-York Historical Society was a valuable resource for scholars in 1857, it never became, as De Peyster anticipated at the opening, "the great central resort for historical investigations of every kind." In fact, the library regulations required that, order to gain access, a nonmember had to obtain a recommendation from a member "to whom the applicant is known."[166] And certainly the library was never intended, in the words of Samuel Osgood at its dedication, "to be an instrument of popular education."[167] The best evidence for this is the collection development policy at the Astor Library, where Washington Irving was president and Joseph Cogswell, a longtime member of the Historical Society, was superintendent. Despite frequent complaints about its service and policies, the Astor did serve, in some cases perhaps begrudgingly, the public. Although Cogswell took care not to duplicate other special libraries in the city, he sought to build a comprehensive collection in American history at the same time that George Henry Moore was doing the same thing at the Historical Society.[168] Cogswell knew that the books Moore collected were not publicly available. To the extent that the Society did serve the public, it was, by 1857, a stratified public. It served the same stratum that paid for its new building, the wealthy citizens of the metropolis.

4

The Biblical Library of the American Bible Society

Evangelicalism and the Evangelical Corporation

In November 1849, President Luther Bradish delivered the annual discourse before the New-York Historical Society. He offered the members and guests a grand narrative of the history of the last century, of "the great progress which the world has made . . . in the physical, intellectual and moral condition of the race." Central of course to his narrative was "the assertion of a new and vital principle of liberty and of free government," which was the "working out of the Great Plans laid by infinite wisdom in the Councils of Eternity." Bradish was also active in and later served as president of the American Bible Society. More than half of his lengthy address was devoted to demonstrating that "above all has the last century been distinguished by the more general diffusion . . . of the religion and morality of the Bible."[1]

The American Bible Society was founded in 1816 to publish and distribute Bibles at cost throughout the United States and abroad.[2] Shortly after its founding, its managers established a reference collection as a resource for the Society's editors and translators. In some respects, the scope and purpose of this public library were rather different from those considered in previous chapters. It was highly specialized, comprising mostly Bibles in a multitude of languages and editions, and relatively small; by the Civil War it held barely two thousand volumes. Although it was accessible to the public, it seems to have been used primarily by employees of the Society. Nonetheless, the library was an essential part of an important public institution. The collection reflected the Protestant values that the Society sought to defend and promote and that were a critical component of republican culture during the antebellum years. It is impossible to understand the history of the United States during this period without considering the pervasive influence of Protestant evangelicalism. At the same time, the development of the library points toward fundamental changes in the economic and public spheres, the import of which did not become wholly evident until later in the century. It reflected values associated with the rise of the national corporation and an emerging liberal, commercial culture.

The British and Foreign Bible Society was organized in 1804. It quickly became the leader of a worldwide movement to bring the Gospel to the poor in purse and spirit. The first Bible society in the United States was the Philadelphia Bible Society, founded in 1809. Within just a few years, more than one hundred state and local organizations had been established. By 1814, Elias Boudinot, president of the New Jersey Bible Society and former president of the Continental Congress, and others began calling for a national institution that would consolidate and coordinate these local societies. Their efforts came to fruition in the Garden Street Dutch Reformed Church in New York City on May 8, 1816. Sixty delegates representing thirty-four organizations convened to listen to stirring oratory, adopt a constitution, and elect a board of thirty-six managers of the American Bible Society. The founding members included many prominent national figures, including Boudinot, who served as the first president; the novelist James Fenimore Cooper; Jedidiah Morse, geographer and the author of popular children's textbooks; and the Reverend Lyman Beecher, later a leader in the temperance movement and numerous other evangelical causes. Representing a variety of Protestant denominations throughout the nation, the delegates stressed repeatedly that their mission excluded "local feelings [and] sectarian jealousies . . . by its very nature" and enshrined in the constitution the principle that "the sole object shall be to encourage a wider circulation of the Holy Scriptures without note or comment."[3] The constitution further pledged the Society would "according to its ability, extend its influence to other countries, whether Christian, Mohammedan, or Pagan."

Clifford Griffin and other historians who viewed the antebellum philanthropies that comprised the "benevolent empire" as instruments of "social control," emphasized the fear that underlay these efforts at evangelical reform. They portrayed the reformers as angst-ridden elites attempting to bolster their moral authority in the face of a rising tide of immigration, a new, divisive style of party politics, and the specter of infidelity. Historians of social control pointed, for example, to Boudinot's *Age of Revelation or the Age of Reason Shewn to be an Age of Infidelity*, published in 1801, as evidence of the reactionary nature of evangelical reform. In it the future Bible Society leader attacked Thomas Paine's *The Age of Reason* and attempted to counteract the morally degenerating effects of Deism.[4] In the case of the American Bible Society, the social control thesis did have a degree of validity. An "Address to the People of the United States" issued at the constituting convention opened with an ominous reference to a "political world [that] has undergone changes stupendous, unexpected, and calculated to inspire thoughtful men with the most boding anticipations." It went on to decry "a period of philosophy, falsely so called . . . which under the imposing names of reason and liberality, [was] attempting to seduce mankind from" the path of true religion.[5] There was without doubt an element of anxiety at the founding convention in 1816.

Yet Griffin's account greatly overstated the extent to which reformers like Boudinot were motivated by fear. Certainly their motives were mixed, but there is a clear and persistent strain of optimism that runs throughout the American Bible Society's founding documents. After the allusion to a political crisis in the opening of the "Address to the People of the United States," there were repeated and dramatic references to a new spirit that was sweeping the Christian world, "an excitement, as extraordinary as it is powerful [that] has roused the nations." Indeed, the "period of philosophy" had passed, succeeded by "the age of Bibles," "auspicious to whatever is exquisite in human enjoyment, or precious to human hope." Granted this is a rhetorical document, intended to rouse the faithful to action (and donation), but there is nonetheless a powerful and genuine sense of confidence that pervades the "Address." Further, these millennial expectations are expressed in the language of community. Terms and phrases such as "unity," "cooperation," "concert," and "national feeling" appear in nearly every other paragraph.[6] Again, this was more than stirring rhetoric designed to elicit support. The Society's founders sincerely sought and expected to achieve a more perfect union based upon the values to be found in the Bible.

The Bible Society's first annual report informed members that "the Managers have commenced a collection of Bibles, especially the earlier editions, in every language." The library was established at the Board of Managers meeting in January 1817, at which they resolved that "a Copy of each edition of the Bible printed for the A.B.S." would "be deposited in this Society's Biblical Library." The following month they expanded the collection policy to include "Copies of the early Editions of the Bible" and encouraged members to make donations.[7] The member who was most responsible for the early development of the library and who served as its de facto librarian during its formative years was the Society's first recording secretary, John Pintard.[8] Pintard, the founder the New-York Historical Society, was responsible for the resolution that established the collection and immediately took a keen interest in developing it. In March 1817, he wrote to his close friend and Bible Society manager Samuel Bayard, "we shall make this an important department—promote it whenever you can. Greek, Latin, Hebrew, any tongue or dialect—ancient or modern—will suit as we want the various Editions of the Scriptures—in one collection."[9] Pintard donated Bibles from his own library, solicited donations from others, arranged for temporary quarters at the Historical Society, and prepared the first catalog.[10] In November, he reported to his daughter Eliza that "the Biblical Library is a child of my own and accumulates beyond my expectations."[11]

In many respects, John Pintard was representative of the generation of patrician New Yorkers who dominated the city's voluntary organizations in the early nineteenth century. His ancestors were Huguenots who had fled France and settled in New Jersey in the seventeenth century. Born in 1759, he was orphaned as an infant and raised by his uncle, Lewis Pintard, a prominent New York merchant. Pintard began his formal schooling at an academy in Hempstead on Long Island and graduated from the College of New Jersey, later Princeton University, in 1776. He was an ardent bibliophile and an avid reader, particularly of theological works. He devoted part of every Sunday to religious reading and read the entire Bible at least once a year throughout his adult life.[12] Pintard served briefly in the New Jersey militia at the outbreak of the Revolution and for most of the war acted as secretary to his uncle, the American commissioner for prisoners of war in New York.[13] In the 1790s he was elected to the New York City Council and the New York State Assembly. As a young man he failed in a series of business ventures, but in 1809 was appointed secretary of the Mutual Insurance Company, a salaried position that was his primary source of income until his retirement in 1829.[14]

Pintard, like many members of New York's first families, also devoted much of his time to philanthropies like the American Bible Society. Indeed, for Pintard and the patrician founders of the Society there was no sharp distinction between commerce, government, and benevolence, between the economic, political, and public spheres. In their minds, all three were inextricably linked components of civic progress, for which the city's elite was peculiarly suited, by education and social position, to provide leadership.[15] Pintard certainly spoke for many of his class and generation when he said that "the motives which activate me . . . arise from a sincere disposition to be useful in my day . . . and to apply the talents with which I am endowed for the benefit of Society."[16] While his earnest attitude toward

John Pintard in 1832

public service was fairly typical, the range of his public activities was extraordinary. In 1817, the year in which he started the Biblical Library, Pintard held office in eleven additional organizations, including the Chamber of Commerce, the Literary and Philosophical Society, and the St. Esprit Church. He was especially interested in libraries and, besides the Bible

Society collection, was instrumental in the development of the New York Society Library, the General Theological Seminary Library, the Mercantile Library Association, the Apprentices' Library, and the libraries of the Society for the Prevention of Pauperism and the Society for the Reformation of Juvenile Delinquents.[17]

John Pintard's involvement in these various public institutions reflects many of the salient characteristics of reform and benevolence in the early nineteenth century. First, books and libraries were an important part of the public sphere. While all of these collections served a variety of purposes and readers, they were all intended in some way to promote public morality and the commonweal. Second, leadership in these organizations was shared within a relatively select group of public-spirited patricians. This is another example of what Thomas Bender terms "interlocking directorates at the top," and these directorates in turn interlocked with the directorates that founded and managed learned institutions such as the Historical Society.[18] Pintard's friend DeWitt Clinton, for example, was a manager of the American Bible Society.[19] Further, extended family connections often reinforced ties within the interlocking directorates. Elias Boudinot, the first president of the Bible Society, was John Pintard's uncle's brother-in-law, and manager Samuel Bayard was married to his cousin. Finally, benevolence, as well as other kinds of elite association during this period, was primarily local and often a source of intense local pride. Pintard wrote to Boudinot in 1817 that the "Grand Canal [Erie Canal], our Colleges, Academies—Theological, Biblical, and Scientific Institutions will proudly elevate the city of New York to that rank which her geographical situation and advantages entitles her to hold."[20] Even the American Bible Society, a national organization, was locally oriented to an extent. Its constitution required that the Board of Managers meet monthly somewhere in New York City and that two-thirds of the managers reside in New York or its environs.[21]

There was a countervailing tendency among Bible-cause supporters to think in terms beyond their immediate locality, to envision more extensive forms of community. One obvious source of this more expansive identity was their ideal of Christian fraternity. The entire Bible movement was premised upon the evangelical belief that Christianity "teaches us that we are all members of the great family of mankind." An intimately related source was the republican veneration of the commonweal, the conviction that a "nation pouring forth its devotion" would secure "the purest interest of the community."[22] A third source was what Thomas Haskell has called the "humanitarian sensibility." Haskell argues that the impetus of antebellum reform was a new "*perception* or *cognitive style*" inspired by reformers' participation in a market economy. The emergence of complex, contractually regulated markets created a heightened sense of moral obligation and a more abstract sense of causality, which, in turn, compelled many elites to feel responsible for the well being of the less fortunate beyond the boundaries of their local communities.[23] This new cognitive style is evident in the "Address to the People" that the Bible Society circulated in 1816. Supporters were assured that Bible work would "satisfy our conviction of duty" by "minister[ing] to the blessedness of . . . tens of thousands, of whom we may never see the faces, nor hear the names."[24] Haskell's argument is particularly relevant to a society that literally marketed its benevolence in the form of cheap Bibles.[25] Indeed, the managers noted occasionally in their annual reports that the "extended commerce of the age" would help ensure the success of their cause.[26]

One key to understanding antebellum reform generally is to consider how individual organizations defined the geographic scope of their benevolence. The American Bible Society was part of a trend toward the nationalization of voluntary association, but the borders of its benevolent evangelical republic were never precisely fixed. From its beginnings, it was also part of a global Bible movement. The varying emphasis placed over time upon national and international efforts is evident throughout the annual reports and other publications. It may also be traced in the catalogs of the Biblical Library.[27] Since the library served as the basis for the Society's scriptural translations, the development of its collection provides evidence of shifting priorities within the organization it served. The earliest surviving catalog, printed in 1837, reflects a relative emphasis upon Bible work within the United States. Although a total of eighty-five languages other than English are represented, this figure is somewhat misleading, since many of the non-English editions were published by foreign Bible societies. In 1823 the board had resolved to purchase from societies abroad "a regular series of Bibles and Testaments . . . other than in the English language, to be deposited in the Biblical Library."[28] Of far greater evidential value is the relatively small number of titles listed under "lexicons, concordances, and bibliographical works," the part of the library that would have enabled the Society to fulfill its constitutional pledge to "extend its influence to other countries." Only twenty-three of a total of 531 titles in the 1837 catalog fell under this heading.[29] Clearly, Bible translations for distribution overseas were not a priority for the Society during its first two decades.

Some of the Bibles in foreign languages in the collection were editions that the Society imported or published for domestic distribution. For example, during its first year alone it purchased from abroad Bibles in German, Gaelic, and Welsh and printed a French Bible.[30] Copies of these were added to the library. This effort to reach the nation's non–English speaking readers reflects the managers' conviction that Bible reading would inculcate the evangelical values upon which to build an inclusive culture for the new republic. They were confident that distributing the Gospel among the foreign born would transmit "the principles of knowledge and virtue so valuable to a republican government."[31] Perhaps the most interesting example of this inclusive spirit and optimism is the Bible Society's early support of missionary activities among Native American tribes. The 1837 catalog lists editions of the Scriptures in nine Indian languages, including the *Epistles of John* in Delaware published by the Society in 1818,[32] and the earliest annual reports stressed that "the Board have not been unmindful of their *brethren of the woods*." Even though the tribes were "divided from us by . . . everything which distinguishes savage from civilized man," the introduction of the Bible would effect an "improvement in civilization" and thus enable them to partake of the blessings of European culture.[33]

This zeal for civilizing "the heathen" can only be understood in an international context. Like republicanism, nineteenth-century evangelicalism was a transatlantic ideology. Indeed, the two shared critical points of convergence, the most important of them an implicit faith in reason, science, and progress. Elias Boudinot's denunciation of Thomas Paine notwithstanding, the leaders of the American Bible Society saw themselves as the vanguard of the Age of Reason. Like the Bible societies in Europe, the American society consistently used the imagery of Enlightenment when describing its efforts to spread the Word to the benighted peoples of Africa and Asia. It conflated the light of the Gospel with the advance of commerce and science, which, allied with the missionary impulse, would bring about an "empire of religion and civilization."[34] The annual report in 1838, for example, reminded Bible workers that "the operations of this Society were never designed for our land alone" and noted the divinely inspired "changes among nations favorable to the introduction of the Scriptures," including an international "commerce [that] is bringing us into contact with almost every people."[35] The catalog published in 1837 solicited donations from members in the hope that the library would become "an extensive repository of the most valuable works relating to . . . Biblical science," which would promote "the spread of the Holy Scriptures among the nations of the earth."[36]

Enjoined by its constitution to "extend its influence to other countries," the Bible Society had always aided missionary work abroad, but during its early years these efforts were relatively modest. Normally this support was in the form of grants to Protestant missions for foreign translations. Between 1816 and 1831, the board appropriated less than $5,300 to overseas organizations.[37] Beginning in the 1830s, however, there was a dramatic shift in the Society's priorities. In 1833 alone, the managers granted a total of $15,000 to support translations of the Bible by missionaries in India, Burma, and Hawaii.[38] At the annual meeting the following year, with the confidence and optimism typical of nineteenth-century evangelicals, the Society resolved to "employ its best endeavors, in concert with similar institutions, toward effecting the distribution of the Bible among all the accessible population of the globe, within the shortest practicable period."[39]

This dramatic resolution "called the attention of missionaries anew to the work of preparing translations" and effected a distinct change in the scope and character of the Biblical Library.[40] From 1837 to 1863 the number of foreign languages represented in the collection rose from 85 to 125, most of them non-European, the translation of which the Society had underwritten. The managers boasted "that more than three-fourths of the entire race, if able to read, could here find the revealed will of their common Creator."[41] There was also a corresponding increase in linguistic reference works. The 1863 catalog classed ninety-six titles under "grammatical works," and "dictionaries and lexikons," again many of them in non-Western languages.[42] Finally, there was an entirely new kind of book that was listed under "miscellany." During this later period, the annual reports occasionally solicited donations of "sketches of travel, or histories of nations," noting that such titles were valuable, "as the Society is now extensively engaged in preparing and distributing books in foreign countries."[43] More than fifty titles in history and travel in exotic lands and biographies or autobiographies of overseas missionaries were included in the 1863 catalog.[44]

There were a number of motives behind this growing enthusiasm for translations and for Bible work overseas from the 1830s onward. Certainly the prospect of converting the heathen in foreign climes was considerably more exotic and dramatic than distributing Bibles to poor immigrants at home. A more compelling reason, however, may lie in fundamental changes in the way that Society members perceived their domestic market. As immigration increased and the country became more ethnically and denominationally heterogeneous, Bible workers were less confident that the Scriptures could serve as the foundation of an inclusive American republic. This diminishing faith in shared values was an important part of the changing emphases within the American Bible Society.

When the Society was founded in 1816, America was on the brink of fundamental social, political, and economic change. The 1820s saw the beginnings of the development of a modern party system, in which professional politicians managed national political organizations fueled by political patronage and cemented by party loyalty rather than adherence to abstract political ideals. Although the country was religiously and ethnically diverse before 1816, that diversity increased markedly in the succeeding decades as immigrants arrived in increasing numbers, and theological divisions arose within the ranks of evangelical Protestantism. Perhaps most significantly, the United States was moving rapidly toward a modern, industrial, nationally integrated economy. All of these changes were aspects of an emerging liberal culture that was reflected in the American Bible Society and the library it developed to sustain its efforts in the Bible cause.

A sharp distinction between republicanism and liberalism tends to distort the history of this critical transitional period. To begin with, republican and liberal values are, in a sense, incommensurable. Republicanism developed historically as a political ideology and liberalism was originally associated with economic theory. Although both were identified with a broader cluster of cultural values, each tended to emphasize different, relatively discrete spheres of human activity. Moreover, certain of the defining republican and liberal values were more complementary than oppositional. The difference between terms such as liberty and rights, or independence and individualism is a matter of nuance that would have meant little to the men and women of the early nineteenth century. To insist upon elaborate distinctions between such keywords imposes our own theories upon real persons and events. The managers of the American Bible Society did not think and act according to paradigms articulated by historians more than a century and a half after the fact. In their eyes, they were simply spreading the word under rapidly evolving circumstances. In doing so, they, in the words of Gordon Wood, "without . . . realizing they were defending 'republicanism' or advancing 'liberalism' . . . cumulatively transformed the culture."[45]

The complex relationship between republicanism and liberalism is well illustrated by a critical event in the life of that most republican of

Bible Society leaders and the founder of its library, John Pintard. In October 1791, Pintard was employed as an agent for William Duer, a wealthy speculator living in New York City. Together they were implicated in the young republic's first financial panic and possibly the first instance of what today would be called insider trading. Duer and a group of associates that included members of such prominent New York families as the Livingstons, the Verplancks, and the Roosevelts conspired to corner the market in the stock of the Bank of the United States and the Bank of New York, having been assured, according to Duer, by his friend, Secretary of the Treasury Alexander Hamilton, that the two institutions were about to merge. Pintard's role was to help finance the operation through loans from small-time investors, laborers, shopkeepers, and artisans. By March 1792, he had borrowed nearly $700,000, a vast sum at the time. When the proposed merger fell through, many of these humble investors lost their life savings, the economy went into a brief but disastrous depression, and William Duer went to jail. The mayor wisely reinforced the guard to discourage the lynch mobs that gathered nightly outside his cell. John Pintard fled with his books and his family across the Hudson to New Jersey. He lived in Newark for the next several years, including more than a year spent in debtor's prison, and did not return to New York until 1797, when Congress passed the first national bankruptcy law.[46] Properly chastened, he wrote years later "he that maketh haste to get rich encompasseth himself in many sorrows. Alas! How sadly I have experienced the truth of this . . . proverb."[47]

Contemporary opinion divided over whether Pintard was a dupe or a knave. The truth probably lies somewhere between these extremes. He was certainly foolish to have associated with a swindler like Duer, but he must also have understood the serious risks to which he was exposing thousands of working-class investors. From our perspective, it is perhaps more to the point to ask whether he was a hypocrite. The stern republicanism to which he ostensibly adhered posed an irreconcilable opposition between speculation and the commonweal, between unearned wealth and republican virtue. Did the John Pintard who during this period signed a letter, "John Pintard, Humble servant is rather an antirepublican phrase," betray his values in associating with a shady speculator like William Duer?[48] The Panic of 1792 is an extreme example, but it shows that, in practice, there was no irresolvable tension between republicanism and the market. John Pintard came of age in a time of unbridled optimism and ambition. He and the other civic-minded leaders of the American Bible Society never felt compelled to live up to later historians' paradigmatic version of republicanism. They celebrated the expansive, exuberant spirit of the age and saw no contradiction between *Homo civitatis* and *Homo economicus*.

A philanthropic association within the public sphere, the Bible Society was, from its inception, at the forefront of innovations in the economic sphere. Two of the earliest additions to the Biblical Library were copies of *The School Bible* and the New Testament, published in 1810 and 1814 respectively, by David and George Bruce of New York, purportedly the first Bibles stereotyped in the United States.[49] Stereotyping is the printing of pages from metal plates produced from molds cast from blocks of moveable type. This revolutionary process significantly reduced labor costs for mass printings and was therefore ideally suited to the purposes of the American Bible Society. In the "Address to the People of the United States" delivered at the organizing convention in 1816, the managers promised to "furnish great districts of the American continent with well executed stereotype plates, for their cheap and extensive diffusion," and subsequent annual reports repeatedly emphasized that "their first exertions ought to be directed towards the procurement of well executed stereotype plates."[50]

When combined with the new, increasingly sophisticated steam presses of the 1830s and 1840s, stereotyping allowed the Society to compete with and in many cases even surpass the capacity of the major commercial printing houses of the era.[51] In 1850, it printed more than 633,000 Bibles and Testaments, and by 1862 annual production had surpassed one million.[52] In May 1853, the Bible Society dedicated a new headquarters, a six-story Bible House that occupied an entire city block at Astor Place in lower Manhattan. The largest building in the city at the time, it included a spacious, fireproof room for the library and enabled the Society to consolidate all of its operations under one roof. The production process was "so planned, that from the delivery of the paper in Ninth Street, it proceeds regularly through its various stages of manufacture, until it arrives in books in the Depository, with but very little labour in hoisting from one story to another." The Society's new home was the culmination of the managers' dedication to efficiency and productivity, in the words of historian Peter Wosh, "a monument to industrial technology."[53]

Just as important as the mechanization of labor during this period was a concomitant revolution in corporate organization. As corporations in both the public and economic spheres grew in size and complexity, they necessarily adopted new and distinctively modern functions and organizational structures. The development of the American Bible Society generally and its library in particular portended changes in the management of bureaucracies that are often associated with large for-profit corporations much later in the century. When John Pintard established the Biblical Library in 1817, his primary goal was to assist the Society's employees in preparing accurate translations of the Scriptures. Annual reports emphasized that "the object was to have the means at hand for comparing one version with another," thus enabling the translators to determine "the true meaning of the Inspired Word."[54] Yet, the library was part of a complex, evolving organization and, as such, it served multiple functions that changed over time. For example, Bible Society publications also noted that it could "be visited, and the books there consulted, by any friend of the Society."[55] In part, this invitation was simply meant to share the library's bibliographic treasures with the evangelical reading public. However, the public nature of the collection served more than one end. In 1896, Corresponding Secretary Edward Gilman prepared a report for Society in which he outlined the history and condition of the library and held that, apart from its practical uses, "consciously or unconsciously," the founders intended that it would function as a "museum or place for exhibiting the results of past and current Bible work with a view to the enlisting of new enthusiasm for the future."[56] The library thus served a very modern purpose. In part it was a public relations tool, a means of enlisting support for the Bible movement. It was part of complex organization and could perform a multiplicity of functions, both internal and external.

From its inception, the library served an internal function that was just as important as its role as a resource for the Society's translators. In 1816, the American Bible Society was one of the few nongovernmental bodies in the United States that was truly national, indeed international, in scope. In order to market the Scriptures throughout the states and territories, as well as to Protestant missions abroad, the Society performed many complex, interrelated activities, including printing and binding, sales and distribution, and fundraising. Coordinating and documenting all of these functions over vast distances required an effective recordkeeping system, what today would be called an archives or a records management center. Shortly after Pintard became recording secretary in 1817, the Board of Managers instructed him to copy the Society's outgoing communications "into books provided for that purpose, one for foreign and the other for domestic correspondence," and "to note in the said Books the time when, and the mode in which he forwarded each letter." He was further charged with maintaining "an Alphabetical Index and such marginal notes as may promote the convenience of reference" for the managers and to make these records available at every meeting of the board.[57] This archival function was later formalized and expanded in 1845 in the Society's first printed by-laws, which stated that "in [the library] shall be placed . . . all manuscripts, and other interesting papers which the Society . . . may deem worthy of preservation."[58] Long before for-profit, national corporations such as the railroads, the Bible Society began developing in its library a modern system of corporate records management.

Not long after the library's archival function was made explicit in the by-laws, there was a critical change in the nature of the records that it archived. The Society's most important administrative documents were the reports transmitted by its Bible agents, each of whom was responsible for a soliciting donations and selling the Scriptures in a state or territory or in an overseas agency.[59] Through the early 1850s, these monthly statements, which were often excerpted in the annual reports, were relatively informal, anecdotal accounts of Bible work throughout the United States and the world. This format allowed agents to "weave the whole into a narrative, which affords an opportunity of introducing anything interesting in the way of incidents, anecdote, remarks or conversation coming under their notice."[60] All of this changed in February 1859, when the board mandated a standardized, printed form for the monthly reports. Designed by Archibald Russell, a founder of the American Geographical and Statistical Society and the author of *Principles of Statistical Inquiry* (1839), the new report required agents to supply weekly figures in twenty-six columns, all culminating in the monthly "total receipts from sales and donations."[61] This format enabled accountants and managers in the Bible House in New York to gauge the effectiveness of individual employees and to summarize the progress of the Bible cause generally in a statistically precise fashion. The substitution of numbers for narrative in the records archived in the Biblical Library marks a decisive transition to a modern corporate model of organization and the ascendancy of impersonal corporate values.

At the same time that the Society was consolidating its operations nationally and internationally, its vision of an inclusive culture based upon evangelical Protestant values was slowly fragmenting. To begin with, this projection of interdenominational harmony was never more than an ideal. From its inception, the Bible cause never presented a truly unified front against infidelity. In 1816, a number of prominent organizations, including, most notably, the Philadelphia Bible Society and the Episcopal Bible and Common Prayer Book Society, declined to send delegates to the constituting convention. In 1823, the same year that John Pintard began to prepare the Biblical Library's first catalog, the Board of Managers directed that he should "procure all such works as have been published . . . or that may hereafter be published, in relation to the controversy on the subject of Bible Socïeties."[62] Pintard himself became embroiled in a bitter debate with the leader of his own church, John Hobart, the Episcopal bishop of New York, over his membership in the Bible Society. The Society's librarian at first hesitated to join because Hobart "at the origin of this Institution . . . alarmed the Episcopalians by holding out that the American Bible Society swallowed them up in the gulph of presbyterianism and warned them against the danger of becoming members." Pintard quickly overcame his misgivings and later complained that "the Episcopalians with our Bishop apprehended that we would be annihilated by associating with other denominations in this great and glorious work."[63] Although such divisions within the ranks of Protestantism were rare in the 1810s and 1820s, the dispute was a harbinger of future interdenominational conflicts. As the country became more diverse ethnically and more divided denominationally, the Society's optimism and its rhetoric of inclusion became increasingly problematic.

The Bible Society hoped to ensure denominational harmony by focusing solely on the lowest common denominator theologically. It sought to avoid controversy by distributing the Bible "without note or comment." However, a seemingly technical point of Biblical translation called into question the unity of purpose within the Bible cause and eventually precipitated a schism within the Society. Baptists believe that the baptism of adults into the church requires literal and complete immersion in water. Reflecting this belief, they read "immersion versions" of the Bible that rendered the Greek word *baptiso* as "to immerse" rather than "to baptize." In 1835, Baptist missionaries requested funds from the American Bible Society to publish an immersion translation of the Scriptures for their mission in Calcutta. When the Board of Managers voted to reject their request, on the grounds that they could "encourage only such versions as conform in the principles of their translation to the Common English Version," the Baptist members of the board resigned and formed a rival organization, the American and Foreign Bible Society.[64] As a result of the controversy, the Society placed renewed emphasis upon its Biblical Library to enhance the authority of its translations. In 1836, it hired George Bush, the chairman of the Oriental Languages Department at New York University, as editor of all its publications. He was instructed to "have care of the Library" and to "have charge of the integrity of the text of the English Scriptures printed by the Society, rendering them all conformable to the standard copy now in use."[65] By the 1830s, the American Bible Society's original vision of pan-denominational unity had faded considerably.

The dispute with the Baptists over immersion translations was relatively minor compared with the Society's conflicts with the Catholic Church. As the number and influence of Roman Catholics in the United States grew in the 1820s and the 1830s, the Society became increasingly distrustful and intolerant. While its publications still referred occasionally to the "better class" of priests who were allies in the Bible cause, the emphasis shifted decidedly to "the more corrupt of the priesthood [who] are opposed the distribution of the Scriptures in any form" or who circulated only Catholic versions of the Bible, "a cunning device for power."[66] All of the annotated catalogs of the Biblical Library published after 1837 carefully noted each title that appeared on the church's *Index of Prohibited Books*. This anti-Catholicism reached its height in 1849 with the publication of William P. Strickland's official *History of the American Bible Society*. Strickland devoted an entire chapter to "Bible Prohibition in Roman Catholic Countries" and included lurid references to American priests burning the Scriptures.[67]

This fear and suspicion of the church was directly related to the ethnicity of its communicants. Especially after the Potato Famine in the late 1840s, an increasing proportion of American Catholics were immigrants from Ireland, a group many within the ranks of the Bible cause deemed unfit for republican government. Even John Pintard, certainly one of the more broad-minded of the Society's leaders, wrote despairingly of a country "overwhelmed with Irish emigrants," poor "Pat and his wife Shelah [who] cannot withstand the temptation" of alcohol, which leads to "thefts, incendiaries, and murders."[68] This same unease over the rising tide of immigration is evident in the Society's publications. At the annual meeting in 1837, a resolution was passed expressing concern over "the rapid influx of foreign emigrants, the great extent to which they are without the Bible, and the consequent danger of their example and influence while in this condition." A year earlier, the annual report had urged members to redouble their efforts to supply newcomers with the Scriptures and added ominously that "in the thorough performance of this duty depends in no small measure the perpetuity of our social institutions."[69] Within twenty years of its founding, the Society's initial optimism had diminished considerably. In the face of rising demographic and denominational diversity, it had, to a considerable extent, lost faith in its vision of an inclusive culture founded upon a set of unifying values.

The Biblical Library is important in the history of nineteenth-century reform because it reflects this gradual shift from a unified republican culture to a fragmented liberal culture earlier than many other associations within the public sphere. In addition, it highlights the pervasiveness of evangelical values throughout the nineteenth century, values that were critical as well to other public libraries in New York City. Finally, the Bible Society and its library are an early example of the rise of the national corporation in the United States. Corporatization within the economic sphere was to have a profound effect on the public sphere later in the century. Large-scale evangelical organizations like the American Bible Society pioneered the new form of organization.

5

Commerce and Culture

Recreation and Self-Improvement in New York's Subscription Libraries

In 1849, the City of New York taxed the New York Society Library. The tax assessor determined that since a considerable portion of its building on Broadway and Leonard Streets was leased to various businesses or rented out for exhibits, concerts, and other performances, the Library was not exempt from taxation as a public institution. The trustees appealed the assessment and lost. In December 1853, Judge Robert Emmett of the Superior Court held that the property was "used and occupied for the purpose of gain and traffic" and therefore taxable real estate.[1] This long and complex legal dispute raises fundamental questions regarding the public character of subscription libraries such as the New York Society Library. Since the Library, in order to maintain its membership and its collection, was required to generate income and attract "customers" just like a commercial concern, to what extent did it fulfill a public purpose? Was it substantially different from a commercial library, "an ordinary circulating library," that the movement party, the pro-Athenaeum faction, referred to in their criticism of the Board of Trustees in the heated elections of the 1830s?[2]

Although later in the nineteenth century commercial circulating libraries simply rented out their books just as video stores today rent DVDs, initially they were in some respects similar to the New York Society Library. Patrons paid an annual, semiannual, monthly, or even a weekly subscription to borrow from their collections. The critical difference was that they operated for profit and their customers did not purchase stock, a share in the library to join a society of readers. Commercial circulating libraries in Great Britain started around 1725. William Rind of Annapolis founded the first in the American colonies in 1762. The first in New York City and the third in North America opened in August 1763, not coincidentally when the Society Library was closed temporarily for renovations. Garrat Noel's library was typical in that it was part of his bookstore next door to the Merchants Coffee House on Wall and Water Streets, but later circulating collections were available in a variety of other establishments, including dry goods stores and millinery shops. Noel's subscription, four dollars annually, was actually rather more expensive that the Society Library's, but the annual fees for the city's circulating libraries varied considerably.[3] At a time when most books were comparatively expensive, a luxury item in the eighteenth century, commercial circulating libraries made print culture accessible to readers of more modest means. William Rind's first advertisement, for example, expressed his desire to "open and extend the fountains of knowledge, which are at present shut against all but men of affluent fortunes."[4]

When the pro-Athenaeum candidates for the Society Library's board referred in 1833 to an ordinary circulating library in a pamphlet criticizing the incumbents, they were not implying that there was an inherent contradiction between commerce and the diffusion of knowledge. The belief that commercialism was by its nature vulgar and therefore inimical to culture emerged later in the century, especially during the Gilded Age. During the early republic, some of the New York's most important cultural institutions were commercial establishments. The city's first museum was founded by John Pintard in 1791 under the auspices of the Tammany Society (later in the nineteenth century better known as Tammany Hall), but not long thereafter it was sold to his friend John Scudder, an amateur naturalist. From 1816 to 1830, Scudder's American Museum was an affiliate of the New York Institution, sharing free quarters provided by the Common Council with the New-York Historical Society, the Academy of Fine Arts, and the Literary and Philosophical Society.[5] Under Scudder's direction and with Pintard's encouragement, the museum developed exhibits that were designed to entertain as well as educate the people. It included, for example, an extensive gallery of unusual shells and rare butterflies, as well as a massive Grand Naval Panorama depicting American victories on the Great Lakes during the War of 1812.[6]

Similarly, the city's earliest commercial circulating libraries were expected both to entertain and to instruct, to provide the reading public with "rational amusement." Garrat Noel's very first advertisement, for example, informed "those who delight in reading" that his collection was available for their "profit and entertainment."[7] Even quite early in the nineteenth century, however, there was a tension between republican values, the expectation that a collection serve an edifying, moralizing public purpose, and the market, the popular demand for purely recreational reading. When Joseph Osborn published a prospectus of his library in 1806, he was somewhat ambivalent, even defensive regarding the provision of fiction. On one hand, he assured prospective customers that "the department of *Novels and Romances (as hitherto obtaining the most substantial patronage)* has been so copiously and so attentively supplied that scarcely a Novel or Romance [is] not included." At the same time, he hoped to "convince those of their error who imagine that Novels and Romances constitute the principal part of this collection, and who, but for the prejudices they entertain against that kind of reading would willingly subscribe to [the] library." Osborn further "assure[d] the public that . . . no books shall be circulated . . . which are generally deemed unfriendly to the cause of virtue" and "parents and heads of families in particular" that young readers would "be supplied with books of instruction and rational amusement."[8]

By the time the pro-Athenaeum candidates for the board charged that the trustees of the Society Library had developed a collection that "scarcely offers more attraction than . . . an ordinary circulating library," it was evidently more profitable to provide entertainment than to diffuse knowledge. In 1841, P. T. Barnum purchased the American Museum from John Scudder's heirs.[9] For just twenty-five cents, New Yorkers could view such "curiosities" as the Swiss Bearded Lady, a dwarf Aztec priest and priestess "from a newly discovered and idolatrous people of Central America" (who had also been on display at the Society Library when the trustees' tax case was before the Superior Court) and, "the most amusing imaginable, as well as the most extraordinary," General Tom Thumb, the smallest man in the world. The *New York Herald* dismissed Barnum as a "moral humbug," but the public flocked to his extravaganzas.[10] Similarly, the city's commercial circulating libraries by this time had abandoned any pretense of developing collections to promote rational amusement. Their advertisements and published catalogs attracted readers almost exclusively with popular novels.[11] In 1840, when the New York Lyceum attempted to found a public library that would offer an alternative to the commercial libraries, the directors circulated a pamphlet that warned that "these are the only collections [that] are open to all classes of people," yet they were not "designed for popular instruction." Instead, they offered "captivating, but dangerous and often disgusting and immoral works of fiction."[12]

The Lyceum's pamphlet was also critical of the city's public libraries. The Society Library, as well as the Mercantile Library Association and the Apprentices' Library, offered far fewer novels than the commercial libraries, but they were nonetheless the most popular, the most highly circulated part of their collections. New York's existing public libraries did not, therefore, promote "the cause of truth and virtue" and advance the "intellectual and moral welfare" of the community.[13] Significantly, however, the Lyceum directors conceded that "these libraries are, to a considerable extent, obliged to comply with the general requirements of their frequenters." They relied largely upon annual subscriptions to develop their collections and competed for readers with the ordinary circulating libraries. In an expanding market for print, public libraries were obliged cater to popular demand. The history of the city's subscription libraries in the ensuing decades sheds light upon a tension between public purpose and presumably private pleasure.

When the City taxed the New York Society Library in 1849, it held not simply that the building was used as a source of gain and traffic, but more fundamentally, that the Library itself was not a public institution. Since it was "owned by certain individuals as stockholders," it was not "of a public character," and therefore not, "in point of public usefulness," a "public library according to the true intent and meaning" of the statute governing taxable property.[14] One way in which to assess the public character of the Library is to examine the manner in which it recruited its stockholders, how it defined the public that it served. Unlike the city's commercial libraries, the New York Society Library rarely advertised. In 1844, the Board of Trustees appointed a special committee to "devise a plan by which this institution may be brought more prominently before the public and its usefulness be extended." The members composed an elaborate address that solicited the "favor and support of their fellow citizens" and confidently predicted that "in this community there must be . . . thousands who would eagerly avail themselves of [the Library's] privileges." The committee recommended that the appeal be published in local newspapers. Instead, a different, shorter address was printed and apparently circulated privately. Rather than welcome thousands to the Library, it simply stated that "an important public interest" would be served if "a fair proportion of the inhabitants of this city who have the means of enjoying the privilege" were to join.[15]

The trustees were torn between the need to raise revenue with which to develop the collection and a desire to maintain the exclusivity of the membership. One obvious way of resolving this dilemma was simply to raise the price of a subscription. When the board voted in 1866 to increase the annual fee from six to ten dollars, they noted that it would ensure a "comparative exclusiveness," which "like all other luxuries . . . must be paid for." The alternative, expanding the membership, would occasion "some inconvenience to the present body of shareholders." Rather than advertising extensively like an "ordinary circulating library" and risk attracting undesirable applicants, the trustees and the librarian sought to recruit suitable members by personal solicitation. The annual report for 1873, for example, urged that "each shareholder is a centre in him or herself, and can, if so inclined, help" increase the number of subscribers and thereby augment the Society's income. Similarly, the report for 1898, called upon "the members to interest such of their acquaintances in the institution as are likely to prove desirable acquisitions."[16] This mode of recruitment certainly preserved the elite status of the Library. By the turn of the century, a circular informed prospective readers that "its books circulate to a select membership who become subscribers by invitation."[17]

In the annual reports and other publications, the collection was often referred to as a "Family Library." They stressed that a share was intended for the use not just of the individual shareholder, but also his entire household. The trustee's report for 1857 stated that, unlike, for instance, the Astor and the Mercantile Library Association, "ours is emphatically the Family Library, sending its treasures to the fireside and closet." This was a means of highlighting its "distinctive character," of setting itself apart as it faced increasing competition from other institutions in the city.[18] Later in the century, however, as the nouveau riche joined the ranks of New York society, the Society Library placed an increasing emphasis upon the lineage of the families that comprised the membership. A circular published in 1876, for example, "presenting the public advantages" of the Library, noted with pride that it had since its founding "fulfilled its duties in meeting the literary wants of successive generations of the best families of the city."[19] Catering especially to the Knickerbockers who traced their ancestry back to the colonial era, the Society Library's membership declined even as New York became the capital of a national elite. In 1856, when the Library moved to its new building on Astor Place, there were 1,087 shareholders. A half-century later there were only 725. By that time, the Library had dropped even the pretense of having a "public character." In 1905, the trustees explained in their annual report that they never "advertise its advantages in the daily papers, as most business concerns do," because "its patronage," comprising "the first families of the first city of America," might "thereby lose its charm."[20]

To the extent that the Library did market its privileges, it made special efforts to attract female readers. The Ladies Reading Room in the new building on Astor Place "answered the best expectations of the Trustees in awakening a lively interest on the part of those whose aid is ever essential" and proved "an agreeable literary resort for those who have the taste and leisure to use" it. In part, this solicitude for the presumed special needs of female subscribers was a reflection of the ideology of domesticity. In the annual report for 1857, for example, "'Woman's Rights' in this sphere of her duty" were "acknowledge[d] to the fullest extent." Fine arts and literature, as well as the education of children, were feminine concerns. The board therefore anticipated that the new reading room "must necessarily exert a good influence in creating a taste for reading."[21] Perhaps more important, marketing to female readers simply made good business sense. By 1900, three-fourths of the visitors to the Library were women. Catering to them was the best way to ensure that the city's first families continued to subscribe.[22]

What the ladies were reading, as well as their husbands, fathers and brothers, was fiction. From 1854 to 1856, novels accounted for slightly more than 45 percent of the volumes loaned by the Library. Although the annual reports rarely provide circulation statistics, that number no doubt increased steadily in the ensuing decades. By 1899, it had reached approximately 78 percent. Moreover, the supply increased to keep up with the demand. In 1850, fiction was just 5 percent of the entire collection.[23] In 1886 alone, 42 percent of the new volumes added were novels. Toward the end of the century, there was certainly a more liberal attitude toward the provision of fiction in libraries generally, but at least some of what was circulated by the Society Library during this period could hardly have been considered uplifting or enlightening. For example, the list of new titles appended to the annual report for 1895 includes not only several entertaining volumes of popular detective fiction, but also the latest work by Ouida, the most notoriously trashy novelist of the day. The following year a member wrote to the chair of the Board of Trustees to complain that her sister had borrowed a lurid fictional biography entitled *Criminals I have Known* (1895). "Surely anyone who desires such a book," she fumed, "can buy it for himself. Why ever admit one to the library?"[24]

To justify the purchase and circulation of popular fiction the trustees during this period made two contradictory arguments. The first was similar to the justifications offered by the managers of the publically funded free circulating libraries that provided recreational reading to New York's working class in the 1880s and 1890s. They held that although the Society Library bought and the shareholders read large quantities of novels, they were only novels of suitable literary quality. The annual report for 1857, for example, stated that "the character of books purchased is fully up to the standard of former years, embracing all the popular works of merit of the day." In 1881, the trustees boasted that during that year there had "been a greater demand for books, particularly works of a higher standard."[25] However, there was a fundamental difference between why the trustees of the Society Library and the managers of the free circulating libraries felt compelled to explain away the popularity of popular novels. In the case of the latter, it was a defense of public libraries as they were coming to be understood. The free libraries had to justify the expenditure of public funds and assure taxpayers that their collections were uplifting the masses thorough the medium of print. For the elites who managed the Society Library, the defense of recreational reading was inextricably related to class and status. The trustees had to contend that the shareholders read only the finest novels in order to maintain the fiction that the true upper class had a natural monopoly on culture. In their report for 1903, they explained that "as the members are persons of refinement and culture, [we are] guided in [our] selections of new books as far as possible by the expressed wishes of the members."[26] The reading of the first families of New York was, by definition, refined, an expression of their cultural superiority.

The second, contradictory argument that the board employed to justify the purchase of popular fiction was eminently practical and reflects the business model upon which the commercial circulating libraries operated. In their report for 1858, a year after they had assured the shareholders that they selected only works of the highest standard, the trustees noted that "complaints have been made that the Novelties of the day are not provided in sufficient number to supply the demand." They recognized that "it is absolutely necessary that several copies of every popular work should be purchased on its first appearance."[27] This was simply a realistic acknowledgment that, in order to retain its membership (and maintain its income) the Library had to obey the law of supply and demand, just as a commercial library did. In fact, since it appealed to a small niche market, New York's most elite families, satisfying the demand for recreational reading was especially imperative.

By the turn of the century, fewer and fewer subscribers were coming to the Library to borrow its books. When the new building opened on Astor Place in 1856, it was considered the "heart of the choice residential section of the city," the "centre of New York society."[28] Yet, in the later decades, the city's first families built their homes farther and farther uptown. As early as 1870 the trustees complained that the Library's "income is becoming more and more affected by the upward movement of the population of the city," and by 1884 they frankly admitted that the collection was "no longer convenient of access" for "that class of citizens for whom it was originally designed." In an effort to maintain the membership, they began to deliver books to the shareholders' homes for a modest fee.[29] Starting in 1904, delivery was offered for free, and the following year it accounted for more than 70 percent of the circulation. In the early twentieth century, the service became a major attraction, an effective means of retaining old members and attracting new ones. A circular published in the 1920s promised prospective readers that the Society Library was "the ideal library, because you do not have to go to its building," and noted that upon request books were even sent by parcel post to elite resorts such as Newport and Palm Beach.[30]

As late as 1888, two years after the State of New York passed the law that permitted the City to appropriate tax monies to the free circulating libraries, the Society Library still referred to itself as a public library. Despite its elite membership and costly annual subscription, it continued fairly late into the nineteenth century to idealize itself as valuable public institution. Yet, by the turn of the twentieth century, as Andrew Carnegie began to build an extensive system of branch libraries for the New York Public Library, the trustees and subscribers were clearly no longer concerned with even the pretense of assuming a public role in the cultural life of the city. The New York Society Library advertised its exclusivity to those "sensitive persons" who, in the words of the annual report for 1905, "object to [the] crowded rooms [and] discomforts of a public library," assuring those who might have concerns about "hygiene and contagion" that "its books have always circulated among a select membership." The first public library in the city of New York "offered to each of its members all the advantages of a private library."[31]

In January 1861, Nathan Appleton Lee, a young lawyer living in New York, wrote home to his sister Harriet Glover in Charleston. Written one month after South Carolina seceded from the Union, his letter made no mention of the secession crisis or an impending civil war. Instead, he described for her subscription libraries in his adopted city. A member of the Society Library, which he termed "a Family Library or one designed for the use of ladies as well as gentlemen," Lee explained that he had joined because he had "been particularly pleased with the description of people who frequent the . . . Library, . . . generally rather old and quiet men [of] gentlemanly demeanor." He had considered membership in one other subscription library, but found its members to be mostly "noisy and rather rowdy young men," who "only come to make displays of themselves." This was the Mercantile Library Association, the Society Library's main competitor and, at the time, the largest circulating library in New York.[32]

The Library was organized with the help of William Wood about the same time that he assisted in the founding of the Apprentices' Library of the General Society of Mechanics and Tradesmen. On November 3, 1820, he posted a notice on the bulletin board of the *Commercial Advertiser* inviting "the young men of South Street, Front, Water, Pearl, Maiden Lane and Broadway," then the main business thoroughfares of the city, to a meeting to discuss the formation of a library for merchants' clerks. On November 27, a group of self-improving aspiring merchants adopted a constitution and elected officers and, on February 12 of the following year, opened the Mercantile Library Association of the City of New York in rented rooms on Fulton Street. The library grew slowly over the next few years, mainly through donations. By 1826 it had a collection of approximately 3,300 volumes and about 700 members, each of whom paid an annual subscription of two dollars. The main obstacles to growth were limited funds with which to purchase books and limited space in which to shelve them. In 1828, a group of benevolent merchants founded the Clinton Hall Association (named for DeWitt Clinton, who died that year) and erected a large building for the Library on Nassau Street, which opened in November 1830. Most of the space was rented out to stores and offices, providing a generous and reliable source of income. By an agreement effected between the two institutions, stockholders of the Clinton Hall Association were permitted to use the collection for free and retained control over their real estate, but only young men employed as clerks could join the Library, vote and hold office.[33]

During its early history, the Mercantile Library served a number of closely related functions beyond simply providing good reading for self-improving young men. The Library was central to the clerks' identity as aspiring merchants and a means of enhancing the reputation and influence of the "commercial class." As the term was understood in the early nineteenth century, *class* did not refer to socioeconomic status, but rather was used somewhat loosely to identify groups of people who shared common aims and activities. The New York Society Library, for example, sought to recruit as subscribers "persons of leisure of every class," including parents, students, and "literary, scientific and professional men."[34] In annual reports and addresses before the Association, the young men of the Mercantile Library were repeatedly reminded that members of the mercantile class traded not solely for mere profit, but for the moral and material advancement of humankind. The Library during this period espoused an ideology that Stuart Blumin has termed the "commercial theory of value" (in opposition to Ricardo's labor theory of value embraced by the mechanic class in the General Society of Mechanics and Tradesmen). It held that the exchange of goods was the source of all value and all progress throughout history. For example, in a lecture in 1836 "On the Benefits and Influence of Commerce," John Gourlie claimed that it "exhibits to us a true picture of the career of man, from a state of barbarism, to a state of cultivated civilization and refinement."[35] Three years later, Noah Webster called it "the instrument by which civilization, learning, arts, science, and religion are conveyed to every part of the globe, and planted in the dark regions of ignorance and paganism." The Mercantile Library served a broader public purpose because it was, according the Association's first annual report, "calculated . . . to extend the sphere of usefulness, and advance the character of the mercantile community."[36]

Although the Mercantile Library was founded as an educational institution, during its early history it was clearly concerned as much with the moral as with the mental improvement of its members. For young clerks eager for advancement, morality and reputation were regarded as the key to rising within the mercantile community. A merchant was considered successful only so far as others of his class trusted him. Echoing what was a commonplace during the period, an early annual report reminded the members that "character is more valuable than capital" in the pursuit of success in business. Supporters of the Library advised prospective employers that membership provided an assurance that a clerk was worthy of confidence, since it betokened a "continual cultivation of moral principles."[37] There was, moreover, an underlying, fundamental assumption that mental and moral development were inextricably linked. One of the earliest catalogs confidently pronounced that the collection would "elevate [the members'] spirits and their morals by familiarizing their moments of leisure with whatever is fair in the actions of other times or excellent in science," while an early history of the Library lauded "that love of literary pursuit, which has sown in their hearts the seed of every noble principle."[38]

In this age of reform, reformers and philanthropists were especially concerned with the moral welfare of young clerks. During the eighteenth century, a young man who aspired to join the mercantile class was trained in a system not unlike the more formal apprenticeship for an aspiring artisan employed by a member of the General Society of Mechanics and Tradesmen. He worked for a number of years for an established merchant, usually a family connection, and boarded in his home, so that he was under constant moral supervision. After he had learned the trade and established his reputation, he then "commenced business on his own account."[39] By the time the Mercantile Library was founded in 1820, this system, like the system of apprenticeships for mechanics, was clearly breaking down. As the pace of business accelerated and the size of mercantile establishments grew, merchants could no longer exercise the moral influence and oversight they had in earlier generations.

At the same time, New York and other cities became magnets for ambitious young men from the countryside seeking to make a fortune and a name for themselves.[40] No longer under the watchful eyes neighbors and family, they came, according to the Mercantile Library's first president at its first meeting, to "a large and populous city, with excitements to pleasure surrounding them on every side, and, burned on by the warmth of early years," were in danger of becoming "the votaries of vice and depravity." This concern over the moral susceptibility of young clerks was a constant refrain in the early publications of the Association. Good books in the Library would provide a potent means of averting moral disaster.[41] The Clinton Hall Association, the merchants' organization, in turn served as a kind of institutional guardian to the Mercantile Library Association and was frequently referred to as such in the Library's annual reports. In the Clinton Hall Association's articles of subscription, its trustees were instructed to "exercise a general and paternal watchfulness" over the clerks and, in the legal agreement between the two institutions, were empowered to evict the Library if it were found to contain "immoral or irreligious books."[42]

The preamble to the Mercantile Library's constitution stated that the Association was founded to "extend our information upon mercantile and other subjects of general utility [and] promote a spirit of useful inquiry." In the early annual reports and in addresses before the membership, the directors and supporters frequently expressed concern that the city's clerks, often boys as young as sixteen, with only a rudimentary common school education, were ill prepared for a career in commerce. They stressed that success as a merchant required far more than bookkeeping and basic literacy.[43] The annual report for 1836, for example, reminded the clerks that "the profession we have chosen is one that requires knowledge before its possessor can maintain an elevated rank in society," and advised them that "the whole surface of the globe—its climate, soil, productions . . . should be familiar to him." Similarly, Charles Edwards, in an address to the members three years later on "What Constitutes a Merchant," dismissed "the idea [that] his intellect is confined to the counting room" and held that the successful prosecution of his trade required a mastery of, among other subjects, mechanics, law, foreign languages, hydrography, and the history of commerce.[44]

"Subjects of general utility" such as these, however, comprised a relatively small proportion of the Library's collection. In the first catalog, published in 1821, for example, books on commerce were just 7 percent of the total, law 5 percent, and technology 1.5 percent. By contrast, titles in history and biography were 22 percent of the collection and literature 11 percent.[45] In part, this difference simply reflects the publishing industry in the early nineteenth century, the kinds of books that were printed and therefore available to the Library for purchase or by donation. More important, the relatively large proportion of titles in the humanities served to advance the broader cultural mission of the Library. It enabled the clerks of New York City, again in the words of the preamble to the constitution, to "qualify ourselves to discharge with dignity . . . the social offices of life." A member of the mercantile class was expected to be more than a mere trader. A merchant was, by definition, a gentleman as well. Through his membership in the Mercantile Library an ambitious, self-improving clerk could acquire a liberal education and thus the refinement that would, according to the introduction to the catalog of 1825, give "to our social intercourse the charm of intelligence." Such elegance, polish would reflect favorably upon a young man aspiring to rise in the profession. Just as important, it would, in the words of the directors' report for 1837, "raise the standard of mercantile character and place the merchant on a par with the most cultivated classes of society."[46]

As the Library increased its membership and expanded its collection, it began offering additional means of mental and moral self-improvement to the members and to the public. In 1838, for example, it introduced evening classes for a nominal tuition in a variety of subjects, including chemistry, bookkeeping, elocution, and music. Almost from the beginning, however, the courses were sparsely attended, and they were finally discontinued in 1870.[47] The lecture series inaugurated in 1827 proved much more popular, both with the members and the general public, and was for many years a lucrative source of income for the Association. However, the subjects addressed in the lectures changed considerably over the years as the directors "endeavored to popularize this valuable auxiliary of our institution," especially as it faced increasing competition from the New York Athenaeum and other associations in the city. The first series, on mercantile law, was described in the annual report for 1827 as a means of improving the "man of business [by] an acquaintance with those branches of science which are, in a measure, connected with commerce." By the 1840s and 1850s, there was very little science and much more entertainment. In 1859, for example, all of the subjects were of an improving, but popular nature, such as "Travels in Africa," "The Magnetic Telegraph," and "The Early Life of Franklin."[48] By this time, the annual reports more often stressed that the Association could extend its usefulness by "combining mental culture with rational amusement."[49]

From its founding, however, the Library served other functions beyond the moral and mental improvement of its members. The preamble to the constitution also stated that the Association would "adopt the most efficient means to facilitate mutual intercourse." Features such as a conversation room and debating societies were designed to appeal to the gregarious nature of young men and to foster community within the mercantile class.[50] More important, for a country boy embarking upon his career in a teeming, impersonal city, membership in the Association offered companionship and a sense of belonging. As the directors explained in their annual report for 1846, "there are many belonging to this Institution, far away from friends and the endearments of domestic life [who] make up for this great privation [by] meeting those of their own class, on one common ground, in one social brotherhood."[51] On a more practical level, the Association also provided a savings bank on the premises, made arrangements for the clerks to have access to a gymnasium and bathing facilities, and even supported a magazine, the *Merchants' Magazine and Commercial Review*. During its early years, it aspired to be as much a fraternal organization as a library.[52]

The activities that most effectively fostered mutual intercourse among the members of the Association were the annual meetings and the annual elections of the Board of Direction. Unlike the Society Library, the campaigns for office were spirited, highly organized, and hotly contested. The candidates formed opposing parties (usually designated the "Regular Ticket" and the "Reform Ticket"), published platforms and broadsides, and debated issues in the local press.[53] Similarly, the annual meetings were rowdy, boisterous events, at which the clerks seem to have taken great delight in amending their constitution.[54] Although the Association's supporters and local editors occasionally admonished them for "exciting faction" and for their "over excited zeal," there seems to have been a consensus that, for the most part, this was all just good, clean fun. *Leslie's Illustrated*, for example, reported after the election in 1859 that "as usual 'the boys' had an uproarious good time," and the trustees of the Clinton Hall Association noted with approval that in all likelihood "both parties will settled down to their accustomed good fellowship."[55] In fact, politics within the Association was sometimes viewed as a practical and useful exercise in popular democracy. Freeman Hunt, editor of the *Merchants' Magazine and Commercial Review*, held that the disputes at the annual meetings were of far more consequence than the "twaddling debates of the academy," since they "sharpen[ed] the facilities" and fostered "an aptitude even for political or other office."[56]

For the young men elected to manage the affairs of the Mercantile Library, their tenure in office certainly enhanced their character and reputation within the mercantile community. By 1855, it was the most extensive and most popular circulating library in the city. Its collection of over 42,000 volumes was slightly larger than the Society Library's and its membership of 4,600 readers was more than four times as large.[57] Just as important, serving on the Board of Direction was considered valuable professional experience. In the same article in which he discussed the benefits of participation in the annual meetings, Freeman Hunt also noted that "management of the society's affairs by the clerks is a means of teaching them order, dignity, self-respect, business tact."[58] The directors' annual reports frequently stressed that the Association's success was a direct result of the sound business principles upon which it was managed. For example, unlike the Society Library, the Mercantile Library advertised extensively in the local newspapers, a "means sanctioned by mercantile usage," which was ultimately a "real economy, a most judicious investment." The annual report for 1850 included a succinct summary of the "system of management," the business model, that the Library had adopted by that period: "active . . . proselytism by means of advertisements and . . . an anxious endeavor to satisfy the wants of the members . . . in the purchase of books they may require, and such as conduce to their intellectual improvement."[59]

By the 1840s, the Mercantile Library Association followed a business plan based largely upon meeting demand, while at the same time it continued to espouse a mission of "combining mental culture with rationale amusement." To expand its membership and increase its income, it provided a generous selection of recreational reading. As early as 1834, fiction was the most extensive class in the catalog, larger than either history or literature.[60] The annual reports usually included an "annual warning against the pernicious tendency and effects of novel reading," as well as praise for the directors' business acumen in adhering to the "system of management" outlined in 1850 and a standard set of arguments to explain away the high demand for novels. By far the most common justification for the generous supply of fiction was that the clerks read only the best, the "standard" authors. The report for 1854 explained that although "the circulation of popular literature has been very large, . . . the facts deductive from extended observation go far to prove the majority of productions to have been of the highest order." It also noted that "it was thought advisable to limit the [purchase] of books merely to those of the greatest importance [i.e., popularity] and latest publication, the demand for which, in a circulating library [like] ours, it is absolutely essential we should supply." The directors also argued frequently that fiction would in itself lead to more substantial reading, that the clerks would start by reading popular titles and thereby develop a taste for the standard authors. In 1832, they explained that the collection would "conduct curiosity through the field of . . . romance to the more useful and instructive knowledge presented by scientific and other works." At the same time, they also "endeavored in the selection of writings to give satisfaction to all concerned."[61] The directors never provided any real evidence that members read only the best fiction or that their reading was progressively improving. During the antebellum years, it was critical to the Association's identity and public image that they gloss over the inherent contradiction between the clerks' business model and the Library's ostensible mission to provide uplifting, rational amusement.

In 1843, the members revised their constitution to allow "persons not engaged in mercantile pursuits" to join the Mercantile Library as "subscribers" for a higher annual fee (originally five dollars instead of three), although they were not permitted to vote or hold office. The directors' report for that year provides no details of the debate over the amendment, but it was evidently adopted to raise revenue in the midst of the severe depression following the Panic of 1837. In the short term, just as at the Apprentices' Library, which began admitting "pay readers" in 1842, creating this new category initially did little to improve the Association's finances. Even ten years later, subscribers were only a very small proportion of the total membership.[62] Moreover, the annual reports and other publications continued to refer to the Library as a means of enhancing the character and reputation of the mercantile community. Nonetheless, admitting persons not engaged in commerce in order to generate income reveals a tension between the clerks' business sense and their sense of community.

The same year that the constitution was amended to create this new category of readers, the Board of Direction issued a special report rejecting "A Plan of Systematic Instruction by Lectures." As first outlined in the annual report for 1838, this ambitious proposal would have created a "Collegiate Institution" by engaging "competent professors," lecturers, in "all the principle departments of knowledge most needful to the accomplished merchant," including "Principles of Commerce," "Natural Philosophy," "Intellectual Philosophy," and "Belles Lettres."[63] The merchants' college became an extremely contentious issue in the ensuing annual elections, a rare instance in which there was actually substantial disagreement between the contenting parties.[64] The board elected in 1843 rejected the plan in its entirety. No doubt caught up in spirit of the faction, it did so in remarkably impolitic language. Most notably, the directors held that members of the Association did not require a broad, liberal education, that "success in trade . . . depend[s] not so much on manly virtues, intelligence and integrity, as on capital, enterprise, love of acquisition, craft and opportunity." Further, the typical merchant's clerk of New York City was in fact not interested in mental and moral self-improvement, but rather "in the leisure hours . . . seeks amusement, relaxation from the toils of business, . . . light and cheerful employments, reading, music, visiting, and the like."[65] Like the change in the constitution the same year that allowed readers from outside the mercantile community access to the collection, the rejection of the merchants' college seems to contradict the very principles upon which the Library was founded and portended fundamental changes in the aims of the Association later in the century.

In 1853, the directors of the Mercantile Library reported that despite "all the external evidences of prosperity, . . . our Institution . . . is not fulfilling all the objects for which it was established," including, in the words of the preamble to the constitution, adopting "the most efficient means to facilitate mutual intercourse." The following year, there was new tenant in Clinton Hall, a new organization that, for a time, proved much more successful in providing companionship and support for its members.[66] One of the most prominent attractions of the Young Men's Christian Association was its circulating library for "moral and religious culture." In addition, like the Mercantile Library, it also provided classes, lectures, a gymnasium and baths. The YMCA, however, was much more comprehensive. Among other services, it provided an employment bureau, financial aid for the unemployed, assistance in choosing a proper church and boardinghouse, and a committee that visited members who were ill. It even offered a final resting place in Woodlawn Cemetery in the Bronx.[67] More important, the YMCA fostered a sense of identity, of community, that was stronger, more attractive than the Mercantile Library's identification with the mercantile class. In 1854, in an address at Clinton Hall, a supporter assured the membership that "Christianity alone gives the true fraternity, within that one great family in heaven and on earth."[68]

The YMCA was established for and appealed primarily to the same class of young men that had founded the Mercantile Library thirty years earlier. During its early history, members were often clerks, many of them from the country, experiencing for the first time the excitements and temptations of the metropolis. In his remarks at the opening of the Association's library and rooms in 1852, Daniel Lord, a member of the Clinton Hall Association (and benefactor of the American Bible Society), described the plight of the "young, who come as strangers into a great city . . . to try their fortune." "Leaving the cheering hearth of the paternal cottage," they encountered New York's "darker phases . . . places of costly, exciting and unsafe pleasures" that "spread abroad their snares and expose the soul."[69] The YMCA thus offered the country lad "lonely in the midst of crowds" and assailed by "new and strange temptations" Christian sympathy and fraternity. Although it was governed and partly funded by benevolent merchants and evangelical ministers, the young men themselves did the real work of the Association. They alone were able to "meet [the stranger's] social want" and "save him from becoming the prey of the self-indulgent—the card and the billiard player and the infidel."[70] And the library played a key role in recruiting new members by providing a sociable, homelike atmosphere. In the words of an early address before the Association, it was "lighted with gas, and what is better than gas, with wholesome reading and . . . Christian sympathy." Members, who at the founding paid an annual subscription of just one dollar, could borrow books, but any young man was welcome to read there for free.[71]

The library's first catalog, published in 1855, certainly reflected a unanimous resolution passed at an early meeting "to place on the shelves . . . such works only that . . . were adapted for the perusal of members of a *Christian Association*."[72] Works of theology, including numerous compilations of sermons and several multivolume titles of biblical commentary, comprised approximately 28 percent of the 1,813 volumes.[73] A roughly equal proportion of the collection was history and biography, a very popular genre in the Mercantile Library and other subscription libraries. Some of these were standard works such as Thomas Macauley's *History of England*, William Prescott's *Conquest of Mexico*, and John Romeyn Brodhead's *History of the State of New York*. A greater number, however, reflect the preoccupations of Protestant evangelicals, for instance, *God in History*, *The History of Temperance*, and *The History of Romanism*.[74] Similarly, many books on other subjects were clearly written for a Christian reading public. The library offered such titles as *The Harmony of Geology and Religion*, *Republican Christianity*, and *The Harmony of Phrenology and the Bible*. Finally, the catalog included numerous works suitable for Christian clerks, for example, *The Bible in the Counting House*, *Mercantile Morals*, and *Useful Lads, or Friendly Advice to Boys in Business*. Unlike the Mercantile Library, the Association provided almost no reading that was purely for the entertainment of its members, the kinds of books that the librarian Reuben Poole dismissed as "a conglomeration of trash." He was determined that "the library should be primarily an educational institution."[75]

The catalog of 1855 included a very small selection of novels, approximately 6 percent. The majority of them were apparently donations from various evangelical publishers and many appear to have been written for children rather than young men.[76] All of them were clearly intended to provide moral and religious instruction in the guise of entertaining narrative. For example, *The Harvey Boys: Illustrating the Evils of Intemperance* and *The Village Boys, or the Sin of Profaneness* were both distributed by the American Sunday School Union.[77] Commercial presses issued other works of fiction in the catalog, and, judging from the number of editions and sequels published, they were highly popular works. *Beatrice, or the Unknown Relatives* claimed to "represent the happiness of a Protestant family circle," while *The Female Jesuit, or the Spy in the Family* purported to be true crime, an account of Catholic espionage.[78] The library also offered a number of works by T. S. Arthur and Susan Warner, two of the most commercially successful authors of the 1850s. In general, the YMCA catalog is representative of an important segment of the publishing industry in the mid–nineteenth century, of the demand for highly sentimental, didactic novels.[79] Fiction was a very small part of the collection, but the largest proportion of the books circulated. It usually accounted for at least 25 percent of the total circulation.[80]

Although it was funded partly through members' subscriptions and appealed primarily to young clerks, the YMCA had more in common with the city's free circulating libraries than with the Mercantile Library Association. Like the "missionaries of literature" in the free libraries, Reuben Poole insisted that librarians must "maintain the purity of their collections and protect them from inundations of worthless books." He forcefully advocated sharply limiting the supply of popular fiction as a means of reducing the demand.[81] Moreover, Poole was a recognized leader of the public library movement in the city, a movement in which the directors of the Mercantile Library showed practically no interest. He was a founding member of both the American Library Association and the New York Library Club, served on the club's executive committee until his death in 1895 and wrote extensively for *Library Journal* and other publications.[82]

It is ironic therefore that when the State of New York passed the law in 1886 permitting the City to fund free circulating libraries, the YMCA was not eligible. When the Association finally opened its own building on Twenty-Third Street in 1869, the Board of Directors decided that the library would no longer circulate its books. Poole and the Library Committee apparently opposed this restriction, which was directly contrary to a central tenet of the emergent public library movement. The board's decision, however, was fully in keeping with the spirit of the evangelical movement. The early YMCA sought to restore the social influence that was lost when a young man moved to the anonymous city from his rural village, where there was a "general knowledge of each other's affairs and neighborly supervision of each other's habits." Requiring young men to read in the YMCA building may be seen as a means of exercising moral oversight, of "bringing into play upon the stranger that gentle restraint which consists of being observed by friends who know us."[83] Reuben Poole's calling as a missionary of literature was at odds with the Association's mission to save souls.

In 1870, the Mercantile Library Association had the highest circulation of any library in the United States and the fourth largest collection.[84] As the result of an ambitious fundraising campaign the previous decade, the Clinton Hall trustees had paid off the mortgage on its building and contributed approximately $15,000 of rental income to the Library's expenses annually.[85] More important, membership had increased dramatically, especially in the years immediately following the Civil War. By 1870, nearly 11,000 clerks and "subscribers" had joined and more than 1,700 merchants held stock in the Clinton Hall Association. The Library's directors attributed the Association's popularity not to a desire for mental and moral self-improvement, but to the "system of management" outlined in the annual report for 1850 and to an expanding market for popular literature. In the report for 1870, they proudly declared that "the first aim and single purpose of our Library is to satisfy the reading public" and that in doing so it was "following only a natural law of making our supply correspond to the demand."[86] As the economy expanded and the city's population increased dramatically, they confidently predicted that "if the present policy be pursued . . . the Mercantile Library will occupy a position second to none in this country."[87]

The Board of Direction also attributed the Association's prosperity to effective and extensive marketing, to what the report in 1850 had referred to as "an active system of proselytism by advertisements." In the 1840s, when the Library first adopted this means of attracting the reading public, the largest amount expended on advertising in a single year was $264. In the 1860s, the annual average was $688.[88] During 1866 and 1867 alone, the membership increased by 44 percent and 30 percent respectively, which the board boasted was a result of its "efforts . . . to keep the library constantly before the public by means of . . . notices in the papers and bulletins judiciously distributed."[89] Moreover, this success was not simply a matter of how much the Association spent on advertising, but also how it advertised. Advertisements in the local newspapers often drew the reader's eye with "Books! Books! Books!" in large, bold print, and circulars assured the public that "every member may feel sure of procuring any book he may wish to read." This proselytism was directed not just to clerks, but also to, among other "classes," heads of families, students, professional men, boys and girls, and even "intelligent young mechanics." Just like the city's new and very popular department stores, the Association's advertising promised something for everyone.[90]

One class that the Library was especially eager to recruit was female readers. Its advertisements often stressed that "ladies are permitted to join upon the same terms as gentlemen," and many of them appealed specifically to women. A circular published in 1861, for example, was addressed to "Ladies, Heads of Families, Students, and Others," but the word *ladies* appears at the very top of the page, in a much larger and more ornate font.[91]

SOCIETY LIBRARY,

67 University Place.

New York, Nov. 5. 1868.

Dear Sir,

I beg to call your attention to the New York Society Library, comprising not only a fine collection of some 60,000 Vols. which circulate among the Shareholders and their families, but an excellent Reading Room with the latest foreign and American periodicals.

Occupying its own building, and being entirely free from debt, it offers a desirable investment as well as one of the most agreeable and select resorts of the kind (for both ladies and gentlemen) to be found in the city.

MERCANTILE LIBRARY,
CLINTON HALL, ASTOR PLACE.

90,000 VOLUMES IN THE LIBRARY.

10,000 MEMBERS.

WE RECEIVE FROM THE PUBLISHERS ALL THE NEW BOOKS AS SOON AS PUBLISHED, AND COPIES ENOUGH OF EACH WORK TO SUPPLY THE DEMAND.

A large and valuable invoice of English Books just received, for which see Catalogue at the desk of the Library.

The Reading-room is regularly supplied with over 400 Periodicals, comprising the best Magazines and Newspapers of ENGLAND, FRANCE, GERMANY, and the UNITED STATES. Also a valuable Reference Library.

OPEN FROM 8 A.M. TO 10 P.M.

THE BRANCH OFFICE,
At 49 Liberty Street, opposite the Post-office,
Contains a Large Assortment of the Most Popular Books and Files of the Daily Papers.

BOOKS ARE DELIVERED TO MEMBERS AT THEIR RESIDENCES.

A Member will provide himself with some of our blank orders, and also "Delivery Stamps," which will be sold at twenty stamps for one dollar. He will fill out one of the orders, put a stamp on it, and drop it in one of our Order Boxes; or *he can send it by Mail.* The book he wants will then be delivered at his residence and the book to be returned taken away at the same time.

TERMS OF MEMBERSHIP.—To Clerks, $1 Initiation and $3 Annual Dues. To all others, $5 a year in advance. Ladies may join as Clerks.

ANY ONE CAN BECOME A MEMBER.

Opposite: A personal invitation from the librarian in 1868 to join the Society Library, "one of the most agreeable and select resorts of the kind" (Courtesy of the New York Society Library)

Above: Advertisement for the Mercantile Library, 1867: "ANY ONE CAN BECOME A MEMBER." (*Round Table, A Saturday Review of Politics, Finance, Literature, Society and Art,* November 9, 1867)

Since the statistics in the annual reports were never broken down by gender, it is difficult to determine how successful the Association was in attracting female readers, but it seems clear from descriptions of the Library in newspapers and magazines that later in the century women comprised a substantial proportion, perhaps even a majority, of the membership. For instance, a letter to the editor of the *New York Times* in 1881 complained at some length that the Library had done nothing for years except build "a vast collection of the very lightest of literature . . . intended to feed the greedy maw of society birds." However, critics of the Association no doubt tended to exaggerate the number of female subscribers simply because they associated the provision of novels, of light reading, with "the weaker sex."[92]

In joining a public library, women were, in certain respects, assuming a public role. The ways in which they made use of a membership sheds light upon gender and public space and public activity later in the nineteenth century. Like the Society Library, the Mercantile Library Association, in order to attract female readers, provided special accommodations for them. The board reported in 1854, for example, that the new "ladies reading room" was "the result of a most pleasing necessity, influenced by the large increase in the list of our lady subscribers" and that, in order to "cause a large and valuable augmentation of our membership from that source," they had adopted "rules and regulations of such a nature as to protect the most modest instincts."[93] Several years later, an article in *Scribner's Monthly* noted that such provisions were unnecessary. The author explained that the segregated reading room was seldom used because "ladies have no hesitation in taking their seats in the main room." He went on to describe the "numbers of young ladies who turn aside from the regular Broadway promenades, and throng the library counters looking over the latest novels," as well as the "young men [who] have no objection to com[ing] for their weekly supply while the hall is still gay with ribbons and bright eyes." This was in marked contrast to the library of the Cooper Union just across the street. Middle-class female readers seldom used the free reading room there, presumably in part because it had a reputation for attracting "loungers" and vagrants. In the later nineteenth century, class as well as gender influenced women's use of public libraries as public spaces.[94]

The Mercantile Library Association encouraged females employed in clerical positions to join the Library as clerks rather than subscribers. Those who did so not only paid a lower annual subscription, but should also have been permitted, according to the constitution, to vote and even to run for office.[95] Newspaper and magazine accounts of the Association's annual elections occasionally noted in passing that women who were "active members" were constitutionally entitled to the franchise, but never exercised it. Reading with males in a public reading room was one thing, but participating in the electoral process was perhaps too public and therefore too masculine an activity for a respectable female to engage in.[96] Just as important, the annual elections for much of the remainder of the century continued to be loud, boisterous, physical events. As the *New York Sun* explained in its account of the contest in 1870: "There are numerous women members, but none voted. The squeeze in the hall was too great and women do not like to be squeezed."[97]

The directors' optimistic report for 1870 failed to note a significant change in the condition of the Association. Support for the Mercantile Library among the clerks of New York City was clearly waning. The number of active members reached its peak in 1868 at approximately 7,600. It decreased every year thereafter, sometimes precipitously, and by the end of the century had dropped to fewer than 750, less than 25 percent of the total membership.[98] Moreover, this decline occurred during a period in which the clerical workforce was rapidly expanding. In 1870, roughly 28,000 men and women were employed as clerks in the city of New York. In 1900, there were more than 123,000.[99] The mercantile community's identification with the Library was eroding at the same time that the community itself was growing at an unprecedented rate.

There were certainly several reasons for the dramatic decline in the number of active members later in the nineteenth century. The annual elections, for example, seem to have become a source of embarrassment rather than a means of mutual intercourse. Once considered a harmless expression of youthful exuberance, by the late 1860s they were seen as divisive, factional, and corrupt. Articles in the local press recounted electoral "outrages of the most atrocious character," committed by "bookworms imitating Tammany," who employed at the polls "Broadway statues [pimps], thieves, gamblers, pickpockets, and keepers of low houses of questionable entertainment."[100] This bad press certainly tarnished the Association's reputation and contributed to its decline. Beyond this, clerks, both men and women, were less likely to join in the late nineteenth century simply because New York offered so many ways for young people to have fun. The Association competed with other forms of recreation. The annual report for 1896 noted that the Library's popularity continued to wane because "the attractions now offered in our city for . . . entertainment and amusement . . . at night are becoming greater and more varied each year."[101]

Police keeping order at the Mercantile Library election (*Scribner's*, February 1871)

Finally, probably most decisively, as subscribers increasingly outnumbered the active members, clerks no longer had a sense of personal attachment to the Association. The board focused increasingly upon recruiting "society birds" and others, and merchants' clerks no longer identified with the Library as a mercantile institution.

Indeed, what was rapidly diminishing as early as the 1860s was not simply clerks' identification with the Mercantile Library Association, but rather their sense of identity as a "class," as a "mercantile community." When the active members wrote a new constitution in 1870, they eliminated altogether the elaborate preamble that set forth the objects of the Library.[102] Presumably this meant that the "merchants' clerks of the city of New York" no longer felt the need to "facilitate mutual intercourse," to "extend [their] information on mercantile . . . subjects," or to "discharge with dignity the duties of [their] profession." In the Gilded Age, a clerk was simply a man or woman who performed clerical tasks for a salary, often in a large establishment with dozens, perhaps hundreds of fellow clerks. As William E. Dodge, a trustee of the Clinton Hall Association, noted with regret in an address in 1880, "now business is in comparatively few hands, with large capital and many clerks," most of whom had no expectation of ever "doing business on their own account."[103] There was no point in forgoing the attractions of the city and retiring to the Library at night for self-improving reading, if one had no reasonable prospect of ever advancing to the rank of merchant. Rather than identifying with an idealized local mercantile community, white-collar workers were developing a consciousness, a sense of themselves as the American middle class.[104]

Similarly, the city's "merchant princes" no longer regarded themselves as the leaders of a mercantile community that included their clerks. Moreover, by the 1870s, their prestige and influence had waned considerably. As New York became the locus of national corporations and large-scale manufacturing increasingly drove the national economy, industrialists like Andrew Carnegie, a member of the General Society of Mechanics and Tradesmen, came to dominate the economic elite. More important, there was no longer a sharp distinction between the merchant prince and the master mechanic. As Sven Beckert has shown, both groups diversified their interests later in the nineteenth century, investing their capital in both trade and industry, and thereby "decisively overcame particularist identities that had been . . . rooted in distinct sectors of the economy." New York's merchants became businessmen, just one part, and not the leading part, of a transnational capitalist class.[105]

Later in the nineteenth century there was also a steady decline in the subscribing members, those who were not clerks and therefore paid a higher subscription and were not entitled to vote or hold office. Their number reached its peak in 1872 at approximately 4,300. Thirty years later there were fewer than 1,700.[106] This decline in the popularity of the Library is attributable in large part to the failure of the "system of management," the business model, outlined in the annual report for 1850 to anticipate and adapt to fundamental changes in the print market. Later reports frequently noted, for example, that all kinds of books, not just sensationalistic dime novels, were widely available at very low prices. In 1881, the directors complained that "the cheap form of publishing . . . heretofore . . . almost exclusively confined to fiction, is now extended [even] to the better, or standard class of literature" and had "seriously effect[ed] the material interests of the Library." They reported, for instance, that Benjamin Disraeli's recently published novel *Endymion* was available in a cheap edition for just twenty cents. The Association had to compete not just with other circulating libraries, but also with bookstores that sold their product at prices that middle-class New Yorkers could quite easily afford.[107]

The crux of the business model that the Association adopted in 1850 was "an anxious endeavor to satisfy the wants of members" by "securing to them . . . full opportunity of obtaining [any book] when called for." Clearly, for both the clerks and subscribers the demand was for popular fiction. In 1867, for example, the circulation of fiction exceeded 70 percent, and the annual report for that year noted that this was in fact lower than in previous years.[108] Moreover, throughout the latter half of the nineteenth century there was a corresponding increase in supply. In 1850, American publishers issued 128 novels by American authors. By 1900, that number had reached 616.[109] More important, the demand for new works of fiction was typically immediate and transitory and therefore inherently difficult to satisfy. "The ephemeral productions of the press are sought for with avidity when first issued . . . but in a few brief months are banished to the seclusion of the shelves," so that, as the directors explained in their report in 1860, "the effort to *satisfy the demand for popular reading* . . . the difficulty of supplying a large constituency of readers with books in special demand, is a problem of no easy solution."[110]

The Library tried its best to solve the problem by purchasing fiction in quantity. It bought, for example, seven hundred copies of Disraeli's most popular novel, *Lothair* (1870).[111] By 1870, however, when the membership began to decline, the directors declared that it had become "impossible" to "cater to the demands of a not always more than reasonable public." And if the Library was unable to do so, members could simply quit and buy what they wanted at any one of the more than one hundred bookstores in the city.[112] In the culture of print of the late nineteenth century, readers did not need to join a library association to become part of a reading community. They simply had to purchase for themselves inexpensive copies of what the Mercantile Library was unable to provide in sufficient quantity, what the annual report for 1859 called "just those books which are most talked of and that everyone is supposed to have read."[113]

Another important reason for the steady decline in the Library's popularity was its inconvenient location. When the Association moved north in 1853 to the renovated Astor Place Opera House, it was considered "the most suitable [site] for a popular public library" in New York, "centrally situated, convenient of access from every quarter of the city." By 1869, as the middle class moved farther and farther up the island of Manhattan, an article in *Leslie's Illustrated* pointed out that the new Clinton Hall had become just as poorly located, just as difficult for the membership to reach, as the old Clinton Hall on Beekman Street had been fifteen years earlier.[114] In their annual reports the directors now noted with regularity and alarm that the collection was "becoming . . . more and more isolated from the great mass of the reading community." Members began to complain that it was cheaper to simply buy a book than to pay the carfare to go to the Library and borrow it.[115]

Beginning in 1866, in an attempt to respond to these complaints, the Association began to deliver books to members' homes. Like the New York Society Library, it charged for the service and over the years tried a number of different pricing models and methods of delivery. All of them lost money.[116] The reason it was not commercially feasible is that the Library's members lived throughout the New York area, and it was simply too expensive to send books anywhere in Manhattan or the surrounding cities and suburbs. The "families of fashion" that patronized the Society Library lived in elite enclaves near each other, within what an article in the *Times* termed "the magic circle of the socially elect." By contrast, the Association's middle-class subscribers were "widely distributed throughout city and country."[117] The delivery service in the short term probably slowed the decline in membership, but it was costly and ineffective in the long term.

Another option that the directors considered was moving uptown to a more central location. In 1883, they reported that, "notwithstanding the low prices at which certain classes of books can be bought, . . . it is possible to greatly enlarge our usefulness were it in our power to bring our collection nearer to the homes of those from whom we may expect support."[118] However, just five years later the board abandoned that plan as too costly and prevailed upon the trustees of the Clinton Hall Association to raze Clinton Hall and erect a new, modern building on Astor Place. When it opened in May 1891, there was no appreciable increase in the membership. The directors then weighed a more innovative option, creating a system of small branches. Yet by 1897, when taxpayers were funding twenty-seven free circulating libraries in the city, they had concluded that, although this was "the best and most popular method of reaching our constituency," it was not a viable business proposition, that "branch libraries maintained on a liberal scale cannot be kept going by the receipts from subscriptions alone."[119] In 1901, the year in which the New York Public Library established its Circulation Department, the Association closed its only uptown location, a small library and reading room on Fifth Avenue and Thirty-Ninth Street.[120]

In 1902, the Mercantile Library in effect ceased to be a mercantile institution. At the annual meeting in January the constitution was amended to allow subscribers as well as active members to vote and run for office. The Association was no longer governed by and for the merchants' clerks of the city of New York. At about the same time, the area the library occupied in the new Clinton Hall was reduced by half. The entire sixth floor was converted to office space. The librarian, William T. Peoples, was given a new title, Superintendent and General Manager, and the annual report for that year commended him for being "always present during business hours to look after the renting of offices . . . and to receive the suggestions or (if any there be) complaints of tenants."[121] In 1903, when the president of the Clinton Hall Association announced that the city's new subway system would have a station on Astor Place with an entrance from the basement of the building, he anticipated a substantial increase not in the membership but in the annual income from rents. By the early twentieth century, the Mercantile Library Association of the City of New York was no longer an institution for the mental and moral improvement of young clerks or even primarily a library that catered to the whims of the reading public. More than anything else, it was prime commercial real estate in lower Manhattan.[122]

6 "Men of Leisure and Men of Letters"

New York's Public Research Libraries

On May 7, 1849, the popular English actor Charles Macready took the stage at the luxurious new Astor Place Opera House to play the title role in *Macbeth.* Hundreds of working-class devotees of his American rival, Edwin Forrest, packed the galleries and promptly began to boo and hiss and pelt the stage with apples, potatoes, copper coins, and rotten eggs. By the third act, the mood had become increasingly violent. After a chair was hurled from the upper tier into the orchestra pit below, Macready quit the stage and vowed to sail home to England.

Only a dramatic public appeal from forty-seven prominent New Yorkers convinced Macready to repeat his performance three days later. While the police made arrests in the galleries, he was able, with considerable difficulty, finish the play, but outside the Opera House a crowd of thousands had gathered to protest. The Seventh Regiment of militia, the city's "Silk Stocking Regiment," was called out to restore order, and when the mob—shouting "Burn the damned den of aristocracy!"—began to throw paving stones through the windows and charge the entrance, the troops open fired. The Astor Place riot was the most violent civil disturbance in the New York before the Civil War. At least twenty-two people were killed, more than 150 were wounded, and 117 were arrested.[1]

It seems incredible today that a feud between two Shakespearean actors could culminate in violence and bloodshed. Ultimately, however, the rivalry between Macready and Forrest was a particularly dramatic manifestation of a broader cultural conflict. The English tragedian's restrained, cerebral performances seemed foppish and aristocratic to Forrest's working-class admirers, who relished his melodramatic, histrionic style, and Macready had made matters worse by commenting in the press upon the boorish behavior of American audiences. More important, the Astor Place Opera House itself had become a symbol of the elite insulating itself from the sometimes rowdy public culture of the city. Opened in November 1847 and financed by a group of 150 wealthy and socially prominent subscribers, its

The Astor Place Riot in *History of the Seventh Regiment of New York, 1806–1889*, vol. 1 (1890)

strictly enforced dress code was pointedly designed to exclude the masses. When the mob in the street on May 10 shouted, "You can't go in there without . . . kid gloves and a white vest, damn 'em!" they were challenging the cultural leadership of the city's privileged class. When the authorities called out the Seventh Regiment, members of that class were insisting upon their right to exclude those they deemed unfit for culture. The Astor Place riot called into question the role that New York's elite would play in defining and disseminating culture in an increasingly fractured and volatile public sphere.[2]

In 1849, the New-York Historical Society was at New York University on Washington Square, just a few short blocks from Astor Place. Members leaving the library on the evening of May 10 could have seen the rioters beginning to gather outside the Opera House before Charles Macready took to the stage.[3] These were prosperous years for the Historical Society, following the period of instability and near insolvency in the 1820s and 1830s. In 1841, to prevent further financial entanglements, the by-laws were amended to limit the circumstances under which the Society could assume new debt, and four years later the Executive Committee reported proudly that "healthy and vigorous action have succeeded indolent and inglorious repose."[4] Between 1849 and 1862, shortly after the move to its new fireproof building on Second Avenue and Eleventh Street, the membership increased from approximately 500 members to more than 1,500.[5] In this newly prosperous condition, the Society was in a position to assume a more active role among the city's cultural institutions. How the New-York Historical Society used its growing resources, how it defined its cultural mission and the public that it served, provides a telling illustration of one elite association's response to the tensions and divisions manifested in the Astor Place riot.

In June 1849, Henry Rowe Schoolcraft, the pioneering Native American ethnologist, delivered an address before the Society on the "Literary and Scientific Institutions of Europe." Having recently returned from a tour abroad, he offered a rather unflattering comparison of scholarly societies in the United States with those he had visited in European cities. He described "the vast libraries [that] overwhelm the mind" in Great Britain and on the Continent and held that "the paucity of our means of similar researches" was "a source of wholesome humiliation." Schoolcraft was especially critical of New York City. He reported that "there is not a prominent city in Europe which, in proportion to population, has so few associations for the cultivation of [arts and] science." Schoolcraft did, however, reserve special praise for the New-York Historical Society as well as the Lyceum of Natural History, claiming they were the only "efficient associations to advance the dominions of science or letters" in the city.[6]

Schoolcraft's most interesting and unexpected observation on the literary and scientific institutions of Europe concerns class relations within the most important and influential of the societies in Great Britain, the British Association for the Advancement of Science. He noted that "it is almost the only area I met with, upon which the extremes of British society meet, where the poor and the rich, the titled and the untitled, freely mingle on the exalted and exalting basis of letters." In a similar vein, he remarked that the "benign effects and influences" of this democratic mingling in the interests of the diffusion of knowledge were "carried home to every corner" of the nation and were "the surest means to keep her free." Although Schoolcraft did not compare the American with the European societies in this respect, there is no evidence that such a spirit of democracy prevailed within the association that he was addressing. From its founding, the New-York Historical Society drew its membership largely from the city's elite, but by the 1840s, it was becoming, like the Society Library during the same period, more purposefully, intentionally exclusive. For example, in

1804 prospective members were elected by ballot by a simple majority vote. When the by-laws were amended in 1846, they could by excluded by three "blackballs."[7] Despite the increase in its membership, the Society was becoming more selective in the face of rising class tensions.

According to Schoolcraft, one important reason for the superiority of the learned societies of Europe was their high degree of specialization. There, he reported, "the whole field of human knowledge is parceled out, studied, and watched over with eager intensity by separate and distinct . . . associations." In its earliest years, the scope of the New-York Historical Society was fairly broad, but this was in part because there were no other organizations in the city at the time to collect and conserve material for scholarly research. For example, its first appeal "To the Public" for donations for the library in 1805 also included a request for "such animal, vegetable and mineral subjects as may be deemed worthy of preservation," and in 1817 it began a series of lectures in zoology, geology, mineralogy, and chemistry. In 1829, however, the Society presented its "cabinet" of specimens in natural history to the Lyceum of Natural History.[8] During this early period, it also developed a modest collection of art. The initial accessions were primarily portraits and busts of Society members or notable Americans, but in 1858, the New York Gallery of the Fine Arts closed its doors and donated its entire collection to the Historical Society. Since most of the nearly one hundred paintings were by American artists, they complemented to some extent the historical works in the library.[9]

Thereafter, however, the Society rapidly began to acquire works of art in a manner quite contrary to the "division of labor" that Schoolcraft observed and admired in the scholarly associations of Europe. In 1858, for example, it accepted a donation from James Lenox, founder of the Lenox Library, of thirteen massive marble relief sculptures from Nineveh from the seventh century BCE. Two years later, it purchased the extensive Abbott Collection of Egyptian Antiquities, including jewelry, sculpture, and three mummified bulls. In 1864, it received from Thomas J. Bryan the Bryan Gallery of Christian Art, mostly paintings by European artists, some dating as far back as the Byzantine period. These acquisitions, and a number of smaller donations over the years, made the Historical Society one of the most notable (and eclectic) museums of art in the United States.[10] This collection was not developed in any deliberate fashion, and there were a number of reasons why it was acquired. On a practical level, it was undoubtedly reassuring for donors to know that their precious gifts would be safe in one of the few fireproof buildings in the city. For its part, the

Society was certainly reluctant to decline extremely valuable donations like Lenox's and Bryan's.

Yet there were more fundamental, consequential reasons why a voluntary association originally devoted to the promotion of local, state, and national history would begin to collect mummified bulls and Byzantine art. During this period, the fine arts were coming to signify a new conception of culture, the uses of which were inextricably linked with class and class-consciousness. For men like John Pintard, founder of the New-York Historical Society, *culture*, and related terms such as *cultivation*, was all-embracing; it denoted the general improvement, both practical and intellectual, of the individual and society. By the time of the Astor Place riot, it was assuming a more restricted, exclusive meaning. Culture signified individual refinement, conversance with a narrowly prescribed artistic and literary canon. The fine arts thus became a principal means by which the individual could demonstrate that refinement and thus set him or herself above those who were uncultivated. Given this significant shift in the uses of culture, elite institutions like the Historical Society could choose between two very different paths, between a private or a public agenda. They could undertake to cultivate, to uplift the working class into the realms of high culture, or they could use culture to insulate themselves, to place themselves above the vulgar, uncultivated masses.[11]

The Historical Society developed its art collection so extensively after moving into the new building that it soon became pressed for space. By the 1870s, the library was severely overcrowded, in part because the gallery above the reading room, which had originally housed the manuscripts, newspapers, maps, and charts, now was hung with paintings. Sculptures, some of them life-sized statues, were displayed on all of the reading tables.[12] Already in the early 1860s, the members began to consider acquiring more spacious quarters, which, in turn, led at least some of them to envision a new and more public role for the Society and its expanding collections. The leader of this movement was Frederic De Peyster, descendant of an old Knickerbocker family who served as president from 1864 to 1866 and from 1873 until his death in 1882. He was also largely responsible for raising the funds to purchase the Abbott Collection. Had De Peyster brought his ambitious plans to fruition, the history of the Historical Society, and indeed of public libraries in New York City would have been markedly different.[13]

In August 1860, the Executive Committee, "mindful of their relations and duties to the citizens of New York," resolved to seek municipal support

Library of the New-York Historical Society (*Andrew's American Queen*, February 1879)

to establish in Central Park a "grand museum of antiquities, science, and art" that would be "accessible to all classes of the community." Five years later, De Peyster elaborated on the proposal in an anniversary address entitled "The Moral and Intellectual Influence of Libraries on Progress." The Society's collection of books and manuscripts in American history would remain in the building on Second Avenue as a "Working Library" for students and scholars. Its treasures of art and antiquities would be placed on display in the abandoned State Arsenal in the southeastern corner of the park and a separate public library would be developed there to "embrace all the departments of literature, science and arts."[14] The "Library, Museum of Antiquities and Science, and Gallery of Art" would help to ensure social order and good government by "substitut[ing] a salutary pleasure for gross indulgences." It would be "a home for the poor," who were "shut out from the refining effects of social intercourse." By "educat[ing] the people into a taste for literary culture and the beautiful productions of art," it would "raise the tone of public thought and feeling."[15] De Peyster proposed that, rather than retreating behind its works of fine art and antiquities, the Society use its treasures to refine and uplift the masses.

In March 1862, the legislature passed an act permitting the Society to take possession of the abandoned State Arsenal near Fifty-Ninth Street and Fifth Avenue, provided that its museum was "accessible to the public under proper regulations" and that the plan was approved by the Commissioners of the Central Park. The commissioners did not authorize use of the building until October 1865, and thereafter the subscription to raise the necessary funds seems to have stalled. In April 1868, a second bill was passed, granting the Society a plot of land on the eastern border of the park between Eighty-First and Eighty-Fourth Streets. Again, the effort failed due to lack of funds. By the early 1870s, the Society had abandoned its plan for a public library and museum of fine art and antiquities.[16]

There were certainly a number of reasons why De Peyster was never able to realize his expansive vision of a more public role for the New-York Historical Society. In part, it was simply a matter of timing. In the immediate aftermath of the Civil War and especially during the depression of 1873, raising funds for any large-scale public project would have been extremely difficult.[17] The site of the proposed museum was problematic as well. In the late 1860s and early 1870s, Central Park was still a fairly remote location, relatively far removed from the homes of many Knickerbocker families on and around Washington Square, just blocks from the Historical Society's building on Second Avenue. The fact that the park was public land also most likely raised fears that administering the museum would require consorting with unsavory Tammany politicians. Librarian Robert Kelby wrote in his history of the Society that the plan failed because the proposed site was city property.[18] The most important reason, however, was simply a lack of enthusiasm. De Peyster failed to raise the necessary funds largely because most of his fellow members did not share his ambition to transform the Society into a more actively public institution dedicated to the cultivation of the working class.

In 1874, another voluntary association of the city's elite began construction of a museum on the same plot of land in Central Park granted to the New-York Historical Society in 1868. The trustees of the Metropolitan Museum of Art, most of whom were also members of the Historical Society, succeeded where De Peyster had failed largely because they were willing to enlist the support of machine politicians. They convinced Tammany boss William M. Tweed not only to construct their building on city property at taxpayers' expense, but also to provide an annual appropriation for its maintenance.[19] Although the contract with the City required that the museum be free to the public four days a week, this meant little in practical terms for most working-class men and women. Since it was not open in the evening or on Sundays, the city's poor, or indeed most New Yorkers, could not enjoy the uplifting influence of its collections in any case.[20] The trustees of the Metropolitan got what most members of the Historical Society probably wanted: public money without actually having to share their treasures with the public. Their museum was a critical component of the effort of elites later in the nineteenth century to create what Sven Beckert has termed a "class-segmented public sphere."[21]

When the Historical Society constructed new and larger quarters later in the century, it made no attempt to secure funding from the City or State of New York. In 1880, a committee was appointed to solicit subscriptions from the membership. The cornerstone was not laid until 1903 and, finally, in December 1908, the Society's new home was opened on Seventy-Seventh Street and Central Park West, opposite the Metropolitan Museum of Art on the other side of the park.[22] By this time, the character of the area around Washington Square in which the old building was located had changed dramatically. The *New York Times* was of course not strictly accurate when it referred in 1901 to its "remoteness from a residential neighborhood." There were many thousands of residences in the vicinity, but for the most part they were no longer the homes of New York's elite. "All the old families [had] moved away," and it had become "the most isolated . . . of all neighborhoods in the city for the class of people who would naturally be interested in [the Society's] work."[23] By contrast, Central Park West was becoming the most fashionable address in New York, the heart of the uptown area to which elite New Yorkers had migrated. In the annual reports and in other publications, the leaders of the Society staunchly denied that it was in any sense "exclusive," indeed insisted that it was "eminently a public institution."[24] But by the early twentieth century, it had physically distanced itself from the masses in lower Manhattan and retreated uptown to an upper-class enclave.

The city's elite employed other means during this period to set itself apart from the lower and middle classes and to assert its social and cultural superiority. One of the most popular was genealogy. Earlier in the century it was "deemed," according to a biographer of John Francis, one of the Society's first librarians, "inconsistent with the . . . sentiment of republican and democratic faith to lay much stress upon genealogical claims."[25] Yet by the 1870s, tracing ones ancestral roots had become a favorite pastime of the upper class. Exclusive voluntary associations, like the Holland Society and the Sons of the American Revolution, founded in 1884 and 1885 respectively, required prospective members to document their pedigrees, and libraries such as the Historical Society's and that of the New York Genealogical and Biographical Society, established in 1869, developed collections that allowed them to do so. This enthusiasm for family history was in large part a reaction of New York's first families to the waves of new immigrants that dramatically altered the demography of the city in the late nineteenth century. As a member of the Genealogical Society explained, its purpose was to provide a "firm foundation on which those who are to come after us can establish the fact that they are the descendants of the original settlers and founders of civilized life upon this continent, not of the hordes of foreigners."[26]

Genealogical research was an important focus of the New-York Historical Society library in the later nineteenth century. Before 1900, by far its largest single endowment was the $15,000 bequeathed in 1882, along with a private library of 1,400 volumes, for the Stephan Whitney Phoenix Collection of Heraldry and Genealogy. The Society's annual reports and other publications frequently highlighted its resources for family history and noted that "this kind of request has enormously increased since the organization of the various [genealogical] associations which have sprung into existence" in the final decades of the century. In the 1880s and 1890s, many of the primary documents reprinted in the Society's *Collections*, such as "Rolls of Freemen of New York City" and the "Muster Rolls of New York Provincial Troops" were tools for tracing and documenting ones descent from the city's first families.[27] Moreover, the Society's librarian during this period, William Kelby, was an avid and noted amateur genealogist. He was a one of the founders and the first registrar of the Sons of the American Revolution and took great interest and pride in developing the genealogical collection.[28] Rather than a resource for the education and uplift of the public, the library during this period was used by the membership at least in part to provide evidence of their hereditary superiority.

In Gilded Age New York, a model of cultural uplift that that relied upon the sponsorship of elite voluntary associations was increasingly problematic. On one hand, the masses that were to be cultivated were more and more willing to assert their independence in matters of culture. On the other, organizations like the New-York Historical Society, always relatively exclusive, had largely abandoned any public role in the dissemination of culture. At a time of cultural as well as economic laissez-faire, from where was the support and direction for public cultural institutions to come? What expressions of culture were to be promoted, for whom and for what ends? Was Henry Schoolcraft's democratic vision of working-class men actively participating in the production and dissemination of knowledge tenable? Was Frederic De Peyster's dream of uplifting the masses through the beauty of art and literature at all possible?

The Astor and the Lenox Libraries were the two most valuable research collections in New York City in the latter half of the nineteenth century. Both were founded by wealthy New Yorkers who devoted a part of their considerable fortunes to the promotion and dissemination of scholarship and culture. In 1895, they merged with the Samuel J. Tilden Foundation to form what is today the New York Public Library's Reference and Research Services. Histories of the Astor and the Lenox illustrate the possibilities and the limitations of individual philanthropy on a large scale in the later nineteenth century. They also reveal the sometimes conflicting expectations that different segments of the public had of public libraries during this period.

James Lenox was born in New York City on August 19, 1800, the only son of Robert Lenox, a wealthy merchant who had emigrated from Scotland shortly after the Revolution. Educated at Columbia and admitted to the bar, he joined the family business as a young man, but shortly after his father's death in 1839, retired and devoted the remainder of his life to amassing an eclectic and extremely valuable collection of rare books and fine art. By all accounts reclusive and unsociable, even his friend and biographer Henry Stevens conceded that most found him "proud, aristocratic, distant, and haughty." Lenox had inherited an extensive tract of prime real estate in upper Manhattan and, as the city's elite moved northward, he acquired a large fortune that allowed him to satisfy his every bibliophilic whim. He never married, and for nearly three decades he filled his mansion on Fifth Avenue and Twelfth Street with his bibliographic treasures, packing room after room from floor to ceiling with rare volumes "corded up like wood." In 1869, approaching his seventieth birthday, and unwilling to expose his beloved collection "to the peril of dispersion in the auction room" upon his death, he announced his plan to create a public library for the city of New York.[29]

The state legislature passed the act of incorporation of the Lenox Library on January 20, 1870. The new corporation was to be exempt from

James Lenox in the 1870s

taxation and was required to make its collections "accessible at all reasonable hours during the day . . . free of expense to all persons resorting thereto." Eight days later, the nine trustees met for the first time and elected James Lenox president, and the following March he conveyed to them a plot of land on Seventy-First Street and Fifth Avenue, opposite the east side of Central Park. Construction on the building began shortly thereafter, but was not completed until the summer of 1875, at a cost of more than a half million dollars. During the course of the following year most of Lenox's priceless collection of books, manuscripts, and works of art was transferred to the Library. In the meantime, George Henry Moore had resigned as the librarian of the New-York Historical Society and in October 1872 was appointed superintendent of the Lenox Library at the princely salary of $5,000 a year.[30]

Founded upon a private library acquired over the course of a quarter-century, the Lenox never had a clearly articulated policy for developing its collection. It represented, according to the annual report published the year after Lenox's death in 1880, "the favorite studies of a lifetime consecrated . . . to the choicest pursuits of literature and art." The focus of the founder's bibliographic interests had varied somewhat over the years. Initially, Lenox, a staunch Presbyterian and president of the American Bible Society from 1864 to 1871, purchased mostly rare early editions of the Bible in various languages, eventually acquiring an extremely valuable collection of approximately 3,500 volumes.[31] Later his acquisitions broadened to include a number of special topics, including angling, early printing, and voyages of discovery, as well as works by and about selected authors, especially John Bunyan, John Milton, and William Shakespeare. Although Lenox's private collection was augmented to a considerable extent after the founding by a number of generous donations, the Lenox Library was of limited use to most scholars, much less to the general public. As Wilberforce Eames, the librarian at the time of the consolidation that created the New York Public Library, explained some years later, it lacked "books on almost every subject besides the few subjects on which Mr. Lenox collected." Moreover, since most of Lenox's monetary gifts to the Library were spent on staffing and on the construction, furnishing, and maintenance of the building, for most years there was little left over to expand the collection. Eames reported that during the early years of the Library there was "some disappointment" that "there was practically nothing that . . . would be used by the ordinary reader."[32]

The library was opened to the public in 1877, but only for exhibitions. In January, a selection of the paintings and sculpture was placed on display, followed by an exhibit of rare books and manuscripts in December. These celebrations of high culture were the most inclusive function of the Lenox, yet practically from the beginning attendance was very sparse. This was explained in part by the fact that most of New York was at work when the exhibits were on view. The Library was always closed on Sundays and in the evening and for many years was opened only two or three days during the week. Also, the uptown location, which the trustees conceded was some "distance . . . from the present centre of population," certainly helped to keep the masses away.[33] Most important, however, in discouraging the general public from attending were "the regulations established . . . to exercise a proper control of the admissions." Prospective visitors were required to apply in writing to the superintendent, who would then send tickets in the mail, provided the request was not deemed "unreasonable."[34] After the initial novelty had worn off, and especially after the opening of the Metropolitan Museum of Art just eight blocks north in 1884, daily attendance for the exhibitions was dismal, seldom averaging more than fifty persons a day in a city that by 1880 numbered well over a million inhabitants. The *New York Times* cogently summed up the public role of the Lenox when it observed that it could "scarcely be looked upon as an educational institution of widespread utility."[35]

The Library itself was not open to the reading public until 1890. Before that time, researchers could apply for permission to use specific books "under the immediate supervision of the Superintendent." And it was not until 1893, more than two decades after the founding and just two years before the Lenox became part of the New York Public Library, that the trustees, in the words of the new librarian, Wilberforce Eames, made "the reading-room service really useful to the public." For most of its history, the Lenox Library was, in fact, not a library, but rather a highly specialized, very exclusive museum. As Eames recounted shortly after the consolidation with the Astor and the Tilden Trust, "the intention of the founder was to establish a museum of book rarities which would . . . supplement . . . other public libraries."[36] It was regarded as a specialized collection of fine art, "rare and precious memorials of the typographic art and the historic past," the "greater proportion [of which] must always be for exhibition in general, rather than for absolute use by the multitude." Every research library, particularly one as valuable as the Lenox, must strike a balance between preservation and utility, making its collection accessible to scholars while ensuring its integrity for future generations. The trustees seem never to have recognized this. They were concerned primarily with hoarding Lenox's treasures. No doubt they were pleased and flattered when the *Literary World* wrote in 1879 that "there is not one volume that does not look . . . as if it had never been touched by human hands."[37]

Few New Yorkers shared the *Literary World*'s admiration for the Lenox Library. Certainly there was considerable resentment of the restrictive regulations established for its use. Superintendent Moore informed the board in a report in 1883 that "the requiring of any ticket has been much criticized . . . by many people who regard all such restraints as a needless abridgement of the liberties of the public." More often, New Yorkers simply enjoyed poking fun at Lenox's "public" library. Even Joseph Choate, one of the founders of the Metropolitan and a leader of New York society, joked at a meeting called in support of the Free Circulating Library in 1882 that he thought it was actually possible to go to the Lenox Library, but "it was never opened when I was unemployed and could go there." A cartoon that appeared in *Life* two years later showed the Library surrounded by cannon to discourage intrepid scholars from trying to gain admittance, and the corpses of those who had failed hanging from gibbets projecting from its roof. Most of the reading public, however, was probably either unaware of or indifferent to Lenox's gift to the city. *Harper's Bazaar* reported shortly before the consolidation that "a great majority of . . . studious New Yorkers, even those who make habitual use of other libraries," never bothered to visit the Lenox. When James Lenox founded his public library, he had no real interest in serving a broadly conceived public, and the public reciprocated his indifference. Lenox aimed for what many members of the New-York Historical Society wanted when they rejected De Peyster's plan for a public library and museum in Central Park: the exhibition of objects of rarity and beauty to an exclusive audience as a means of affirming and displaying their cultural superiority.[38]

Unlike James Lenox, John Jacob Astor was not a scholar. Nor did he inherit his wealth. Born in Waldorf, Germany, in 1763, and largely self-educated, the founder of New York's most extensive research library in the nineteenth century immigrated to the United States at the end of the American Revolution. Astor soon became a leader in the fur trade in the West and by the turn of the century had amassed a considerable fortune. Most of this he shrewdly invested in Manhattan real estate, so that by the time he retired from active business around 1834, he was by far the wealthiest man in America and the largest landlord in New York. In his declining years he considered various means of "perpetuating his memory" in "the city of his adoption." In 1838, he decided to devote a portion of his vast wealth to the founding of a public library.[39]

The person most responsible for shaping the character of the Astor Library was not John Jacob Astor, but rather a New England scholar-librarian named Joseph Green Cogswell. Born in Ipswich, Massachusetts, in 1786, Cogswell graduated from Harvard in 1806, and later served briefly as assistant librarian there. As a young man, he made an extensive tour of Europe that included visits to the great libraries of the continent, as well as two years of study at Göttingen University. In Germany, he became fast friends with Edward Everett and George Ticknor, who helped found the Boston Public Library shortly before the Astor opened in New York. He moved to the city in 1836 to tutor the children of a local banker and while there met John Jacob Astor. After persuading Astor to perpetuate his memory with a public library, Cogswell lived with him in his opulent mansion on lower Broadway and began to plan and purchase books for it. Originally, Astor agreed to present his gift to the people of the city of New York during his lifetime, but in 1839 he added a codicil to his will that would bequeath a plot of land and an endowment upon his death.[40]

John Jacob Astor died on March 29, 1848. Of a fortune estimated at over $20 million, he left $400,000 for the Astor Library, his only major benefaction. The following January the state legislature passed an act of incorporation for a "Public Library in the City of New York" dedicated to "the advancement of useful knowledge and the general good of society."[41] At their first meeting in April 1848, the trustees elected Astor's friend Washington Irving president and appointed Cogswell superintendent, and in September, they selected a site on Lafayette Place, a short distance from the Astor Place Opera House. Construction of the building began in the spring of 1850, a year after the Astor Place riot, and was completed in the summer of 1853. In the meantime, Cogswell was authorized to make several trips to Europe to purchase books. Taking advantage of the unsettled state of the continent after the revolutions of 1848, he was able to acquire an impressive collection at reasonable prices. When the Astor opened to the public in January 1854, it held approximately 80,000 volumes and was already the largest library in the city and the second largest in the nation. Only Harvard's collection was more extensive.[42]

Unlike James Lenox and the trustees of the Lenox Library, Cogswell followed a cogently articulated policy in purchasing books and from the very beginning set out to "mark, as clearly as possible, the character of the [collection]." First, his selections were "governed more by intrinsic value than by the accident of rarity, believing that the Astor Library should be a . . . useful one, rather than a mere museum of curiosities."[43] Second, the Astor was to be a general research library. As such, while "no one department of learning [was] overlooked in laying the foundation," it was "not to be expected that it [would] be found complete in any one department."[44] For example, Cogswell purchased comparatively few medical and legal texts, on the grounds that other, specialized libraries in the city were better suited to provide them. There were, nonetheless, a few select fields in which the library would attempt, as nearly as possible, to develop comprehensive collections. In particular, the Astor aimed to collect all works published on the history of the United States (despite that this was ostensibly the object of the Historical Society), bibliography, and "practical industry." Throughout its history, the trustees adhered to the collection development policy established by Cogswell at the founding and, despite chronic underfunding, the Library grew steadily over the years. When it became part of the New York Public Library in 1895, it contained 271,394 volumes and was still by far the largest in the city.[45]

Despite the novelty of a library on such a grand scale open freely to the public, there was frequent, sometimes pointed criticism of Astor's gift to the city. The *Times*, for example, complained not long after the opening that "too much had . . . been sacrificed to the bibliomaniac," while *Gleason's Pictorial Drawing-Room Companion* wrote about the same time that "the librarian has been most unfortunate in his selections," which "certainly do not embody that amount and variety of popular and general information" of interest to the average reader. Most of the objections raised in the press, however, concerned the policies that the trustees established regarding access to the collection. The Astor was a "reference library," intended for consultation rather than circulation; unlike, for example, the Boston Public Library, it did not loan its volumes for use outside the building under any circumstances. In April 1854, a letter to the *Times* referred to the widespread "disappointment caused by learning that no books, even of the most popular character . . . could be taken from the premises." The most serious and persistent complaint, however, concerned the hours of the library. The Astor, like the Lenox, was closed in the evening and on Sundays. Thus, according to the *Galaxy*, "this great treasury of knowledge and storehouse of scientific and literary wealth [was] as a sealed book" to most New Yorkers.[46] Over the years there was a growing sense that the collections and policies of Astor's public library were not designed to serve the public.

The trustees staunchly defended their administration of Astor's legacy. In a resolution passed in July 1857 intended to "prevent further agitation on the subject," they declared that it was the founder's intention and the "settled and unchangeable basis of administering the library" that books

The Astor Library (*Life*, January 7, 1892)

would not circulate. Such a policy, they explained, was not only necessary for the "preservation and safety of the library," but it also ensured that scholars traveling great distances to use the collection would have access to the volumes they needed. The following year, Superintendent Cogswell wrote a letter to the *New York Times* in response to the "silly clamor" over the public's access to the Astor. As to the hours of the library, he claimed, certainly with some justification, that it simply could not afford to remain open in the evening. Even if it did, he added, most of the reading public, who had to work during the day, would be too tired to read the books at night anyway. In fact, Cogswell forthrightly explained that the Astor was not intended for the use of the "great mass of the people." Rather its collections were developed and its policies formulated to meet the needs of a "small class of the population," the "men of leisure and the men of letters." He and the trustees appear to have considered the frequent complaints from the public as a sign of ingratitude, if not impertinence. The Astor had hardly been opened before they reminded their critics in an annual report that "[we] only are the constituted judges of the proper mode of effecting" the public purposes of the library.[47]

Given this attitude toward the reading public on the part of its management, it is hardly surprising that the library's employees acquired a reputation for decidedly poor public service. The entire collection was shelved in closed stacks, and there were chronic, pointed complaints in the press regarding the brusqueness and discourtesy of the attendants from whom readers requested books. In the summer of 1855, for example, the *Times* received an "avalanche" of letters that it referred to as "another Astor Place riot."[48] Correspondents, men and women from all walks of life, related essentially the same tale of the "dragons" who guarded the treasures of the Library and chased away the public with "rudeness, incivility, and insult." In one particularly telling example, "Rusticus" wrote that he frequently "observed that there is a great difference in the manner of [the attendants] to different people," that "on calling at the Library when dressed for a dinner party, I found myself very differently treated from what I was when I came in my traveling clothes."[49] The *Times* agreed with the new Astor Place rioters that there was a "stifling air of reserve and repulsion" that discouraged certain readers from using the collection. The Astor Library was never a place where "the capitalist and the mechanic [sat] side by side in honourable community of thought."[50]

Nonetheless, the editors of the *Critic* overstated the case somewhat when they dismissed the Astor as "not, strictly speaking, a public library at all," but rather "a private library to which outsiders are occasionally admitted." While it never fostered the democratic mingling of classes that Henry Schoolcraft so admired in his address on the scientific and literary associations of Europe, there was always a significant number of New Yorkers with the time, patience, and fortitude that were often necessary to gain access to the collection. Frederick Saunders, a librarian at the Astor for nearly four decades, recalled, for example, many "strange people" who frequented the library, the "bibliomaniacs and bohemians who . . . haunt these precincts."[51] Moreover, use of the Astor increased steadily over the years, from approximately twenty-three thousand visitors in 1865, the first year in which statistics were reported, to over eighty-five thousand in 1895, when it became part of the New York Public Library.[52] Not all users, however, were accorded the same status. Each year, a relatively small number of favored readers were granted "alcove privileges," which allowed them to enter and conduct research in the closed stacks. This required a letter of recommendation from a trustee or "some other well known and responsible citizen" and was, according to the *Times*, very difficult to obtain. Although the treasures of the Library were free to all members of the reading public, some of them were more equal than others.[53]

Clearly, those with alcove privileges were Cogswell's preferred readers. They were the "men of leisure and the men of letters" to whom he referred in his letter to the *Times* in 1858 as the intended beneficiaries of Astor's legacy. They also represented a new generation of social and intellectual leaders that Thomas Bender has called the "metropolitan gentry." The earlier generation comprised men from a fairly well-defined, generally recognized patrician caste. Their influence derived from personal relationships and from their leadership in local scholarly associations. They were gentlemen scholars like John Pintard and DeWitt Clinton, those who George Folsom described in his early history of the Historical Society as "gentlemen . . . esteemed in their day for professional skill, literary taste, and classical or scientific attainments." Often the metropolitan gentry were also well-to-do gentlemen (or, in some cases, gentlewomen), but they were writers as well, professionals at work in the rapidly expanding publishing industry. Unlike the earlier generation, their influence was exercised throughout the nation through the medium of print. In his *New York by Gaslight* (1882), James D. McCabe Jr. included a fascinating taxonomy of the city's elite in which he praised its "artists, authors . . . scientific men, and others of kindred pursuits" as "the saving element of the society of the metropolis."[54] It was in this light that some supporters of the Astor viewed the public purpose of a public library that was not intended for "the great mass of the people." The alcove readers would use its resources to produce books, and articles for newspapers and popular magazines that would in turn be used to instruct the masses. The *Home Journal*, for example, explained that the reading public would "take the . . . Library through the [*New York*] *Sun* [and] through the 'Entertaining-Knowledge' books, popular biographies, and other useful dilutions" of its scholarly treasures.[55]

Cogswell and the Astor trustees dismissed out of hand the possibility of a public library as it was coming to be understood in the latter half of the nineteenth century, one that loaned for use in the home more popular works that appealed to the average reader. In the first place, they deemed the "great mass of the people" rather too dishonest to allow them to remove books from the building. Cogswell, in a defense of the Astor's status as a library of reference, patiently explained that "a free library of circulation is a practical impossibility in a city as populous as New York." He assumed that readers would simply steal the loaned volumes and the entire collection "would be dispersed to the four winds within five years." More importantly, he held that such an institution simply did not fulfill a public purpose. "Popular libraries," a term he used disparagingly, were not for "the lasting welfare and progressive improvement . . . of the community," but rather for its "mere momentary gratification." As such, they were "the proper concerns of clubs and private societies."[56]

The critics of the Astor and the supporters of the growing public library movement in New York had a more expansive, liberal vision of what a public library could accomplish and whom it could serve. A correspondent to the *Times* wrote in 1854 that there was always "a large class, toiling through the dreary course of a city life" that was eager to "leave daily pains and troubles, and wander in the temples of imagination and . . . store the mind in the realms of science." Other editorials over the years reiterated and expanded upon the moral and practical benefits of popular libraries. On one hand, it was urged that "a great library ought to" enable "everyone [to] pursue in it researches peculiar to his trade or business." On the other, since "the booklover [is] not confined to any favored class in this free community," even the masses could improve themselves if they were exposed to the refining influence of good reading. They might not borrow the same weighty tomes perused by the Astor's alcove readers, but they could still be uplifted if granted free access to good literature. The proponents of the public library movement firmly believed that reading "standard authors" such as Sir Walter Scott, James Fenimore Cooper, and Charles Dickens (whose works Cogswell privately dismissed as "trashy") would refine and thereby exert a powerful moral influence upon the working class. This, in their view, was the public purpose that a public library was intended to fulfill.[57]

The history of John Jacob Astor's legacy, particularly the public's reception of it, reveals some of the shortcomings and pitfalls of large-scale, individual philanthropy in the Gilded Age and Progressive Era. First, the character of an institution founded upon a personal fortune was usually determined by a single individual, whose intentions may have been at odds with the desires and expectations of the community. In the case of the Astor, the guiding influence, Joseph Green Cogswell, was also an incredible snob who was temperamentally ill-suited to manage a public li-

Joseph Cogswell, probably around 1870

brary.[58] Moreover, the public's perception of the Astor Library was colored in part by the reputation of the founder and his family. Even before Astor's death in 1848, there was considerable class resentment of the immense fortune that he had amassed, a sense that he had made "his money by unfair means or that it [was] unfair that [he] should be so rich." His son, William B. Astor, inherited his father's vast real estate holdings, including property in the city's worst slums and was popularly known as the "landlord of New York."[59] Critics were fond of pointing out that Astor's gift represented a mere fraction of his unprecedented wealth, and some argued that he ought to have given more to the city that made its accumulation possible.[60] Finally, because succeeding generations sat on the Board of Trustees and played a direct role in the management of the Library, the Astor was frequently referred to as a "family monument," a form of familial vanity rather than a truly public benefaction. When the great-grandson, William Waldorf Astor, declined to serve, he explained that he did so because of "complaints . . . that it was an appendage of the Astor family which controlled it for the purposes of self-glorification to the detriment of the public interest."[61]

Chronic underfunding proved to be another limitation of large-scale philanthropy during the Gilded Age. The original endowment for a privately funded public institution was not always sufficient in the long term to carry out the founder's intentions. The $400,000 that John Jacob Astor bequeathed to the Astor Library, for example, was a considerable fortune in 1848. However, nearly half of it was spent on the land, the building, and the original collection of books. Even with generous contributions from his son and grandson, and occasional support from other trustees and affluent, public-spirited New Yorkers, the annual income of the Library was comparatively limited.[62] The collection grew at an impressive rate, but by the 1890s other libraries with more substantial funding, such Harvard University's and the Library of Congress, were the most important institutions nationally. The superintendent in his annual reports made frequent appeals to the generosity of the city's elite, but they were reluctant to contribute to the Astor family's monument. As the *New York Times* explained, "Croesus will give his gold, [only] if the gold will bring glory to Croesus."[63]

The most severe criticism of the Astor was that it stood in the way of a truly public institution. Its detractors charged that its mere existence meant that neither the City of New York nor a more generous philanthropist would ever provide a library that would meet the needs of the entire citizenry.[64] As it happened, the creation of the New York Public Library required the combined collections and endowments of both the Astor and the Lenox, an enormous gift from the country's greatest Croesus, Andrew Carnegie, and annual appropriations from the City. By the beginning of the twentieth century, New Yorkers finally had a great library that served both "the great mass of the people" as well as the "men of leisure and the men of letters." By the end of the nineteenth century, however, public libraries generally were much less important for scholarly research. Leadership within the scholarly community had passed from the men of leisure toiling in the alcoves of the Astor to professional academics working in a university library.

7

Scholars and Mechanics
Libraries and Higher Learning in Nineteenth-Century New York

On January 20, 1847, Townsend Harris, the president of the Board of Education, presented the report of a special committee that recommended a radical departure in public education for the city and state of New York. It urged the board to petition the legislature for a new law that would reserve a portion of the state's Literature Fund to establish and annually fund a "free College or Academy for the instruction of students who have been pupils in the Public Schools."[1] The annually elected Board of Education was established just five years earlier, shortly before the City took over the privately managed and largely tax-supported Public School Society. Created in 1790 and amended in 1834, the Literature Fund appropriated state monies from the sale and lease of public lands to support private academies, including the grammar schools run by Columbia College and New York University. Among other things, it provided modest funding for books, maps and globes, and other educational materials.[2] Harris's committee proposed the new school as a democratic alternative to Columbia College and New York University. The Free Academy of the City of New York, renamed the College of the City of New York in 1866, and known informally as City College, would be publicly supported, open to rich and poor alike, and offer a modern, progressive curriculum. The committee's report raised fundamental questions regarding the role of higher learning in a democracy. What public and private purposes does it fulfill? What segments of a community does it serve and how? Should it be supported or assisted through public funds? The establishment of City College, its curriculum, and its library reflect various answers to these questions throughout the latter half of the nineteenth century.

Many of the arguments advanced in favor of the College of the City of New York echoed those used by William Livingston at the founding of Columbia in 1754 and by the founders of New York University in 1830.[3] Harris and others portrayed both institutions as outmoded bastions of aristocracy. They argued that, since both did little more than teach dead languages to the children of the elite, the city sorely need a school "more congenial with our republican institutions," one that bore "a close analogy to the life of the nation" and that would pursue the "greatest good for the greatest number."[4] At times, their rhetoric recalled Edward Schoolcraft's plea for scholarly and cultural institutions that would bring together the rich and the poor on equal terms.[5] More often, however, it reflected the rising class tensions and aggressive egalitarianism of Jacksonian New York. Harris's report to the board, for example, demanded to know "if the wealthy part of the community seek instruction to enlarge the minds of their children, why should not an opportunity be given to the sons of toil to give the same advantages to their children?"[6] The "People's College" would teach new, practical subjects, such as chemistry and physics, to the masses and thereby create a class of intelligent, productive mechanics, well prepared to "meet the varied needs of our busy community."[7]

The promoters of City College emphasized that it was to be a tax-supported institution. It would be paid for by the people and managed by their representatives, the Board of Education, for the benefit of the public. The school would belong to the citizens of New York and thus avoid the stigma of pauperism associated with charity scholarships in private schools.[8] City College supporters were especially critical of the fact that Columbia College and New York University received an annual appropriation from the Literature Fund. They argued that public funds should be expended for public purposes, not to "secure the opportunity of growing pale and sickly in classical and less useful studies" to the children of wealthy families.[9] The practical instruction offered at City College would certainly help young men of modest means secure respectable, gainful employment, but its founders more often emphasized its value to the entire community. The well-educated, productive mechanic would be a responsible, intelligent citizen. The school would thus be "imminently useful to society," ensuring "the permanency of our free institutions" and the preservation of "social quiet and order."[10] Supporters also stressed the benefits to the artisanal community in particular. The City College graduate would "become extensively useful to his class" by fostering intelligent, efficient craftsmanship, thereby "making industry honorable" and "adding dignity to labor."[11]

Much of the criticism aimed at Columbia College and New York University was well founded. Despite the university's ambitious plans at its founding for a more practical and popular approach to higher education, and certain concessions to public opinion made by the college at the same time, there was little real change at either institution in the 1830s and 1840s. Both remained small, elitist, and traditional.[12] In 1847, the year that Harris proposed a publicly supported school, twenty-two students graduated from Columbia College. Five years later, more than twenty years after its founding, New York University had a total of only 455 graduates.[13] Despite founder Albert Gallatin's progressive vision of school that would educate the sons of artisans and shopkeepers as well as the patriciate, the university's first chancellor, James M. Mathews, boasted in an early annual report that it had become "the resort of young men whose names have long been identified with the history of our State and country."[14] New York University did offer a nonclassical course that did not require Latin and Greek, but students who completed it did not earn a bachelor's degree. Columbia discontinued its alternative to the classical curriculum, started in 1830, in 1843. What *Putman's Monthly* wrote of the university in 1853 certainly applied equally to the college: its "halls which could give convenient room to six hundred students . . . look melancholy and deserted."[15]

The libraries of Columbia College and New York University were relatively neglected for most of the nineteenth century.[16] Access was limited. They were generally open fewer than ten hours a week and then only to sophomores, juniors, and seniors.[17] The catalogs were usually unwieldy manuscripts that were often out of date.[18] For much of the century the librarian was a faculty member who was given charge of the library as an additional duty and who may or may not have been interested in library matters. At Columbia, for many years, the janitor served as assistant librarian.[19] The collections were small compared to other libraries in the city and grew largely through donations from professors and alumni. In 1862, New York University had 2,281 volumes, and in 1868, Columbia had 13,795 while the Astor Library, the largest in the city, had a total of 137,533 volumes.[20] In fact, librarians at neither institution aimed at building large, comprehensive collections. As Williams Jones, the librarian at Columbia, explained in an article in 1862, "the ideal of a College Library . . . does not seem to include a vast number of volumes. Selectness rather than great extent . . . appear to us to be the governing principle." Jones was "inclined to disbelieve the expediency . . . of accumulating new, elementary scientific publications," described the holdings in American history as "by no means a specialty," and emphasized that the collection contained practically no contemporary prose fiction, even of the most highly regarded authors.[21] He did collect as comprehensively as possible in the classics, however, including "all writings of a fictitious character left by the ancients." Much like Columbia alumnus James Lenox, Jones also took particular pride in his library's bibliographic "rarities" and "curiosities," describing, for example, all the works autographed by the famous and nearly famous of past centuries.[22]

Libraries of such limited scope and access had limited appeal for the students. In 1865, Columbia's new president, Frederick A. P. Barnard, complained in his annual report that the library was "so little frequented," because "it continues to be doubtful whether a journey [there] would reward the inquirer with any information more satisfactory than that the authority he seeks is not to be found."[23] Typically, a student made more extensive use of the collection developed by his literary society. Most American colleges in the nineteenth century had two literary societies, which honed their members' skills in debate, oratory, and composition through friendly intramural competition. Like most such associations, the Philolexian and the Peithologian at Columbia, and the Eucleian and Philomathean at New York University maintained fairly well-organized, well-rounded libraries that circulated, among other works, current belles-lettres and periodicals. Most students belonged to one or the other and used their collections for recreational reading and to prepare for debates and orations. When Lyman Abbott, for example, looked back on his days at New York University in the 1850s, he had no clear memory of the college library, although he did borrow extensively from the library of the Eucleian Society.[24] Lyman and others also made use of the city's major public libraries. In 1793, when Robert R. Livingston purchased a subscription to the Society Library for Columbia's seniors, representatives of the class wrote a letter thanking him for providing access to "a collection of books far more general and extensive than any we might have reason to expect in a library particularly belonging to the College."[25] As late as 1890, the New York University annual catalog provided a very brief description of the library, then advised current and prospective students that the Astor Library, with its extended hours and more than 200,000 volumes, was a five-minute walk from campus.[26]

Judging from the reception of Townsend Harris's arguments in 1847 for publicly supported higher education, New Yorkers in the 1840s saw a need for a more practical and less exclusive alternative to Columbia College and New York University. Harris's report was adopted by the Board of Education in February 1847, and he and two others were assigned to draft a memorial to the legislature calling for a bill to authorize a local tax levy for the Free Academy and an annual appropriation from the Literature

Fund. The law passed in May of that year required a ballot referendum at the next election of the Board of Education. The referendum passed overwhelmingly on June 7, 1847, and nine days later the board formally established the Free Academy of the City of New York by a vote of twenty-eight to one. On January 19, 1849, the school was officially opened in a new building on the corner of Lexington Avenue and Twenty-Third Street.[27]

Townsend Harris had resigned from the board and from his position as chair of the Executive Committee of the Free Academy before classes began. Despondent over the death of his mother, he liquidated his business interests in early 1849 and left the country to travel in the Far East.[28] It is impossible to know whether the curriculum at City College would have developed differently had Harris remained as its guiding force during its formative years. Yet, just as with the founding of New York University almost two decades earlier, the original vision of providing a pragmatic education for young men of humble means was greatly compromised. The school did offer a five-year course in modern languages (French, German, and Spanish), as well as a traditional classical course, and both included such modern, practical subjects as chemistry, civil engineering, and commercial law. Further, students were allowed to take a "partial course" in either the modern or ancient language courses. Unlike New York University, City College awarded from its inception a bachelor of science degree to those completing the modern course, as well as a bachelor of arts degree to those who took Latin and Greek.[29]

Nonetheless, a preference for the classics was evident through much of the nineteenth century. For example, in his address delivered at the first anniversary of the college, Erastus C. Benedict, the new president of the Board of Education, was at best ambivalent about the value of the modern languages within the curriculum. While granting that the community should "insist that the practical and useful ought to triumph," he cautioned that "our opinion as to what is the practical and the useful is by no means agreed to." He held that "we do much by placing the modern and the ancient side by side in inevitable comparison" and warned that City College would be "vulgarized and degraded" if it excluded "those branches of knowledge . . . considered the proper education for scholars, for professional men, for men of wealth and leisure."[30]

The curriculum at City College and changes in the curricula at New York University and at Columbia in the 1850s did reflect the beginning of a gradual but critical shift in the focus of higher education in the United States. In 1857, Columbia established an undergraduate School of Science.

Although it was discontinued just four years later, a graduate School of Mines was founded in 1864 that provided instruction in a broad range of the physical sciences. In 1855, New York University finally began awarding the Bachelor of Science, as well as the Bachelor of Arts degree. It required German, modern history, and English literature, as well as courses in mathematics and science, but not Latin or Greek.[31] Similarly, the instruction at City College was part of a movement away from a rigidly classical curriculum, designed to turn young men into young gentlemen, toward what we would recognize today as a liberal arts education. In his address at the opening of the college, Horace Webster, its first principal, explained that "the object of education . . . has not in view so much to give information" as to promote "the practical application of the intellectual powers to any given subject."[32] By current standards, instruction at City College, with its emphasis upon recitation and no elective courses, seems rigid and uninspired. In 1849, it was comparatively progressive.

Perhaps the most significant difference between the publicly supported college and its two rivals was the fact that most of its students enrolled in the partial course and never intended to take a degree. As the Board of Trustees explained in 1873, in response to criticism in the press of the low graduation rate, "the majority . . . [were] from families depending for their support upon their own industry," so "they [came] to school just as long as they [could] be spared from productive pursuits" and then "enter[ed] counting-rooms and various spheres of business."[33] Thus, City College boys were not "rich loafers," as John W. Burgess, a professor of political science at Columbia, described his undergraduates in the 1870s, but neither were most of them the sons of sturdy mechanics that Townsend Harris in 1847 had hoped would fill the classrooms.[34] Although the skilled trades were fairly well represented, very few of the students were sons of common laborers, who could not be "spared from productive pursuits" even for a brief period, and nearly half were the sons of clerks, merchants, and professionals, presumably those of more modest means who could not afford the tuition at Columbia or New York University. Even those from more humble backgrounds were far more likely to become businessmen or professionals upon graduation, so that Harris's vision of an institution that would "add dignity to labor" was never truly realized. City College served at best as a means of upward mobility for the middle or lower-middle classes in the city.[35] As well, the majority of City College students chose the classics course. Of the first three classes, for example, only about 25 percent took modern languages.[36] Moreover, the traditional, classical curriculum there changed more slowly than at Columbia or New York University. By the end of the nineteenth century, City College was larger and less exclusive than its private rivals, but pedagogically more conservative.[37]

The City College Library was similar in many respects to Columbia's and New York University's. In the 1850s and 1860s its collection was, like theirs, relatively small. In 1860, the year the first printed catalog appeared, it held approximately nine thousand volumes.[38] However, despite two generous private endowments, it grew more slowly later in the century than the collections at the other schools. By 1900, for example, Columbia had approximately 260,000 volumes, while City College had fewer than 34,000.[39] Perhaps the most notable feature of the library was that it circulated multiple copies of the titles that were required for the students' coursework. In 1876, in addition to the regular collection of nearly 20,000 volumes, it also made available a total of approximately 13,000 textbooks. This was an important part of the library, since the students of more modest means would have been unable to afford them. On the whole, the City College Library seems to have been rather more catholic than Columbia's. It had relatively weaker holdings in the classics, which included some works in translation, and was strongest in history, biography, and travel. It also had a reasonably complete collection of scientific periodicals, the subscriptions for which consumed much of its annual budget. Unlike Columbia, it did collect fairly extensively in contemporary literature, although, of course, it offered no popular fiction.[40] For more ephemeral works and also for "books considered improper for the eyes of the innocent," one of the literary societies, the Clionian, maintained a small collection for its members. The other society, the Phrenocosinia, apparently had no library.[41]

Access to the collection was considerably more restricted than at Columbia or New York University. During the early years, the library was only open every other Friday, from 8:30 to 9:00 in the morning. Moreover, to borrow a book, a student had to present a permission slip signed by three professors testifying to the fact that he was currently in good academic standing. He could also be expelled for not paying for a lost or damaged volume.[42] The library's most serious limitation was a lack of space. A special report by the Board of Trustee's Library Committee in 1872 found it to be "far from satisfactory" and described "books . . . crowded away on the shelves without order or any proper arrangement" or "piled away" in darkened corners.[43] Little use was made of the collection. Lewis Mott, class of 1883, remembered the library mostly as a detention hall. Located across the corridor from the president's office, students were sent there as a punishment when found guilty of '"gross disorder, insubordination, and impertinence.'" According to Mott, "a large majority of the students did not take out a single book . . . from the beginning to the end of the course."[44]

The conditions in the City College Library (and in Columbia's and New York University's as well) were not so much shortcomings as a reflection of the state of higher education for much of the nineteenth century. The city's public college taught, even in its modern languages course, a comparatively narrow, static curriculum to a relatively select group of students. They were expected to be consumers of a limited canon, so that an extensive collection of titles in a wide range of subjects was not essential. Later, with fundamental changes in curricula and the rise of the modern research university, academic libraries would change dramatically, but during this early period the City College Library was adequate, given the goals of the institution. In the meantime, however, Townsend Harris's vision of a practical public education for intelligent mechanics was largely realized at a privately funded school. Its library served not only a much larger and more inclusive student body, but, to an unprecedented extent, the city's rapidly expanding reading public as well.

In 1825, Peter Cooper, a wealthy inventor and manufacturer, began buying parcels of land in what was then an outlying district of Manhattan to build an institute for the improvement of the working classes of New York City. By 1854, he was able to acquire the entire block between Third and Fourth Avenues, Astor Place, and Seventh Street, a short distance from the Historical Society, the Astor Library, the New York Society Library, the Mercantile Library Association, and the American Bible Society's Bible House. That same year he began construction on a six-story building to house the Cooper Union for the Advancement of Science and Art. Cooper then conveyed the property to a five-member Board of Trustees that included himself as president, his only son Edward, and his business partner and son-in-law Abram Hewitt. The deed of gift specified that a portion of the premises was to be leased to shops and businesses and that the income was to "be forever devoted to the instruction and improvement of the inhabitants of the United States in practical science and arts."[45] Opened in 1859, just ten years after City College, the most important feature of the Cooper Union was a night school to provide instruction "close to the practical life and remunerative employment of each student."[46] In addition, the deed also called for a free reading room with books and periodicals for the improvement and rational amusement of the people of New York.[47] The library of the Cooper Union became the most popular and most publicly accessible collection in the city in the second half of the nineteenth century.

Born in 1791, Peter Cooper began work at the age of eight in his father's hat factory in Peekskill, New York. Later he also worked in a family brickmaking business and brewery before moving to New York City to apprentice himself to a coach maker in 1808. Despite having had almost no formal schooling, he then engaged in a succession of highly successful businesses, most notably a glue factory, a grocery, and an iron foundry. He also patented a number of lucrative inventions, including a cloth-shearing machine, a rotary steam engine, and the country's first steam locomotive, the Tom Thumb.[48] According to one biographer, Cooper was barely literate. He deeply regretted his lack of formal education and, in the words of an early annual report of the Cooper Union, "became satisfied early in his life that the working class of this city required greater opportunities for instruction and rational amusement than were afforded by the existing institutions."[49] As Cooper recalled years later, the idea for the form this instruction was to take was suggested to him in 1828 by an acquaintance who had recently returned from Paris. His friend spoke glowingly of the Ecole Polytechnique there and of the practical education it imparted to the city's young men. Cooper then decided that the institution he would found would have as its core a technical school to teach the mechanics of New York the practical, scientific knowledge they needed to advance in their vocations.[50]

In certain respects, Peter Cooper's career in philanthropy resembled that of the most notable philanthropist for American public libraries, Andrew Carnegie. Like Carnegie, Cooper regarded "his wealth as a sacred trust to be used for the welfare of his fellow man" and was, in the words of his obituary in the *New York Times*, "his own Executor"; he personally directed the charitable dispensation of his fortune during his lifetime, rather than bequeathing it, like John Jacob Astor, in his will.[51] In fact, Carnegie called himself "a humble follower of Peter Cooper," and praised him for being "among the first of our disciples of the Gospel of Wealth."[52] Both men also insisted that true charity provided only the means for self-help and that education was the key that would lead workers to "a better knowledge of the true relations between labor and capital and their mutual dependence on each other."[53] Cooper, however, seems to have identified more sincerely with the working class than did Carnegie, whose frequent references to his humble origins seem rather affected. Cooper had a genuine empathy

Peter Cooper, photograph by Mathew Brady, probably the early 1860s

for the plight of poor in the face of industrialization. While he regarded unions as an ill-advised panacea, he nonetheless deplored the fact that "much capital is employed in maintaining servile and unskilled forms of labor and . . . in supporting a great many without any productive industry." He feared that "the greater the refinement and wealth of the few, the greater the pauperism . . . in proportion to the whole people."[54]

Cooper recognized that, with the industrialization of the trades and the consequent decline of the apprentice system, a new approach to education was needed to prevent workers from falling "into servile forms of . . . labor."[55] The "mere scholastic" curriculum emphasized at City College and elsewhere would send "a great many helpless scholars . . . yearly into the world," but it would do nothing to "lift [them] above the reach of abject poverty."[56] The Cooper trustees emphasized that the practical instruction provided in the night school was not intended to train young men for the trades. Rather, it would improve those already engaged in industry and thus educate competent managers, foremen, and employers.[57] Most of the five-year course was taught within six departments: chemistry, mechanics, and mathematics; and architectural, mechanical, and freehand drawing.[58] Like the students at City College, the majority who enrolled at the Cooper Union never intended to graduate from the full program. They took only "those special branches for which they felt the need in their daily business." Although both schools were absolutely free, the fact that instruction at the Cooper Union was offered mainly in the evening was a critical difference. Since its students were generally of more modest means and had to work during the day to support themselves, that was the only time they could set aside for self-improvement.[59]

The Cooper Union did make one notable concession to a "mere scholastic" curriculum. From the beginning there was an extracurricular "oratory and debating class" on Saturday nights, in which students wrote essays and organized formal debates under the guidance of one of the instructors. In 1872, this was expanded into an elective "English Literary Department" that also included courses in elocution, rhetoric, and literature.[60] Directed for many years by J. C. Zachos, the curator of the library, the aim of the department was imminently practical and markedly different from the program in modern languages taught at City College. Rather than making mechanics into gentleman, it was designed to help the students "meet . . . the requirements of business among gentlemen." Realizing that ambitious young men from poor families often lacked the cultural capital, the verbal, literary, and social skills expected of them in the business world, the literary department provided "some liberal culture beyond the technicalities of the mechanical arts" and thus "qualified [them] to take leading places in the superintendence of manufactures and workshops." Like the other courses in the night school, and like the General Society's Apprentices' Library, the department was intended to enable young mechanics to rise within their class their rather than out of it.[61]

Perhaps the most progressive feature of the Cooper Union was the expanded educational opportunities it offered to young women. Female students were enrolled in the English Department, a special music class, and, at least in the earliest years, and in relatively small numbers, courses in the night school.[62] In 1866, the only graduate from the night school was Rosalinda H. Palmer, and Peter Cooper took special pleasure at the annual commencement in presenting her with the Cooper Medal and lauding her accomplishment as an example "of how great and uncommon difficulties can be met and overcome."[63] Most of the instruction for women, however, focused on vocational training for newly emerging, feminized occupations. According to the Cooper Union's annual reports, its founder had a "deep interest . . . in all that can advance the happiness and better the condition of the female portion of the community" and was especially sympathetic toward the "daughter, left by her natural guardians, either by death or neglect, to buffet with the difficulties of getting an honest livelihood in the world."[64] The school thus offered day classes in telegraphy, stenography and typewriting, bookkeeping, and domestic economy.[65] There was also a daytime School of Design for Women that taught subjects such as freehand drawing, lithography, and painting on china, which enabled young women to support themselves through the "application of art to the practical purposes of life."[66] It had a special library solely for the use of its students and was one of the most popular and effective programs offered by the Cooper Union.[67]

The general library and reading room, Peter Cooper's "special delight," was free to the entire community without restriction.[68] Unlike the library of the General Society of Mechanics and Tradesmen and the free circulating libraries that were founded in the 1880s and 1890s, the Cooper Union Library did not require a reference from a "responsible person" to use the collection, and there was no minimum age for admission.[69] Like the Astor, it was a noncirculating "reference library," but it was considerably more welcoming and accessible to the public. It was open from 8:30 a.m. to 10:00 p.m. Monday through Saturday and, beginning in 1872, from 9:00 a.m. to 9:00 p.m. on Sundays. The trustees boasted that the Cooper Union Library was the most popular in the city, the "favored resort . . . of the working class."[70] Use of the collection increased steadily through the years, from 219,710 "visitors" in 1860 to 402,685 in 1880 to 516,986 in 1900. The Astor Library, by comparison, had only 62,778 readers in 1890, shortly before it was incorporated into the New York Public Library.[71] An article in *Frank Leslie's Popular Monthly* in 1894 noted that "an important element of this success is the feeling on the part of the populace that the institution is designed for their use, and that they are entirely welcome."[72]

As outlined in Peter Cooper's deed of gift and elsewhere, the library played a distinct role within the overall plan of the Cooper Union. For the most part it was not intended as a complement to the vocational training provided in the night school and in the School of Design, although it did provide some textbooks for students.[73] Nor was it, like the very popular public lecture series sponsored by the Cooper Union, designed primarily for the moral or civic improvement of the working class, to guide them "in the glorious yet fearful power of framing and carrying on the government of our choice."[74] The library was certainly a means of individual self-culture, a useful supplement to the instruction in the public schools, in which "the mind is [made] ready to assimilate knowledge through . . . books, newspapers, [and] magazines."[75] However, it was also meant simply to offer working men and women a form of wholesome, constructive leisure. Recognizing that "in great cities there is a necessity for recreation and amusement intermediate between that provided by the theatre and . . . the churches," Cooper sought to provide them with "comfortable repose and relaxation from the labors of the day."[76]

The number of periodicals published in the United States increased fivefold between 1865 and 1885.[77] While the trustees acknowledged that they lacked the financial resources to keep pace with this explosion of print, the Cooper Union nonetheless made every effort to "furnish the fullest and most desirable information on all the topics of current interest, in the political, social, literary and scientific world."[78] The reading room's collection of newspapers and magazines was the most widely used and one of the most extensive in the city. By 1897, there were subscriptions to 436 periodicals, including eighty-four dailies from across the United States and thirty-one foreign-language journals. While there was a very wide selection of titles, including commercial, evangelical, and scientific publications, visitors to the reading room seem to have been more interested in amusement than instruction. The trustees reported that "no tables are so constantly filled than those which contain the illustrated periodicals," which were liberally provided "with a view of affording the working class an attraction from less desirable places of resort."[79] Also, in a city with a very large population of immigrants and migrants, foreign journals and newspapers from outside of New York City were undoubtedly a welcome source of news from home.

The noncirculating reference library was developed as an "adjunct" to the reading room. It was not established until the year after the founding of the Cooper Union, grew relatively slowly, and was used less extensively than the collection of current periodicals.[80] Most of the annual appropriation went toward journal subscriptions, and for some years practically the only additions to the reference library were bound, noncurrent periodicals transferred from the reading room.[81] The collection started with approximately four thousand volumes in 1860, had grown to fifteen thousand by 1880, and to thirty-seven thousand by 1900. This was, of course, considerably smaller than the Astor Library, which opened in 1854 with 80,000 volumes and had 283,000 by 1895, the year it was incorporated into the New York Public Library.[82] The aims of the two institutions, however, were obviously very different. It was not, the trustees explained, "the object of the founder to establish a great Library for learned consultation, but a . . . well furnished and commodious reading room for the use of that intelligent class, so numerous in every large city, that are engaged in the business of life [and have] very limited leisure."[83]

The first annual report of the Cooper Union noted that, despite its impressive collections, the Astor Library was of little practical use to the average mechanic, because it was closed in the evenings. However, since "his range of reading and his requirements [were] more limited," it would "not . . . be difficult to supply his ordinary wants." The Cooper Union Library held "little . . . that a specialist, in any department of science or literature, would find of much service," but was nonetheless a popular adjunct to the reading room.[84] Of the 33,259 volumes in the library in 1895, nearly 25 percent were noncurrent bound periodicals. There was a comparatively large selection of "miscellaneous literature and collected works" (20 percent) and a rather smaller one of history and travel (8 percent). Science holdings were also very limited (7 percent), but there was a fairly extensive collection of government documents (15 percent), which included a complete set of the *Reports of the United States Patent Office*. There was also a small selection of theology (2 percent); poetry (.2 percent); and economics and political science (4 percent). Fiction was approximately 13 percent of the entire collection, roughly half of what was found in a typical free circulating library during this period.[85]

As in the reading room, the periodicals were the most heavily used volumes in the library, accounting for nearly half of the 350,182 titles requested in 1894. Literature, history, and science were considerably less popular (12 percent, 6 percent, and 5 percent, respectively), and poetry and political economy were used hardly at all. Predictably, fiction was the second most popular category, accounting for 27 percent of the books read that year.[86] This was lower than the average in most libraries with circulating collections, but requests for novels evidently declined somewhat after 1886, when most of New York's free circulating libraries were established. In earlier years, for which the library reports do not provide detailed statistics on the number of books used, fiction was usually estimated at around 50 percent.[87] Like the librarians in the city's free libraries, J. C. Zachos, the curator of the Cooper Union, frequently referred to the "high standard . . . maintained in the selection of books," insisting that only novels of "acknowledged merit are added to the Library."[88] At the same time, however, Zachos was less preoccupied with the moral and intellectual uplift of the working class. He often pointed out that the appeal of light fiction was "not surprising in a library visited by many overworked men and women," that it could be "the solace and the refuge of those who have to grapple with the sterner and more repulsive facts of the world."[89] Compared with the free circulating libraries, the library of the Cooper Union was more willing to develop a collection in which "the useful and practical [could] be mixed with the agreeable and recreative."[90]

The library was one of the most public spaces in the city, "free to all without ticket or introduction." Measuring 125 by 80 feet, it accommodated approximately fifteen hundred to two thousand readers per day.[91] Many of them were "regular" users, and there was a consistent pattern to the use of the room during the course of a day. In the early morning, the unemployed came to scour the employment advertisements in the newspapers. During the daytime, the hall was filled with the chronically unemployed, people who worked at night, and those with the financial means to "lead a life of leisure." In the evening, visitors were of a more "serious character," students, clerks, and businessmen who made more extensive use of the books in the library.[92] According to an article in the *New York Times*, the library, like the Astor, had its cast of odd characters, such as the "long haired poets greedily devouring volumes of verse" and "obscure geniuses making grimaces over the books." It was also a refuge for the homeless in a crowded city in which "almost every spot belongs to someone and is guarded by a jealous eye." While the attendants took special care to exclude those who were intoxicated or disorderly, they were sympathetic toward those destitute persons who, "stunned by a succession of misfortunes," read the books and periodicals at the Cooper Union because they had nowhere else to go.[93] In contrast to the haughty, unwelcoming reception given the public by the attendants at the Astor, the trustees of the Cooper Union took great pride in a library that was "more free and hospitable, and easy of access to them than are many of the churches."[94]

The Cooper Union's library and reading room were almost exclusively male public spaces. The curator and trustees seem to have been sincerely interested in promoting the use of the collections by female readers, but met with little success. Beginning in 1887, for example, a special alcove was reserved solely for women, although they were free to read in any part of the room.[95] Despite this change, however, females as a proportion of the total annual visitors seldom rose above 2 percent. Evidently there was considerable reluctance to enter into a masculine space within the public sphere and thereby render themselves, in the words of Abigail Van Slyck, "vulnerable to the symbolic violations of the male leer and the impertinent comment."[96] One of the teachers in the school, for example, complained about the "'loafers and idlers who swarm about, staring at . . . the women.'" Significantly, the only time that use by females increased was when use by males decreased. In 1879, dismayed by the unruly conduct of some readers and the occasional defacement or theft of the books, the trustees began requiring visitors to apply for "tickets of admission." In the next two years, before the policy was discontinued, the number of female readers increased for the first time in the nineteenth century to over 10 percent, while the overall readership plummeted by more than 30 percent.[97] When the tickets were no longer required, use by women returned to its former level. The city's free circulating libraries were more gender-neutral spaces. In its first annual report, for example, the New York Free Circulating Library estimated that one-third of its readers were female. This may have been, in part, because they were required to venture into a public space only briefly to borrow books, before returning to their homes to read them. Yet the librarians of the free libraries, most of whom were women, also consciously fostered more intimate, domestic spaces in their small, neighborhood branches.[98]

By the 1880s, the Cooper Union Library, a relatively large, centralized, noncirculating collection, was contrary to the trend in public libraries represented by the city's free circulating libraries. Yet Peter Cooper, inspired by the establishment of the Boston Public Library in 1854, had always intended that it would provide the foundation for an extensive lending library. This was first proposed in the second annual report. The trustees explained that, while they lacked the resources to fund a circulating collection, they would "cooperate heartily with whomever may be disposed to provide the requisite means." Ten years later, on his eightieth birthday, "admonished of the uncertainty of life, and of the propriety of doing what I can while I have the health," Cooper offered $50,000 toward the creation of a circulating library and an endowment of $100,000, half of the income of which was to be used to develop the collection.[99] As it happened, additional support was not forthcoming, and the interest from the entire $150,000 was thereafter appropriated for the annual support of the reading room and reference library. Even with this stable source of income, most of which was used for periodical subscriptions, the Cooper Union Library was severely under funded.[100] While a few smaller gifts and endowments were offered in subsequent years, the trustees frequently complained that "the Library . . . has received . . . from the public very few evidences of appreciation, other than the incessant use of its privileges and the consequent destruction of its contents."[101]

The trustees' various attempts over the years to establish a large lending library illustrate how support for cultural institutions evolved throughout the nineteenth century. When it was first proposed in 1860, they outlined "three plain methods by which the library may be established and maintained." The first possibility, tax support from and presumably administration by the City of New York, they dismissed as the least desirable. A staunch supporter of civil service reform, Peter Cooper apparently believed, like the founders of the New York Free Circulating Library years later, that Tammany Hall was not to be trusted with the operation of a public library. The second option was individual donations, "a general subscription among the citizens." Usually solicited from the wealthier portion of the community, this was the most common means of funding cultural and charitable enterprises until the later nineteenth century and was how the New York Circulating Library was founded in 1878. It is not clear why the trustees never initiated a subscription drive for their lending library. In 1865, however, they did attempt to create a collection that, like the New York Society Library's, would circulate to subscribers who paid an annual membership fee. Unlike the Society Library, the members' yearly subscription was to be very modest and the books would have been made be available for reference to the public. This plan, too, never came to fruition.[102]

The third option for funding the proposed circulating library in 1860 was large-scale philanthropy, a "special gift of some citizen who desires to render a great service to the community." This was the benevolence characteristic of the Gilded Age, when men such as Charles Pratt and Anthony Drexel amassed unprecedented wealth with which they created major public institutions, like the Pratt Institute in Brooklyn and the Drexel Institute in Philadelphia, devoted to the public weal.[103] Peter Cooper's fortune was rather more modest than the typical Gilded Age philanthropist's.[104] In order to establish a lending library in connection with the Cooper Union, the trustees sought to cooperate with the city's other notable library benefactors. In 1895, when the Tilden Trust and the Astor and Lenox Libraries consolidated to form the New York Public Library, they hoped that their books would become the circulating collection of the new institution. Unfortunately, the board of the new library had little interest in providing home reading for the masses at that time. In 1901, when Andrew Carnegie and the City of New York agreed to create a system of branch libraries for the New York Public Library, the Cooper Union expected to become part of this new Circulation Department.[105] The Carnegie gift was a new kind of benevolence that first emerged in the Progressive Era. More complex and on a larger scale, it combined public and private funding and public and private governance. Again, the public library declined to incorporate the Cooper Union Library.

The Cooper Union was a pioneering philanthropic institution for the education of the working class, and its library and reading room were a great benefit to New York City's reading public. By the late nineteenth century, however, it was out of the mainstream in regards to major developments in public librarianship. By the time the free circulating libraries were founded, the new field of "library economy" was developing to serve this new type of library. It emerged with a range of new professions and in New York was fostered in a new kind of university. In the 1880s, the city suddenly became a center for both library education and the public library movement. One of the focal points of the movement was an institution that had remained on the periphery of the public sphere for most of the century.

When Melvil Dewey was appointed chief librarian at Columbia College in 1883, he was already one of the leading librarians in the country. He had helped found the American Library Association in 1876, served as editor of the association's official organ, *Library Journal,* from 1876 to 1881, and as a student at Amherst College created the Dewey Decimal Classification, the system by which most public libraries still organize their collections. During the brief period in which he worked in New York, he founded the New York Library Club, the first professional organization in the country devoted to promoting local library interests and cooperation, and lobbied for the state Library Law of 1886, which provided tax support for the city's free circulating libraries. As chief librarian at Columbia, he organized the

Melvil Dewey in 1888

world's first school for the training of librarians and transformed a small, neglected college library into, among other things, a resource for the public library movement in New York City.[106]

The transformation of the Columbia College Library was largely a collaboration between Dewey and Columbia's president, Frederick A. P. Barnard. In 1883, Dewey was eager to put his ideas regarding modern library methods and services into practice, and Barnard was in the midst of a long and difficult campaign to evolve the conservative, insulated college into a modern research university. Barnard's predecessor, Charles King, had shown little interest in forging an active, public role for the city's oldest college. When Peter Cooper proposed in 1859 that Columbia cooperate with the Cooper Union to create a "thorough school of practical science," King and the Board of Trustees curtly rejected the idea.[107] Similarly, Dewey's predecessor in the library, Beverly Betts, had placed little value on public service and saw no need to develop an extensive collection for research and instruction. He was proud that he frugally returned as much as half of his annual appropriation for books every year, and when the Library Committee proposed the construction of a new building, he informed them that it was unnecessary. Barnard recalled toward the end of his tenure that Betts frequently complained to him that the presence of students in the library annoyed him.[108]

Frederick A. P. Barnard was inaugurated as president of Columbia College in May 1864. Earlier, he had served five years as president and chancellor of the University of Mississippi before the outbreak of the Civil War. Although he began his career as a professor of mathematics and natural science, his most important writings were on the reform of higher education. At Columbia, Barnard advocated abandoning the rigidly classical curriculum and the adoption of a more flexible, practical approach to collegiate instruction. In one of his earliest annual reports, he urged that "the first business of education is to find out what the individual is fit for, the next is to make the most of him in that for which he is fit."[109] He placed particular emphasis upon the expansion of the scope of subjects taught and the introduction of elective courses. As president, Barnard had limited powers and throughout his tenure he struggled against a powerful conservative faction on the Board of Trustees. Nonetheless, he gradually introduced significant reforms during his nearly twenty-five years at Columbia. For example, the college introduced a system of limited electives for seniors in 1872 and expanded it to juniors in 1880.[110] Barnard also had a keen appreciation of the library as integral part of the curriculum. He served as chairman of the trustee's Library Committee, personally donated hundreds of his own books to the collection, and bequeathed in his will a generous endowment for purchases in physics and astronomy.[111]

In February 1881, after Barnard complained repeatedly about a lack of space in the library, the Board of Trustees approved the construction of a new building. Two years later, when it was near completion, they requested the Library Committee to recommend any changes necessary to make full use of the new accommodations. The report adopted in April 1883 called for longer hours, increased appropriations for collections, a complete reorganization of the staff, and the appointment of a "chief librarian" who was "an expert in his vocation [and would] get the library in good working order and afterwards run it economically and actively and successfully."[112] Betts, realizing that he was clearly not the librarian the board had in mind, submitted his resignation under protest. Barnard had already written to Melvil Dewey a few days earlier encouraging him to apply, and Dewey immediately began lobbying for support among the country's leading librarians. On May 7, 1883, the board appointed him chief librarian of Columbia College Library.[113]

Dewey was attracted to the new position not because of the prestige it conferred—Columbia's reputation in the library community was decidedly mediocre at the time—but because of the opportunity it afforded him to advance his ideas regarding library education and modern library management. In urging him to come to New York, Barnard had assured him that it was a chance to put into practice "whatever plans you have for being useful on a large scale."[114] In June 1883, the board approved Dewey's proposals for the reorganization of the library, and he began the process of consolidating the collections in the new building and recataloging all of the books according to the Dewey Decimal System. He also rewrote the college statutes regarding the library, creating new policies and regulations designed to "grant every practical privilege" and to "remove every possible obstacle from the path of the reader."[115]

The hours of the library were increased nearly tenfold, from 8:00 a.m. until 10:00 p.m. Monday through Saturday, including holidays.[116] The staff was expanded to five librarians and twenty-one assistants, whose "aim [was] to make the library as useful as possible to the greatest number." For the first time, there was a reference librarian available at all times to assist readers in identifying and locating sources in the collection for their research.[117] The library also began to offer a number of specialized services, including photographic reproduction, rush cataloging for specially requested books, free pencils and paper for note taking, and telegraph messages and typewriting at cost. There was a pleasant lobby for quiet conversation that featured comfortable settees, ice water, and bulletin boards with information about the college and the library.[118] In the words of an official history written several years later by one of his successors, Dewey's arrival "mark[ed] the beginning of the library of today."[119]

Barnard and Dewey envisioned an entirely new mission for the university library. In his first annual report as chief librarian, Dewey enthused that "the library has been given its true rank as a distinct university department, essential to and serving all" the other departments. In particular, it was to play a direct role in instruction. The reference librarians, rather than simply providing a student with the necessary resources for an assignment, would always try "whenever possible, [to show him] . . . how and where to find for himself what he seeks . . . so that [he] may thereafter work by himself in any great library."[120] Yet the library's instructional responsibilities were to extend far beyond simply teaching how to locate the appropriate books or articles on a given topic. Its staff would work side by side with the other departments, imparting critical scholarly skills, such as the proper arrangement and indexing of sources, and instilling a "spirit of accuracy," so that students' work in the library would provide "instruction for the rest of their lives." In elaborating on this expanded educational role,

Columbia College Library (*Harper's New Monthly Magazine*, November 1884) (Picture Collection, The New York Public Library, Astor, Lenox and Tilden Foundations)

Dewey drew a direct parallel between what he was trying to accomplish at Columbia and the public library movement in which he was so deeply interested. He held that the "library is the real university of the future, for the people as well as the scholar."[121]

For Dewey the appointment at Columbia was an opportunity to put into practice his ideas regarding the synergistic relationship between popular libraries and the modern university library. In an introduction to a special issue of *Library Journal* on higher education, he wrote that the "importance [of a college or university library] will be doubly emphasized" if it "anchors itself in the esteem of the local community." Dewey sought to make Columbia a model of public service not just for its faculty and students but also for the entire city of New York. In a "Circular of Information" issued in 1886, he stressed that "any . . . visitor, though an entire stranger, is always received cordially" and given a tour of the library, and the new library regulations permitted "literary and scientific people" to apply for "readers' tickets" that would allow them access to the reference collection.[122] A correspondent to the *Literary World* (most likely either Barnard or Dewey himself) pointed out that "though this is not a Free Circulating Library, it is really more public than the Astor, for to its greatly increased hours and facilities every scholar is welcome." Moreover, the example of public service set at Columbia would energize the movement for public libraries. In the special issue of *Library Journal* referred to above, Dewey expressed confidence that the "student who is made to understand . . . the full usefulness of an open library, comes back into his community a missionary for the library cause."[123]

For President Barnard, the real value of the new library for the future of Columbia lay in its service to the graduate programs. Although he was interested in reforming collegiate education, mainly through the introduction and expansion of elective courses, he devoted much of his tenure to promoting, in the face of stiff opposition from many of the trustees and a conservative faction within the faculty, the "idea of a grand university."[124] When he arrived at Columbia in 1864, there were already three professional courses: the School of Law, the School of Medicine, and the School of Mines. Barnard recognized that his expansive plans would only "advance by small degrees," and it was not until 1880 that Columbia took its first decisive step in what he termed its "manifest destiny." The School of Political Science established that year was essentially a graduate department of social sciences, offering such subjects as history, public law, sociology, and economics.[125] Its longtime dean and Barnard's chief ally in the campaign for graduate education at Columbia was John Burgess, who had been Dewey's professor at Amherst College and who had lobbied for his appointment as chief librarian.[126]

When he retired in 1889, the selection of Barnard's successor revolved around the future of the school's graduate programs. The board's election of Seth Low, a wealthy businessman and later a reform mayor of New York City, signaled a victory for the faction allied with Barnard and Burgess.[127] Low completed what they had started in the development of graduate instruction. In 1890, the School of Philosophy was created, offering courses in philosophy, literature, and philology. The School of Pure Science was established in 1892, and the School of Mines was renamed the School of Practical Science in 1896. Later that year, Columbia College officially changed its name to Columbia University.[128] By the close of the century,

Columbia had evolved the structure of a modern university and was one of the nation's leading institutions in graduate education.

The library was an integral part of what Nicholas Butler, dean of the School of Philosophy and later president of the university, called the "Barnard-Burgess-Dewey revolution." Dewey recognized that the future of Columbia lay largely in its graduate programs and developed the library's collections especially to meet the research needs of graduate students and faculty. In his annual report for 1884, he noted that "the wants of undergraduates are . . . comparatively simple, but now that our scope is that of the university our field seems practically limitless."[129] That same year, he instituted for the first time a detailed collection development policy that was carefully designed to meet the varying demands that the different departments would place upon the library. For example, in subjects designated as "class A," which included library science and higher education, Dewey would collect comprehensively, while for those in "class D," such as agriculture and the mechanical trades, he would buy only the most exceptional works. According to the new policy, the library would now accept as gifts "the highest grade of recreative reading," since "the old rule [barring fiction] was carried to such an extreme that while we had able professors lecturing on our famous authors, we had of many of them not a page in our library." In another notable departure from past practices, the library would no longer purchase "rarities" and "curiosities."[130] With substantially increased annual appropriations for books, Dewey was able to able to expand the library significantly during his brief tenure at Columbia. When he arrived in 1883, the collection totaled approximately fifty thousand volumes. When he left less than six years later, it had grown to nearly twice that number.[131]

Dewey anticipated the active collaboration of the faculty in creating a library that was adequate to the needs of a modern university. He proposed in 1886 the appointment of a standing committee, with elected representatives from each of the schools, that would advise the Board of Trustees on "general library interests and further the more direct cooperation of the library and the chairs of instruction."[132] He also recruited faculty members to participate in a series of lectures on library research. While librarians would give general instruction in "bibliographic apparatus" and "right methods," professors would give "specific guidance in their respective departments . . . with representative books before them as illustrations."[133] Most significantly, Dewey encouraged the faculty to assume primary responsibility for the development of the library's collections. To encourage their active participation, he assigned to each professor a mailbox in the library in which to place requests for new titles. He even suggested that the faculty members in the each of the schools apportion among themselves the annual appropriation for books.[134]

That Dewey expected to rely primarily upon the expertise of the faculty in building the collection had fundamental implications for the development of librarianship as a profession.[135] His arrival at Columbia coincided roughly with the period in which the academic disciplines were developing the means of organization and communication necessary for the professionalization of higher education. For example, Columbia University Press was established in 1893. It published such journals as the *Political Science Quarterly* for the School of Political Science, *Comparative Literature* for the School of Philosophy, and *Contributions from the Geological Department* for the School of Pure Science.[136] Between 1876 and 1905 thirteen national academic societies were founded in the United States. These new organizations provided, as Thomas Bender has observed, an "important sense of 'we-ness,'" as well as "social guarantees of competence, certification."[137] The Modern Language Association, for instance, organized at Columbia in 1883, welcomed "all earnest workers in modern education," but pointedly rejected "the indiscriminate admission" of "erratic and unfortunate applicants" who "would impair the utility of any educational body."[138] By the 1890s, the typical scholarly producer in the United States was no longer the gentleman of leisure who toiled away in the alcoves of the Astor Library, but rather a professional academic, based locally in a university and its extensive library and connected translocally to like-minded professionals through a scholarly society and scholarly journals.

This transformation of American scholarship was integrally connected with the development of graduate education. The college statute that created the School of Political Science in 1880 described it as a means of preparing "young men for the duties of public life." Approximately two decades later, an official history of the university explained that while a minority of its graduates did in fact become civil servants, journalists, or "directors of organized charities," most became professional academics.[139] This was a rapid and dramatic shift in purpose and to an extent it was market driven. Between 1880 and 1900, the number of students enrolled in institutions of higher learning in the United States more than doubled, from less than fifty thousand to approximately one hundred thousand.[140]

In part, graduate schools at Columbia and elsewhere developed to meet a growing demand for college and university instructors.

The fact that the faculty in a sense was using graduate education to reproduce itself also meant that securing an academic position conferred a special kind of authority, that expertise in certain fields became the exclusive province of the university. When Peter Cooper inaugurated an annual series of lectures in political science at the Cooper Union in 1859, he was inspired by the amateur reformer's zeal for moral uplift and universal education.[141] The new class of professional academics, particularly in the emerging social sciences, had different priorities and concerns. This is not to say that they were indifferent to the problems of modern society. For example, Franklin Giddings, the first chair of sociology at Columbia, lectured at the Cooper Union and arranged for his graduate students to do fieldwork in the city's charities.[142] Yet he was not, like Cooper, a philanthropist and reformer working within the community. Rather he was an expert, an impartial authority offering to it, as he explained in an address before the American Social Science Association in 1894, "the scientific groundwork on which philanthropy must build."[143]

The American Library Association, organized in 1876, certainly provided librarians with a sense of professional identity, but it was a "we-ness" that was rather different from that which brought together the members of the emerging academic societies. Melvil Dewey, writing in *Library Journal* on the founding convention, reported that "there was not one who had not felt that he or she belonged to a philanthropic profession." They were also convinced, according to Dewey, that "library management rested upon a science."[144] However, unlike a professional academic such as Giddings, a public librarian worked in and ideally was part of the neighborhood in which a branch library was located. The public library movement expanded and shaped a profession that, like other "helping professions" such as nursing and social work, provided service and expertise within rather than to the community.

From the beginning, however, the nature of its expertise, of its professional authority, was problematic. Just as at Columbia, where Dewey expected to cede responsibility for developing its collection to professional academics, the librarians in the city's free circulating libraries had to rely to a great extent upon the expert knowledge of others in selecting books. There were so many titles published on so many topics that, even in a small neighborhood library, it was clearly not possible to read everything. Thus, as Dewey's successor at Columbia, George H. Baker, noted at a meeting of the New York Library Club, although "any systematic attempt at reading is almost impossible . . . even in a public library [one could] find men and women with specific literary taste and knowledge who will help."[145] Yet, apart from selecting books, and despite Dewey's insistence that there was "work beneath the surface that only the [librarian] and not the casual observer appreciates," much of library work in the late nineteenth century was routine and not especially demanding intellectually. Dewey himself, for example, in a speech to group of prospective library school students, explained that while it was useful to have a general background in the humanities, "a very legible handwriting is practically more important to most applicants . . . than a half dozen sciences."[146] As opposed to the emerging academic disciplines, librarianship had more to do with neatness and order than professional expertise.

Columbia's School of Library Economy admitted its first class in January 1887. For Dewey, and for most library leaders at the time, a student's intellectual abilities were less important than the personal qualities that were deemed essential in a librarian. The primary purpose of the school was to train men and women for the public library movement, and the mission of the modern public library was the education of the working class. That educational work, however, was moral rather than practical. Dewey was confident that, by "develop[ing] the taste for better books," the modern librarian would "elevate the masses and make their lives better worth living," thereby exercising a "far-reaching influence for good."[147] "Mere intellectual industry" was therefore of secondary importance. He stressed to potential applicants to the school that "the best work will always be done on the moral plane, where the librarian puts his heart and life into his work," that the "natural qualities most important in a library are . . . earnestness and enthusiasm."[148] A philanthropic spirit was more essential than a finely honed mind.

There were three men and seventeen women in the first class of the School of Library Economy.[149] Dewey intended the two-year course in part as one answer to the question posed in an article that appeared in *Harper's Bazaar* shortly after his arrival at Columbia: "What Shall We Do with Our Young Women?" This was a pertinent and perplexing issue "in these days of higher and broader education for women" and in a society that was beginning, albeit slowly, to reject "the notion that the only thing we can do . . . is to marry them."[150] Dewey was particularly interested in recruiting "college-bred women," since they had the social and educational background necessary to carry out the enculturating mission of the public library movement. Although in certain respects his acceptance of female librarians was somewhat patronizing, in general his attitude toward women in the profession was fairly progressive at the time. He held that "there is almost nothing in the higher branches which she cannot do quite as well as a man of equal training" and, writing of the qualifications of the "ideal librarian," predicted that in the future "most of the men who will achieve this greatness will be women."[151] However, although Dewey never really acknowledged it, his motives in recruiting females were partly economic. The public library movement created a pressing need for dedicated, well-educated library workers. Women, largely because they had so few professional opportunities open to them, were willing to work for less than men. Dewey and other (mostly male) library administrators took advantage of this fact in order to run their libraries as cheaply as possible.[152]

Although Dewey enjoyed President Barnard's unqualified support, a conservative faction on the Board of Trustees and within the faculty adamantly opposed higher education for females. He later described his "whole five years at Columbia [as] a constant struggle against the Anti-Women element."[153] The year before he came to New York, in response to considerable public pressure, the board had approved a "Collegiate Course for Women." Students were allowed to take examinations leading to a bachelor's degree, but not to attend classes. An official history of the university, published in 1904, commented, apparently without a hint of irony, that "these women found increasing difficulty in passing examinations upon lecture courses which they could not attend." This problem was resolved in 1889 with the founding, with strong support and encouragement from Melvil Dewey, of Barnard College, an affiliated institution of Columbia.[154] However, when the board discovered that women had been admitted into the Library School in 1887, the Committee on Buildings refused to provide a classroom for the students. Dewey was forced to clear out a storeroom above the college chapel. Matters came to a head in May 1888, when Barnard, now nearly eighty years old, resigned. Dewey was suspended, and three separate committees were appointed to investigate various aspects of his tenure as chief librarian and director of the school. He was allowed to resign on December 20, 1888. By that time he had already accepted the position of State Librarian of New York, and he moved his library school to Albany the following year.[155]

Dewey's brief tenure at Columbia had an enduring impact upon the public library movement in New York City and the United States. Under his leadership, the university library's public services were a model not just for academic libraries, but for popular libraries as well. His protégé and successor as chief librarian, George Hall Baker, remained active in the New York Library Club, founded by Dewey in 1885, and later served as its president. One of his students in the first class of the School of Library Economy, Mary Wright Plummer, established in 1895 at the Pratt Institute in Brooklyn the third library school in the United States. Most important, Dewey was instrumental in the passage of the state Library Law of 1886, which provided public funding for free circulating libraries.[156] By the time he left New York in 1889, the public library movement, which was just beginning in 1883, had created a system of privately managed public libraries throughout the city to educate and uplift the masses.

8

New York's Free Circulating Libraries

The Mission of the Public Library in the Gilded Age

What Mordecai Noah said at the reopening of the library of the General Society of Mechanics and Tradesmen in 1850 remained true for more than a quarter of a century.[1] The Apprentices' Library was still the only collection in the city of New York available to the "poor, little ragged apprentice boy . . . disposed to drink deep at the Pierian Spring." While other large cities such as Boston and Chicago established municipal systems that were free to every resident, leaders in the profession both locally and nationally increasingly regarded New York as a backwater of public library development. Reference libraries such as the Astor and the Lenox welcomed scholars and writers, the metropolitan gentry, and subscription libraries such as the Mercantile Library Association and the Society Library were open to those who could afford to pay an annual fee. But as late as 1878, most New Yorkers still lacked, in the words of the *New York Times*, the "advantage of free and easy access to books as a means of moral and social culture."[2] The Apprentices' Library was the only substantial free lending library in the city, and even it was free only to young men and women employed in industry.

The decades after the Civil War were prosperous years for the General Society. Due in part to judicious investments in Manhattan real estate, it had ample resources to carry out its "mission . . . to all the working classes."[3] In 1878, it moved uptown to a refurbished mansion on Sixteenth Street and supplemented its annual income by leasing the building on Crosby Street. The following year, it discontinued the annual subscriptions for "pay readers," which had never been a significant source of revenue. It expanded, however, the definition of free readers to include journeymen, as well as all boys, girls, and women who were "employed at any legitimate business."[4] Like Peter Cooper, the leaders of the General Society of Mechanics and Tradesmen believed that, in an industrializing economy, its mission should focus in particular upon "that portion of the community most in need of information and the least able to pay for it."[5]

The Society's by-laws required that voting on a proposed member would not "proceed to ballot . . . unless four brothers shall have previously vouched for his character . . . and also for his being a mechanic or tradesman."[6] By the time of the move uptown, however, the initiation fee was fifty dollars, more than twice the cost, for example, of a share in the New York Society Library. The membership included some of the city's wealthiest industrialists, men like Andrew Carnegie and Columbia graduate Abram Hewitt, who had never served formal apprenticeships. Apparently this was a matter of concern for at least some of the brothers. At a meeting in February 1874, a special committee reported that the "words 'Mechanics and Tradesmen,' as they were connected by the founders of our Society, simply mean that it was never intended that any one but a mechanic, or one who has learned a trade, should become a member." Yet, according to the official *Annals of the General Society*, it "[did] not appear that any decisive action was taken on this subject."[7] Even late into the nineteenth century, some of New York's most prominent manufacturers, employers who had no direct contact with workers on the shop floor, continued to identify with the ethos expressed in the Society's motto "By Hammer and Hand All Arts Do Stand." Carnegie, for example, in an article in 1896 entitled "How I Served My Apprenticeship," claimed that the $1.20 he earned his first week as a "bobbin boy" in a cotton factory gave him more "genuine satisfaction" than the "many millions of dollars [that] have since passed through my hands," since it was "the direct result of honest manual labor."[8] This rather vaguely defined yet nonetheless sincerely expressed producerism allowed some Gilded Age captains of industry to extol the harmony of capital and labor during a period of rising class tensions and unprecedented disparities of wealth.[9]

In August 1886, the Apprentices' Library became a free library. Any resident of the city was granted access and borrowing privileges.[10] Although it seems likely that the collection would eventually have been opened to anyone "employed at any legitimate business," this change in policy did not reflect a change in the mission of the General Society. Rather, it was a response to legislation passed in Albany the previous month. Under the provisions of "An Act to encourage the growth of free public libraries and free circulating libraries in the cities of the State," any library organization in the city of New York that made its collection freely accessible to the public was entitled to apply to the Board of Estimate for up to $5,000 for every 100,000 volumes it circulated.[11] The Library Law of 1886 changed entirely the direction of library development in the city. It resulted in the founding of a wide range of free circulating libraries, private associations that were funded largely with public money. These new libraries were the first step toward a public library system as the term is understood today and were eventually consolidated to form the Circulation Department of the New York Public Library. The free circulating libraries were established by the city's elite as a means of bridging the economic, social, and religious divisions of late nineteenth-century New York. In some respects, however, the libraries were themselves a reflection of those divisions.

Although the first large, tax-supported public library in the United States, the Boston Public Library, was established in 1848, contemporaries regarded the founding of the American Library Association in 1876 as the true beginning of the "public library idea."[12] The Apprentices' Library was a pioneering effort in that it circulated its collection for free for home use. The crux of the public library idea, however, was that libraries should circulate freely to *everyone* in the community and, just as important, that they should be conveniently located. Rather than one imposing central building far from a city's residential neighborhoods, as in Boston, the public library idea favored small branches within walking distance of readers' homes. According to one of the founders of New York's free circulating libraries, "as the people are not likely to come to a central library, we must scatter them among the people."[13] Beyond this, there was a spirit of service that pervaded the circulating libraries that was lacking in the more established organizations, particularly the noncirculating reference libraries. For example, whereas the Lenox and the Astor were closed in the evenings, when working people might use their collections, almost all of the free circulating libraries remained open until nine or ten o'clock at night, as well as on Sundays. Similarly, librarians at the "book museums" tended to regard books as sacred artifacts that would be desecrated by contact with the irreverent masses. Librarians at the new free circulating libraries abandoned entirely the idea that their collections needed to be shielded from the public and often reported proudly that their books were "read to pieces."[14]

The first free circulating library in New York City was actually founded before the passage of the Library Law of 1886. In 1878, a group of benevolent ladies from Grace Episcopal Church taught a free sewing class to young girls in a poor neighborhood in lower Manhattan. One day before class began, a teacher heard overheard one of the students reading to her classmates a hair-raising tale from one of the city's many cheap weeklies of serialized fiction. Distressed that the children should be enjoying such lurid fare, their teacher offered to lend each of them a book of wholesome literature once a week "on condition that she should never again buy a sensational story paper."[15] This proved so effective that the women raised a collection of about five hundred donated books and opened a small library on Fourteenth Street and Fourth Avenue. In March 1880, after soliciting advice and assistance from "gentlemen upon whose judgment and charitable disposition reliance was placed," they incorporated as the New York Free Circulating Library.[16] It became the largest and most influential of the city's circulating libraries. By 1900, it operated eleven branch libraries throughout Manhattan and circulated approximately 1,635,000 books that year from an aggregate collection of nearly 167,000 volumes. The New York Free Circulating Library was instrumental in the passage of the Library Law of 1886, and when it eventually consolidated with the New York Public Library in 1901, formed the nucleus of the new Circulation Department.[17]

The free circulating libraries were founded during a period of rising class conflict. From the national railroad strikes of 1877, one year before the founding of the New York Free Circulating Library, to the unrest surrounding the Haymarket trials in 1886, to the severe depression of the early 1890s, tensions between rich and poor escalated throughout the Gilded Age. The republican ideal of a unified public defined by shared values became increasingly elusive. The free circulating libraries in New York were a sustained attempt to reconstruct a republic fractured by the economic disparities and dislocations of the late nineteenth century. This was the predominant theme, for example, at a meeting held in support of the New York Free Circulating Library in 1882. The Reverend Henry Potter, rector of Grace Church and bishop of the Episcopalian Diocese of New York, reminded his audience that "in the Old World, the classes are bound together by ties not existing among us," that "the relations here of indifferent wealth to the poor may reach out until they become so distant that it may be hard to unite them." On a more optimistic note, John Hall, president of New York University, assured them that if "rich men [will] aid in this work by bridging over the chasm between themselves and the less fortunate or wealthy classes, . . . they will lay broader and deeper the foundations of society with a regulated liberty."[18]

Amidst of the economic and political unrest of late nineteenth-century New York, the maxim that an informed public is the mainstay of republican government acquired particular urgency. At the American Library Association conference in 1894, Ellen Coe of the New York Free Circulating Library warned that "in these troublous times popular ignorance is invested with terrors unknown before."[19] Yet the mission of the free libraries went well beyond merely protecting the working class from the wiles of socialists and anarchists. The libraries intended to civilize, to cultivate among the poor an appreciation of beauty and refinement. This was fundamentally different from the aim of libraries such as the New-York Historical Society in which use of the collections set their readers apart from the masses and served as a means of affirming their presumed status as scholars and gentlemen. It was rather different too from the ethic of mutual, communal improvement that inspired the founders of the New York Society Library in 1754. Uplift in the Gilded Age was animated not by what William Livingston termed "a united Harmony of public Spirit," but rather by elites' desire to elevate the ignorant masses toward "their" cultural level.[20]

Although the promoters of the public library idea frequently stressed that the circulating libraries were free to the entire community, that "the benefits of the institutions were to be shared by all persons, regardless of class and color, race and religion," in practice they were clearly created to serve, to "civilize" the poor.[21] When Catherine Bruce, who provided the funds to construct the George Bruce branch of the Free Circulating Library, saw a carriage standing in the street outside the library, she angrily declared that it was "not for carriage people."[22] The elites who founded the free libraries sought to ease class tensions by uplifting the masses, so that those who walked and rode the trolley cars shared the same refined values as the carriage people. Reading the proper books in the proper atmosphere would do more than simply foster good citizenship. It would reconstruct a fractured community. The founders reported optimistically that the libraries were inculcating "habits of quiet, neatness, and decorum," that "such a place is civilizing and improving to manners as well as mind."[23] For New York's elite in the late nineteenth century, the key to a "harmony of public spirit" was this effort to remake the masses in their own image.

The free circulating libraries were just one strand in a web of mutually reinforcing middle- and upper-class voluntary associations working to uplift the urban poor. At the meeting in support of the New York Free Circulating Library in 1882, for example, one of the speakers referred approvingly to the links between the Library and the local Charity Organization Society (COS).[24] Groups like the COS, which sent "friendly visitors" into the homes of the poor to determine whether they were financially and morally entitled to charity, were once viewed by many historians as instruments of "social control."[25] Rather than philanthropic, humanitarian enterprises, they were dismissed as tools by which an anxious elite sought to regulate the behavior an unruly working class. Among library historians, Michael Harris was particularly critical of late nineteenth-century public libraries as a means of social control.[26] There was certainly an element of control in organizations like the COS and, to a lesser extent, the free circulating libraries. Even though membership in the libraries was of course entirely voluntary, terms such as *control, supervision,* and *regulation* were, in fact, used with some frequency in the annual reports and other publications.[27] The word used most often, however, was *influence.*[28] It is unlikely that the elites who founded the free libraries would have taken comfort in the fact the poor were coerced into adopting their values. Rather, they could feel secure knowing that they exercised influence, that the poor were willingly guided into the higher realms of elite culture. In any case, the founders were convinced that their values were self-evidently superior. The movement to establish free circulating libraries was inspired by the optimistic assumption that the less fortunate would naturally embrace a higher cultural standard if they were exposed to the elevating influence of good books.

However, it was not simply the volumes on the shelves, but the branches themselves, the physical environment of the library, that would exert a wholesome, uplifting influence on the reader. The free libraries were consciously designed to inculcate by example a fundamental value of Gilded Age reformers: domesticity. Reference libraries like the Astor and the Lenox were constructed as imposing public monuments to high culture, which often discouraged New Yorkers of more humble means from using their collections. The circulating collections by contrast were often sited in converted houses and storefronts, and their interiors were carefully designed to foster a more intimate, welcoming atmosphere. They were to serve as model homes, as both an example and a refuge for the poor crowded into dark and noisy tenements. The New York Free Circulating Library, for example, strove to provide "cheerful and homelike library buildings," "places of rest and comfort" for "those having no quiet homes."[29] In addition to books, supporters of the Library also donated works of art, and plants and flowers, so that the poor could read in an uplifting milieu of middle-class domesticity.[30]

This emphasis upon values associated with the domestic sphere sheds light on the central role that women played in the founding and management of the New York Free Circulating Library. As noted earlier, the first branch of the Library was organized entirely by women, and even later, after "men of standing in the community" ostensibly assumed leadership of the most important committees, they continued to take the most active part in the direction of the branches. As Joseph Choate, who had lost his seat on the Board of Trustees for failing to attend the monthly meetings, explained at the rally in support of the Library in 1882, "those who appear as officers of the institution are only ornamental; the real work is done by the ladies."[31] Further, for most of the Library's history the chief librarian was female, as were practically all of her assistants.[32] Both as an educational institution and as a model of domesticity, the free library was a deemed a woman's place. Employment or philanthropic work there was considered an acceptable extension of her nurturing, maternal role from the private into the public sphere.[33]

With its emphasis upon homelike branches in poor neighborhoods, there was a marked affinity between the public library movement and the settlement house movement. Probably all of the settlement houses in New York City had a library, or at least a reading room, and two of them, University Settlement and East Side House, had circulating collections substantial enough to receive tax monies under the terms of the Library Law of 1886. The Webster Library of East Side House in particular became one of the most innovative and influential free libraries in the city. First established in 1892 as a "distribution station" for the New York Free Circulating Library, the Webster opened in a separate building in early 1894, and by the time of its consolidation with the New York Public Library in 1903, it had approximately 12,000 volumes and an annual circulation of over 106,000.[34] Its librarian, Edwin Gaillard, was an influential voice in local library circles and later coordinated relations between the public library and the public schools.[35] Inspired by the lofty ideals of the social gospel movement, the Webster, like the Free Circulating Library, sought to recreate community, to foster harmony between the rich and the poor. In its first annual report, the settlement was described as "the home of some men of education, who desire to become acquainted with their neighbors, become their friends," to assist them "not as superiors to inferiors, but as brethren, as children of one Father."[36]

For Gilded Age voluntary associations such as the free circulating libraries and the settlements, the locus of uplift and reform was the neighborhood.[37] They hoped to exercise a pervasive influence by creating institutions that were part of the social fabric of the local community, by forging "this bond of neighborhood, . . . one of the most human, yea, of the most Divine, of all bonds."[38] Since the poor neighborhoods of New York were often home to immigrants and their children, this emphasis upon locality meant that reformers were often forced to come to terms with ethnic as well as class differences. Readers of German descent, for example, made extensive use of the Ottendorfer branch of the New York Free Circulating Library, its second branch, established in 1884.[39] More troubling for elite and middle-class New Yorkers, however, were the new waves of immigrants who arrived in the 1890s and later, newcomers from southern and eastern Europe who seemed more alien, more threatening than earlier groups. In 1898, for instance, the Webster reported a sharp decrease in the number of Germans using the Library and a corresponding increase in Czech readers. To an extent, the free circulating libraries, particularly those in the settlement houses, accorded a degree of respect to the cultures of these new immigrants. The Webster Library, for example, purchased a small collection of books in Czech.[40] Yet, at the same time, the libraries clearly expected that their influence would contribute to the "Americanization" of the foreign population. The Free Circulating Library, for example, reported proudly that its collections helped to "make them acquainted with their adopted country, and to fit them to become intelligent American citizens."[41]

The Webster and the New York Free Circulating Library were products of mainstream Anglo-Protestantism. There were other free libraries that thrived somewhat apart from the dominant culture. In fact, the public library idea as it developed in New York reflected the diversity and complexity of the city's ethnic and religious composition. There were, for example, two Jewish libraries. Founded by B'nai B'rith in 1850, the Maimonides Library developed a more scholarly, less popular collection, and at the turn of the century chose to close its doors rather than be absorbed by the Circulation Department of the New York Public Library.[42] The Aguilar Free Library, founded in 1886, was second in size and popularity only to the Free Circulating Library. The first circulating library established in response to the new library law, by the time it consolidated with the public library in 1903, the Aguilar operated four branches and had a collection of approximately 85,000 volumes, with an annual circulation of nearly 800,000.[43]

Founded by a group of men and women "who were then actively interested in Jewish communal affairs," the Aguilar in many ways paralleled the New York Free Circulating Library.[44] The name of the Library itself referred to the virtues of domesticity. Grace Aguilar was a Jewish poet, novelist, and theologian who died in 1847.[45] According to a Library newsletter, her writings, in particular her most popular novel, *Home Influence*, expressed in "a chaste and beautiful moral tone" the "beautiful home influences of . . . [the] family circle."[46] Founded mostly by German-American Jews, the Aguilar sited its "branches in localities where the Jewish population was dense" and served a growing reading public of Russian and eastern European Jewish immigrants. The directors stressed in their annual reports that, particularly in the East Broadway branch in lower Manhattan, the "immigrant population here . . . imbibes their patriotic ardor through these books, and the library thus aids the making of good citizens."[47] However, during a period of rising anti-Semitism, Americanization at the Aguilar was rather different from Americanization at the Free Circulating Library, and it certainly never meant a dilution of the newcomers' identity as Jews. The East Broadway branch, for example, purchased books in Hebrew and subscribed to Jewish periodicals such as the *American Hebrew* and the *American Israelite*.[48] Culture-building associations such as the Aguilar were expected to reinvigorate Judaism in the United States, in fact. As one supporter explained: "The constant recruits we draw from abroad are acclimated within one generation, are made worthy Americans, and more than make good the vacancies created in our ranks by backsliders."[49]

The Cathedral Free Circulating Library, the branch system maintained by the Catholic Church, was the third largest in the city. Began in 1888 as a small collection in the Cathedral School of Cathedral Parish, the Library grew steadily and eventually opened to the public in 1893, although it did not apply for and receive funds from the City until 1897. By the time it consolidated with the New York Public Library in 1904, the Cathedral Library comprised a main library on Amsterdam Avenue, four branches, and five distribution stations, including one in a Catholic settlement house. The previous year it circulated over 350,000 volumes from a collection of approximately 50,000.[50] Although its director, Father Joseph McMahon, stressed that the Library welcomed readers of all faiths, it was created and closely supervised by the Catholic Church.[51] Of all the circulating libraries in the city, terms such as *control* and *regulate* appeared most frequently and emphatically in the publications of the Cathedral Library.[52] The Cathedral was also the last to join the New York Public Library and fiercely resisted consolidation for almost four years.

In the midst of the bitter controversy over the takeover, the Cathedral Free Circulating Library declared that it was "established to counter the evil influences of public libraries in general." In part, this antagonism was founded on the fact that public library collections included works that reflected the pervasive anti-Catholicism of the period. A "Statement of the Position of the Cathedral Library" issued in 1901 maintained, certainly with some justification, that "on the shelves of these libraries can be found books which are calumnies of Catholic doctrine, faith, and practice." Just as important, however, church officials were concerned that the free circulating libraries were not sufficiently selective in developing their collections, that they provided access to "works . . . injurious to the morals of the average reader."[53] Yet, despite the rather heated rhetoric it employed as it fought to remain independent of the New York Public Library, the Cathedral Library was by no means opposed to public libraries per se. Just as much as their counterparts in the Protestant and Jewish free circulating libraries, the supporters of the Cathedral were putting "into practical form their belief in good literature as a civilizing and elevating influence."[54] The public library idea, the free lending of books from branch libraries for home use, was widely accepted. What librarians and library leaders differed over was how best to develop collections that would civilize and elevate the masses.

The debate in the 1880s and 1890s within New York's free circulating libraries centered on the provision of fiction. A consensus within local library circles recognized "a great distinction between matters of opinion and matters of taste" and held that, in matters of opinion, in subjects such as philosophy, religion, and politics "it should be the desire of the library boards to have each side fairly and, if possible, evenly represented."[55] Even the most conservative of the free libraries, the Cathedral Library, held copies of, for example, Karl Marx's *Das Kapital,* Henry George's *Progress and Poverty,* and Charles Darwin's *Origin of Species.*[56] Rather than trying to exercise control or influence, the libraries for the most part promoted critical, wide-ranging reading in matters of opinion. The Free Circulating Library, for example, printed bibliographies on important public issues such as the tariff and the free coinage of silver, as did the Aguilar, including one entitled simply "Questions of the Day."[57]

Fiction, however, was a matter of taste.[58] There was no firm consensus regarding how much and what kinds to collect. The late nineteenth century was a period of change and conflict in this respect. The older prejudice against fiction as intrinsically inferior or even immoral had faded, and there was a greater willingness within local library circles to accommodate to some degree popular tastes in reading. Some library leaders argued that certain kinds of fiction at least were essentially harmless and that the provision of recreational reading was a legitimate function of a public library. One of the speakers at the meeting in 1882 in support of the New York Free Circulating Library, for example, described "the joy and relief it would furnish to the tired working class."[59] Some even argued that fiction could instruct as well as amuse. The newsletter of the Aguilar Library referred to the "librarians' . . . especial favorite, the 'subject reader,'" who read, for example, historical novels to lend "vividness and color to his mental picture" of historical events, and an article in the *New York Post* on the Free Circulating Library held that "no one who realizes how stimulating ideas and knowledge are most readily absorbed will be disposed either to lament or apologize for" the circulation of fiction.[60] Yet, for most librarians, fiction was neither for amusement nor instruction. Fiction was a matter of taste, and the mission of the public library in the Gilded Age was to cultivate good taste among and thereby civilize and morally uplift the masses.

The parameters of the debate over fiction in free circulating libraries were sharply defined at the American Library Association's annual conference in 1894 by two members of the New York Library Club's Executive Committee. In a paper entitled "Common Novels in Public Libraries," Ellen Coe, the head librarian of the New York Free Circulating Library, urged her audience never to forget that they were "'missionaries of literature.'" While conceding somewhat grudgingly that it was sound policy to supply "books [that] are extremely light, entertaining, amusing," in order to attract the "unlettered, half-educated classes" to the library, she insisted that "a certain unmistakable good literary quality should be maintained," that it was possible to purchase attractive works "which still unquestionably possess the desirable qualities of literary and moral excellence." Quoting from the presidential address that year by J. N. Larned, she rallied her colleagues to "'defend our shelves.'"[61]

At the same session, George Watson Cole presented "Fiction in Libraries: A Plea for the Masses." Cole appealed to his audience to recognize that "'what is trash to some, is, if not nutrient, at least stimulus to others.'" He advised them that "the librarian should not carry his head so high in the clouds so as to forget that the vast majority of people are bowed down by their cares and burdens, and care more for mental relaxation than instruction."[62] Most provocatively, Cole argued that libraries that were supported by public funds had an obligation to meet the public's demand for popular fiction. He held that "the library is in existence by the grace of the public, and it is its duty to cater" to the "wants of the masses who bear the burden of taxation."[63]

These two papers represented two competing ideals of public library development. In practice, the collections of New York's free circulating libraries reflected a tension between the need to attract the working class with "trash" and the desire to uplift them with works of "literary and moral excellence." Few of his colleagues agreed with Cole that they were to cater to the masses. Librarians and trustees viewed library work as a calling, as a noble mission not to provide private amusement, but to promote public refinement and morality. In fact, Cole's argument that public monies should support collections that satisfied the public's demand for popular fiction was sometimes turned on its head. At a meeting of the New York Library Club in 1889, for example, one member insisted that free libraries had no "right . . . to spend funds . . . given to us to benefit the public, on books that do not benefit."[64] At the same time, however, many librarians would have disagreed with Coe that they should purchase only refined and uplifting works. As a practical matter, they understood that free libraries, just like the Mercantile Library earlier in the century, were popular largely because they provided popular fiction. Moreover, since the City's appropriations were tied to the number of volumes circulated annually, more fiction meant more generous funding.

Few librarians believed at heart that a collection of what Coe called "pure fiction" was even possible.[65] In practice, they recognized that it was, in the words of one library supporter, "baby-talk" to "suppose that everything can be ticketed with 'bad' or 'good.'" They realized that books were "first-rate, second-rate, and so on," and that second-rate works were the best means of attracting the masses to free libraries. They purchased "impure" fiction in the belief, or at least the hope, that reading the second rate, or possibly even the third rate, would eventually lead to the first rate.[66] This belief that popular fiction could serve as a stepping-stone to more refined, uplifting reading was fundamental to the development of public libraries and was widely held for much of the nineteenth century. When Mordecai Noah spoke at the reopening of the Apprentices' Library in 1850 of his "poor, little ragged apprentice boy" who would begin with "books of fiction, wit, and humor" and eventually "slide insensibly into a course of *belles-lettres* and polite literature," he was making essentially the same argument advanced at a meeting of the New York Library Club more than a half century later, when one member advised that "the public . . .

is attracted first by poor and cheap things, but [its] mind must naturally expand and reach to higher aims in literature."[67]

The catalogs of the free circulating libraries make it clear that even the self-styled missionaries of literature failed to practice what they preached. In Ellen Coe's own library, for example, the New York Free Circulating Library, less than 10 percent of the collection in 1895 was classed as literature, while more than 25 percent was classed as fiction.[68] Because of the different ways that they defined and reported statistics, it is difficult to generalize, but in approximate terms the city's free libraries probably held between 40 and 50 percent juvenile books and popular fiction.[69] There was a general agreement that certain types of works should be excluded. For instance, dime novels and the sensational story papers that so alarmed the ladies of Grace Church in 1878, "blood and thunder" fiction that tended to "speak lightly of virtue and connive at bold or polished villainy," was considered beyond the pale.[70] Beyond this, however, there was ample room for disagreement. Librarians excluded books because they were sensationalistic or overly sentimental, because they glamorized wrongdoers or gave readers unrealistic expectations of life, or simply because they were poorly written.[71] Yet if the purchase of popular works was predicated on the assumption that reading the second rate would lead eventually to the first rate, then, in the words of Arthur Bostwick, Coe's successor at the Free Circulating Library, "difference of opinion will always exist" over "where a line must be drawn to separate . . . the desirable from the undesirable."[72]

In 1881, a committee of the American Library Association conducted a national survey of fiction in public libraries. It asked in particular whether libraries circulated the works of twenty-one authors, "all or some of whose works are sometimes excluded . . . by reason of sensational or immoral qualities."[73] The list was somewhat dated by the time the free libraries in New York began to publish their catalogs. For example, by the 1890s, the popular English writer Wilkie Collins, as well as Edward Bulwer-Lytton, who is most remembered today for writing that "it was a dark and stormy night," may not have been considered first rate, but they were no means controversial.[74] Nonetheless, whether these twenty-one presumably suspect authors appear in the surviving catalogs of the free circulating libraries gives some idea of where they drew the line on the question of popular fiction.[75] Only the Apprentices' Library, for example, held works by all twenty-one, including even G. W. M. Reynolds, E. D .E. N. Southworth, and the infamous Ouida, one of whose most memorable characters had "a thousand lovers, from handsome marquesses of the Guides to tawny black-brown scoundrels in the Zouaves." Most librarians considered all three little better than dime novelists.[76] Predictably, the Cathedral Library was the most conservative of the free libraries. Its catalog listed only five of the authors in the ALA survey. The Aguilar and the Bond Street branch of the Free Circulating Library fell somewhere between these extremes, holding fifteen and sixteen, respectively. There was considerable variation among New York's free libraries regarding the collection of popular fiction, but all of them drew a line that included the second rate.

The demand for popular novels was always much greater than the supply. In all of the libraries, fiction as a proportion of the total circulation was considerably higher than fiction as a proportion of the total collection. For example, in the New York Free Circulating Library in 1895, fiction was approximately 26 percent of the volumes on the shelves, but accounted for 40 percent of the volumes circulated.[77] Again, because of the different ways that they reported statistics, it is difficult to make generalizations about the free libraries' circulation, but overall fiction was at least 40 and often more than 50 percent.[78] Moreover, the proportion of literature circulated was very low, usually 6 percent or less, and more important, these numbers changed very little over time. For example, the Aguilar circulated 63 percent novels in 1890 and 63 percent again ten years later.[79] The free circulating libraries' own statistics belie the claim that the lending of popular fiction would lead to more refined, uplifting reading.

In their annual reports and other publications, the librarians and trustees tended to use a stock set of arguments to explain to their supporters, and probably to themselves as well, why the character of the circulation failed to improve appreciably over time. Most commonly, they simply claimed, often with little or no evidence, that although their readers were perhaps not developing an appreciation of fine literature, they were still reading the very best, the most uplifting popular fiction.[80] The librarian of the Apprentices' Library, for example, noted in 1879 that even though "works of fiction and juvenile literature are still the most sought after, it is gratifying to report that a perceptible improvement is apparent in the demand for books of a standard character," that is, titles by the "standard," first-rate authors such as Charles Dickens or Sir Walter Scott.[81] Another argument stressed that, although popular fiction circulated more frequently, readers actually spent more time reading the more improving, uplifting works of literature. In 1889, William Appleton, chairman of the Free Circulating Library, referring to the circulation statistics for that year, cautioned that "a light novel may be read and given out ten times where a serious standard work is circulated only once, and yet the actual time spent by the reader may be the same." Six years later, shortly after taking charge of the Library, Arthur Bostwick put this argument to the test by conducting a brief experiment in which the circulation of books in the various classes in the collection was calculated in terms of the number of days each volume was checked out. He discovered that, on average, fiction and literature actually circulated for approximately the same amount of time, about one week, but then cited this as evidence that "the users of the library draw out many of the solider works . . . which require more time to read."[82]

Despite the confidence that the missionaries of literature expressed in public, by the 1890s the assumption that reading the second-rate would lead to the first-rate was becoming rather less tenable. In 1893, Ellen Coe conducted for *Library Journal* a national survey of librarians' opinions on the provision of fiction in public libraries. Asked whether "you believe the reading of light fiction leads to more serious reading," less than 25 percent of the respondents said "yes," approximately 25 percent believed it was "doubtful," and over half said "no."[83] This did not mean, however, that the library community was prepared to abandon its mission of uplift. Rather librarians were simply losing faith in the power of reading to improve the reader naturally, "insensibly." They now began to emphasize the need to take an active role in developing and refining the literary tastes of the masses.

Again, the key term used was not *control,* but *influence.* The librarians of the free libraries recognized that they could never force working-class readers to rise above popular fiction, but for the most part they remained confident that they might over time guide them to finer, more uplifting reading. For example, when the members of the New York Library club discussed the question, "How far should reading be controlled in libraries?" the word *control* was used hardly at all. Instead, the general tenor of opinion was that "we should not dictate, but influence their choices."[84] This emphasis on nurturing the reading of individual users meant that the success of a public library depended to a large extent upon the personality of the librarian, upon her ability to develop personal relationships with the people of the neighborhood in which the branch was located. This was emphasized in the Library Club's discussion as well as the annual reports of the different libraries. The New York Free Circulating Library, for instance, referred glowingly to a librarian in one of the smaller branches whose "readers" were "personally know to her," which allowed her "better opportunities for guiding the reading of those applying for books, and thus a great improvement has . . . been made in the character of the books read." Another was singled out for her ability "to make friends . . . and help them, without seeming to dictate."[85]

In the later 1890s, most of the free libraries adopted two very significant changes in policy. Although they would seem, at first glance, to have given readers greater scope and freedom in the selection of books, both were often described as ways to augment the influence of the librarians in the branches. The first of these was the "two-book system." Until about 1895, readers were allowed to borrow only one volume at a time. Under the two-book system, they could check out two, provided that one of them was a work of nonfiction. It was stressed repeatedly in the annual reports and elsewhere that the new policy would provide an opportunity to develop an appreciation of works of a more substantial, uplifting character, that it would encourage users to "enjoy other kinds of reading when proper guidance is furnished by the librarian."[86] The second change, the "open-shelf system" was considered even more "radical." From the beginning, the free circulating libraries were "closed-shelves" collections; readers chose a book with the help of a catalog or a librarian, then filled out a request slip and submitted it at a circulation desk.[87] Under the new plan, they were free to browse among the books on "open shelves." The annual reports occasionally held that simply offering the public direct access to the collection in this way would naturally, automatically result in an improvement in reading habits. It would "afford" a direct "familiarity with books of culture" and thus "stimulate a taste for standard works of literature."[88] Just as often, however, the reports stressed that it allowed librarians to provide friendly guidance as readers selected their books. "Personal aid" was "the natural adjunct of open shelves," the best way to forge "cordial and sympathetic relations between borrowers and librarians."[89]

Open shelves and the two-book system were just part of a wide range of changes in the city's free libraries in the 1890s. These dramatic innovations did not mean that librarians and trustees had lost faith in the public library movement as it was originally conceived. In the words of Ellen Coe, quoting from First Corinthians at a meeting of the New York Library Club in 1895, the missionaries of literature were still prepared to "believe all things, hope all things, endure all things," firmly convinced that the "reward will seldom fail."[90] Nonetheless, there was an underlying sense that the influence of the public library could and should be enhanced. There was growing conviction among the supporters of New York's free libraries of the need to somehow augment the basic idea of providing books for home use in branches in the city's poorer neighborhoods.

In 1888, there was a sharp exchange in the pages of *Library Journal* between Jacob Schwartz of the Apprentices' Library and Max Cohen of the Maimonides Library that in many ways paralleled the argument six years later between Ellen Coe and George Watson Cole over the provision of fiction in free libraries. In a contribution entitled "Business Methods in Libraries," Schwartz challenged librarians to abandon their "Utopian day dreams" and recognize the "practical fact" that "library management . . . is principally and primarily a business, and must be managed on business principles." He then enumerated a list of "sound business principles" that echoed the Mercantile Library Association's "system of management" and included, shockingly, "advertise your wares," and "buy only what your customers want."[91] In a heated reply, Cohen was "mortified" that Schwartz had given "public expression to such a low ideal of the librarian's vocation." He insisted that "the librarian [is] an educator, not a cheap-john," a peddler of shoddy, worthless goods, and declared that business principles were "fatal to the principle of the Public Library" and to "the cause of higher culture."[92]

Schwartz was stating his case in a deliberately provocative fashion, and Cohen was certainly not the only public librarian in New York who took offense. Nonetheless, Schwartz's article embodied much of the spirit of what came to be known, in the later 1890s and the early twentieth century, as the "modern library idea." In its last annual report in 1901, the New York Free Circulating Library summed up the progress of public libraries in the city since its founding and in doing so made a distinction between the public library idea and the modern library idea. The modern library idea encompassed all of the defining features of the public library idea, free books circulated from small branches located throughout the city. Yet the modern library idea also included such innovations as open shelves, the two-book system, and a host of other changes, "all in the direction of providing greater facilities for the public."[93] Nine years later, Arthur Bostwick, now head of the Circulation Department of the New York Public Library, wrote *The American Public Library*, the classic exposition of the modern library idea. Like Schwartz, Bostwick made an explicit analogy between public libraries and commerce. He wrote that "the modern . . .

library idea is simply tantamount to a confession that the library, as a distributor, must obey the laws that all distributors must obey, if they are to succeed."[94] Although Schwartz and Bostwick were careful to point out that they were simply advocating sound principles of management for libraries, the business analogy they both used was very appropriate.[95] At the heart of the modern library idea were new kinds of library services and aggressive efforts to expand the market of library users by promoting those services to new classes of readers.

Librarians such as Ellen Coe and Max Cohen found troubling the mere suggestion that the libraries might share anything in common with the business world. For them, the high ideals of the public library, the mission of literature, transcended the sordid world of commerce. This view clearly predominated during the years in which the public library idea gained momentum in the city. For example, in their earliest annual reports, both the Aguilar and the Free Circulating Library stressed that they were merely responding to a "natural and great demand for good reading," that readers flocked to the branches "without resort to advertising or any artificial methods."[96] By the time Arthur Bostwick took charge of the Free Circulating Library in 1895, however, those he described as the "old-fashioned librarians" were clearly in the minority, and there was a greater willingness to adopt a more commercial attitude toward the promotion of public libraries. By 1898, for instance, his library had developed an extensive advertising campaign using posters, handbills, and other "means of giving the public information about us."[97] The Webster in particular embraced business methods to promote good reading and advertised its collection in stores, the elevated railcars, factories, churches, and saloons. It explained in its annual report for 1902 that in order to be successful, it had to make itself known in the neighborhood, that "even shoe stores endeavor to do as much."[98]

Perhaps the most characteristic feature of the modern library idea was its focus on serving a new market of library users, children.[99] The reference and subscription libraries were open only to adults, but the free circulating libraries not only welcomed younger readers, but, whenever space and funds allowed, established separate children's libraries or reading rooms.[100] For example, at the time of its consolidation with the New York Public Library, the Free Circulating Library had separate facilities for children in eight of its eleven branches, and over half of its readers were juveniles.[101] Recognizing the special needs of younger readers, especially those from tenement neighborhoods, the free libraries took pride in

Bond Street branch of the New York Free Circulating Library, 1899 (Picture Collection, The New York Public Library, Astor, Lenox and Tilden Foundations)

providing "large, light, and airy rooms, wherein dwell cheerfulness and a spirit of content, much to the satisfaction of our little patrons." They assigned as children's librarians women who were not only "well read and well educated," but also "attractive to children in manner and person."[102] This special care and effort was considered a wise investment in the future of the library. Librarians at the more established branches noted proudly that many of their most loyal adult readers first developed sound reading habits as juvenile users, "so that this library . . . as it were . . . created it own readers."[103] Central to the modern library idea was the conviction that "there is no more important work in the building . . . than that with children," since it "pays so well in immediate and far-off results."[104]

Librarians also worked with children outside the building. Another distinctive feature of the modern library idea was cooperation between the public library and the public school. From the beginning, supporters of the public library idea had considered the educational mission of both institutions to be inextricably linked, and they proudly referred to the public library as the People's University.[105] At a time when most students left school at around age twelve, the library would provide the means for further self-cultivation, "thus carrying forward the work of civilization which is commenced in the primary school."[106] However, while the public library idea saw the branch library as simply a "necessary supplement of our common-school system," the modern library idea envisioned a direct, proactive role for librarians in the education of young children.[107] As Ellen Coe explained in an article in *Library Journal*, "it is not only nor chiefly in the way of this post-graduate education that the library should be considered as an ally of the school; its help . . . is absolutely necessary in the actual class-room work."[108] Cooperation between schools and libraries took many forms, but most commonly a branch librarian would select for a class, with the help of the teacher, a small collection of titles dealing with topics the students were currently studying. The books would be sent on loan to the school for a semester, and they would circulate from the classroom rather than the branch. The Webster Library in particular was very active in "school work," and its librarian, Edwin Gaillard, later supervised relations with the public school system in the Circulation Department of the New York Public Library.[109]

Many of the most innovative services associated with the modern library idea were an outgrowth of these cooperative activities with the primary schools. For example, when the free circulating libraries were first established, it was assumed that reference collections would be the exclusive province of the large reference libraries such as the Astor and the Lenox. Yet once they began collaborating with the schools, it became evident that reference books were not just for scholars, that other library users, particularly children writing essays or doing homework for their classes, had need of them as well. All of the free libraries developed at least a basic reference collection of dictionaries, encyclopedias and yearbooks, but the Aguilar in particular devoted special care and attention to reference service, even listing in its annual reports all the new reference titles added at each branch. It described the reference collection as "the most valuable feature of a library" and noted with pride "the crowd of children . . . who eagerly wait their turn to get a seat at the reference table."[110]

This new interest among public librarians in reference service reflected critical shifts in the field of education. For most of the nineteenth century, children learned primarily through memorization and recitation, from, in the words of John Shaw Billings, the first director of the New York Public Library, "dry manuals in mechanically taught elementary schools."[111] Beginning in the 1890s, however, new approaches emerged that valued creativity and individuality, that stressed the active acquisition of knowledge, rather than learning facts and dates by rote.[112] Librarians applauded these changes and saw reference service in public libraries as a means of invigorating the learning process. As the Aguilar Free Library explained in its final report, they considered "the habit of looking up information, each one for himself, one of the most desirable habits to cultivate among our rising generation."[113] The modern library idea valued the child as a "moral, reasoning being, not as automaton," and stressed that children should be "encouraged to investigate," since "it is 'digging' that leaves a permanent impression on the mind."[114]

The free libraries' work with the schools was also part of a larger effort to forge stronger links between the branches and the neighborhoods they served. The libraries were eager to cooperate with other local organizations to supply good reading to the masses, and to this end, many of them established a "Traveling Library Department." A traveling library was a small collection of carefully selected books, like those sent on loan to the public schools, that circulated outside of the branch from potentially any location in the neighborhood.[115] The Free Circulating Library had a particularly extensive and successful traveling library program that, by 1900, loaned out more books that many of its branch libraries. That year, for example, nearly 140,000 volumes were circulated from 153 traveling libraries, operating out of locations that included, besides the public schools, three telegraph offices, five public playgrounds, six Sunday schools, twenty-five firehouses, and a variety of neighborhood clubs.[116] In addition, the traveling collections of the free circulating libraries also included "home libraries." These were boxes of ten to fifteen volumes that actually circulated from apartments in the tenement districts. Typically, an older boy or girl in the family would assume responsibility for loaning the books to his or her friends in the neighborhood, and each week a "visitor" from the branch library would replenish the collection and meet with the children to get "acquainted with the little ones [and] lead them to the reading of better books."[117] The traveling library departments, and the home libraries in particular, were emblematic of the modern librarian who, in the words of Arthur Bostwick, did "not sit down and wait for customers."[118]

In addition to these efforts to reach out to potential readers in the neighborhoods, the modern library idea also encompassed a variety of services beyond the free circulation of books. From the beginning, photography

Traveling library of the New York Free Circulating Library on board the St. John's Guild Floating Hospital (The New York Public Library Archives, The New York Public Library, Astor, Lenox and Tilden Foundation)

and artwork were an important part of the refining influence of the branch library. By the late 1890s, however, the free circulating libraries began to envision themselves as "a centre not only for books, but for all the learning which helps to develop a true culture."[119] Some of them began to lend out prints and photographs so that users could experience the uplifting influence of art as well as literature in their homes. In 1899, for example, the Free Circulating Library loaned out over one thousand reproductions from one of its branches.[120] Artwork on the walls of the libraries was also used to inspire and to guide readers to the best books. Next to an engraving of George Washington, for instance, the librarian might place a brief bibliography of titles in the library relating to his life and times.[121] Eventually these became much more elaborate and incorporated more than just pictures and photographs, so that the display itself served an educational purpose. This feature of the modern library idea was developed most extensively and creatively in the Webster Library's Department of Practical Illustration. Designed to supplement its work with the public schools, the Webster's displays used a wide range of physical objects to illustrate subjects of interest to its readers. In 1901, for example, its librarians created a display on North American Indians that included, among other items, a loom, a tepee, and casts of prehistoric tools donated by the Smithsonian Institution.[122] While the Webster was "primarily a good Circulating Library," it believed "it could add immensely to its helpfulness were it also a museum of fine and useful arts."[123]

Despite the modern library idea's emphasis upon actively seeking out "customers," the free circulating libraries actually served only a part of the city's reading publics. Because they were viewed as private charities (albeit supported largely through public funds), in practice they excluded New York's rising middle class. By the close of the century there was a growing public sentiment for a public library that served the entire city. Created in a complex series of negotiations and consolidations over the course of several years, the New York Public Library was a civic institution in which all New Yorkers could feel a sense of ownership and identity. Because it served a broader, more inclusive reading public, the new library pursued a more diverse and expansive mission beyond refining and uplifting masses.

9 The Founding of the New York Public Library

Public and Private in the Progressive Era

In *Triumphant Democracy, or, Fifty Years' March of the Republic* (1886), Andrew Carnegie compared material conditions in the United States near the close of the nineteenth century with conditions half a century earlier. He marveled that "we might almost conclude that we were upon another planet and subject to different primary conditions." Dedicated to "the beloved Republic under whose equal laws I am made the peer of any man," his best seller explained at great length and with an abundance of statistics why America "leads the civilized world." For Carnegie, republicanism was the critical constant in American history. The essential change in the republic over the course of fifty years was the increased prosperity of all of her citizens.[1]

Not all Americans in 1886 shared Carnegie's optimism. The fifty years' march of the republic also saw the rise of the corporation, rapid industrialization, massive immigration, divisive party politics and political corruption, and alarming disparities of wealth. By the end of the nineteenth century, the cumulative effect of these changes and dislocations challenged the republican ideal of a homogeneous community of virtuous, independent, civic-minded citizens. By around 1910, the various and sometimes contradictory reactions to these changes came to be known as "progressivism." The New York Public Library was founded, in part with Andrew Carnegie's money, amidst the tumult of the Progressive Era, and its founding sheds light on critical strains of progressive thought. The creation of a public library as we understand the term today necessarily revolved around what was meant by the word *public* and how that public was best served. These questions were raised repeatedly, although not always answered, in the long series of negotiations and accommodations that eventually resulted in one of the world's great public libraries.

The founding of the New York Public Library took place in two phases over the course of nearly two decades. The first phase created the Reference Department, a noncirculating collection catering primarily to scholars. The second established the Circulation Department, an extensive system of branch libraries sited in neighborhoods throughout the city. During both phases there were extensive and sometimes divisive discussions not only of the kinds of books a public library should provide and the public it should serve, but also regarding who should pay for the library and who should govern it. The institution that resulted from this long and complex process served multiple publics, was publicly and privately funded, and was administered by both public officials and private citizens. The structure, governance, and financing of the New York Public Library were and are unique, but this blending of the public and the private was an important and characteristic feature of the Progressive Era. There was a new fluidity and permeability of the boundary between the public and the private that reflected a significant reconfiguration of the public sector at all levels of government.

In 1838, for the first time, the City of New York taxed the New York Society Library, on the grounds that it was a private institution and therefore did not qualify for the exemption granted to public libraries under state law. The Society's board appealed and was eventually upheld by Peter A. Cowdrey, the corporation counsel. Cowdrey based his decision upon the definition of a public library that prevailed when the Society Library was founded nearly a century earlier. He held that in order to be tax exempt, a library had only to demonstrate that it had "something of a public character," that it was "common to many." The Society Library was a public library in the same sense that a railroad was a public conveyance or a tavern was a public house.[2] Just eleven years later, the State of New Hampshire passed the first law permitting municipalities to tax their residents to support a library. This inaugurated the movement for public libraries as the term is understood today, tax-supported, circulating collections free to all members of the public and governed by public officials.[3]

The debate over a municipal library system for New York City did not begin in earnest for another half-century. A number of factors account for this comparatively late development. By 1880, New York had more than one million residents, and the task of creating a public library for such a large and heterogeneous population was a formidable and expensive undertaking.[4] Moreover, subscription libraries like the Mercantile Library Association and a constellation of voluntary organizations such as the Aguilar and the New York Free Circulating Library already provided reasonably adequate library services for many New Yorkers. The most formidable obstacle to the creation of a modern public library in New York City, however, was the profound reluctance of professional librarians and supporters of the public library movement to share power with elected public officials. Although by 1880s they regularly applied to the City for public monies for the free libraries, they were convinced that the direct involvement of the city's politicians would render the public library yet another source of graft and corruption for Tammany Hall.

Yet, by the 1890s, strong public sentiment gradually overcame these obstacles. It hurt New Yorkers' civic pride that their city still lacked a modern public library, particularly when rivals such as Boston and Chicago had already built impressive municipal systems. Additionally, to progressives preoccupied with system and efficiency New York's uncoordinated patchwork of subscription and free circulating libraries seemed haphazard and anachronistic. But the critical factor in the creation of both the Reference Department and the Circulation Department was money. In both cases, it was the generosity of a private citizen that made a public library possible.

The gift that spurred the establishment of the Reference Department was bequeathed to the citizens of New York by Samuel J. Tilden. Tilden was a corporate lawyer and anti-Tammany Democratic who rose to political prominence in the early 1870s in the legal and political fight that ended the rule of "Boss" William Tweed in the city.[5] He was elected governor of the state in 1875 and in 1876 lost the disputed presidential election to Rutherford B. Hayes. He died in August 1886 and left the bulk of his estate, more than $5 million, to "establish and maintain a free public library and reading room in the city of New York and to promote . . . scientific and educational objects." In March of the following year, his executors, his law partner Andrew Haswell Green, his private secretary George W. Smith, and the writer, journalist and politician John Bigelow, obtained from the legislature an act incorporating the Tilden Trust. In April, they appointed two additional trustees, Alexander E. Orr and Stephen A. Walker, and elected Bigelow president. The powers of the trust were limited to the establishment and maintenance of a public library.[6]

Tilden never married and was survived by his sister, Mary B. Pelton, and the six children of his brother Henry. All of the nieces and nephews received generous trust funds under the terms of the will. The same day it was admitted to probate, one of the nephews, George H. Tilden, filed suit to overturn it, contesting a clause that granted the trustees discretion to devote all or part of the estate to any "charitable, educational or scientific purposes" that would be "widely and substantially useful to the interests of mankind." His lawyers argued that the will was "invalid because of the indefiniteness and uncertainty in its objects and purposes, and because it substitutes for the will of the testator the will of the trustees." George Tilden and his brothers also lobbied successfully to include in the act incorporating the Tilden Trust a clause stipulating that the incorporation would not affect their claim to the estate, pending the settlement of the lawsuit. In October 1891, after more than five years of litigation, amid charges of corruption and malfeasance, the state Court of Appeals decided in favor of the heirs and declared the will invalid.[7]

Before the case was resolved in the courts, the Tilden Trust had reached a separate agreement with Laura P. Hazard, the granddaughter of Tilden's sister, who died shortly after her brother. As Mary Pelton's only heir, Hazard would have been entitled to one-half of Tilden's property when the will was declared invalid. In May 1891, she agreed instead to sell her interest for $975,000. As a result, in spite of the Court of Appeal's decision, the trust still had an endowment of one half of the Tilden estate, less the cost of the settlement, slightly more than $2 million. It could still establish a public library, but with considerably less than half the amount that Samuel Tilden had bequeathed to the city.[8]

Predictably, everyone except the heirs was disappointed and angry over the outcome of the suit, particularly after it was revealed that the creditors of the spendthrift nephews were lobbying on their behalf in Albany. The local press covered the case extensively. Editorial pages lavished praise upon Tilden's generosity and public spirit. The *Commercial Advertiser* boasted that the new library would be even better than the public libraries in Chicago and Boston, that the bequest would become "the foundation of the greatest public library in the world thus far." The *Daily Tribune* called the Tilden Trust "one of the most far-reaching and beneficent purposes ever conceived by an individual in the interest of society." When the courts finally decided in favor of the nieces and nephews, the "vultures" were roundly criticized for their greed and selfishness.[9]

The editorials in the *New York Times* were especially critical, drawing upon the language of republicanism to paint a sharp contrast between Tilden and his heirs. The heirs were "persons whose interests were opposed to those of the public." While "most men . . . would prefer to have less money and more reputation," they forsook reputation in a "greedy eagerness to lay hands on money which they had not earned." The state legislature, which was supposed to serve as the "custodian of the interests of the people," had, by adding the clause in the Tilden Trust legislation protecting the rights of the heirs, "endanger[ed] the rights of the people." The nieces and nephews had no "natural right" to be "supported in idleness." Indeed, it was un-American and typically English to "'found a family,'" that is, to lay the foundation of a hereditary fortune and thus "enable a line of descendants to live without doing any work." Tilden, by contrast, had earned his money and set a commendable example by devoting it, upon his death, to the public weal. A public library on the monumental scale envisioned in his will was hardly likely in a monarchy, since "no Prince ever has or ever could, from his own property, acquired in his own lifetime by his own energy and skill, make such a gift."[10]

Republicanism was just one language that was used in the late nineteenth century to express discontent and enlist support for change. The broad constellation of organizations and causes that historians generally label "progressive" drew upon and were influenced by other traditions and languages as well. The gospel of efficiency, for example, played a critical role later in the founding of the New York Public Library.[11] Republicanism, however, was one of the most venerable and resonant languages available to would-be reformers, and by the 1880s and 1890s it was more and more effective and appealing. Throughout the century there had always been a degree of tension between liberalism and republicanism, between the pursuit of individual interest and the claims of the larger community.[12] Liberalism lost some of its allure amid the rampant greed and excessive individualism of the Gilded Age. Republicanism, with its emphasis on moderation and the public weal, enjoyed a renascence during the Progressive Era.

Neither, however, eclipsed the other, and late nineteenth-century Americans never consciously weighed one against the other. Indeed, republican values remained an essential part of the public sphere in an age of conspicuously unrepublican consumption. As the lawsuit over Tilden's will made its way through the courts, this paradox was abundantly evident during one of the city's most important civic celebrations of the century, the centennial of George Washington's inauguration at City Hall in April 1789. This was, of course, a momentous occasion for the entire nation, but in New York, the first home of the national government, the festivities lasted three days and were accompanied by a tremendous outpouring of patriotism. All of the local newspapers covered the numerous parades and public addresses in effusive detail, and none of them lost the opportunity to impart a civics lesson along with the news. The *Daily Tribune* intoned that "the adoption of the Constitution demonstrated the capacity of the people to maintain the liberties they had won," while the *Sun*, in a lengthy history of the founding, concluded that America's "grand political experiment" was to create "a Union that was at once republican and steadfast." The editors of the *Herald* were indignant when President Benjamin Harrison appeared in public wearing a Prince Albert jacket, deeming it a "concession to royalty" and an "offense against the Republic." The *World*, quoting a speech by Episcopal Bishop (and Astor Library trustee) Henry Potter, bemoaned the fact that "'merchantable ideas rule[d] the hour'" and reminded New Yorkers that "Plutocracy [has] no place in the Republic as founded by the fathers."[13]

Yet, at the same time, these same newspapers described in tones of awe and admiration perhaps the most opulent gathering of plutocrats in the history of the city. The Centennial Ball on April 29, 1889, "pal[ed] all of the assemblies . . . before it, . . . shin[ing] out in the triumphs of society like the Edison light among tallow dips." While a large crowd of the curious and the envious jostled outside, approximately six thousand of the nation's very wealthiest citizens gathered in the Metropolitan Opera House to celebrate the centennial and parade their wealth. They enjoyed an eight-course dinner served by three hundred liveried waiters, danced to music by a hundred-piece orchestra, and consumed five thousand bottles of champagne. The opera box from which President Harrison observed the spectacle was referred to as his throne, while Ward McAllister, the reigning prince of New York society, was said to have once again proved himself worthy of his crown. Reporters described in extravagant detail the sumptuous array of jewels on display. Mrs. John Wysung wore diamonds "the size of her thumbs." Caroline Astor, the queen of high society and wife of William Astor, grandson of the founder of the Astor Library, was "literally loaded with diamonds." The press also described at length the costumes worn by the most socially prominent women present. A few honored the occasion by wearing modest dresses from the colonial period, but many more wore styles inspired by the courts of Louis XV and Louis XVI. No one seems to have found it ironic that the nation's elite celebrated the birth of the American republic dressed as French aristocrats.[14]

The revelers at the Centennial Ball constructed a new, purposefully exclusive definition of *society*. Before the Gilded Age, the term had a specific and a general sense, but both connoted inclusivity and mutuality. The New York Society Library was founded as a society in its specific sense, as an association or company of readers. Such an association could conceivably be inclusive or exclusive, but when the Library was established in 1754 it was intended to serve an extensive reading public. By contrast, society as defined and reigned over by Caroline Astor included only the fashionable few listed in the *Social Register* and chronicled in the society pages. It was not simply exclusive; exclusivity was the crux of its definition.[15] The Tilden Trust, incorporated the same year the *Social Register* began publication, was created to found a library to serve society its older and more general sense.[16] The Tilden Library was to be an institution "widely and substantially beneficial to the interests of mankind." Samuel Tilden had intended to provide the city with a library that included a broad reading public and promoted the common weal of the republic amid the exclusivity and excesses displayed at the Centennial Ball.

After the Court of Appeals decided in favor of the heirs, the Tilden Trust was left with an endowment of only $2,025,000, enough to establish a substantial library, but not one of the depth and breadth that Samuel Tilden had envisioned.[17] In May 1892, at their first meeting after the will was declared invalid, the trustees weighed their options. All of the alternatives discussed involved some degree of cooperation or consolidation with existing organizations. They appointed a Plan and Scope Committee, which over the next two years met with representatives of a number of scholarly institutions in the city, including Columbia College, New York University, and the Scientific Alliance, a federation of societies that promoted research and popular education in the sciences.[18] During this same period, the trustees also prevailed upon the legislature to pass legislation permitting libraries in New York City to consolidate.[19] The board apparently never even considered requesting funds from the City. As L. V. F. Randolph explained in a letter to fellow trustee Andrew Haswell Green, "the moment the Tilden Trust asks aid of any sort from the city of New York it begins to put in danger from political and demagogic influences the integrity and usefulness of its administration."[20]

By early 1894, talks with various library and scholarly associations had stalled. In the spring of that year, "after dinner, while waiting for the ladies to put on their wraps, on the way to the opera," Tilden trustee Lewis Cass Ledyard mentioned this casually to Astor Library trustee John Cadwalader. This exchange was the genesis of negotiations that eventually led to the creation of the New York Public Library.[21] In November, the Astor and Tilden boards appointed committees to confer on the question of consolidation. The following January, representatives of the Lenox Library learned of a probable merger and appointed their own committee to join the discussions.[22] The three institutions complemented one another in important respects, and merging them offered obvious mutual advantages. The Tilden Trust had a fairly generous endowment, but no books and no building. To buy an initial collection of books and to construct a building would have reduced its income considerably. The Astor and the Lenox, on the other hand, had very rich collections, but relatively smaller endowments with which to develop them.[23] The combined income of all three institutions presumably would be sufficient to found a public library on the scale that New Yorkers had anticipated since the announcement of the Tilden bequest more than eight years earlier.

On May 23, 1895, the three corporations formally agreed to merge to create the New York Public Library. The consolidation agreement itself was a relatively simple legal instrument that revealed little about the kind of library the founders intended, apart from the rather vague stipulation that it would "continue and promote the several objects and purposes set forth in the respective acts of incorporation."[24] The full legal title of the new corporation was the New York Public Library, Astor, Lenox, and Tilden Foundations. The conference committees had recognized that the only fitting name would be the New York Public Library, but they also agreed that the original benefactors deserved formal recognition.[25] The new Board of Trustees would have twenty-one members, with approximately equal representation from the three constituent boards.[26] They were broadly empowered to establish regulations regarding "the general custody, care, conduct and management of the affairs" of the new library. However, the agreement added the significant proviso that the trustees would make "appropriate provisions with reference to the limitations . . . under which any of the funds or property of the said several corporations are now held." This clause referred primarily to certain restrictions on the use of the Astor and Lenox bequests and was elaborated in a set of resolutions agreed to by the consolidation committees and passed by the new board at its first meeting on May 27. The Astor Library would remain a noncirculating reference collection and an amount of money at least equal to the income of the Astor endowment in 1894, approximately $47,000, would be devoted each year to purchasing books for reference only. Similarly, the Bibles in the Lenox Library were designated a special, noncirculating collection to be shelved separately from the regular collections of the new library.[27]

The founding of the New York Public Library was a national event that was extensively covered and commented upon not just in the local press, but in literary and professional journals and popular magazines as well. *Library Journal* considered it "one of the most important steps in library matters ever taken in this country," while *Peterson's Magazine* called it "one of the most important steps in educational matters . . . in many years." *Harper's Weekly* deemed it "one of the most important events in the whole history of the island of Manhattan."[28] Local newspapers boasted that New York was now poised to take its rightful place among the cultural capitals of the civilized nations. The *Times* wrote that the Library "puts the city, in an important essential of civilization, among the chief cities of the world" and would surpass the public collections in Chicago and Boston, while the *World* brashly predicted that it would rival the British Museum and the Bibliothèque Nationale.[29] *Harper's Weekly* aptly summed up the public's response when it wrote that news of the consolidation was greeted with "the general delight and approval of the great public which is most concerned."[30]

Ever since Samuel Tilden's death almost nine years earlier, New York's politicians, editors, and civic and cultural leaders had agreed that the public of the great city of New York deserved a great public library. This does not mean, however, that there was consensus on even the most fundamental matters, including the definition of a public library. Now that the New York Public Library was an accomplished fact, its new board was obliged to address the critical question of what they actually meant by the term. There was considerable ambiguity arising from the different ways that the twenty-one trustees conceived the Library's public and how that public was to be served by its Library. This ambiguity was reflected even in the agreement of consolidation itself. Both in the agreement and in their respective acts of incorporation, the Astor and Lenox Libraries were designated public libraries. This no longer meant of course, as Peter Cowdrey had written of the Society Library in 1838, that their collections were merely "common to many," that any member of the public could use them for a fee. When the Astor and the Lenox Libraries were established, they were considered public libraries in the sense that any member of the public could use them, under certain conditions, without charge.

Yet by the time the New York Public Library was founded, a public library implied much more than simply free access. For most laypersons as well as library professionals, it had become synonymous with the "public library idea," with the collections and services provided in the branches of the city's free circulating libraries. This meant not only that the public could take books home to read for free, but also that the books were of a popular, albeit an edifying nature, that they were written for the general, self-improving reader rather than for scholars.[31] Further, public libraries were widely expected to serve not the privileged few, not Joseph Cogswell's "men of leisure and . . . men of letters," but the "masses," the presumably self-improving working people who flocked to the free circulating libraries. According to the *Tribune*, "the idea that branch libraries should be established [by the New York Public Library] in the centres of dense population, where the plain, everyday workingman can derive some benefit from them, seems to predominate."[32]

The consolidation agreement was intentionally ambiguous regarding this fundamental issue. It simply stated that "the new corporation shall establish and maintain a free public library . . . with such branches as may be deemed advisable."[33] Similarly, in their comments to the press in the weeks before the merger, some members of the consolidating committees suggested that the new system would or might include small lending libraries, possibly by absorbing the city's free circulating libraries, but the new board refused to commit to such a policy.[34] No doubt there was a range of opinion among the trustees. However, sixteen of them were from the Astor and Lenox Libraries, both of which were noncirculating collections with decidedly poor reputations for public service. The only board member who actively championed the public library idea was Andrew Haswell Green, a former Tilden trustee who was firmly committed to his friend Tilden's vision of a more popular library. At a meeting of the board in January 1896, he introduced a resolution to establish circulating branch libraries that was soundly rejected. At a meeting the following month, an alternative resolution passed merely committing the Library to "the broadest possible policy . . . in reference to the nature and scope of [its] work."[35]

One of the most important decisions that the new board faced in the months following the consolidation, and one that would decisively shape the character of the new library, was the appointment of its first director. In December 1895, the trustees hired John Shaw Billings. Then fifty-eight years of age, Billings was a physician and leading member of the older generation of self-trained scholar-librarians. After serving as a field surgeon in the Union Army during the Civil War, he was posted to the Office of the Surgeon-General, where he spent more than thirty years developing the most extensive medical library in the nation. Before joining the New York Public Library, he had acquired an international reputation as the founder and director of the National Library of Medicine, the designer and organizer of the hospital of John Hopkins University, and the creator of

Index Medicus, the standard index to medical literature still in use today.[36] Although Arthur Bostwick later accused Billings of having "no sympathy" with the public library idea, this was something of an overstatement.[37] As director of the New York Public Library, and during his tenure as president of the American Library Association, Billings does seem to have gained some appreciation of the role that neighborhood lending libraries could play in advancing popular education.[38] Nonetheless, he never showed any marked enthusiasm for them. Like his friend John Cadwalader, the Astor trustee who recruited him as director, he regarded the development of a great reference collection for scholars as the "distinctive business" of the New York Public Library.[39]

Even more fundamental than the appointment of the Library's director was the location of its central building. Where the New York Public Library was located was intimately related to the question of the public it was intended to serve. Everyone, including the former Astor trustees, recognized that the Astor Library was not suitable. The building was not fireproof and was too small for the extensive collections that the board planned to develop. The Lenox Library was in some respects a more eligible location. Its property included an adjacent lot, bequeathed by James Lenox's sister Henrietta, upon which the New York Public Library could expand in the future.[40] However, Henrietta Lenox's will stipulated that the lot could be used only for an extension to the library. This meant that if the trustees built on the property, and then later moved the library to new location, they would be legally prohibited from selling the property, unless they obtained releases from all of Henrietta Lenox's heirs. In part because of this restriction, the board was divided over the issue of the site for the new library. At its first meeting in May 1895, it passed a compromise resolution selecting the Lenox site, but only on the condition that the heirs agreed to sign releases.[41]

This restriction in Henrietta Lenox's will was not the only reason some of the trustees considered the Lenox Library an unsuitable location for the New York Public Library. The Lenox was far uptown on Fifth Avenue and Seventieth Street. While it was conveniently near such elite cultural institutions as the Museum of Natural History and the Metropolitan Museum of Art, it was far from the homes of the city's working-class readers. The trustees recognized that in establishing a library of reference, its location would be a less critical issue, since most scholars would be willing to travel some distance in order to consult its unique collections. On the other hand, according to the board's Site Committee, "a library for popular use, intended to reach the people, with a circulating department as an essential feature of it . . . would present at once as one of the main questions to be considered that of accessibility."[42] Because of this, most of the city's newspapers opposed the Lenox site. The *Herald*, for example, doubted whether "the property of the Lenox Library would be a wise selection," since "the usefulness and practical value of the consolidated library depend so greatly upon its . . . accessibility."[43]

The location of the Lenox Library raised fundamental issues beyond even the public's ease of access. A decision to locate near the Museum of Natural History and the Metropolitan Museum of Art might have meant a less public, more exclusive library. Despite occasional rhetoric to the contrary, both of these museums were intended for the use of citizens of wealth and refinement, terms that their founders assumed to be largely synonymous. The Metropolitan, for example, whose board included six New York Public Library trustees, was not opened in the evenings or on Sundays, the only times that New Yorkers of more modest means could enjoy the collection.[44] The museum purposefully sought to create a realm of "high culture" that would define the city's elite in contradistinction to the masses who were unfit to appreciate true art. Like the nearby Lenox Library, which was frequently described as a "book museum," the founding of the Metropolitan Museum was part of a larger effort to create a public sphere segregated by class.[45] As such, it was the object of pointed criticism in the popular press. The *Herald* declared that "from the very beginning it has been an exclusive social toy, not a great instrument of education." The *Times* complained that it was "less available" to the public than "similar institutions in monarchical Europe."[46]

Just as important within the context of the founding of the New York Public Library was the relationship between the City of New York and both the Metropolitan and the Museum of Natural History. Both institutions were built in the 1870s on public land at the public expense. The City annually appropriated public funds for the maintenance of the buildings. This support was provided despite the forthrightly exclusive nature of both museums and the fact that city officials were permitted only a nominal role on their governing boards. At first glance, their relationship with the City calls to mind the New York Institution, which, with municipal support in the 1810s and 1820s, sought to consolidate and invigorate the learned societies of the city's elite.[47] The critical difference was that the founders of the New York Institution may have been naive and presumptuous, but they were nonetheless sincere in their conviction that under their direction the arts and sciences would promote the welfare of the entire community. The trustees of the Metropolitan and the Museum of Natural History, despite an occasional rhetorical flourish in their public statements, never really believed this. For example, it was not until 1891, and only after intense public pressure, that the Metropolitan opened its galleries on Sundays, thus attracting patrons that Director Louis P. di Cesnola found "repulsive and unclean."[48] Locating the New York Public Library near the Metropolitan Museum of Art and the Museum of Natural History and attempting to establish a similar relationship with the City would have implied a model of culture building that by 1895 was no longer tenable. Such a decision, in the words of Councilman James Roosevelt when the City finally ended its support of the New York Institution in 1831, would have "been the subject of frequent and . . . just animadversion."[49]

Most of the trustees and many of the city's newspapers seemed to favor the site of the old Croton Water Reservoir. Located on Fifth Avenue between Fortieth and Forty-Second Streets, it was not only closer to the more densely populated districts farther downtown, but was also conveniently accessible by public transportation from all parts of the city.[50] In January 1896, when it was finally determined that Henrietta Lenox's heirs would not sign releases on the Lenox property, John Bigelow, the first president of the Library, confided to his diary that it was "the most comforting piece of news" he had "heard for many a day."[51] No longer bound by their resolution to use the Lenox Library, the trustees were now free to consider other sites. Perhaps the most attractive feature of the reservoir was that it was public property. No longer in use since the construction of the New Croton Aqueduct in 1893, it would be an ideal location, if the City could be persuaded to raze it and donate the land to the New York Public Library.[52]

The possibility of financial support from the City of New York and the conditions under which it might be secured were central issues from the founding of the Library. The trustees recognized that, even if they were able to build on the Lenox property, the cost of an addition to the Lenox building would substantially reduce the Library's endowment and therefore restrict the development of its collections. If, on the other hand, the City agreed to provide the building, the Library could dedicate most of its financial resources to purchasing books. Thus, the resolution passed by the board in February 1896 that committed the Library to the "broadest possible policy" stipulated that "the nature and scope of [its] work" would be limited by "the funds at the disposal of the Corporation, or which can be obtained." The trustees clearly hoped to obtain such funds from the City of New York. At the same meeting they further resolved to make a formal, public application to the City to build and maintain a new library on the reservoir site.[53]

The board understood that the municipal authorities would be unwilling to appropriate tax monies for a "library of reference purely on the old lines," one that did not include a more popular, circulating collection.[54] The ensuing negotiations with the City thus raise the critical question of whether the trustees, in considering the scope of the new library, were motivated more by the need for municipal support than by a sincere desire to create a more inclusive, public institution. In their public statements, they frankly acknowledged that without public funds for a building, the reduced endowment would be inadequate to develop an extensive reference collection for scholars.[55] Yet even in its internal communications, the board expressed at least some interest in becoming more useful to a wider public. The committee that originally recommended seeking support from the City was "impressed by the necessity of attempting to do more than merely to establish a library of reference" and by "the larger measure of usefulness which would be gained by the adoption of a plan involving a broader scope."[56] The board's formal address to Mayor William Strong in April 1896 went considerably further. It enthused that libraries "within the reach of every man's home" were "in a very real sense a part of the educational system" of the city and hinted that the New York Public Library would either cooperate or consolidate with the free circulating libraries.[57]

In the contract between the Library and the City of New York, signed on December 8, 1897, the City agreed to raze the reservoir and construct an 87,500-square-foot building designed by an architectural firm selected by the Library's board.[58] The City also committed to maintaining the building and grounds. The structure itself cost slightly more than nine million dollars, while the annual maintenance averaged approximately thirty-six thousand dollars during the first five years that it was open.[59] The City was not granted representation on the board. The New York Public Library agreed not only to make its reference collection freely accessible to the public, but also to operate a circulating library in the new building. Both collections were to be open evenings and on Sundays. Thus, even in this first phase of the founding, the creation of what became known as the Reference Department, there was a provision for circulation, even though the demand was clearly for branch libraries, and a centrally located collection

The Croton Reservoir (*top*, 1899) on Forty-Second Street and Fifth Avenue became the site of the Marble Palace for Booklovers, the New York Public Library's Central Building (*bottom*, 1911).

could never bring books "within the reach of every man's home." In part, the trustees did it for the money. The City of New York would never have agreed to finance the new building without a circulating collection. On the other hand, as the Executive Committee of the board reported about the time that the City made its first appropriation for construction, the New York Public Library was prepared to "at least sympathize with the general public," while "preserving the character of the Library as a library of reference."[60] The reservoir site, both geographically and in terms of public utility, was located somewhere between the free circulating libraries in lower Manhattan and the Lenox Library uptown, but rather closer to the latter.

Throughout the negotiations over the reservoir site, and particularly in their formal address to the mayor in 1896, the library trustees had publicly expressed their support for the ideals embodied in popular libraries. Once the City began construction of a magnificent reference library for scholars, there was a general expectation that the New York Public Library would absorb the various free circulating libraries into a comprehensive system embracing both reference and circulation. Yet for nearly two years after the contract for the Central Building was signed, neither the Public Library board nor the leaders of the smaller library associations took any definite steps toward consolidation. There were a variety of reasons on both sides for this initial hesitancy, but to a considerable extent both were torn between two central and, in this case, conflicting preoccupations of progressivism: a desire for efficiency and the fear of corruption. Everyone recognized that, despite the impressive statistics marshaled each year by the free circulating libraries, it was inefficient for so many different organizations to pursue the same goals in an uncoordinated fashion. It would be vastly more efficient and economical for all of these libraries to at least centralize basic functions such as binding, cataloging, and book selection.[61] At the same time, a truly comprehensive system of circulating collections serving all of the city's neighborhoods would cost more than the combined resources of all the free circulating libraries. Since the New York Public Library's endowment was barely sufficient to maintain its reference collections, a system of branches for circulation would require guaranteed, ongoing support from the City. By the late 1890s, such a substantial commitment was highly unlikely unless municipal authorities were granted at least a limited role in the governance of the Library. This would mean consorting with machine politicians presumed to be irredeemably, contagiously corrupt, the introduction of what President John Bigelow called "the Tammany bacillus" into the public library system.[62]

It was in part this fear of political corruption that had ended an earlier attempt to create a New York Public Library. Even before the announcement of the Tilden bequest in 1886, some prominent New Yorkers had been dissatisfied with the city's inefficient patchwork of privately managed institutions and sought to create a publicly supported public library. In January of that year, Adolph Sanger, president of the Board of Aldermen, introduced a bill in the state legislature to establish, "as a monument to the homage paid by the people to self-culture," a free public library "on the most liberal and well-considered basis." The City would construct a central building on the Croton Reservoir site and appropriate $40,000 annually to "furnish free reading to the people of the city." The mayor, the city comptroller, the president of the Board of Alderman, and the president of the Department of Public Parks were to serve ex officio on the Board of Trustees.[63] When asked why the City could not simply allocate funds to the New York Free Circulating Library, Sanger responded that it was inappropriate to grant tax monies to "gentlemen to run a private library," that "a public library should be public in every sense of the word."[64]

Supporters of the public library movement were convinced that any plan that allowed elected officials a role in the governance of the proposed library would "encounter the practical certainty of its becoming one more corruptionist engine in the hands of city rulers."[65] Melvil Dewey and representatives of the New York Free Circulating Library appeared before the senate's Committee on Cities to oppose the Sanger bill. They argued that the City should focus on establishing small branch libraries, rather than a large, central building, and that public monies would be more wisely appropriated to a "society already chartered and actively engaged in this work," presumably the New York Free Circulating Library. As a result of their lobbying effort, the Sanger bill died in committee, and the legislature passed their substitute bill that permitted municipalities to fund privately managed circulating libraries. Such appropriations were merely discretionary, however, and in New York City the maximum amount that could be appropriated to any one library was $40,000.[66] By the mid-1890s, the city government paid most of the operating expenses of most of the free circulating libraries.[67]

The state Library Law of 1886 was a partial victory for the free circulating libraries. On one hand, they received significant public funding, while avoiding the direct involvement of public officials in the administration of private library associations. The legislation did not *require* appropriations from the city government, however. The New York Free Circulating Library, for example, each year received only about half of the maximum amount permitted by the law.[68] Moreover, after 1897, the year in which the City contracted with the New York Public Library to maintain the Central Building on Forty-Second Street, city officials were increasingly critical of this private management of public funds. Robert Van Wyck, who succeeded William Strong as mayor later that year, called it "a system of fostering private control of public institutions . . . a sort of auxiliary government by societies." In October of the following year, he threatened to take over the free circulating libraries altogether.[69] By 1899, the libraries were clearly on the defensive. In their annual report for that year, the trustees of the New York Free Circulating Library conceded that certain efficiencies could be achieved through closer cooperation between the city's lending libraries. They also recognized that the City had a right to "supervise" the expenditure of public monies appropriated to privately managed institutions. They concluded, however, that "today a union of public scrutiny with private management seems to be the best solution." Such a policy would provide "the individual [with] the opportunity to work for the public good," while at the same time avoiding "the introduction of politics" into the administration of the libraries.[70]

In late 1899, the New York Public Library, likewise concerned over the possibility of a City takeover of the branches, began tentative steps toward incorporating the free circulating libraries. In November, Director Billings wrote a memorandum to the Board of Trustees outlining possible courses of action. He never considered as an option a system of branch libraries as a department of the municipal government and advised against the immediate merging of the free libraries into the public library. He recommended instead that for the present it would be "best to preserve . . . the interest felt by many persons in each of the . . . volunteer organizations." Billings stressed that any reorganization should proceed gradually and that the board should "avoid all appearance of grasping for power or of interfering with the work" of the smaller libraries. As an initial step, he suggested that the City charge the New York Public Library with investigating and reporting on the management of the free circulating libraries.[71]

In June 1900, City Comptroller Bird Coler formally requested that the board undertake a comprehensive study of the lending libraries.[72] Billings surveyed the various library associations during the course of the summer, and the Executive Committee presented a report to Coler in September. By this time, the trustees had evidently rejected the gradualist policy outlined in Billings's memo the previous year. They concluded that although each individual library was managed in an efficient and professional manner, "the great defect in the present method of supplying the free circulation of books to the people of New York is the want of a . . . uniform system of expenditure, cataloging, accountability, and inspection." The city therefore needed a centralizing agency to coordinate these functions across all of the circulating libraries. Implicitly rejecting the creation of such an office within the municipal government, the trustees advised that "the most effective and economical method for providing such a central authority will be to place this work under the direction of some one of the organizations now in existence."[73] At the next meeting of the Board of Estimate, the body responsible for the municipal budget, Billings proposed that the New York Public Library act as the coordinating agency for the circulating libraries. About this same time, the New York Free Circulating Library, no doubt recognizing the inevitable, began negotiating the terms of a merger.[74]

The agreement between the New York Public Library and the New York Free Circulating Library was signed January 11, 1901. This consolidation of the reference library and the largest of the lending libraries was a marriage of convenience in which both parties got what they wanted. Primarily, both sides wished to prevent presumably corrupt public officials from meddling in public library affairs. Second, the agreement ensured that the reference library and the circulating libraries would function as relatively independent entities within a consolidated corporation. All of the income and property that the New York Free Circulating Library ceded to the New York Public Library was to be devoted solely to the operation of branches.[75] After more than twenty years as the city's leading lending library, the Free Circulating Library's board cherished its independence and was extremely reluctant to relinquish complete control to another organization. For their part, Billings and the Public Library board had no experience and little interest in managing lending libraries.[76] Thus, at their meeting the following month, the trustees created a separate Circulation Department. Headed by a chief of circulation and a Circulation Committee that formally reported to the library director and the Board of Trustees, in practice the Circulation Department operated as a semi-independent unit within the larger organization. Leaders of the New York Free Circulating Library were appointed to all seven seats on the Circulation Committee, giving them a significant degree of autonomy within the new corporation.[77]

What the consolidation did not provide for and what the Circulation Department badly needed was a reliable source of income. The Free Circulating Library had avoided public governance, but it still had no guarantee of public funding. Aside from its contractual agreement to maintain the Central Building on Forty-Second Street, the City of New York was not legally required to support the New York Public Library. Its annual appropriation for circulation was still discretionary. Just as money from a private individual, the Tilden bequest, had led to the founding of a great public library devoted to reference, an equally generous benefaction from a private citizen was instrumental in ensuring the success of its new Circulation Department. On March 12, 1901, Andrew Carnegie wrote to John Shaw Billings offering $5.2 million for the construction of "Branches for the special benefit of the masses of the people."[78] It was Carnegie's gift that finally secured from the City an ongoing commitment to support circulating libraries.

For much of the nineteenth century, charitable institutions in the public sphere were supported by philanthropy on a relatively modest scale. The New York Free Circulating Library, for example, before the state Library Law of 1886, relied mostly upon smaller donations and an annual membership fee of ten dollars.[79] Carnegie himself, who joined in 1881 and served on the board from 1893 to 1901, gave about $10,000 over the course of twenty years. The latter part of the century was the age of big philanthropy, when wealthy men like John Jacob Astor and James Lenox devoted entire fortunes to creating monuments to their memory and the public good. Andrew Carnegie's gift giving, however, was of a different magnitude. It was huge philanthropy. Both Carnegie and Samuel Tilden, for example, offered approximately $5 million for a public library in New York, but for Carnegie this was just one library in one city. Worldwide, his gifts for libraries alone totaled approximately $56 million, and by the time of his death in 1919 he had given away in total more than $333 million.[80] The charitable trusts founded by Andrew Carnegie and other huge philanthropists such as John D. Rockefeller transformed American philanthropy. Through them the benevolence of a single individual or family could influence public policy, as in the case of Carnegie's gift to the New York Public Library, or even, in effect, create policy in the absence of public funding.[81]

Andrew Carnegie's life spanned and embodied the transition from an economy based upon household and artisanal production to an industrial economy dominated by national and transnational corporations. His fa-

Andrew Carnegie (*Judge*, July 25, 1903)

ther was a prosperous master weaver in Dunfermline, Scotland, who sank into respectable poverty after the introduction of steam-loom weaving. Carnegie, born in 1835, was raised in a family he proudly described as "staunch republicans, wild, with Burns, for the "'Royalty of Man.'"[82] Later in life, of course, he became a symbol of the excesses of industrial capitalism, the coolly calculating robber baron who amassed a fortune by exploiting the labor of his fellow man. Carnegie was an enthusiastic disciple of Herbert Spencer, advocating, in an influential, widely read essay on "The Gospel of Wealth," "great inequality . . . the concentration of business . . . in the hands of a few; and the law of competition . . . as being not only beneficial, but essential to the future progress of the race."[83] At the same time, he remained sincerely, emotionally attached to the republicanism of his youth. His book *Triumphant Democracy* is essentially an extended argument designed to remind the citizens of his adopted land and convince the subjects of his native land that "the republican form [of government] and not the government of a class through the monarchical form is the surest foundation of individual growth and national greatness."[84] Carnegie even commissioned his own republican coat of arms, featuring an inverted crown, with a liberty cap above it, and below it the Carnegie motto, "Death to Privilege."[85]

Andrew Carnegie was not a hypocrite, and he was not self-deluded. That he could sincerely espouse both republicanism and "great inequality" reveals some of the complexities and ambiguities of republican and liberal thought. Republicanism in particular defies definition, but certainly within it there were two dominant coexisting themes, liberty and independence on one hand and civic engagement and community on the other. In the simple, relatively homogeneous, agrarian society of the late eighteenth and early nineteenth centuries, these two strands of republican thought had rarely clashed. By the late nineteenth century, however, sturdy republican independence increasingly became synonymous with the liberal notion of individualism. Unbridled individualism in the economic sphere could, and did, erode community in the public sphere.

Carnegie's "Gospel of Wealth" sought to resolve this contradiction, to reconcile republicanism and liberalism, community and individualism. Originally published in the *North American Review* in 1889, it wholeheartedly embraced the Spencerian doctrine of the survival of the fittest, the "law [to which] we owe our wonderful material development." At the same time, it frankly acknowledged the corrosive effects of unrestrained individualism, conceding that vast economic disparities meant that "human society loses its homogeneity" and "rigid castes are formed."[86] Wisely directed, personally administered philanthropy was the one "true antidote for the temporary unequal distribution of wealth," ensuring "the reconciliation of the rich and the poor—a reign of harmony." For Carnegie the

Gospel of Wealth differed from conventional philanthropy in two critical respects. First, the true philanthropist was to personally oversee the redistribution of his surplus income during his own lifetime, not bequeath it posthumously in his will. Mindful of the fate of Samuel Tilden's bequest to the people of New York, Carnegie admonished his fellow millionaires that "he who dies rich, dies disgraced."[87] Second, true philanthropy was devoted to "uses which give nothing for nothing, which require cooperation, self-help," whereas mere charity, simply distributing alms to the poor, "tend[ed] to sap the spirit of manly independence."[88] Libraries were therefore one of the best uses of surplus wealth. They helped only those who helped themselves.[89]

In the case of public libraries, the Gospel of Wealth also required that communities help themselves. In return for the gift of a library building, Carnegie insisted that the local government appropriate tax monies annually to maintain the collection. This not only ensured ongoing public support and public interest, but, just as important, it also meant that "all taint of charity is dispelled."[90] Even the humblest citizens could enter a Carnegie library with an empowering sense of ownership, knowing that as taxpayers they contributed to its maintenance. Carnegie's offer of $5.2 million for public libraries in New York was, even for him, an unprecedented sum, but his contracts with the City and with the New York Public Library, signed in the spring of 1902, were typical of the conditions attached to all of the Carnegie libraries worldwide. In return for fifty buildings constructed in Manhattan, Staten Island, and the Bronx, the City of New York agreed to provide each year at least 10 percent of his total gift to maintain and develop circulating collections. Tax monies were to be appropriated annually to the New York Public Library, which was designated as Carnegie's agent for library services in those boroughs.[91] Thus, for the first time, the City committed to ongoing support of branch lending libraries.

For the most part, New Yorkers responded to Carnegie's benefaction with enthusiasm and gratitude. Mayor Robert Van Wyck called Carnegie "the greatest human product of the nineteenth century," while John Shaw Billings predicted that his generosity would "result in the greatest free public library system in the world."[92] The *New York World* reported that "Tammany officials, reformers, capitalists, philanthropists, workingmen join in . . . a genuine public spirit, something that has not been known here for fully half a century."[93] Only the *Sun* actively opposed accepting the gift. It pointed out that since the City was obliged to support the libraries he built, Carnegie's offer was in fact "a proposition to the people to spend their own money," a "costly change in public policy" that would result in "ruinous prodigality."[94] The *Herald* praised Carnegie's generosity, but argued that a public institution such as the New York Public Library should be governed by public officials, that "since the people are to support these libraries the people's direct representatives should have their management and control."[95]

Carnegie instead chose the New York Public Library to manage the Carnegie libraries, and the City of New York agreed to fund them through the new Circulation Department. Since the City was now understandably unwilling to subsidize collections that would compete with the Public Library, this in effect meant an end to the independence of the remaining free circulating libraries. In the fall of 1902, Comptroller Edward M. Grout began to pressure these private institutions to dissolve and be absorbed into the Circulation Department. Most of them were extremely reluctant to do so, but the Carnegie agreements furnished Grout with both a carrot and a stick. His stick was the imminent loss of municipal support. In October, he announced that after 1903 the City would fund lending libraries only through the New York Public Library.[96] His carrot was a new building paid for by Andrew Carnegie. Once a free circulating library agreed to join the Circulation Department, it was understood that Carnegie funds would be used to build a new branch named after the old library, and that members of the board would be appointed to the Public Library's Circulation Committee.[97]

Besides the New York Free Circulating Library, which formed the nucleus of the Circulation Department in January 1901, the largest independent system in the city was the Aguilar Free Library. Even before the announcement of the Carnegie gift, the board of the Jewish library had appointed a committee to investigate cooperation with the other lending libraries, and actual consolidation with the New York Public Library was largely a matter of, in the words of Chief of Circulation Arthur Bostwick, "the smoothing down of ruffled plumage."[98] While Aguilar President Samuel Greenbaum was willing to acquiesce to a merger, Henry Leipziger, chairman of the Library Committee, fiercely resisted the loss of the Library's independence. In the annual report for 1901, Greenbaum recognized that the time was "very near at hand when the free circulating libraries will necessarily come under one general control." Leipziger, in the same report, simply referred to a "closer relationship between the existing libraries." However, once Grout announced that the City would soon fund only the Circulation Department, Leipziger bowed to the inevitable and agreed to the consolidation. In February 1903, the Aguilar ceded its property to the New York Public Library, and Greenbaum was elected to the Library's board. Leipziger's plumage was smoothed by an appointment to the Circulation Committee.[99]

Negotiations with the third largest system, the Cathedral Library Association, were considerably more contentious. Since the Catholic library was founded as an antidote to the pernicious influence of public libraries, resistance to joining the New York Public Library involved more than mere pride and sentimentality. Particularly after losing state support for parochial schools in a new constitution adopted in 1894, the church in New York City was determined to prevent what it viewed as an intrusion into clerical affairs. In the spring of 1901, shortly after Carnegie made his offer to the City and long before Grout threatened to cut off City funds, the Cathedral Library Association took the offensive. Anticipating the change in municipal policy, the Association circulated a "Statement of the Position of the Cathedral Library" that outlined its argument for continued independence. It contended that consolidation with the Circulation Department would defeat the very purpose of the Library, which "was established in order to counteract the evil influences of public libraries in general," and "would mean the establishment of so many new instruments for the propagation of opposition to our Church." It further argued that to compel a merger would be undemocratic. The New York Public Library was essentially a private organization managed by Protestants. As members of the voting, taxpaying public, Catholics, who comprised "the majority of the religious element of the city," were entitled to libraries that represented their own theological and intellectual interests.[100]

Most of city's newspapers opposed separate appropriations for the Cathedral Library that would allow it to remain independent of the Public Library. In part, their arguments were based upon the separation of church and state, "one of the foundation stones of the Republic,"[101] but there was certainly an element of anti-Catholicism in the debate as well. The *Evening Post*, for example, wrote that the Catholics' demand for public support was an expression of "medievalism."[102] More important, many held that the issue was not democracy, as the "Statement of the Cathedral Library" had argued, but rather the public good that transcended the demands of any particular political constituency. The *Tribune* insisted that "public money should be used for the public and not for any part of it," while the *Times* assured its readers that the New York Public Library would represent "the general and not any special public."[103] Such arguments on behalf of the public weal call to mind the republican fear of factions, but with a critical difference. Here the danger came not from small cabals of selfish, conspiring individuals, but from large, powerful organizations selfishly pursuing interests contrary to those of the people. The public good was eroded by "special interests," a term that entered the American vocabulary about this time.[104]

For his part, Billings saw no need to force the issue. In his inaugural address to the American Library Association in 1902, he suggested that "the question will . . . be decided . . . by political party requirements," and assured his audience that "there is no immediate danger to the free public library system from this particular form of opposition."[105] His assessment of the controversy proved quite clear sighted. While Father Joseph McMahon, the director of the Cathedral Library, insisted that he would resist consolidation at any cost and warned that it was "now purely a question of politics," the municipal authorities made a number of critical concessions.[106] Two Catholics were elected trustees of the New York Public Library, thus assuring at least minimal representation on the board, and in late 1903 Comptroller Grout (who coincidentally was up for reelection) announced that the City would fund the Library for one more year.[107] After delicate negotiations for most of the following year, and faced with the certain loss of municipal support in 1905, McMahon and Archbishop John Farley finally relented. The Cathedral Library Association ceded its property to the New York Public Library on December 31, 1904.[108]

By this time, most of the other lending libraries had already consolidated.[109] Only a very few were able to remain independent. The New York Society Library and the Mercantile Library had never received appropriations from the City. They were able to rely upon rents, endowments, and a small but loyal membership for support. Both are still in operation today.[110] A number of the smaller circulating libraries simply refused to join the New York Public Library and were forced to close for lack of funds. B'nai B'rith, for example, after trying to find a "wide-minded philanthropist" who would "rescue" its Maimonides Library, finally sold the collection in early 1906.[111] The General Society of Mechanics and Tradesmen, on the other hand, was rescued by its most famous member. Andrew Carnegie, a brother since 1888, donated more than half a million dollars about this time, a portion of which was used to expand and endow the library. The

Apprentices' Library is still a lending library and is still an integral part of the Society's activities.[112]

When Andrew Carnegie wrote to John Shaw Billings offering to finance the construction of branch libraries for the New York Public Library, he observed, with characteristic modesty, that the project "probably breaks the record, but this is the day of big operations."[113] Having just sold the Carnegie Steel Company to J. P. Morgan to create U.S. Steel, America's first billion-dollar corporation, Carnegie knew as much about operating on a large scale as anyone in the country. Certainly by the time the Central Building opened in 1911, the New York Public Library was a big operation. That same year the Circulation Department loaned more than 7.5 million books, a world record according to *Library Journal,* and the collection of the Reference Department had more than doubled in size since its creation in 1895 to approximately 800,000 volumes.[114] Yet the Library was more than just big. Rather than simply an aggregation of the city's research and circulating libraries, it had become a very different kind of public institution once the Carnegie gift guaranteed ongoing support from the taxpaying public.

In fact, this change was evident even before the City agreed to construct the Central Building on Forty-Second Street. In the fall of 1896, shortly after the trustees formally petitioned Mayor Strong, both the Astor and Lenox Libraries made a portion of their reference books, mostly dictionaries and encyclopedias, accessible on open shelves and installed electric lights in order to extend their hours into the early evening.[115] By the time the new building finally opened in 1911, there was clearly an emphasis on public service that had been conspicuously absent during the decades in which the research libraries catered to "men of leisure and . . . men of letters." As Billings explained in an article in *Library Journal,* it had "been planned [so that] great facilities can be given to the general public . . . without interfering with those required by scholars and special students." The trustees and the director clearly understood that the future success of the new library now depended in large measure upon, in the words of Governor John Dix at the opening ceremony, "the good will and support of all the people."[116] This meant not simply that the "taint of charity" had been dispelled or even that the public felt an ordinary sense of ownership. What the Library most needed and what the "marble palace for booklovers" engendered was civic pride. An article in *Harper's Monthly* in March 1911 described an incident that occurred while the building was still under construction that aptly illustrates the extraordinary "enthusiasm and devotion" it inspired. A careless workman scratched a newly polished floor when he dragged a heavy ladder across the room. A fellow citizen working nearby rushed over, grabbed the ladder, and indignantly declared: "This floor belongs to the people of New York!"[117]

Although the people's palace in midtown Manhattan attracted the most public attention, more dramatic and fundamental changes were transforming the branch libraries. In its final annual report in 1901, the New York Free Circulating Library described the "shifting of the burden of support from private to public shoulders" as "the progress of the Library from a private charity to a public necessity." It explained that "the idea that this system of circulating libraries is only for the use of the very poor has been superseded by the belief that it is an important adjunct of the city's educational system."[118] But because the Circulation Department was a tax-supported rather than a charitable institution, it emphasized a rather different kind of education. This shift in purpose was evident in a pamphlet published by the City shortly before the opening of the Central Building entitled *Results Not Shown by Statistics in the Work of the Public Libraries of Greater New York.* Mostly a collection of testimonials from satisfied taxpayers, it stressed the ways in which the reading public could use the books for economic rather than cultural self-improvement. "A young woman, a clerk, found that the library contained a fine collection of books on business, . . . used them continually for one winter and was able to better her position." A group of ambitious young men consulted the collections to prepare for the debates organized by their debating club, and three of them later graduated from prestigious law schools. The pamphlet included an entire section on "Aids to Those Studying for College Regents, Civil Service, and Promotion Examinations."[119] Now that the branches had progressed from a private charity to a public necessity, the mission shifted from uplifting the masses with, in the words of Ellen Coe of the Free Circulating Library, works of "literary and moral excellence" to a focus, in part, on providing the middle class, or those who aspired to join the middle class, with the means for upward mobility. This change in the construction of the reader was apparent in an address by Arthur Bostwick before the American Library Association in 1903. The chief of the new Circulation Department told his colleagues that tax monies should be used to develop collections for the "average man or woman of good education and good taste," that "the great reading public" is "just you and I and some other fellows."[120]

Bostwick's address was entitled "The Purchase of Current Fiction." That the branches were now explicitly tax-supported also influenced a shift in the Library's policy toward the provision of recreational reading. In part, this change simply reflected American society's more liberal, less censorious attitude toward the popular novel, a moderation of the prejudice typified by those whom Bostwick referred to as the "old-fashioned librarians." For example, at the ceremony marking the laying of the cornerstone of the Central Building in 1902, Mayor Seth Low observed that "indeed . . . many will read only that which amuses instead of that which deepens and instructs, but [this] is not to be despised, for there is a place in life for amusement as well as work."[121] Moreover, some public librarians came to believe that even popular fiction could serve a constructive, educative purpose, that it could provide what their counterparts in the early republic termed rational amusement. Bostwick, for example, claimed "we should be glad" that "a large proportion of our people prefer to get their history and travel, their sociology and psychology in the form" of novels. He held that reading fiction "may strengthen the critical facility and stimulate the intellect."[122]

A more important reason for this more liberal policy regarding the provision of popular novels was a fundamental change in the relationship between the reading public and the Public Library once it became an explicitly tax-supported institution. As Bostwick explained in a later address on "The People's Share in the Public Library," in language that in many ways echoed the annual reports of the Mercantile and Society Libraries many years earlier, the new library was obligated to respond to the demand for recreational reading because "its customers [were] the citizens at large, who pay, through the agency of taxation, for what they receive." He described the public as a "stockholder," the "boss and beneficiary" of the public librarian.[123] Like the city's subscription libraries, the New York Public Library was now obliged at least to an extent to supply what its members demanded.

Of course, not all of the funding for the Library was provided by the taxpaying public. The New York City Board of Estimate appropriated monies each year for the Circulation Department, while the Reference Department was supported by individual donations and the income from the Astor, Lenox, and Tilden endowments. The governance of the New York

Public Library was still mostly private. Most of its twenty-five trustees were elected by the board and served for life. However, once the City committed to providing ongoing support, the public was granted a degree of representation. In February 1899, while the board was engaged in a lengthy dispute with the City over funding for the Central Building, the by-laws were amended to include the city comptroller ex officio. Three years later, shortly after the contract with Andrew Carnegie guaranteed annual funding for branches, the state legislature passed a bill that added the mayor and the president of the Board of Aldermen as well.[124]

Representation on the Board of Trustees, however, was more than simply a matter of statutes and by-laws. Certain segments of the reading public were accorded a kind of informal representation and others were excluded altogether. Women, for example, had founded and played a major role in managing the free circulating libraries. Once their branches became a "public necessity" and were consolidated with the New York Public Library, they immediately lost all power. Initially, they were not even appointed to the Circulation Committee. In a remarkably diverse city, the trustees were mostly wealthy, white, male Protestants. However, wealthy, white, male Jews and Catholics served as well. When the Aguilar and Cathedral Libraries joined the New York Public Library, Samuel Greenbaum and Morgan O'Brien were elected to the board, and since then it has always included at least one Jewish member and a number of Catholics. For most of the twentieth century, the Archbishop of New York served in a kind of unofficial ex officio capacity.[125] Moreover, although only three elected officials represented the taxpaying public, the fact that they held one of the Library's purse strings, the funding for the Circulation Department, meant that they could exercise considerable influence. Carnegie's requirement that the City appropriate at least 10 percent of his total gift annually for the branches proved to be grossly inadequate. Although circulation was always funded at a much higher level, the mayor and other public officials wielded significant power by virtue of their control of public monies.[126]

The New York Public Library in 1911 was a large, complex, modern organization, emblematic of a day of big operations. It was, both in terms of governance and funding, a mix of public and private. Like other "public corporations," such as the city's Metropolitan Transit Authority, it was one means by which the scope of government expanded dramatically during the Progressive Era.[127] The Library performed multiple functions that included facilitating scholarly research, enabling cultural and economic self-improvement, and circulating harmless recreational reading.[128] It served multiple reading publics: men, women, and children; immigrants of various nationalities and the native born; Jews, Catholics, and Protestants; scholars and devourers of popular fiction; the masses and the middle class. It was a new kind of public library and a new kind of public institution for a new century.[129]

Afterword

Public Libraries and New York's Elusive Reading Publics

In her 2007 article "Ideologies and Practices of Reading," Barbara Sicherman observes that while there is an extensive literature on production and distribution, "the consumption of books is almost wholly unchartered territory."[1] This is due in part to a paucity of evidence. Even with the increasing availability of online, searchable, full-text sources, it is difficult to find firsthand accounts not just of what readers read, but also of how and why they read, of their intimate encounters with print. This is particularly true for research on public libraries in the eighteenth and nineteenth centuries. There are few surviving sources that shed light on how individual users of New York City's early public libraries made use of the collections, that document what Wayne Wiegand terms "the library in the life of the user."[2] The history of public libraries nonetheless has the potential to leaven our understanding of the history of reading. As Sicherman, Wiegand, and others have argued, reading is fundamentally a social activity.[3] Accounts of individual reading experiences, when they are available, combined with institutional data such as circulation records and statistics, where they have survived, can show how print helped construct social identities and how it functioned within and across groups, including but not limited to socioeconomic classes. The history of New York's early public libraries can help chart the territories of America's elusive reading publics.

> In works of fiction I have indulged very sparingly, not from want of relish, but from a firm conviction that such reading is, in general, time greatly misspent, and that the indulgence is productive of many evil consequences.
>
> John H. Griscom, M.D., *Memoir* (1859)

John Griscom, the son of a middling farmer, was born in Salem County, New Jersey, in 1774 and moved to New York City in 1807. He was a member of the New York Society Library and the New-York Historical Society and a vice president of the American Bible Society.[4] He was also active in a number of local reform organizations, including the Public School Society, and founded the Society for the Prevention of Pauperism. Griscom supported himself and his family for most of his life as a teacher. Beginning in 1812, he served briefly as chair of chemistry at Columbia and when the New York Institution opened three years later, he became professor of mechanical and chemical philosophy and maintained a chemical laboratory there. He also helped establish the Mechanics Institute, which offered the means for self-improvement to the city's artisans, and lectured to aspiring merchants in courses sponsored by the Mercantile Library Association. He wrote, among other works, *Monitorial Instruction*, a how-to book for Lancasterian instruction in the new public schools.[5] Rather than a gentleman scholar, like his friends John Pintard and Dewitt Clinton, Griscom is best described as a public scholar. Perhaps more than other any public figure in early nineteenth-century New York, he sought to make education, the opportunity for self-improvement, available beyond the children of the gentry, to ensure, as he remarked in a lecture before the Mechanics Institute, that higher learning was more than "a thing of patrician acquirement."[6]

Griscom's *Memoir* includes an entire chapter on "The Character and Manner of His Reading" and throughout provides historical perspective on prescriptive reading in the early decades of the century, on what and how cultural authorities expected readers to read. He warned of the danger of giving "way to desultory, and, more especially, to *unprofitable* reading" and recommended instead books of "durable merit and value, or which required *study*, rather than simple perusal." Reading served "the important purpose of the acquisition of solid and accurate science" and helped in "preparing the individual for more enlarged usefulness and influence in society." Mere popular fiction, on the other hand, such as the works of Sir Walter Scott, was indulgent, since it was written "without any good or useful object in view."[7] Griscom valued reading according to the extent to which it served a moral, productive, public purpose.

The early charge ledgers of the New York Society Library provide clear evidence that not all of Griscom's fellow readers followed his advice. Trustee Samuel Mitchell, for example, checked out Henry Fielding's *Tom Jones*, and trustee Samuel Bard borrowed an English translation of Alain-René Lesage's *Gil Blas*.[8] Griscom, a devout Quaker, would have considered both works, with their depictions of low society and allusions to sexual promiscuity, scandalous. Yet, evidence of how the subscribers read the books, how they experienced reading, is very limited. The few surviving accounts from the early decades of the nineteenth century provide very little detail and refer, perhaps predictably, mostly to the kinds of prescriptive reading, to the works of durable merit, of which Griscom would have approved. For instance, subscriber Maria Trumbull in 1801 wrote home to her father in Connecticut that she had convinced a young man of her acquaintance to set aside a novel on the Sabbath and read a collection of sermons instead.[9]

Sources that cast novel reading in a positive light during this period are rare. Hocquet Caritat, a Society Library member and proprietor of the city's most popular circulating library, in his "General Defense of Modern Novels," argued that good fiction was superior to, for example, history and biography. He held that it provided "amusement and instruction," that while certain older works, such as Fielding's, were "polluted with oaths and impurity," many modern novels provided edifying "models of heroic virtue, invincible chastity, and noble disinterestedness." Caritat's defense is interesting and noteworthy not only because he criticized certain categories of prescribed reading, such as history, but also because he praised the public utility of popular fiction: "By their fruits ye shall know them. When was this nation so distinguished for courage, generosity, and delicacy?"[10] By contrast, cultural authorities like John Griscom viewed novel reading as a private, indulgent, escapist. Griscom would certainly have agreed, for example, with "On the Cause of the Popularity of Novels," which appeared in the *Literary Magazine* in 1807. The author wrote that the "reason for the high favor in which such compositions are held" was simply "the tameness and insipidity of . . . common events."[11] Readers read fiction to escape real life.

> In the wide department of fictitious writing, let your consciences restrain and direct your inclination, and rectify your taste. . . . Its captivation should put you on your guard, my young friends, and teach you that temperance, if not abstinence is your duty.
>
> Catharine Maria Sedgwick, *Means and Ends, or Self-Training* (1839)

Catharine Maria Sedgwick, the daughter of Federalist politician and jurist Theodore Sedgwick, was born in Stockbridge, Massachusetts in 1789. Beginning in 1821, she spent half her time in New York City, "wintering" with her brother Robert, a prominent local attorney. She had access to the Society Library's collection through his subscription. Unlike many women writers in the nineteenth century, Sedgwick wrote as an avocation and, like John Griscom, she was active in local reform associations, including the Free School of the First Congregational Church. In a career spanning four decades, she wrote historical romances and domestic fiction, as well as *Means and Ends*, a conduct book for teenage girls, and stories and sketches for popular magazines.[12] In an article in *Godey's Lady's Book*, "Literati of New York City," Edgar Allan Poe wrote that she was "the first female prose writer of her country," and he praised the "tone of thoughtful morality" that informed her work.[13] Her literary reputation waned in later decades, but she remained popular throughout the nineteenth century. The New York Free Circulating Library and the Apprentices' Library held her books as late as the 1890s.[14]

In *Means and Ends*, Sedgwick offered her readers earnest counsel on such matters as dress, manners, music, conversation, cooking, and skin care. Her advice on reading was in many respects similar to John Griscom's. In a chapter entitled "Books—What to Read, How to Read," she urged her "dear young friends" to read "thoroughly and understandingly," and to select history, biography, and English literature in lieu of "the trash that fills the circulating libraries." The important difference between *Means and Ends* and Griscom's *Memoir* is the greater emphasis that she placed upon taste. Works of durable merit were, of course, still essential, but even romance could be improving, morally uplifting, provided one avoided "poor novels and trashy tales," and read instead tasteful writers such as Sir Walter Scott.[15] Historians of reading have argued that this increasing social value attached to culture, refinement, taste, to a canon that included "standard" authors of fiction, was a critical component of the emergence of the American middle class and the construction of a middle-class identity.[16] Conversely, poor taste in reading, "trashy" books, were associated with a soulless consumerism, with low-class, market-driven desires. According to Nan Enstad and others, middle-class "ideology distinguished consumption with values (i.e. 'tasteful' consumption) from consumption seen as lacking values and deriving solely from crass market interests."[17]

At first glance, the history of New York's most popular public library in the mid–nineteenth century would seem not to support this construction of the city's reading publics. Especially after 1850, the Mercantile Library was nothing if not market driven. Managed by clerks, the quintessential middle-class profession, it recruited new members through "an active system of proselytism by advertisements" and retained their patronage by "following . . . a natural law of making our supply correspond to the demand."[18] By contrast, the Society Library, catering to the "first families" of the city, rarely advertised and assured subscribers that its reading room was "an agreeable literary resort for such as have the taste and leisure to use its privileges."[19] The histories of these two libraries, however, do not controvert current scholarship on the history of reading, but rather suggest how multifarious and elusive New York's reading publics were. For example, the fact that even later in the century the Mercantile Library, unlike the city's commercial libraries, continued to supply a generous selection of the kinds of tasteful, self-improving books that Catharine Sedgwick recommended to her dear young friends shows that there was a demand for all kinds of reading.[20] Some of the members wanted what Sedgwick dismissed as the "insidious romances of the present day," while others clearly read the "standard authors." Most likely, many read both. As the directors noted in their report for 1883, "the public is a multiple personage."[21]

None of the Mercantile Library's charge ledgers from the later nineteenth century have survived, so we have no record of what readers actually borrowed. Moreover, firsthand accounts of reading from members of either library are rare and often not particularly revealing. A typical entry from George Templeton Strong's diary reports: "Tonight at the Society Library awhile to look through magazines, and to the Union League Club."[22] When readers did write about their reading and their use of libraries, they usually referred to the kinds of authors and texts that Catharine Sedgwick would have considered tasteful and improving. L. Frank Tooker, for example, wrote in his autobiography that he borrowed the Mercantile Library's copy of Horace in order to edit an article for *Century Magazine*.[23] The most interesting and telling account I have found of a library user's experience of an author is from Philip Hone's diary and describes a real-life encounter, Charles Dickens's visit to New York in 1842. Hone, a member of the Society Library and a trustee of the Clinton Hall Association, was on the committee that planned the "Boz ball" and described in detail the "Boz mania" that swept the city. For example, Catharine Sedgwick and a group of her friends crashed the male-only Boz dinner; they slipped in and observed the festivities from the back of the stage on which the after-dinner speeches were delivered.[24] New York's reading publics were crazy for Dickens not because he was tasteful, a standard author, but because he was a supremely entertaining writer.

This is not to say that some members of a nascent middle class did not use taste, high culture as a means of forging a distinctive, exclusive identity. But for many readers, I think, the standard was more permissive, less prescriptive. There was a large reading public that read a range of works that fell somewhere between the *Odes* of Horace and the insidious romances that Sedgwick warned against in *Means and Ends*. They wanted to be amused in a respectable manner—and what helped determine respectability for this broad, middling reading public was more often public opinion than the opinions of cultural authorities. The Mercantile Library sought to provide (among other classes of reading) the newest, the most popular titles, "just those books which are most talked of and that everyone is supposed to have read."[25] The Boz mania that Philip Hone described in his diary was driven in part by the conspicuous consumption of current fiction to claim a kind of identity, to show that one was smart, in style, fashionable.

The Mercantile Library Association's promise to supply the most talked-of titles raises two critical, related questions. Elizabeth Long and other historians have explored the social nature of reading, the power of books to create communities of readers. For example, in *Means and Ends*, Catharine Sedgwick advised young girls to "make your reading a social blessing by communicating liberally" with family and friends.[26] To what extent did New York's public libraries foster or constitute such reading communities? In the case of the Mercantile Library, there is certainly some evidence to support this. For instance, an illustration entitled "Saturday Night," which accompanied an article on the Library in *Scribner's Monthly* in 1871, shows a reading room crowded with groups of readers socializing over texts.[27] On the other hand, later in the century both the Mercantile Library and the Society Library delivered books to members' homes, which must have constrained the sociability of reading. As shared collections of reading, all of New York's public libraries served as reading communities. But there is unfortunately little surviving evidence that sheds light on the nature, depth, and functions of those communities.

A more complex and interesting question is the role that public libraries played in constructing "interpretive communities." According to Janice Radway, these are broader, more diffuse "collections of people who, by virtue of a common social position and demographic character, unconsciously share certain assumptions about reading as well as preferences for reading material."[28] Since these interpretive communities are, by their nature, amorphous, ill defined, it is inherently difficult to determine

Saturday night at the Mercantile Library (*Scribner's*, February 1871)

and document how they function and are constituted. Nonetheless, New York's public libraries, by providing books that everyone in a given community was supposed to have read, certainly provided an infrastructure that supported them. In fact, the Mercantile Library, with its extensive, aggressive advertising and its consumer-driven business plan, not only catered to but also helped to form an interpretive community. Its "system of management" fostered a middling reading public that shared a preference for works of popular fiction that were entertaining, well written and well plotted, and, above all, current. As the directors' remarked in their annual report for 1904, there was "always a feverish demand for something newer . . . than the newest."[29]

A careful reading of the Society Library's surviving records shows that it followed an essentially identical business plan. Like the Mercantile Library, it too purchased and circulated what the annual report for 1858 termed the "novelties of the day." As an institution that catered to the city's first families, however, the trustees insisted that its members were all "persons of refinement and culture" and therefore read only the finest, the most refined literature.[30] This seems similar to those members of the middle class who used good books, a reputation for tasteful consumption, to forge an exclusive middle-class identity. There was, however, a critical difference. For the middle class, refinement was something one earned. One became cultured by, among other things, reading the prescribed books that cultural authorities deemed standard, edifying. For the subscribers of the Society Library, culture was an entitlement, a birthright of the first families. One inherited one's culture in the same way that one inherited one's social position. The fiction that the Library circulated only the finest authors was an essential element of Knickerbocker identity.

> The happiest epoch of a young girl's life is the daydreams she has of the lover who shall come to her some day, and the roseate future stretching away beyond. I should not like to destroy those girlish fantasies.
>
> Laura Jean Libbey, *That Pretty Young Girl* (1889)

This third New York writer, Laura Jean Libbey, was the antithesis of a standard author. She was a dime novelist. Arbiters of culture considered her books, written for adolescent girls, especially harmful, not simply because they were poorly written, but because they presented a "false view of life."[31] Libbey's plots seldom varied. Typically, a pretty young girl, the titular heroine, through some tragic reversal of fortune, finds herself alone and defenseless in the world. But through a combination of virtue and pluck, and often with the aid of a handsome hero, she foils a wicked seducer and lives happily ever after, usually married to the true-hearted hero. Typical plot devices include duels, druggings, kidnappings, and being buried alive. What did vary somewhat was the socioeconomic status of the heroine. In some stories she was a plucky heiress (*The Silver King's Daughter, or The Startling Secret of the Old Mine*) and in others she was a plucky working-class adolescent (*Leonie Locke, or The Romance of a Beautiful New York Working Girl*).[32] Libbey never wrote a best seller, but she was remarkably prolific and extremely popular. From 1883 to 1903 she wrote more than eighty novels, and total sales at her death in 1924 were estimated at between ten to fifteen million copies. A review of *That Pretty Young Girl* in the *Catholic World* began: "Miss Laura Jean Libbey is so absurd when considered as a novelist, that nothing but her vogue could excuse mention of her last preposterously silly story."[33]

Contemporary arbiters of culture (and some book historians as well) tended to classify fiction by class. They presumed that dime novels and the story papers were read only by the uncultured, tasteless masses. The *Catholic World*'s review of *That Pretty Young Girl*, for example, held that "books like [these are] pabulum for the multitude," consumed by girls "standing behind counters," rather than the middle- and upper-class women on the other side of the shop counter. Arthur Bostwick, in an address delivered before the American Library Association on the "Uses of Fiction," observed that "we are disconcerted and the effect is depressing" when a "tastefully dressed woman [is] reading, we shall say, Laura Jean Libbey." But he claimed that this merely showed that "our masses are moving upward and progress along the more material lines is often more rapid than in matters of the intellect."[34] There is ample evidence, however, that dime novels had no class, yet they were read avidly by all classes. A reviewer in the *New York Times* of *Miss Middleton's Lover*, one of Libbey's more popular titles, wrote that "the number of horrors that she contrives to introduce into one volume is really exceedingly credible to her powers of compression," and added that "of course it pleases the clubmen." Although it is not clear whether the New York Society Library collected "Laura Jean Libbeys," it did provide a generous selection of, for example, The Duchess (Margaret Wolfe Hungerford), another very popular dime novelist of the period.[35]

Conversely, there also is ample evidence that many of the city's working-class readers read the kinds of books of which Arthur Bostwick and the trustees of the New York Free Circulating Library would have approved. In the late nineteenth and early twentieth centuries, middle- and upper-class reformers were especially concerned with assimilating and acculturating new immigrants. In part as a result of the Americanization movement, we have firsthand descriptions not just of their experiences of, for example, emigration and work, but also of reading. These accounts show that especially the children of newcomers were often passionate about books and the libraries that provided them for free. Melech Epstein wrote in an autobiographical sketch of the "serious young immigrants who filled the evening classes and crowded the libraries . . . eager to read." But for young people like Epstein, these first encounters with print meant much more than simply adopting the middle-class values espoused by the Americanization movement. Reading represented freedom, limitless possibilities, the opportunity to forge a new identity in a new land. For Sophie Ruskay, "books, avidly devoured, were more than food to us. They stimulated our dreams and enlarged our world. . . . The library was the most wonderful place in the world."[36]

Reading could be used to fashion multiple identities, identities that may have been alien, even threatening to elite Protestants in the Americanization movement. Rose Pastor was a Jew and a socialist. She wrote an English-language advice column, "Just Between Ourselves Girls," for the *Yiddisches Tageblatt*, a Yiddish daily newspaper. For her, libraries were both a means of nurturing "a profounder respect for Judaism" and promoting self-improvement more generally, of rising within, not out of the working class. In July 1903, Pastor wrote, "With our free circulating libraries what excuse is there other than ignorance for any girl who reads the crazy phantasies from the imbecile brains of Laura Jean Libbey, The Duchess, and others of their ilk! . . . I appeal to you—if you read those books—stop! stop!"

Elizabeth Hasanovitz loved the New York Public Library's Central Building, the "sacred temple" on Forty-Second Street. She wrote in her autobiography, *One of Them*, that "a worshipping mood often possessed me as I crossed its threshold." But she "hated New York . . . for its many capitalists . . . and if my eye was sometimes disturbed when looking up the front entrance at the carved names, Astor, Lenox, I said to myself, 'Never mind Astor, never mind Lenox, —'t is ours—everybody's!'" Public libraries could be used in a transgressive fashion, in ways that subverted core values upon which middle-class identity was based.[37]

Moreover, readers did not always read in the prescribed manner. Sophie Ruskay, for instance, wrote in her autobiography that the librarian was "happily unaware of the generous number of pages that I hurriedly skimmed—pages of description, long arid stretches that interrupted the more exciting and romantic narrative." Of course, by the time the free circulating libraries were founded, some public librarians had a more permissive attitude toward popular fiction. For example, George Watson Cole, in an address before the American Library Association, reminded his colleagues that "the vast majority of people are bowed down by their cares and burdens, and care more for mental relaxation than instruction." Yet, his "Plea for the Masses" in 1894, an argument in favor of romantic narrative, was essentially very similar to the argument against it in "On the Cause of the Popularity of Novels" in 1807. Popular fiction was seen as escapist, nonproductive reading that provided fantasy, daydreams instead of tasteful, rational amusement.[38]

Historians of reading, however, have recognized that popular fiction can serve a constructive, "rational" purpose. It can, in the words of Barbara Sicherman, furnish "opportunities for self-creation."[39] The *New York Times* reported that as late as 1924 Laura Jean Libbey's romantic narratives "have become Americanization" in "the crowded cities . . . where there are great lumps of population but one remove from Europe."[40] But Libbey's novels did something more essential than promoting the middle-class values espoused by the Americanization movement. Her plucky working-class heroines could instill a sense of self-respect, self-worth for young immigrants who were often looked down upon by those who sought to uplift them. Contrary to the creed of most public librarians, popular fiction was not merely recreational, a private indulgence. By providing reading publics with the means of forging positive, constructive identities, it served a valuable public purpose.

Appendix A: Timeline

June 1698	First consignment of 220 volumes for the Society for the Propagation of the Gospel's New York library arrives from England and is kept in the vestry of Trinity Church.
March 1754	New York Society Library founded.
August 1763	Garrat Noel opens the city's first commercial circulating library.
November 1772	New York Society Library granted a royal charter.
September 1776	British troops occupying Manhattan loot the New York Society Library.
November 1785	General Society of Mechanics and Tradesmen founded.
December 1788	New York Society Library reconstituted after the Revolution.
April 1795	New York Society Library moves to its own building on Nassau Street. The first public library building in the city.
April 1796	New York State passes the first law in the new nation for establishing public libraries.
November 1804	New-York Historical Society founded.
May 1816	American Bible Society founded. Biblical Library established the following January.
July 1816	New York Institution opens in Brideswell. New York City provides free accommodation to the Historical Society and other learned societies.

November 1820	Apprentices' Library of the General Society of Mechanics and Tradesmen opens.
November 1820	Mercantile Library Association of the City of New York founded.
January 1822	New state constitution grants franchise to all adult white males.
December 1824	New York Athenaeum founded.
May 1825	New-York Historical Society advertises the sale of its library. Only a grant from the state government two years later saves the Society from bankruptcy.
October 1825	Erie Canal opens. Key to New York City's commercial supremacy.
November 1830	Mercantile Library Association's Clinton Hall opens on Nassau Street.
May 1831	Common Council evicts the associations affiliated in the New York Institution from Brideswell, including the New-York Historical Society.
September 1832	New York University opens in Clinton Hall.
April 1833	Peterborough, New Hamphire, opens as the first tax-supported library in the United States.
September 1833	First issue of the *New York Sun*. Beginning of the penny press in the United States.
Spring 1838	New-York Historical Society revives, begins to recover from its brush with bankruptcy the previous decade.
May 1838	City of New York taxes the New York Society Library for the first time. The Library successfully appeals on the grounds that it is a public library.
July 1838	New York Society Library merges with the New York Athenaeum.
February 1842	Charles Dickens visits New York. "Boz mania" sweeps the city.

February 1842	Apprentices' Library opens to "pay readers," members of the reading public who are not apprentices or members of the General Society of Mechanics and Tradesmen.
October 1843	Mercantile Library's board rejects a plan to create a "Collegiate Institution" for the city's clerks. Holds that the true "cause of mercantile success" is not "manly virtues, intelligence," but "love of acquisition, craft, and opportunity."
January 1844	Mercantile Library amends its constitution to allow persons not employed as clerks to join the library as "subscribers." Subscribers pay a higher annual subscription and cannot vote or hold office.
January 1849	Classes begin at the Free Academy of the City of New York, later City College, on Lexington Avenue and Twenty-Third Street.
March 1849	City of New York taxes the New York Society Library on the grounds that it is not a public library. The Library appeals and loses in court.
May 1849	Astor Place riot.
July 1849	New Hampshire passes the first law permitting municipalities to levy taxes to support public libraries.
April 1852	New York Young Men's Christian Association founded. A major attraction is a circulating library offering wholesome reading to members.
May 1853	American Bible Society opens its Bible House on Astor Place. By 1859, the Cooper Union, the Astor Library, the Society Library, the Mercantile Library, and the New-York Historical Society are all located on or near Astor Place as well.
June 1853	Board of Education assumes control of schools managed by the Public School Society. Like the free circulating libraries later in the century, the Society was publicly funded and privately managed.

January 1854	Astor Library opens to the reading public.
March 1854	Boston Public Library opens, the first large, tax-supported public library in the United States.
June 1855	General Society of Mechanics and Tradesmen opens its Apprentices' Library to all young men employed in industry.
November 1857	New-York Historical Society Library dedicates its new building on Second Avenue and Eleventh Street.
November 1859	Classes begin at the Cooper Union. It includes a noncirculating library free to all residents.
August 1860	New-York Historical Society board proposes establishing a public library and museum in Central Park "accessible to all classes of the community." The plan fails due to a lack of support among the members.
February 1861	General Society of Mechanics and Tradesmen opens its Apprentices' Library to all young women employed in industry.
November 1866	Mercantile Library Association begins offering home delivery of books for a fee.
November 1869	New York YMCA opens its first building on Twenty-Third Street. Library becomes a noncirculating collection.
1870	Mercantile Library Association has the highest circulation of any library in the United States. Records its highest total membership, nearly 13,000 readers.
January 1870	Lenox Library incorporated.
October 1876	American Library Association founded.
November 1878	New York Free Circulating Library founded.
November 1878	General Society opens its Apprentices' Library to journeymen and all girls, boys, and women "employed at any legitimate business."

1883	Society Library begins delivery of books to members' homes for a fee.
October 1883	Columbia College opens it new library building under the direction of newly appointed Chief Librarian Melvil Dewey.
June 1885	New York Library Club founded by Melvil Dewey and other leading librarians in the city.
January 1886	Adolph Sanger, president of the Board of Aldermen, introduces in the state legislature a bill to create a New York Public Library funded and managed by the City. The bill dies in committee in the face of opposition from the New York Free Circulating Library and the New York Library Club.
July 1886	State legislature passes "An Act to Encourage the Growth of Free Public Libraries." It permits the City of New York to provide funds to privately managed free circulating libraries.
August 1886	Samuel J. Tilden dies and leaves the bulk of his estate to establish a public library in New York City. His will is contested by his heirs, who later receive approximately half of the money intended for the library.
November 1886	Aguilar Free Library incorporates.
January 1887	Columbia opens its School of Library Economy, the world's first library school.
December 1888	Melvil Dewey forced to resign as chief librarian at Columbia. Library school closes.
June 1889	Andrew Carnegie publishes his "Gospel of Wealth" in the *North American Review.*
November 1892	State of New York passes legislation codifying the procedures by which municipalities may establish tax-supported public libraries.
1893	Cathedral Library, founded in 1888, opens to readers of all faiths. Begins receiving an annual appropriation from the City in 1897.

February 1893	Lenox Library reopens after renovations and becomes reasonably accessible to the reading public for the first time since its founding.
April 1895	Arthur Bostwick, an influential proponent of the "modern library idea," appointed chief librarian at the New York Free Circulating Library.
May 1895	Astor and Lenox Libraries and the Tilden Trust combine to create the New York Public Library.
December 1897	City of New York and the New York Public Library contract to build the Central Building on Forty-Second Street and Fifth Avenue.
January 1901	New York Free Circulating Library consolidates with the New York Public Library and becomes the nucleus of the Circulation Department.
May 1901	Andrew Carnegie offers the New York Public Library $5.2 million for branch libraries. By 1904 most of the free circulating libraries are forced to consolidate.
January 1902	Mercantile Library Association ceases to be a mercantile association. All members, not just those employed as clerks, can vote and run for office.
May 1911	New York Public Library's Central Building, the "marble palace for booklovers," opens to the city's reading publics.

Appendix B: New York Libraries, circa 1900

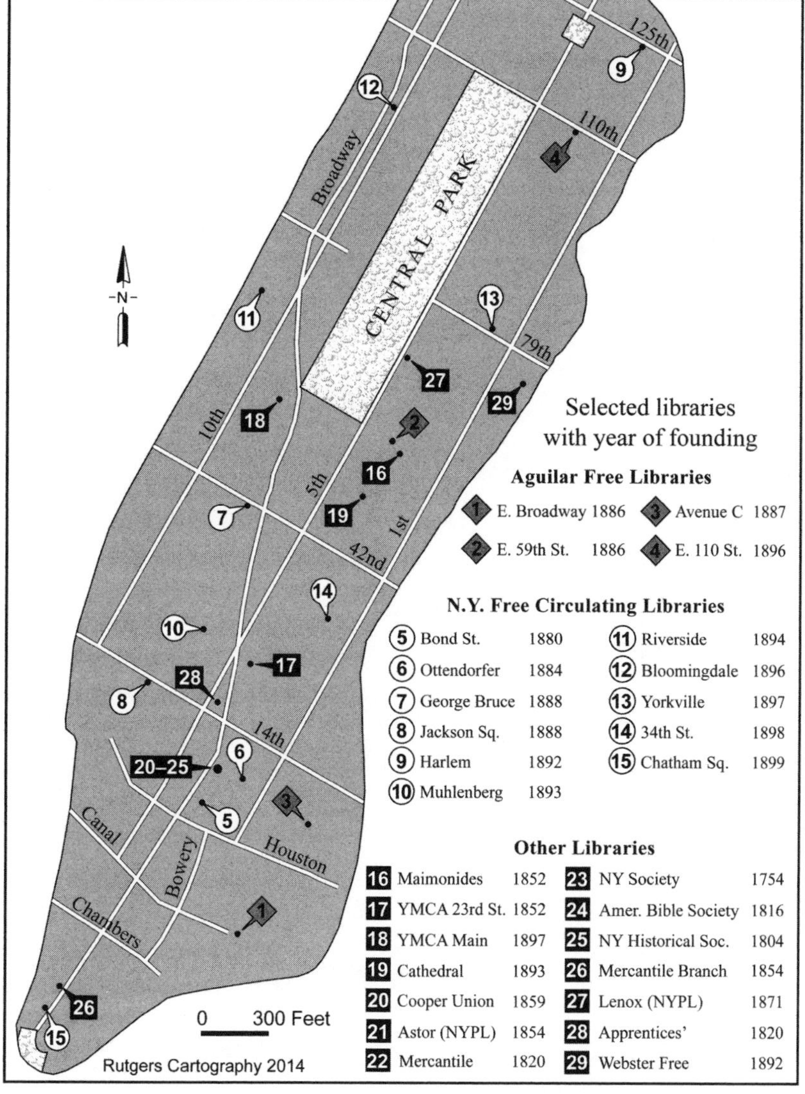

Notes

Introduction: Readers, Libraries, and New York City Before 1911

1. "City's $29,000,000 Library Is Opened," *New York Times*, May 24, 1911; *Library Journal* 36 (May 1911): 217. In 2008, the name was changed to the Stephen A. Schwarzman Building.

2. "Proceedings at the Opening of the New Building of the New York Public Library, Astor, Lenox and Tilden Foundations," *Bulletin of the New York Public Library* 15 (June 1911): 347.

3. Montrose J. Moses, "The Efficiency of the New York Public Library," *The Independent*, May 25, 1911, 1100; David Gray, "A Modern Temple of Education: New York's Public Library," *Harper's Monthly Magazine*, March 1911, 570; *The Dial* 50 (January–June 1911): 431; Hildegarde Hawthorne, "Books and Reading," *St. Nicholas*, September 1911, 1051.

4. "Great Crowds at Library," *New York Times*, June 1, 1911. The quote is from "City's $29,000,000 Library," 3. The *Times* reported that the next day "apparently almost everyone who was in the neighborhood of Fifth Avenue and Fortieth to Forty-Second stopped to inspect the new building." "50,000 Visitors See New Public Library: Attendants Busy Preventing Confusion as They Inspect the Great Building," *New York Times*, May 25, 1911.

5. Greater New York City was established in 1898 by the creation and consolidation of five boroughs: Manhattan, the Bronx, Staten Island, Queens, and Brooklyn. Before consolidation, New York City included only the present-day borough of Manhattan and the south Bronx. The libraries whose histories are explored in this book were all in the city of New York before consolidation.

6. Jesse H. Shera, *Foundations of the Public Library: The Origins of the Public Library Movement in New England, 1629–1855* (Chicago: University of Chicago Press, 1949; repr., n.p.: Shoestring Press, 1965), 156–57. Shera used William F. Poole's definition in the report on public libraries published by the Bureau of Education in 1876: A public library is free, tax-supported, and "managed as a public trust." But he went on to explain that "the meaning of 'public library' varied as the institution evolved under the impact of social and economic changes." Haynes McMullen, *American Libraries Before 1876* (Westport, Conn.: Greenwood Press, 2000), 121, 168. McMullen uses a similar definition but also acknowledges

that the term was defined differently before 1876. Both authors mention only briefly that the definition changed over time and do not explore the significance of these changes. Most other public library historians do not acknowledge or recognize that that the definition changed at all.

7. "Population of the 24 Urban Places, 1790," table 2 in Campbell J. Gibson, *Population of the 100 Largest Cities and Other Urban Places in the United States: 1790 to 1990* (Washington, D.C.: Government Printing Office, 1999), 553. The extensive and very interesting report on New York includes a series of maps showing the growth of the city from 1642 to 1836. One of the maps is for 1782.

8. On patricians and cultural leadership in early republican New York, see Thomas Bender, *New York Intellect: A History of Intellectual Life in New York City, from 1750 to the Beginnings of Our Own Time* (New York: Knopf, 1987), 48–62.

9. Austin Baxter Keep, *History of the New York Society Library, with an Introductory Chapter on Libraries in Colonial New York, 1698–1776* (New York: New York Society Library, 1908), 43–63. The quote is at page 54.

10. An Act to Incorporate Such Persons as May Associate for the Purpose of Procuring and Erecting Public Libraries in this State, The Revised Statutes of the State of New York, as Altered by Subsequent Legislation, ch. 18, tit. 9 (Gould, Banks 1852) (passed April 1, 1796). The type of libraries incorporated under the terms of this Act were often referred to as "social libraries." An individual purchased stock, a "share," in the society and paid an annual subscription to borrow books. Shares could be sold or inherited just like stock in any corporation. As noted previously, this was the first law in the United States governing the establishment of public libraries. Shera, *Foundations of the Public Library*, 62.

11. Charles C. Jewett, *Notices of Public Libraries in the United States* (Washington, D.C.: Printed for the House of Representatives, 1851), 84–97. This report was an appendix to the Smithsonian's annual report to Congress in 1850.

12. Carl F. Kaestle, *The Evolution of an Urban School System: New York City, 1750–1850* (Cambridge, Mass.: Harvard University Press, 1973), 80–88. The association was incorporated as the Free School Society. The name was changed to the Public School Society in 1825, the same year in which schools managed by religious denominations ceased receiving public funds. The history of the Public School Society parallels in some ways the history of the free circulating libraries discussed later. Both were supported with public funds but were managed by private boards until they became public institutions as the term is understood today.

13. The royal charter is reprinted in Keep, *History of the New York Society Library*, 538–47. The charter was not granted until 1772.

14. New York Society Library, *A Catalogue of the Books Belonging to the New-York Society Library* (New York: H. Gaine, 1758).

15. A Subscriber to the New-York Society Library, "On the Utility of Public Libraries," *New-York Magazine; or, Literary Repository*, June 1791, 307–9.

16. “Mercantile Library Association,” *The Merchants' Magazine and Commercial Review*, July 1839, 78.

17. Milton M. Klein, ed., *The Independent Reflector or Weekly Essays on Sundry Important Subjects More Particularly Adapted to the Province of New-York by William Livingston and Others* (Cambridge, Mass.: Harvard University Press, 1963), 220. This essay, “Of Patriotism,” was written in 1753, a year before the New York Society Library was founded, but it is a clear statement of the views of its founders. *The Independent Reflector* was a weekly periodical that was published largely as a result of the controversy that surrounded the establishment of Columbia College. As will be seen below, the founding of the library was directly related to the founding of the college.

18. The 1822 constitution abolished the requirement that voters own property; adult white males could vote if they paid taxes, served in the militia, or helped maintain public roads. All restrictions for whites were dropped in a constitutional amendment in 1826. The property requirement was retained for blacks, which effectively disenfranchised practically all freedmen in New York City. Edwin G. Burrows and Mike Wallace, *Gotham: A History of New York City to 1898* (New York: Oxford University Press, 1999), 512–14.

19. Barbara Shupe, Janet Steins, and Jyoti Pandit, *New York State Population, 1790–1980: A Compilation of Federal Census Data* (New York: Neal-Schuman, 1987), 200–2; “Nativity of the Population for Urban Places Ever Among the 50 Largest Urban Places Since 1870: 1850 to 1990,” table 22 in Campbell J. Gibson and Emily Lennon, *Historical Census Statistics on the Foreign-born Population of the United States: 1850–1990* (Washington, D.C.: U.S. Bureau of the Census, 1999), www.census.gov/population/www/documentation/twps0029/twps0029.html.

20. Ronald J. Zboray, *A Fictive People: Antebellum Economic Development and the American Reading Public* (New York: Oxford University Press, 1993), 9–11, 31, 65; John Tebbel, *A History of Book Publishing in the United States, Vol. 1: The Creation of an Industry, 1630–1865* (New York: R. R. Bowker, 1972), 262–364.

21. “The Thinker: Fictitious Reading,” *New York Evangelist*, July 10, 1841, 112. This article is a review of and excerpt from a lecture on “Popular Reading” delivered before the Mercantile Library Association.

22. New-York Lyceum (1840). Available in Readex American Broadsides, WorldCat accession no. 438040095. The Lyceum was founded in 1838 to establish a public library with a subscription “rate sufficiently low to meet the necessities of the great majority.” The reference to excitable French lunatics is part of a long quote from Horace Mann's third annual report to the Massachusetts Board of Education (1840).

23. This brief article is quoted in its entirety in “Libraries,” *Philadelphia Album and Ladies' Literary Port Folio*, September 20, 1826, 6. See also David Kaser, *Books*

for a Sixpence: The Circulating Library in America (Pittsburgh: Beta Phi Mu, 1980).

24. On women and recreational reading, see, for example, Elizabeth Long, *Book Clubs: Women and the Uses of Reading in Everyday Life* (Chicago: University of Chicago Press, 2003), especially 4–7; and Barbara Sicherman, "Ideologies and Practices of Reading," in *A History of the Book in America, Vol. 3, The Industrial Book, 1840–1880*, ed. Scott E. Jasper, Jeffrey D. Groves, Stephen W. Nissenbaum, and Michael Winship (Chapel Hill: University of North Caroline Press, 2007), 289.

25. Mercantile Library Association, *Thirtieth Annual Report of the Board of Direction of the Mercantile Library Association* (New York: Mercantile Library Association, 1851), 16; Zboray, *A Fictive People*, 156–210.

26. On the beginnings of penny newspapers in New York City, see William Huntzicker, *The Popular Press: 1833–1865* (Westport, Conn.: Greenwood Press, 1999), 19–34. Newspapers during this period frequently printed serialized fiction. The "paperback revolution" began in New York City in 1839. Tebbel, *A History of Book Publishing, Vol. 1*, 242–51.

27. New York Society Library, *Annual Report of the Trustees of the New York Society Library* (New York: New York Society Library, 1857), 2.

28. [Defendant's, the City of New York's, answer to plaintiff's, the Society Library's, complaint], June 25, 1851; [Plaintiff's reply to Defendant's answer to complaint], October 13, 1851; both part of New York Superior Court, "Trustees of the New York Society Library against The Mayor, Alderman, and Commonalty of the City of New York, Judgment Roll," New York County Clerk, Division of Old Records. For a summary of this complex legal dispute, see Keep, *History of the New York Society Library*, 422–26. It began in 1849 and the Library finally paid the tax in 1856. Keep's claim that the Superior Court held that "this institution was a public library" yet dismissed the complaint on a technicality is not true. After the court case, the Board of Councilmen voted to remit the tax, but the Board of Aldermen sided with the city. Legal jargon aside, the case revolved around the question of whether the Library was a public institution and therefore tax exempt. The city taxed the Library in 1838, 1839, 1849, 1850, and 1887 (507). The Library appealed each time, and this was the only instance it was required to pay the assessment.

29. The phrase "free of expense to persons resorting thereto" appears both in Astor's will and in the act of incorporation. The New York Public Library, Astor, Lenox and Tilden Foundations, *Book of Charters, Wills, Deeds and Other Official Documents* (New York: New York Public Library, 1905), 4, 11. U.S. Bureau of Education, *Public Libraries in the United States of America: Their History, Condition and Management*, Special Report, Pt. 1 (Washington: U.S. Government Printing Office, 1876), 762–72; see also Harry Miller Lydenberg, *History of The New York Public Library, Astor, Lenox and Tilden Foundations* (New York: New

York Public Library, 1923), 1–94. The opening of the Boston Public Library, also in 1854, was another reason for the shift in the popular conception of a public library. It was the first extensive, tax-supported library in the country.

30. Sydney Ditzion, *Arsenals of a Democratic Culture: A Social History of the American Public Library Movement in New England and the Middle States from 1850 to 1900* (Chicago: American Library Association, 1947), 142–64. Astor's gift was different from other instances of big philanthropy in one important respect. Peter Cooper, for example, bequeathed his entire fortune to the Cooper Union. Astor's $400,000 gift for the New York Public Library was a small part of an immense fortune estimated at more than $20,000,000. It was his only major public bequest.

31. Astor Library, *Annual Report of the Trustees of the Astor Library* (New York: Astor Library, 1854), 28.

32. "Dr. Cogswell and the Astor Library," *New York Times*, September 22, 1858; "The Astor Stumbling-Block," *The Critic*, April 22, 1882, 114.

33. Joseph Green Cogswell, "Resources of the Astor Library," *New York Times*, September 22, 1858. "Silly clamor" referred to complaints that there was not a complete catalog of the library, but it reflects Cogswell's attitude toward the public generally. Astor Library, *Annual Report* (1854), 28. In the annual report, Cogswell also claimed that the library served the public because it was open to teachers in the public schools.

34. Shupe, Steins, and Pandit, *New York State Population, 1790–1980*, 200; Bender, *New York Intellect*, 171.

35. Quoted in Sven Beckert, *Monied Metropolis: New York City and the Consolidation of the American Bourgeoisie, 1850–1896* (Cambridge: Cambridge University Press, 2001), 270. On "*the* Mrs. Astor," see, for example, Eric Homberger, *Mrs. Astor's New York: Money and Social Power in Gilded Age New York* (New Haven, Conn.: Yale University Press, 2002); and Greg King, *A Season of Splendor: The Court of Mrs. Astor in Gilded Age New York* (Hoboken, N.J.: John Wiley & Sons, 2009).

36. Beckert, *Monied Metropolis*, 267–71; Bender, *New York Intellect*, 172. Raymond Williams regarded *culture* as "one of the two or three most complicated words in the English language." Williams, *Keywords: A Vocabulary of Culture and Society*, rev. ed. (New York: Oxford University Press, 1983), 87–93, especially 90–91. On the "class-linked model of culture," see Sicherman, "Ideologies and Practices of Reading," 287, 295. Sicherman argues this is just one of four "models of reading" during the middle to later nineteenth century (283–88) and adds fiction as an "anti-model" (288–92).

37. Bender, *New York Intellect*, 265–93.

38. "The Poor Taste of the Rich: The Bradley-Martin House," *House Beautiful*, December 1904, 20–23; "Poor Taste of the Rich: House of Mr. A. C. Burrage," *House Beautiful*, February 1905, 21.

39. Lydenberg, *New York Public Library*, 216–18. This includes the text of the law.

40. The largest of the free circulating libraries, the New York Free Circulating Library, was founded in 1879, and its supporters were largely responsible for the passage of the Library Law of 1886. Before it was absorbed by the New York Public Library in 1901, it managed eleven branch libraries in Manhattan. Lydenberg devotes a chapter to each of the larger free circulating libraries. Although these libraries were free to all, the Free Circulating Library was managed by Protestants, the Aguilar Free Library by Jews and the Cathedral Library Association by the Catholic Church. In all, the City funded fourteen separate private library associations in 1900. Lydenberg, *New York Public Library*, 400, 416. "Tammany bacillus" is from John Bigelow Diary, December 2, 1898, John Bigelow Papers, New York Public Library Archives and Manuscripts Division.

41. For a succinct contemporary definition of the public library idea, see New York Free Circulating Library, *Twenty-First and Final Report of the New York Free Circulating Library, With a Sketch of Its History* (New York: New York Free Circulating Library, 1900), 23–24.

42. Dee Garrison, *Apostles of Culture: The Public Librarian and American Society, 1876–1920* (New York: Free Press, 1979; repr., Madison: University of Wisconsin Press, 2003), 173–85. On the role of women in the public library movement, see Paula D. Watson, "Founding Mothers: The Contribution of Women's Organizations to Public Library Development on in the United States," *Library Quarterly* 64 (July 1994): 233–71.

43. Lyle H. Wright, *American Fiction, 1774–1850: A Contribution Toward a Bibliography*, 2d rev. ed. (San Marino, Calif.: Huntington Library, 1969), 365–85. Lyle H. Wright, *American Fiction, 1876–1900: A Contribution Toward a Bibliography* (San Marino, Calif.: Huntington Library, 1966), 617–83. This includes only fiction by American authors and does not include the substantial number of pirated editions of British novels. See also John Tebbel, *A History of Book Publishing in the United States, Volume II: The Expansion of an Industry, 1865–1919* (New York: Bowker, 1975), 675–708, for titles in all categories from 1880 through 1918.

44. For example, a national survey of public libraries in 1893 conducted by the head librarian of the New York Free Circulating Library estimated that the average circulation of fiction was 56 percent. Ellen Coe, "Fiction," *Library Journal* 18 (July 1893): 250–51.

45. Williams, *Keywords*, 183–88. Like culture, literature is a very complex word. One reason is that, in certain contexts, it retains its older, broader meaning. For example, articles in the sciences or social sciences often include a "review of the literature."

46. The annual reports of the free circulating libraries often noted approvingly that their readers borrowed history, science, and other works of nonfiction. But

more often they proudly referred to the increased circulation of Scott, Dickens, and the other "standard authors." Neither the free circulating libraries nor the Mercantile Library offered any real proof of an improvement in the kinds of books circulated.

47. Both quotes are from Ellen M. Coe, "Common Novels in Public Libraries," *Library Journal* 19 (Conference Proceedings 1894): 23–24.

48. New York Free Circulating Library, *Library Meeting at the Union League Club, Jan. 20, 1882*, 3–4. This was appended to New York Free Circulating Library, *Third Annual Report* (New York: New York Free Circulating Library, 1882). The speaker was John Hall, pastor of the Fifth Avenue Presbyterian Church. Hall also held that a "society of regulated liberty" would help keep the wealthy "safe from crime and violence." Gilded Age reform was a mix of fear and optimism. Hall argued for the provision of fiction in the Free Circulating Library. "The imagination is a fact of human nature. . . . What we want is to make people seek the first-rate."

49. Max Cohen, "The Librarian an Educator, and not a Cheap-John," *Library Journal* 13 (December 1888): 366–67. A "cheap john" was a purveyor of shoddy merchandise. This was Cohen's response to an article the previous month by Jacob Schwartz of the Apprentices' Library urging his colleagues to adopt "business methods" in managing public libraries. Cohen was especially "mortified" that Schwartz advised "buy[ing] only what your customers want." Jacob Schwartz, "Business Methods in Libraries," *Library Journal* 13 (November 1888): 334. In 1888, most public librarians certainly sided with Cohen. New York Free Circulating Library, *First Annual Report of the New York Free Circulating Library* (New York: New York Free Circulating Library, 1880), 19; Aguilar Free Library Society, *First Annual Report of the Aguilar Free Library Society* (New York: Aguilar Free Library Society, 1889), 6.

50. New York Free Circulating Library, *Twenty-First and Final Report of the New York Free Circulating Library, With a Sketch of Its History* (New York: New York Free Circulating Library, 1900), 23. The report is dated 1900, but it was published in February 1901, immediately after the consolidation with the New York Public Library.

51. The reference to "pushing" libraries is from a discussion of "Catalogs and Methods of Making the Library Known" at the New York Library Club. "New York Library Club," *Library Journal* 17 (March 1892): 99. Arthur E. Bostwick, *The American Public Library* (New York: D. Appleton & Co., 1910), 3–4. "New York Library Club," *Library Journal* 25 (March 1900): 131.

52. Act to Revise and Consolidate the Laws Relating to the University, ch. 378, secs. 38, 42, 1895 N.Y. Laws 783, 784. The entire act is reprinted in New York State Library, *New Library Law of the State of New York* (Albany: New York State Library, 1892).

53. Carnegie's agreements with the City are reprinted in New York Public Library, *Book of Charters*, 238–45. Originally, there were to be forty-two branches,

but that was later increased to fifty. The clause requiring municipal funding is found on page 242. Around the time of the consolidation of Greater New York, Brooklyn and Queens had already established separate public libraries and Carnegie, in the same agreements, made separate gifts to those systems. This is why there are now three public libraries in New York City. Phyllis Dain, *The New York Public Library: A History of Its Founding and Early Years* (New York: New York Public Library, 1972), 223–28.

54. New York Public Library, *Facts for the Public* (New York: New York Public Library, 1911), 3. Lydenberg, *New York Public Library*, 416.

55. Andrew Carnegie, "Best Uses of Wealth," in *Miscellaneous Writings of Andrew Carnegie*, ed. Burton J. Hendrick (Freeport, N.Y.: Books for Libraries Press; repr., New York: Doubleday & Co., 1933), 2:211.

56. New York Public Library, *Results Not Shown by Statistics in the Work of the Public Libraries of Greater New York* (New York: New York Public Library, 1910), 6. "I picked up a book in the meat market while a woman wasn't lookin' and saw your sign inside—so I come in."

57. New York Public Library, *Results Not Shown by Statistics*, 5–7, 10. The pamphlet also frequently referred to different religions and ethnicities, again stressing service to a broad reading public. In their final report, the trustees of the New York Free Circulating Library explained that "the idea that this system of circulating libraries is only for the use of the very poor has been superseded by the belief that it is an important adjunct of the city's educational system." Consolidation with the New York Public Library "mark[ed] the progress of the Library from a private charity to a public necessity." New York Free Circulating Library, *Final Report*, 23.

58. New York Public Library, *Results Not Shown by Statistics*, 9, 11. These stories are from the section entitled "The General Effect." The pamphlet also included an entire section entitled "Aid to Those Studying for College Regents, Civil Service, and Promotion Examinations."

59. See, for example, New York Public Library, *Results Not Shown by Statistics*, 4, 6, and especially 8: "A tired little woman said she had read all . . . the standard authors, [but] now she had to work so hard during the day, and had so many worries, that when night came she just wanted a light novel to keep her mind off her troubles."

60. Arthur E. Bostwick, "The Purchase of Current Fiction," in American Library Association, *Twenty-fifth Annual Conference, Niagara Falls, June 22–27, 1903* (Philadelphia: American Library Association, 1903), 31–33. Bostwick also argued that recreational reading could be educational as well. It is clear here that Bostwick's conception of the "public" of the public library was far different from Ellen Coe's. He seemed to equate its readers with the middle class. For example, he held that librarians should develop collections for "the average man or woman of good education and good taste" and that "'the public' is just you and

I and some other fellows." On new public services, see, for example, "New York's Recreation Piers Well Worth Their Cost," *New York Times*, June 25, 1905.

61. During 1910–11, the library spent $308,857 of income from the endowments on the Reference Department in the Central Building, and the City appropriated $678,847 to the Circulation Department for the branches. New York Public Library, *Facts for the Public*, 3.

62. Until 1950 all of the trustees were men. The women who had founded and to a large extent managed the free circulating libraries were marginalized as soon as those libraries were incorporated in the new public institution.

63. John Shaw Billings, "Public Library Systems of Greater New York," *Library Journal* 36 (October 1911): 490.

64. Carleton Bruns Joeckel, *The Government of the American Public Library* (Chicago: University of Chicago Press, 1935), 77–80.

65. Coe, "Common Novels in Public Libraries," 23.

66. On a public library in a rural community, see Christine Pawley, *Reading on the Middle Border: The Culture of Print in Late-Nineteenth Century Osage, Iowa* (Amherst: University of Massachusetts Press, 2001), 61–116.

1. The New York Society Library: Books, Authority, and Publics in Colonial and Early Republican New York

1. John Adams, for example, claimed that he "never understood" what republicanism meant and that "no other man ever did or will." Quoted in Bernard Bailyn, *Ideological Origins of the American Revolution* (Cambridge, Mass.: Harvard University Press, 1967), 283 n. 50.

2. There is a vast literature on and in reaction to the "republican synthesis." The seminal works that laid the foundation for a historiography that stressed the centrality of republicanism in early American history are: Bernard Bailyn, *Ideological Origins of the American Revolution; Gordon S. Wood, The Creation of the American Republic, 1776–1787* (Chapel Hill: University of North Carolina Press, 1969); J. G. A. Pocock, *The Machiavellian Moment: Florentine Political Thought and the Atlantic Republican Tradition* (Princeton: Princeton University Press, 1975). A good example of the scholarship in reaction to the republican synthesis is Joyce Appleby, *Republicanism and Liberalism in the Historical Imagination* (Cambridge, Mass.: Harvard University Press, 1992). A somewhat dated but still very useful of overview is Daniel T. Rodgers, "Republicanism: the Career of a Concept," *Journal of American History* 79 (June 1992): 11–38.

3. On the beginnings of public libraries in the United States, see Jesse H. Shera, *The Foundations of the Public Library: The Origins of the Public Library Movement in New England, 1629–1855* (Chicago: University of Chicago Press, 1949), and Sidney H. Ditzion, *Arsenals of a Democratic Culture: A Social History of the American Public Library in New England and the Middle States from 1850 to 1900* (Chicago: American Library Association, 1947). On the founding of the

New York Public Library, see Harry Miller Lydenberg, *History of the New York Public Library: Astor, Lenox and Tilden Foundations* (New York: New York Public Library, 1923). And Phyllis Dain, *The New York Public Library: A History of Its Founding and Early Years* (New York: New York Public Library, 1972).

4. Austin Baxter Keep, *History of the New York Society Library, with an Introductory Chapter on Libraries in Colonial New York, 1698–1776* (New York: De Vinne Press, 1908), 150. This is the official history of the Society Library. It is better than most official institutional histories. Keep footnoted some of his sources and was occasionally, albeit mildly, critical of the library's leadership. The introduction and chapters 1–3, which dealt with the history of the library through the Revolution, were his dissertation in political science for Columbia University.

5. Gordon S. Wood, *The Radicalism of the American Revolution* (New York: Knopf, 1992), 181–82.

6. Charles T. Laugher, *Thomas Bray's Grand Design: Libraries of the Church of England in North America, 1695–1785* (Chicago: American Library Association, 1973), 8–16. See also *The Dictionary of National Biography*, s.v. "Bray, Thomas," by John Henry Overton. To place the Society for Promoting Christian Knowledge in the context of contemporary organizations, see Meyer Reinhold, "The Quest for 'Useful Knowledge' in Eighteenth-Century America," *Proceedings of the American Philosophical Society* 119 (April 1975): 108–32.

7. In New York, the establishment of the church meant only that the colonists were taxed to support it. There are no reliable statistics for the various denominations during this period. One of the founders of the Society Library, William Livingston, estimated that during the period in which the library was founded, one in ten persons in the colony was Anglican. Livingston, a Presbyterian, may have exaggerated somewhat, but the Anglicans were certainly a small minority. Milton M. Klein, ed., *The Independent Reflector or Weekly Essays on Sundry Important Subjects More Particularly adapted to the Province of New-York By William Livingston and Others* (Cambridge, Mass.: Harvard University Press, 1963), 183 n. 2.

8. Thomas Bray, *Bibliotheca Parochialis: Or, a Scheme of such Theological Heads both General and Particular, as Are More Peculiarly Requisite to be Well Studied by Every Pastor of a Parish, Together with A Catalogue of Books which May be Read upon each of those Points, Part I* (London: E. Holt, 1697), reprinted in *Rev. Thomas Bray: His Life and Selected Works Relating to Maryland*, ed. Bernard C. Steiner (New York: Arno Press, 1972; repr., Baltimore: Maryland Historical Society, 1901), 191–208. The extensive catalog Bray outlined in part I and promised to publish as part II was never compiled. However, many of the catalogs of the actual parochial libraries sent to the North American parishes have survived. A number of these are reproduced in Laugher, *Bray's Grand*

Design, 92–101. Laugher claims that in practice books in the parochial libraries often circulated. Laugher, *Bray's Grand Design*, 47.

9. Bray's ideas for the lending libraries are explained most fully in Thomas Bray, *Several Circular Letters to the Clergy of Maryland, Subsequent to Their Late Visitation, to Enforce Such Resolutions as Were Taken Therein* (London: William Downing, 1701), reprinted in *Rev. Thomas Bray*, 123–55.

10. Thomas Bray, *Apostolick Charity, Its Nature and Excellence Considered, in a Discourse . . . Preached at St. Paul's, Decemb. 19 1697 . . .* (London: W. Downing, 1698), reprinted in *Rev. Thomas Bray*, 76. This includes a summary of the libraries founded in North America up to that time. *Rev. Thomas Bray*, 73–76.

11. For a history of the Bray library in New York, see Keep, *Society Library*, 8–42. For an overview of Bray's extensive writings on libraries see Bernard C. Steiner, "Rev. Thomas Bray and His American Libraries," *American Historical Review* 2 (October 1896), 59–75. In all, Bray founded five provincial libraries, thirty-eight parochial libraries, and thirty-seven layman's libraries. For a tabular overview, see Laugher, *Bray's Grand Design*, 82–86. Bray's most elaborate description of the library plan is the "prefatory epistle" in Thomas Bray, *Bibliotheca Parochialis* (London: E. Holt, 1697), available online in EEBO–Early English Books Online.

12. Thomas Bray, "*Bibliotheca Americanae Quadripartitae*, or, Catalogues of the Libraries Sent into the Several Provinces Belonging to the Crown of England, in Order to Promote All the Parts of Usefull and Necessary Knowledge Both Divine and Humane," manuscript at the Library of Sion College, London, 2–14. The New York Public Library, Research Division, and the University of California Berkeley Library have microform copies of a handwritten copy. The quote is from page 14. This was probably written around 1701 or after. The New York catalog is not one of the catalogs included.

13. Trinity Church, Vestry Minutes, April 4, 1698. Word-processed transcription courtesy of the Trinity Church Archives. For the other provincial libraries, see Laugher, *Bray's Grand Design*, 82–83.

14. Bray, "*Bibliothecae Americanae*," 14. Thomas Bray, *An Essay Towards Promoting All Necessary and Useful Knowledge, Both Divine and Human, In All the Parts of His Majesty's Dominions, Both at Home and Abroad* (London: E. Holt, 1697), reprinted in *Rev. Thomas Bray*, 53.

15. On the SPG bookplate, see John Chalmers, "The Cover," *Journal of Library History* 18 (Fall 1983): 473–75.

16. A facsimile of the bookplate is in Keep, *Society Library*, 100. Instructions for labeling the books are in Bray, "Bibliotheca Americanae."

17. Vestry Minutes, April 4, 1698. Laugher, *Bray's Grand Design*, 34. Bray himself was ambiguous at times on this important point. In "*Bibliotheca Americanae*," under "Directions For the Use . . . of the Library . . . [in] New York"

he wrote that "the Chief Design of this Library is for the use of the Church of England Minister belonging to the . . . City." Bray, "*Bibliotheca Americanae*," n.p.

18. Keep, *Society Library*, 35. For other libraries in New York in the early eighteenth century, see Keep, *Society Library*, 43–117.

19. Bailyn, *Ideological Origins of the American Revolution*, xi. For examples see, Bernard Bailyn, ed., *Pamphlets of the American Revolution* (Cambridge, Mass.: Belknap Press of Harvard University, 1965).

20. The Zenger case set a landmark precedent for freedom of the press in the United States. See for example, William Lowell Putnam, *John Peter Zenger and the Fundamental Freedom* (Jefferson, N.C.: McFarland & Co., 1997); David Paul Nord, "The Authority of Truth: Religion and the John Peter Zenger Case," *Journalism Quarterly* 62 (Summer 1985): 227–35; and Cathy Covert, "'Passion Is Ye Prevailing Motive': the Feud Behind the Zenger Case," *Journalism Quarterly* 50 (Spring 1973): 3–10. James Alexander's account of the trial has been widely reprinted. For example, James Alexander, *A Brief Narrative of the Case and Trial of John Peter Zenger, Printer of the New York Weekly Journal*, ed. Stanley Nider Katz (Cambridge, Mass.: Belknap Press of Harvard University Press, 1972).

21. Edwin G. Burrows and Mike Wallace, *Gotham: A History of New York City to 1898* (New York: Oxford University Press, 1999), 179. Richard M. Ketchum, *Divided Loyalties: How the American Revolution Came to New York* (New York: Henry Holt & Co., 2002), 56–58. My brief description overly simplifies the often-byzantine politics of the colony during this period. The key is to think of the De Lancey and Livingston factions not as political parties, but as the loci of shifting alliances. For a more detailed history of the Livingstons in New York politics, see Milton M. Klein, *The American Whig: William Livingston of New York*, rev. ed. (New York: Garland, 1993), 181–228.

22. Dorothy Rita Dillon, *The New York Triumvirate: A Study of the Legal and Political Careers of William Livingston, John Morin Scott, and William Smith, Jr.* (New York: Columbia University Press, 1949). The quotes are from the Reverend Samuel Johnson, the president of King's College, quoted in William Smith, Jr., *Historical Memoirs from 16 March 1763 to 9 July 1776 of William Smith*, ed. William H. W. Sabine (New York: New York Times and the Arno Press, 1956), 1:3; and an anonymous newspaper correspondent quoted in Dillon, *New York Triumvirate*, 47. See also, Thomas Bender, *New York Intellect: A History of Intellectual Life in New York City, from 1750 to the Beginnings of Our Own Times* (New York: Knopf, 1987), 14–18.

23. Quoted in Klein, *American Whig*, 187.

24. *Independent Reflector*, 18. William Smith, Jr., *History of the Province of New-York*, ed. Michael Kammen (Cambridge, Mass.: Harvard University Press, 1972), 1: xxiii. Rheinhold, "Quest for 'Useful Knowledge,'" 114. Among the Society's members were James Alexander and William Smith, Sr.

25. For the early history of Kings College, see David C. Humphrey, *From Kings College to Columbia, 1746–1800* (New York: Columbia University Press, 1976); and Horace Coon, *Columbia: Colossus on the Hudson* (New York: Dutton, 1946), 36–57.

26. Board of King's College to James De Lancey, Lt. Governor, 5 May 1754, in William Smith, "Memoirs, vol. 2, ~1753, Oct. 5 ~1760, Dec. ~1777, May 5–July 5." William Smith Papers, ca. 1631–1883, bulk (1770–1780), New York Public Library, Manuscripts and Archives Division. Parts of Smith's memoirs, which include copies or transcripts of various public documents, were published in 1956. See note 19. See also William Smith Jr., *Historical Memoirs from 26 August 1778 to 12 November 1783 of William Smith*, ed. William H. W. Sabine (New York: New York Times and the Arno Press, 1956).

27. Bender, *New York Intellect*, 17–25. Bender stresses that "much that was said in connection with the controversy over the founding of King's College was said as well in the Society Library elections." Bender, *New York Intellect*, 19.

28. Milton M. Klein, the editor of 1963 edition of the *Independent Reflector*, notes in an appendix eleven specific passages that obviously paraphrase the *Independent Whig*. *Independent Reflector*, 450–52. An essay on "The Vanity of Birth and Titles" quotes an extensive passage directly from the *Independent Whig*. *Independent Reflector*, 365.

29. Ibid., 57.

30. The *Independent Reflector* advised, for example, that the incorporating act should include a provision guaranteeing free access to the library for all students. Ibid., 203.

31. Ibid., 41–42, 442.

32. This issue set forth the Independent Reflector's "creed." Ibid., 393. This particular article of faith was evidently a paraphrase of the *Independent Whig*. Ibid., 452.

33. Ibid., 208, 359.

34. Gordon Wood has described this as a critical shift to "new . . . ideals of gentility." Wood, *Radicalism of the American Revolution*, 194–97.

35. *Independent Reflector*, 193,175, 172. Klein includes an appendix that attempts to identify the authors of the individual essays, all of which were simply signed with a pseudonymous initial. He concludes that well over half of the total were written by Livingston, the acknowledged leader of the triumvirate; that "the journal was essentially his in design and execution." A small number of the essays were written by persons other than Livingston, Scott, and Smith. Ibid., 446–49.

36. Smith, *History of New York*, 1:209–10, 2:150. The private friends included Livingston's brother Philip, his cousin Robert, and William Alexander, the son of James Alexander.

37. On the early history of the Library Company, founded in 1731, see James Green, "Subscription Libraries and Commercial Circulating Libraries in Colonial Philadelphia and New York," in eds. Thomas Augst and Kenneth Carpenter, *Institutions of Reading: The Social Life of Libraries in the United States* (Amherst: University of Massachusetts Press, 2007), 53–71. See also Keep, *Society Library*, 149–50 and especially 150 n. 2, which lists "proprietary libraries" founded in the other colonies. For the evolution of public libraries during the colonial period, see Shera, *Foundations of the Public Library*, 30–40, 51–53.

38. The "Articles" are reprinted in Keep, *Society Library*, 535–37. The Articles remained in force into the twentieth century.

39. Smith, *History of New York*, 2:150.

40. [William Livingston], "Watchtower, No. XXV," *New-York Mercury*, May 12, 1755. The Watchtower was a regular column the triumvirate began after the De Lancey faction pressured the printer of the *Independent Reflector* into refusing to print it. *Independent Reflector*, 40–41. This contribution was almost certainly written by Livingston. It is signed with the same initial he used in the *Independent Reflector*, B., and shows his inimitable tact, restraint, and discretion. The dirty schemer was probably Justice John Chambers of the Supreme Court. Dillon, *Triumvirate*, 41. "Defeats of High-Church on the Subject of the College" is rather an exaggeration. *Independent Reflector*, 44–45.

41. Keep, *Society Library*, 554–60, lists chronologically all of the trustees who served through 1908. I was able to determine the political affiliations of most of the trustees either in Keep's history or in Appendix B of Smith, *History of New York*, a biographical directory compiled by the editor. It is possible, given the neat balance between the two factions, that some sort of informal agreement had been reached, although there is no surviving evidence for this.

42. Keep, *Society Library*, 152, 166. Page 168 is a facsimile of the first bookplate. In all six Livingstons served on the board during the colonial period.

43. De Lancey was only elected twice, in 1754 and 1756. It is possible that he was too distracted by the French and Indian War to seek a charter for the Society. It seems more likely that he was so embittered by the battle over the College that he took little interest in the library once elected.

44. "New York Society Library, First Minute Book, 1754–1772," May 7, 1754, New York Society Library. Hereafter, Minutes of the Board. The second manuscript volume covers the period from 1788 when the library reopened after the Revolution through 1832. Both are at the New York Society Library. After these initial lists were solicited from all of the subscribers, it seems that only the trustees submitted lists for approval by the board for later acquisitions.

45. New York Society Library, *A Catalogue of the Books Belonging to the New-York Society Library* (New York: H. Gaine, 1758). The Society printed a facsimile of this catalog in 1954 to commemorate its two hundredth anniversary. It is orga-

nized first by size (folio, quarto, octavo, and duodecimo), then roughly alphabetically by first letter; that is, for example, all of the titles beginning with the letter "A" are grouped together but not alphabetically. The first titles the board ordered in 1754 are listed in Minutes of the Board, May 29, 1754.

46. Austin Baxter Keep counts ten merchants and thirteen lawyers serving on the board before 1760. Keep, *Society Library*, 163.

47. Ibid., 153.

48. Aside from one title in French and a few in Latin, all of the collection was in English.

49. Wood, *Radicalism of the American Revolution*, 193–96. The quote is at page 195. On refinement in the context of colonial New York, see Burrows and Wallace, *Gotham*, 172–75.

50. *Independent Reflector*, 219–20, 345.

51. See the Spectator Project at Rutgers University Libraries (www2.scc.rutgers.edu/spectator) for the full text of the *Spectator* and other eighteenth-century periodicals.

52. *Independent Reflector*, 345.

53. Ibid., 39, 20–21.

54. Bailyn, *Ideological Origins*, 22–54.

55. Gordon's translations included lengthy introductions relating the decline of Rome to the principles of English Whiggery. Bailyn, *Ideological Origins*, 42. History and biography were the largest genres in the 1758 catalog.

56. In all, the catalog includes about one-third of the approximately one hundred authors that Bailyn identified as the most important sources of revolutionary thought.

57. The same list of subscribers appears in Minutes of the Board, May 29, 1754, along with the list of the first books ordered from London.

58. James Raven, *London Booksellers and American Customers: Transatlantic Literary Community and the Charleston Library Society, 1748–1811* (Columbia: University of South Carolina Press, 2002), 72.

59. These five were a surgeon, an apothecary, a printer, and two distillers. The majority of the members were either lawyers (36) or merchants (22). The charter is reprinted in Keep, *Society Library*, 538–47.

60. Dillon, *Triumvirate*, 199–203. Livingston became the first governor of the state of New Jersey and signed the Constitution. For divisions in the city during the Revolution see Ketchum, *Divided Loyalties* and Judith L. Van Buskirk, *Generous Enemies: Patriots and Loyalists in Revolutionary New York* (Philadelphia: University of Pennsylvania Press, 2002).

61. Smith, *Historical Memoirs from 1763 to 1776*, 2:278.

62. Minutes of the Board, December 21, 1788. The act validating the charter is reprinted in Keep, *Society Library*, 547–48.

63. Keep, *Society Library*, 212, 239. *The Charter, Bye-Laws, and the Names of the Members of the New-York Society Library: With a Catalogue of the Books Belong to the Said Library* (New York: T. & J. Swords, 1793).

64. A Subscriber to the New-York Society Library, "On the Utility of Public Libraries," *New-York Magazine; or, Literary Repository*, June 1791, 307–9. For more on postrevolutionary learned societies, see Rheinhold, "Quest for 'Useful Knowledge,'" 124–29. For circulation statistics by subject category, 1789–90, see Shera, *Foundations of the Public Library*, 122.

65. Keep, *Society Library*, 289.

66. Keep, *Society Library*, 225, 402.

67. *Minutes of the Common Council of the City of New York, 1784–1831* (New York: The City, 1917), VII: 738 (May 2, 1814); VIII: 232–36 (June 18, 1815). The quotes, from pages 232, 233, and 235, are part of an ad hoc committee's report on the societies' petition. Mayor DeWitt Clinton and most of the members of the committee were Society members.

68. Bender, *New York Intellect*, 62–66. The quote is at page 65. Brideswell became available when the new almshouse at Bellevue opened. Washington Irving quipped that the City's plan was to "give the rich in brains/The worn-out mansion of the poor in pocket." Quoted in Bender, *New York Intellect*, 64.

69. *Minutes of the Common Council*, VIII: 686 (November 18, 1816). Minutes of the Board, November 16, 1816.

70. Keep, *Society Library*, 299–300.

71. By 1827, the writing was clearly on the wall. That year the organizations comprising the New York Institution and others, including the Society Library, campaigned unsuccessfully to have the City grant a ninety-nine-year lease on Brideswell. See, for example, "Minutes of the American Academy of Fine Arts from January 1817," May 5, 1827, New-York Historical Society. See also Keep, *Society Library*, 299–300; Bender, *New York Intellect*, 76.

72. *Minutes of the Common Council*, XIX:78 (May 31, 1830).

73. Keep, *Society Library*, 247, 250, 304, 406–7. Each increase in the annual subscription required an act of the assembly and these are reprinted in Keep, *Society Library*, 548–51. Shera estimates that approximately half of the subscription libraries in New England charged an annual subscription of less than a dollar. Shera, *Foundations of the Public Library*, 77.

74. Tom Glynn, "Books for a Reformed Republic: The Apprentices' Library of New York City, 1820–1865," *Libraries & Culture* 34 (Fall 1999): 355–56. The number of pay readers in the Apprentices' Library was comparatively small. Thomas Augst, "Making Society Out of Books: The New York Mercantile Library and the Enterprise of Reading," in *The Clerk's Tale: Young Men and Moral Life in Nineteenth Century New York* (Chicago: University of Chicago Press, 2003), 158–206. From 1754 to 1761, the Society Library allowed nonsubscribers to pay one to four shillings to borrow a book for a month, depending upon the size. It

was not until 1878 that it allowed "temporary subscriptions," but by the turn of the century these annual subscriptions from nonshareholders generated substantially more revenue than subscriptions from the members holding shares. Keep, *Society Library*, 156, 171, 522.

75. According to the by-laws in force between 1789 and 1812, the board was not required vote on new members. Since they never voted anyway, the change in 1812 had no practical effect, but it would seem to indicate greater exclusivity. Although my description of the board may seem unduly harsh, even the Society's official historian referred to "a spirit of exclusiveness [to which] must be attributed to some degree the languor, approaching atrophy, into which at times the institution has sometimes lapsed." Keep, *Society Library*, 404.

76. This is the average of the complete terms of service of the thirty-four trustees who served at any time between 1800 to 1830. The average is skewed somewhat by Verplanck, who served a total of fifty-eight years.

77. Aside from the bitter elections around the time of the founding, through 1833 there appears to have been only one other election in which rival candidates vied for office. In 1795, members ousted the trustees who served on the building committee, probably because of cost overruns. Keep, *Society Library*, 226.

78. Kent's entire opinion is included in Minutes of the Board, May 2, 1825. His argument is involved, highly legalistic, and based largely on his interpretation of the spirit of the charter, rather than its actual words. See also Keep, *Society Library*, 280–86, who called the election a "lesson in arbitrament by law and the prevention of disorder."

79. Nonetheless, one of the recurring complaints in the election disputes of the next decade was that the board was unable or unwilling to furnish a complete list of the current shareholders. There is no record in the minutes of a prospective member being rejected by the board.

80. Keep, *Society Library*, 284–85. John I. Morgan and Evert A. Bancker, *Address* (n.p., 1833), 9. This is one of the first pamphlets circulated in the heated election campaigns of the 1830s discussed below. The explanation that the newcomers hoped to turn the library into a bank may not have seemed so far-fetched in 1825. New York State did not have a general incorporation law at that time. Each corporation was formed by a special act of the legislature. Getting control of a previously incorporated organization may have been seen as a way to bypass the legislature, particularly on such a sensitive political issue as the chartering of a bank. On the other hand, the corporate powers conferred in the Society's charter were very limited.

81. For the constitutional convention, see Burrows and Wallace, *Gotham*, 512–15.

82. General Society of Mechanics and Tradesmen, *Report of the Special Committee . . . to which was Referred the Resolution for Extending the Usefulness*

of that Institution (New York: Wm. A. Mercein, 1831). Not all of the report's recommendations were adopted immediately, but from the 1830s the library increased in importance until, by the Civil War, it was the Society's most important function and one of the most popular libraries in the city.

83. Peter J. Wosh, *Spreading the Word: The Bible Business in Nineteenth-Century America* (Ithaca, N.Y.: Cornell University Press, 1994), 151–75.

84. In the case of these two libraries, changes were made in part for financial reasons. The merchants' clerks in the MLA, for example, entered into an agreement with a merchants' organization, the Clinton Hall Association, in which the latter agreed to provided a building for the library. The Historical Society experienced a period of financial instability when it lost its rooms in Brideswell with the other organizations of the New York Institution.

85. Richard D. Brown, *Knowledge Is Power: The Diffusion of Information in Early America, 1700–1865* (New York: Oxford University Press, 1989), 280.

86. For the founders' ambitions for the new university, see [Jonathan Mayhew Wainwright], *Considerations Upon the Expediency and Means of Establishing a University in the City of New-York* (New York: Grattan, 1830); *Journal of the Proceedings of a Convention of Literary and Scientific Gentlemen Held in the Common Council Chamber of the City of New York, October, 1830* (New York: Jonathan Leavitt and G. & C. & H. Carvill, 1831). This meeting was organized by NYU to solicit advice on policies and curricula from scholars and educational leaders across the country. See also Thomas J. Frusciano and Marilyn H. Pettit, *New York University and the City: An Illustrated History* (New Brunswick, N.J.: Rutgers University Press, 1997), 1–15.

87. *Address to the Citizens of New-York, on the Claims of Columbia College and the New University, to their Patronage* (New York: n.p., 1830). See also Coon, *Columbia*, 69–70. "The promoters [of NYU] echoed what the Livingstons . . . had said at the founding of King's College . . . [that it] was not democratic . . ."; Bender, *New York Intellect*, 89–104. By the 1840s, NYU was more like Columbia than a "new university." In 1843, when NYU no longer posed a threat, Columbia abandoned its revised curriculum.

88. See, for example, "Report of William Gracie and Others Relative to the Expediency of Establishing an Athenaeum," New-York Historical Society, Misc. Mss Box 23, no. 14A.

89. Minutes of the Board, May 16, 1824.

90. Henry Wheaton, *An Address Pronounced at the Opening of the New York Athenaeum, December 14, 1824*, 2nd ed. (New York: J. W. Palmer, 1825), 23. Although its officers vigorously denied it, the disputed election of 1825 may have been connected in some way with the Athenaeum. April 1825 was the first Society Library election after the Athenaeum's founding. James Renwick, one of the old trustees who was reelected, was a vice president of the Athenaeum. That the new members wanted to combine with the Athenaeum is at least as plausible

as that they were stealth bankers. On lectures as a means of popular education in the nineteenth-century, see Donald M. Scott, "The Popular Lecture and the Creation of a Public in Mid–Nineteenth Century America," *Journal of American History* 66 (March 1980): 791–809.

91. The constitution, by-laws, and list of the lectures for 1825, as well as the aims of the founders, were circulated in James Renwick, et al., *To the Public* (New York: J. W. Palmer & Co., 1825). This and the Wheaton address are both at the New York Public Library.

92. Wheaton, *New York Athenaeum*, 58.

93. Keep, *Society Library*, 335.

94. Robert W. July, *The Essential New Yorker: Gulian Crommelin Verplanck* (Durham, N.C.: Duke University Press, 1951). Bender, *New York Intellect*, 135–39.

95. The most substantial collection of Verplanck's speeches is Gulian C. Verplanck, *Discourses and Addresses on Subjects of American History, Arts, and Literature* (New York: J. & J. Harper, 1833). An accessible and representative speech is "The Advantages and Dangers of the American Scholar," in *American Philosophic Addresses, 1700–1900*, ed. Joseph L. Blau (New York: Columbia University Press, 1946), 115–50. A complete bibliography of Verplanck's writings and published addresses may be found in July, *Verplanck*, 291–94.

96. The first series of lectures was delivered in the winter of 1827. Mercantile Library Association, *Seventh Annual Report* (New York: Mercantile Library Association, 1828), 40–41. The MLA "made the charge for the tickets so small that no one need be deterred from attending on the ground of expense" and the board stressed that their aim was to provide informal education for ambitious young men rather than to generate revenue. Nonetheless, by 1838 they reported that "no other single cause has contributed in a greater degree to the unexampled growth and prosperity of our institution than the popularity of the lectures." Mercantile Library Association, *Eighth Annual Report* (1829), 47; and Mercantile Library Association, *Seventeenth Annual Report* (1838), 14.

97. Gulian C. Verplanck, "Lecture Introductory to the Several Courses Delivered before the Mercantile Association of New York," in Gulian C. Verplanck, *Discourses and Addresses on Subjects of American History, Arts, and Literature* (New York: J. & J. Harper, 1833), 233–54.

98. Ibid., 241, 243.

99. Ibid., 243, 246. It is significant that Verplanck said that citizens "feel" their duties. There are distinct overtones of romanticism throughout his oratory. In one address he pictured his listeners' "future lives . . . winding their quiet way through the green pastures and shaded vales of domestic life . . . gladdening the land and clothing it with fruitfulness, and beauty, and joy." Gulian C. Verplanck, *The Right Moral Influence and Use of Liberal Studies. A Discourse Delivered after the Annual Commencement of Geneva College, August 7th, 1833* (New York: Henry Ludwig, 1833), 47.

100. Ibid., 237, 241.

101. Ibid., 242, 250–51. Priestley was an English chemist who migrated to the United States after the Revolution.

102. Ibid., 257, 246–47. On Roscoe, see *The Dictionary of National Biography*, s.v. "Roscoe, William," by Warwick William Wroth. Thomas Bender argues that the Liverpool Athenaeum was key to the founding of the Apprentices' Library, as well as the New York Athenaeum and the Mercantile Association. Bender, *New York Intellect*, 73.

103. Ibid., 246. The following year Verplanck split with the Democrats over the chartering of the second Bank of the United States. Bender, *New York Intellect*, 136.

104. Ibid., 242–43.

105. Both Keep and Bender argued that the primary reason the Athenaeum failed was its inconvenient location, that it was too far downtown and therefore too distant from the homes of its wealthy supporters. Keep, *Society Library*, 362; Bender, *New York Intellect*, 74–75. Its complex organizational structure and expense were certainly equally important factors.

106. Keep, *Society Library*, 334, 336.

107. Morgan and Bancker, *Address*, 6. My argument here is not that the collection itself was mismanaged. The Society Library was the most extensive in the city at this time. But the Society was continually in debt, while the membership slowly declined.

108. Morgan and Bancker, *Address*, 3, 6–7. Although the pro-Athenaeum faction occasionally stooped to sarcasm, they never went so far as to suggest that their opponents were not gentlemen.

109. John J. Morgan, et al., *To the Members of the New-York Society Library* (n.p., [1838]), 2.

110. *To the Stock Holders of the New-York Society Library* (n.p., 1833), 5.

111. Ibid., 4, 14.

112. Ibid., 5, 6.

113. Ibid., 16; E[dward] W. Laight et al., *Statement of the Trustees of the New-York Society Library* (n.p., [1838]), 14–15.

114. Ibid., 6. Circulating libraries originated in Great Britain in the late eighteenth century and competed with other types of libraries in the United States through the first half of the nineteenth. For circulating libraries, see David Kaser, *A Book for a Sixpence: The Circulating Library in America* (Pittsburgh: Phi Beta Mu, 1980); Shera, *Foundations of the Public Library*, 127–55.

115. Laight, *Statement of the Trustees*, 14; *To the Stock Holders of the New-York Society Library*, 16.

116. Laight, *Statement of the Trustees*, 13; *To the Stock Holders*, 16.

117. Laight, *Statement of the Trustees*, 13; *To the Stock Holders*, 14.

118. See for example, *New York American*, April 18, 1838. This newspaper and two other large-circulation dailies, the *New York Advertiser* and the *New York Post*, printed numerous letters from both sides, particularly in the two weeks leading up to the 1838 election on April 24.

119. *To the Stock Holders*, 10. Besides the pamphlets quoted thus far, two others were circulated during this period. Edward W. Laight, et al., *To the Shareholders of the New-York Society Library* (n.p., 1835), a pro-Athenaeum pamphlet. It lists James Kent and Washington Irving as pro-Athenaeum candidates. And Plebeian, *Reply to the Manifesto of the Trustees of the City Library* (n.p., [1833]), a pro-Athenaeum pamphlet by an unknown author. This one is so riddled with sarcasm that it is often difficult to follow. All of the pamphlets are at the New York Public Library.

120. *New York Post*, May 1, 1833.

121. Laight, *Statement of the Trustees*, 4.

122. For a detailed history of the years of negotiations and the election of 1838, see Keep, *Society Library*, 339–58.

123. Ibid., 451. For an enumeration of the reforms advocated, see *To the Stock Holders*, 14–15.

124. In 1838, eight of twelve of the candidates on both the anti- and pro-Athenaeum ballots, or members of their families, appeared in [Moses Yale Beach], *Wealth and Biography of the Wealthy Citizens of New York City: Comprising an Alphabetical Arrangement of Persons Estimated to be Worth $100,000 and Upwards*, 5th ed. (New York: New York Sun, 1845; reprint, New York: Arno Press, 1973). This volume in the Big Business: Economic Power in a Free Society series reprinted Beach's fifth (1845) and twelfth (1855) editions. See also Edward Pessen, *Riches and Class before the Civil War* (Lexington, Mass.: D. C. Heath, 1973), 256–61, on New York, and 310–19 on Moses Beach. See also Edward Pessen, "Philip Hone's Set: The Social World of the New York City Elite in the 'Age of Egalitarianism,'" *New-York Historical Society Quarterly* 56 (October 1972): 285–308.

125. Laight, *Statement of the Trustees*, 15. Wosh makes a similar point regarding elites' philanthropic work. Wosh, *Spreading the Word*, 50–53.

126. Keep, *Society Library*, 402. These statistics are complicated by the fact that individuals sometimes owned multiple shares. Before the election, for example, the 420 members held 480 shares. A member with more than one share had extended borrowing privileges, but still had only one vote at the annual elections.

127. Keep, *Society Library*, 307. Barbara Shupe, Janet Steins, and Jyoti Pandit, eds., *New York State Population, 1790–1980: A Compilation of Federal Census Data* (New York: Neal-Schuman Publishers, 1987), 200–202.

128. General Society of Mechanics and Tradesmen, *Annual Report of the Finance Committee* (New York: General Society of Mechanics and Tradesmen,

1843), 12. Mercantile Library Association, *Twenty-Second Annual Report* (New York: Mercantile Library Association, 1843), 6.

129. Keep, *Society Library*, 406–7. The increase in the annual subscription was certainly prompted by an increase in the debt. The Society sold the building on Nassau Street in 1836 and was out of debt for the first time since 1795. Then it promptly amassed an even greater debt as a result of its new building and a series of unwise investments. Keep, *Society Library*, 426–31. To put the price of a share in context, twenty-five dollars was perhaps a month's wages for a skilled laborer.

130. Minutes of the Board, December 18, 1839.

131. New York Society Library, *Alphabetical and Analytical Catalogue of the New-York Society Library with the Charter, By-Laws, etc., of the Institution* (New York: James Van Norden, 1838). New York Society Library, *Alphabetical and Analytical Catalogue of the New-York Society Library with the Charter, By-Laws, etc., of the Institution* (New York: R. Craighead, 1850). The Society published a supplement to the 1813 catalog in 1825. New York Society Library, *Supplement to the Books Belonging to the New-York Society Library* (New York: C. S. Van Winkle, 1825). The collection had approximately 12,500 volumes in 1813 and approximately 17,000 in 1825. In 1838, before the new catalog was printed, the library received at least 1,600 volumes from the Athenaeum, in addition to its newspapers and periodicals. Keep, *Society Library*, 337.

132. Charles C. Jewett, *Notices of Public Libraries in the United States* (Washington, D.C.: Printed for the House of Representatives, 1851), 84–97. Jewett was the librarian of the Smithsonian Institution. His report was the first real attempt to survey libraries in the United States and was appended to the Smithsonian's annual report for 1850. For nineteenth-century library statistics generally, see Robert V. Williams, "The Making of Statistics of National Scope on American Libraries, 1836–1986: Purposes, Problems, and Issues," *Libraries & Culture* 26 (Spring 1991): 465–67. The Astor Library was founded by John Jacob Astor and later became the nucleus of the Research Division of the New York Public Library. See Lydenberg, *New York Public Library*, 1–95; Dain, *New York Public Library*, 3–10.

133. For 1838, I counted the titles under each subject and calculated the percentage of novels. For 1850, I relied upon, Ronald J. Zboray, "Appendix 2: Categories in the Analytical Catalogue (1850) of the New York Society Library," in *A Fictive People: Antebellum Economic Development and the American Reading Public* (New York: Oxford University Press, 1993), 202–10. If two additional categories, Anglo-American and foreign "Romance and Facetiae," are included, fiction was approximately 10 percent in 1838 and five percent in 1850.There were 8,690 total titles in 1838 and 11,737 in 1850. See also Ronald J. Zboray, "Gender and Boundlessness in Reading Patterns," in *Fictive People*, 156–79, which analyzes the circulation records of the Society Library for two periods in the 1840s and 1850s.

134. Glynn, "Apprentices' Library," 364–66. For fiction in public libraries later in the century see, see Esther Jane Carrier, *Fiction in Public Libraries, 1876–1900* (New York: Scarecrow Press, 1965).

135. A similar argument is developed in Bender, *New York Intellect*, 121–22; and Wood, *Radicalism of the American Revolution*, 349–50. See also Lawrence W. Levine, *Highbrow/Lowbrow: The Emergence of Cultural Hierarchy in America* (Cambridge, Mass.: Harvard University Press, 1988).

2. Books for a Reformed Republic: The Apprentices' Library in Antebellum New York

1. Lawrence Martin, *The General Society of Mechanics and Tradesmen of the City of New York* (New York: General Society of Mechanics and Tradesmen, 1960), 3; General Society of Mechanics and Tradesmen (hereafter, also GSMT), *Charter and Bye-Laws of the General Society of Mechanics and Tradesmen* (New York: General Society of Mechanics and Tradesmen, 1798), 1.

2. GSMT, *Charter and Bye-Laws*, 10–11.

3. Thomas Earle and Charles T. Congdon, *Annals of the General Society of Mechanics and Tradesmen of the City of New York, from 1785 to 1880* (New York: General Society of Mechanics and Tradesmen, 1882), 242. This is a history commissioned by the Society that consists mostly of primary documents. Earle was the Society's president in 1857.

4. GSMT, *Charter and Bye-Laws*, 12.

5. Earle and Congdon, *Annals*, 243.

6. Sean Wilentz, "Artisan Republican Festivals and the Rise of Class Consciousness in New York City, 1788–1837," in Michael H. Frisch and Daniel J. Walkowitz, eds., *Working-Class America: Essays on Labor, Community, and American Society* (Urbana: University of Illinois Press, 1983), 45.

7. Robert E. Weir and James P. Hanlan, eds., *Historical Encyclopedia of American Labor* (Westport, Conn.: Greenwood, 2004), s.v. "Labor Theory of Value," by Robert E. Weir.

8. Earle and Congdon, *Annals*, 303. This is from Dobbs's inaugural address in 1878. That he was still drawing upon the labor theory of value in the midst of the Gilded Age shows its adaptability and popularity.

9. The seminal works on republicanism in early American history are Bernard Bailyn, *The Ideological Origins of the American Revolution* (Cambridge, Mass.: Harvard University Press, 1967); Gordon S. Wood, *The Creation of the American Republic, 1776–1787* (Chapel Hill: University of North Carolina Press, 1969); and J. G. A. Pocock, *The Machiavellian Moment: Florentine Political Thought and the Atlantic Republican Tradition* (Princeton: Princeton University Press, 1975). For an excellent discussion of the historiographical debate surrounding their work, see Daniel T. Rodgers, "Republicanism: The Career of a Concept," *Journal of American History* 79 (June 1992): 11–38.

10. Wilentz, "Artisan Republican Festivals," 50.

11. Earle and Congdon, *Annals*, 326.

12. There is a substantial literature on various aspects of the industrial revolution. Some important works include George Rogers Taylor, *The Transportation Revolution, 1815–1860* (New York: Rinehart, 1951); Charles Sellers, *The Market Revolution: Jacksonian, 1815–1846* (New York: Oxford University Press, 1991); Paul E. Johnson, *A Shopkeeper's Millennium: Society and Revivals in Rochester New York, 1815–1837* (New York: Hill and Wang, 1978); *Bruce Laurie, Artisans into Workers: Labor in Nineteenth-Century America* (New York: Noonday Press, 1989); Alan Dawley, *Class and Community: The Industrial Revolution in Lynn* (Cambridge, Mass.: Harvard University Press, 1976); and Paul G. Faler, *Mechanics and Manufacturers in the Early Industrial Revolution: Lynn, Massachusetts, 1780–1860* (Albany: State University of New York Press, 1981).

13. The seminal study of liberal thought in the United States is Louis Hartz, *The Liberal Tradition in America: An Interpretation of American Political Thought since the Revolution* (New York: Harcourt, Brace, 1955). For a later work that responds, in part, to Bailyn, Wood, and Pocock, cited earlier, see Joyce Appleby, *Liberalism and Republicanism in the Historical Imagination* (Cambridge, Mass.: Harvard University Press, 1992).

14. Marchette Chute, *The First Liberty: A History of the Right to Vote in America* (New York: Dutton, 1969), 298.

15. There is an extensive literature on various facets of the antebellum reform movement. Some important monographs are Alice Felt Tyler, *Freedom's Ferment: Phases of American Social History to 1860* (Minneapolis: University of Minnesota Press, 1944); Clifford S. Griffin, *The Ferment of Reform, 1830–1860* (New York: Crowell, 1967); Thomas Bender, *Toward an Urban Vision: Ideas and Institutions in Nineteenth-Century America* (Lexington: University of Kentucky Press, 1975); Paul S. Boyer, *Urban Masses and Moral Order in America, 1820–1860* (Cambridge, Mass.: Harvard University Press, 1978); Ronald G. Walters, *American Reformers, 1815–1860* (New York: Hill and Wang, 1978); Lori D. Ginzberg, *Women and the Work of Benevolence: Morality, Politics, and Class in the Nineteenth-Century United States* (New Haven: Yale University Press, 1990); and Anne Firor Scott, *Natural Allies: Women's Associations in American History* (Urbana: University of Illinois Press, 1991).

16. W. David Lewis, "The Reformer as Conservative: Protestant Counter-Subversion in the Early Republic," in Stanley Coben and Lorman Ratner, eds., *The Development of an American Culture* (Englewood Cliffs, N.J.: Prentice-Hall, 1970), 67.

17. Ibid., 79–82.

18. Quoted in ibid., 82–83.

19. The concept of social control was once a central theme in the scholarship on reform and charity in the nineteenth century. Frances Fox Piven and

Richard A. Cloward, *Regulating the Poor: The Functions of Public Welfare* (New York: Pantheon Books, 1971), is a seminal work. For a well-rounded discussion of its strengths and weaknesses, see the essays in Walter I. Trattner, ed., *Social Welfare or Social Control? Some Historical Reflections on Regulating the Poor* (Knoxville: University of Tennessee Press, 1983).

20. Richard D. Brown, *The Strength of a People: The Idea of an Informed Citizenry in America* (Chapel Hill: University of North Carolina Press, 1996), 133–51.

21. Brown, *Strength of the People*, 126–32.

22. General Society of Mechanics and Tradesmen, *Some Memorials of the Late William Wood, Esq., the Eminent Philanthropist, with Resolutions of Respect for his Memory* (New York: General Society of Mechanics and Tradesmen, 1858), 16–19. This is a special report by the Apprentices' Library Committee investigating Wood's role in establishing the library. The Society's school closed in 1858.

23. Ibid., 19–20; Earle and Congdon, *Annals*, 60–61. For a brief biography of William Wood, see "The New York Mercantile Library," *Scribner's Monthly*, February 1871, 354.

24. Thomas Mercein, "An Address upon the Opening of the Apprentices' Library," reprinted in Paul A. Gilge and Howard B. Rock, eds., *Keepers of the Revolution: New Yorkers at Work in the Early Republic* (Ithaca, N.Y.: Cornell University Press, 1992), 52–54.

25. Mercein, "Address upon the Opening of the Apprentices Library," 52–53.

26. General Society of Mechanics and Tradesmen, *Catalogue of the Apprentices' Library* (New York: General Society of Mechanics and Tradesmen, 1820). Hereafter cited as GSMT, *Catalogue* (1820).

27. GSMT, *Catalogue* (1833), 168.

28. General Society of Mechanics and Tradesmen, *Report of the Special Committee to Whom was Referred the Resolution for Extending the Usefulness of that Institution* (New York: General Society of Mechanics and Tradesmen, 1830), 1.

29. GSMT, *Report of the Special Committee* (1830), 4–7.

30. Earle and Congdon, *Annals*, 277; Martin, *General Society of Mechanics and Tradesmen*, 7.

31. General Society of Mechanics and Tradesmen, "Report of the Library Committee, 1830," reprinted in *Report of the Special Committee* (1830), 21–22.

32. GSMT, *Report of the Special Committee* (1830), 16–18.

33. Ibid., 9. The regulations published in 1855 stated that members could use the library for free. GSMT, *Catalogue* (1855), ix.

34. General Society of Mechanics and Tradesmen, *Report of the Finance Committee*, (New York: General Society of Mechanics and Tradesmen, 1848), 4. This reports on finances for 1847; all of the reports cited below were published

the year following the year on which they reported. Hereafter cited as GSMT, *Annual Report* (1848). GSMT, *Annual Report,* (1855), 5; *Annual Report* (1866), 7.

35. "Inaugural Address of President Noah Norwall, Delivered January 14th, 1862," in Earle and Congdon, *Annals,* 342.

36. Earle and Congdon, *Annals,* 95, 105.

37. Ibid., 272.

38. GSMT, *Catalogue* (1855), ix; *Catalogue* (1865), 9.

39. GSMT, *Annual Report* (1852), 12; *Annual Report* (1855), 8; *Annual Report* (1861), 12; *Annual Report* (1865), 13.

40. Earle and Congdon, *Annals,* 107.

41. GSMT, *Annual Report* (1855), 8.

42. GSMT, *Catalogue* (1855), viii–ix.

43. Earle and Congdon, *Annals,* 320.

44. GSMT, *Catalogue* (1855).

45. Earle and Congdon, *Annals,* 320.

46. GSMT, *Annual Report* (1851), 7. In 1849, Elizabeth Demilt also donated $3,000 to the Mercantile Library Association and $5,000 to the New-York Historical Society Library. Charles C. Jewett, *Notices of Public Libraries in the United States* (Washington, D.C.: Printed for the House of Representatives, 1850), 86, 93. This was printed as an appendix to Congress, Fourth Annual Report of the Smithsonian Institution, 31st Cong., 1st sess., 1850, S. Doc. 120, Serial Set 564. William Rhees drew upon Jewett's work extensively for his report ten years later. See note 58.

47. Martin, *General Society of Mechanics and Tradesmen,* 8.

48. Earle and Congdon, *Annals,* 278.

49. Ibid., 273–74.

50. Ibid., 278–79.

51. Ibid., 274–75.

52. GSMT, *Catalogue* (1855), viii.

53. Earle and Congdon, *Annals,* 319.

54. GSMT, *Annual Report* (1863), 12–13.

55. Ibid., 12; *Annual Report* (1864), 11; *Annual Report* (1865), 11; *Annual Report* (1866), 13.

56. Earle and Congdon, *Annals,* 322.

57. GSMT, *Annual Report* (1861), 10–12; *Annual Report* (1866), 10–13.

58. William J. Rhees, *Manual of Public Libraries, Institutions, and Societies in the United States and the British Provinces of North America* (Urbana: University of Illinois Press, 1967 [1859]), 255–97.

59. Ibid., xxvi–xxvii; Jewett, *Notices of Public Libraries,* 190–91.

60. Rhees, *Manual of Public Libraries,* 585–650. These numbers are probably underestimated. Rhees included a list of libraries by state at the end of the Manual, not all of which are described in the text. I simply counted all the librar-

ies with "mechanic" or "apprentice" in their names and others that Rhees described and that were clearly for workers. However, there are others, such as the ubiquitous "Franklin Libraries," that are not described, but may well have served working-class readers. Sean Wilentz, *Chants Democratic: New York City and the Rise of the American Working Class, 1788–1850* (New York: Oxford University Press, 1984), 272–74.

61. Harris, *History of Libraries*, 168; Elmer D. Johnson, *Communication: An Introduction to the History of Writing, Printing, Books and Libraries* (Metuchen, N.J.: Scarecrow Press, 1973), 150, 157.

62. Mercantile Library Association, *Thirty-First Annual Report of the Board of Direction of the Mercantile Library Association of the City of New-York* (New York: Mercantile Library Association), 17.

63. George Burwell Utley, ed., *The Librarians' Conference of 1853: A Chapter in American History* (Chicago: American Library Association, 1951) reprints the proceedings from Norton's Literary and Educational Register.

64. Quoted in full in Rhees, *Manual of Public Libraries*, xi–xvii.

65. GSMT, *Some Memorials of the Late William Wood*, 18.

66. Earle and Congdon, *Annals*, 257.

67. GSMT, *Catalogue* (1855), vii–viii. It is interesting to note that the librarian was paid considerably less than his counterparts at other institutions. Rhees estimated in 1859 that the average annual salary of a library was $450 and the General Society's librarian was paid $350. Rhees, *Manual of Public Libraries*, xxiii, 259.

68. James Ranz, *The Printed Book Catalogue in American Libraries: 1723–1900* (Chicago: American Library Association, 1964), 3, 7.

69. Quoted in John Tebbel, *A History of Book Publishing in the United States, Volume 1: The Creation of an Industry, 1630–1865* (New York: R. R. Bowker, 1972), 227.

70. Ranz, *The Printed Book Catalogue*, 23–30.

71. As early as 1850, Charles C. Jewett had started work on a union catalog of the largest libraries in the United States. A union catalog brings together all the holdings of several libraries. Jewett also proposed using stereotyped cards for producing card catalogs, instead of printed catalogs, so that the preparation of a new catalog would require only inserting the cards for new acquisitions and rearranging the old ones. Both of these ideas were abandoned when Jewett left the Smithsonian, but they were adopted later in the century.

72. GSMT, *Catalogue* (1855), v.

73. GSMT, *Report of the Special Committee* (1830), 12; *Annual Report* (1856), 9; *Annual Report* (1866), 12.

74. Political science comprehended several subclasses that would be classified elsewhere in modern catalogs, including bookkeeping, statistics, and various areas of the law.

75. Nicholas Truebner, *Bibliographical Guide to American Literature* (Detroit: Gale Research Company, 1969) [1859], 198–202, 261–98.

76. Earle and Congdon, *Annals*, 276.

77. Lyle H. Wright, "A Statistical Survey of American Fiction, 1774–1850," *Huntington Library Quarterly* 2 (April 1939): 309.

78. Earle and Congdon, *Annals*, 74–75. The committee reported that it would be "inexpedient" to discontinue the circulation of fiction, but suggested that any member could instruct the librarian not to allow his employees to borrow it. See also Thompson, *Evolution of the American Public Library*, 91.

79. Rhees, *Manual of Public Libraries*, 260.

80. Lyle H. Wright, "Propaganda in Early American Fiction," *Papers of the Bibliographical Society of America* 33 (1939): 104–5.

81. Earle and Congdon, *Annals*, 276.

82. Ibid.

3. The Past in Print: History and the Market at the New-York Historical Society Library

1. The address is reprinted in R. W. G. Vail, *Knickerbocker Birthday: A Sesqui-Centennial History of the New-York Historical Society, 1804–1954* (New York: New-York Historical Society, 1954), 452–54. It was also circulated privately to prospective members.

2. Ibid., 453.

3. The only full-length biography of Pintard is David L. Sterling, "New York Patriarch: A Life of John Pintard, 1759–1844" (Ph.D. diss., New York University, 1958). See also James Grant Wilson, *John Pintard, Founder of the New-York Historical Society* (New York: New-York Historical Society, 1902); Joseph A. Scoville [Walter Barrett, pseud.], *Old Merchants of New York* (New York: Carleton, 1863–1870; repr., New York: Greenwood Press, 1968), 2:217–44; Dumas Malone, ed., *Dictionary of American Biography* (New York: Scribner's, 1934), s.v. "John Pintard," by Robert Greenhalgh Albion; John Pintard, *Letters from John Pintard to his Daughter Eliza Noel Pintard Davidson, 1816–1833*, ed. Dorothy C. Barck (New York: New-York Historical Society, 1940–41), 1:ix–xx; and James J. Heslin, "John Pintard," in Clifford L. Lord, ed., *Keepers of the Past* (Chapel Hill: University of North Carolina Press, 1965), 30–39.

4. The first minutes are reprinted in Vail, *Knickerbocker Birthday*, 23; the original constitution is at pages 451–52, and the original by-laws at 465–67. "Men of taste and refinement" is Vail's phrase (30).

5. Ibid., 481.

6. Ibid., 34. Minutes of the New-York Historical Society, vol. 1 (1804–1837) September 15, 1809, New-York Historical Society Archives, New-York Historical Society Library, 29. Hereafter, also NYHS. Minutes, vol. 1.

7. Vail, *Knickerbocker Birthday*, 35–36.

8. Leonard Louis Tucker, *Clio's Consort: Jeremy Belknap and the Founding of the Massachusetts Historical Society* (Boston: Massachusetts Historical Society, 1990); Stephen T. Riley, "Jeremy Belknap" in *Keepers of the Past*, ed. Clifford L. Lord (Chapel Hill: University of North Carolina Press), 19–29.

9. David V. Van Tassel, *Recording America's Past: An Interpretation of the Development of Historical Studies in America, 1607–1884* (Chicago: University of Chicago Press, 1960), 95–102 (the quote is at page 100); Leslie W. Dunlap, *American Historical Societies, 1790–1860* (Madison, WI: Cantell, 1944), vii.

10. Dunlap, *American Historical Societies*, 22–24, 27–28, 41–42.

11. George H. Callcott, *History in the United States, 1800–1860: Its Practice and Purpose* (Baltimore: John Hopkins University Press, 1970), 35.

12. See Chapter 4 for Pintard's role in the Panic of 1792 and his subsequent bankruptcy. Edward Pessen estimated that about 60 percent of the Society's approximately five hundred members in 1846 were from New York's wealthiest families, which he defined as the upper one percent of the city's wealth holders. Edward Pessen, *Riches, Class, and Power before the Civil War* (Lexington, Mass.: D.C. Heath and Company), 276.

13. Vail, *Knickerbocker Birthday*, 15–20, has succinct biographical sketches of the founders, as does Robert Hendre Kelby, *The New York Historical Society, 1804–1904* (New York: New-York Historical Society, 1905), 3–15. Not all of the founders trained in the law were practicing lawyers. Clinton, for example, was a one of the new republic's first professional politicians. George Folsom, "Historical Sketch of the Society," in New-York Historical Society, *Collections of the New-York Historical Society*, 2nd ser., vol. 1 (New York: New-York Historical Society, 1841), 459. Hereafter, NYHS, *Collections* (1841).

14. Thomas Bender, *New York Intellect: A History of Intellectual Life in New York City, from 1750 to the Beginnings of Our Own Time* (New York: Knopf, 1987), 66. The most recent biography of Clinton is Evan Cornog, *The Birth of Empire: DeWitt Clinton and the American Experience* (Oxford: Oxford University Press, 1998). Shortly after his death, his friend Hosack wrote *Memoir of DeWitt Clinton: with an Appendix, Containing Numerous Documents, Illustrative of the Principal Events of his Life* (New York: J. Seymour, 1829).

15. Callcott, "The Personal Uses of History," in *History in the United States*, 193–204.

16. Vail, *Knickerbocker Birthday*, 359.

17. "Domestic Literary Intelligence," *Analectic Magazine*, October 1814, 349. "Shine in the dignity of the F.R.S" is a quote from Alexander Pope's poem "The Dunciad."

18. Hugh Williamson, "A Discourse on the Benefits of Civil History," in NYHS, *Collections* (1814), 29. "Rational amusement" and similar terms were used frequently in addresses before the Society, especially in its earliest years.

19. Gouverneur Morris, "An Inaugural Discourse Delivered before the New-York Historical Society, at Their Annual Meeting, 6th December, 1812," in NYHS, *Collections* (1814), 27; Gulian C. Verplanck, "An Annual Discourse Delivered Before the New-York Historical Society, December 7, 1818" in NYHS, *Collections* (1821), 44; James Kent, "An Anniversary Discourse, Delivered before the New-York Historical Society," in NYHS, *Collections* (1814), 12.

20. Dunlap, "State Relations and Finances," in *American Historical Societies*, 48–64.

21. New-York Historical Society, *Semi-Centennial Celebration: Fiftieth Anniversary of the Founding of the New-York Historical Society, Monday, November 20, 1854* (New York: New-York Historical Society, 1854), 52.

22. The memorial is reprinted in NYHS, *Collections* (1814), v–xii. The quote is at pages v–vi. See also Bender, *New York Intellect*, 57.

23. George Folsom, "Historical Sketch of the Society," 463.

24. Vail, *Knickerbocker Birthday*, 453.

25. NYHS, *Collections* (1811), vi. Emphasis in the preface. NYHS, *Collections* (1814), i.

26. New-York Historical Society, *Proceedings of the New York Historical Society, at the Dedication of the Library, Tuesday, November 3, 1857* (New York: New-York Historical Society, 1857), 6. See also, for example, William Campbell, "Historical Inquiry in the Last 25 Years" (1850), New-York Historical Society Addresses, Box 2, New-York Historical Society Archives, New-York Historical Society, 1. "To ally the present and the future with the past is one of the chief objects of history."

27. New-York Historical Society, *Proceedings of the New-York Historical Society for the Year 1849* (New York: New-York Historical Society, 1849), 115. Hereafter, NYHS, *Proceedings* (1849). Williamson, "The Benefits of Civil History," 27. The address "To the Public" warned that "without the aid of . . . authentic documents, history will be nothing more than . . . ingenious conjectures and amusing fables." Vail, *Knickerbocker Birthday*, 452.

28. NYHS, *Semi-Centennial Celebration*, 49; NYHS, *Collections* (1841), iii. Emphasis in Folsom's preface. Morris, "Inaugural Discourse, 1812," 28.

29. NYHS, *Collections* (1814), vii. The word *oblivion* appears four times in the petition. It is used frequently in the Society's publications and addresses and those of other historical societies as well, especially during this early period. See, for example, William Beach Lawrence, "Purposes and Attainments of the New-York Historical Society (1842)," NYHS Addresses, Box 2, NYHS Archives, 7: "the object of our Society is to . . . procure, as materials for history, those documents of the olden time that, without such aid, might pass into oblivion." On the use of the term by other organizations and individuals, see Callcott, *History in the United States*, 112.

30. There were twenty-three queries in total. Vail, *Knickerbocker Birthday*, 454–56. The queries appear to be based in large part upon a letter that Samuel

Miller circulated privately in 1798 for a proposed history of the state. It is available online and in microfilm in Early American Imprints, Series 1, no. 34110.

31. Williamson, "Benefits of Civil History," 35; Joseph Blunt, *An Anniversary Discourse Delivered Before the New-York Historical Society, on Thursday, Dec. 13, 1827* (New York: G. and C. Carvill, 1828), 7.

32. "Dust and obscurity of private archives" is from "To the Public." Vail, *Knickerbocker Birthday*, 452. Rescuing the "fast perishing memorials" is from the preface to the second volume of the second series of the *Collections*. NYHS, *Collections* (1849), v. By this point, the editors were "point[ing] with becoming pride to their successful endeavors" to do so.

33. This is from the librarian's report in 1843. NYHS, *Proceedings* (1843), 25–26. In the address in 1805 the founders were confident that individuals would "cheerfully confide [primary sources] to a public institution in whose custody they would be preserved for the general benefit of society." Vail, *Knickerbocker Birthday*, 452.

34. Ibid., 45, 49.

35. NYHS, Minutes, vol. 1, December 6, 1818, 153–54; September 8, 1818, 146–47; Dunlap, *American Historical Societies*, 41.

36. Pamela Spence Richards, *Scholars and Gentlemen: The Library of the New-York Historical Society, 1804–1982* (Hamden, Conn.: Archon Books, 1984), 11; John Pintard, *Letters to His Daughter*, 1:13, 18, 107 (June 10, 1816; July 5, 1816; and January 27, 1818). The quote is from the latter date.

37. NYHS, *Collections* (1814). To save money, the catalog was added to the end of the second volume of the *Collections*, with separate pagination, totaling 139 pages. The Gates Papers were actually acquired shortly after the catalog was published. Vail, *Knickerbocker Birthday*, 50. The address "To the Public," which requested donations, was reprinted in local papers in 1809. A similar circular was published in 1817. For the full text, see "Transactions of Learned Societies," *The American Monthly Magazine and Critical Review*, July 1817, 193.

38. This is from Francis's remarks at the fortieth anniversary celebration, which, with separate pagination, were added to the end of NYHS, *Proceedings* (1844). The quote is at pages 84–85. A report some years later to the legislature made a similar point. Although less than half of the collection in 1829 were works of American history, in the early years many books were acquired (by donation), because they were "deemed expedient at the time to secure, for the benefit of science and literature." Frederic De Peyster Jr., J. Delafield, and Henry M. Francis, *In Assembly, March 2, 1829, Report of the New-York Historical Society* (New York: Edwin Croswell, 1829), 3. It was not until the late 1830s or early 1840s that additions to the library were strictly limited to American history. NYHS, *Proceedings* (1843), 29.

39. *Analectic Magazine*, "On the Means of Education and the Scientific Institutions of New York," June 1819, 457–58.

40. Van Tassel, *Recording America's Past*, 103–10. The quote is at page 103. Callcott, *History in the United States*, 42. Callcott counted "major publications," which he defined as volumes of more than two hundred pages. In all, the historical societies issued more than five hundred separate works, including constitutions, lists of members, etc. Dunlap, *American Historical Societies*, 95–96. The fifth volume of the Society's second series was the second catalog of the library.

41. NYHS, *Collections* (1811), iv. This apparently was a paraphrase of Thomas Jefferson, "multiplication of copies shall place them beyond the reach of accident." The phrase "multiply the copies" was used very frequently by the documaniacs. Walter Muir Whitehill, *Independent Historical Societies* (Boston: Boston Athenaeum, 1962), 4.

42. John Romeyn Brodhead, ed., *Documents Relative to the Colonial History of the State of New York* (New York: Weed, Parsons & Co., 1856), 1:v. This fifteen-volume set is discussed later herein. It was published for the State of New York but was largely a project of the Historical Society.

43. Van Tassel, *Recording America's Past*, 54–59, 115; Callcott, *History in the United States*, 38.

44. NYHS, *Collections* (1841), 12. NYHS, *Dedication of the Library*, 17.

45. James Green, "The Rise of Book Publishing," in *An Extensive Republic: Print, Culture, and Society in the New Nation, 1790–1840*, Robert A. Gross and Mary Kelley, eds., vol. 2 of *A History of the Book in America* (Chapel Hill, NC: University of North Carolina Press, 2010), 79. The phrase "original contributions" is used in the preface to NYHS, *Collections* (1849), iii. "Original works" is sometimes used interchangeably, and both are used in contradistinction to original documents.

46. E A D[uyckinck], "Literary Prospects of 1845," *The American Review: A Whig Journal of Politics, Literature, Art and Science*, February 1845, 148, 151. Duyckinck was nonetheless cautiously optimistic: "The old is worn out, the reign of the humbug is extinct" (147).

47. "Taunts of transatlantic rivals" is from George Tucker of the American Philosophical Society at the fiftieth anniversary. NYHS, *Fiftieth Anniversary of the Founding*, 65. For similar language see Verplanck, "Annual Discourse," 83 and especially remarks at the fiftieth anniversary by Joseph Blunt: "thirty years ago it was tauntingly asked by the Edinburgh Review, Who reads an American book" (80). This criticism in the *Edinburg Review* in 1820 was frequently cited and proudly refuted by cultural nationalists. "The American mind must be up and doing" is from John W. Francis, *New York During the Last Half Century: A Discourse in Commemoration of the Fifty-Third Anniversary of the New York Historical Society, and the Dedication of Their New Edifice* (New York: John F. Trow, 1857), 73.

48. Francis, *New York During the Last Half Century*, 72–74.

49. Luther Bradish, "The Progress of History," (1849), New-York Historical Society Addresses, Box 2, New-York Historical Society Archives, New-York Historical Society, 2. "He who simply notes the passing events of his Age, without investigating their causes . . . is a mere chronicler."

50. NYHS, *Collections* (1841), 283.

51. NYHS, *Proceedings* (1848), 74; NYHS, *Collections* (1829), vi.

52. I have borrowed the phrase "grand narrative" from Allan Megill, "'Grand Narrative' and the Discipline of History," in *A New Philosophy of History*, ed. Frank Ankersmit and Hans Kellner (London: Reaktion Books, 1995). It is particularly apt in this context, since Megill distinguishes master narrative, an "account of some segment of history," from grand narrative, an "account of history generally" (152). Americans' conception of their place in history and in the world during this period was certainly grand, if not grandiose. See also, for example, Dorothy Ross, "Historical Consciousness in Nineteenth-Century America," *American Historical Review* 89 (October 1984): 910–13.

53. David Hosack, "An Inaugural Address Delivered before the New-York Historical Society, on the Second Tuesday of February, 1820," in NYHS, *Collections* (1821), 274; Blunt, "Anniversary Discourse," 51. American republicanism as an example to the world was a very frequent theme in the annual discourses and other publications. See, for example, "is it nothing for the universal good of mankind to have carried into successful operation a system of self-government . . . such as before had existed before only in the utopian dreams of philosophers?" Verplanck, "Annual Discourse," 100.

54. The annual report in NYHS, *Proceedings* (1848), 25; Blunt, Anniversary Discourse," 9; remarks of William Adams at NYHS, *Dedication of the Library*, 21. See also, for example, Callcott, "Interpreting the Past," in *History in the United States*, 151–74.

55. Alexander W. Bradford, "A Discourse Delivered Before the New York Historical Society, at its Forty-First Anniversary, 20th November, 1845," in NYHS, *Proceedings* (1845), 8–9, 31. This is appended to the end of the *Proceedings*, with separate pagination. NYHS, *Dedication of the Library*, 19. See also Ross, "Historical Consciousness," 910–11.

56. Quoted in Milton Halsey Thomas, "Mid–Nineteenth Century Life in New York: More Revelations from the Diary of George Templeton Strong," *New-York Historical Society Quarterly* 37 (January 1953): 19. The date for the entry is May 3, 1858. This article appeared shortly after the publication of excerpts from Strong's diary in four volumes in 1952.

57. Williamson, "Benefits of Civil History," 25. Another interesting example of nineteenth-century historical silliness was the widespread belief that the American Indians descended from the ancient Hebrews. See, for example, an address by William L. Stone published, with citations, in NYHS, *Proceedings* (1845),

80. DeWitt Clinton, however, rejected this theory and argued that their ancestors were probably the ancient Scythians. NYHS, *Collections* (1814), 56.

58. NYHS, *Proceedings* (1845), 115–24. Quotes are at pages 115 and 119. See below for more on the reaction to this rather comical effort. Other historical societies also took part in the movement for a more poetic national name. The Massachusetts society, for example, preferred Columbia to Alleghania. Dunlap, *American Historical Societies*, 117–19.

59. George Templeton Strong, *Diary of George Templeton Strong: The Turbulent Fifties, 1850–1859*, ed. Allan Nevins and Milton Halsey Thomas, (New York: Macmillan, 1952), 57 (June 30, 1851).

60. For a history of the term, see Elizabeth L. Bradley, *Knickerbocker: The Myth Behind New York* (New Brunswick, N.J.: Rivergate Books, 2009). Irving himself commented on the widespread use of the term in an "Author's Apology" that he wrote for the 1848 edition, *A History of New* York, vol. 7 of *Complete Works of Washington Irving*, ed. Michael L. Black and Nancy B. Black (Boston: Twayne, 1984), 5.

61. Irving, *History of New York*, 16, 10, 167, 882–83, 286. Irving poked good-natured fun at the Historical Society in a number of passages. For example, Knickerbocker left his fortune to the Society and, "it is rumored that [they] have it mind to erect a wooden monument to his memory" (15).

62. "New York Historical Society," *New York Spectator*, April 5, 1838. This is from a review of a lecture before the Society on Governor Edmund Andros. Irving's *History of New York* was frequently criticized by the members. See, for example, Verplanck, "Annual Discourse, 1818," 44.

63. Privately published works are different from self-published works, in which the author pays for the publication, but offers them for sale in the market. Some privately published works were no doubt intended to be widely circulated. Further, many titles during this period were privately or publicly circulated either anonymously or under a pseudonym. This was at least ostensibly meant to show the author's modesty.

64. [Gulian Verplanck], *Procès Verbal of the Ceremony of Installation of President of the Historical Society, as It Will Be Performed February 8, 1820* (New York: Printed for the Members, 1820), 5–6, 12, 14, 4, 13. Santa Claus refers to Saint Nicholas, the patron saint of the Knickerbockers and the Society. Verplanck circulated this immediately after a heated election at the Society in which his slate of candidates was defeated. Vail, *Knickerbocker Birthday*, 60–61.

65. "Bucktail Bards," *Analectic Magazine*, March 1, 1820, 220–22. This reviews *Procès Verbal. Bucktail Bards* is another anonymous work, probably coauthored by Verplanck, but the *Analectic* declined to print the review submitted to the editors because "the sentiments it holds forth are so much in discordance with our own."

66. [Dewitt Clinton], *An Account of Abimelech Coody and the Other Celebrated Writers of New York: In a Letter from a Traveller to His Friend in South Carolina, January 1815* (New York: Privately printed, 1815), 4, 22, 18, 17. Coody was the pseudonym under which Verplanck attacked Clinton in print, so his faction within the New York Federalist party came to be known as the Coodies. See also Bender, *New York Intellect*, 69–71. It is significant that almost all of the names that Clinton uses to refer to the wits and literary worthies, besides Coody and Knickerbocker, are working-class occupations: Ironmonger, Cordwainer, Lady's Shoemaker. Verplanck's family was in fact more Knickerbocker than Clinton's.

67. [Clinton], *Coody*, 18, 9, 8, 6, 9. Clinton's clumsy satire included a lengthy and fulsome description of himself, for example: "few men have read more and few men can claim more extensive knowledge" (21). Presumably he was embarrassed when the Traveller's identity became public knowledge soon after *Coody* was printed. Cornog, *Clinton*, 127–28.

68. Hosack, "Inaugural Address, 1820," 274–75; Francis, *New York During the Last Half Century*, 50.

69. "A Brief Sketch of These Periodical Works Commonly Called Magazines; with a Short Biographical Account of Their Projector Mr. Edward Cave," *The New York Magazine and General Repository of Useful Knowledge*, May 1, 1814, 5–8. Quotes are at pages 5 and 8.

70. For a good overview of this period, see Andie Tucher, "Newspapers and Periodicals," in *An Extensive Republic*, 389–407. Frank Luther Mott provides a useful chart of the era's most successful magazines in Mott, *A History of American Magazines, Volume 1, 1741–1850* (Cambridge, Mass.: Harvard University Press, 1966), 215, as well as brief histories of many of the magazines. See Vail, *Knickerbocker Birthday* for the literary careers of Mitchell, Miller, and others.

71. Francis, *New York During the Last Half Century*, 221. Francis was quoting the playwright George Colman.

72. John D. Stevens, *Sensationalism and the New York Press* (New York: Columbia University Press, 1991), 15; Mott, *American Magazines, 1741–1850*, 156; Tucher, "Newspapers and Periodicals," 396. On newspapers and political parties, see, for example, Gerald D. Baldasty, *The Commercialization of the Press in the Nineteenth Century* (Madison: University of Wisconsin Press, 1992), 11–35; Tucher, "Newspapers and Magazines," 399–404; and John Nerone, "Newspapers and the Public Sphere," in *The Industrial Book, 1840–1880*, ed. Scott E. Casper et al., vol. 3 of *A History of the Book in America* (Chapel Hill: University of North Carolina Press, 2007), 232–34.

73. Lawrence, "Purposes and Attainments of the Society," 6. "New-York Historical Society," *The New York Magazine and General Repository of Useful Knowledge*, May 1, 1814, 26.

74. Stevens, *Sensationalism and the New York Press,* 15. Much of the news in the newspapers was copied from Washington or Europe. Since postal regulations allowed editors to receive copies of papers postage-free, it was easier to fill the columns with news from other towns or cities than to collect news locally. Tucher, "Newspapers and Periodicals," 396–97. On these "exchanges," see also Nerone, "Newspapers and the Public Sphere," 233. Magazines and newspapers also published fiction and essays from British periodicals, despite the widespread criticism of "vampers of English matter." Tucher, "Newspapers and Periodicals," 398.

75. "Bucktail Bards," 220–21.

76. [Duyckinck], "Literary Prospects of 1845," 148–49. Duyckinck joined the Historical Society in 1837 and served as domestic corresponding secretary from 1873 to 1878.

77. Eric Lupfer, "The Business of American Magazines," in *The Industrial Book,* 248–50. Frank Luther Mott, *A History of American Magazines, Volume 2, 1850–1865* (Cambridge, Mass.: Harvard University Press, 1938), 253–55; Mott, *A History of American Magazines, Volume 1, 1741*–1850, 494–502, 608. The reference to Irving's sociable chats is from Mott's history of the *Knickerbocker* in which Mott quotes from his first contribution to the magazine. For an interesting contemporary reference to the "magazine mania," see "The Magazines," *New York Times,* January 23, 1861, 2. It sketches brief histories of the most popular titles and claims that "amid the hurry and bustle of the day, people . . . infinitely prefer the little-of-everything to be found in periodicals" to books.

78. Robert A. Gross, Introduction: An Extensive Republic," in *An Extensive Republic,* 36–37; Tucher, "Newspapers and Periodicals," 398–99.

79. Tucher, "Newspapers and Periodicals," 404. For a much more detailed discussion of new technologies, most of which were used in periodical as well as book production, see Michael Winship, "Manufacturing and Book Production," in *The Industrial Book,* 40–69.

80. The subscription papers sold single copies only at their offices, usually for six cents. Although it is considered the beginning of the newspaper revolution, the *Sun* was not the first penny paper, just the first to survive for an extended period and circulate widely. William E. Huntzicker, *The Popular Press, 1833–1865* (Westport, Conn.: Greenwood, 1999), 13. See also, for example, George H. Douglas, *The Golden Age of the Newspaper* (Westport, Conn.: Greenwood, 1999), 1–10. The quote from the first issue is at page 6. See also Stevens, *Sensationalism and the New York Press,* 18–28. A very useful bibliography, with brief descriptions of all the newspapers, is Louis H. Fox, *New York City Newspapers, 1820–1850* (Chicago: University of Chicago Press, 1927). A summary table by year is at pages 120–131. There were twelve newspapers in the city in 1820 and forty-eight in 1850.

81. Philip Hone, *The Diary of Philip Hone, 1828–1852,* rev. ed. (New York: Dodd, Mead, 1936), 275 (September 22, 1837).

82. On advertising in the *Sun*, see Huntzicker, *Popular Press*, 6–9.

83. James L. Crouthamel, *Bennett's New York Herald and the Rise of the Popular Press* (Syracuse, N.Y.: Syracuse University Press, 1989); Douglas, *Golden Age of the Newspaper*, 22–35. Stevens, *Sensationalism and the New York Press*, 29–41.

84. For examples, see "New York Historical Society," *New York Herald*, January 20, 1843; "Historical Society," *New York Herald*, May 3, 1849; "New York Historical Society." *New York Herald*, December 25, 1856. The quote is from "Meeting of the New York Historical Society Last Evening," *New York Herald*, November 8, 1843.

85. "Solons" is from "New York Historical Society—Important Proceedings," *New York Herald*, June 8, 1849. "Savants" was used more frequently. See, for example, "Great Debate in the Historical Society," *New York Herald*, June 15, 1845. "Ridiculous puffery" and "newspaper toadies" are from "New York Historical Society—Our Country Without a Name," *New York Herald*, March 7, 1845. At times, the *Herald* could be nasty: "The Historical Society is made up of small lawyers and smaller physicians, with a sprinkling of very small parsons, and nondescripts who loaf about the outer courts of literature." "The Historical Society," *New York Herald*, May 15, 1845. More often it was just funny, as when it reported that President Tyler was detained and unable to attend a meeting of the Society and thus "providentially saved from being bored to death . . . , and therefore . . . preserved to live out his . . . term of office." "Transactions of the Historical Society," *New York Herald*, June 16, 1843.

86. "Great Excitement Among the Savans [*sic*] of the Historical Society—Important Discussion," *New York* Herald, April 3, 1845. See also "Great Debate in the Historical Society on the New Name of the Country," *New York Herald*, May 15, 1845. This is the meeting in which the members voted not to adopt the report of the committee that recommended changing the name to Alleghania. It actually gives a much more detailed account of the proceedings than the Society's *Proceedings.*

87. "We Have No News from Europe, Who Cares?" *New York Herald*, April 15, 1836. "In a short time, Europe will be like an old woman, without a tooth or a touch of sensibility. This continent is a fresh blooming young maiden—not yet knocked in the head with an axe, and disfigured in her lovely limbs."

88. "N.Y. Historical Society (By Our Own Reporter)," *John Donkey*, January 1, 1848. This article also made fun of Horace Greeley, editor of the *New York Tribune*, the *Sun*'s editor Moses Beach, and other local newspaper and magazine editors who supposedly attended and interrupted each other to make absurd and pointless remarks.

89. The full text of the letter was reported (without comment) in "New York Historical Society," *New York Herald*, October 6, 1847. The proceedings of the Society simply state that the letter was presented by a member, but they make no reference to the founder's roomy seat. New-York Historical Society, *Proceedings* (1847), 129.

90. John Donkey claimed to have inherited the breeches from his grandfather and donated them to the Society. "General Washington's Leather Breeches," *John Donkey,* January 1, 1848, 1. "Wearing the Breeches," *John Donkey,* January 29, 1848, 5. "New York Historical Society," *John Donkey,* March 11, 1848, 11. Most of the quotes from this article are taken directly from New-York Historical Society, *Proceedings* (1848), 24–25. But John Donkey makes them ridiculous by adding references to the breeches. And part of the joke was that the local newspapers had reported inaccurately on the meeting and he was "happy in being able to lay before the public a correct and corrected version."

91. For a brief history of *John Donkey,* see Mott, *History of American Magazines, vol. 1,* 780–83.

92. "Scoundrels and cheats" and "the revolution that has taken place in a great portion of the public mind" is from "Another Revolution Approaching—The New York Press," *New York Herald,* April 15, 1839. Bennett equated selling a newspaper by subscription to the credit system upon which Wall Street was based and that had ruined the American economy in the Panic of 1837. This was not entirely logical, since a newspaper subscription was certainly cancelled if the subscriber did not pay. But the analogy gave Bennett the opportunity to extoll "the astonishing power, both political and moral, of the newspaper press of New York." See also "The *Washington Globe* versus *New York Herald,*" *New York Herald,* September 26, 1836 and "Newspaper Revolution," *New York Herald,* October 10, 1842.

93. NYHS, Minutes, vol. 1, July 12, 1814, 50.

94. NYHS, Minutes, vol. 1, July 14, 1818, 138. The quote is from New-York Historical Society, *To the Honourable the Legislature of the State of New York; The Memorial of the New-York Historical Society* (New York: New-York Historical Society, 1827), 5. This also includes the report on the memorial from the state senate Committee on Literature. The Society also used the loan to set up the library in the New York Institution when it moved there in 1815. NYHS, Minutes, vol. 1, January 13, 1818, 129.

95. NYHS, Minutes, vol. 1, September 18, 1818, 146–47.

96. NYHS, Minutes, vol. 1, March 9, 1824, 267. NYHS, Minutes, vol. 1, January 13, 1829, 373. The only source of income during this period was the membership dues. Members were to pay two dollars a year, although it appears that for some years during this period they were not collected at all. NYHS, *Collections* (1821), 7–13, lists 231 resident members. NYHS, Minutes, vol. 1, July 8, 1828, 335–49. This includes the report of another committee appointed to settle the Society's debts and is the best account of the extremely confused state of the Historical Society's finances during this period. Besides the loan from the insurance company, on which Society paid 7 percent interest annually, most of the debt was owed to three members, David Hosack, John Francis, and John Pintard.

97. NYHS, *Memorial* (1827), 12.

98. Hugh G. J. Aikten, "Yates and McIntyre: Lottery Managers," *Journal of Economic History* 13 (Winter 1953): 39–40. This is an excellent, detailed history of Eliphalet Nott and the lottery act of 1814 in all its complexity. On Nott, Codman Hislop, *Eliphalet Nott* (Middleton, Conn.: Wesleyan University Press, 1971). Most states had banned lotteries by 1830. Dennis P. Rudd and Frank R. Flanegin, "A Historical Perspective of the Lottery," *Financial History* 65 (1999): 13. In 1818, John Pintard wrote to his daughter that a means "to regulate lotteries with the least possible injury to the public morals, considering the prevailing appetite for desperate gambling, is . . . quite beyond my comprehension." Pintard, *Letters to his Daughter*, 1:157 (November 28, 1818).

99. On Nott and the lottery, see George Wise, "Reckless Pioneer," *American Heritage of Invention & Technology* (January 1990): 26–31.

100. The lotteries laws from 1814 and 1822 are reprinted in Union College, *Documents Relative to the Dispute between the Trustees of Union College and Yates and McIntyre* (Schenectady, N.Y., 1834). This collection of documents has no pagination, but numbers the paragraphs of each document consecutively. The two laws are paragraphs 1–26. This complex controversy over Nott and the lottery actually stretched in the 1850s. The law granting $12,000 to the library is reprinted in NYHS, *Collections* (1814), xi–xii.

101. Aitken, "Yates and McIntyre," 39, 41–42; Wise, "Reckless Pioneer," 28. The quote is from "An Act to Limit the Continuation of Lotteries," Union College, *Documents Relative to the Dispute*, paragraph 19.

102. Richards, *Scholars and Gentlemen*, 13; NYHS Minutes, vol. 1, May 11, 1824, 273.

103. NYHS, Minutes, vol. 1, December 14, 1824, 286, and February 8, 1825, 290. The minutes simply state that in December representatives of the Athenaeum asked to confer with representatives of Columbia, the Society Library, and the Historical Society and that in February a "project is contemplated to be laid before the several institutions for the purpose of effecting this union." There is no explanation later as to why the plan was abandoned. The minutes of the directors of the Athenaeum in March explained that they considered it "indelicate to go forward in the unsettled state of affairs of the Athenaeum." Quoted in Austin Baxter Keep, *History of the New York Society Library* (New York: New York Society Library, 1908), 297–98. Apparently the Athenaeum's affairs were "unsettled" because it had been in existence only since December 1824.

104. NYHS, Minutes, vol. 1, April 12, 1825, 292–93. The full text of the advertisement is in Vail, *Knickerbocker Birthday*, 65.

105. NYHS, Minutes, vol. 1, May 28, 1825, 296–300 and June 4, 1825, 300–2. The vote was ten to six. Vail, *Knickerbocker Birthday*, 65–67. Vail quotes extensively from two editorials, including: "upon the subject of selling this valuable library, there is but one sentiment entertained by the press of this city." The *Daily*

National Journal in Washington warned that "the fact of this sale . . . will be greedily laid hold of by the scoffers at American taste and literature." "Washington," *Daily National Journal*, May 10, 1825.

106. New-York Historical Society, *To the Legislature* (1827). This includes the Society's petition, the first report of Committee on Literature, the law itself, and an address before the Society by David Hosack after its passage. The quote is from a second report of the committee. *Report from the Committee on Literature on the Memorial of the New-York Historical Society*, Senate Document 45 (Albany, 1827), 3. Clinton's remarks on the Society in his annual message to the legislature in 1827 are reprinted in Vail, *Knickerbocker Birthday*, 67–68.

107. NYHS, Minutes, vol. 1, January 13, 1829, 372. On Francis's debt, NYHS, Minutes, vol. 1, July 8, 1828, 339 and NYHS, Minutes, vol. 1, January 13, 1829, 344. These two reports of the committee explain how the debt was reduced or paid off. They give the best evidence of how confused and mismanaged the financial affairs of the Society were during this period. The committee had "great difficulty" just figuring out how much the Society owed.

108. NYHS, Minutes, vol. 1, July 8, 1828, 339, 341. The body of the report says that Pintard was offered the stock, but refused to sign a release. A small marginal note on page 341 says: "A release was duly executed on Jan. 7 1829 and forwarded to the committee."

109. "Historical Society," John Pintard Papers, Box 7, Folder 2, NYHS Library. This brief document is John Pintard's version of his dispute with the Society over money owed to him for books. It is written in the third person, and it is unclear who wrote it. The handwriting is probably not Pintard's. In all fairness to the special committee, which in its report in July 1828 referred to the "informality in former proceedings," Pintard, who served from 1819 to 1827, seems to have been at best an ineffective treasurer. The committee claimed, for example, that he collected no dues at all in 1821 and 1822, when the Society was heavily in debt. NYHS, Minutes, vol. 1, July 8, 1828, 339, 337.

110. Vail, *Knickerbocker Birthday*, 78. Folsom, "Historical Sketch," 467; Lawrence, "Purposes and Attainments of the Society," 11–12.

111. John Pintard to John W. Francis, September 1, 1831, John Pintard Papers, Box 11, New-York Historical Society Library. Francis was about the only early member of the Society left by 1831.

112. Vail wrote that officers would lend the keys to members and their friends "to the confusion of the Society's collections." Vail, *Knickerbocker* Birthday, 76. William Dunlap was able, for example, to conduct research for his history of the American theater with the help of his friend John Francis. William Dunlap, *Diary of William Dunlap (1766–1839): The Memoirs of a Dramatist, Theatrical Manager, Painter, Critic, Novelist, and Historian*, vol. 3, March 16, 1832–December 31, 1834 (New York: New-York Historical Society, 1930), 805 (July 19, 1834). Hone, *Diary*, 275–76 (September 28, 1837).

113. Campbell, "Historical Inquiry," 6. School district libraries were pioneered in New York State beginning in 1835 and were free to the entire community. See, Sidney H. Ditzion, "The District School Library, 1835–55," *Library Quarterly* 10 (Spring 1940): 545–77. It is not entirely clear why history became so popular around 1830. David D. Van Tassel, for example, cited George Templeton Strong, who remarked in his diary that Americans "crave a history" because "we have not, like England and France, centuries of achievements and calamities to look back on." Van Tassel, *Recording America's Past,* 100. And George H. Callcott held that "the American people . . . gloried in [history] as a sign of cultural maturity." Callcott, *History in the United States,* 25. However, neither of them, nor Levin and Pfitzer, cited later, explained satisfactorily why the rise in the popularity of history did not occur earlier in the century or why it declined after 1860. Moreover, the popularity of history during this period was a European as well as an American phenomenon.

114. For a chronological list of the societies established through 1890, see Van Tassel, *Recording America's Past,* 181–90. Some of these were mainly for genealogy and many lasted only a short time. Van Tassel included the St. Nicholas Society of the City of New York, founded by Washington Irving, which was really a social club rather than an historical society.

115. "The extraordinary actions of these men, while they rival the exploits recorded in chivalric tale, have the additional interest of verity." Washington Irving, *Voyages and Discoveries of the Companions of Columbus* (Philadelphia: Carey and Lea, 1831), 6.

116. Callcott, *History in the United States,* 33. Callcott's table is based upon Frank Luther Mott, *Golden Multitudes: The Story of Best Sellers in the United States* (New York: Bowker, 1947), appendixes A and B, 303–31. Mott's lists are arranged by date of publication and author, not by genre. Callcott included what Mott termed "better sellers" in appendix B. Mott defined a best seller as a book with sales equal to at least one percent of the population (303), according to "estimates based upon data drawn from a variety of sources," but concedes that "records are often faulty or nonexistent" (9).

117. John Tebbel, *A History of Book Publishing in the United States, Volume 1: The Creation of an Industry, 1630–1865* (New York: R. R. Bowker, 1972), 221. Tebbel identifies 1842 as "the great leap forward." There was a dramatic increase in the 1830s of both new books and books by American authors, but those gains were largely erased by the Panic of 1837. Green, "The Rise of Book Publishing," 124–27.

118. Pintard, *Letters to His Daughter,* 3:239 (April 2, 1831). Pintard referred specifically to the tendency to "amplify & throw into romance" the events of the Revolution and also to his "pains to correct such errors." Mott, *Golden* Multitudes, 306–8, 317–20. In certain instances it is difficult to distinguish between fiction and nonfiction on Mott's lists. For example, I counted Solon Robinson's "better

seller," *Hot Corn: Life Scenes in New York Illustrated* (1854) as nonfiction, but Robinson's "tales of truth" are probably a mix of fact and fiction.

119. Callcott, *History in the United States,* 34–35.

120. Ibid., 33. There were nine best sellers in history from 1800 to 1829.

121. Ibid., 13; Mott, *Golden Multitudes,* 88. Irving's historical works are: *History of the Life and Voyages of Christopher Columbus* (1828); *Chronicle of the Conquest of Grenada* (1829); *Voyages and Discoveries of the Companions of Columbus* (1831); *Astoria, or Anecdotes of an Enterprize Beyond the Rocky Mountains* (1836); *Oliver Goldsmith* (1849); *Mahomet and His Successors* (1849–50); and *Life of George Washington* (1855–59).

122. For the connections between romantic literature and history during this period, see, for example, David Levin, *History as Romantic Art: Bancroft, Prescott, Motley, and Parkman* (Stanford: Stanford University Press, 1959); Callcott, *History in the United States,* 11–13; and Gregory M. Pfitzer, *Popular History and the Literary Marketplace, 1840–1920* (Amherst: University of Massachusetts Press, 2008), 33–40.

123. George Bancroft, *History of the United States of America, from the Discovery of the Continent* (repr., Port Washington, N.Y.: Kennikat Press, 1967), 1: 1–3. This is a reprint of the last edition before Bancroft's death, published in 1885. He adds at the end of the introduction that he did not change a word of it because the nearly fifty "intervening years have justified their expression of confidence in the progress of our republic." This very brief introduction is a good summary of the grand narrative in American historiography.

124. John Warner Barber, *Incidents in American History: Being a Selection of the Most Important and Interesting Events which Have Transpired Since the Discovery of America, to the Present Time,* 3RD ed. (New York: Cooledge, 1847), 1.

125. Pfitzer, *Popular History,* 37–40; Stanley T. Williams, *The Life of Washington Irving* (New York: Oxford University Press, 1935), 1:323, 2:297. There are few detailed, reliable primary sources for these two key events. Irving certainly manufactured certain details solely to heighten the drama and romance of his narrative.

126. On the role of facts in history and the relationship between facts and moral truth, see Callcott, *History in the United States,* 177–78; Pfitzer, *Popular History,* 29–31. "Romantic colouring" and "intrinsic truth" are from Washington Irving to Thomas Aspinwall, August 31, 1828, in Washington Irving, *Letters, Volume II, 1823–1838,* vol. 24 of *The Complete Works of Washington Irving,* ed. Ralph M. Alderman, Herbert L. Kleinfield, and Jennifer S. Banks (Boston: Twayne, 1979), 330. This letter refers to his *Conquest of Granada.* Irving's frequent references to fact and fiction in his correspondence are complex and inconsistent. For example, in another letter from this same period, to his publisher Henry Carey, he wrote that the *Conquest of Grenada* was based upon "old

Spanish historians [but] colored and tinted by the imagination so as to have a romantic air, without destroying the historical basis . . . of events." But in the very next sentence he claims his history is "as near the truth as any of the [early] chronicles [with] the advantage of containing the striking facts . . . true or false, of all of them." Washington Irving to Henry Carey, October 11, 1828, *Letters*, 2:347.

127. *The Critic, a Weekly Review of Literature, Fine Arts, and the Drama*, June 13, 1829, 86. *Monthly Review of Literature*, April 1828, 407–10 [available in Early English Periodicals]. Washington Irving, *The Life and Voyages of Christopher Columbus*, vol. 11 of *The Complete Works of Washington Irving*, ed. John Harmon McElroy (Boston: Twayne, 1981), 31.

128. William Cullen Bryant, *A Discourse on the Life, Character and Genius of Washington Irving, Delivered Before the New York Historical Society, at the Academy of Music in New York, on the 3d of April, 1860* (New York: G. P. Putnam, 1860), 30.

129. Williams, *Washington Irving*, 1:292–93, 2:75–86. Williams called *Astoria* a "stupendous piece of hack work" (75). See also James P. Ronda, "Washington Irving's West," *Historian* 66 (Fall 2004): 546–51.

130. [Washington Irving], "From the Elbow-Chair of Launcelot Langstaff, Esq," *Salmagundi; or, the Whim-Whams and Opinions of Launcelot Langstaff, Esq., and Others* January 24, 1807, 8. In 1807, Irving's family supported him. The family business went bankrupt in 1819.

131. John McWilliams, "The Almighty [unmentionable] Dollar": Washington Irving and Money," *Literature in the Early American Republic: Annual Studies on Cooper and His Contemporaries* 2 (2010): 202–27. By the time of his death, Washington Irving's works had sold approximately 800,000 copies and he had earned more than $200,000. Tebbel, *History of Book Publishing*, 1:222. Pierre Munro Irving, "Literary Statistics," in *Life and Letters of Washington Irving*, reprinted in Andrew B. Myers, ed., *A Century of Commentary on the Works of Washington Irving* (Tarrytown, N.Y.: Sleepy Hollow Restorations, 1976), 34–37. For a good example of Irving as literary entrepreneur, see a letter to his agent, Thomas Aspinwall, August 31, 1828. Of *The Conquest of Granada* he wrote, "if it succeeds the subject is one of permanent interest and must make the book something of a stock book. This publishers will take into consideration when making a bargain." Irving, *Letters*, 2:331. Such discussions of the market for print are common in Irving's correspondence. I am not arguing that Irving was not a genial man of letters, but he also had a shrewd appreciation of and catered to the reading public.

132. For what David Van Tassel termed "the raid on foreign archives" and similar documentary projects, see Van Tassel, *Recording America's Past*, 104–8; Callcott, *History in the United States*, 49–51; and Dunlap, *American Historical*

Societies, 54–60. The quote is from a petition of the New-York Historical Society to the state legislature in 1846 for a grant to publish collections of state documents. NYHS, *Proceedings* (1846), 98.

133. For an account of Brodhead's raid, see Brodhead, *Documents Relative to the Colonial History of New York,* xxii–xxxvi. This is the report that he submitted to the governor upon his return from Europe. His report to the Society is appended to NYHS, *Proceedings* (1844), 1–55. See also Nicholas Falco, "The Empire State's Search in European Archives," *American Archivist* 32 (Spring 1969): 109–23. The reference to ransacking archives is NYHS, *Proceedings* (1844), 48. There were similar projects in England, France, and Prussia around the same time to collect and publish government documents. Van Tassel, *Recording America's Past,* 105.

134. E. B. O'Callaghan, ed., *Documentary History of the State of New York* (Albany: Weeds, Parsons, 1849–51); *Journals of the Provincial Congress, Provincial Convention, Committee of Safety and Council of Safety* (Albany: Weeds, 1842) in two volumes. E. B. O'Callaghan, ed., *Journal of the Legislative Council of the Colony of New York* (Albany: Weeds, Parsons, 1861) two volumes. The New-York Historical Society petitioned the legislature to published the first two: NYHS, *Proceedings* (1843), 8–9; (1849), 37.

135. Callcott, *History in the United States,* 51 n. 57; Francis, *New York During the Last Half Century,* 227.

136. The law passed in 1849 for the publication and distribution of *Documents Relative to the Colonial History of the State of New York* specified that the volumes were to be sold for no less than 25 percent of the cost of production. Another law passed seven years later required that they were to be sold for not less than $2.50. Brodhead, *Documents Relative to the Colonial History of New York,* xliii–xlv. Both laws reserved copies for "literary exchanges and distribution," which presumably included distribution to public libraries.

137. "*Collections of the New York Historical Society,* Second Series, Volume I," *New York Review,* January 1842, 96. The reviewer was actually posing a rhetorical question, asking whether in a large, prosperous city like New York (the "haunts of commerce") a publication so valuable should meet with public indifference. The Historical Society's financial accounts were in such a confused state in the early years that it is difficult to determine how much money they lost by publishing the *Collections,* but it may have been one reason the Society nearly folded in the early 1820s. A "Memorandum of Publications of the Society on hand, 1848," for example, shows hundreds of unsold volumes from the first series. "Memorandum of Publications of the Society on hand, 1848," Official Papers, 1846–1849, Folder 6, NYHS Archives, NYHS Library. Moreover, a number of the addresses before the Society make reference to the duty of each member to purchase every volume of the *Collections.* The *Proceedings* of the Society ceased publication in 1849 because they lost money.

138. De Peyster, *In Assembly, March 2, 1829, Report*, 4.

139. NYHS, *Collections* (1849), iv, NYHS, *Proceedings* (1849), 33. In 1858, the Society established an endowment, the Publication Fund, to pay for future *Collections*. For the terms of the fund, see NYHS, *Circular to Members* (n.p., 1864), 2–3 and Kelby, *New York Historical Society*, 132. The Society published thirty volumes between 1868 and 1897.

140. "The New-York Historical Society," *American Monthly Magazine*, February 1838, 197.

141. Campbell, "Historical Inquiry," 6; "The New-York Historical Society," *New Yorker*, November 17, 1838, 141.

142. For the full text of the agreement to share the collections, see Vail, *Knickerbocker Birthday*, 84. See also LeRoy E. Kimball, "The Old University Building and the Society's Years on Washington Square," *New-York Historical Society Quarterly* 32 (July 1948): 149–219. The Society moved from the Remsen Building to rent-free rooms in the Stuyvesant Institute in 1837, but it was forced to move again when the Institute defaulted on its mortgage during the Panic of 1837. Peter Gerard Stuyvesant was president of the Society from 1836 to 1839. Vail, *Knickerbocker Birthday*, 78–82.

143. NYHS, *Proceedings* (1849), 20. NYHS, *Proceedings* (1846), 9. The 230 members in 1827 are listed in NYHS, *Memorial* (1827), 23–26. The Society began meeting monthly rather than quarterly in 1816. Vail, *Knickerbocker* Birthday, 58.

144. Vail, *Knickerbocker Birthday*, 86; NYHS, Minutes, vol. 2, October 4, 1842.

145. NYHS, *Proceedings* (1843), 95; NYHS, *Proceedings* (1848), 19.

146. "Daniel Webster's Address Before the New York Historical Society," *Weekly Herald*, February 28, 1852, 6. *Evening Mirror*, November 20, 1854, quoted in Vail, *Knickerbocker Birthday*, 387–88. NYHS, *Dedication of the Library*, 25–26. Many women may have attended meetings in earlier decades, but this is the first time that their presence was frequently remarked upon in the press and the Society's publications. In 1846, apparently for the first time, they were invited to partake of the refreshments after a meeting. NYHS, *Proceedings* (1846), 30.

147. NYHS, *Proceedings* (1843), 95; Folsom, "Historical Sketch," 468. See also Donald M. Scott, "The Popular Lecture and the Creation of a Public in Mid-nineteenth Century America," *Journal of American History* 66 (March 1980): 791–809; Robert J. Greef, "Public Lectures in New York, 1851–1878: A Cultural Index of the Times" (PhD diss., University of Chicago, 1941); Waldo W. Braden, "The Lecture Movement: 1840–1860," *Quarterly Journal of Speech* 34 (April 1948): 206–12.

148. Philip Hone commented in his diary on the popularity of public lectures generally and specifically on the course delivered by Sparks. Hone, *Diary*, 572–73 (November 15, 1841). "New York Historical Society," *New York Spectator*, October 27, 1841. "The celebrity of Dr. Sparks as a historical writer . . . renders it unnecessary . . . to say one word in support of his eminent qualifications."

149. The lectures for 1838 through the first part of 1841 are listed in NYHS, *Proceedings* (1841), 470. Folsom remarked upon the success of the series in 1838 and 1839. Folsom, "Historical Sketch," 468–69. Vail wrote that the series in 1840 "was discontinued for lack of support." Vail, *Knickerbocker Birthday*, 86. This may have had as much to do with competition from other lectures and other forms of entertainment as the subject matter of the lectures.

150. NYHS, *Proceedings* (1844), 21. This is from the annual report.

151. Folsom, "Historical Sketch," 469; NYHS. *Proceedings* (1847), 8, 50. The "subscription" for the library raised $1,000 in $50 contributions.

152. Lenox donated, for example, a copy of Davis Peterson De Vries, *Voyages from Holland to America, a.d. 1632 to 1644*, "one of the rarest [books] to be found." NYHS, *Collections* (1857), 4. John Brodhead, in an address in 1844, remarked that the new class of corresponding members was "of great importance, . . . we hope [they] will become valuable contributors to our Institution." NYHS, *Proceedings* (1844), appendix, 44. New-York Historical Society, *Constitution and By-Laws of the New York Historical Society, Founded November 20th, 1804* (New York: The Society, 1844), 5. Corresponding members resided outside of New York City, and some lived abroad.

153. NYHS, *Proceedings* (1843), 20; NYHS, *Collections* (1859). This volume of the *Collections* was the first printed catalog since 1814. See also James J. Heslin, "Library Acquisitions policy of the New-York Historical Society," *New-York Historical Society Quarterly* 46 (January 1962): 90.

154. Lawrence, "Purposes and Attainments of the New-York Historical Society," 13.

155. For the specific hours, see NYHS, *Proceedings* (1843), 32. Although the days are not specified, the library would not have been opened on Sundays during this period. "Persons introduced by a member, during [these] hours, have free access to the library." Introductions were apparently relatively informal. A circular published in 1862 states that "visitors may be introduced to the library, etc., by the private card of a Member, or written note of introduction." New-York Historical, "Circular to Members," (n.p.: 1862), 2.

156. Richard, *Gentlemen and Scholars*, 34–37. The office of librarian remained an elected position until 1937, when the by-laws were amended to include a director of the Society.

157. NYHS, *Proceedings* (1846), 35–36; (1847), 62; (1848), 13. The catalog was the fourth volume of the second series of the *Collections*.

158. NYHS, *Proceedings* (1846), 31; Charles C. Jewett, *Notices of Public Libraries in the United States* (Washington, D.C.: Printed for the House of Representatives, 1851), 93. This report was an appendix to the Smithsonian's annual report to Congress in 1850.

159. NYHS, *Proceedings* (1843), 19; (1849), 35, 69. The proceedings and other publications of the Society during this period refer frequently the fact that the library was not safe in a building that was not fire proof.

160. NYHS, *Proceedings* (1847), 83–85. An extensive account of the Building Committee's work is in NYHS, Minutes, vol. 2, January 15, 1850.

161. New York State, Senate, "Memorial of the New York Historical Society, Jan. 7, 1850," 2–3 (WorldCat accession no. 44089817). This includes the petition, as well as the report of the senate committee on colleges, academies, and common schools. NYHS, Minutes, vol. 2, January 15, 1850 refers to a favorable report in the assembly. The bill was tabled in the assembly in April 1849. *Journal of the Assembly of the State of New York* (1849), 1189.

162. NYHS, Minutes, vol. 2, January 15, 1850. This extensive report from the committee makes no mention of a public appeal in local newspapers. "Appeal" [1848], Official Papers, 1846–1849, Folder 2, New-York Historical Society Archives, New-York Historical Society Library.

163. NYHS, *Proceedings* (1847), 85. William B. Astor was John Jacob Astor's son. He took over his father's business interests after his death and served on the board of the Astor Library. Field was later president of the Historical Society and the New York Free Circulating Library.

164. George Bancroft said essentially the same thing, that "the building [was] the endowment for history by the citizens and especially by the merchants of New York." NYHS, *Dedication of the Library*, 10, 16. Francis, *New York During the Last Half Century*, 232.

165. NYHS, *Dedication of the Library*, 16.

166. Ibid., 13; New-York Historical Society, *Catalogue of the Printed Books in the Library of the New-York Historical Society*, Collections of the New-York Historical Society, ser. 2, vol. 4 (New York: The Society, 1859), v–vi.

167. NYHS, *Dedication of the Library*, 25.

168. Cogswell joined in 1838. New-York Historical Society, *The Charter and By-Laws of the New York Historical Society, Revised January 1858, With a List of Members* (New York: New-York Historical Society, 1862), 49. For the collection development policy at the Astor Library, see a report by Cogswell reprinted in Harry Miller Lydenberg, *History of the New York Public Library Astor Lenox and Tilden Foundations* (New York: New York Public Library, 1923), 24–32. The history collection policy is at page 31. "This department is fuller perhaps than any other." Cogswell specifically did not want extensive collections in theology, law, and medicine, because there were specialized collections elsewhere in the city (26–27, 35).

4. The Biblical Library of the American Bible Society: Evangelicalism and the Evangelical Corporation

1. Luther Bradish, "The Progress of History," (1849), New-York Historical Society (hereafter also NYHS) Addresses, Box 2, NYHS Archives, 3, 32, 2, 10.

2. The most comprehensive critical history of the American Bible Society to date is Peter J. Wosh, *Spreading the Word: The Bible Business in Nineteenth-Century America* (Ithaca, N.Y.: Cornell University Press, 1994). Other second-

ary works include Creighton Lacy, *The Word-Carrying Giant: The Growth of the American Bible Society (1816–1966)* (South Pasadena, Calif.: William Carey Library, 1977), and two official histories, William P. Strickland, *History of the American Bible Society from Its Organization to the Present Time* (New York: Harper Bros., 1856), and Henry Otis Dwight, *The Centennial History of the American Bible Society* (New York: Macmillan, 1916).

3. American Bible Society, *Constitution of the American Bible Society . . . together with their Address to the People of the United States* (New York: G. F. Hopkins, 1816), 9, 16.

4. On social control and the benevolent empire, see, for example, Clifford S. Griffin, "Religious Benevolence as Social Control," *Mississippi Valley Historical Review* 44 (December 1957): 423–44. On the founding of the American Bible Society, Clifford S. Griffin, *Their Brothers' Keeper: Moral Stewardship in the United States, 1800–1865* (New Brunswick, N.J.: Rutgers University Press, 1960), 25–29.

5. American Bible Society (hereafter also ABS), *Constitution and Address* (1816), 13–14. "Stupendous political changes" is, at least in part, a reference to the moribund state of the Federalist Party. The year following the founding of the American Bible Society, the Federalists declined to run a gubernatorial candidate in New York State, overwhelmed by "the Irish and that class who were brought in by the Democrats to break down Federalism." John Pintard, *Letters from John Pintard to His Daughter Eliza Noel Pintard Davidson, 1816–1833*, ed. Dorothy C. Barck (New York: New York Historical Society, 1940–41), 1:63 (May 1, 1817).

6. ABS, *Constitution and Address* (1816), 13–20.

7. American Bible Society, *First Annual Report* (New York: American Bible Society, 1817), 30; ABS, Minutes of the Board of Managers, January 15, 1817, and February 5, 1817, ABS Archives.

8. The Society did not employ a librarian until 1836. The office of recording secretary was its first paid position, although Pintard later claimed he donated the annual salary of $400 to charity. Pintard, *Letters to His Daughter*, 4:24 (March 2, 1832). He served as recording secretary until 1836, when he was elected a vice president. He held that office until his death in 1844.

9. John Pintard to Samuel Bayard, March 22, 1817, John Pintard Papers, New-York Historical Society. Quoted in Peter J. Wosh and Lorraine A. Coons, "A 'Special Collection' in Nineteenth-Century New York: The American Bible Society and Its Library," *Libraries & Culture* 32 (Summer 1997): 326.

10. "Status of Bibles Donated to ABS 1817/1818," typewritten manuscript dated January 31, 1941, ABS Archives; ABS, Minutes of the Board of Managers, January 15, 1817, and February 6, 1823.

11. Pintard, *Letters to His Daughter*, 1:89 (November 7, 1817).

12. For Pintard's reading habits, see Larry E. Sullivan, "Books, Power, and the Development of Libraries in the New Republic: The Prison and Other Journals of John Pintard of New York," *Journal of Library History* 21 (Spring 1986): 407–24.

13. John Pintard, "Reflections of John Pintard, L.L.D., Transcribed by his daughter, Louis Hall Pintard Servoss," John Pintard Papers, Box 16, NYHS. This autobiographical fragment is a fascinating, charming document. It describes Pintard as a youth of seventeen, "imbued with the principles of liberty," quitting college and rushing to the defense of New York City.

14. The most detailed biography of Pintard available is David L. Sterling, "New York Patriarch: A Life of John Pintard, 1759–1844" (Ph.D. diss., New York University, 1958). See also, James Grant Wilson, *John Pintard, Founder of the New-York Historical Society* (New York: New-York Historical Society, 1902); and Dumas Malone, ed., *Dictionary of American Biography* (New York: Scribner's, 1934), s.v. "John Pintard," by Robert Greenhalgh Albion.

15. Wosh makes a similar point in *Spreading the Word*, 13. He also stresses, as I do below, the importance of localism in elite civic involvement during this early period.

16. Pintard, *Letters to His Daughter*, 1:94 (December 2, 1817). Pintard's wife teased him that he had "an insatiable itch to be always occupied with everyone's business but [his] own."

17. Ibid., 1:47–48, 197 (January 3, 1817; June 8, 1819). See also Sullivan, "Books, Power, and the Development of Libraries," 409.

18. Thomas Bender, *New York Intellect: A History of Intellectual Life in New York City, from 1750 to the Beginnings of Our Own Time* (New York: Knopf, 1987), 66.

19. Clinton was a founder of the Society and served on the board of managers and as a vice president. See Evan Cornog, *The Birth of Empire: DeWitt Clinton and the American Experience* (Oxford: Oxford University Press, 1998).

20. John Pintard to Elias Boudinot, May 20, 1817, ABS Archives, Recording Secretary's Papers.

21. ABS, *Constitution and Address* (1816), 11–12. There were obviously practical reasons for these constitutional requirements as well. Requiring that a majority of the managers live in New York made it easier for the board to conduct its business in a regular and timely fashion. But at the same time, New Yorkers took pride in the fact that the Society was headquartered in their city. In a speech at the constituting convention, manager George Griffin called New York "the London of America" that would "electrify the Western continent." American Bible Society, *Proceedings of a Meeting . . . of the American Bible Society . . . with the Speeches . . .* (New York: J. Seymour, 1816), 8.

22. ABS, *Proceedings of a Meeting* (1816), 10–11, 14–15.

23. Thomas L. Haskell, "Capitalism and the Origins of Humanitarian Sensibility, Part I," *American Historical Review* 90 (April 1985): 339–61, and "Capitalism and the Origins of Humanitarian Sensibility, Part II," *American Historical Review* 90 (June 1985): 547–66. The quote is at page 342, and the emphasis is Haskell's.

24. ABS, *Constitution and Address* (1816), 20.

25. Assuming that free Bibles would not be read, the local societies normally sold Bibles at cost. The Society produced Bibles very cheaply and sold them to its constituent societies at cost and to societies that were not affiliated at five percent above cost. ABS, Minutes of the Board of Managers, January 15, 1817.

26. See, for example, ABS, *Twenty-Fifth Annual Report* (1841), 118.

27. Between 1816 and 1863, the Society published four catalogs, in 1823, 1837, 1855, and 1863. There are no surviving copies of the catalog prepared by John Pintard in 1823. ABS, Minutes of the Committee on Versions, March 26, 1896, ABS Archives.

28. ABS, Minutes of the Board of Managers, February 6, 1823.

29. American Bible Society, *Catalogue of the Editions of the Holy Scriptures in Various Languages, and Other Biblical Works, in the Library of the American Bible Society* (New York: Daniel Fanshaw, 1837), 26–27. These titles included reference works for modern European languages as well as Hindi, Persian, Burmese, Chinese, Arabic, and Ethiopic.

30. ABS, *First Annual Report* (1817), 29; and *Annual Report* (1818), 53–54. The French Bibles were distributed in the newly acquired Louisiana Territory. John Pintard in particular was very interested in Louisiana. See Sterling, "John Pintard," 216–41.

31. ABS, *Second Annual Report* (1818), 53. The quote is part of an account of a joint lobbying effort undertaken by the American Bible Society and the Philadelphia Bible Society. The societies petitioned Congress without success to lift the import duty on Bibles in foreign languages.

32. ABS, *Catalog* (1837), 5–6.

33. ABS, *Second Annual Report* (1818), 48–51. The emphasis is in the report.

34. ABS, *Proceedings of a Meeting* (1816), 8.

35. ABS, *Twenty-Second Annual Report* (1838), 980–81.

36. ABS, *Catalogue of the Library* (1837), endleaf.

37. Wosh, *Spreading the Word*, 152.

38. ABS, *Seventeenth Annual Report* (1833), 681.

39. ABS, *Eighteenth Annual Report* (1834), 708. The resolution as originally proposed aimed at supplying the entire world within the space of twenty years. The managers prevailed upon the members to be somewhat less ambitious. ABS, *Twenty-Fourth Annual Report* (1840), 54–55.

40. Ibid., 55.

41. Ibid. (1856), 41.

42. American Bible Society, *Catalogue of Books Contained in the Library of the American Bible Society, Embracing Editions of the Holy Scriptures in Various Languages, and Other Biblical and Miscellaneous Works* (New York: American Bible Society, 1863), 127–33. There were 1,339 editions of the Bible in the 1863 catalog.

43. ABS, *Forty-Sixth Annual Report* (1862), 26.

44. ABS, *Catalogue* (1863), 135–60.

45. Gordon S. Wood, "Republicanism and the Political History of Colonial America: Afterword," *Proceedings of the American Antiquarian Society* 102 (April 1992): 213. This is the concluding essay in a special issue entitled "The Republican Synthesis Revisited."

46. David L. Sterling, "William Duer, John Pintard, and the Panic of 1792," in Joseph R. Frese and Jacob Judd, eds., *Business Enterprise in Early New York* (Tarrytown, N.Y.: Sleepy Hollow Press, 1979), 99–132. This article is based largely on his dissertation, "John Pintard," 134–70. Edwin G. Burrows and Mike Wallace, *Gotham: A History of New York City to 1898* (New York: Oxford University Press), 309–10. Burrows and Wallace contend that Duer's plan was to hype the stock by circulating rumors of the merger and then sell at a handsome profit.

47. John Pintard to Lewis Marsden Davidson, May 6, 1833, Pintard Papers, New-York Historical Society. Quoted in Sterling, "John Pintard," 143.

48. John Pintard to Jeremy Belknap, August 26, 1798, in Massachusetts Historical Society, *Collections Massachusetts Historical Society*, 6th series (Boston: Massachusetts Historical Society, 1891), 4:446–48. Pintard would have been expected, of course, to close the letter with "Your humble servant, John Pintard."

49. "Biblical Library of the American Bible Society," *Christian Herald*, July 12, 1817, 256.

50. ABS, *Constitution and Address* (1816), 17; *First Annual Report* (1817), 23.

51. Wosh, *Spreading the Word*, 18–24; David Paul Nord, "The Evangelical Origins of Mass Media in America," *Journalism Monographs* 88 (May 1984): 7–11, 17.

52. Dwight, *Centennial History of the American Bible Society*, 577.

53. ABS, *Thirty-Seventh Annual Report* (1853), 774–76; Wosh, *Spreading the Word*, 17. The claim that it was the largest building in the city is in "The New Bible House," *Scientific American*, April 9, 1853, 234.

54. ABS, *Thirty-Eighth Annual Report* (1854), 34–35.

55. ABS, *Thirty-Ninth Annual Report* (1855), 36.

56. ABS Library, Minutes of the Committee on Versions, March 26, 1896, 258–59. Gilman also noted a third purpose, "the opening for Bible students of a library for reference and consultation."

57. ABS Library, Minutes of the Board of Managers, May 15, 1818. Pintard wrote to his daughter that indexing the correspondence "made my head snap." Pintard, *Letters to his Daughter*, 1:316 (August 21, 1820).

58. ABS, By-Laws, 1845, Article XII, American Bible Society Archives.

59. In 1853, the Society employed thirty-seven agents. For the development of the agency system, see Wosh, *Spreading the Word,* 175–99.

60. ABS, Minutes of the Committee on Agencies, February 2, 1859, ABS Archives.

61. Instructions for agents were set forth in: American Bible Society, *Bible Agents Guide* (New York: American Bible Society, 1860). The form is reprinted in Peter J. Wosh, "Bibles, Benevolence, and Bureaucracy: The Changing Nature of Nineteenth Century Religious Records," *American Archivist* 52 (Spring 1989): 174. The change to the new format was not effected without opposition. William Forrest, the chairman of the Agency committee complained that it was "an attempt to bring within the computation of a business transaction the worth of truth or the gain of godliness" (175). This mania for tabulation apparently effected even the descriptions of the library in the annual reports. From 1858 to 1861, the library section simply lists the books added for that year with no accompanying text.

62. ABS, Minutes Board of Managers, February 6, 1823.

63. Pintard, *Letters to His Daughter,* 1:44, 91 (January 2, 1817). Pintard's relations with his bishop became increasingly strained over the years, especially after Hobart opposed the establishment of the General Theological Seminary. When he died in 1830, Pintard wrote to his daughter: "I hope he is better off than I trust our Diocese will be." Pintard, *Letters to his Daughter,* 3:175 (September 9, 1830).

64. ABS, Minutes of the Board of Managers, November 19, 1835.

65. Ibid., April 7, 1836.

66. ABS, *Twenty-Third Annual Report* (1839), 39; *Twenty-Fourth Annual Report* (1840), 53.

67. Strickland, *History of the American Bible Society,* 75, 201.

68. Pintard, *Letters to His Daughter,* 3:52, 152 (December 17, 1828; June 11, 1830).

69. ABS, *Twenty-First Annual Report* (1837), 888; *Twentieth Annual Report* (1836), 840.

5. Commerce and Culture: Recreation and Self-Improvement in New York's Subscription Libraries

1. The quote is from [Plaintiff's reply to Defendant's answer to complaint], October 13, 1851; part of New York Superior Court, "Trustees of the New York Society Library against The Mayor, Alderman, and Commonalty of the City of New York, Judgment Roll," New York County Clerk, Division of Old Records. For a summary of the case, see Austin Baxter Keep, *History of the New York Society Library* (New York: New York Society, 1908), 422–26. Interestingly, Keep, in this official history of the Library, claimed that the judge ruled in favor of the City on

a technicality, "on the ground that the Library had not pursued the proper remedy" (423). This is not true. The City levied a tax in 1838, 1839, 1849, 1850, and 1887 (507) and the Library appealed each time. It only paid the real estate tax in 1849 and 1850, by court order. The Mercantile Library Association was taxed each year and never appealed.

2. See Chapter 1.

3. Keep, *New York Society Library*, 101–11; Jesse H. Shera, *Foundations of the Public Library: The Origins of the Public Library Movement in New England, 1629–1855* (Chicago: University of Chicago Press, 1949; repr., n.p.: Shoestring Press, 1965), 127–55. Noel closed his circulating library soon after the Society Library reopened.

4. Quoted in David Kaser, *A Book for a Sixpence: The Circulating Library in America* (Pittsburgh: Beta Phi Mu, 1980), 19.

5. On the New York Institution, see Chapter 1. See also Thomas Bender, *New York Intellect: A History of Intellectual Life in New York City, from 1750 to the Beginnings of Our Own Time* (New York: Knopf, 1987), 62–66.

6. Lloyd Haberly, "The American Museum from Baker to Barnum," *New-York Historical Society Quarterly* 43 (July 1959): 273–80. The Tammany Society first sold the museum to Gardiner Baker in 1795, and it was sold two more times before John Scudder purchased it in 1810. After Scudder's death in 1821, it became increasingly more popular and less educational.

7. *New-York Gazette*, August 29, 1763.

8. Joseph Osborne, *Prospectus of J. Osborn's Circulating Library (Formerly H. Caritat's)* (New York: s.n, 1806), 4–5. Available online from Early American Imprints, Second Series. Fiction comprised 41 percent of the collection in the catalog that Caritat published two years earlier. Kaser, *Books for a Sixpence*, 174.

9. *To the Stock Holders of the New-York Society Library* (n.p., 1833), 6. Bluford Adams, *E Pluribus Barnum: The Great Showman and the Making of U.S. Popular Culture* (Minneapolis: University of Minnesota Press, 1997), 75–115.

10. The Swiss Bearded Lady: *New York Times*, September 10, 1853. The "Aztec Children" at the Society Library: *New York Daily Times*, December 16, 1851; and at Barnum's American Museum: James W. Cook, ed., *The Colossal P. T. Barnum Reader: Nothing Else Like It in the Universe* (Urbana: University of Illinois Press, 2005), 174. Tom Thumb: *New York Times*, January 10, 1854. "Moral humbug" is quoted in A. H. Saxon, *P. T. Barnum: The Legend and the Man* (New York: Columbia University Press, 1989), 210.

11. See, for example, *New York Evening Post*, July 11, 1839, with front-page advertisements from three circulating libraries, all of which emphasize the selection of novels. Very few catalogs survive from this period, but see *Catalogue of the Irving Circulating Library, 120 Nassau Street, Conducted by William H. Attree* (New York: n.p., 1842). It lists only the novels in the collection.

12. New-York Lyceum, *New-York Lyceum* (New York: n.p., 1840). Available online in Readex's American Broadsides and Ephemera, Series I, 1760–1900.

13. Ibid.

14. [Plaintiff's, New York Society Library's, summons and complaint] March 25, 1851; [Defendant's, the City of New York's, answer to plaintiff's complaint], June 25, 1851, New York Superior Court, "Trustees of the New York Society Library against The Mayor, Alderman, and Commonalty of the City of New York, Judgment Roll." The reference to stockholders is from the defendant's answer to the complaint. The reference to the true intent and meaning of the law is from the complaint. The references to public character and public usefulness are from an opinion by the City Counsel in a separate case against the Library in 1839, which is attached as Schedule K of the complaint.

15. The original address is in "New York Society Library Minutes, March 1842 to April 1846," February 17, 1845, New York Society Library Archives. The address actually circulated is: "The Trustees of the New-York Society Library respectfully ask the attention of the public to the following statement" [1846], G. NYSL Circulars, Box 1, New York Society Library Archives. A draft is in "New York Society Library Minutes, May 1846 to June 1852," November 11, 1846, New York Society Library Archives. The same committee wrote both addresses and the board approved publishing the first in local newspapers. It seems that the board had a change of heart and later wanted a less inclusive address and one that was not as widely distributed. I have searched extensively and found only one newspaper advertisement from the nineteenth century, from the September 26, 1836 edition of the *New-York Spectator.*

16. New York Society Library, *Annual Report of the Trustees of the New York Society Library* (New York: New York Society, 1866), 4–5; NYSL, *Annual Report* (1873), 3; *Annual Report* (1898), 5. See also "To Shareholders," NYSL Circulars, Box 1, NYSL Archives. This is a printed letter sent to shareholders from the Committee of the Shareholders with the dated handwritten in as February 25, 1856. "They take the liberty of asking you to procure among your friends at least one additional shareholder." More often the task of personally recruiting new members fell to the librarian and the trustees. See, for example, Butler, W. S.—misc., Correspondence and Librarian's Papers, Series 2, Box 1, 1860–1890, NYSL Archives. This has copies of a number of letters written by the librarian to individuals asking them to join the Library. Committee on Library Funds—List of Names Invited to be Members, Trustee Committee Reports, 1842–1884, NYSL Archives. This fairly extensive list has an address and occupation for each name, which presumably helped determine that they were "suitable."

17. New York Society Library, *New York Society Library, A membership in the library makes the reading of books . . .* (New York: New York Society, c. 1910) (copy at the New-York Historical Society).

18. NYSL, *Annual Report* (1857), 12–13. In 1856, an entirely new board was elected that for a time took a much more active role in trying to increase the usefulness of the Library. The report for 1856 contains very similar language. In fact, it stresses that the Library was particularly important for families of the nouveau riche. "Let the sons and daughters who are to represent this opulence be cultivated so that they may grace it by their intelligence." NYSL, *Annual Report* (1856), 7–8.

19. New York Society Library, *The New York Society Library, In presenting to the public the advantages . . .* (New York: New York Society, 1876) (copy at the New-York Historical Society). The annual report for 1904 included a list of families that were members during the colonial period and still held shares in 1904. NYSL, *Annual Report* (1904), 12.

20. A list of members in 1856 is included in John MacMullen, *A Lecture on the Past, Present and Future of the New-York Society Library* (New York: John F. Trow, 1856), 29–42. Membership for 1908—725 members—is given in Austin Baxter Keep, *History of the New York Society Library* (New York: De Vinne Press, 1908), 522. In this official history of the NYSL, Keep also emphasized the patronage of the first families. By 1908, the Library offered "temporary" annual subscription for $15 that did not require the purchase of a share. These generated more income than the proprietary subscriptions (521–22). On the national elite in New York City, see Sven Beckert, *Monied Metropolis: New York City and the Consolidation of the American Bourgeoisie, 1850–1896* (Cambridge: Cambridge University Press, 2002), 237–39. In 1892, 1103 of the 4047 millionaires in the United States lived in New York City. Tribune Association, *American Millionaires: The Tribune's List of Persons Reputed to be Worth a Million or More* (New York: Tribune Association, 1892), 90–91.

21. NYSL, *Annual Report* (1857), 5. See also, for example, MacMullen, *Lecture*, 19. "The mother and the daughter need a quiet place . . . apart from the rush of the multitude."

22. NYSL, *Annual Report* (1900), 3. It is unclear if there was still a separate reading room for women in 1900. If there was, it probably saw little use. Over the years, the space was occasionally rented out to various tenants. Keep, *Society Library*, 475–76. For a seminal work on the cult of domesticity, see Nancy F. Cott, *Bonds of Womenhood: "Women's Sphere" in New England: 1780–1835* (New Haven, Conn.: Yale University Press, 1977).

23. Ronald J. Zboray, *Fictive People: Antebellum Economic Development and the American Reading Public* (New York: Oxford, 1993), 163, 203–5. Zboray estimates that the circulation of novels more than doubled from 1847–49 to 1854–56, from 21.13 percent to 45.40 percent. I think this is because there was a new catalog in 1850. It had less fiction than the 1838 catalog (see Chapter 2), but it was *new* fiction. NYSL, *Annual Report* (1899), 4.

24. NYSL, *Annual Report* (1886); (1895), 18–35. Henry S. F. Cooper Jr. and Jenny Lawrence, eds., *The New York Society Library: 250 Years* (New York: New York Society, 2004), 92–93. This is a collection of documents and excerpts of documents from the Library's archives. On Ouida, see, for example, Dee Garrison, *Apostles of Culture: The Public Librarian and American Society, 1876–1920* (New York: Free Press, 1979; repr., Madison: University of Wisconsin Press, 2003), 85–86.

25. NYSL, *Annual Report* (1857), 9; *Annual Report* (1881), 3.

26. NYSL, *Annual Report* (1903), 4.

27. NYSL, *Annual Report* (1858), 4.

28. Keep, *History of the New York Society Library*, 476; "Finding the Centre of New York Society, *New York Times Sunday Magazine*, December 19, 1909. The second is a fascinating article that reports on how the *Social Register* tracked the movement of the families listed in the register as they moved north, displacing working-class and middle-class residents as they went. Until the turn of the century, the average was one block per year. The center in 1859 was Fourteenth Street.

29. NYSL, *Annual Report* (1870), 8; *Annual Report* (1884), 3; *Annual Report* (1883), 4.

30. NYSL, *Annual Report* (1904), 5; NYSL, *Annual Report*(1905), 5; New York Society Library, *The New York Society Library in Wall Street in 1754 . . .* (New York: New York Society, [1927]). Copy at Columbia University Library, tipped into the back of National Bank of North America in New York, *The Old Wall Street, Number 41, Number 43* (New York: National Bank of North America, 1903). The Society Library finally caught up with New York society when it moved to East Seventy-Ninth Street in 1937.

31. NYSL, *Annual Report* (1888), 4; *Annual Report* (1905), 4–5; *Annual Report* (1903), 4. Of course, how the Library conceived its public role later in the century is a complex question. For example, the annual report for 1870 states that although "its associations have tended to confine it to the wealthier portion of society" . . . "the result must be an improved sentiment and higher tone in the community at large." The "diffusion of information in one class in the community is a benefit to all classes." NYSL, *Annual Report* (1870), 4–5. I call this the trickle-down theory of the public good.

32. "N. Appleton Lee Letters to His Sister Mrs. Harriet Glover: New York City, 1861 Jan 20 and 23," Bancroft Library, University of California Berkeley Library, 1, 4. It is remarkable that Lee never referred to the secession crisis in his letter. This was certainly not because he considered it outside of Harriet's sphere, since he also discusses the family's finances at some length. William J. Rhees, *Manual of Public Libraries, Institutions, and Societies in the United States and the British Provinces of North America* (Urbana: University of Illinois Press, 1967 [1859]), 278–87.

33. One fairly detailed and reasonably accurate account of the Association's founding is John H. Gourlie, *An Address Delivered Before the Mercantile Library Association at its Eighteenth Annual Meeting January 8, 1839 Embodying a History of the Association* (New York: James Van Norden, 1839). The original agreement between the Clinton Hall Association and the Mercantile Library Association is included in Mercantile Library Association of the City of New York, *The Constitution, Rules, Regulations, &c., of the Mercantile Library Association, Clinton Hall, New-York* (New York: Mercantile Library Association, 1836), 11–12. Every early history of the Mercantile Library Association claimed that the Clinton Hall Association was founded specifically to aid the Library. In fact, it was founded to promote learning and literature generally in New York City and to honor the memory of DeWitt Clinton. The Association first attempted to consolidate with the New York Athenaeum, but the Athenaeum declined the offer. "[Minutes of the] Clinton Hall Association," Mercantile Library Association Archives. The final "communication" from the Athenaeum is copied in the minutes for March 25, 1829.

34. New York Society Library, *The New York Society Library Was Founded in 1700 and is One of the Oldest Literary Institutions in New York—One of the Oldest in the United States* (New York: New York Society Library, 1856), 1.

35. Stuart M. Blumin, *The Emergence of the Middle Class: Social Experience in the American City, 1760–1900* (Cambridge: Cambridge University Press, 1989), 127–28; John H. Gourlie, "On the Benefits and Influences of Commerce," in *Lectures Delivered Before the Mercantile Library Association, Clinton Hall* (New York: Mercantile Library Association, 1836), 27. The commercial theory of value and variations on that theme run throughout the Association's publications and lectures. See, for example, Daniel D. Barnard, "Commerce, as Connected with the Progress of Civilization," *Merchants' Magazine and Commercial Review*, July 1839, 3. This was a lecture before the Association.

36. Noah Webster, *Observations on Language, and on the Error of Class-Books; Addressed to the Members of the New York Lyceum. Also, Observations on Commerce, Addressed to the Members of the Mercantile Library Association, in New York* (New Haven: S. Babcock, 1839), 34. "First Annual Report," [1821] in Mercantile Library Association of the City of New York, *Annual Reports of the Board of Direction of the Mercantile Library Association of the City of New York, from 1821 to 1838* (New York: James Van Norden, 1868), 6.

37. "Ninth Annual Report," [1829] in MLA, *Annual Reports*, 54. Daniel Lord, "Popular Principles Relating to the Law of Agency," *Merchants' Magazine and Commercial Review*, October 1839, 338. One of the early annual reports proudly noted that no member of the Association had ever been accused of defrauding his employer. "Tenth Annual Report," [1830] in MLA, *Annual Reports*, 63.

38. Mercantile Library Association of the City of New York, *Systematic Catalogue of the Books in the Collection of the Mercantile Library Association of*

the City of New York (New York: Harper & Brothers, 1837), iii. Gourlie, *Address Embodying a History of the Association*, 17.

39. See, for example, Daniel Lord, "Popular Principles Relating to the Law of Agency," *Merchants' Magazine and Commercial Review*, October 1839, 325. This was an address delivered before the Library. Lord briefly outlines three steps in a merchant's career—a clerk, an agent, and a partner—which seem to parallel the steps in a mechanic's career—an apprentice, a journeyman, and a master. See also "Mercantile Education," *Merchants' Magazine and Commercial Review*, February 1, 1844, 143–44. "Commencing business on his own account" was a common phrase during the period and appears in the Library's constitution. A member who did so, who became a merchant, could continue to use the library, just as a journeyman could continue to use the Apprentices' Library after he had completed his apprenticeship.

40. Allan Stanley Horlick, *Country Boys and Merchant Princes: The Social Control of Young Men in New York* (Lewisburg, Pa.: Bucknell University Press, 1975), 83–105.

41. For President Lucius Bull's remarks at the first meeting, see "At a Meeting of the Subscribers to the Mercantile Library Association," *National Advocate for the Country*, November 27, 1820. See also, for example, Mercantile Library Association of the City of New York, *Thirty-Second Annual Report of the Board of Direction of the Mercantile Library Association in the City of New York* (New York: Baker, Godwin & Co., 1853), 13: "Most of the young men who are engaged in mercantile pursuits in this city are strangers from the country, . . . surrounded by glittering allurements and incitements to pleasure on every hand," without "the gentle restraints of home and kindred upon him." Hereafter, MLA, *Thirty-Second Annual Report* (1852). The library's fiscal year varied over the years. This report, for example, covers January to December 1852 and was published in January 1853.

42. "Thirteenth Annual Report" [1833], in MLA, *Annual Reports*, 85. "The Directors are satisfied that, in thus publicly acknowledging the obligations due to their guardian Institution, they echo the unanimous sentiments of their fellow members." The Clinton Hall Association's constitution, its articles of subscription, are reprinted in MLA, *Thirty-Third Annual Report* (1853), 37–39. Shares in the Association cost one hundred dollars and, like shares in the Society Library, could be transferred, sold or inherited. "Agreement between the Clinton Hall Association . . . and the Mercantile Library Association," in MLA, *Constitution* (1836), 12.

43. The original constitution is reprinted in "At a Meeting of the Subscribers to the Mercantile Library Association." On the "deficiencies of education " in the mercantile community, see, for example, MLA, *Seventeenth Annual Report* (1837), 8, and *Thirty-Second Annual Report* (1852), 31.

44. "Sixteenth Annual Report" [1836], in MLA, *Annual Reports*, 117. Charles Edwards, "What Constitutes a Merchant," *Merchants' Magazine and Commercial Review*, October 1839, 291. Most of the address is devoted to catalog of all the subjects a merchant (as opposed to an farmer or a "mere working man") must master.

45. William Douglas Boyd Jr., "Books for Young Businessmen: Mercantile Libraries in the United States, 1820–1865" (Ph.D. dissertation, Indiana University, 1975), 151. This table compares the catalogs of the mercantile libraries in New York, Boston, Philadelphia, and Cincinnati in the early nineteenth century.

46. Mercantile Library Association, *Catalogue of the Books Belonging to the Mercantile Library Association of the City of New York* (New York: Hopkins & Morris, 1825), 12. MLA, *Seventeenth Annual Report* (1837), 7. Former mayor Philip Hone, in an address before the members in 1841, predicted that the library would "elevate the mercantile character of our city by uniting in a happy union the refinement of literary taste with the spirit of trade." Philip Hone, "Commerce and Commercial Character," *Merchants' Magazine and Commercial Review*, February 1841, 146.

47. MLA, *Eighteenth Annual Report* (1838), 6; *Forty-Ninth Annual Report* (1869–70), 37. Each annual report lists the classes offered and number of pupils attending. The reports frequently noted that "these means of instruction are not duly appreciated." MLA, *Thirty-Third Annual Report* (1853).

48. The very first course of lectures was on mercantile law. "Seventh Annual Report" [1827], in MLA, *Annual Reports*, 40–41. One way the directors popularized the lectures was to offer free tickets to pupils in the female academies in the city. MLA, *Thirty-Eighth Annual Report* (1858–59), 22–23.

49. MLA, *Twenty-Eighth Annual Report* (1848), 9. By 1872, when Mark Twain delivered the Association's most lucrative lecture ever, he amused his audience by solemnly assuring them that his remarks were intended only to improve them. Mark Twain, *Mark Twain's Letters*, ed. Lin Salamo and Harriet Elinor Smith (Berkeley: University of California Press, 1997), 5:33–34.

50. An article in *Scribner's Monthly* reported that the conversation room was seldom used. "The New York Mercantile Library," *Scribner's Monthly*, February 1871, 357. The room may have been rented out during certain periods. In 1847, it was set aside for "monthly meetings for Conversational, Literary, and other Exercises," but by 1853, the directors reported that the literary societies "maintained a languishing existence." MLA, *Twenty-Seventh Annual Report* (1847), 20–21; *Thirty-Third Annual Report* (1853), 34. In the nineteenth century, a literary society usually referred to a debate club. See Chapter 8 on the literary societies in the city's colleges.

51. MLA, *Twenty-Sixth Annual Report* (1846), 4.

52. On the savings bank, see MLA, *Twenty-Eighth Annual Report* (1848), 22. The library's president, vice president, and treasurer served *ex officio* on the board.

Statistics for "bathing" and "gymnastics" were included in the annual reports in the section on classes. The report for 1856 gives the total attendance for the classes from their inception in 1838 and access to the baths and gym were clearly more popular than most of the classes. MLA, *Thirty-Fifth Annual Report* (1855–56), 35–36. The annual report for 1839 claimed that the Association had "brought into existence" the magazine edited and published by Freeman Hunt. Mercantile Library, *Nineteenth Annual Report* (1839), 17. Often referred to as *Hunt's Magazine*, the *Commercial Review* reported regularly on the Library and for some years Hunt also printed the library's annual reports.

53. For typical press coverage of an annual election, see, for example, "Mercantile Library—The Opposition Ticket—Great Meeting," *New York Herald*, January 5, 1841. The opposition charged that the regular ticket's candidate "'knew no more about books than a stove.'" Of the election in 1836, the *Herald* wrote that "in the midst of the fog raised by both sides, we must confess, we cannot see clearly the difference between the belligerent parties." "A Meeting of the Mercantile Library, Friendly to the Rolfe Ticket," *New York Herald*, January 11, 1836.

54. Accounts of the annual meeting were part of the annual report. Between 1825 and 1864, the constitution was amended at least six times and there were frequently debates over amendments that never passed. The annual report for 1840 noted, apparently without irony, that "the amended constitution . . . was passed after much examination . . . no material features having been changed therein." MLA, *Twentieth Annual Report* (1840), 14. Henry Patterson described in his diary the meeting in 1842, at which there were "several motions to amend our constitution, which gave rise to some sharp debating and caused a great deal of uproar and confusion, but they were all happily lost." Henry A. Patterson Diary, January 15, 1842, Manuscript Division, New-York Historical Society.

55. "Mercantile Library Association," *Frank Leslie's Illustrated Journal*, May 28, 1859; "Trustees of the Clinton Hall Association," *New-York Spectator*, January 21, 1839, where the trustees referred to "exciting faction" and "over excited zeal." They also expressed concern over the "injudicious publications of both parties in the newspapers." See also, for example, "Election of Officers for the Mercantile Library Association," *Morning Herald*, January 11, 1838. "Prevent youthful excitement? Binding the winds, chaining the sea were an easy task in comparison. The free, wild, buoyant spirit of youth must and will have vent." The article also gives examples of the how "buoyant" the elections could become. After a tussle between partisans of the two tickets: "Is there a Phenologist here? A young man got a new bump on his nose, can anyone tell what it is?"

56. "Mercantile Library Associations," *Merchants' Magazine and Commercial Review*, October 1853, 445. This quote refers specifically to the New York association.

57. NYSL, *Annual Report* (1856), 4, 6; MLA, *Thirty-Fifth Annual Report* (1855–56), 12, 17.

58. "Mercantile Library Associations," 445. In an address before the MLA a number of years later, a Mr. Lathers, probably one of the "guardians" in the Clinton Hall Association, praised the officers for their "practical knowledge of business affairs." MLA, *Forty-First Annual Report* (1861–62), 43.

59. MLA, *Twenty-Sixth Annual Report* (1846), 11; *Twenty-Ninth Annual Report* (1849), 14; *Thirtieth Annual Report* (1850), 9–10.

60. MLA, *Twenty-Eighth Annual Report* (1848), 9. Boyd, "Books for Young Businessmen," 151. In 1834 fiction was still a small proportion of the entire collection. Fiction was 16.3 percent; literature was 12.5 percent; and history was 10 percent. Commerce was 1.9 percent. For Boyd's methodology, see 143–46.

61. MLA, *Thirty-Third Annual Report* (1853), 15. This report also notes that fiction was improving from a moral standpoint, that novels of the day had less "literary merit," but "generally inculcate[d] correct principles of conduct or some great moral principle." MLA, *Thirty-Fourth Annual Report* (1854), 12, 16. The purchase of fiction for this year was over 38 percent. "Twelfth Annual Report," [1832] in MLA, *Annual Reports*, 77. The same justifications for the provision and high circulation of fiction used in the 1830s and 1840s by the Mercantile Library were used half a century later by the city's free circulating library.

62. MLA, *Twenty-Third Annual Report* (1843), 4. The amendment was proposed by a member of the board and in their report (18) they "suggested measures which . . . will enable [the Association] to regain all, and more than all that it has lost during the late unparalleled depression and distress." Subscribers were about 2 percent of the total membership (which also included honorary members and Clinton Hall stockholders) in 1853. MLA, *Thirty-Third Annual Report* (1853), 9. In 1870, the annual subscription for clerks was increased to four dollars. MLA, *Forty-Ninth Annual Report* (1869–70), 44.

63. MLA, *Eighteenth Annual Report* (1838), 18–26; *Nineteenth Annual Report* (1839), 13–16. All of the quotes are from the former report at pages 20–21.

64. See, for example, "The Mercantile Library Association and Their Lectures," *New York Herald*, November 23, 1843.

65. Mercantile Library Association of the City of New York, *Report of the Board of Directors of the Mercantile Library Association on a Systematic Plan of Instruction by Lectures* (New York: Hunt's Merchants' Magazine, 1843), 4–6. This report is remarkable. It flatly contradicts all of the lofty sentiments expressed at the addresses before the membership during this period. See for example, Edwards, "What Constitutes a Merchant" (1839); and John Sergeant, "Mercantile Character," *Merchants' Magazine and Commercial Review*, July 1840, 9–22.

66. MLA, *Thirty-Third Annual Report* (1853), 34. The following year the directors reported that the YMCA tenancy was "a pleasing feature of their administration, as likely to be conducive of mutual benefit to both institutions." MLA, *Thirty-Fourth Annual Report* (1854), 33.

67. New-York Young Men's Christian Association, *A Memorandum Respecting New-York as a Field for Moral Christian Effort among Young Men* (New York: YMCA, 1866). This is a pamphlet that was circulated to raise money to finance a building for the Association. It is a good summary of the early work of the YMCA. "Moral and religious culture" is at page 7. Pages 10–14 provide a list of the different services and committees. More interesting, the memorandum is essentially an extensive moral survey of the city in 1866. In that year there were, for example, nearly as many "'pretty waiter girl' saloons" as Protestant churches in New York. They employed 1,191 "priestesses of sin" (6). The Mercantile Library is reported to have had "limited moral usefulness" (9). On Woodlawn Cemetery, see, for example, New-York Young Men's Christian Association, *Thirty-First Annual Report of the New-York Young Men's Christian Association* (New York: YMCA, 1884), 30.

68. YMCA, *Second Annual Report* (1854), 45. For a history of the New York association, see Pamela Bayless, *The YMCA at 150: A History of the YMCA of Greater New York, 1852–2002* (New York: YMCA, 2002).

69. Daniel Lord, *An Address Delivered on the Opening of the Rooms of the New-York Young Men's Christian Association, September 20th, 1852* (New York: Theo. H. Gray, 1852), 5–6. The addresses and reports from this early period often refer to clerks as the young men of the Association and appeal to the city's merchants for support. A report from 1881 lists the membership by occupation. Clerks were far larger than any other category and over twenty-five percent of the total. YMCA, *Twenty-Eighth Annual Report* (1881), 20–21. An address reprinted in the annual report for 1854 refers to the "middling classes." YMCA, *Second Annual Report* (1854), 42. See also Horlick, *Country Boys and Merchant Princes*, 226–43. Later, when the Association started branches, young men from the working class were segregated in the Bowery Branch and the Railroad Men's Branch. By contrast, the city's YWCA served working-class women. Helen Bittar, "The Y.W.C.A. of the City of New York, 1870–1920" (Ph.D. dissertation, New York University, 1979).

70. Letter written to the Association in 1866, excerpted in Bayless, *YMCA at 150*, 11. Isaac Ferris, *Address Delivered at a Meeting of Young Men, Convened for the Formation of the Young Men's Christian Association* (New York: Theo. H. Gray, 1852), 10. From the same address: "Seniors for counsel, the young for effort" (10). The Association's early reports and other publications make frequent references to the loneliness of strangers in the city and using the natural sociability of young men to relieve it.

71. "Address of Rev. Theodore L. Cuyler," reprinted in YMCA, *Second Annual Report* (1854), 37–38. For an indication of the important role the library played during this early period, see, for example, *A Selection from the Late Correspondence of the New-York Young Men's Christian Association, Tending to Illustrate Its Mode of Working and Show Its Efficiency* (New York: YMCA, 1866).

This is a collection of excerpts from letters from grateful members and was published in conjunction with the *Memorandum* of the same year. There are frequent references to the library. In almost all of the early publications that include a list the Association's committees and activities, the library and reading room are listed first. An early annual report noted that the very low annual subscription for membership made it "absolutely necessary for the Association to ask the assistance of the Christian public." YMCA, *Second Annual Report* (1854), 16. Later the subscription was raised to two dollars and then five dollars.

72. YMCA, *Second Annual Report* (1854), 19.

73. Young Men's Christian Association of the City of New York, *Catalogue of the Library of the New-York Young Men's Christian Association, Clinton Hall, Astor Place* (New York: John A. Gray, 1855). Since the Library Committee estimated spending approximately ninety cents per volume, slightly less than half of the books were donations. The rest were purchased with the one thousand dollars raised by a special subscription for the library. YMCA, *Second Annual Report* (1854), 19. This was the only printed catalog until 1900. In that year most of the collection was moved to the new headquarters on Fifty-Seventh Street and, for the first time since 1870, was made available for circulation. Young Men's Christian Association of the City of New York, *Catalogue of the Library of the Young Men's Christian Association of the City of New York, Circulating Department, July 1900* (New York: YMCA, 1900).

74. YMCA, *Catalogue* (1855), 27, 15, 28, 24, 54, 28. Many of the biographical or autobiographical works were the lives of ministers and missionaries.

75. YMCA, *Catalogue* (1855), 25, 14, 44; R. B. Poole, "Selection of Books, No. 2," *Watchman*, July 1, 1877, 5. Poole was the librarian from 1864 to 1895. Born Reuben Pool, he changed his last name because he hated to see his name on signs that read "Pool and Billiards." Biographical sketch in the Kautz Family YMCA Archives, University of Minnesota Libraries. The *Watchman* article is second in a seven-part series, mostly on selecting books for YMCA libraries. Judging from this series, this library probably became somewhat more scholarly and less evangelical under Poole's direction, although there is no surviving catalog from this period. In 1880, the Association received a bequest of approximately $150,000 in the will of William Niblo, which made the library less dependent on donations. YMCA, *Twenty-Seventh Annual Report* (1880), 40.

76. The year after the catalog was published, the Library Committee thanked a number of evangelical publishers for donations. YMCA, *Third Annual Report* (1856), 19. The proportion of novels was apparently even smaller later in the century. In 1894, Poole wrote that fiction was less than four percent. Reuben B. Poole, "Books in Demand in a City Library," *Christian Thought* 11 (1893–94): 447–48.

77. YMCA, *Catalogue* (1855), 26, 56. The catalog lists only abbreviated titles and authors. *The Harvey Boys* (http://catalog.hathitrust.org/Record/008597202)

was published in 1834 and *Village Boys* in 1847. Some of the works of fiction are not really even narratives, but rather thinly disguised sermons. For example, *Family Conversations on the Evidences of Revelation* (Philadelphia: American Sunday School Union, 1830).

78. YMCA, *Catalogue* (1855), 10, 22. *Beatrice, or the Unknown Relative* (London: Bentley, 1852). Jemina Luke, *Female Jesuit, or the Spy in the Family* (New York: Dodd, 1851).

79. On T. S. Arthur, see Horlick, *Country Boys and Merchant Princes*, 188–209. On Susan Warner, Edward Halsey Foster, *Susan and Anna Warner* (Boston: Twayne, 1978). David S. Reynolds, *Faith in Fiction: The Emergence of Religious Literature in America* (Cambridge, Mass.: Harvard University Press, 1981).

80. The annual reports do not include circulation statistics until 1870. In the 1870s, the average circulation for fiction was 26.75 percent. YMCA, *Twenty-Seventh Annual Report* (1880), 45. This report gives statistics for each class of the collection for each year of the decade. After 1881 there is a dramatic decline in the circulation of fiction. I can find no reason to account for this and suspect that they were either cooking the books, changing how titles in the collection were classified to minimize the circulation of fiction, or actively discouraging members from reading it. After 1870, members were not allowed to take books out of the building on Twenty-Third Street.

81. Reuben Poole, "The Librarian and His Constituents," *Library Journal* 11 (August–September 1886): 354. R. B. Poole, "Fiction in Association Libraries," *Young Men's Era*, April 30, 1891, 280. Ellen Coe, the librarian of the New York Free Circulating Libraries, used the phrase "missionaries of literature" to describe public librarians in an address at the American Library Association in 1894. She was quoting from the presidential address that year by J. N. Larned. Ellen M. Coe, "Common Novels in Public Libraries," *Library Journal* 19 (1894): 23–24.

82. William Peoples, the librarian at the Mercantile Library, was also a founding member of the New York Library Club and was active in local professional circles. The management of the Association however seemed to take no notice of the profound changes that were going around it in the 1880s and 1890s, as the city's free circulating libraries were founded and expanded. The directors stated unequivocally that, although they "cordially welcome that which would . . . educate the masses of the people," they would never make their collection free in exchange for funding from the City under the Library Law of 1886. MLA, *Sixty-Fifth Annual Report* (1885–86), 13. Since it is hardly mentioned in the annual reports, it is difficult to determine how the public library movement affected the Mercantile Library. On the New York Library Club, see Tom Glynn, "The Professionalization of a Calling: Mission and Method at the New York Library Club," *Libraries & the Cultural Record* (Fall 2006): 438–61.

83. Verranus Morse, "The Work of the Young Men's Christian Association and How to Do It," in *An Analytical Sketch of the Young Men's Christian Association's*

in North America from 1851 to 1876 (New York: International Committee of the Young Men's Christian Associations, 1901), 46. The *Sketch* is a collection of addresses and essays by Morse, an early leader of the Association. This address was delivered before the New York YMCA in 1862. YMCA, *Eighteenth Annual Report* (1872), 16. There is no explanation in the 1870 annual report of the decision not to circulate books outside of the building. The Library Committee in a number of subsequent reports mentions that it planned in future to circulate the collection, to create a free circulating library, but I suspect that the board never sanctioned these statements. Curiously, the last time that Poole or the committee mentioned a circulating collection was shortly before the passage of the Library Law of 1886. Possibly the boards made it clear at this point that they would never apply for money from the City. R. B. Poole, "Libraries of the Young Men's Christian Associations," *Library Journal* 10 (September–October 1885): 223.

84. MLA, *Forty-Ninth Annual Report* (1869–70), 17.

85. MLA, *Forty-Fifth Annual Report* (1865–66), 37. The Clinton Hall Association raised the funds to pay the mortgage by issuing additional stock. The rental income varied considerably from year to year. In 1866, rents and other income totaled approximately $14,000 (p. 41). In 1870, it was more than $18,000. MLA, *Forty-Ninth Annual Report* (1870), 49.

86. MLA, *Forty-Ninth Annual Report* (1869–70), 18, 22.

87. MLA, *Fifty-Third Annual Report* (1873–74), 20–21.

88. MLA, *Twenty-Ninth Annual Report* (1849), 8. In 1866–67 alone, the library spent $2,087 on advertising. MLA, *Forty-Sixth Annual Report* (1866–67), 5.

89. MLA, *Forty-Fourth Annual Report* (1864–65), 8. The quote is at page 9. Since the library's fiscal year closed in April during this period, the large increase in membership for this year was not young men returning from the Civil War. The number of subscribers increased approximately 37 percent from the previous year. MLA, *Forty-Fifth Annual Report* (1865–66), 8.

90. *New York Evening Post*, September 8, 1866; *Bulletin No. 3 of the Mercantile Library Association of the City of New York* [probably March 1859], 1. These and many other ads and circulars are from Mercantile Library Association Archives, Box 6, which contains two scrapbooks. One is untitled and covers the middle 1860s through the early 1870s. The other is titled "MLA Scrapbook, 1858–1863." Both also contain extensive election material, including leaflets distributed by the rival "tickets." John William Ferry, *A History of the Department Store* (New York: Macmillan, 1960).

91. "Mercantile Library Association of the City of New York" [Bulletin No. 5, circa 1861]. "Mercantile Library Association, Clinton Hall (Astor Place)" [November 1854] noted that "we already have a large number of Lady Subscribers . . . and we would gladly see this list increased." Both circulars are in Mercantile Library Association Archives, box 6, "MLA Scrapbook, 1858–1863."

92. "Mercantile Library Management," *New York Times,* May 12, 1881. An article a year later claimed that circulating libraries "represent the tastes of the weaker sex," since "the majority of persons who draw books are ladies." "What the People Read," *New York Times,* January 22, 1882. What the people read, of course, was novels.

93. MLA, *Thirty-Fourth Annual Report* (1854), 24. "Report of the Directors of the Mercantile Library Association," in *Addresses of John Romeyn Brodhead, esq., and His Excellency, Gov. Horatio Seymour, Delivered before the Clinton Hall Association and Mercantile Library Association at their Celebration, Commemorative of the Removal of the Library to Astor Place* (New York: Nesbit & Co., 1854), 32.

94. "The New York Mercantile Library," *Scribner's Monthly,* February 1871, 357–58, 363. On the reading room in the Cooper Union, see Chapter 7.

95. For example, "First Bulletin of the Mercantile Library Association," December 1858, Mercantile Library Association Archives, box 6, "MLA Scrapbook, 1858–1863." From the first page: "Regular dues: to Clerks (Female Clerks included), $4." Most of the bulletins and a number of advertisements in this scrapbook use identical or very similar language.

96. "The New York Mercantile Library," *Scribner's Monthly,* 366.

97. "The School for Repeaters," *New York Sun,* May 18, 1870.

98. MLA, *Forty-Seventh Annual Report* (1867–68), 7; *Eightieth Annual Report* (1900), 5.

99. "Table XXXII: Number of Persons in Thirty Principal Cities Engaged in Each Class of Occupations, with Distinctions of Age, Sex, and Nativity, in the Census of 1870," in *Ninth Census—Volume I: Statistics of the Population of the United States . . .* (Washington, D.C.: Government Printing Office, 1872), 793. "Table 42: Total Males and Females Ten Years of Age and Over Engaged in Each of 140 Groups of Occupations . . ." in *Special Reports: Occupations at the Twelfth Census* (Washington, D.C.: Government Printing Office, 1904), 456–57 (www2.census.gov/prod2/decennial/documents/00173559ch9.pdf). The definitions of occupations under "trade" changed and were more detailed in the later census. In each case, I counted only the occupations that seemed to be clearly clerical, such as "clerks and copyists" and "salesmen and saleswomen." My totals are therefore incomplete and do not include clerks employed in certain sectors, for example, in banks and insurance companies.

100. "How the Mercantile Library Election was Carried" (*New York Sun*?), May 22, 1870. "The Mercantile Library Fuss," *New York Sun,* May 1871. "Mercantile Library Matters" (*New York Sun*?), May 9, 1871. All of these are clippings from Mercantile Library Association Archives, box 6, untitled scrapbook. Many of the articles about the elections in this scrapbook are from 1870 and 1871. These were remarkably contentious contests that revolved around whether the library should open on the Sabbath. Typically, both tickets supported this.

The bad press the Library received during this period was certainly influenced by a general disgust and disillusionment with local politics. But if half of what the bookworms were accused of was true, their annual elections were just as corrupt as the fights between Republicans and Tammany Hall.

101. MLA, *Seventy-Sixth Annual Report* (1896), 10. See also Lewis A. Erenberg, *Steppin' Out: New York Nightlife and the Transformation of American Culture, 1890–1930* (Westport, Conn.: Greenwood, 1981).

102. MLA, *Forty-Ninth Annual Report* (1869–70), 39–44.

103. William E. Dodge, *Old New York: A Lecture* (New York: Dodd, Mead & Co., 1880), 41. For an example of the scale of clerical work in the Gilded Age, see the description of the city's largest department store, A. T. Stewart's, in James D. McCabe Jr., *Great Fortunes and How They Were Made; or the Struggles and Triumphs of Our Self-Made Men* (Philadelphia: Maclean, 1870; repr., Freeport, NY: Books for Libraries Press, 1972), 107–8. Stewart employed 470 clerks in the sales department alone.

104. Blumin, *The Emergence of the Middle Class*, especially 68. Blumin stresses, among other factors, the alignment of nonmanual work with salaried employment. Significantly, the new constitution in 1870 also included a new definition of an active member, a "person employed on a salary as a clerk."

105. Beckert, *Monied Metropolis*, 242–45. The quote is at page 244. See also Horlick, *Country Boys and Merchant Princes*, 179–80. "It seemed increasingly difficult to maintain that the "Merchant Prince" was anything more than a successful businessman." *On the Mercantile Library*, 252–59.

106. MLA, *Fifty-First Annual Report* (1871–72), 13; *Eighty-Second Annual Report* (1902), 7.

107. MLA, *Sixtieth Annual Report* (1880–81), 5–6. The report for 1886 exaggerated only slightly when it claimed that every annual report since 1870 had attributed the steady decline in membership in part to "cheap literature." MLA, *Sixty-Fifth Annual Report* (1885–86), 7.

108. MLA, *Thirtieth Annual Report* (1850), 10; *Forty-Sixth Annual Report* (1866–1867), 12–13.

109. Lyle H. Wright, *American Fiction, 1774–1850: A Contribution Towards a Bibliography*, 2d rev. ed. (San Marino, Calif.: Huntington Library, 1969), 384–85; John Tebbel, *A History of Book Publishing in the United States, vol. 2, The Expansion of an Industry, 1865–1919* (New York: R. R. Bowker, 1975), 692. These numbers do not include the significant number of novels by foreign authors that were available to American readers, including pirated editions of British works.

110. MLA, *Forty-First Annual Report* (1861–62), 22; *Thirty-Ninth Annual Report* (1859–60), 38–39.

111. MLA, *Sixtieth Annual Report* (1880–81), 5. Even for the Mercantile Library this was an especially high number. But of most popular works it typically

purchased at least one hundred copies. The report for 1859 explained that the directors hoped to emulate Mudie's, the very popular British circulating library, purchasing many copies of popular works, then selling them later, while they were still in demand. The problem, of course, was that by the time they were offered for sale, they were no longer popular and could only be sold at a very low price. For this modification of the library's business plan: MLA, *Thirty-Eighth Annual Report* (1858–59), 15–17. It included the creation of a "Department of Duplicate Books." Some of the library's circulars during this period included lists of books for sale.

112. MLA, *Forty-Ninth Annual Report*, (1869–70), 7, 23; Henry A. Martin, ed., *Gouldings Business Directory of New York, Brooklyn, Newark, Paterson, Jersey City, Hoboken and Elizabeth* (New York: L. G. Goulding, 1873), 83–85. There are 120 booksellers listed for New York. Books were sold at other kinds stores as well, and the directory probably does not include every bookseller in the city.

113. MLA, *Thirty-Eighth Annual Report* (1858–59), 15. On communities of readers during this period, see, for example, Barbara Sicherman, "Ideologies and Practices of Reading," in *A History of the Book in America*, Scott E. Casper et al., eds., vol. 3, *The Industrial Book, 1840–1880*, 294–95.

114. MLA, *Thirty-Third Annual Report* (1853), 32–33; "The New York Mercantile Library," *Frank Leslie's Illustrated Newspaper*, September 18, 1869, 13.

115. The quote is from MLA, *Sixty-First Annual Report* (1881–82), 10. "After paying ten cents for car fare, they could only obtain a ten cent book." MLA, *Sixtieth Annual Report* (1880–81), 7. The report two years later claimed this was the most frequent complaint from the members. Mercantile Library, *Sixty-Second Annual Report* (1882–83), 14–15. Since Clinton Hall was owned and controlled by the Clinton Hall Association, the Library's directors had no say over the location of the library. This was frequently a source of conflict between the two boards later in the century.

116. MLA, *Forty-Sixth Annual Report* (1866–67), 13. For examples of changes in the service in attempts to make it self-sustaining, see MLA, *Forty-Ninth Annual Report* (1869–70), 13–14; *Sixty-Third Annual Report* (1883–84), 11; *Seventy-Eighth Annual Report* (1898), 11. In 1904, the directors reported that the Association spent $2.50 for every dollar it received from subscribers using the service. MLA, *Eighty-Fourth Annual Report* (1904), 8–9.

117. "Finding the Centre of New York Society," 1; MLA, *Seventy-Sixth Annual Report* (1896), 10.

118. MLA, *Sixty-Second Annual Report* (1882–83), 15. Since the Clinton Hall Association owned Clinton Hall, its trustees had complete control not only over the location of the building, but also its maintenance and the space allocated to the library. These issues were often a source of conflict between the two boards.

119. MLA, *Seventy-First Annual Report* (1891–92), 10. For an account of the reopening and a history of the Library, see 40–46 and 34–39. Mercantile Library,

Seventy-Seventh Annual Report (1897), 12–13. The directors advised that "in lieu of more branch libraries" the "omnivorous readers" should make more extensive use of the delivery service.

120. MLA, *Eighty-First Annual Report* (1901), 10–12. At different times after 1867, the Association maintained a small branch at four different locations in this general vicinity. All of them were closed because "the public failed . . . to give sufficient support." In 1901, the downtown branch that was opened in 1853 after Clinton Hall moved north to Astor Place was converted to a delivery station. Members were only allowed to pick up and return books. MLA, *Eighty-Second Annual Report* (1902), 8. It is interesting that during this period, from the mid-1880s to the end of the century, the annual reports make practically no mention of the city's free circulating libraries. It is unclear whether or to what extent those libraries competed with the Mercantile Library. They offered much less fiction and presumably catered to the working class. But they were free. The Association's annual report in 1897 made a clear distinction between readers in the free circulating libraries and "the classes composing our membership." MLA, *Seventy-Seventh Annual Report* (1897), 12.

121. MLA, *Eighty-First Annual Report* (1901), 16–17, 19–20.

122. MLA, *Eighty-Second Annual Report* (1902), 15; *Eighty-Third Annual Report* (1903), 17. From a practical point of view, these changes were eminently sensible. Higher rents meant that the Clinton Hall Association could both pay off its mortgage more quickly and devote more money to building the collection. Nonetheless, after 1901, when the Association elected a new and more active board, there was a marked change in the tone of the annual reports, with less of a focus on books and a greater emphasis on managing the Association's property.

6. "Men of Leisure and Men of Letters": New York's Public Research Libraries

1. The most recent account of the riot is Nigel Cliff, *The Shakespeare Riots: Revenge, Drama, and Death in Nineteenth-Century America* (New York: Random House, 2007). See also Lawrence W. Levine: *Highbrow/Lowbrow: The Emergence of Cultural Hierarchy in America* (Cambridge, Mass.: Harvard University Press, 1988), 63–69; John F. Kasson, *Rudeness & Civility: Manners in Nineteenth-Century Urban America* (New York: Hill and Wang, 1990), 222–28; and Edwin G. Burrows and Mike Wallace, *Gotham: A History of New York City to 1898* (New York: Oxford University Press, 1999), 761–66. For an extensive, albeit biased, contemporary account, see An American Citizen, *A Rejoinder to "The Replies from England, etc. to Certain Statements in the Country Respecting Mr. Macready," Together with an Impartial History and Review of the Lamentable Occurrences at the Astor Place Opera House, on the 10th of May, 1849* (New York: Stringer & Townsend, 1849). This includes newspaper accounts of the riot and extensive excerpts from the coroner's inquest. The letter to Macready is reprinted on page 49.

2. The quote is from Levine, *Highbrow/Lowbrow*, 64. Nativism was also important factor in the riot. The mob's leaders, who styled themselves the "American Committee," had distributed handbills earlier in the day asking "Shall Americans or English Rule in this City?" Yet, because Macready was English, the mob seems to have been composed of an unlikely mix of Irish and nativists. Seven of the twenty-two killed were Irish laborers. Burrows and Wallace, *Gotham*, 763, 764.

3. On the Society's years at New York University, see LeRoy E. Kimball, "The Old University Building and the Society's Years on Washington Square," *New-York Historical Society Quarterly* 32 (July 1948): 149–219.

4. Minutes of the New-York Historical Society (hereafter also NYHS), vol. 2, November 2, 1841, NYHS Archives, 129; New-York Historical Society, *Proceedings of the New York Historical Society for the Year 1845* (New York: New-York Historical Society, 1846), 27.

5. New-York Historical Society, *Proceedings of the New York Historical Society for the Year 1849* (New York: New-York Historical Society, 1849), 20; *The Charter and By-Laws of the New York Historical Society, Revised January 1858, with a List of Members* (New York: New-York Historical Society, 1862), 45–73.

6. Henry Rowe Schoolcraft, "The Literary and Scientific Institutions of Europe," Official Papers of the New-York Historical Society, Box 6, NYHS Library. This is a manuscript, and quotes are from pages 2–4 and 23. On Schoolcraft, see Richard G. Bremer, *Indian Agent and Wilderness Scholar: The Life of Henry Rowe Schoolcraft* (Mount Pleasant: Central Michigan University, 1987). Schoolcraft was elected an honorary member in 1819, but he was active in the affairs of the Society during the periods in which he resided in New York. He served on the Executive Committee from 1845 to 1847. Vail, *Knickerbocker Birthday*, 482.

7. Schoolcraft, "The Literary and Scientific Institutions of Europe," 21–23; Vail, *Knickerbocker Birthday*, 451. This is a reprint of the original constitution. Prospective members had to be nominated by a current member. New-York Historical Society, *Charter and By-Laws of the New York Historical Society, Revised March 1846* (New York: New-York Historical Society, 1846), 15.

8. Schoolcraft, "The Literary and Scientific Institutions of Europe," 5; Vail, *Knickerbocker Birthday*, 454. The quote on "mineral subjects" is from a reprint of "To the Public," which appeared in newspapers in 1805 and again in 1809. Robert Hendre Kelby, *The New-York Historical Society, 1805–1904* (New York: New-York Historical Society, 1905), 31–32. George Folsom, "Historical Sketch of the Society," in New-York Historical Society, *Collections of the New-York Historical Society*, second series, vol. 1 (New York: New-York Historical Society, 1841), 465.

9. Before acquiring the collection of the Gallery of Fine Arts, the Society had seventy-four paintings, mostly portraits, all by American artists. NYHS, "Annual Report of the Committee on the Fine Arts, January, 1862," Official Papers of the New-York Historical Society, Box 6, folder 3, NYHS Library, New York. Kelby,

NYHS, 52. On the Gallery of the Fine Arts, see Winifred Howe, *A History of the Metropolitan Museum of Art* (New York: Gilliss Press, 1913–46), 1:62–67.

10. New-York Historical Society, *Report of the Executive Committee* (New York: New-York Historical Society, 1889), 15–16; Kelby, *New-York Historical Society*, 52–53, 108–11, 126–28. An interesting description of the collection during this period is: "Relics of Antiquity," *New York Times*, April 5, 1871: "The works of art probably exceed in value those of any other library in the United States." United States Bureau of Education, *Public Libraries in the United States of America: Their History, Condition and Management*, Special Report, Pt 1 (Washington, D.C.: Government Printing Office, 1876), 928.

11. Arguments along these lines are made by, among others, Levine, *Highbrow/Lowbrow*, esp. 206–7; Thomas Bender, *New York Intellect: A History of Intellectual Life in New York City, from 1750 to the Beginnings of Our Own Time* (New York: Knopf, 1987), 121–22, 171–72; and Sven Beckert, *Monied Metropolis: New York City and the Consolidation of the American Bourgeoisie, 1850–1896* (New York: Cambridge University Press, 2001), 267–68. See also Gordon S. Wood, *The Radicalism of the American Revolution* (New York: Knopf, 1992), 349–51; Raymond Williams, *Keywords: A Vocabulary of Culture and Society*, rev. ed. (New York: Oxford University Press, 1983), s.v. "culture"; Tony Bennett, "Culture," in *New Keywords: A Revised Vocabulary of Culture and Society*, ed. Tony Bennett, Lawrence Grossberg, and Meaghan Morris (Malden, Mass.: Blackwell, 2005), 63–69.

12. Pamela Spence Richards, *Scholars and Gentlemen: The Library of the New-York Historical Society, 1804–1982* (Hamden, Conn.: Archon Books, 1984), 29–30. See also Vail, *Knickerbocker Birthday*, 103, 118, for illustrations of the gallery and library at this time. By about 1868, the "Department of Art" held more than five hundred paintings. NYHS, "Museum of History, Antiquities, and Art, in the Central Park," Official Papers, Box 8, folder 4, NYHS Library, New York.

13. For brief biographical sketches of De Peyster, see Kelby, *New-York Historical Society*, 56–57; and Vail, *Knickerbocker Birthday*, 122. Trained as a lawyer, although he never practiced law, De Peyster was involved in a very wide range of civic and scholarly associations, including a term as chairman of the New York Society Library.

14. The original resolution is reprinted in Kelby, *New-York Historical Society*, 53–54. See Frederic De Peyster, *The Moral and Intellectual Influence of Libraries upon Social Progress* (New York: New-York Historical Society, 1866), 48, 84. The extensive library may have been De Peyster's idea. It is not referred to in the resolution of the Executive Committee or in the enabling acts subsequently passed by the legislature.

15. De Peyster, *Moral and Intellectual Influence of Libraries*, 80, 81, 90.

16. Richards, *Scholars and Gentlemen*, 32–34; Kelby, *New-York Historical Society*, 53–55. The act passed in 1862 is reprinted in De Peyster, *Moral and*

Intellectual Influence of Libraries, 41–42. The commissioners authorized use of the building little more than a month before De Peyster's address (44). The second act, passed in 1868, is reprinted in NYHS, "Museum of History, Antiquities, and Art."

17. De Peyster himself claimed that if the commissioners had approved the plan a year earlier, the subscription for funds would have been successful. De Peyster, *Moral and Intellectual Influence of Libraries*, 44.

18. Kelby wrote that the plan failed "owing to the great cost of the proposed building, and the erection of the same on city property." Kelby, *NYHS*, 55.

19. An interesting firsthand account of the meeting with Tweed is quoted in Howe, *History of the Metropolitan*, 138–39. The petition presented to the Tammany boss was "signed by owners of more than one-half of the real estate of New York City." The annual appropriation from the City was $15,000 for the first year and had risen to ten times that by the turn of the century. Calvin Tompkins, *Merchants and Masterpieces: The Story of the Metropolitan Museum of Art*, rev. and updated ed. (New York: Henry Holt, 1989), 45, 87. At least 64 percent of the trustees between 1870 and 1896 were members of the Historical Society. Beckert, *Monied Metropolis*, 268. For the founding documents of the museum, see Metropolitan Museum of Art, *Charter, Constitution, By-Laws, Lease, Laws; together with the Original Constitution and a Summary of its Amendments* (New York: Metropolitan Museum of Art, 1910).

20. The museum was finally open on Sundays in 19891 after the legislature threatened to block construction of a new wing. Before that time, the trustees claimed it was closed for religious reasons on the one day that most New Yorkers could attend. Burrows and Wallace, *Gotham*, 1082. Although the trustees stressed the educational aims of the museum repeatedly in their annual reports, it was clear they had a very limited conception of art education. From the fifth annual report, 1875: "The educational importance of the Institution receives the constant consideration of the Trustees. They have every desire . . . to make its collections available for scholars and students." Metropolitan Museum of Art, *Annual Report of the Trustees, 1871–1894* (New York: Metropolitan Museum of Art, 1894), 63.

21. For an insightful discussion of elite cultural institutions during this period, see Beckert, *Monied Metropolis*, 267–71. The quote is at page 267.

22. Kelby, *NYHS*, 70–71; Vail, *Knickerbocker Birthday*, 154, 184, 192.

23. "An Up-Town Home for the Historical Society," *New York Times*, March 9, 1901; "Historical Society's Novel Entertainment," *New York Times*, December 8, 1901.

24. "Report of the Librarian, 1884," Official Papers of the New-York Historical Society, Box 12, NYHS Library, New York. "Circular" dated December 15, 1885, ibid. New-York Historical Society, *Report of the Executive Committee* (New York: New-York Historical Society, 1902), 21. However, the annual report that reported

on the purchase of land for the new building did note that "new methods of rapid transit will insure its convenience of access." New-York Historical Society, *Report of the Executive Committee* (New York: New-York Historical Society, 1891), 12.

25. Henry T. Tuckerman, "A Memoir of the Author," introduction to John W. Francis, *Old New York, or Reminiscences of the Past Sixty Years* (New York: W. J. Widdleton, 1866), ix. Francis's history is an expanded version of his anniversary address before the Society in 1857. In his biography, Tuckerman points out that "among other secondary influences of progress in liberal tastes and scientific truth, is the new interest in race and family as related to character."

26. Quoted in Beckert, *Monied Metropolis*, 270. See also Burrows and Wallace, *Gotham*, 1083–84. In his description of New York "society," James D. McCabe, referred to a "College of Heraldry" that would "manufacture" pedigrees and coats of arms for the newly rich. James D. McCabe, Jr., *New York by Gaslight: A Work Descriptive of the Great American Metropolis* (New York: Greenwich House, 1984; repr., Philadelphia: Hubbard Brothers, 1882), 197–200.

27. Vail, *NYHS*, 150. For a complete list of the Society's publications, see 491–504. For a complete list of the endowments at the turn of the century, see, New-York Historical Society, *Report of the Executive Committee* (New York: New-York Historical Society, 1900), 9–11. For glowing references to the genealogical collection, New-York Historical Society, *Report of the Executive Committee* (New York: New-York Historical Society, 1889), 16; (1897); 15, (1898), 16. The quote regarding use of the collection by genealogists is from John Austin Stevens, *Memoir of William Kelby, Librarian of the New York Historical Society, Read Before the Society, November 1, 1898* (New York: New-York Historical Society, 1898), 20. See also Richards, *Scholars and Gentlemen*, 47–49.

28. Stevens, *William Kelby*, 20, 24, 32, 36. Kelby's is a very interesting case of the city's elite accepting into their ranks a son of the working class. His father was the Society's janitor and he began work there at the age of sixteen in 1861. He was not officially elected librarian until 1893, although before that time he had served as assistant librarian and de facto librarian. He emigrated from Ireland as a child, although Stevens was quick to point out that the Kelbys "belonged to what is termed the Englishry of Ireland" (3). Stevens also graciously omitted mentioning his father's occupation. Kelby died in 1898.

29. Henry Stevens, *Recollections of James Lenox and the Formation of His Library*, revised and elucidated by Victor Hugo Paltsits (New York: New York Public Library, 1951 [1886]), 3–9. Stevens was Lenox's agent for nearly a quarter-century and was largely responsible for developing the collection before the incorporation of the Library. Most of his biography is actually an account of his acquisition of various bibliographic "nuggets." "Corded up like wood" is from page 7 and the reference to his reputation as "distant and haughty" is from page 5. Stevens went on to state, however, that Lenox was "communicative as a

child to his intimates." The quote regarding the "peril of dispersion" is from his obituary. "Death of James Lenox," *New York Times*, February 19, 1880. Lenox's father shrewdly bought thirty acres of land, the "Lenox farm" in upper Manhattan, for approximately $7,000 in 1817 and 1818. At the time of Lenox's death in 1880, the *Times* estimated that it was worth $10,000,000. The obituary details Lenox's other gifts to the city, the most important of which, besides the Lenox Library, was the Presbyterian Hospital. He had five sisters, one of whom, Henrietta, also never married and bequeathed a sizable endowment and a valuable plot of land to the Library.

30. The act of incorporation is reprinted in George Lockhart Rives and Charles Howland Russell, comps., *The New York Public Library, Astor, Lenox, and Tilden Foundations, Book of Charters, Wills, Deeds and Other Official Documents* (New York: New York Public Library, 1905), 49–52. Details regarding the progress of the Library during these first few years are found in the annual reports that the Lenox Library was required to submit to the legislature. Lenox Library, *Annual Report of the Trustees of the Lenox Library, New York, January 5, 1871* (New York: New York Public Library, 1871), 5–7, for the initial organization and other matters. The by-laws are reprinted on pages 12–14. Title varies; hereafter, Lenox Library, *Annual Report* (1870). For the completion of the building and the transfer of the collections, Lenox Library, *Annual Report* (1875), 5; for the appointment of Moore, *Annual Report* (1872), 7–8; for a detailed description of the building, *Annual Report* (1874), 3–6. See also Harry Miller Lydenberg, *History of the New York Public Library: Astor, Lenox and Tilden Foundations* (New York: New York Public Library, 1923), 99–101. This is the official history of the New York Public Library and includes an extensive chapter on the Lenox as well as the Astor Library.

31. Lenox Library, *Annual Report* (1880), 7; Henry Otis Dwight, *The Centennial History of the American Bible Society* (New York: Macmillan, 1916), 269, 348.

32. Wilberforce Eames, "The Lenox Library and Its Founder," *Library Journal* 24 (May 1899): 199–201. Quotes are at page 100. This was a paper that Eames read before the New York Library Club. It is an interesting discussion of how the Library's policies and collections developed over time, although large sections of it are plagiarized from Steven's biography. A good description of the various gift collections that made up the Library, with the number of volumes in each, may be found in Lenox Library, *Annual Report* (1893), 19–20. Lenox left only $50,000 to the Library upon his death. Lenox Library, *Annual Report* (1881), 8. The collection developed more fully after his sister Henrietta bequeathed $100,000 in her will, the interest on which was to be used only for purchasing books. Lenox Library, *Annual Report* (1887), 6. For the total amounts devoted to collection development in each year of the Library's existence, see Lydenberg, *New York Public Library*, 523.

33. In 1877, when the exhibitions began, the Library was open from 11:00 a.m. to 4:00 p.m. on Monday and Thursday. Lenox Library, *Annual Report* (1877), 5. By 1883, it was open from 11:00 a.m. to 4:00 p.m. Tuesday through Saturday, Lenox Library, *Annual Report* (1883), 5. By 1889, the hours were 10:00 a.m. to 5:00 p.m. Monday through Saturday. Lenox Library, *Annual Report* (1889), 14. The quote is from Lenox Library, *Annual Report* (1877), 6. For a detailed description of the art on exhibit, see "Fine Arts, Picture Gallery of the Lenox Library, First Notice," *New York Times*, January 18, 1877, and "Fine Arts, Picture Gallery of the Lenox Library, Second Notice," *New York Times*, January 18, 1877.

34. "Proper control of the admissions" is from Lenox Library, *Annual Report* (1876), 6; "unreasonable" is from *Annual Report* (1877), 6. The report never explains what was considered reasonable, but I suspect that requests with spelling or grammatical errors or from an "unreasonable" address were rejected. The use of tickets was discontinued in 1887. Lenox Library, *Annual Report* (1887), 5.

35. "The Park Institutions," *New York Times*, January 6, 1878. The *Times* reported that Lenox had "erected barriers which render entrance to the building exceedingly difficult." The annual attendance for the exhibits, with a few exceptions, declined steadily as the city's population increased. For attendance statistics, see Lydenberg, *New York Public Library*, 523. For population statistics, see Barbara Shupe, Janet Steins, and Jyoti Pandit, eds., *New York State Population, 1790–1980, A Compilation of Federal Census Data* (New York: Neal-Schuman Publishers, 1987), 200–2.

36. The trustees finally published regulations for the use of the Library in 1890. Lenox Library, *Annual Report* (1889), 14–15. In the context of the times, they were not especially onerous. Researchers had to register before they could use the books and could be required to "give references or furnish such guarantees of responsibility as shall be satisfactory to the Superintendent." "Under the immediate supervision of the Superintendent" is from: Lenox Library, *Annual Report* (1882), 7. The two quotes by Eames are from: Eames, "The Lenox Library and Its Founder," 200, 201.

37. Lenox Library, *Annual Report* (1881), 8; *Annual Report* (1880), 7; "The Lenox Library," *Literary World*, June 21, 1879, 200.

38. Moore's report, which outlines for the trustees his conception of the public role of the Library, is reprinted in Lydenberg, *New York Public Library*, 108–113. The quote is at page 110. New York Free Circulating Library, *Library Meeting at the Union League Club, Jan. 20, 1886* (New York: New York Free Circulating Library, 1886), 5. Choate stressed the "ample provision for the rich and educated in the way of books." The cartoon and accompanying "skit" from Life is reprinted in Lydenberg, *New York Public Library*, 113–16. The skit is hilarious. It begins with a humble applicant applying to the superintendent for admission, and follows the application through various Lenox functionaries, until it "goes to the

Commissioner of Vital Statistics" in order "to ascertain if the applicant is still living." "The Lenox Library," *Harper's Bazaar*, September 16, 1893, 759.

39. The most recent biography is Axel Madsen, *John Jacob Astor: America's First Multimillionaire* (New York: John Wiley, 2001). On Astor's business career, see John D. Haeger, *John Jacob Astor: Business and Finance in the Early Republic* (Detroit: Wayne State University Press, 1991). The Astor rags-to-riches story is largely true. He arrived in the United States with twenty-five dollars to his name. However, marrying into the Brevoort family certainly improved his prospects. The quote is from a resolution passed at the second meeting of the Board of Trustees. Astor Library, Board of Trustees Minutes, June 1, 1848 [microfilm], Record Group 1: Astor Library Records, 1839–1911, Series I: Administration, 1839–1904, New York Public Library, Manuscripts and Archives Division, New York.

40. Orie William Long, *Literary Pioneers: Early American Explorers of European Culture* (Cambridge, Mass.: Harvard University Press, 1935), 77–108. There are also chapters on Everett and Ticknor. On their role in the public library movement, see Sidney Ditzion, *Arsenals of a Democratic Culture: A Social History of the American Public Library Movement in New England and the Middle States from 1850 to 1900* (Chicago: American Library Association, 1947), 13–18. Joseph Green Cogswell, *Life of Joseph Green Cogswell as Sketched in his Letters* (Cambridge, Mass.: Riverside Press, 1874), is an excellent source for the founding of the Library and includes many letters to Ticknor and his wife regarding Cogswell's relations with Astor and the early development of the Library. Cogswell was sometimes impatient with Astor's reluctance to firmly commit to a public library, but he found him "not the mere accumulator of dollars I had supposed him," well-versed "on many subjects, [with] a great interest in the arts and literature" (213).

41. The codicils to the will relating to the library and the act of incorporation are reprinted in Rives and Rowland, *NYPL, Book of Charters*, 3–8, 9–13. The quote is from Astor's will, page 3. The $400,000 did not include the land. According to the terms of the will, the trustees were required in effect to purchase either of two sites in lower Manhattan from the Astor estate.

42. A concise history of events leading up to the opening of the Library in 1854 may be found in Astor Library, *Annual Report of the Trustees of the Astor Library of the State of New York, Made to the Legislature on the 1st of February, 1854* (New York: Astor Library, 1854), 5–8. Hereafter, Astor Library, *Annual Report* (1853). See also Lydenberg, *New York Public Library*, 9–22. For a comparison of libraries in the city and in the United States about this time, see William J. Rhees, *Manual of Public Libraries, Institutions, and Societies in the United States and the British Provinces of North America* (Urbana: University of Illinois Press, 1967 [1859]), 623–24. The trustees explained in their first annual report that in sending Cogswell on a buying trip to Europe in 1848, it was their intention "to

avail themselves of the opportunity afforded by the distracted political condition of Europe and the reduction of prices consequent upon it." Astor Library, *Annual Report* (1849), 5.

43. Cogswell to Ticknor, May 6, 1839, in Cogswell, *Letters*, 220. Joseph Green Cogswell, "Letter from Dr. Cogswell," *Literary World*, February 24, 1849, 169.

44. Cogswell, "Letter from Dr. Cogswell," 169; Astor Library, *Annual Report* (1853), 29.

45. On collection development for law and medicine, industry, and American history, respectively, see Lydenberg, *New York Public Library*, 26–27, 31. This is a reprint of most of an extensive article that appeared in the *Home Journal* describing the collection. It was also widely reprinted in the local newspapers. Joseph Green Cogswell, "The Astor Library: A Letter from Dr. Cogswell," *Home Journal*, January 7, 1854, 1. Cogswell donated his own funds to develop the bibliography collection, as did Astor's son, William B. Astor, for the industry and technology collection. Astor Library, *Annual Report* (1853), 29–30. On the growth of the collection throughout the Library's history, see Lydenberg, *New York Public Library*, 520.

46. "Dr. Cogswell and the Astor Library," *New York Times*, September 22, 1858; *Gleason's Pictorial Drawing-Room Companion*, January 28, 1854, 61; Lector (pseud.), "The Astor Library," *New York Times*, April 18, 1854; Frank H. Norton, "The Astor Library," *The Galaxy: A Magazine of Entertaining Reading* 7 (April 1869): 527. Initially the Library was open from 10:00 a.m. until 5:00 p.m. Monday through Saturday. Readers had to be fourteen years or older. Astor Library, Annual Report (1853), 23–24. The age limit was raised to sixteen in 1854, and after 1865 the Library opened at 9:00 a.m. Lydenberg, *New York Public Library*, 17.

47. Astor Library, *Annual Report* (1857), 7. Here and elsewhere, the trustees stressed that they were following John Jacob Astor's wishes in regards to the policies and collections of the Library. Joseph Green Cogswell, "Resources of the Astor Library," *New York Times*, September 22, 1858. "Silly clamor" actually refers to the lack of a subject catalog for the Library, another frequent complaint, but it reflects the tenor of the letter generally. "Dr. Cogswell and the Astor Library" (note 46) was the editorial response to Cogswell's defense and concludes with a plea to place the Library under "vigorous, living management." Astor Library, *Annual Report* (1853), 28–29.

48. "Another Astor Place Riot," *New York Times*, July 24, 1855. For examples of the "avalanche," see: "Want of Gallantry at the Astor Library," July 18, 1855; "Complaint of a Poor Scholar," July 19, 1855; "The Astor Library," July 20, 1855; "The Astor Library," July 23, 1855. Many of the complaints seem to have been about the same attendant, who seems to have delighted in making readers wait for their books and making snide remarks about their requests. President Washington Irving's response to the "Astor Place Riot" was hardly conciliatory.

Although he assured the public that the trustees would make every effort to render the Library a "free and open resort," he noted the "diffidence and sensitiveness of the studious," implying the critics were partly at fault. "The Astor Library," *New York Times*, August 3, 1855. Most public libraries before the mid-1890s had closed stacks.

49. Rusticus's letter is "Astor Library," July 23, 1855. "Dragons" is from an editorial response to Cogswell's letter in defense of the Library (note 47): "Dr. Cogswell and the Astor Library," New York Times, September 22, 1858. "Rudeness, incivility, and insult" is from another editorial: "The Astor Library," *New York Times*, July 21, 1855.

50. "Dr. Cogswell and the Astor Library," 4. Several years later, the *Times* changed its editorial stance, referring to the critics of the Astor as "grumblers" and "wiseacres." "The Astor Library," *New York Times*, June 26, 1874; Norton, "The Astor Library," 538.

51. "The Astor Stumbling-Block," *Critic*, April 22, 1882, 114; "A Book Lover's Memories: Some Reminiscences by Librarian Frederick Saunders," *New York Times*, July 18, 1895; Frederick Saunders, "Our Metropolitan Library," *The Independent*, August 12, 1875. Saunders joined the Astor in 1858 and retired in 1896, shortly after the consolidation with the Lenox and the Tilden Foundation. His accounts of the "strange people" he encountered at work are rather good-natured, if somewhat condescending. For other descriptions of the Astor's users, see "At the Astor Library," *Library Journal* 15 (January 1890): 20–21 (reprinted from the *New York Tribune*); and Cromwell Childe, "Odd Characters Seen at the Astor Library," *New York Times: Illustrated Magazine Supplement*, September 25, 1898. The *National Police Gazette* claimed it was where schoolgirls went to flirt with "nobby young men." "Classical Art," *National Police Gazette*, December 12, 1880, 6. The article quotes a (probably fictional) "disgusted spinster" who remarked "they ought to be spanked . . . the little hussies."

52. Lydenberg, *New York Public Library*, 521. Still, these figures are less impressive when taking into account that by 1890 the greater metropolitan area, the five boroughs that currently comprise the city of New York, had over 2,500,000 inhabitants. Even Saunders admitted that "its great work is . . . but little suspected . . . by the denizens of the populous city in which it stands." Saunders, "Our Metropolitan Library," 2.

53. Childe, "Odd Characters," 4. Alcove readers are seldom discussed in the annual reports, but the requirements are described briefly in Astor Library, *Annual Report* (1882), 8–9. The reports rarely give the number of alcove privileges outstanding in any given year, but alcove readers usually accounted for between 10 and 20 percent of the daily visitors. Lydenberg, *New York Public Library*, 521. In 1875, there were 1,286 alcove readers and 5,871 daily admissions to the alcoves. Astor Library, *Annual Report* (1875), 15. By 1889, two letters from "reputable and

responsible citizens" were required for alcove privileges. "Books Thefts at the Astor Library," *Library Journal* 13 (August 1889): 348.

54. Bender, *New York Intellect*, 168–206; George Folsom, "Historical Sketch of the Society," in New-York Historical Society, *Collections of the New-York Historical Society*, second series (New York: H. Ludwig, 1841), 1:459; McCabe, *New York by Gaslight*, 195–96.

55. McCabe, *New York by Gaslight*, 195–96. "Topics Astir: The Astor Library," *Home Journal*, January 21, 1854, 2. Cogswell and the trustees made similar arguments when they deigned to justify their management of the Library. In an early annual report, for example, they explained that its collections were "great reservoirs of science and learning . . . indispensable for feeding the streams which diffuse the blessings of knowledge to every dwelling." Astor Library, *Annual Report* (1853), 28.

56. Astor Library, *Annual Report* (1854), 6; *Annual Report* (1853), 27–28. Cogswell did not actually use the word "steal," but that was clearly his meaning.

57. Lector, "The Astor Library"; "The Astor Library," *New York Times*, September 17, 1873; "The Astor Library," *New York Times*, November 20, 1885. These editorials criticized the Astor specifically, especially with regard to the limited hours, but, as will be seen in Chapter 7, they also echoed in many respects arguments made by the leaders of the public library movement. The public library movement also placed great emphasis upon the circulation of books and upon small branch libraries throughout the city's neighborhoods. Cogswell referred to Scott, Cooper, and Dickens as trash in a letter to Ticknor. Cogswell, *Letters*, 264–65. The Astor held a small number of novels, but the trustees in the annual reports took great pains to point out that almost nobody read them. Astor Library, *Annual Report* (1869), 5–6. In this report, they also compare their readers favorably with those of the circulating libraries. Astor Library, *Annual Report* (1871), 3; *Annual Report* (1875), 6.

58. This was, of course, even truer of the Lenox Library. James Lenox never intended to build a public library in any real sense of the term, and he turned a deaf ear to the public's criticism of its management. Interestingly, it was not at all true of the third part of what was to become the New York Public Library, the Tilden Foundation created by Samuel J. Tilden. As will be seen in Chapter 8, not only was Tilden's will legally contested by his heirs (which eventually led to the alliance with the Astor and the Lenox), but there was also some disagreement among the trustees as to what kind of library would best serve the public.

59. "The Astor Library," *Critic*, December 17, 1881. The *Critic* had changed its editorial stance by this date and was referring ironically to the notion that the Astor fortune was "unfair." The editors dismissed it as "communism." Dain, *New York Public Library*, 9. The public response to Andrew Carnegie's library philanthropy was also colored by his unsavory business reputation. Robert

Sydney Martin, ed., *Carnegie Denied: Communities Rejecting Carnegie Library Construction Grants, 1898–1925* (Westport, Conn.: Greenwood, 1993).

60. C. A. Bristed, "The Astor Library and Its Founder's Fortune," *New York Times*, October 3, 1869. Bristed was Astor's grandson and he argued that the family owed nothing to New York. He also pointed out that the Astor Library represented, not two percent of his grandfather's fortune, but rather 5 percent. Lector, "The Astor Library." Lector argued that the family did owe a considerable debt to the city.

61. "Family monument" is from "The Astor Library Stumbling Block," 114. The *Critic*'s editors had again changed their editorial stance. The term "monument" occurred frequently in the press in reference to the Lenox as well as the Astor. At times it was used in a positive sense; rich men were encouraged to give to public purposes and the incentive was that a public institution would be a monument to them after their death. The quote from William Waldorf Astor is from a letter to the board about the time of the consolidation, quoted in full in Lydenberg, *New York Public Library*, 309–10. See pages 517–19 for the trustees and officers throughout the Library's history. Many family members sat on the board, including in-laws. This was also the case for the Lenox Library. See pages 522–23 for the officers and trustees. In all fairness, the Astors probably would have been criticized for indifference if they had not served. William Waldorf Astor was writing from his home in London. The British branch of the family was later granted two titles of nobility, a viscountcy and a barony.

62. For a summary of the Library's finances after the building had been completed and its doors opened, see Astor Library, *Annual Report* (1855), 7–8. The son, William Backhouse Astor, gave a total of $550,000. Astor Library, *Annual Report* (1875), 10. The grandson, John Jacob III, gave $850,000. Astor Library, *Annual Report* (1890), 20. However, the Astor fortune grew substantially in the decades following the death of its founder.

63. "The Astor Library," *New York Times*, July 18, 1875. Both the Lenox Library and the Cooper Union made similar complaints about the ingratitude of the city's "Croesuses." Andrew Carnegie's gifts to public libraries proved adequate, because the municipalities that accepted them were contractually required to provide funding annually.

64. "The Astor Library," *New York Times*, September 17, 1873. The editors suggested that the City provide annual appropriations to the Astor trustees to "enable them to extend their usefulness." "The Astor Stumbling-Block," 114. The *Critic* thought that the state legislature would have funded a public library were it not for the Astor "stumbling block." "A Suggestion to Mr. Vanderbilt," *Critic*, May 6, 1882, 128. Cornelius Vanderbilt later gave money to the YMCA to help develop its libraries.

7. Scholars and Mechanics: Libraries and Higher Learning in Nineteenth-Century New York

1. "Report of the Select Committee Appointed to Inquire into . . . the Literature Fund" is reprinted in Mario Emilio Cosenza, *The Establishment of College of the City of New York as the Free Academy in 1847, Townsend Harris, Founder: A Chapter in the History of Education* (New York: The Alumni Association of the College, 1925), 15–33. This is mostly a collection of primary documents.

2. On the creation of the board, see Carl F. Kaestle, *The Evolution of an Urban School System: New York City, 1750–1850* (Cambridge, Mass.: Harvard University Press, 1973), 160–61. See also S. Willis Rudy, *The College of the City of New York: A History, 1847–1947* (New York: Arno Press, 1977), 5–6. The early history of public education in the city revolved in part around a conflict between Catholics and Protestants over the version of the Bible used in the schools. The Public School Society was dissolved and the Board of Education assumed responsibility for its schools in 1853. On the Literature Fund, *Laws of the State of New York for 1790*, chap. 38; *Laws of the State of New York for 1834*, chap. 140.

3. On the founding of Columbia and the New York Society Library, and on the rivalry between Columbia and New York University when the latter was founded in 1830, see Chapter 1. On the founding of City College, see Thomas Bender, *New York Intellect* (New York: Knopf, 1987), 101–6. See also Rudy, *College of the City of New York*, 1–21.

4. "Report of the Select Committee," 25, 30; *Addresses Delivered upon the Occasion of the Opening of the Free Academy, January 27, 1849* (New York: Wm. C. Bryant, 1849), 18. As with the founding of New York University, instruction in Greek and Latin was a critical issue. At the ceremony marking the first anniversary, Erastus C. Benedict, President of the School Board, claimed that from "ancient and dead tongues" there was created a "learned class . . . of the most exclusive aristocracy." Erastus C. Benedict, *An Address Delivered at the First Anniversary of the Free Academy of the City of New York* (New York: Bryant & Co., 1850), 12.

5. For example, Benedict enthused that the classes would be "mingled all together on a footing of republican equality." Benedict, *Address at the First Anniversary*, 14.

6. "Report of the Select Committee," 31. In the press, supporters and opponents of the proposed school seem to have split largely along party lines. For a sampling of Whig and Democratic editorials, see Cosenza, *Establishment of the College*, 38–51, 60–88, 129–64, 191–99, and 205–20.

7. Free Academy of the City of New York, *Second Annual Report of the Free Academy of the City of New York* (New York: Free Academy, 1851), 3; "Report of the Select Committee," 30; Benedict, *Address at the First Anniversary*, 17. Of all the useful, modern subjects, chemistry was most emphasized. It was, for

example, frequently referred to in a series of editorial exchanges between Harris and a supporter of New York University, with the latter arguing that City College was unnecessary, in part because of the excellence of the chemistry faculty at his alma mater.

8. *Addresses Delivered on the Opening of the Free Academy*, 5; Benedict, *Address at the First Anniversary*, 8; *New York Courier*, March 15, 1847, reprinted in Cosenza, *Establishment of the College*, 81. Another important argument made use of by the supporters of City College was that a public college would strengthen the public schools by stimulating competition for admission to the former. "The Memorial and Draft of a Bill Presented to the State Legislature . . ." reprinted in Cosenza, *Establishment*, 94.

9. Cosenza, *Establishment of the College*, 42.

10. "The Memorial and Draft of a Bill," 93. The editor of the *New York Subterranean* predicted the school would allow poor young men to compete in the "race of life." Cosenza, *Establishment*, 131. And Harris's report stressed the curriculum would "effectually fit them for various departments of labor and toil." "Report of the Select Committee," 30.

11. "Report of the Select Committee," 30; *Addresses Delivered on the Opening of the Free Academy*, 10.

12. On the founding of New York University and its brief rivalry with Columbia in the early 1830s, see Bender, *New York Intellect*, 89–104. See also Thomas J. Frusciano and Marilyn H. Pettit, *New York University and the City: An Illustrated History* (New Brunswick, N.J.: Rutgers University Press, 1997), 1–14.

13. "Report of the Select Committee," 28; Louise L Stevenson, "Preparing for Public Life: The Collegiate Students at New York University, 1832–1881," in *The University and the City: From Medieval Origins to the Present*, ed. Thomas Bender (New York: Oxford University Press, 1988), 151.

14. Frusciano and Petit, *New York University*, 20. Gallatin envisioned the halls of the college crowded with "those brave men who constitute our fire and military forces." Quoted in Stevenson, "Preparing for Public Life," 162. He was the leading proponent of the new university, but resigned from the governing council before the opening ceremony, charging that the council had abandoned the original plan. He wrote of Mathews "he is . . . a perfect monarch and I do not like Monarchy." Quoted in Frusciano and Petit, *New York University*, 15.

15. *Putman's Monthly* 2 (July 1853): 7–8. Quoted in Stevenson, "Preparing for Public Life," 151.

16. This neglect is reflected in a dearth of primary sources for most of the century. For most years either the librarian did not submit an annual report or those reports have not survived. The libraries are rarely mentioned in the college or university annual reports, except occasionally to lament a lack of funding and the meager growth of the collections. The same holds true for City College Library.

17. In 1799, the Columbia library was open one hour every Saturday. In 1853, it was open from 1:30 to 3:00 p.m. on Monday, Wednesday, and Friday. In 1863, the hours were 1:00–3:00 p.m. every weekday. James H. Canfield, "The Library," in *History of Columbia University, 1754–1904*, ed. Brander Matthews et al. (New York: Macmillan, 1904), 433, 438. William A. Jones, *Statement of the Librarian* (1857), 4. This is a printed response by the college librarian to a series of questions from the Board of Trustees. Before 1835, only juniors and seniors could use the Columbia Library. Between 1838 and 1883, freshman could use it with special permission. Canfield, "The Library," 435. Melvil Dewey, "The New Library Regulations," *School of Mines Quarterly* (November 1883): 69. As late as 1890, the New York University Library was open from 2:00 p.m. to 4:00 p.m. Monday through Saturday and "three evenings each week." University of the City of New York, *Catalogue and Announcements* (New York: New York University, 1890), 70.

18. Columbia's first printed catalog appeared in 1874. Canfield, "The Library," 439. It is unclear when a card catalog was introduced, but it was probably in the early 1880s, around the time that Melvil Dewey became chief librarian.

19. Columbia's first full-time librarian was Nathaniel F. Moore, who served from 1837 to 1839 and who was president of the university from 1842 to 1849. Rowe Weeks was assistant librarian and janitor from 1847 to 1883. Canfield, "The Library," 435–36. Apparently the first full-time librarian at New York University was Leslie J. Tompkins, who began in 1894.

20. Jones, "The College Library," 11; Henry M. Baird, "Report of the Librarian for the Year 1861–1862," New York University Archives, Elmer Holmes Bobst Library, New York. Baird's entire, handwritten "report" is the number of volumes added that year, the total number of volumes in the collection, and its value. Canfield, "The Library," 438; Harry Miller Lydenberg, *History of the New York Public Library: Astor, Lenox, and Tilden Foundations* (New York: New York Public Library, 1923), 520.

21. William A. Jones, *Columbia College Library: An Article Originally Published in the University Quarterly, January, 1861* (New York: n.p., 1861), 19, 26, 28. The only exceptions that Jones made for fiction were the works of the college's celebrated alumnus, Washington Irving and Sir Walter Scott's Waverly novels, which he considered "literary illustrations of History." Jones was actually a fairly progressive and conscientious librarian for his day. The fact that he wrote an article describing the collection shows that he was more interested in promoting the use of the library than most of his predecessors.

22. Jones, *The College Library*, 21, 28, 31–32. Jones also highlighted the rarities within each particular subject within the library; see 16, 18, 21, 22, 25, 26, 29, 30.

23. Columbia College, *Annual Report of the President Made to the Board of Trustees, June 5, 1865* (New York: Columbia College, 1865), 20–21. Barnard was complaining in particular about the lack of a printed catalog, but he also pointedly referred to the "deficiencies in modern literature and modern science."

24. Frusciano and Pettit, *New York University*, 106–8; Horace Coon, *Columbia: Colossus on the Hudson* (New York: Dutton, 1947), 325–27; Edward G. Holley, "Academic Libraries in 1876," *College & Research Libraries* 37 (January 1976): 26–28. In 1846, for example, the Eucleian Society at New York University printed a classed and alphabetical catalog of its collection, before the college library had a printed catalog. Archival collections for both are available in the New York University Archives. On the debates at New York University, see Stevenson, "Preparing for Public Life: New York University," 164–66. For the history of literary societies generally, see Thomas S. Harding, *College Literary Societies: Their Contribution to Higher Education in the United States, 1815–1876* (New York: Pageant Press, 1971). After 1876, the college libraries began to eclipse the literary society libraries.

25. Letter from George Clinton Jr. et al. to Robert R. Livingston, July 21, 1806, Library Subject Files, Box 6, folder 4, Columbiana Library, Columbia University, New York. William Jones wrote in 1861 that any books that students could not access in the Columbia Library were available the Astor, the Society Library, the Historical Society, the Mercantile Library and elsewhere. Jones, Columbia College Library, 5.

26. New York University, *Catalogue* (1890), 71.

27. Rudy, *College of the City of New York*, 10–29; Sandra Shoiock Roff, Anthony M. Cucchiara, and Barbara J. Dunlap, *From the Free Academy to CUNY, Illustrating Public Higher Education in New York City, 1847–1997* (New York: Fordham University Press, 2000), 6. Cosenza, *Establishment*, 221–23. The memorial, the state senate and assembly bills, and the law establishing the Free Academy are preprinted at 89–128. The referendum passed by a vote of 19,305 to 3,409.

28. Rudy, *College of the City of New York*, 24–25. Harris later became the first Consul General to Japan in 1855 and negotiated the first commercial treaty with that country in 1858.

29. Board of Education of the City of New York, *Report of the Executive Committee on the Free Academy, July 7, 1852* (New York: Board of Education, 1852). All of the early reports of the Board of Education, the president, and the faculty, and the extant early library catalogs and reports are available in the City College Archives. Rudy, *College of the City of New York*, 13–19. The courses were identical, except for the language classes. The power to confer degrees was granted in a law passed by the legislature in April 1854. The Board of Education created the two separate degrees the following June (38–40). For the rest of the century, practically any change in the curriculum occasioned a struggle between a traditional, classically oriented faction and a more progressive, modernizing faction within the student body, faculty, trustees, and alumni. In 1878, for example, after the introduction of a nondegree commercial course, a student newspaper complained that it "lowers the tone of the College" (166). See also

Richard Rogers Bowker, "College Days and College Ways II: The Old Building and the Early Curriculum." *City College Alumnus* 22 (June 1926). Bowker was the first publisher of *Library Journal* and the first president of the New York Library Club.

30. Benedict, *Address at the First Anniversary*, 11–15. Part of Benedict's argument was that the college would be exclusive if it excluded men of wealth and leisure. Taken as a whole, his speech is a case study in vacillation. This is probably explained in part by the fact that he was a (Whig) politician defending a novel and radical public policy. This odd ambiguity is also evident in the addresses at the opening of the school. One speaker criticized "studies . . . far removed from the cares of ordinary mortals," then went on to prove his point by quoting from Virgil in Latin. *Addresses at the Opening of the Free Academy*, 17.

31. Munroe Smith, "The University and the Non-Professional Graduate Schools," in *History of Columbia University*, 210–17; Frusciano and Pettit, *New York University*, 46–47; University of the City of New York, *Catalogue of the University of the City of New York, March, 1859* (New York: Hosford, 1859), 19. It is difficult to determine whether the founding of City College prompted the changes at NYU and Columbia or if it was just another manifestation of larger changes occurring in higher education at the time.

32. *Addresses Delivered on the Opening of the Free Academy*, 32–33.

33. College of the City of New York, *Minutes of the Board of Trustees, January 22, 1873* (New York: The College, 1873), 3. The graduation rate for the class 1858 was approximately 17 percent. Kaestle, *Evolution of an Urban School System*, 107.

34. Coon, *Columbia*, 83; Burgess, *Reminiscences of an American Scholar* (New York: Columbia University Press, 1934), 179–80. The average age of a first-year student in the early years was just fourteen. Rudy, *College of the City of New York*, 70.

35. Kaestle, *Evolution of an Urban School System*, 107–8. Kaestle provides very interesting tables derived from the Board of Education annual reports that give, among other statistics, the occupations of the students' parents and their occupations upon graduation. Some of the statistics are problematic. For example, artisans are grouped together with factory workers. All of the graduates of the classes of 1858, 1859, and 1860 took up clerical, mercantile, or professional positions. Frusciano and Pettit, *New York University*, 105–6; Rudy, *College of the City of New York*, 68–69.

36. Board of Education of the City of New York, *Report on the Organization of the Free Academy* (New York: Board of Education, 1851), 3. In the first three years, 569 students had entered the school, and 330 were still enrolled as of the date of the report.

37. Rudy, *College of the City of New York*, 128, 160–72, 223–28. City College did not introduce electives, for example, until 1901.

38. Free Academy of the City of New York, *Catalogue of the Library of the Free Academy of the City of New York* (New York: Free Academy, 1860), preface.

39. Allen Kent and Harold Lancour, eds., *Encyclopedia of Library and Information Science* (New York: Marcel Dekker, 1968), s.v. "Columbia University Libraries," by Alice H. Bonnell, 5:69; College of the City of New York, *Annual Library Report for the Year Ending June 30, 1900 of the Librarian of the City College of New York to the Regents of the State of New York* (New York: College of the City of New York), 10. The endowments, totaling $35,000, are described in *Catalogue of the Free Academy* (1860). See also, Nathaniel J. Stewart, "A History of the Library of the College of the City of New York" (M.S. thesis, College of the City of New York, 1935): 36–37, 62–64. I was unable to find a record for this in any catalog or database, but a copy is available in the City College Archives. The Free Academy library lost its support through the Literature Fund when it changed its name to the College of the City of New York. The fund was limited to the state's academies.

40. United States Bureau of Education, *Public Libraries in the United States of America: Their History, Condition and Management*, Special Report, Pt 1 (Washington, D.C.: Government Printing Office, 1876), 945–46. Students borrowed few books from the library and the majority of these were novels. For example, in 1877 an average of sixty-nine volumes circulated each week; of these, thirty-nine were novels. Stewart, "History of the Library," 62. On collection development at City College, see also, Charles H. Herbermann, "First Annual Report of the Librarian," in College of the City of New York, *Minutes of the Board of Trustees of the College of the City of New York, October 2, 1874* (New York: College of the City of New York, 1874), 8.

41. Stewart, "History of the Library," 68–70. Rudy, College of the City of New York, 141–142. Lewis F. Mott, "The College Library," *City College Quarterly* 17 (June 1921): 4–5. Mott gives as examples of books to be found only in the Clionian Library *Tom Jones* and *The Decameron.* As late as 1905, there was apparently a list of titles, such as the works of Algernon Charles Swinburne, that were held by the library but not to be used by the students. "Topics of the Times," *New York Times*, November 7, 1905.

42. "By-Laws of the Board of Education Concerning the Library of the Free Academy," in *Catalogue of the Free Academy* (1860), v–vii. Book requests were accepted during the half-hour in the morning and delivered at three in the afternoon. It is unclear how long these very restrictive rules were in effect. The by-laws issued in 1871, for example, stated simply that "students . . . shall be entitled to the use of the Library under such conditions as may be imposed by the President." College of the City of New York, *Twenty-Second Annual Register of the College of the City of New York, 1870–1871* (New York: College of the City of New York, 1871), 30. In 1881, the teachers and principals of the city's public schools were granted access to the library. Steward, "History of the Library," 66–67.

43. College of the City of New York, *Minutes of the Board of Trustees of the College of the City of New York, December 26, 1872* (New York: College of the

City of New York, 1872), 2–4. This problem was alleviated somewhat the following year, when one of the classrooms was remodeled and fitted with shelves for the science reference books. Nonetheless, space was limited even when the campus moved to its present location on St. Nicholas Heights in 1907. A separate library building was not constructed until 1929, and even that proved inadequate. Stewart, "History of the Library," 54; Rudy, *College of the City of New York*, 376–77, 444.

44. Mott, "The College Library," 4–5. Mott was hired as a professor of English in 1897 and retired in 1934. His article is, in part, a plea for a new library building.

45. The cost of the land and building was $630,000. Rossiter W. Raymond, *Peter Cooper* (Boston: Houghton, Mifflin, 1901), 66. The entire deed is reprinted in *First Annual Report of the Trustees of the Cooper Union for the Advancement of Science and Art* (New York: Cooper Union, 1860), 33–39; the title varies, but hereafter Cooper Union, *Annual Report* (1859). The quote is at page 34. Documents from the archives of the Cooper Union, including the early annual reports, are available online at: http://library.cooper.edu/archive/cooper_archives_page.html. Allan Nevins, *Abram S. Hewitt, with Some Account of Peter Cooper* (New York: Harper and Brothers, 1935), 113–14; Edward C. Mack, *Peter Cooper: Citizen of New York* (New York: Duell, Sloan and Pearce, 1949), 243–52. Mack claimed the first plot of land was not purchased until 1839, while Nevins claimed it was 1825.

46. Cooper Union, *Annual Report* (1874), 7.

47. Ibid. (1859), 36. The same provision also called for an art gallery. The Bryan Collection that was eventually displayed at the New-York Historical Society was initially at the Cooper Union. Bryan moved the collection after he saw Peter Cooper noting the merits of one of the paintings to a visitor with the point of his umbrella. R. W. G Vail, *Knickerbocker Birthday: A Sesqui-Centennial History of the New-York Historical Society* (New York: New-York Historical Society, 1954), 127–28.

48. The most substantial biography of Cooper is Mack, *Peter Cooper.* Nevins, *Abram S. Hewitt*, has considerable material on Cooper. Raymond, *Peter Cooper*, is a slim eulogy, but an interesting primary source, written by a close friend and associate, and an employee of the Cooper Union. Another interesting primary source is J. C. Zachos, *A Sketch of the Early Days and Business Life of Peter Cooper* (New York: Cooper Union, 1877). Zachos was also a friend and the curator of the Cooper Union Library. The "autobiography" is partly Zachos's narrative and partly a transcript of Cooper's reminiscences. Zachos "edited" a number of books for Cooper, which "breathe[d] his spirit, but not always his expression." Zachos, *Peter Cooper*, 24. I suspect the same holds true for Cooper's speeches and letters that appear in the annual reports.

49. He "never had more than a year or so of schooling and . . . could not spell the simplest English." C. Sumner Spalding, *Peter Cooper: A Critical Biography of*

His Life and Works (New York: New York Public Library, 1941), 5; Cooper Union, *Annual Report* (1859), 7.

50. Cooper Union, *Annual Report* (1873), 18–19. This story appears more than once in the annual reports and it is somewhat suspect. Raymond claimed in his biography that originally Cooper wanted a museum for the instruction and amusement of the masses and had to be talked out of it. The room that was to serve as the main hall of the museum became the library. Raymond, *Peter Cooper*, 69–75. Beginning in 1858, the General Society of Mechanics and Tradesmen also had a night school, although it was comparatively small until Andrew Carnegie offered funds for its expansion in 1900. Lawrence Martin, *The General Society of Mechanics and Tradesmen of the City of New York* (New York: General Society of Mechanics and Tradesmen, 1960), 15; Thomas Earle and Charles T. Congdon, *Annals of the General Society of Mechanics and Tradesmen of the City of New York, from 1785 to 1880* (New York: General Society of Mechanics and Tradesmen, 1882), 136.

51. Cooper Union, *Annual Report* (1870), 18. This is from a speech Cooper made to students and graduates on his eightieth birthday. "A Practical Philanthropist," *New York Times*, April 5, 1883.

52. Cooper Union, *Annual Report* (1899), 11. This is from a letter from Carnegie to the trustees offering the Cooper Union $300,000 to start a day school to complement its night school. The founding of the day school was one of the most notable events in the Cooper Union's history. This occurred about the same time that Carnegie began his large-scale philanthropy for public libraries.

53. See, for example, Cooper Union, *Annual Report* (1873), 12; *Annual Report* (1880), 15; *Annual Report* (1870), 12. This quote refers in particular to the Cooper Union's annual lecture series.

54. Cooper Union, *Annual Report* (1873), 5; *Annual Report* (1880), 17. The quotes are from J. C. Zachos. Nonetheless, as president of the Cooper Union, Cooper was actively involved in its affairs until his death in 1883. It seems highly unlikely that he never read (or had read to him) the annual reports written by the friend who "edited" his autobiography and other works. Zachos seems to have been strongly influenced by the labor theory of value as it was expressed in the late nineteenth century. For Cooper's views on labor unions, see Mack, *Peter Cooper*, 361–62.

55. Cooper Union, *Annual Report* (1872), 6.

56. Cooper Union, *Annual Report* (1874), 6; *Annual Report* (1878), 6.

57. Cooper Union, *Annual Report* (1899), 14. A fundamental contradiction in the Cooper Union's aim to elevate the working class was that not everyone could be employed as a manager, foreman, or employer.

58. Cooper Union, *Annual Report* (1859), 10–11. There was an additional department or "course" in the night school, music. The music course, however, was intended to train teachers and choir singers (14).

59. Cooper Union, *Annual Report* (1868), 9. During the early years, the school did not grant a bachelor's degree but rather the "Medal of the Cooper Union." In 1891, by which time the possession of an academic degree carried more weight in terms of employment or admission to the new graduate schools, the Cooper began offering the degree. Cooper Union, *Annual Report* (1891), 9–10. Students could also obtain a "certificate" after they had completed all of the classes within a department or "course." The minimum age for admission was sixteen. Students were also required to provide a "certificate of good moral character." Cooper Union, *Annual Report* (1859), 11.

60. Cooper Union, *Annual Report* (1865), 17; *Annual Report* (1872), 12.

61. Cooper Union, *Annual Report* (1875), 10.

62. It is unclear when and why women stopped attending the night school. In the earliest annual reports, the trustees stressed that the Cooper Union was coeducational and even provided statistics on their attendance in the night school. See for example, Cooper Union, *Annual Report* (1859), 8, 17; *Annual Report* (1882), 14. But the annual report in 1886 states that there were no women in the night school, and there are no further references in later reports. It may be that the policy was changed after Cooper's death. Cooper Union, *Annual Report* (1886), 10.

63. Cooper Union, *Annual Report* (1865), 22.

64. Cooper Union, *Annual Report* (1863), 38; *Annual Report* (1874), 8.

65. Cooper Union, *Annual Report* (1893), 10–11; *Annual Report* (1897), 14.

66. Cooper Union, *Annual Report* (1859), 17–18; *Annual Report* (1896), 15. The fact that instruction was only offered during the day must have limited the number of poor women who could afford to attend, but Cooper, recognizing this difficulty, arranged for modest scholarships for the neediest students. Cooper Union, *Annual Report* (1863), 38. The trustees also admitted a small number of paying students to the School of Design. They justified this exception to the rule that instruction at the Cooper Union was to be free on the grounds that the "presence of ladies of leisure and refined taste tend to raise the standard of art and give to the friendless associations of value in reference to their future careers." Cooper Union, *Annual Report* (1859), 17. Later the school added a department of "normal teaching" to prepare young women for positions as drawing teachers in public and private schools. Cooper Union, *Annual Report* (1883), 15.

67. On the art library, see for example, Cooper Union, *Annual Report* (1897), 36.

68. Raymond, *Peter Cooper*, 85.

69. Since readers were allowed to take books to their homes for free, all of the free circulating libraries required such a reference. It is seldom referred to in their annual reports and later on may have been more of a formality. They often stressed how few books were lost as a result of free circulation. Librarians at the New York Free Circulating Library, in its earliest years, actually visited applicants' homes, probably just to confirm the address. See for example, New York Free

Circulating Library, *First Annual Report of the New York Free Circulating Library* (New York: New York Free Circulating Library, 1880), 19–20; New York Free Circulating Library, *Third Annual Report of the New York Free Circulating Library* (New York: New York Free Circulating Library, 1882), 11.

70. Cooper Union, *Annual Report* (1872), 14; *Annual Report* (1860), 22. The report for this year pointed out that "the working class of this city, being employed at their business during the day, can rarely avail themselves of the rich treasures of the Astor Library."

71. Cooper Union, *Annual Report* (1868), 33; *Annual Report* (1880), 12; *Annual Report* (1900), 41; Harry Miller Lydenberg, *History of the New York Public Library, Astor, Lenox, and Tilden Foundations* (New York: New York Public Library, 1923), 521. It is problematic to compare the Cooper Union Library with the free circulating libraries, since users at the latter could read the books at home and because they were small neighborhood libraries, rather than large, centralized collections like the Cooper Union.

72. James Bassett, "Libraries of New York, First Article," *Frank Leslie's Popular Monthly*, January 1894, 22.

73. Cooper Union, *Annual Report* (1900), 41.

74. Cooper Union, *Annual Report* (1863), 42. The deed specified that the lectures should "have for their constant object . . . the means necessary and appropriate to remove the physical and moral evils that afflict our city, our county and humanity." In practice, the lectures delivered were sometimes in a rather lighter vein, including, for example, humor and travelogue. Cooper Union, *Annual Report* (1878), 27–30 lists all the lectures from 1868 to 1879.

75. Cooper Union, *Annual Report* (1868), 14.

76. Cooper Union, *Annual Report* (1865), 18; *Annual Report* (1860), 22.

77. John Y. Cole, "Storehouses and Workshops: American Libraries and the Uses of Knowledge," in *The Organization of Knowledge in Modern America, 1860–1920*, ed. Alexandra Oleson and John Voss (Baltimore: Johns Hopkins University Press, 1979), 367.

78. Cooper Union, *Annual Report* (1867), 23; *Annual Report* (1886), 12.

79. Cooper Union, *Annual Report* (1859), 23.

80. Cooper Union, *Annual Report* (1886), 12. The annual reports refer repeatedly to the fact that newspapers and periodicals were used more extensively than books.

81. See, for example, Cooper Union, *Annual Report* (1865), 17.

82. Cooper Union, *Annual Report* (1860), 22; *Annual Report* (1880), 13; *Annual Report* (1900), 50; Lydenberg, *New York Public Library*, 520.

83. Cooper Union, *Annual Report* (1886), 12.

84. Cooper Union, *Annual Report* (1859), 23; *Annual Report* (1886), 13.

85. Cooper Union, *Annual Report* (1895), 29–30. A national survey of circulating libraries in 1893 found that fiction as a proportion of the entire collection

averaged 24 percent. Ellen Coe, "Fiction," *Library Journal* 18 (July 1893): 250–51. However, comparing collections during this period is problematic, because of the different ways and the varying levels of detail with which libraries reported statistics. For fiction in New York's free circulating libraries about this time, see Chapter 8.

86. Cooper Union, *Annual Report* (1894), 29–22.

87. Cooper Union, *Annual Report* (1872), 14; *Annual Report* (1873), 11. It is possible that these earlier estimates for fiction are somewhat overstated. The report for 1876, for example, gives statistics for one month, in which fiction accounted for 37 percent of the volumes requested. Cooper Union, *Annual Report* (1876), 9. The survey conducted in 1893 reported the average circulation of fiction nationally as 56 percent. Coe, "Fiction," 250–51.

88. Cooper Union, *Annual Report* (1872), 14; *Annual Report* (1901), 48.

89. Cooper Union, *Annual Report* (1898), 38; *Annual Report* (1874), 9.

90. Cooper Union, *Annual Report* (1859), 9.

91. Cooper Union, *Annual Report* (1869), n.p.; *Annual Report* (1891), 22; Mack, *Peter Cooper*, 85.

92. Cooper Union, *Annual Report* (1897), 44.

93. "Not What It Should Be," *New York Times*, November 10, 1889; "Medicine of the Mind," April 7, 1872.

94. Cooper Union, *Annual Report* (1874), 10. The reference to churches was made in regard to the opening hours on Sunday. The annual reports did make frequent mention of excluding "undesirable" persons, but, in context, I think this refers mostly to people who were clearly disorderly or intoxicated. See note 97, for example, for Cooper's reluctance to introduce the use of "tickets" for admission. Attendants were also very strict about napping in the library. Use of the reading room and library was directly affected by economic conditions. For example, during the very severe depression of the early 1890s, the "capacity of the room was taxed to its fullest extent." Cooper Union, *Annual Report* (1895), 29.

95. Cooper Union, *Annual Report* (1887), 19. The fact that the annual reports for certain years give statistics for female readers in the first place would seem to indicate an interest in promoting use by women. In 1897, the trustees considered eliminating the women's alcove in light of the low use but decided to continue it.

96. Abigail A. Van Slyck, "The Lady and the Library Loafer: Gender and Public Space in Victorian America," *Winterthur Portfolio* 31 (Winter 1996): 221–41. The quote is at page 225. Mack, *Peter Cooper*, 330. Another reason for the low use by women may have been the selection of magazines to which the library subscribed. Many of them were oriented toward the trades or commerce, rather than the home. It did subscribe, however, to the *Ladies' Repository*, as well as *Godey's Ladies Book*, an immensely popular title during this period. Cooper Union, *Annual Report* (1868), 32.

97. Cooper Union, *Annual Report* (1879), 13–15; *Annual Report* (1880), 13. In his biography, Raymond wrote that the board discussed requiring tickets but claimed that Cooper was not "willing (and his fellow trustees agreed with him) to impose any restriction or censorship upon admittance." This is not true, but the policy only lasted two years. Raymond, *Peter Cooper,* 87.

98. New York Free Circulating Library, *First Annual Report of the New York Free Circulating Library* (New York: New York Free Circulating Library, 1880), 19–20. Most of these female readers were between the ages of twelve and twenty-one, while the Cooper users were "men and women of maturity." Cooper Union, *Annual Report* (1876), 9. On the city's free circulating libraries as domesticized spaces, see Chapter 8.

99. Cooper Union, *Annual Report* (1860), 47–50. The report refers to the Liverpool Public Library as well as the Boston Public Library, as an example to be emulated by New York City. On the founding of the Boston Public Library, generally regarded as the beginning of the public library movement in the United States, see Jesse H. Shera, *Foundations of the Public Library: The Origins of the Public Library Movement in New England, 1629–1855* (Chicago: University of Chicago Press, 1949; repr. n.p.: Shoestring Press, 1965): 170–81; Cooper Union, *Annual Report* (1870), 12.

100. Cooper Union, *Annual Report* (1875), 7; *Annual Report* (1890), 9.

101. Cooper Union, *Annual Report* (1896), 16. On gifts and endowments to the library, see for example, Cooper Union, *Annual Report* (1863), 11; *Annual Report* (1888), 24–27; *Annual Report* (1891), 7; *Annual Report* (1901), 47.

102. Cooper Union, *Annual Report* (1860), 47–50; *Annual Report* (1865), 17–19. On Cooper and civil service reform, see Mack, *Peter Cooper,* 380.

103. Charles Pratt founded the Pratt Institute in Brooklyn in 1887. Anthony Drexel founded the Drexel Institute (now Drexel University) in Philadelphia in 1891. Both were originally devoted to the industrial education of the working class. The Cooper trustees were probably correct when they claimed that both philanthropists were inspired by the Cooper Institute. Cooper Union, *Annual Report* (1890), 9.

104. For a summary of Cooper's expenditures for the Cooper Union, see Raymond, *Peter Cooper,* 67 n. 1. He not only gave a much larger proportion of his entire fortune to charity, but his children also bequeathed their inheritances to the Cooper Union upon their deaths. For Cooper in comparison to other philanthropists of the period, see "A Great Philanthropist," *New York Times,* May 12, 1895.

105. Cooper Union, *Annual Report* (1894), 11; *Annual Report* (1900), 16. It is not clear from this report whether the trustees wanted to become part of the new library or whether they simply hoped that Carnegie would provide them with a new building. If the latter, they misunderstood the terms of Carnegie's gift.

106. The best biography of Dewey is Wayne A. Wiegand, *Irrepressible Reformer: A Biography of Melvil Dewey* (Chicago: American Library Association, 1996). See also Dee Garrison, *Apostles of Culture: The Public Librarian and American Society, 1876–1920* (New York: Free Press, 1979; repr., Madison: University of Wisconsin Press, 2003), 105–72. An interesting hagiography by a Dewey disciple, which includes primary documents, is Grosvenor Dawe, *Melvil Dewey: Seer, Inspirer, Sage, a Biographic Compilation* (Essex, N.Y.: Lake Placid Club, 1932). On the founding and early years of the New York Library Club, see Tom Glynn, "The Professionalization of a Calling: Mission and Method at the New York Library Club, 1885–1901," *Libraries & the Cultural Record* 41 (Fall 2006): 438–61.

107. Cooper Union, *Annual Report* (1859), 26–28, 36. The possibility of cooperating with another local institution to create a polytechnic school is actually referred to in the Deed of Trust, reprinted in this first annual report. Mack, *Peter Cooper*, 263–66; Nevins, *Hewitt*, 276.

108. Garrison, *Apostles of Culture*, 274 n. 2; John William Burgess, *Reminiscences of an American Scholar* (New York: Columbia University Press, 1934), 74–75; Frederick A. P. Barnard to Seth Low, December 15, 1888, reprinted in Dawe, *Dewey*, 327.

109. From Barnard's report for 1872, quoted in Coon, Columbia, 81. The only full-length biography of Barnard is John Fulton, *Memoirs of Frederick A. P. Barnard, Tenth President of Columbia College in the City of New York* (New York: Macmillan, 1896). The official account of Barnard's tenure is John Howard Van Amringe, "President Frederick A. P. Barnard, 1864–1889," in *History of Columbia University*, 140–51.

110. A good example of Barnard's views on college education can be found in Columbia College, *Annual Report of the President of Columbia College Made to the Board of Trustees* (New York: Columbia College, 1877), 20–25. An interesting and more accessible source is William F. Russell, ed., *The Rise of a University, vol. 1, The Later Days of Old Columbia College* (New York: Columbia University Press, 1937), a collection of extensive excerpts from his annual reports. See in particular, "Changes in Curriculum," 66–115, and "Electives," 156–79.

111. Van Amringe, "President Frederick A. P. Barnard, 1864–1889," 148. During Dewey's first three years as chief librarian, Barnard donated 778 books and 8,773 pamphlets. Columbia College Library, *Second and Third Annual Reports of the Chief Librarian, June 30, 1886* (New York: Columbia College, 1886), 57.

112. Canfield, "The Library," 439. Winifred B. Linderman, "History of the Columbia University Library, 1876–1926" (Ph.D. diss., Columbia University, 1959), 71–73, 78–84. The quote is at page 40.

113. Garrison, *Apostles of Culture*, 126–28; Wiegand, *Dewey*, 77–79.

114. Quoted in Wiegand, *Dewey*, 80. In 1881, Columbia's library was the thirty-eighth largest in the country, much smaller than, for example, the Astor,

the New-York Historical Society Library, the Mercantile Library Association, and the Apprentices' Library. Columbia College Library, *Second and Third Annual Reports*, 54–55.

115. Columbia College Library, *First Annual Report of the Chief Librarian, May 31, 1884* (New York: Columbia College, 1884), 8, 11; Columbia College, Library, *School of Library Economy, Circular of Information, 1886–1887* (n.p., n.d.), reprinted in Columbia University School of Library Service, *School of Library Economy of Columbia College: Documents for a History* (New York: Columbia University, 1937), 69, 71.

116. Melvil Dewey, "The New Library Regulations," *School of Mines Quarterly* 5 (November 1883): 69.

117. Columbia College, *Circular of Information*, 69, 77–78.

118. Dewey, "New Library Regulations," 70; Columbia College Library, *First Annual Report*, 13; Columbia College, *Circular of Information*, 10.

119. James Canfield, "The Library," *History of Columbia University*, 439.

120. Columbia College Library, *First Annual Report*, 10, 21.

121. Columbia College, *Circular of Information*, 78, 80; Columbia College Library, *Second and Third Annual Report*, 6.

122. Melvil Dewey, "Development of College Libraries," *Library Journal* 2 (October 1877): 63; Columbia College, *Circular of Information*, 80. Dewey, "Library Regulations," 67.

123. "Correspondence: The Columbia College Library," *Literary World*, May 15, 1886: 169; Dewey, "Development of College Libraries,", 63.

124. Columbia College, *Annual Report of the President of Columbia College, Made to the Board of Trustees, June 4, 1866* (New York: Columbia College, 1866), 27.

125. Munroe Smith, "Development of the Professional Schools, 1858–1979," in *History of Columbia University*, 219; Munroe Smith, "Graduate Schools and University Organization, 1880–194," in ibid., 223–29; Columbia College, *Annual Report of the President* (1866), 3.

126. Garrison, *Apostles of Culture*, 126–27.

127. Bender, *New York Intellect*, 281–84; Coon, *Columbia*, 86–89. After leaving Columbia, Low served from 1901 to 1904 as the first mayor of the newly consolidated Greater New York.

128. Smith, "Graduate Schools and University Organization," 237, 245, 254–56.

129. Nicholas Murray Butler, *Across the Busy Years: Recollections and Reflections* (New York: Scribner's, 1939), 1:76, 94–95; Columbia College Library, *First Annual Report*, 15.

130. Columbia College Library, *First Annual Report*, 14–17; *Second and Third Annual Reports*, 39.

131. In 1882, the year before Dewey's appointment, the budget for collection development was $2,645.21. In 1885–1886, it was $11,807.76. Columbia College

Library, *First Annual Report*, 34; *Second and Third Annual Report*, 52; Wiegand, *Dewey*, 107–8.

132. Columbia College Library, *Second and Third Annual Report*, 20.

133. Columbia College, *Circular of Information*, 18–19, 31–32. The lectures were delivered in the Library School but were open to other students and the public.

134. Columbia College Library, *First Annual Report*, 15; *Second and Third Annual Report*, 20.

135. Wiegand, *Dewey*, 95; John Y. Cole, "Storehouses," 372.

136. Smith, "Graduate Schools and University Organization," 254; Smith, "The Graduate Schools," in *History of Columbia University*, 274–75, 281, 284.

137. Bender, *New York Intellect*, 278; Bender, "Culture of Intellectual Life," 4, 13.

138. "School and College," *Independent*, January 3, 1884, 8; T. W. Hunt, "Modern Language Association of America," *Independent*, January 8, 1885, 6–7.

139. Smith, "The Graduate Schools," 267, 270. Beginning in 1894, the annual reports of the dean of the school included the number of graduates placed at institutions of higher learning (295); Burgess, *Reminiscences of an American Scholar*, 244.

140. Bender, *New York Intellect*, 276–78.

141. Cooper Union, *Annual Report* (1859), 36. For a sample of the lectures delivered, see Cooper Union, *Annual Report* (1881), 25, which lists titles from 1868 to 1882.

142. Smith, "The Graduate Schools," 277. In 1892, Columbia began cooperating with the Cooper Union to deliver weekly lectures in political science and other topics. Giddings delivered four lectures in 1895 on "The Evolution of Society." Cooper Union, *Annual Report* (1895), 38.

143. F. H. Giddings, "Relation of Sociology to Other Scientific Studies," *Journal of Social Sciences* 32 (November 1894): 145. On the ASSA, see Thomas L. Haskell, *The Emergence of Professional Social Science: The American Social Science Association and the Nineteenth-Century Crisis of Authority* (Urbana: University of Illinois Press, 1977). See also Thomas Bender, "The Erosion of Public Culture: Cities, Discourses, and Professional Disciplines," in *The Authority of Experts: Studies in History and Theory*, ed. Thomas L. Haskell (Bloomington: Indiana University Press, 1984), 98–100.

144. Melvil Dewey, "Conference a Success," *American Library Journal* (November 1876): 90.

145. "Joint Meeting with the N. Y. Library Club," *Library Journal* (October 1897): 34. Dewey also spoke at this meeting. He disagreed with practically everyone else present, insisting that librarians should read outside of work if need be, in order to be able to advise readers properly. Arthur Bostwick of the New York Free Circulating Library suggested an idea that did not come to fruition

until the twentieth century, book reviews that were written by librarians for librarians.

146. Columbia College Library, *First Annual Report*, 9; Melvil Dewey, *Librarianship as a Profession for College-Bred Women: An Address Delivered Before the Association of College Alumnae* (Boston: Library Bureau, 1886), 21.

147. Ibid., 3, 5, 18.

148. Ibid., 18, 19, 21.

149. Columbia College, School of Library Economy, "Annual Register, 1886–1887"; reprinted in School of Library Economy, *Documents for a History*, 201. All of the students had college degrees or prior experience in libraries. They were to receive a certificate of completion after two years, although Dewey petitioned the trustees unsuccessfully (and unrealistically) for the authority to grant a BLS, MLS, and DLS. Wiegand, *Dewey*, 96, 98.

150. "What Shall We Do with Our Young Women," *Harper's Bazaar*, October 25, 1884, 679. The article was actually reprinted from a British journal, *The Whitehall Review*. Much of it applies to gender and professionalization in the United States as well. The one significant difference is that women did not enter librarianship in large numbers in the United Kingdom during this period.

151. Melvil Dewey, "The Ideal Librarian," *Library Journal* (January 1899): 14. Dewey, *Librarianship as a Profession for College-Bred Women*, 19–21. Much of Dewey's speech concerns the public library movement generally. For a concise statement of his views on women in the profession, which is taken verbatim from the speech, see Melvil Dewey, "Women and Libraries: How They Are Handicapped," *Library Notes* (October 1886): 89–90. Women began to predominate in public libraries, at least in rank-and-file positions, even before the opening of the school. From its founding in 1878, for example, the New York Free Circulating Library hired mostly women.

152. Dewey was somewhat inconsistent. In his speech before the Association of College Alumnae, he predicted that women's salaries would rise as they became more educated and experienced. But he also said that their salaries would remain lower than men's, in part because a woman "almost always receives, whether she exacts it or not, much more waiting on and minor assistance." Dewey, *Librarianship as a Profession for College-Bred Women*, 19–22. Dewey hired Walter S. Biscoe at a thousand dollars a year to head the recataloging project when the books were consolidated in the new building. He paid the "Wellesley Half Dozen," the six young female college graduates who assisted him, five hundred dollars. Wiegand, *Dewey*, 84–85.

153. Dewey to Brownell, about 1894. Quoted in Annie Nathan Meyer, *Barnard Beginnings* (Boston: Houghton Mifflin, 1935), 145. For Barnard's views on higher education for women, excerpted from his annual reports, see *Rise of a University*, 249–87. John Burgess parted ways with Dewey and Barnard on this issue. He argued that admitting women would drive away boys and thus "make the college

a female seminary, and a Hebrew female seminary . . . at that." Burgess boasted in his autobiography that this argument was very effective with the trustees and faculty. Burgess, *Reminiscences*, 241–42.

154. Van Amringe, "President A. P. Barnard," 145; Smith, "Graduate Schools and University Organization," 247–49; Smith, "Graduate Schools," 285–86; William Peterfield Trent, "Barnard College," in *History of Columbia University*, 397–408; Meyer, *Barnard Beginnings*. Meyer was one of the founders, and she credits Dewey for his encouragement and support. Among other matters, he helped write the memorial to the board that resulted in the resolution establishing the college (48). Shortly after he left Columbia, he wrote to Meyers expressing his "very warm personal interest in Barnard College which in its pre-natal days was probably discussed more in my private office . . . than anywhere else" (145). Columbia did not become coeducational until 1983.

155. Wiegand, *Dewey*, 96–108; Garrison, *Apostles of Culture*, 131–35. The presence of women in the Library School was not the only reason for Dewey's dismissal and perhaps not the major one. Dewey made little effort to enlist support among the trustees and faculty and his ego prevented him from resolving any conflicts with the opposition in a diplomatic fashion. For example, his claim in an annual report that "it is quite possible to make a great university of a library without professors" certainly did not endear him to his colleagues in other departments. Columbia College Library, *Second and Third Annual Report*, 7. For an enumeration of all the specific grievances against Dewey, see Wiegand, *Dewey*, 107.

156. On Baker, see Linderman, "History of the Columbia University Library," 184–253. Bohdan S. Wynar, ed., *Dictionary of American Library Biography* (Littleton, Colo.: Libraries Unlimited, 1978), s.v. "Plummer, Mary Wright," by Robert A. Karlowich and Nasser Sharify. Plummer was subsequently the director of the library school at the New York Public Library. On the passage of the Library Law of 1886, see Chapter 8.

8. New York's Free Circulating Libraries: The Mission of the Public Library in the Gilded Age

1. On the reopening of the Apprentices' Library, see Chapter 3.

2. "Shall We Have a Public Library?" *New York Times*, February 26, 1871.

3. Quoted in Chapter 3, this is from Mordecai Noah's address at the rededication of the library in 1850. Thomas Earle and Charles T. Congdon, *Annals of the General Society of Mechanics and Tradesmen of the City of New York, from 1785 to 1880* (New York: General Society of Mechanics and Tradesmen, 1882), 276. Some years later, a member explained to historian Martha Lamb that the Society enjoyed such prosperity "because it never sold a piece of real estate that it once got possession of." Martha J. Lamb, "The Career of a Beneficent Enterprise," reprinted from the *Magazine of American* History in General Society of Mechanics and

Tradesmen of the City of New York, *Manual of the General Society of Mechanics and Tradesmen* (New York: Lotus Press, 1895), 122. In 1884, for example, $29,494 of an annual income of $38,308 was from rents. Only $1,000 came from the members' initiation fees. General Society of Mechanics and Tradesmen of the City of New York (hereafter also GSMT), *Annual Report of the General Society of Mechanics and Tradesmen of the City of New York* (New York: GSMT, 1885), 6.

4. GSMT, *Annual Report* (1880), 12; Earle and Congdon, *Annals of the General Society*, 394.

5. GSMT, *Annual Report* (1874), 9.

6. In 1856, the state legislature passed a law permitting the Society to increase the initiation fee to fifty dollars. Reprinted in GSMT, *Manual* (1895), 19. The new by-laws passed in 1866 raised the fee and are reprinted in Earle and Congdon, *Annals of the General Society*, 291–300. Unlike the Society Library, members of the GSMT did not pay an annual fee to maintain their membership at this time.

7. Earle and Congdon, *Annals of the General Society*, 186. A minority report was also presented that simply held that "all persons directly connected with a mechanical business should be eligible." This definition would obviously include men like Carnegie and Hewitt.

8. "How I Served My Apprenticeship" first appeared in *Youth's Companion* in April 1896 and was reprinted Andrew Carnegie, *The Gospel of Wealth and Other Timely Essays* (New York: Century, 1901). The quote is at page ix. Carnegie was relating his apprenticeship as a businessman. On Carnegie and the GSMT, see Robert Rutter, "Mr. Carnegie and the Society of Mechanics and Tradesmen," *New York Times*, March 22, 1902.

9. Expressions of producerism can be found as well in the presidential addresses later in the century. For example, William Otis Monroe in 1875: "Recognizing the relations of skilled handicrafts to the prosperity of a nation, our Society, among an industrious and free people, has done its part to assert and maintain the dignity of labor." GSMT, *Annals of the General Society*, 362.

10. GSMT, *Annual Report* (1886), 24.

11. The law is reprinted in Harry Miller Lydenberg, *History of the New York Public Library, Astor, Lenox and Tilden Foundations* (New York: New York Public Library, 1923), 216–17. At a meeting of the New York Library Club the following year, Robert Rutter, a member of both the General Society and the club, claimed there was no connection between the change in policy and the new law, that he was surprised to learn the Apprentices' Library fell under its provisions. Considering the timing of the change, this seems highly unlikely. "New York Library Club," *Library Journal* 12 (April 1887): 165.

12. The seminal works on the development of public libraries in the United States are Sidney Herbert Ditzion, *Arsenals of a Democratic Culture: A Social History of the American Public Library Movement in New England and the Middle*

States from 1850 to 1900 (Chicago: American Library Association, 1947); Jesse H. Shera, *Foundations of the Public Library: The Origins of the Public Library Movement in New England, 1629–1855* (Chicago: University of Chicago Press, 1949); and Dee Garrison, *Apostles of Culture: The Public Librarian and American Society, 1876–1920* (New York: Free Press, 1979; repr., Madison: University of Wisconsin Press, 2003). For a succinct description of the public library idea, see New York Free Circulating Library, *Twenty-First and Final Report of the New York Circulating Library, with a Sketch of Its History* (New York: New York Free Circulating Library, 1900), 23–24. Hereafter, NYFCL, *Annual Report* (1901). This report is dated 1900 but was published in early 1901, immediately before the Free Circulating Library was absorbed by the New York Public Library.

13. Henry Leipziger one of the founders of the Aguilar Free Library, at a discussion of the New York Library Club, *Library Journal* 17 (April 1892): 132. In 1867 and 1868, the General Society discussed establishing reading rooms (as opposed to circulating collections) in lower Manhattan, but decided that sufficient funds were not available. Earle and Congdon, *Annals of the General Society of Mechanics and Tradesmen*, 161–62.

14. See, for example, East Side House (Webster Free Circulating Library), *Eleventh Annual Report for the Year Ending January 31, 1902* (New York: East Side House, 1903), 12–13. Hereafter, East Side House, *Annual Report* (1902). New York Free Circulating Library (hereafter NYFCL), *Annual Report* (1886), 11. Aguilar Free Library Society, *Fourteenth Annual Report of the Aguilar Free Library Society of the City of New York* (New York: Aguilar Free Library Society, 1903), 10. Hereafter, AFL, *Annual Report.*

15. On story papers, which were similar to dime novels, see, for example, Michael Denning, *Mechanic Accents: Dime Novels and Working-Class Culture in America* (New York: Verso, 1987), 10–11.

16. NYFCL, *Annual Report* (1901), 20–21. "The Free Circulating Library," *New York Evening Post*, March 18, 1889, reprinted in Lydenberg, *New York Public Library*, 203–5. The act of incorporation is reprinted in George Lockhart Rives and Charles Howland Russell, eds., *The New York Public Library, Astor, Lenox, and Tilden Foundations, Book of Charters, Wills, Deeds and Other Official Documents* (New York: NYPL, 1905), 163–64. This includes all of the legal documents associated with the founding of the New York Public Library, including the acts of incorporation of each of its constituent parts.

17. NYFCL, *Annual Report* (1901), 20–25, 29, 37; Lydenberg, *New York Public Library*, 199–240, is a concise history of the Library.

18. NYFCL, *Library Meeting at the Union League Club, Jan. 20, 1882*, 4, 6–7. This was appended to NYFCL, *Annual Report* (1882).

19. Ellen M. Coe, "Common Novels in Public Libraries," *Library Journal* 19 (1894): 23. Coe was quoting the presidential address of that year by Josephus N. Larned of the Buffalo Public Library.

20. On this quote from the *Independent Reflector*, see Chapter 1.

21. NYFCL, *Library Meeting, 1882*, 3.

22. Arthur E. Bostwick, *A Life with Men and Books* (New York: H. W. Wilson Co., 1939), 169.

23. NYFCL, *Annual Report* (1889), 10–11.

24. NYFCL, *Library Meeting, 1882*, 4. The president of the Free Circulating Library at this time, Henry Pellew, was also one of the founders of the COS. There were other important connections. Otto Ottendorfer, for example, was active in the COS and also donated money for the second branch of the NYFCL, the Ottendorfer Branch. During the severe depression of the early 1890s, the NYFCL employed assistants through the local COS Relief Committee. NYFCL, *Annual Report* (1894), 14–15.

25. Historians of social control were especially critical of the COS. For a discussion of social control historiography as it relates to the COS and for a more nuanced account of the history of the COS in New York, see Joan Waugh, "'Give This Man Work!': Josephine Shaw Lowell, the Charity Organization Society of New York, and the Depression of 1893," *Social Science History* 25 (Summer 2001): 219–21.

26. See for example, Michael H. Harris, "The Purpose of the American Public Library: A Revisionist Interpretation of History," *Library Journal* 98 (September 17, 1973): 2509–2514.

27. See, for example, a discussion at the New York Library Club of "How Far Should Reading Be Controlled in Libraries?" "New York Library Club, Fifteenth Regular Meeting," *Library Journal* 14 (March 1889), 93–94.

28. See Ann Douglas, *The Feminization of American Culture* (New York: Avon Books, 1977), 51–55, on "the doctrine of feminine influence."

29. Bostwick, *Life with Men and Books*, 2; NYFCL, *Annual Report* (1894), 12. See also, for example, NYFCL, *Annual Report* (1900), 16; AFL, *Annual Report* (1901), 18. The settlement libraries discussed in this chapter were, of course, literally in settlement houses.

30. See, for example, NYFCL, *Annual Report* (1885), 24; *Annual Report* (1890), 27; *Annual Report* (1900), 56. See also AFL, *Annual Report* (1895), 36; *Annual Report* (1900), 58.

31. NYFCL, *Library Meeting, 1882*, 5.

32. The historical sketch in the final report took special note of the role played by both the female trustees and librarians. Of the fifty-one trustees throughout the Library's history, nineteen were women. Ellen Coe served as chief librarian from 1881 until her marriage in 1895. As will be seen, she was active in professional circles both locally and nationally.

33. On the role of women in the public library movement nationally, see Paula D. Watson, "Founding Mothers: The Contribution of Women's Organizations to Public Library Development in the United States," *Library*

Quarterly 64 (July 1994): 233–71. In the New York libraries founded by non-Protestants, women played a less prominent role. They were employed as librarians and even chief librarians but generally did not serve as trustees. Once the NYFCL was consolidated with the NYPL, the new Circulation Department was managed exclusively by men.

34. Lydenberg, *New York Public Library*, 263–68, 534; East Side House, *Annual Report* (1892), 7–8; *Annual Report* (1893), 5; *Annual Report* (1894), 6. On the University Settlement Library, see Lydenberg, *New York Public Library*, 255–62, 534. On settlement libraries in New York City generally, see "New York Library Club," *Library Journal* 21 (January 1896): 24–25.

35. Phyllis Dain, *The New York Public Library: A History of Its Founding and Early Years* (New York: New York Public Library, 1972), 298–99.

36. East Side House, *Annual Report* (1891), 1.

37. For an analysis of the neighborhood as a "workable unit for social reform," see Don S. Kirschner, "Ambiguous Legacy: Social Justice and Social Control in the Progressive Era," *Historical Reflections* 2 (Summer 1975): 81–86.

38. East Side House, *Annual Report* (1896), title page. This is a quote from the English clergyman and writer Charles Kingsley.

39. NYFCL, *Annual Report* (1885), 11.

40. East Side House, *Annual Report* (1897), 14; (1898), 16–17.

41. NYFCL, *Annual Report* (1886), 12. See also Plummer Alston Jones Jr., *Libraries, Immigrants, and the American Experience* (Westport, Conn.: Greenwood Press, 1999).

42. Dain, *New York Public Library*, 18, 264–66; Ada Sterling, "To Rescue an Old Library," *New York Times*, February 19, 1906; Allegra Eggleston, "Plea for the Maimonides Library," *New York Times*, February 23, 1906.

43. AFL, *Annual Report* (1902), 30, 36. This is the last annual report. A brief history of the Library is at pages 8–12.

44. AFL, *Annual Report* (1902), 8.

45. See Michael Galchinsky, *The Origin of the Modern Jewish Woman Writer: Romance and Reform in Victorian England* (Detroit: Wayne State University Press, 1996), 135–90.

46. "Grace Aguilar," *Voice of the Aguilar Free Library* 1 (November 1891), 2. For Victorian readers and library organizers, the fact that Aguilar died young and "was a delicate child from birth" no doubt enhanced her appeal.

47. AFL, *Annual Report* (1903), 9; *Annual Report* (1890), 9.

48. AFL, *Annual Report* (1895), 29; *Annual Report* (1903), 36. I do not argue that the founders of the NYFCL, for example, were anti-Semitic, but they certainly tended to conflate Protestantism and Americanism. On anti-Semitism in late nineteenth-century New York, see Moses Rischin, *The Promised Land: New York's Jews, 1870–1914* (Cambridge, Mass.: Harvard University Press, 1962), 265–67. On anti-Semitism among New York elites, see Sven Beckert, *Monied*

Metropolis: New York City and the Consolidation of the American Bourgeoisie, 1850–1896 (Cambridge: Cambridge University Press, 2001), 265–66. Henry Leipziger, one of the founders of the Aguilar, was instrumental in forcing Melvil Dewey from his position as New York State Librarian. Dewey was clearly anti-Semitic. Wayne A. Wiegand, "'Jew Attack': The Story behind Melvil Dewey's Resignation as New York State Librarian in 1905," *American Jewish History* 83 (September 1995): 359–79.

49. "Judaism in New-York," *New York Times*, January 23, 1887. This is a quote from the president of the Young Men's Hebrew Association, who referred to the Aguilar as one of the institutions promoting the Americanization of the immigrant.

50. Joseph H. McMahon, *Final Report of the Director of the Cathedral Free Circulating Library* (New York: Cathedral Library Association, 1905), 5–19.

51. McMahon, *Final Report of the Cathedral Library*, 7.

52. See, for example, McMahon, *Final Report of the Cathedral Library*, 9. Cathedral Library Association (hereafter, also CLA), "Statement of the Position of the Cathedral Library with Reference to the Proposed Action of the City of New York in the Matter of the Carnegie Library Proposition," [4], Record Group 4, Free Circulating Libraries, Cathedral Library Association, New York Public Library Archives and Manuscripts Division. This was a pamphlet published by the Library in 1901, when it was fighting consolidation by the New York Public Library.

53. CLA, "Statement of the Position of the Cathedral Library," [3–4]. As an example of "calumnies" against Catholicism, in 1904 the *New York Daily News* printed a petition to remove John Hay's *Castilian Days* from the New York Public Library and quoted passages that very clearly denigrated the church. "Petition," *New York Daily News*, November 9, 1904.

54. McMahon, *Final Report of the Director*, 10.

55. "New York Library Club, Fifteenth Regular Meeting," 93. The quote is from William Eaton Foster of the Providence Public Library, who participated as a visitor in the club's discussion of how far reading should be controlled in libraries. Significantly, no one challenged this statement, and the discussion thereafter focused on fiction. Arthur Bostwick, the librarian of the Free Circulating Library, held that "the exclusion of nonfiction is generally on the score of incorrect statement or bad treatment of the subject." Arthur E. Bostwick, *The American Public Library* (New York: D. Appleton & Co., 1910), 131. However, Bostwick apparently did consider public opinion a factor in book selection. He advised that a book might be held "objectionable" to "a class of readers" because of "political or religious aspersions." A. E. Bostwick, W. A. Bardwell, and Wilberforce Eames, "What Should Librarians Read?" *Library Journal* 25 (February 1900): 58.

56. Cathedral Library Association, *Author and Title Catalog of the Cathedral Library Association of New York* (New York: Cathedral Library Association, 1899).

However, these three titles and others were starred in the catalog; readers had to request permission to borrow them.

57. NYFCL, *Annual Report* (1895), 27; AFL, *Annual Report* (1896), 28. Since none of the "bulletins" have survived, it is impossible to judge how well the different sides of any given issue were represented, but all the available evidence indicates the libraries avoided taking sides. Many of the bulletins were clearly intended to promote patriotic reading. Both the NYFCL and the Aguilar printed bulletins on Washington and Lincoln practically every year.

58. On the reception of fiction in public libraries during this period, see Evelyn Geller, *Forbidden Books in Public Libraries, 1876–1939: A Study in Cultural Change* (Westport, Conn.: Greenwood Press, 1984); Esther Jane Carrier, *Fiction in Public Libraries, 1876–1900* (New York: Scarecrow Press, 1965); Garrison, *Apostles of Culture*, 67–87; Patrick Williams, *The American Public Library and the Problem of Purpose* (New York: Greenwood Press, 1988), 9–24. This was also a period of great change in the novel itself, with the emergence of naturalism and what one New York librarian called "novels presenting studies of modern social conditions." *Library Journal* 25 (March 1900): 128. See also "Priest Denounces Realistic Novels," *New York Times*, January 27, 1903. The priest was Joseph McMahon, director of the Cathedral Library.

59. NYFCL, *Library Meeting, 1882*, 3–4. Another speaker explained that "the imagination is a fact of human nature; it has its cravings and has to be dealt with wisely." On changing attitudes toward fiction during this period, see, for example, Barbara Sicherman, "Ideologies and Practices of Reading," in *A History of the Book in America*, ed. Scott E. Casper et al., vol. 3, *The Industrial Book, 1840–1880* (Chapel Hill: University of North Carolina Press, 2007), 292; Garrison, *Apostles of Culture*, 88–104.

60. *Voice of the Aguilar Free Library* 1 (November 1891): 4. The *Post* article, "A Study of the New York Circulating Library," was reprinted in *Library Journal* 11 (May 1886): 142–43. It is a study of the Library's most popular titles by subject, including fiction.

61. Coe, "Common Novels in Public Libraries," 23–24.

62. George Watson Cole, "Fiction in Libraries: A Plea for the Masses," *Library Journal* 19 (Conference Proceedings 1894): 20. "What is trash to some" is a quote from Frederick Beecher Perkins, the librarian of the Boston Public Library. Cole was the director of the Jersey City Free Public Library, but he lived in Manhattan and was an active member of the club. New York Library Club, *Libraries of Greater New York, Manual and Historical Sketch of the New York Library Club* (New York: New York Library Club, 1902), 109, 173.

63. Cole, "Fiction in Libraries," 18–19. "Masses who bear the burden of taxation" is a quote from former ALA president William Frederick Poole, the librarian of the Boston Public Library, the Boston Atheneum, and other institutions. It is significant that Cole quotes at great length from three older library leaders,

all from New England, Poole, Perkins, and Samuel Swett Green, of the Worcester Free Public Library. This was an attempt, I think, to lend weight and respectability to what many considered a radical argument.

64. "New York Library Club, Fifteenth Regular Meeting," *Library Journal* 14 (March 1889): 93.

65. Coe, "Common Novels in Public Libraries," 23.

66. NYFCL, *Library Meeting, 1882*, 4.

67. "New York Library Club," *Library Journal* 26 (April 1901): 219.

68. NYFCL, *Annual Report* (1895), 25. Juvenile literature was reported as approximately 14 percent. When the Library was absorbed into the New York Public Library in 1901, juvenile literature was 17 percent, fiction was 29 percent, and literature was 9 percent. NYFCL, *Annual Report* (1901), 38.

69. The Apprentices' Library reported approximately 46 percent fiction and juvenile literature. GSMT, *Annual Report* (1879), 11. The Aguilar reported 43 percent, which probably includes juvenile fiction, but probably not, for example, history written for children. AFL, *Annual Report* (1895), 41. The Webster and the Cathedral never published collection statistics. A national survey conducted by Ellen Coe for *Library Journal* reported an average of 24 percent fiction, which apparently did not include juvenile works. Ellen Coe, "Fiction," *Library Journal* 18 (July 1893): 250–51.

70. R. B. Poole, "Fiction in Libraries," *Library Journal* 16 (January 1891): 9. Poole, librarian of the YMCA Library, was one of the city's most conservative librarians, but even the most progressive librarians would never have considered purchasing works of the "blood and thunder" variety.

71. Barbara Sicherman, "Ideologies and Practices of Reading," 291.

72. Arthur E. Bostwick, "The Purchase of Current Fiction," in *Papers and Proceedings of the Twenty-Fifth General Meeting of the American Library Association Held at Niagara Falls, NY* (Boston: American Library Association, 1903), 31–33.

73. *Library Journal* 6 (December 1881): 314. "The A.L.A. Co-operation Committee's Report on Exclusion," *Library Journal* 7 (February 1882): 28–29. The list comprises twenty-eight authors, but I have excluded seven writers of juvenile fiction, since fiction for children and adults involved somewhat different issues. Interestingly, Horatio Alger was considered objectionable in 1881, probably on the grounds that he gave young boys unrealistic expectations of life. In all of the surviving catalogs, however, Alger is well represented, and in 1889 he was the most popular juvenile author in all of the branches of the New York Free Circulating Library. NYFCL, *Annual Report* (1889), 20.

74. In fact, even in 1881 Collins and Bulwer were probably not considered especially controversial, and it is interesting that their names appear on the list. All of the thirty libraries that responded to the survey collected them. In the catalog of the Aguilar Free Library, both were starred as recommended authors.

75. The catalogs are CLA, *Author and Title Catalog* (1899); General Society of Mechanics and Tradesmen of the City of New York, *Finding List of the Apprentices' Library Established and Maintained by the General Society of Mechanics and Tradesmen of the City of New York* (New York: J. J. Little & Co., 1888); New York Free Circulating Library, *Catalogue of the New York Free Circulating Library, Bond Street Branch, English Books* (New York: New York Free Circulating Library, 1892); and Aguilar Free Library Society, *Fiction List of the Aguilar Free Library* (New York: New York Free Circulating Library, 1895). There is also a surviving catalog of the Bruce branch of the Free Circulating Library, but I chose the Bond Street catalog, since it was the first branch founded and therefore more likely to hold the authors in the 1881 survey. The Bruce branch held thirteen of the twenty-one. Comparing these catalogs from the 1890s with the survey in 1881 is somewhat problematic, since some of the authors had declined in popularity and a few were probably not in print when the free circulating libraries were founded. However, the most suspect authors tended also to be the most popular and were available in the 1890s and even later. E. D. E. N. Southworth, for example, who was considered rather trashy, was still in print in the 1940s. Garrison, *Apostles of Culture,* 81. All of the libraries solicited donations, too, and might have accepted older works that were out of print.

76. The authors in the ALA survey are discussed in Garrison, *Apostles of Culture,* 75–87; and Williams, *The American Public Library,* 13–14.

77. NYFCL, *Annual Report* (1895), 23–24. These numbers sometimes varied widely by branch. For example, in the Ottendorfer branch, fiction was only 17 percent of the collection but accounted for 54 percent of the circulation. Owing to the way the statistics were reported, here and elsewhere I calculated the percentage of fiction circulated as an average of the percentages for each individual branch. This is different from calculating the fiction circulation systemwide as a percentage of the total circulation systemwide.

78. Coe's national survey in 1893 reported an average annual circulation of fiction of 56 percent. Coe, "Fiction," 251. According to Arthur Bostwick, by 1910, "a library that circulates less than sixty percent considers that is doing fairly well." Bostwick, *American Public Library,* 126.

79. AFL, *Annual Report* (1890), 13; *Annual Report* (1900), 37–38. Literature was 3 percent in 1890 and 6 percent in 1900. In the Free Circulating Library, fiction was 42 percent in 1890 and 39 percent in 1900. Juvenile books were 29 and 28 percent, respectively. Literature was approximately 6 percent both years. NYFCL, *Annual Report* (1890), 18; *Annual Report* (1901), 39. The Apprentices' Library reported 79 percent fiction and juvenile books in 1890 and 64 percent fiction in 1900. I think this drop means that nonfiction juvenile books, history for example, were assigned to other classes. Literature was 2 percent in 1890 and 6 percent in 1900. GSMT, *Annual Report* (1890), 22; *Annual Report* (1900), 16. The Webster Library reported circulation statistics only in 1903: 28 percent

adult fiction and 46 percent juvenile fiction. Poetry and literature was 5 percent. East Side House, *Annual Report* (1903), 21. The Cathedral Library never reported circulation statistics.

80. Since detailed circulation records have not survived, it is difficult to assess these arguments. There is, however, limited evidence that at least some readers were reading the "standard" works. The NYFCL reported occasionally on its most popular books and authors in fiction and other classes, and Charles Dickens was consistently the most popular author and *Uncle Tom's Cabin* was always the most popular title. However, that certain standard authors or titles circulated frequently does not mean that overall the "first-rate" circulated more frequently than the "second-rate." NYFCL, *Annual Report* (1886), 27–32; *Annual Report* (1889), 19–26; "Study of the New York Free Circulating Library," 142–43 (reprinted from the *New York Post*); "New York (N.Y.) F.C.L." *Library Journal* 17 (December 1892): 499–500. Jules Verne's *Mysterious Island* and Alexandre Dumas's *Count of Monte Cristo* were usually the second and third most popular titles in fiction. Both Wilkie Collins and Edward Bulwer Lytton were lower on the lists, but still very popular. The Aguilar also reported on "some of the titles most frequently circulated," with similar results. AFL, *Annual Report* (1895), 26–28.

81. GSMT, *Annual Report* (1879), 23. Variants on this argument appear with great frequency in the annual reports. See, for example, AFL, *Annual Report* (1896), 8. "The novels circulated are of the kind which merit wide circulation and tend to instruct, and to improve the literary tastes of the readers." The term "standard works" also appears quite often. In an interview with the *Harlem Reporter* in 1892, Ellen Coe stressed that "each year there is a greater demand for the standard works of fiction," that authors like Mary J. Holmes, who was in the ALA survey in 1881, "are giving way to Dickens, Scott, and Dumas." *Library Journal* 17 (December 1892): 500.

82. NYFCL, *Annual Report* (1889), 12; *Annual Report* (1895), 28–32. The "Experiment on a New Method of Stating Circulation" is also described in Arthur E. Bostwick, *Library Journal* 21 (March 1896): 96–98; see also Bostwick, *American Public Library*, 127–28. Overall, works of fiction circulated for 6.8 days, while titles classed as literature circulated for 7.4 days. In another experiment ("modern" public librarians like Bostwick loved experimentation), however, he reached a different conclusion. In 1901, in a study of the circulation of large, multivolume works, he found that readers would often borrow only the first or the second volume, but that "circulation decreases steadily from volume to volume." From this he concluded that readers in his library did not actually read what they borrowed, since "what is true of books in more than one volume is presumably also true, although perhaps in a less degree, of one-volume works." "Do Readers Read?" *Library Journal* 26 (November 1901): 803–4. Significantly,

Bostwick did not report on his study in *Library Journal*, but in a literary journal, the *Critic. Library Journal* reprinted excerpts from the article.

83. Coe, "Fiction," 230–31.

84. "New York Library Club, Fifteenth Regular Meeting," 93–94.

85. NYFCL, *Annual Report* (1893), 12–13; *Annual Report* (1899), 27.

86. The Free Circulating Library adopted the two-book system in 1895 and reported that it had "materially improved the character of reading." NYFCL, *Annual Report* (1895), 15. *Library Journal* credited the policy with a 50 percent increase in the circulation of nonfiction. E. A. Birge, "The Effect of the 'Two-Book System' on Circulation," *Library Journal* 23 (March 1898): 99. "When proper guidance is furnished" is from Birge's report (100). The Aguilar also adopted the policy in 1895 and reported that "the result is gratifying." AFL, *Annual Report* (1895), 11. The Webster waited until 1897; East Side House, *Annual Report* (1898), 16. The Cathedral Library and the Apprentices' Library apparently never adopted it. Interestingly, Jacob Schwartz, librarian of the Apprentices' Library, denounced it as "a fraud and expressly devised to get a larger grip on the public pap." Birge, "Effect of the Two-Book System," 101. That is, Schwartz felt it was used to inflate circulation in order to get a larger appropriation from the City, which appropriated money based on volumes circulated. As will be seen the below, Schwartz was one of the most "liberal" of the free circulating librarians in terms of the circulation of fiction.

87. Bostwick, *American Public Library*, 292, has a great photograph of the "old closed shelf system" in which the librarians are actually behind a cage.

88. NYFCL, *Annual Report* (1899), 31.

89. NYFCL, *Annual Report* (1898), 25; (1899), 31. See also Arthur E. Bostwick, "The Duties and Qualifications of Assistants in Open-Shelf Libraries," *Library Journal* 25 (1900): 40–41. Since open shelves supposedly encouraged book theft, he argued that assistants had to have "first, greater readiness and ability to aid the public in selection, and, second, greater watchfulness in guarding against abuse." The Webster adopted open shelves in 1897, the Free Circulating Library in 1898, and the Aguilar in 1899. Initially, this was considered a truly radical innovation. In 1894, Henry Leipziger said it would be impossible in the Aguilar. "New York Library Club," *Library Journal* 19 (April 1894): 133. The Cathedral Library never had open shelves.

90. "New York [State] Library Association and New York [City] Library Club," *Library Journal* 20 (January 1895): 23. Coe used the same quote in Ellen M. Coe, "What Can Be Done to Help a Boy to Like Good Books after He has Fallen into the 'Dime Novel Habit,'" *Library Journal* 20 (April 1895): 119.

91. Jacob Schwartz, "Business Methods in Libraries," *Library Journal* 13 (November 1888): 334.

92. Max Cohen, "The Librarian an Educator, and not a Cheap-John," *Library Journal* 13 (December 1888): 366–67.

93. NYFCL, *Annual Report* (1901), 23–24.

94. Bostwick, *The American Public Library,* 1–4. The quote is at page 3. Bostwick also called the modern library idea the "American library idea" because British librarians were apt to dismiss it as "American tomfoolery" (3).

95. Bostwick, for example, stressed that "the comparison of library work with trade holds, of course, only in so far that both are systems of distribution," and that libraries should distribute only wholesome literature. Bostwick, *American Public Library,* 4. Schwartz responded to Cohen in a later issue of *Library Journal,* arguing that libraries could not properly serve an educational purpose unless they were properly managed. John [*sic*] Schwartz, "The Librarian as Educator, Mr. John Schwartz Replies to Mr. Cohen," *Library Journal* 15 (January–February 1889): 5–6.

96. NYFCL, *Annual Report* (1885), 11; AFL, *Annual Report* (1903), 10. The second quote is from the historical sketch in the Aguilar's final report. See also NYFCL, *Annual Report* (1880), 19; AFL, *Annual Report* (1889), 6. These are the first reports issued by the AFL and NYFCL.

97. NYFCL, *Annual Report* (1898), 18–19. In *The American Public Library,* Bostwick frequently described the opponents of the modern library idea as "the old-fashioned librarians." He referred to "'library advertising'" as one of the "distinctively 'modern' features of American public libraries." Bostwick, *American Public Library,* 9.

98. East Side House, *Annual Report* (1903), 18.

99. Most of the free libraries required borrowers to be at least twelve years of age, although in 1895 the NYFCL lowered the limit to ten. NYFCL, *Annual Report* (1895), 13. The NYPL did not remove the age limit until 1906, and even then it was considered a fairly radical change in policy. Dain, *New York Public Library,* 301. As late as 1927, approximately half of the large public library systems in the United States had an age restriction. American Library Association, *A Survey of Libraries in the United States* (Chicago: American Library Association, 1927), 3–5. Typically, the Webster was ahead of its time in having no restriction except for basic literacy. East Side House, *Bulletin of the New Books of the Webster Free Library* 1 (December 1899). Surprisingly, there is no evidence that the Cathedral Library had an age limit. All of the libraries, including the Webster, required borrowers of any age to have a "responsible person" sign the reader's application as a guarantor.

100. For a good discussion of the issues involved in service to children in free libraries, see a paper read before the New York Library Club: Mary Wright Plummer, "The Work for Children in Free Libraries," *Library Journal* 22 (November 1897): 679–86. See also Bostwick, *American Public Library,* 11–13, 76–94. Bostwick held that by the late 1890s "a separate children's room became a component part of every properly constructed and operated public library" (13).

From the beginning, the Circulation Department of the New York Public Library had a "Supervisor of Children's Rooms" and the Library was nationally renowned for its services to children. Dain, *New York Public Library*, 299–306.

101. NYFCL, *Annual Report* (1901), 15–17, 40. In two of the branches, Bond Street and Jackson Square, the Library could only afford or make room for a "children's table." My estimate of the total number of children is based upon the number of new readers who were children, since the total number of readers is not broken down by age. What is perhaps more revealing is the trend in new readers who were children: in 1890 it was 39 percent (*Annual Report*, 20); in 1895 it was 50 percent (*Annual Report*, 26); and in 1900 it was 58 percent (*Annual Report*, 40).

102. NYFCL, *Annual Report* (1899), 28; Plummer, "Work for Children in Free Libraries," 681.

103. AFL, *Annual Report* (1898), 16; *Annual Report* (1901), 14. Librarians often used the metaphor of cultivation when referring to young readers. In 1884, the chairman of the library committee of the General Society wrote: "The husbandman must patiently await the operation of those silent forces in nature which first cause growth, then fruitage; so with those who seek the best interest of the young in endeavoring to train their thoughts to higher and nobler aims and objects in life." GSMT, *Annual Report* (1884), 14. The metaphor was a staple among educators throughout the century. See Robert Wiebe, "The Social Functions of Public Education," *American Quarterly* 21 (Summer 1969): 149–50.

104. Plummer, "Work with Children in Free Libraries," 681.

105. There is a significant parallel between the development of public libraries and public schools in the United States. The public library was often preceded by the free library society, and the public school was often preceded by the free school society. Both the free library societies and the free school societies were privately managed, eventually received public funds, and were then taken over by local governments. Moreover, the GSMT also ran a free school before the establishment of the public school system in New York, and the Aguilar Library was for several years connected with the Hebrew Free School Association. AFL, *Annual Report* (1903), 20–21.

106. AFL, *Annual Report* (1892), 14.

107. NYFCL, *Library Meeting, 1882*, 8. This was one of three resolutions passed by the meeting. For background on the new approach to working with schools, see Josephine A. Rathbone, "Cooperation between Libraries and Schools: An Historical Sketch," *Library Journal* 26 (April 1901): 187–91.

108. Ellen M. Coe, "The Relation of Libraries to Public Schools," *Library Journal* 17 (June 1892): 193. Although Bostwick would probably have described Coe as an "old-fashioned librarian," the "missionaries of literature" and the "modern librarians" agreed on many points, especially work with schools and the traveling libraries.

109. Dain, *New York Public Library*, 298. The Webster went even further than the other circulating libraries to accommodate public school teachers. See, for example, a circular the Webster sent to teachers, explaining special privileges available to them. Edwin White Gaillard, "To the Teachers, From the Library," Record Group 4, Free Circulating Libraries, Webster Library, New York Public Library Manuscripts and Archives Division. Schoolwork was always highlighted in all of the libraries' annual reports and a frequent topic of discussion and papers presented at the New York Library Club. See, for example, Henry L. Elmendorf, "Public Library Books in Public Schools," *Library Journal* 25 (April 1900): 163–65. See also NYFCL, *Annual Report* (1895), 19–20. This was Bostwick's first year as chief librarian, and his report includes a good description of the kinds of activities undertaken in the schools.

110. AFL, *Annual Report* (1895), 10; and, for example, *Annual Report* (1900), 43–46, during which year alone well over one hundred reference titles were added to the reference collections.

111. John S. Billings, "Some Library Problems of To-Morrow: Address of the President," *Library Journal* 27 (Conference Proceedings 1902): 3. Billings was quoting from James Bryce, *Studies in History and Jurisprudence* (1901).

112. See, for example, Wiebe, "Social Functions of Public Education," 154–56. See also Lawrence A. Cremin, *American Education: The Metropolitan Experience, 1876–1980* (New York: Harper & Row, 1988): 153–322.

113. AFL, *Annual Report* (1903), 14.

114. Rathbone, "Cooperation between Libraries and Schools," 187; Plummer, "Work with Children in Free Libraries," 685. Rathbone was actually quoting Charles Francis Adams, one of the earliest proponents of cooperation between public schools and public libraries." See Charles F. Adams Jr., *The Public Library and the Common Schools: Three Papers on Educational Topics* (Boston: Estes & Lauriet, 1879).

115. Many states also ran traveling library systems to serve rural areas where it was not economically feasible to establish permanent collections. Bostwick, *American Public Library*, 108–16. See also "Traveling Libraries, a Symposium," *Public Libraries* 2 (February 1897): 47–51, 54–55.

116. NYFCL, *Annual Report* (1901), 38, 43–46. The librarian's report for the department is quoted in full, with many interesting examples, in NYFCL, *Annual* Report (1899), 34–40. My favorite example is the libraries on the St. John's Guild "Floating Hospitals." These were charity hospitals that plied New York's rivers and harbor, offering medical care and fresh air to the city's poor. Bostwick expanded the program in the NYPL, and by 1908 it had 717 traveling collections and circulated nearly a million volumes. Bostwick, *American Public Library*, 109.

117. NYFCL, *Annual Report* (1898), 27–28. By 1900, there were eighteen home libraries in the NYFCL alone. NYFCL, *Annual Report* (1901), 45. "N.Y.L.A. and N.Y.L.C.," *Library Journal* 21 (January 1896): 24–25. This is a report of a paper

read at the New York Library Club on home libraries. Its interesting that they used the same term as the Charity Organization Society, "visitor." The author of the paper called the home libraries part of "the movement known as the new philanthropy," which combined "scientific study" and "a spirit of friendliness." See also "N.Y.F.C.L.," *Library Journal* 24 (January 1899): 34; Bostwick, *American Public Library*, 112–14.

118. Bostwick, *American Public Library*, 3.

119. East Side House, *Annual Report* (1900), 12.

120. NYFCL, *Annual Report* (1898), 19; *Annual Report* (1899), 32. In this "experiment," the reproductions were circulated with brief bibliographies on the artist and his or her work.

121. NYFCL, *Annual Report* (1889), 13. See also, for example, Pauline Leipziger, "Picture Bulletins and Their Use in the Aguilar Free Library," *Library Journal* 24 (June 1899): 257–58.

122. Edwin White Gaillard, "An Extension of the Picture Bulletin," *Library Journal* 26 (December 1901): 874–75. See also Edwin White Gaillard, "The Outcome of the Picture Bulletin," *Library Journal* 26 (April 1901): 192–93. Gaillard described the displays as "a greater development in what we call the 'modern library movement.'"

123. East Side House, *Annual Report* (1900), 12. From its Department of Practical Illustration the Webster loaned to public schools, among other things, bark, birds' eggs, coral, and anatomical models. East Side House, *Annual Report* (1903), 19. On the relationship between public libraries and museums generally, see Bostwick, *American Public Library*, 303–15.

9. The Founding of the New York Public Library: Public and Private in the Progressive Era

1. Andrew Carnegie, *Triumphant Democracy or Fifty Years' March of the Republic* (New York: Charles Scribner's Sons, 1886), 92.

2. Quoted in Austin Baxter Keep, *History of the New York Society Library* (New York: De Vinne Press, 1908), 422–23.

3. Sidney Ditzion, *Arsenals of a Democratic Culture: A Social History of the Public Library Movement in New England and the Middle States from 1850 to 1900* (Chicago: American Library Association, 1947), 30. The New Hampshire law is quoted in full in Jesse H. Shera, *Foundations of the Public Library: The Origins of the Public Library Movement in New England, 1629–1855* (Chicago: University of Chicago Press, 1949; repr., New York: Shoe String Press, 1965), opposite 192.

4. Barbara Shupe, Janet Steins, and Jyoti Pandit, eds., *New York State Population, 1790–1980* (New York: Neal-Shuman, 1987), 200.

5. Edwin G. Burrows and Mike Wallace, *Gotham: A History of the City of New York to 1898* (New York: Oxford University Press, 1999), 1008–11. On the rise

and fall of Boss Tweed, see Seymour J. Mandelbaum, *Boss Tweed's New York* (San Diego: Blackbirch Press, 2002). For biographies of Tilden, see John Bigelow, *The Life of Samuel J. Tilden* (New York: Harper & Bros., 1895) and Alexander Clarence Flick, *Samuel Jones Tilden: A Study in Political Sagacity* (Dodd, Mead & Co., 1939; repr., Westport, Conn.: Greenwood Press, 1973). Green was one of the founders of Central Park and one of the architects of the plan to consolidate the boroughs into Greater New York in 1898. See John Foord, *The Life and Public Services of Andrew Haswell Green* (Garden City, N.Y.: Doubleday, Page & Co., 1913). For biographies of Tilden, see John Bigelow, *The Life of Samuel J. Tilden* (New York: Harper & Bros. Co., 1895) and Alexander Clarence Flick, *Samuel Jones Tilden: A Study in Political Sagacity* (Dodd, Mead & Co., 1939; repr., Westport, Conn.: Greenwood Press, 1973).

6. Harry Miller Lydenberg, *History of the New York Public Library, Astor, Lenox and Tilden Foundations* (New York: New York Public Library [hereafter, also NYPL], 1923), 129–33. This is the official history of the founding and comprises chapters that originally appeared in the *Bulletin of the New York Public Library.* It includes the full text of many of the key documents and an extensive appendix of statistics. Lydenberg was the first head of the Reference Department. Phyllis Dain, *The New York Public Library: A History of Its Founding and Early Years* (New York: NYPL, 1972), 36–39. Dain's is a more scholarly, critical work, although she relies heavily on Lydenberg on certain key points, including her assessment of John Shaw Billings, the first director, and of various elected officials involved in the founding. George Lockhart Rives and Charles Howland Russell, eds., *The New York Public Library, Astor, Lenox, and Tilden Foundations, Book of Charters, Wills, Deeds and Other Official Documents* (New York: NYPL, 1905), 71–73. This is an excerpt of the clauses in Tilden's will relating to the Library. *Book of Charters* is a compilation of all the legal documents pertaining to the founding, including those relating to the various free circulating libraries that were absorbed after 1900.

7. Lydenberg, *New York Public Library*, 132–40; Dain, *New York Public Library*, 38–42. The text of the final ruling is in *Book of Charters*, 86–88. Bigelow, *Tilden*, 2:359–66; Flick, *Tilden*, 508–19. Flick provides a good summary of the provisions of the will in plain English at pages 511–13. He claims that Governor D. B. Hill, who was seeking an appointment as U.S. senator, assigned judges to hear the case on appeal who were likely to decide in favor of the heirs (515).

8. *Book of Charters*, 89–94. For contemporary summaries of the Tilden case, see, for example, "Tilden Heirs to Get Fund Left to Charity," *New York Herald*, October 28, 1891; "The Tilden Will Contest," *New York Times*, October 28, 1891; and "Tilden's Will Broken," *New York Daily Tribune*, October 28, 1891. The trust also received Tilden's personal library of approximately 20,000 volumes. For a description, see *Bulletin of the New York Public Library* 3 (December 1898): 4–8.

9. *New York Commercial Advertiser* quoted in Charles Amni Cutter, *Library Journal* 13 (December 1888): 378. "Tilden Will Decision," *New York Daily Tribune*, October 28, 1891; "Trying to Thwart a Beneficent Purpose," *New York Times*, March 16, 1887.

10. *New York Times*, October 24, 1886; January 16, 1887; March 16, 1887; March 29, 1887; March 6, 1888; October 29, 1891.

11. Historians of progressivism disagree over what these "languages" were and how to define them, but this is still a fruitful means of exploring the complexities of the Progressive Era. See Daniel T. Rodgers, "In Search of Progressivism," *Reviews in American History* 10 (December 1982): 121–27. For a different formulation and one that is particularly relevant to the founding of the NYPL, see Susan Tenenbaum, "The Progressive Legacy and the Public Corporation: Entrepreneurship and Public Virtue," *Journal of Policy History* 3 (November 1991): 309–30. John Patrick Diggins argues that republicanism was peripheral in the discourse of public intellectuals during the Progressive Era. John Patrick Diggins, "Republicanism and Progressivism," *American Quarterly* 37 (Autumn 1985): 572–98. This does not mean, however, that it was irrelevant in the broader public discourse.

12. A similar point is made in Daniel T. Rodgers, *Contested Truths: Keywords in American Politics since Independence* (New York: Basic Books, 1987), 8–11.

13. *New York Daily Tribune*, April 28, 1889; *New York Sun*, April 28, 1889; *New York World*, May 1, 1889; *New York Herald*, April 30, 1889. The *Herald*, with characteristic modesty, claimed that "the future historian of this great event will not be equipped for his task until he consults our files."

14. *New York Daily Tribune*, April 30, 1889; *New York Sun*, April 30, 1889; *New York World*, April 30, 1889. The prose used by the society reporters was often a curious mix of staunchly republican and rather unrepublican language. The *World* wrote that Mrs. Edward Cooper "looks like a Roman matron," but added that "an Englishmen would say she looked like a duchess." For an excellent exploration of New York's elite during this period, see Sven Beckert, *Monied Metropolis: New York City and the Consolidation of the American Bourgeoisie, 1850–1896* (New York: Cambridge University Press, 2002).

15. On the *Social Register*, see Burrows and Wallace, *Gotham*, 1072–73. On Caroline Astor, see Eric Homberger, *Mrs. Astor's New York: Money and Social Power in Gilded Age New York* (New Haven: Yale University Press, 2002); and Greg King, *A Season of Splendor: The Court of Mrs. Astor in Gilded Age New York* (Hoboken, N.J.: Wiley, 2009).

16. Raymond Williams, *Keywords: A Vocabulary of Culture and Society*, rev. ed. (New York: Oxford University Press, 1983), s.v. "Society." Mitchell Dean, "Society," in *Keywords: A New Vocabulary of Culture and Society*, ed. Tony Bennett, Lawrence Grossberg, and Meaghan Morris (Malden, Mass.: Blackwell, 2005), 326–29.

17. Bigelow, *Tilden*, 2: 367.

18. Lydenberg, *New York Public Library*, 143–50, 301–4; Dain, *New York Public Library*, 42–58. Andrew Haswell Green outlined the trust's options in a letter he read to the board at the May 1892 meeting. Lydenberg quotes the relevant passages at pages 141–43. See also John Bigelow, "The Tilden Trust Library: What Shall It Be?" *Scribner's Magazine* 12 (September 1892): 287–300. It outlines options similar to those in Green's letter.

19. The act passed May 13, 1892. Reprinted in *Book of Charters*, 113–17.

20. Quoted in Dain, *New York Public Library*, 45.

21. Lydenberg, *New York Public Library*, 304–5. Lydenberg based his account of the genesis of the negotiations "largely on talks with the men who effected the consolidation."

22. The reports of the Tilden, Astor, and Lenox consolidation committees are reprinted in Lydenberg, *New York Public Library*, 313–16, 316–28, and 331–35, respectively. A brief discussion of the issues involved in the merger is included in the "Introductory Statement" of the trustees in the first issue of the *Bulletin of the New York Public Library* 1 (January 1897): 10–11.

23. The endowments of the Astor and the Lenox in 1895 stood at $941,000 and $500,000 respectively. By this time the Tilden endowment had grow to between $2,225,000 and $2,500,000. Lydenberg, *New York Public Library*, 313, 317, and 322. These figures come from the reports of the Tilden Trust and Astor Library committees on consolidation. Negotiating with two libraries also probably placed the Tilden trustees in a rather more favorable bargaining position. Confident that they would consolidate with the Astor, they were in a position to moderate certain demands of the Lenox trustees, especially in regard to the future location of the library.

24. The text of the agreement is in *Book of Charters*, 118–22.

25. Apparently there was no wrangling over the order of the names. It was convenient that the alphabetic order of Astor, Lenox, and Tilden was also the chronological order of the incorporation of the two libraries and the Tilden Trust.

26. The original board comprised eight trustees from the Astor Library, eight from the Lenox, and all five trustees of the Tilden foundation. The Astor and Lenox boards each elected seven of their members. The Tilden trustees then elected an additional NYPL trustee from among the remaining Astor trustees and the remaining Lenox trustees. Dain, *New York Public Library*, 67.

27. Minutes of the Board of Trustees of the New York Public Library, May 27, 1895, vol. 1, 32–40, Record Group 5, New York Public Library Board of Trustees, New York Public Library Manuscripts and Archives Division. Hereafter, Minutes of the NYPL Board. The negotiations over these resolutions are detailed in the reports of the consolidation committees. See note 20.

28. *Library Journal* 20 (March 1895): 84; S. Turner Willis, "The Proposed Public Library of New York," *Peterson's Magazine* 5 (June 1895): 638; Laurence Hutton,

"The New York Public Library, Astor, Lenox, and Tilden Foundations," *Harper's Weekly* 34 (23 March 1895): 274.

29. *New York Times*, March 3, 1895; *New York World*, March 14, 1895.

30. *Harper's Weekly* 34 (March 16, 1895): 259. News of the impending consolidation leaked out a few weeks before the formal agreement was signed.

31. For an example in the contemporary literature, see R. R. Bowker, "Libraries and the Library Problem in 'Greater New York,'" *Library Journal* 21 (March 1886): 99. Bowker was the publisher of *Library Journal*. Reprinted from a talk he gave to the New York Library Club, his article argues that a "free public library in a great city" must have both scholarly, reference collections and popular, circulating collections. See also, George Putnam, "The Great Libraries of the United States," *Forum* 19 (June 1895): 485. Putnam was at this time Director of the Boston Public Library and later Librarian of Congress. Putnam added that a public library, as well as being popular and circulating, should also be publicly funded and publicly governed.

32. "Many Suggestions as to Carrying out the Consolidation Scheme," *New York Daily Tribune*, March 8, 1895. The *World* offered similar advice: "Now give us more libraries for the plain people where the plain people can easily get at them." Of the local newspapers that specifically addressed the issue, only the *Times* seems to have been noncommittal. Regarding circulating collections like those of the New York Free Circulating Library and libraries of reference like the Astor, it simply wrote that "there is much to be said on each side of the question." *New York Times*, March 3, 1895.

33. *Book of Charters*, 120. Similarly, the state law authorizing the consolidation stated that "the new Corporation . . . shall be permitted to . . . carry on any form of library." *Book of Charters*, 117.

34. For example, John Cadwalader, one of the prime movers behind the consolidation and the second president of the Library, spoke favorably of absorbing the free circulating libraries and other organizations at some time in the future. *New York Daily Tribune*, March 14, 1895; *New York World*, March 14, 1895. One member of the consolidation committee claimed the Library definitely planned on branch libraries. This was probably Andrew Haswell Green. *New York Daily Tribune*, March 4, 1895.

35. Minutes of the NYPL Board, 1:98, 119–20. Green's support of popular lending libraries was rather oddly coupled with his plan to have the Library set up laboratories for the city's scientific societies. See, for example, *New York Daily Tribune*, March 4, 1895. In his comments to the press, he claimed that the consolidation committees had agreed that this was "one of the most important features" of the consolidation. This had no basis in fact. Public statements such as this and his aggressive advocacy of branch libraries alienated him from his colleagues on the board. Library President John Bigelow, for example, derided his support of circulating libraries as his "lending library fad." John Bigelow Diary, January 27,

1896, John Bigelow Papers, New York Public Library Archives and Manuscripts Division.

36. Fielding H. Garrison, *John Shaw Billings: A Memoir* (New York: G. P. Putnam's Sons, 1915); Harry Miller Lydenberg, *John Shaw Billings, Creator of the National Medical Library and Its Catalogue, First Director of the New York Public Library* (Chicago: American Library Association, 1924); Carleton B. Chapman, *Order out of Chaos: John Shaw Billings and America's Coming of Age* (Boston: Boston Medical Library, 1994). The National Library of Medicine is still the nation's leading medical library, and *Index Medicus*, now online as PubMed, is still the standard bibliography of medical literature. On the founding of the National Library of Medicine, see "Who Founded the National Medical Library?" in *Selected Papers of John Shaw Billings*, ed. Frank Bradway Rogers (Philadelphia: Medical Library Association, 1965), 115.

37. Arthur E. Bostwick, *A Life with Men and Books* (New York: H.W. Wilson, 1939), 182.

38. See, for example, John Shaw Billings, "Some Library Problems of Tomorrow," *Library Journal* 27 (Conference Proceedings 1902): 1–7. See also John Shaw Billings, "The Public Library: Its Uses to the Municipality," *Library Journal* 28 (June 1903): 203–4.

39. "Memorandum," December 28, 1911, presumably by Cadwalader; quoted in Dain, *New York Public Library*, 360.

40. "Introductory Statement," 16–18. Report of the Site Committee, February 5, 1896, 3–4, Record Group 3, Tilden Trust, box 2, New York Public Library Archives and Manuscripts Division.

41. The relevant clause from Henrietta Lenox's will is reprinted in *Book of Charters*, 58–59. The provisional acceptance of the Lenox site was worked out by the respective committees of consolidation before the merger. See note 20 and Minutes of the NYPL Board, May 27, 1895, 1:38–40.

42. Report of the Site Committee, 5–6.

43. *New York Herald*, May 25, 1895.

44. For the connections between the Metropolitan and the New York Public Library, see Dain, *New York Public Library*, 82. For histories of the Metropolitan, see Winifred Howe, *A History of the Metropolitan Museum of Art* (New York: Gilliss Press, 1913–46). See also Calvin Tompkins, *Merchants and Masterpieces: The Story of the Metropolitan Museum of Art*, rev. ed. (New York: Henry Holt, 1989).

45. Beckert, *Monied Metropolis*, 267–69. On the interesting connections between both the Metropolitan and the Museum of Natural History and Central Park, see Roy Rosenzweig and Elizabeth Blackmar, *The Park and the People: A History of Central Park* (Ithaca, N.Y.: Cornell University Press, 1992), 349–66. On the creation of "high culture" generally, see Lawrence Levine, *Highbrow/Lowbrow:*

The Emergence of Cultural Hierarchy in America (Cambridge, Mass.: Harvard University Press, 1988).

46. *Herald* quoted in Burrows and Wallace, *Gotham*, 1082; see also 963–65; *New York Times*, July 10, 1881.

47. See Chapter 1 and Thomas Bender, *New York Intellect: A History of Intellectual Life in New York City, from 1750 to the Beginnings of Our Own Time* (New York: Knopf, 1987), 62–66.

48. Quoted in Tomkins, *Merchants and Masterpieces*, 78. According to Tomkins, the leadership of the Metropolitan was divided over the question of Sunday hours, and Cesnola and some of the younger trustees supported it from the beginning (75–79).

49. New York City, *Minutes of the Common Council*, XIX, 78 (May 31, 1830). See Chapter 1 on Roosevelt and the City's ending its support for the New York Institution.

50. The only paper actively to campaign against the reservoir site was the *Tribune*, which feared that the Library would encroach upon Bryant Park adjacent to it. See, for example, "Keep off the Grass," *New York Tribune*, March 24, 1895. Green, one of the founders of Central Park, opposed the reservoir for the same reason. As it happened, the Library was built adjacent to Bryant Park, and today it is one of the most popular public places in midtown Manhattan. On the question of public transportation in relation to the site, see, for example, Bowker, "The Library Problem," 99–100.

51. John Bigelow Diary, January 16, 1896. Minutes of the NYPL Board, January 8, 1896, 1:96–97. Report of the Site Committee, 4–5.

52. Burrows and Wallace, *Gotham*, 1229.

53. Minutes of the NYPL Board, February 14, 1896, 1:119–23.

54. "Report of the Executive Committee," *Bulletin of the New York Public Library* 3 (March 1899): 108. This is a brief review of the development of the Library from its founding until the first appropriation of City money.

55. "Introductory Statement," 108. This first issue of the *Bulletin of the New York Public Library* appeared in January 1897, in the midst of the negotiations with the City. It was at least in part an effort to make the Library appear more open and welcoming to the public when the trustees needed public money.

56. "Report of the Site Committee," 6.

57. The "Address to the Mayor, Aldermen and Commonalty of the City of New York," delivered on March 26, 1896, is reprinted in *Book of Charters*, 125–33. The quote is at page 129, and references to the free circulating libraries are at pages 129 and 130.

58. The agreement is reprinted in *Book of Charters*, 147–52. The construction of the Central Building was a complex process legally, requiring a series of nine separate laws or contracts between the Library, the State of New York, and vari-

ous municipal agencies. All of these documents are reprinted in *Book of Charters*, 134–55.

59. Lydenberg, *New York Public Library*, 546. This is a table summarizing all the contracts for the Central Building. The original estimate was $2.5 million. When complete, the building cost $2 million more than the Library of Congress, completed about the same time. Dain, *New York Public Library*, 324. The average annual appropriation from the City was calculated from: "Director's Report," *Bulletin of the New York Public Library* 17 (February 1913): 98; 18 (March 1914): 213; 19 (March 1915): 207; 20 (February 1916): 208; and 21 (March 1917): 159.

60. "Report of the Executive Committee," *Bulletin of the New York Public Library* 3 (March 1899): 108.

61. See, for example, G. L. Rives to Bird S. Coler, September 24, 1900, reprinted in New York Public Library, *Correspondence Relating to the Question of a Consolidation of Free Circulating Libraries with the New York Public Library* (New York: NYPL, 1900). Rives's letter is a report to the city comptroller on the results of the Public Library's survey of the free circulating libraries referred to herein. The discussion of efficiency is at pages 22–24.

62. John Bigelow Diary, December 2, 1898.

63. The bills to incorporate the Library and authorize city support are reprinted in Lydenberg, *New York Public Library*, 292–96.

64. From an interview with Sanger published in the *Commercial Advertiser*, February 3, 1886, reprinted in *Library Journal* 10 (February 1886): 46–47. It is not clear in the bill itself if Sanger intended to include branch libraries and even his public statements at the time were somewhat vague on this important point. In this particular interview, he claimed that the free circulating libraries could become branches of his proposed library.

65. Frederic Beecher Perkins, "Public Libraries and the Public," in *Library and Society*, ed. Arthur Bostwick (New York: H. W. Wilson, 1921; repr., Freeport, N.Y.: Books for Libraries, 1968), 233. This is an address that was delivered in 1885 at the American Library Association annual conference.

66. The statement presented to the committee is reprinted in Lydenberg, *New York Public Library*, 298–300. The law authorizing grants to free circulating libraries is reprinted in Lydenberg, *New York Public Library*, 216–17. About the time of the Astor, Lenox, Tilden merger, a new law was passed that changed the formula for discretionary appropriations to ten cents per volume circulated. Lydenberg, *New York Public Library*, 218.

67. See, for example, New York Free Circulating Library, *Twenty-First and Final Report of the New York Free Circulating Library, with a Sketch of Its History* (New York: New York Free Circulating Library, 1900), 23. By 1899, City money accounted for four-fifths of its operating expenses. New York Free Circulating Library, *Twentieth Annual Report of the New York Free Circulating Library* (New York: New York Free Circulating Library, 1899), 12.

68. Lydenberg, *New York Public Library*, 528 and 530, gives the annual appropriation from the City and circulation statistics, respectively, for the New York Free Circulating Library (hereafter, also NYFCL). Based on these figures, from 1887 to 1900, it received $417,250 from the City. The maximum amount it could have received was $801,815.

69. *New York World*, July 12, 1898, quoted in Dain, *New York Public Library*, 175. Van Wyck held up City appropriations for the Central Building and was continually at odds with the circulating libraries. Van Wyck was a Tammany mayor who defeated Strong, a reform mayor. There was no love lost on either side. Several leaders of the libraries were active in the Citizens Union that opposed his administration and worked for nonpartisan elections. See, for example, "Mayor on Libraries," *New York Times*, October 15, 1898.

70. New York Free Circulating Library, *Twentieth Annual Report of the Free Circulating Library* (New York: New York Free Circulating Library, 1899), 12–13.

71. [John Shaw Billings], "Memorandum on the Library Consolidation Question," Record Group 5, New York Public Library Board of Trustees, Committees, Consolidation Committee, New York Public Library Archives and Manuscripts Division.

72. NYPL, *Correspondence Relating to a Consolidation of Free Libraries*, 5–6. This pamphlet includes many of the important documents connected with the consolidation, including the cover letter Billings used in his survey of the libraries, a table summarizing his findings, and his report to the board, which was the basis of the board's report to Coler.

73. NYPL, *Correspondence Relating to a Consolidation of Free Libraries*, 21–26. Quotes are from at pages 22–23 and 24. Unofficially, influential members of the NYPL board had decided as early as July that the best course of action was to take over the circulating libraries. Billings and Cadwalader wrote a "confidential minute" to that effect for the Executive Committee and sent copies to certain representatives of the lending libraries. The minute stresses the danger of political control of the libraries, and that fear probably accounts for this rather abrupt change in policy. Billing's memo the previous fall had sought to avoid responsibility for the circulating libraries. Dain, *New York Public Library*, 195–98.

74. Dain, *New York Public Library*, 201.

75. The agreement is reprinted in *Book of Charters*, 219–24.

76. Arthur Bostwick, *A Life with Men and Books*, 185. Bostwick, the first head of the Circulation Department, quotes Billings as saying: "The trustees and I are running a reference library for scholars. We know nothing about circulating libraries and branches, and we want those to be operated by the same persons who have been doing so in the past with such success."

77. John Shaw Billings, "Report of the Director," *Bulletin of the New York Public Library* 5 (October 1901): 396–98; John Shaw Billings, "The Organization of the New York Public Library," *Library Journal* 26 (Conference Proceedings 1902):

215–17; Dain, *New York Public Library*, 201–4. The current designations are Library Sites and Services and Reference and Research Services.

78. *Book of Charters*, 231.

79. Documentation of the bequests to the NYFCL is reprinted in *Book of Charters*, 165–218. A summary of donations is in NYFCL, *Twenty-First and Final Report* (1900), 57–64.

80. Robert M. Lester, *Forty Years of Carnegie Giving: A Summary of the Benefactions of Andrew Carnegie and of the Philanthropic Trusts which He Created* (New York: Charles Scribner's Sons, 1941), 6, 93. In 1941, the total value of the various Carnegie benevolent trusts was $319,000,000.

81. For a good overview of American philanthropy, see Robert H. Bremmer, *American Philanthropy*, 2nd ed. (Chicago: University of Chicago Press, 1988). On library philanthropy generally, see Ditzion, *Arsenals of a Democratic Culture*, 129–64. On Carnegie's library philanthropy in particular, see Abigail Van Slyck, *Free to All: Carnegie Libraries & American Culture, 1890–1920* (Chicago: University of Chicago Press, 1995), 1–43.

82. Andrew Carnegie, *The Autobiography of Andrew Carnegie* (Boston: Northeastern University Press, 1986; repr., New York: Houghton Mifflin, 1920), 1–13. Andrew Carnegie, "A Confession of Religious Faith," in *Miscellaneous Writings of Andrew Carnegie*, ed. Burton J. Hendrick (Freeport, N.Y.: Books for Libraries Press; repr., New York: Doubleday & Co., 1933), 2:296.

83. Andrew Carnegie, "The Gospel of Wealth," in *The Gospel of Wealth and Other Timely Essays*, ed. Edward C. Kirkland (Cambridge, Mass.: Belknap Press of Harvard University Press, 1962), 16–17.

84. Carnegie, *Triumphant Democracy*, vi.

85. "Andrew Carnegie at Home," *Current Literature* 23 (March 1898): 221.

86. Carnegie, "Gospel of Wealth," 16.

87. Ibid., 19–24, 49.

88. Andrew Carnegie, "The Best Use of Wealth," in *Miscellaneous Writings*, 2:210. This was a speech delivered at the opening of the Carnegie Library in Pittsburgh in 1895.

89. Ibid., 210–11; Carnegie, "Gospel of Wealth," 36–40. Here and elsewhere, Carnegie recalled fondly Colonel James Anderson, who opened his small personal library to the working boys of Pittsburgh on Saturday afternoons. Carnegie devoted an entire chapter in his autobiography to Anderson and his library. Carnegie, *Autobiography*, 43–51.

90. Carnegie, "Best Uses of Wealth," 211.

91. John Shaw Billings, "Report of the Director," *Bulletin of the New York Public Library* 5 (October 1901): 395–96. All of the documents related to the Carnegie gift are reprinted in *Book of Charters*, 231–58. These include a contract between the City and the NYPL at pages 238–48, and between the NYPL and Carnegie at pages 254–58. This rather complicated series of legal instruments was further

complicated by the fact that, in 1898, Manhattan had consolidated with the four outlying boroughs to create Greater New York. Carnegie entered into separate agreements with the Queens Borough Public Library and the Brooklyn Public Library, each founded about the time of the consolidation, so that there were and are three separate public library systems in what is now New York City. Dain, *New York Public Library*, 223–28.

92. "City Will Accept Mr. Carnegie's Gift," *New York Times*, March 17, 1901. "Five Millions for the New York Public Library from Andrew Carnegie," *Library Journal* 26 (March 1901): 134.

93. *New York World*, March 18, 1901, quoted in Dain, *New York Public Library*, 218.

94. *New York Sun*, March 22, 1901; March 19, 1901. The latter editorial in particular is a good summary of the various arguments used against accepting Carnegie's offer. The *Sun* argued, for example, that the City would be wiser to spend its money on public schools and tenements rather than on public libraries, which simply encouraged the reading of trashy fiction. It also argued, rather self-servingly, that the daily newspaper provided the average citizen with all the good reading he needed. The other argument that was frequently advanced against accepting the gift was that Carnegie's money was tainted, earned at the expense of the working class. See, for example, A. M. Baugh, "Workingmen's View Point," *New York Times*, March 24, 1901. A number of cities did in fact reject Carnegie grants under pressure from organized labor. Robert Sidney Martin, *Carnegie Denied: Communities Rejecting Carnegie Library Construction Grants* (Westport, Conn.: Greenwood, 1993). For a good summary of the arguments against Carnegie, see Van Slyck, "Free to All," 19–22, and Dain, *New York Public Library*, 219–21. For a good laugh, see [Finley Peter Dunne,] "The Carnegie Libraries," in *Dissertations by Mr. Dooley* (New York: Harper & Co., 1906), 177–81. "If ye write him f'r an autygraft he sinds ye a libry."

95. *New York Herald*, March 22, 1901.

96. *New York Times*, October 30, 1902.

97. Bostwick, *Life with Men and Books*, 184; Dain, *New York Public Library*, 203–4, 232. Shortly after the consolidation of the NYFCL and the NYPL, the legislature passed a law allowing the remaining free circulating libraries simply to convey their property to the Public Library. This simplified the rest of the consolidations. It meant the New York Public Library would not have to enter into separate agreements with each of the remaining library corporations. *Book of Charters*, 227–30.

98. Aguilar Free Library, *Fourteenth and Final Report of the Aguilar Free Library Society of the City of New York* (New York: Aguilar Free Library Society, 1903), 22. Hereafter, AFL, *Annual Report*. Bostwick, *Life with Men and Books*, 186.

99. AFL, *Eleventh and Twelfth Annual Report* (1901), 8–10, 14; AFL, *Annual Report* (1903), 22. The deeds transferring the Aguilar's property to the NYPL are

in *Book of Charters*, 300–6. Along with Greenbaum, Oscar Strauss was elected to the NYPL board, and Mark Ash was also appointed to the Circulation Committee. Dain, *New York Public Library*, 255–58. Bostwick described Billings and Leipziger as "two autocrats [who] disliked each other at sight." He claimed that ex-Major Billings nearly sabotaged his negotiations with the Aguilar by "throwing the monkey wrench of militarism into the machinery of peaceful adjustment." Bostwick, *Life with Men and Books*, 186–87.

100. Cathedral Library Association, *Statement of the Position of the Cathedral Library with Reference to the Proposed Action of the City of New York in the Matter of the Carnegie Library Proposition* (n.p., n.d.), Record Group 4, Free Circulating Libraries, Cathedral Library Association, NYPL Archives and Manuscripts Division. This sums up the arguments used by the CLA over the course of the next two years. Public remarks by Archbishop Corrigan in April 1901 on the Carnegie offer were taken verbatim from this pamphlet, and the church's stand was covered extensively in the press. See, for example, "The New York Public Library and the Cathedral Library," *Library Journal* 26 (May 1901): 276–77. "Roman Catholics and the Public Library," *New York Times*, April 18, 1901. "Sectarianism and Public Aid," *New York Daily Tribune*, February 24, 1903. After the CLA was absorbed, there seem to have been few complaints about anti-Catholicism in the NYPL, but in 1904, the *Daily News* circulated a petition to remove a book "assailing the Catholic Church." "Petition," *New York Daily News*, November 9, 1904.

101. H. Clay Peters, "Catholic Libraries," *New York Times*, May 12, 1901. Clay was a Catholic who argued the issue with his archbishop in a series of letters published in the *Times*. For other uses of the church-state argument, see, for example, *New York Times*, May 19, 1901, and *New York Tribune*, February 19, 1903. These and other editorials also compared the library merger with the controversy over public support for parochial schools.

102. The *Post* also argued that if the collections did not reflect the needs of Catholic readers, it was simply because "other demands are more urgent." *New York Evening Post*, April 14, 1901.

103. *New York Times*, February 12, 1903; *New York Tribune*, February 19, 1903.

104. For use of the term *interests*, see the Peters editorial, note 101. "Special interests" was a keyword in the progressives' vocabulary and came into use around 1905. In the Progressive Era, it often referred to economic interests. Daniel T. Rodgers, *Contested Truths: Keywords in American Politics since Independence* (New York: Basic Books, 1987), 178–87.

105. Billings was ostensibly referring to Catholic opposition to public libraries generally, but he obviously had in mind the controversy in New York. John Shaw Billings, "Some Library Problems of To-morrow," 6. Particularly in light of his "militarism" in regard to the Aguilar (see note 99), Billings was rather conciliatory in his dealings with the church generally. See, for example, Billings to

Fr. Joseph McMahon, Director of the Cathedral Library, February 14, 1901, Record Group 6, NYPL Central Administration, Director's Office, John Shaw Billings, Subseries 1.4, Letterbooks, Circulation Department, vol. I, New York Public Library Archives and Manuscripts Division. "I don't object to the autonomy you indicate." Generally, the NYPL policy during this period seems to have been to not get involved in the fights between the City and the circulating libraries over consolidation.

106. McMahon pointedly reminded the City that "we represent 1,200,000 people in" New York. *New York Sun,* February 18, 1903.

107. Dain, *New York Public Library,* 252.

108. Ibid., 260–64; *Book of Charters,* 351–54; Joseph H. McMahon, *Final Report of the Director of the Cathedral Library* (New York: Cathedral Library Association, 1905), 3.

109 *Book of Charters,* 259–88, 307–48. Most of the smaller free circulating libraries held out to the last possible day and transferred their property to the NYPL on December 31, 1903.

110. Given the elite character of the Society Library, a merger with a truly public library was out of the question. Even before the creation of the Circulation Department, it had declined offers to negotiate with the fledgling NYPL, "'preferring to die a natural death to strangulation.'" Keep, *History of the New York Society Library,* 502–5.

111. Dain, *New York Public Library,* 264–66; Ada Sterling, "To Rescue an Old Library," *New York Times,* February 19, 1906.

112. Dain, *New York Public Library,* 267–68.

113. *Book of Charters,* 231.

114. [Untitled], *Library Journal* 36 (May 1911): 217; John S. Billings, "The New York Public Library," *Library Journal* 36 (May 1911): 233.

115. Lydenberg, *New York Public Library,* 363, 368, 389. In the fall of 1896, both libraries were open only until 6:00 p.m., but the Astor extended its hours until 9:00 p.m. in 1905.

116. "Proceedings at the Opening of the New Building of the New York Public Library, Astor Lenox and Tilden Foundations," *Bulletin of the New York Public Library* 15 (June 1911): 346.

117. David Gray, "A Modern Temple of Education," *Harper's Monthly Magazine,* March 1911, 567.

118. New York Free Circulating Library, *Twenty-First and Final Report of the New York Free Circulating Library, With a Sketch of Its History* (New York: New York Free Circulating Library, 1900), 23. The report is dated 1900, but it was published in February 1901, immediately after the consolidation with the NYPL.

119. New York Public Library, *Results Not Shown by Statistics in the Work of the Public Libraries of Greater New York* (New York: New York Free Circulating Library, 1910), 9, 10, 11–13. The pamphlet also stressed how economical a library

membership could be: "Your Library has saved me many a dollar" (4). In the entire fifteen-page pamphlet, I find only one reference to "uplifting influence" and one to "refining influence" (both at page 4). Such language was ubiquitous in the annual reports of the free circulating libraries. On the other hand, the Circulation Department continued their focus on children. *Results Not Shown by Statistics* also included sections on "Cooperation with the Schools" and "Help to Children."

120. Arthur E. Bostwick, "The Purchase of Current Fiction," in American Library Association, *Twenty-Fifth Annual Conference, Niagara Falls, June 22–27, 1903* (Philadelphia: American Library Association, 1903), 32.

121. New York Public Library, *Ceremonies on the Laying of Its Cornerstone* (New York: R. W. Crothers, 1902), 27.

122. Bostwick, Purchase of Current Fiction," 31, 32. See also Arthur E. Bostwick, "The Uses of Fiction," in *A Librarian's Open Shelf: Essays on Various Subjects* (New York: H. W. Wilson, 1920), 35–44. An address, delivered at the ALA conference in 1907. On changing attitudes within the profession and the larger society toward fiction, see Dee Garrison, *Apostles of Culture: The Public Librarian and American Society, 1876–1920* (New York: Free Press, 1979; repr., Madison: University of Wisconsin Press, 2003), 88–101.

123. Bostwick, "The People's Share in the Public Library," in *A Librarian's Open Shelf*, 198, 201. This was delivered to the Chicago Woman's Club in 1915. Bostwick left the New York Public Library in 1909 to head the St. Louis Public Library. Attitudes toward fiction among public librarians changed slowly. In this talk, Bostwick claimed that some referred to his attitude toward the taxpaying public as the "'commercial-traveler theory' of the library." In response, Bostwick said that the traveling salesman was "the advance guard of civilization" (198).

124. Dain, *New York Public Library*, 79, 177–79. According to Dain, the ex officio members rarely attended the board meetings. The state law is reprinted in *Book of Charters*, 363.

125. Dain, *New York Public Library*, 78–86, 229–30, 263. See also Phyllis Dain, "Public Library Governance in a Changing New York City," *Libraries & Culture* 26 (Spring 1991): 219–50. The first woman did not join the board until 1950, the first African American in 1970. All but two of the original board members were listed in the *Social Register*.

126. Ten percent of the Carnegie gift was $520,000. The average annual appropriation for the first five years after the completion of the original Carnegie branches was approximately $765,000. "Director's Report," *Bulletin of the New York Public Library* 19 (March 1915): 209; 20 (February 1916): 210; 21 (March 1917): 161; 22 (March 1918): 161; 23 (April 1919): 183; Dain, *New York Public Library*, 310–15.

127. On public corporations during this period, see Tenenbaum, "The Progressive Legacy and the Public Corporation" 309–30. For a more general treatment, Albert S. Abel, "The Public Corporation in the United States," in *Government*

Enterprise: A Comparative Study, ed. W. G. Friedman and J. F. Garner (New York: Columbia University Press, 1970), 181–200.

128. I argue in the following chapter that "recreational reading" serves an important, productive purpose as well.

129. African Americans were only 2 percent of the population of New York City in 1910. Dain, *New York Public Library*, 229. W. E. Burghardt Du Bois, *Some Notes on Negroes in New York City, Compiled from the Reports of the United States Census and Other Sources* (Atlanta: Atlanta University Press, 1903). Little more than a decade later, in the third edition of *The American Public Library*, Bostwick noted "the remarkable transformation of that part of the Harlem district into a Negro city of some 130,000 inhabitants." Arthur E. Bostwick, *The American Public Library*, 3rd ed. (New York: D. Appleton & Co., 1923), 59. Three years later, Arturo Alfonso Schomburg donated the collection that later became the Schomburg Center for Research in Black Culture.

Afterword: Public Libraries and New York's Elusive Reading Publics

1. Barbara Sicherman, "Ideologies and Practices of Reading," in *A History of the Book in America*, vol. 3, *The Industrial Book, 1840–1880*, ed. Scott E. Jasper, Jeffrey D. Groves, Stephen W. Nissenbaum, and Michael Winship (Chapel Hill: University of North Carolina Press, 2007), 279. See also Sicherman's bibliographical essay on the history of reading, 502–4.

2. Wayne Wiegand, "Introduction: 'On the Social Nature of Reading,'" in *Genreflecting: A Guide to Popular Reading Interests*, 6th ed., ed. Wayne Wiegand (Westport, Conn.: Libraries Unlimited, 2007), 11–12.

3. See for example, Sicherman, "Ideologies and Practices of Reading," 294; Wiegand, "Introduction: On the Social Nature of Reading"; Janice Radway, "Interpretive Communities and Variable Literacies: The Functions of Romance Reading," *Daedalus* 113 (Summer 1984): 49–73; Elizabeth Long, "On the Social Nature of Reading," in *Book Clubs: Women and the Uses of Reading in Everyday Life* (Chicago: University of Chicago Press, 2003); Christine Pawley, "Beyond Market Models and Resistance: Organizations as a Middle Layer in the History of Reading," *Library Quarterly* 79 (January 2009): 73–93.

4. John H. Griscom, *Memoir of John Griscom . . . Compiled from an Autobiography and Other Sources* (New York: Robert Carter and Brothers, 1859), 45. John H. Griscom was his son. Besides the autobiography, the memoir also includes extensive selections from the elder Griscom's correspondence. See also Edgar F. Smith, *John Griscom, 1774–1852: Chemist* (Philadelphia, 1927).

5. On Griscom and the Public School Society, see Griscom, *Memoir*, 202–17; on the Society for the Prevention of Pauperism, 157–66; on the New York Institution and the Mechanics Institute, 320–25. See also Thomas Bender, *New York Intellect: A History of Intellectual Life in New York City, from 1750 to the Beginnings of Our Own Time* (New York: Knopf, 1987), 65, 84–85. Monitorial

or Lancasterian instruction was used in the new public schools in part to reduce costs. Older students—monitors—instructed the younger students, and many fewer teachers were hired. John Griscom, *Monitorial Instruction: An Address Pronounced at the Opening of the New-York High-School, with Notes and Illustrations* (New York: Mahlon Day, 1825).

6. Quoted in Bender, *New York Intellect*, 85.

7. Griscom, *Memoir*, 394, 44–45, 47. Most of these quotes are from the autobiography. The first is from a letter to "a young friend, who was inclined to infidelity" (391). The last is from a review of Scott's works in the *Christian Observer*, which, Griscom wrote, "ably stated" his views (45). "Review of New Publications. The Pirate . . ." *Christian Observer*, March 1822, 157–72; April 1822, 237–50. The quote is from March 1822 at page 161. For an account of Griscom's reading, see Harvey J. Graff, "Literacy, Libraries, Lives: New Social and Cultural Histories," *Libraries and Culture* 26 (Winter 1991): 30–32.

8. The Society Library's charge ledgers for 1789–92 are searchable online at www.nysoclib.org//collection/ledger/circulation-records-1789-1792/people. It is possible that either book was borrowed by a member of Bard's or Mitchell's household. Who borrowed a book is usually not noted in the charge ledger.

9. Harriet Trumbull and Maria Trumbull, *A Season in New York, 1801: Letters of Harriet and Maria Trumbull*, ed. Helen M. Morgan (Pittsburgh: University of Pittsburgh Press, 1969), 83. These two teenage young girls spent the winter with the family of James Watson, who was a subscriber to the Society Library (72). During this same period, John Pintard kept a "Journal of Studies," an account of his reading. See Larry E. Sullivan, "Books, Power, and the Development of Libraries in the New Republic: The Prison and Other Journals of John Pintard of New York," *Journal of Library History* 21 (Spring 1986): 406–24.

10. Hocquet Caritat, "General Defense of Modern Novels," in *Explanatory Catalogue of H. Caritat's Circulating Library, No. 1 City Hotel, Broadway, New York* (New York: G & R Waite), 150–54, 158, 156.

11. "On the Cause of the Popularity of Novels," *Literary Magazine, and American Register*, June 1807, 410. The *Literary Magazine* started in New York City, but by 1807 it was published in Philadelphia. The article was actually pirated from the *Edinburgh Review*, January 1799, 33–36.

12. See Catharine Maria Sedgwick, *Means and Ends, or Self-Training* (Boston: Marsh, Capen, Lyon, & Webb, 1839). The most recent biography is Edward Halsey Foster, *Catharine Maria Sedgwick* (New York: Twayne, 1974). A good, concise discussion of her literary career is Nina Baym, *Women's Fiction: A Guide to Novels by and about Women in America, 1820–1870* (Urbana: University of Illinois Press, 1993), 53–63. On her work in reform organizations, see Charlene Avallone, "Catharine Sedgwick and the Circles of New York," *Legacy* 23 (June 2006): 122–24.

13. Edgar Allan Poe, "Literati of New York City—No. V," *Godey's Magazine and Lady's Book*, September 1846, 130.

14. New York Free Circulating Library, *Catalogue of the New York Free Circulating Library, Bond Street Branch, English Books* (New York: New York Free Circulating Library, 1892); General Society of Mechanics and Tradesmen of the City of New York, *Finding List of the Apprentices' Library Established and Maintained by the General Society of Mechanics and Tradesmen of the City of New York* (New York: J. J. Little & Co., 1888). The copy at the New York Public Library includes supplements with more of Sedgwick's work. Some of these books may have been donated, but at least two of her novels, *Mary Dyre* and *Home: A Story of New England Life*, were republished in the 1890s.

15. Sedgwick, *Means and Ends*, 249, 243–46, 247. Sedgwick, of course, advised tasteful consumption not just in reading, but also, for example, art (258), dress (191), and handwriting (28).

16. See, for example, Barbara Sicherman, "Reading and Middle-Class Identity in Victorian America: Cultural Consumption, Conspicuous and Otherwise," in *Reading Acts: U.S. Readers' Interactions with Literature, 1800–1950*, ed. Barbara Ryan and Amy M. Thomas (Knoxville: University of Tennessee Press, 2002), 137–60. I am greatly simplifying a very complex sociocultural shift, of course. In "Ideologies and Practices of Reading," Sicherman outlines four "models" of prescribed reading in the nineteenth century: evangelical, civic, self-improving, and cultural; and contends that reading for culture, taste, became more prominent after the Civil War (283–87). Griscom, I would argue, was concerned mostly with the first three models, and Sedgwick's writings point to an increasing emphasis upon the fourth.

The emergence of the middle class, when and how it happened, and what constituted a middle-class identity, is even more complex and elusive. The best work on this critical subject is still Stuart M. Blumin, *The Emergence of the Middle Class: Social Experience in the American City, 1760–1900* (Cambridge: Cambridge University Press, 1989). Blumin argues that middle-class identity began forming in roughly the two decades before the Civil War but emerged most clearly after the war (258).

17. Nan Enstad, *Ladies of Labor, Girls of Adventure: Working Women, Popular Culture, and Labor Politics at the Turn of the Twentieth Century* (New York: Columbia University Press, 1999), 23. Barbara Sicherman makes a similar point in *Well-Read Lives: How Books Inspired a Generation of American Women* (Chapel Hill: University of North Carolina Press, 2010), 43.

18. Mercantile Library Association of the City of New York (MLA), *Thirtieth Annual Report of the Board of Direction of the Mercantile Library Association* (New York: Baker & Godwin, 1851), 9–10. This is the report for 1850 that outlines the Association's business plan, its "system of management." Mercantile

Library Association of the City of New York, *Forty-Ninth Annual Report of the Board of Direction of the Mercantile Library Association of the City of New York* (New York: Jordan, Comes, & Seymour, 1870), 22. The MLA was not an exclusively middle-class institution. Probably all of the members of the Clinton Hall Association were members of the upper class. And the annual subscription of five dollars for subscribers, members who were not clerks, meant that it was accessible to more prosperous artisans.

19. New York Society Library, *Annual Report of the Trustees of the New York Society Library* (New York: John F. Trow, 1857), 5.

20. The annual report for 1870, for example, the same one that referred to a natural law of supply and demand, stated that "purchases have also been made with a view to answer the demands made upon the Library for the works of certain standard authors." MLA, *Forty-Ninth Annual Report*, 22.

21. Sedgwick, *Means and Ends*, 247. Mercantile Library Association of the City of New York, *Sixty-Second Annual Report of the Board of Direction of the Mercantile Library of the City of New York* (New York: Bowne, 1883), 15. This is a quote from an article entitled "Libraries and Readers" that I have not been able to locate. It is quoted in the context of the difficulty of finding a location for the Library that would suit the public.

22. George Templeton Strong, *Diary of George Templeton Strong: The Civil War, 1860–1865*, ed. Allan Nevins and Milton Halsey Thomas (New York: Macmillan, 1952), 465 (July 9, 1864). Although he makes few references to his use of the Society Library and the library of the New-York Historical Society, Strong (and Philip Hone, cited in note 24) did write extensively in his diary about his reading and his experience of various, mostly standard authors.

23. L. Frank Tooker, *The Joys and Tribulations of an Editor* (New York: Century Co., 1924), 165. Tooker began as an assistant editor at the *Century Magazine* in 1880. His autobiography is an interesting, chatty account of a popular periodical in the late nineteenth and early twentieth century.

24. Philip Hone, *The Diary of Philip Hone, 1828–1852*, rev. ed. (New York: Dodd, Mead, 1936), 582–606 (January 27–June 8, 1842). Sedgwick and her friends' crashing the stag party is described on pages 589–90. Hone socialized with Dickens several times during the visit and was among the party that saw him off when the left the country. When Dickens made fun of his American hosts the following year in *Martin Chuzzlewit*, Hone declared the book a "libel," and one "from which he will not obtain credit as . . . a man of good taste" (666; July 29, 1843).

25. MLA, *Thirty-Eighth Annual Report* (1858–59), 15.

26. Elizabeth Long, "On the Social Nature of Reading," in *Book Clubs: Women and the Uses of Reading in Everyday Life* (Chicago: University of Chicago Press, 2003), 1–30; Sedgwick, *Means and Ends*, 250.

27. "The New York Mercantile Library," *Scribner's Monthly*, February 1871, 363. Alisa Wade Harrison, in her dissertation-in-progress on "learned femininity" in early national New York, has found evidence in the charge ledgers of women visiting the Society Library in groups and also of their borrowing books checked out earlier by their friends.

28. Radway, "Interpretive Communities and Variable Literacies," 54. Radway suggests using more specific, formally constituted reading communities to explore the nature of interpretive communities. See also Janice A. Radway, *Reading the Romance: Women, Patriarchy, and Popular Literature* (Chapel Hill: University of North Carolina Press, 1984).

29. Mercantile Library Association, *Eighty-Fourth Annual Report of the Board of Direction of the Mercantile Library Association* (n.p., 1904), 6.

30. New York Society Library, *Annual Report of the Trustees of the New York Society Library* (n.p., 1858), 4; New York Society Library, *Annual Report of the Trustees of the New York Society Library* (n.p., 1903), 4.

31. Laura Jean Libbey, *That Pretty Young Girl* (New York: American News Company, 1889), preface, n.p. See Robert Morss Lovett, "A Boys Reading Fifty Years Ago," *New Republic* 48 (November 10, 1926): 334–36. Quoted in Sicherman, "Ideologies of Reading," 299. This criticism was common throughout the nineteenth century. See, for example, "On the Cause of the Popularity of Novels," 410. It was "worth while to consider whether the events of romantic life are capable of being realized without danger and disappointment."

32. For an explication of dime-novel plots, based upon Libbey's work, see Enstad, *Ladies of Labor*, 70–77.

33. "Laura Jean Libbey Hoped to Achieve Immortality," *New York Times*, November 2, 1924; "Talk About New Books," *Catholic World*, October 1889, 128.

34. "Talk About New Books," 130, 128; Arthur Bostwick, "The Uses of Fiction," *Bulletin of the American Library Association* 1 (January–November 1907): 186–87. Bostwick did add that "it is our duty, as it is our pleasure, to help these people to grow, but we cannot force them and we should not try" (187). On book historians classifying fiction by class, see Sicherman, "Ideologies of Reading," 296–97.

35. "Is the New Novel, 'Miss Middleton's Lover,' Immoral?" *New York Times*, July 26, 1888. The Society Library published its last catalog in 1850, but some of the annual reports later in the nineteenth century include lists of new titles. I found a total of thirteen novels by The Duchess between 1885 and 1896. These were probably reprints of dime novels in hardcover.

36. Melech Epstein, "Pages from My Stormy Life—An Autobiographical Sketch," *American Jewish Archives* 14 (November 1962): 138. Epstein emigrated from Byelorussia in 1913, when he was twenty-four years old. Sophie Ruskay, *Horsecars and Cobblestones* (New York: Beechhurst Press, 1948), 64. Available online in North American Immigrant Letters, Diaries, and Oral Histories. Ruskay

was born in New York in 1893. Her parents were Russian immigrants. Many immigrants during this period were Jews from Eastern Europe. See Sicherman, *Well-Read Lives*, 193–220, on the reading of young Jewish women in New York around the turn of the century.

37. [Rose Pastor], "Something to Read," *Yiddisches Tageblatt*, July 10, 1903; [Rose Pastor], "Just Between Ourselves, Girls," *Yiddisches Tageblatt*, July 12, 1903. Enstad explores attitudes about the uses of reading among labor leaders and female garment workers in New York in *Ladies of Labor*, 49–60.

38. George Watson Cole, "Fiction in Libraries: A Plea for the Masses," *Library Journal* 19 (1894): 20.

39. Sicherman, "Reading and Middle-Class Identity," 138. See also, for example, Sicherman, "Ideology of Reading," 295; Long, *Book Clubs*; and Radway, *Reading the Romance*.

40. "Libbey Hoped to Achieve Immortality," 11.

Bibliography

Selected Primary Sources

MANUSCRIPT COLLECTIONS

American Bible Society Archives.

New-York Historical Society. Official Papers of the New-York Historical Society

New-York Historical Society. John Pintard Papers.

New York Public Library. Manuscripts and Archives Division. Record Group 1, Astor Library.

New York Public Library. Manuscripts and Archives Division. Record Group 2, Lenox Library.

New York Public Library. Manuscripts and Archives Division. Record Group 3, Tilden Trust.

New York Public Library. Manuscripts and Archives Division. Record Group 4, Free Circulating Libraries.

New York Public Library. Manuscripts and Archives Division. Record Group 5, New York Public Library Board of Trustees.

New York Public Library. Manuscripts and Archives Division. Record Group 6, New York Public Library Central Administration.

New York Society Library Archives.

NEWSPAPERS

New York American

New York Commercial Advertiser

New York Daily Tribune

New York Herald

New York Post

New York Sun

New York Times

New York World

SERIAL PUBLICATIONS

Annual Report of the American Bible Society (title varies)

Annual Report of the General Society of Mechanics and Tradesmen (title varies)

Annual Report of the Trustees of the Cooper Union (title varies)
Bulletin of the New York Public Library
Annual Report of the Trustees of the New York Society Library
Collections of the New-York Historical Society for the Year . . .
East Side House Report for . . . (title varies)
First Annual Report of the Aguilar Free Library (1889), et seq.
First Annual Report of the Trustees of the Cooper Union for the Advancement of Science and Art, et seq.
First Annual Report of the Mercantile Library Association (1821), et seq. (title varies)
First Annual Report of the New York Free Circulating Library (1880), et seq.
Proceedings of the New-York Historical Society for the Year . . .

BOOKS AND PAMPHLETS

Adams, Charles F., Jr. *The Public Library and the Common Schools: Three Papers on Educational Topics.* Boston: Estes and Lauriat, 1879.
Address to the Citizens of New-York, on the Claims of Columbia College and the New University, to their Patronage. New York: n.p., 1830.
Addresses Delivered upon the Occasion of the Opening of the Free Academy, January 27, 1849. New York: Wm. C. Bryant, 1849.
Aguilar Free Library. *Fiction List of the Aguilar Free Library.* New York: Aguilar Free Library, 1885.
Alexander, James. *A Brief Narrative of the Case and Trial of John Peter Zenger, Printer of the New York Weekly Journal,* edited by Stanley Nider Katz. Cambridge, Mass.: Belknap Press of Harvard University Press, 1972.
American Bible Society. *Bible Agents Guide.* New York: American Bible Society, 1860.
———. *Catalogue of Books Contained in the Library of the American Bible Society, Embracing Editions of the Holy Scriptures in Various Languages, and Other Biblical and Miscellaneous Works.* New York: American Bible Society, 1863.
———. *Catalogue of the Editions of the Holy Scriptures in Various Languages, and Other Biblical Works, in the Library of the American Bible Society.* New York: Daniel Fanshaw, 1837.
———. *Constitution of the American Bible Society . . . together with their Address to the People of the United States.* New York: G. F. Hopkins, 1816.
———. *Proceedings of a Meeting . . . of the American Bible Society . . . with the Speeches. . . .* New York: J. Seymour, 1816.
American Library Association. *Survey of Libraries in the United States.* Chicago: American Library Association, 1927.
Barnum, P. T. *The Colossal P. T. Barnum Reader: Nothing Else Like It in the Universe,* edited by James W. Cook. Urbana: University of Illinois Press, 2005.

[Beach, Moses Yale, comp.]. *Wealth and Biography of the Wealthy Citizens of New York City: Comprising an Alphabetical Arrangement of Persons Estimated to be Worth $100,000 and Upwards*, 5th ed. New York: New York Sun, 1845; repr., New York: Arno Press, 1973.

Benedict, Erastus C. *An Address Delivered at the First Anniversary of the Free Academy of the City of New York.* New York: Associate Alumni of the College, 1850.

Bigelow, John. *The Life of Samuel J. Tilden.* New York: Harper & Bros., 1895.

Billings, John Shaw. *Selected Papers of John Shaw Billings.* Compiled by Frank Bradway Rogers. Philadelphia: Medical Library Association, 1965.

Board of Education of the City of New York. *Report on the Organization of the Free Academy.* New York: Board of Education, 1851.

Bostwick, Arthur E. *The American Public Library.* New York: D. Appleton & Co., 1910.

———. *A Life with Men and Books.* New York: H. W. Wilson, 1939.

Bray, Thomas. *Apostolick Charity, Its Nature and Excellence Considered, in a Discourse . . . Preached at St. Paul's, Decemb. 19, 1697. . . .* London: W. Downing, 1698.

———. *Bibliotheca Parochialis: Or, a Scheme of such Theological Heads both General and Particular, as Are More Peculiarly Requisite to be Well Studied by Every Pastor of a Parish, Together with A Catalogue of Books which May be Read upon each of those Points, Part I.* London: E. Holt, 1697. Reprinted in *Rev. Thomas Bray: His Life and Selected Works Relating to Maryland*, edited by Bernard C. Steiner. Baltimore: Maryland Historical Society, 1901; repr., New York: Arno Press, 1972.

———. *An Essay Towards Promoting All Necessary and Useful Knowledge, Both Divine and Human, In All the Parts of His Majesty's Dominions, Both at Home and Abroad.* London: E. Holt, 1697. Reprinted in ibid..

———. *Several Circular Letters to the Clergy of Maryland, Subsequent to Their Late Visitation, to Enforce Such Resolutions as Were Taken Therein.* London: William Downing, 1701. Reprinted in ibid.

Brodhead, John Romeyn. *Addresses of John Romeyn Brodhead, esq., and His Excellency, Gov. Horatio Seymour, Delivered before the Clinton Hall Association and Mercantile Library Association at their Celebration, Commemorative of the Removal of the Library to Astor Place.* New York: Nesbit & Co., 1854.

Brodhead, John Bromeyn, ed. *Documents Relative to the Colonial History of the State of New York*, 15 vols. New York: Parsons, Weeds, 1856.

Butler, Nicholas Murray. *Across the Busy Years: Recollections and Reflections.* New York: Scribner's, 1939.

Carnegie, Andrew. *The Autobiography of Andrew Carnegie.* New York: Houghton Mifflin, 1920; repr., Boston: Northeastern University Press, 1986.

———. *The Gospel of Wealth and Other Timely Essays.* Edited by Edward C. Kirkland. Cambridge, Mass.: Belknap Press of Harvard University Press, 1962.

———. *Miscellaneous Writings of Andrew Carnegie.* Edited by Burton J. Hendrick. New York: Doubleday & Co., 1933; repr., Freeport, N.Y.: Books for Libraries Press, 1968.

———. *Triumphant Democracy or Fifty Years' March of the Republic.* New York: Charles Scribner's Sons, 1886.

Catalogue of the Irving Circulating Library, 120 Nassau Street, Conducted by William H. Attree. New York: n.p., 1842.

Cathedral Library Association. *Author and Title Catalog of the Cathedral Free Library of New York.* New York: Cathedral Library Association, 1899. (In Record Group 4, New York Public Library Manuscripts and Archives Division.)

———. *Statement of the Position of the Cathedral Library with Reference to the Proposed Action of the City of New York in the Matter of the Carnegie Library Proposition.* New York: Cathedral Library Association, [1901]. (In Record Group 4, New York Public Library Manuscripts and Archives Division.)

Clinton, DeWitt. *An Account of Abimelech Coody and the Other Celebrated Writers of New York: In a Letter from a Traveller to His Friend in South Carolina, January 1815.* New York: privately printed, 1815.

Cogswell, Joseph Green. *Life of Joseph Green Cogswell as Sketched in His Letters.* Cambridge, Mass.: Riverside Press, 1874.

Columbia University School of Library Service. *School of Library Economy of Columbia College: Documents for a History.* New York: School of Library Service, 1937.

Common Council of the City of New York. *Minutes of the Common Council of the City of New York, 1784–1831,* 19 vols. New York: Common Council of the City of New York, 1917.

Cooper Jr., Henry S. F. and Jenny Lawrence, eds. *The New York Society Library: 250 Years.* New York: New York Society, 2004.

Cosenza, Mario Emilio. *The Establishment of College of the City of New York as the Free Academy in 1847, Townsend Harris, Founder: A Chapter in the History of Education.* New York: Alumni Association of the College, 1925.

De Peyster, Frederic. *The Moral and Intellectual Influence of Libraries upon Social Progress.* New York: New-York Historical Society, 1866.

de Toqueville, Alexis. *Democracy in America.* Edited by J. P. Mayer. Garden City, N.Y.: Anchor Books, 1969 [1835].

Dewey, Melvil. *Librarianship as a Profession for College-Bred Women: An Address Delivered Before the Association of College Alumnae.* Boston: Library Bureau, 1886.

Dodge, William E. *Old New York, A Lecture.* New York: Dodd, Mead & Co., 1880.

Dwight, Henry Otis. *The Centennial History of the American Bible Society.* New York: Macmillan, 1916.

Earle, Thomas, and Charles T. Congdon. *Annals of the General Society of Mechanics and Tradesmen of the City of New York, from 1785 to 1880*. New York: General Society of Mechanics and Tradesmen, 1882.

Ferris, Isaac. *Address Delivered at a Meeting of Young Men, Convened for the Formation of the Young Men's Christian Association*. New York: Theo. H. Gray, 1852.

Foord, John. *The Life and Public Services of Andrew Haswell Green*. Garden City, N.Y.: D. D. Page and Co., 1913.

Francis, John W. *New York During the Last Half Century: A Discourse in Commemoration of the Fifty-Third Anniversary of the New York Historical Society, and the Dedication of Their New Edifice*. New York: John F. Trow, 1857.

Gaillard, Edwin White. *To the Teachers, From the Library*. New York: East Side House, 1900. (In Record Group 4, New York Public Library Manuscripts and Archives Division.)

Garrison, Fielding H. *John Shaw Billings: A Memoir*. New York: G. P. Putnam's Sons, 1915.

General Society of Mechanics and Tradesmen. *Catalogue of the Apprentices' and De Milt Libraries, New-York*. New York: John W. Amerman, 1855.

———. *Catalogue of the Apprentices' Library for the Years 1833–34, Instituted by the Society of Mechanics and Tradesmen of the City of New-York*. New York: E. B. Clayton, 1833.

———. *Catalogue of the Apprentices' Library in New-York, Established and Supported by the General Society of Mechanics and Tradesmen*. New York: A. W. King, 1865.

———. *Catalogue of the Apprentices' Library, Instituted by the Society of Mechanics and Tradesmen of the City of New-York*. New York: William A. Mercein, 1820.

———. *Charter and Bye-Laws of the General Society of Mechanics and Tradesmen*. New York: General Society of Mechanics and Tradesmen, 1798.

———. *Finding List of the Apprentices' Library Established and Maintained by the General Society of Mechanics and Tradesmen of the City of New York*. New York: J. J. Little & Co., 1888.

———. *Report of the Special Committee . . . to Whom was Referred the Resolution for Extending the Usefulness of that Institution. Also the Annual Reports for 1830 of the Library and School Committees*. New York: Wm. A. Mercein, 1831.

———. *Some Memorials of the Late William Wood, Esq., the Eminent Philanthropist, with Resolutions of Respect for his Memory*. New York: General Society of Mechanics and Tradesmen, 1858.

Gilge, Paul A., and Howard B. Rock, eds. *Keepers of the Revolution: New Yorkers at Work in the Early Republic*. Ithaca, N.Y.: Cornell University Press, 1992.

Gourlie, John H. *An Address Delivered Before the Mercantile Library Association at its Eighteenth Annual Meeting January 8, 1839 Embodying a History of the Association*. New York: James Van Norden, 1839.

Griscom, John. *Memoir of John Griscom . . . Compiled from an Autobiography and Other Sources.* New York: Robert Carter and Brothers, 1859.

———. *Monitorial Instruction: An Address Pronounced at the Opening of the New-York High-School, with Notes and Illustrations.* New York: Mahlon Day, 1825.

Hone, Philip. *The Diary of Philip Hone, 1828–1852,* edited by Allan Nevins. New York: Dodd, Mead, and Co., 1936.

Irving, Washington. *A History of New York.* Complete Works of Washington Irving 7, edited by Michael L. Black and Nancy B. Black. Boston: Twayne, 1984.

Jewett, Charles C. *Notices of Public Libraries in the United States of America.* Washington, D.C.: Printed for the House of Representatives, 1851.

Joeckel, Carleton Bruns. *The Government of the American Public Library.* Chicago: University of Chicago Press, 1935.

Jones, William A. *The College Library: An Article Originally Published in the University Quarterly, January, 1861.* New York: Columbia College, 1861.

Journal of the Proceedings of a Convention of Literary and Scientific Gentlemen Held in the Common Council Chamber of the City of New York, October, 1830. New York: Jonathan Leavitt and G. & C. & H. Carvill, 1831.

Keep, Austin Baxter. *History of the New York Society Library, with an Introductory Chapter on Libraries in Colonial New York, 1698–1776.* New York: De Vinne Press, 1908.

Klein, Milton M., ed. *The Independent Reflector or Weekly Essays on Sundry Important Subjects More Particularly adapted to the Province of New-York By William Livingston and Others.* Cambridge, Mass.: Harvard University Press, 1963.

Laight, Edward W. et al. *Statement of the Trustees of the New-York Society Library.* n.p.: [1838].

———. *To the Shareholders of the New-York Society Library.* n.p.: 1835.

Libbey, Laura Jean. *That Pretty Young Girl.* New York: American News Company, 1889.

Library Meeting at the Union League Club, Jan. 20, 1882. Appended to: New York Free Circulating Library, *Third Annual Report of the New York Free Circulating Library, 1881–1882.* New York: New York Free Circulating Library, 1882.

Lord, Daniel. *An Address Delivered on the Opening of the Rooms of the New-York Young Men's Christian Association, September 20th, 1852.* New York: Theo. H. Gray, 1852.

Lydenberg, Harry Miller. *History of the New York Public Library: Astor, Lenox and Tilden Foundations.* New York: New York Public Library, 1923.

MacMullen, John. *A Lecture on the Past, Present and Future of the New-York Society Library.* New York: John F. Trow, 1856.

Martin, Henry A. *Goulding's Business Directory of New York, Brooklyn, Newark, Paterson, Jersey City, Hoboken and Elizabeth.* New York: L. G. Goulding, 1873.

McCabe, James D. Jr. *Great Fortunes and How They Were Made; or the Struggles and Triumphs of Our Self-Made Men.* Philadelphia: Maclean, 1870; repr., Freeport, N.Y.: Books for Libraries Press, 1972.

———. *New York by Gaslight: A Work Descriptive of the Great American Metropolis.* Philadelphia: Hubbard Brothers, 1882. Reprint, New York: Greenwich House, 1984.

McMahon, Joseph H. *Final Report of the Director of the Cathedral Free Circulating Library.* New York: Cathedral Library Association, 1905. (In Record Group 4, New York Public Library Manuscripts and Archives Division.)

Mercantile Library Association of the City of New York. *Catalogue of the Books Belonging to the Mercantile Library Association of the City of New York.* New York: Hopkins & Morris, 1825.

———. *The Constitution, Rules, Regulations, &c., of the Mercantile Library Association, Clinton Hall, New-York.* New York: Mercantile Library Association, 1836.

———. *Report of the Board of Directors of the Mercantile Library Association on a Systematic Plan of Instruction by Lectures.* New York: Hunt's Merchants' Magazine, 1843.

———. *Systematic Catalogue of the Books in the Collection of the Mercantile Library Association of the City of New York.* New York: Harper & Brothers, 1837.

———. *To the Honourable the Legislature of the State of New York; The Memorial of the New-York Historical Society.* New York: Mercantile Library Association, 1827.

Meyer, Annie Nathan. *Barnard Beginnings.* Boston: Houghton Mifflin, 1935.

Morgan, John I., and Evert A. Bancker. *Address of the Trustees of the New York Historical Society, to the Members of the Society, Relative to the Management and Present Condition of that Institution.* n.p., 1833.

Morgan, John I. et al. *To the Members of the New-York Society Library.* n.p. [1838].

Morse, Verranus. *An Analytical Sketch of the Young Men's Christian Association's in North America from 1851 to 1876.* New York: International Committee of the Young Men's Christian Associations, 1901.

New York Free Circulating Library. *Catalogue of the New York Free Circulating Library, Bond Street Branch, English Books.* New York: New York Free Circulating Library, 1892.

———. *Library Meeting at the Union League Club, Jan. 20, 1886.* New York: New York Free Circulating Library, 1886.

———. *Twenty-First and Final Report of the New York Circulating Library, with a Sketch of Its History.* New York: New York Free Circulating Library, 1900.

New-York Historical Society. *The Charter and By-Laws of the New-York Historical Society.* New York: New-York Historical Society, 1846.

———. *Proceedings of the New York Historical Society at the Dedication of the Library, Tuesday, November 3, 1857.* New York: New-York Historical Society, 1857.

———. *To the Honourable the Legislature of the State of New York; The Memorial of the New-York Historical Society.* New York: New-York Historical Society, 1827.

New York Library Club. *Libraries of Greater New York, Manual and Historical Sketch of the New York Library Club.* New York: n.p., 1902.

New-York Lyceum. *New-York Lyceum.* New York: s.n., 1840. (Available in Readex, American Broadsides [438040095]).

New York Public Library. *Correspondence Relating to the Question of a Consolidation of Free Circulating Libraries with the New York Public Library.* New York, 1900.

———. *Facts for the Public.* New York: New York Public Library, 1911.

———. *Results Not Shown by Statistics in the Work of the Public Libraries of Greater New York.* New York: New York Public Library, 1910.

New York Society Library. *Alphabetical and Analytical Catalogue of the New-York Society Library with the Charter, By-Laws, etc., of the Institution.* New York: James Van Norden, 1838.

———. *Alphabetical and Analytical Catalogue of the New-York Society Library with the Charter, By-Laws, etc., of the Institution.* New York: R. Craighead, 1850.

———. *A Catalogue of the Books Belonging to the New-York Society Library.* New York: H. Gaine, 1758.

———. *The Charter, Bye-Laws, and the Names of the Members of the New-York Society Library: With a Catalogue of the Books Belong to the Said Library.* New York: T. & J. Swords, 1793.

New-York Young Men's Christian Association. *A Memorandum Respecting New-York as a Field for Moral Christian Effort among Young Men.* New York: YMCA, 1866.

Osborne, Joseph. *Prospectus of J. Osborn's Circulating Library (Formerly H. Caritat's).* New York: s.n., 1806.

Pintard, John. *Letters from John Pintard to his Daughter, Eliza Noel Pintard Davidson, 1816–1833.* Edited by Dorothy C. Barck, 4 vols. New York: New York Society, 1940–41.

Plebeian. *Reply to the Manifesto of the Trustees of the City Library.* n.p.: [1833].

Raymond, Rossiter W. *Peter Cooper.* Boston: Houghton Mifflin, 1901.

Renwick, James, et al. *Address from the Committee of the New-York Athenaeum, to the Public.* New York: J. W. Palmer & Co., 1825.

Rhees, William J. *Manual of Public Libraries, Institutions, and Societies in the United States and the British Provinces of North America,* University of Illinois

Graduate School Monograph Series, no. 7. Urbana: University of Illinois Press, 1967 [1859].

Rives, George Lockhart, and Charles Howland Russel, comps. *The New York Public Library, Astor, Lenox, and Tilden Foundations, Book of Charters, Wills, Deeds and Other Official Documents.* New York: New York Public Library, 1905.

Ruskay, Sophie. *Horsecars and Cobblestones.* New York: Beechhurst Press, 1948.

Sedgwick, Catharine Maria. *Means and Ends, or Self-Training.* Boston: Marsh, Capen, Lyon, & Webb, 1839.

Smith, William, Jr. *Historical Memoirs from 16 March 1763 to 9 July 1776 of William Smith.* Edited by William H. W. Sabine. New York: New York Times and the Arno Press, 1956.

———. *Historical Memoirs from 26 August 1778 to 12 November 1783 of William Smith.* Edited by William H.W. Sabine. New York: New York Times and the Arno Press, 1956.

———. *History of the Province of New-York.* Edited by Michael Kammen. Cambridge, Mass.: Harvard University Press, 1972 [1757].

Stevens, Henry. *Recollections of James Lenox and the Formation of His Library.* Revised and elucidated by Victor Hugo Paltsits. New York: New York Public Library, 1951 [1886].

Strickland, William P. *History of the American Bible Society from its Organization to the Present Time.* New York: Harper & Co., 1856.

Strong, George Templeton. *Diary of George Templeton Strong.* Edited by Allan Nevins and Milton Halsey Thomas. 4 vols. New York: Macmillan, 1952.

Tooker, L. Frank. *The Joys and Tribulations of an Editor.* New York: Century Co., 1924.

To the Stock Holders of the New-York Society Library. New York: n.p., 1833.

Truebner, Nicholas. *Bibliographical Guide to American Literature: A Classed List of Books Published in the United States During the Last Forty Years.* Detroit: Gale Research Company, 1969 [1859].

Trumbull, Harriet, and Maria Trumbull. *A Season in New York, 1801: Letters of Harriet and Maria Trumbull,* edited by Helen M. Morgan. Pittsburgh: University of Pittsburgh Press, 1969.

University of the City of New York. *Catalogue of the University of the City of New York, March, 1859.* New York: Hosford, 1859.

Verplanck, Gulian C. *Discourses and Addresses on Subjects of American History, Arts, and Literature.* New York: J. & J. Harper, 1833.

———. *Procès Verbal of the Ceremony of Installation of President of the Historical Society, as It Will Be Performed February 8, 1820.* New York: n.p., 1820.

———. *The Right Moral Influence and Use of Liberal Studies. A Discourse Delivered after the Annual Commencement of Geneva College, August 7th, 1833.* New York: Henry Ludwig, 1833.

[Wainwright, Jonathon Mayhew]. *Considerations Upon the Expediency and Means of Establishing a University in the City of New-York.* New York: Grattan, 1830.

Wheaton, Henry. *An Address Pronounced at the Opening of the New York Athenaeum, December 14, 1824,* 2nd ed. New York: J. W. Palmer, 1825.

Wilson, James Grant. *John Pintard, Founder of the New-York Historical Society: An Address Delivered before the New-York Historical Society, December 3, 1901.* New York: New-York Historical Society, 1902.

Young Men's Christian Association of the City of New York. *Catalogue of the Library of the New-York Young Men's Christian Association, Clinton Hall, Astor Place.* New York: John A. Gray, 1855.

———. *Catalogue of the Library of the Young Men's Christian Association of the City of New York, Circulating Department, July 1900.* New York: YMCA, 1900.

———. *A Selection from the Late Correspondence of the New-York Young Men's Christian Association, Tending to Illustrate Its Mode of Working and Show Its Efficiency.* New York: YMCA, 1866.

Zachos, J. C. *A Sketch of the Early Days and Business Life of Peter Cooper.* New York: Cooper Union, 1877.

ARTICLES

"The A.L.A. Co-operation Committee's Report on Exclusion." *Library Journal* 7 (February 1882): 28–29.

"Andrew Carnegie at Home." *Current Literature* 23 (March 1898): 221–22.

"Another Astor Place Riot." *New York Times,* July 24, 1855.

"The Astor Library." *Critic,* December 17, 1881, 358.

"Astor Library." *Gleason's Pictorial Drawing-Room Companion,* January 28, 1854, 61.

"The Astor Stumbling-Block." *Critic,* April 22, 1882, 114.

"At a Meeting of the Subscribers to the Mercantile Library Association." *National Advocate for the Country,* November 27, 1820.

"At the Astor Library." *Library Journal* 15 (January 1890): 20–21.

Bassett, James. "Libraries of New York, First Article." *Frank Leslie's Popular Monthly,* January 1894, 20–28.

Bigelow, John. "The Tilden Trust Library: What Shall It Be?" *Scribner's,* September 1892, 287–300.

Billings, John Shaw. "The Organization of the New York Public Library." *Library Journal* 26 (Conference Proceedings 1901): 215–17.

———. "The Public Library: Its Uses to the Municipality." *Library Journal* 28 (June 1903): 203–4.

———. "Public Library Systems of Greater New York." *Library Journal* 36 (October 1911): 489–92.

———. "Some Library Problems of To-Morrow: Address of the President." *Library Journal* 27 (Conference Proceedings 1902): 1–10.

"A Book Lover's Memories: Some Reminiscences by Librarian Frederick Saunders." *New York Times,* July 18, 1895.

Bostwick, Arthur. "Do Readers Read?" *Library Journal* (November 1901): 805–6.

———. "The Duties and Qualifications of Assistants in Open-Shelf Libraries." *Library Journal* 25 (Conference Proceedings 1900): 40–41.

———. "Experiment on a New Method of Stating Circulation." *Library Journal* 21 (March 1896): 96–98.

———. "The Purchase of Current Fiction." *Library Journal* 28 (July 1903): 31–33.

———. "The Uses of Fiction." *Bulletin of the American Library Association* 1 (January–November 1907): 183–87.

Bostwick, Arthur E., W. A. Bardwell, and Wilberforce Eames. "What Should Librarians Read?" *Library Journal* 25 (February 1900): 57–61.

Bowker, R. R. "Libraries and the Library Problem in 'Greater New York.'" *Library Journal* (March 1886): 99–100.

"A Brief Sketch of These Periodical Works Commonly Called Magazines; with a Short Biographical Account of Their Projector Mr. Edward Cave." *New York Magazine and General Repository of Useful Knowledge,* May 1, 1814, 5–8.

Bristed, C. A. "The Astor Library and Its Founder's Fortune." *New York Times,* October 3, 1869.

Canfield, James H. "The Library." In *History of Columbia University, 1754–1904,* edited by Brander Matthews et al., 427–42. New York: Macmillan, 1904.

Caritat, Hocquet. "General Defense of Modern Novels." In *Explanatory Catalogue of H. Caritat's Circulating Library, No. 1 City Hotel, Broadway, New York,* 149–58. New York: G & R Waite, 1804.

Childe, Cromwell. "Odd Characters Seen at the Astor Library." *New York Times: Illustrated Magazine Supplement,* September 25, 1898.

"City's $29,000,000 Library Is Opened," *New York Times,* May 24, 1911.

Coe, Ellen M. "Common Novels in Public Libraries." *Library Journal* 19 (December 1894): 23–24.

———. "Fiction." *Library Journal* 18 (July 1893): 250–51.

———. "The Relation of Libraries to Public Schools." *Library Journal* 17 (June 1892): 193–94.

———. "What Can Be Done to Help a Boy to Like Good Books after He has Fallen into the 'Dime Novel Habit.'" *Library Journal* 20 (April 1895): 118–19.

Cogswell, Joseph Green. "The Astor Library: A Letter from Dr. Cogswell." *Home Journal,* January 7, 1854.

———. "Resources of the Astor Library." *New York Times,* September 22, 1858.

Cohen, Max. "The Librarian an Educator, and not a Cheap-John." *Library Journal* 13 (December 1888): 366–67.

Cole, George Watson. "Fiction in Libraries: A Plea for the Masses." *Library Journal* 19 (Conference Proceedings 1894): 18–20.

"Correspondence: The Columbia College Library." *Literary World* (May 15, 1886), 169.

Dewey, Melvil. "Conference a Success." *American Library Journal* (November 1876): 90.

———. "Development of College Libraries." *Library Journal* 2 (October 1877): 63.

———. "The Ideal Librarian." *Library Journal* 24 (January 1899): 14.

———. "The New Library Regulations." *School of Mines Quarterly* 5 (November 1883): 66–70.

"Dr. Cogswell and the Astor Library." *New York Times,* September 22, 1858.

[Dunne, Finley Peter]. "The Carnegie Libraries." in *Dissertations by Mr. Dooley* (New York: Harper & Co., 1906), 177–81.

D[uyckinck], E. A. "Literary Prospects of 1845." *American Review: A Whig Journal of Politics, Literature, Art and Science* 1 (February 1845): 146–51.

Eames, Wilberforce. "The Lenox Library and Its Founder." *Library Journal* 24 (May 1899): 199–201.

Eggleston, Allegra. "Plea for the Maimonides Library." *New York Times,* February 23, 1906.

Elmendorf, Henry L. "Public Library Books in Public Schools." *Library Journal* 25 (April 1900): 163–65.

Epstein, Melech. "Pages from My Stormy Life—An Autobiographical Sketch." *American Jewish Archives* 14 (November 1962): 129–74.

"Five Millions for the New York Public Library from Andrew Carnegie." *Library Journal* 26 (March 1901): 133–134.

Gaillard, Edwin White. "An Extension of the Picture Bulletin." *Library Journal* (December 1901): 874–75.

———. "The Outcome of the Picture Bulletin." *Library Journal* (April 1901): 192–93.

Giddings, H. F. "Relation of Sociology to Other Scientific Studies." *Journal of Social Sciences* 32 (November 1894): 144–49.

Gourlie, John H. "On the Benefits and Influences of Commerce." In *Lectures Delivered Before the Mercantile Library Association, Clinton Hall.* New York: The Association, 1836.

Hone, Philip. "Commerce and Commercial Character." *Merchants' Magazine and Commercial Review,* February 1841, 129–47.

"Is the New Novel, 'Miss Middleton's Lover,' Immoral?" *New York Times,* July 26, 1888.

"Judaism in New-York." *New York Times,* January 23, 1887.

"Laura Jean Libbey Hoped to Achieve Immortality." *New York Times,* November 2, 1924.

Lector [pseud.]. "The Astor Library." *New York Times,* April 18, 1854.

Leipziger, Pauline. "Picture Bulletins and their Use in the Aguilar Free Library." *Library Journal* 24 (June 1899): 257–58.

"The Lenox Library." *Harper's Bazaar,* September 16, 1893, 759–60.

Lord, Daniel. "Popular Principles Relating to the Law of Agency." *Merchants' Magazine and Commercial Review* (October 1839): 325–39.

Moore, Annie Carroll. "Library Membership as a Civic Force." *Library Journal* 33 (July 1908): 269–70.

"New York Historical Society." *John Donkey.* January 29, 1848, 5.

"New York Library Club, Fifteenth Regular Meeting [discussion of 'How Far Should Reading Be Controlled in Libraries?']." *Library Journal* 14 (March 1889): 93–94.

"The New York Mercantile Library." *Scribner's Monthly,* February 1871, 353–68.

"The New York Public Library and the Cathedral Library." *Library Journal* 26 (May 1901): 276–77.

Norton, Frank H. "The Astor Library." *Galaxy: A Magazine of Entertaining Reading,* April 1869, 527–38.

"N.Y.L.A. and N.Y.L.C. [Report on Traveling Libraries]." *Library Journal* 21 (January 1896): 24–25.

"On the Cause of the Popularity of Novels." *Literary Magazine, and American Register* (June 1807): 410–12.

Pastor, Rose. "Just Between Ourselves, Girls." *Yiddisches Tageblatt,* July 12, 1903.

———. "Something to Read." *Yiddisches Tageblatt,* July 10, 1903.

Perkins, Frederic Beecher. "Public Libraries and the Public." In *Library and Society,* edited by Arthur Bostwick. New York: H. W. Wilson, 1921; repr., Freeport, N.Y.: Books for Libraries, 1968.

Plummer, Mary Wright. "The Work for Children in Free Libraries." *Library Journal* 22 (November 1897): 679–86.

Poe, Edgar Allan. "Literati of New York City—No. V." *Godey's Magazine and Lady's Book,* September 1846, 126–32.

Poole, R. B. "Fiction in Association Libraries." *Young Men's Era.* April 30, 1891, 280.

———. "Fiction in Libraries." *Library Journal* 16 (January 1891): 8–10.

———. "The Librarian and His Constituents." *Library Journal* 11 (August/September 1886): 229–32.

———. "Selection of Books, No. 2." *Watchman,* July 1, 1877, 5.

"A Practical Philanthropist." *New York Times,* April 5, 1883.

"Proceedings at the Opening of the New Building of the New York Public Library, Astor Lenox and Tilden Foundations," *Bulletin of the New York Public Library* 15 (June 1911): 327–48.

Rathbone, Josephine A. "Cooperation between Libraries and Schools: An Historical Sketch." *Library Journal* 26 (April 1901): 187–91.

"Review of New Publications. The Pirate. . . ." *Christian Observer,* March 1822, 157–72; April 1822, 237–50.

Rutter, Robert. "Mr. Carnegie and the Society of Mechanics and Tradesmen." *New York Times,* March 22, 1902.

Saunders, Frederick. "Our Metropolitan Library." *Independent,* August 12, 1875, 3–4.

Schoolcraft, Henry Rowe. "The Literary and Scientific Institutions of Europe." Official Papers of the New-York Historical Society, Box 6, New-York Historical Society Library, New York.

Schwartz, Jacob. "Business Methods in Libraries." *Library Journal* 13 (November 1888): 333–34.

———. "The Librarian as Educator, Mr. John [*sic*] Schwartz Replies to Mr. Cohen." *Library Journal* 14 (January–February 1889): 5–6.

"Shall We Have a Public Library?" *New York Times,* February 26, 1871.

"A Study of the New York Circulating Library." *Library Journal* 11 (May 1886): 142–43.

A Subscriber to the New-York Society Library. "On the Utility of Public Libraries." *New-York Magazine; or, Literary Repository* (June 1791): 307–9.

"Talk About New Books." *Catholic World* (October 1889): 123–31.

"The Thinker: Fictitious Reading." *New York Evangelist* 12, July 10, 1841, 112.

"Topics Astir: The Astor Library." *Home Journal,* January 21, 1854, 2.

"Travelling Libraries: A Symposium." *Public Libraries* 2 (January 1897): 47–51, 54–55.

"What Shall We Do with Our Young Women." *Harper's Bazaar,* October 25, 1884, 679.

Williamson, Hugh. "A Discourse on the Benefits of Civil History." In *Collections of the New-York Historical Society for the Year 1814,* 23–36. New York: New-York Historical Society, 1814.

Secondary Sources

BOOKS AND DISSERTATIONS

Appleby, Joyce. *Liberalism and Republicanism in the Historical Imagination.* Cambridge, Mass.: Harvard University Press, 1992.

Appleby, Joyce, Lynn Hunt, and Margaret Jacob. *Telling the Truth about History.* New York: Norton, 1994.

Augst, Thomas. *Clerk's Tale: Young Men and Moral Life in Nineteenth-Century America.* Chicago: University of Chicago Press, 2003.

Bailyn, Bernard. *Ideological Origins of the American Revolution.* Cambridge, Mass.: Harvard University Press, 1967.

Bayless, Pamela. *The YMCA at 150: A History of the YMCA of Greater New York, 1852–2002.* New York: YMCA, 2002.

Beckert, Sven. *Monied Metropolis: New York City and the Consolidation of the American Bourgeoisie, 1850–1896.* Cambridge, Mass.: Harvard University Press, 2001.

Bender, Thomas. *New York Intellect: A History of Intellectual Life in New York City, from 1750 to the Beginnings of Our Own Times.* New York: Knopf, 1987.

———. *Toward an Urban Vision: Ideas and Institutions in Nineteenth-Century America.* Lexington: University Press of Kentucky, 1975.

Blackmar, Elizabeth, and Roy Rosenzweig. *The Park and the People: A History of Central Park.* Ithaca, N.Y.: Cornell University Press, 1992.

Blumin, Stuart M. *The Emergence of the Middle Class: Social Experience in the American City, 1760–1900.* Cambridge: Cambridge University Press, 1989.

Boyd, William Douglas, Jr. "Books for Young Businessmen: Mercantile Libraries in the United States, 1820–1865." PhD diss., Indiana University, 1975.

Boyer, Paul S. *Urban Masses and Moral Order in America, 1820–1920.* Cambridge, Mass.: Harvard University Press, 1978.

Bremmer, Robert. *American Philanthropy,* 2nd ed. Chicago: University of Chicago Press, 1988.

Brown, Richard D. *Knowledge Is Power: The Diffusion of Information in Early America, 1700–1865.* New York: Oxford University Press, 1989.

———. *The Strength of a People: The Idea of an Informed Citizenry in America.* Chapel Hill: University of North Carolina Press, 1996.

Burrows, Edwin G., and Mike Wallace. *Gotham: A History of New York City to 1898.* New York: Oxford University Press, 1999.

Calhoun, Craig, ed. *Habermas and the Public Sphere.* Cambridge, Mass.: Harvard University Press, 1992.

Callcott, George H. *History in the United States, 1800–1860: Its Practice and Purpose.* Baltimore: Johns Hopkins University Press, 1970.

Carrier, Esther Jane. *Fiction in Public Libraries, 1876–1900.* New York: Scarecrow Press, 1965.

Chapman, Carleton B. *Order out of Chaos: John Shaw Billings and America's Coming of Age.* Boston: Boston Medical Library, 1994.

Chute, Marchette. *The First Liberty: A History of the Right to Vote in America.* New York: Dutton, 1969.

Cliff, Nigel. *The Shakespeare Riots: Revenge, Drama, and Death in Nineteenth-Century America.* New York: Random House, 2007.

Cloward, Richard A. and Frances Fox Piven. *Regulating the Poor: The Functions of Public Welfare.* New York: Pantheon Books, 1971.

Coon, Horace. *Columbia: Colossus on the Hudson.* New York: Dutton, 1947.

Cornog, Evan. *The Birth of Empire: DeWitt Clinton and the American Experience.* New York: Oxford University Press, 1998.

Creighton, Lacy. *The Word-Carrying Giant: The Growth of the American Bible Society (1816–1966).* South Pasadena, Calif.: William Carey Library, 1977.

Cremin, Lawrence A. *American Education: The Metropolitan Experience, 1876–1980.* New York: Harper & Row, 1988.

Dain, Phyllis. *The New York Public Library: A History of Its Founding and Early Years.* New York: New York Public Library, 1972.

Dawley, Alan. *Class and Community: The Industrial Revolution in Lynn.* Cambridge, Mass.: Harvard University Press, 1976.

Denning, Michael. *Mechanic Accents: Dime Novels and Working-Class Culture in America.* New York: Verso, 1987.

Dillon, Dorothy Rita. *The New York Triumvirate: A Study of the Legal and Political Careers of William Livingston, John Morin Scott, and William Smith, Jr.* New York: Columbia University Press, 1949.

Ditzion, Sidney. *Arsenals of a Democratic Culture: A Social History of the American Public Library Movement in New England and the Middle States from 1850 to 1900.* Chicago: American Library Association, 1947.

Douglas, Ann. *The Feminization of American Culture.* New York: Avon Books, 1977.

Douglas, George H. *The Golden Age of the Newspaper.* Westport, Conn.: Greenwood, 1999.

Dunlap, Leslie W. *American Historical Societies, 1790–1860.* Madison, Wisc.: Cantell, 1944.

Enstad, Nan. *Ladies of Labor, Girls of Adventure: Working Women, Popular Culture, and Labor Politics at the Turn of the Twentieth Century.* New York: Columbia University Press, 1999.

Faler, Paul G. *Mechanics and Manufacturers in the Early Industrial Revolution: Lynn, Massachusetts, 1780–1860.* Albany: State University of New York Press, 1981.

Flick, Alexander Clarence. *Samuel Jones Tilden: A Study in Political Sagacity.* New York: Dodd, Mead & Co., 1939; repr., Westport, Conn.: Greenwood Press, 1973.

Foster, Edward Halsey. *Catharine Maria Sedgwick.* New York: Twayne, 1974.

Frusciano, Thomas J., and Marilyn H. Petit. *New York University and the City: An Illustrated History.* New Brunswick, N.J.: Rutgers University Press, 1997.

Galchinsky, Michael. *The Origin of the Modern Jewish Woman Writer: Romance and Reform in Victorian England.* Detroit: Wayne State University Press, 1996.

Garrison, Dee. *Apostles of Culture: The Public Librarian and American Society, 1876–1920.* New York: Free Press, 1979; repr. Madison: University of Wisconsin Press, 2003.

Geller, Evelyn. *Forbidden Books in Public Libraries, 1876–1939: A Study in Cultural Change.* Westport, Conn.: Greenwood Press, 1984.

Ginsberg, Lori D. *Women and the Work of Benevolence: Morality, Politics, and Class in the Nineteenth-Century United States.* New Haven, Conn.: Yale University Press, 1990.

Griffin, Clifford S. *Ferment of Reform, 1830–1860.* New York: Thomas Y. Crowell Co., 1967.

———. *Their Brothers' Keepers: Moral Stewardship in the United States, 1800–1865*. New Brunswick, N.J.: Rutgers University Press, 1960.

Haeger, John D. *John Jacob Astor: Business and Finance in the Early Republic.* Detroit: Wayne State University Press, 1991.

Hall, Peter Dobkin. *The Organization of American Culture, 1700–1900: Private Institutions, Elites, and the Origins of American Nationality.* New York: New York University Press, 1982.

Harding, Thomas S. *College Literary Societies: Their Contribution to Higher Education in the United States, 1815–1876.* New York: Pageant Press, 1971.

Harris, Michael. *The Purpose of the American Public Library in Historical Perspective: A Revisionist Interpretation.* (ERIC Document 071668.) Washington, D.C.: ERIC Clearinghouse on Library and Information Science, 1972.

Hartz, Louis. *The Liberal Tradition in America: An Interpretation of American Political Thought since the Revolution.* San Diego: Harcourt Brace Jovanovich, 1991.

Haskell, Thomas L. *The Emergence of Professional Social Science: The American Social Science Association and the Nineteenth-Century Crisis of Authority.* Urbana: University of Illinois Press, 1977.

Horlick, Allan Stanley. *Country Boys and Merchant Princes: The Social Control of Young Men in New York.* Lewisburg, Penn.: Bucknell University Press, 1975.

Howe, Winifred. *A History of the Metropolitan Museum of Art,* 2 vols. New York: Gilliss Press, 1913–1946.

Humphrey, David C. *From Kings College to Columbia, 1746–1800.* New York: Columbia University Press, 1976.

Huntzicker, William. *The Popular Press: 1833–1865.* Westport, Conn.: Greenwood Press, 1999.

Johnson, Paul E. *A Shopkeeper's Millennium: Society and Revivals in Rochester New York, 1815–1837.* New York: Hill & Wang, 1978.

Jones, Plummer Alston, Jr. *Libraries, Immigrants, and the American Experience.* Westport, Conn.: Greenwood Press, 1999.

July, Robert W. *The Essential New Yorker: Gulian Crommelin Verplanck.* Durham, N.C.: Duke University Press, 1951.

Kaestle, Carl F. *The Evolution of an Urban School System: New York City, 1750–1850.* Cambridge, Mass.: Harvard University Press, 1973.

Kaser, David. *A Book for a Sixpence: The Circulating Library in America.* Pittsburgh: Beta Phi Mu, 1980.

Ketchum, Richard M. *Divided Loyalties: How the American Revolution Came to New York.* New York: Henry Holt, 2002.

Klein, Milton M. *The American Whig: William Livingston of New York,* rev. ed. New York: Garland, 1993.

Laugher, Charles T. *Thomas Bray's Grand Design: Libraries of the Church of England in North America, 1695–1785*. Chicago: American Library Association, 1973.

Laurie, Bruce. *Artisans into Workers: Labor in Nineteenth-Century America.* New York: Noonday Press, 1978.

Lester, Robert M. *Forty Years of Carnegie Giving: A Summary of the Benefactions of Andrew Carnegie and of the Philanthropic Trusts which He Created.* New York: Charles Scribner's Sons, 1941.

Levine, Lawrence. *Highbrow/Lowbrow: The Emergence of Cultural Hierarchy in America.* Cambridge, Mass.: Harvard University Press, 1988.

Linderman, Winifred B. "History of the Columbia University Library, 1876–1926." PhD diss., Columbia University, 1959.

Long, Elizabeth. *Book Clubs: Women and the Uses of Reading in Everyday Life.* Chicago: University of Chicago Press, 2003.

Lydenberg, Harry Miller. *John Shaw Billings, Creator of the National Medical Library and Its Catalogue, First Director of the New York Public Library.* Chicago: American Library Association, 1924.

Mack, Edward C. *Peter Cooper: Citizen of New York.* New York: Duell, Sloan and Pearce, 1949.

Madsen, Axel. *John Jacob Astor: America's First Multimillionaire.* New York: John Wiley, 2001.

Mandelbaum, Seymour J. *Boss Tweed's New York.* New York: J. Wiley, 1965.

Martin, Lawrence. *The General Society of Mechanics and Tradesmen of the City of New York.* New York: General Society of Mechanics and Tradesmen, 1960.

Martin, Robert Sidney, ed. *Carnegie Denied: Communities Rejecting Carnegie Library Construction Grants.* Westport, Conn.: Greenwood, 1993.

Mott, Frank Luther. *Golden Multitudes: The Story of Best Sellers in the United States.* New York: Bowker, 1947.

———. *A History of American Magazines, 1741–1850,* 5 vols. Cambridge, Mass.: Harvard University Press, 1930–68.

Nevins, Allan. *Abram S. Hewitt, with Some Account of Peter Cooper.* New York: Harper and Brothers, 1935.

Pandit, Joyoti, Barbara Shupe, and Janet Steins, comps. *New York State Population, 1790–1980: A Compilation of Federal Census Data.* New York: Neal-Schuman Publishers, 1987.

Pawley, Christine, *Reading on the Middle Border: The Culture of Print in Late Nineteenth Century Osage, Iowa.* Amherst: University of Massachusetts Press, 2001.

Pessen, Edward. *Riches and Class before the Civil War.* Lexington, Mass.: D. C. Heath, 1973.

Pfitzer, Gregory M. *Popular History and the Literary Marketplace, 1840–1920.* Boston: University of Massachusetts Press, 2008.

Pocock, J. P. A. *The Machiavellian Moment: Florentine Political Thought and the Atlantic Republican Tradition.* Princeton: Princeton University Press, 1975.

Putnam, William Lowell. *John Peter Zenger and the Fundamental Freedom.* Jefferson, N.C.: McFarland & Co., 1997.

Radway, Janice A. *Reading the Romance: Women, Patriarchy, and Popular Literature.* Chapel Hill: University of North Carolina Press, 1984.

Ranz, Jim. *The Printed Book Catalog in American Libraries, 1723–1900.* Chicago: American Library Association, 1964.

Raven, James. *London Booksellers and American Customers: Transatlantic Literary Community and the Charleston Library Society, 1748–1811.* Columbia: University of South Carolina Press, 2002.

Richards, Pamela Spence. *Scholars and Gentlemen: The Library of the New-York Historical Society, 1804–1982.* Hamden, Conn.: Archon Books, 1984.

Rischin, Moses. *The Promised Land: New York's Jews, 1870–1914.* Cambridge, Mass.: Harvard University Press, 1962.

Rodgers, Daniel T. *Keywords in America Politics since Independence.* New York: Basic Books, 1987.

Roff, Sandra Shoiock, Anthony M. Cucchiara, and Barbara J. Dunlap. *From the Free Academy to CUNY, Illustrating Public Higher Education in New York City, 1847–1997.* New York: Fordham University Press, 2000.

Rudy, S. Willis. *The College of the City of New York: A History, 1847–1947.* New York: Arno Press, 1977.

Russell, William F., ed. *The Rise of a University: The Later Days of Old Columbia College 1.* New York: Columbia University Press, 1937.

Ryan, Nancy P. *Civic Wars: Democracy and Public Life in the American City during the Nineteenth Century.* Berkeley: University of California Press, 1997.

Saxon, A. H. *P. T. Barnum: The Legend and the Man.* New York: Columbia University Press, 1989.

Scott, Anne Firor. *Natural Allies: Women's Associations in American History.* Urbana: University of Illinois Press, 1991.

Sellers, Charles. *The Market Revolution: Jacksonian America, 1815–1846.* New York: Oxford University Press, 1991.

Shera, Jesse H. *Foundations of the Public Library: The Origins of the Public Library Movement in New England.* Chicago: University of Chicago Press, 1949; repr., n.p.: Shoestring Press, 1965, 1949.

Sicherman, Barbara. *Well-Read Lives: How Books Inspired a Generation of American Women.* Chapel Hill: University of North Carolina Press, 2010.

Smith, Edgar F. *John Griscom, 1774–1852: Chemist.* Philadelphia, 1927.

Spalding, C. Sumner. *Peter Cooper: A Critical Biography of His Life and Works.* New York: New York Public Library, 1941.

Steiner, Bernard C. *Rev. Thomas Bray: His Life and Selected Works Relating to Maryland.* Baltimore: Maryland Historical Society, 1901; repr., New York: Arno Press, 1972.

Sterling, David L. "New York Patriarch: A Life of John Pintard, 1759–1844." Ph.D. diss., New York University, 1958.

Stewart, Nathaniel J. "A History of the Library of the College of the City of New York." Master's thesis, College of the City of New York, 1935.

Taylor, George Rogers. *The Transportation Revolution, 1815–1860.* New York: Rinehart, 1951.

Tebbel, John. *A History of Book Publishing in the United States,* 4 vols. New York: R. R. Bowker, 1972–81.

Tompkins, Calvin. *Merchants and Masterpieces: The Story of the Metropolitan Museum of Art,* rev. and updated ed. New York: Henry Holt, 1989.

Trattner, Walter I., ed. *Social Welfare or Social Control? Some Historical Reflections on Regulating the Poor.* Knoxville: University of Tennessee Press, 1983.

Tucker, Louis Leonard. *Clio's Consort: Jeremy Belknap and the Founding of the Massachusetts Historical Society.* Boston: Massachusetts Historical Society, 1990.

Tyler, Alice Felt. *Freedom's Ferment: Phases of American Social History to 1860.* Minneapolis: University of Minnesota Press, 1944.

Vail, R. W. G. *Knickerbocker Birthday: A Sesqui-Centennial History of the New-York Historical Society, 1804–1954.* New York: New-York Historical Society, 1954.

Van Buskirk, Judith L. *Generous Enemies: Patriots and Loyalists in Revolutionary New York.* Philadelphia: University of Pennsylvania Press, 2002.

Van Slyck, Abigail A. *Free to All: Carnegie Libraries & American Culture, 1890–1920.* Chicago: University of Chicago Press, 1995.

Van Tassel, David D. *Recording America's Past: An Interpretation of the Development of Historical Studies in America, 1607–1884.* Chicago: University of Chicago Press, 1960.

Walters, Ronald G. *American Reformers, 1815–1860.* New York: Hill & Wang, 1978.

Wiegand, Wayne A. *Irrepressible Reformer: A Biography of Melvil Dewey.* Chicago: American Library Association, 1996.

Wilentz, Sean. *Chants Democratic: New York City & the Rise of the American Working Class, 1788–1850.* Oxford: Oxford University Press, 1984.

Williams, Patrick. *American Public Library and the Problem of Purpose.* New York: Greenwood Press, 1988.

Williams, Raymond. *Keywords: A Vocabulary of Culture and Society,* rev. ed. New York: Oxford University Press, 1983.

Wood, Gordon S. *The Creation of the American Republic, 1776–1787.* Chapel Hill: University of North Carolina Press, 1969.

———. *The Radicalism of the American Revolution.* New York: Knopf, 1992.

Wosh, Peter J. *Spreading the Word: The Bible Business in Nineteenth-Century America.* Ithaca, N.Y.: Cornell University Press, 1994.

Wright, Lyle H. *American Fiction, 1774–1850: A Contribution Towards a Bibliography,* 2nd rev. ed. San Marino, Calif.: Huntington Library, 1969.

———. *American Fiction, 1851–1875: A Contribution Towards a Bibliography.* San Marino, Calif.: Huntington Library, 1965.

———. *American Fiction, 1876–1900: A Contribution Towards a Bibliography,* 2nd rev. ed. San Marino, Calif.: Huntington Library, 1966.

Zboray, Ronald J. *A Fictive People: Antebellum Economic Development and the American Reading Public.* New York: Oxford University Press, 1993.

ARTICLES

Abel, Albert S. "The Public Corporation in the United States." In *Government Enterprise: A Comparative Study,* edited by W. G. Friedman and J. F. Garner, 181–200. New York: Columbia University Press, 1970.

Aitken, Hugh G. J. "Yates and McIntyre: Lottery Managers." *Journal of Economic History* 13 (Winter 1953): 36–57.

Avallone, Charlene. "Catharine Sedgwick and the Circles of New York." *Legacy* 23 (June 2006): 115–31.

Bennett, Tony. "Culture." In *New Keywords: A Revised Vocabulary of Culture and Society,* edited by Tony Bennett, Lawrence Grossberg, and Meaghan Morris. Malden, Mass.: Blackwell, 2005.

Cole, John Y. "Storehouses and Workshops: American Libraries and the Uses of Knowledge." In *The Organization of Knowledge in Modern America, 1860–1920,* edited by Alexandra Oleson and John Voss, 364–85. Baltimore: Johns Hopkins University Press, 1979.

Coons, Lorraine A., and Peter J. Wosh. "A 'Special Collection' in Nineteenth-Century New York: The American Bible Society and Its Library." *Libraries & Culture* 32 (Summer 1997): 324–36.

Covert, Cathy. "'Passion Is Ye Prevailing Motive': The Feud behind the Zenger Case." *Journalism Quarterly* 50 (Spring 1973): 3–10.

Dain, Phyllis. "Ambivalence and Paradox: The Social Bonds of the Public Library." *LJ: Library Journal* 100 (February 1, 1975): 261–66.

———. "Public Library Governance in a Changing New York City." *Libraries & Culture* 26 (Spring 1991): 219–50.

Diggins, John Patrick. "Republicanism and Progressivism." *American Quarterly* 37 (Autumn 1985): 572–98.

Garrison, Dee. "The Tender Technicians: The Feminization of Public Librarianship, 1876–1905." *Journal of Social History* 6 (Winter 1972): 131–59.

Glynn, Tom. "The Professionalization of a Calling: Mission and Method at the New York Library Club." *Libraries & the Cultural Record* (Fall 2006): 438–61.

Graff, Harvey J. "Literacy, Libraries, Lives: New Social and Cultural Histories." *Libraries and Culture* 26 (Winter 1991): 24–45.

Green, James. "The Rise of Book Publishing." In *A History of the Book in America, vol. 2, An Extensive Republic: Print, Culture, and Society in the New Nation, 1790–1840,* edited by Robert A. Gross and Mary Kelley, 75–127. Chapel Hill: University of North Carolina Press, 2010.

———. "Subscription Libraries and Commercial Circulating Libraries in Colonial Philadelphia and New York." In *Institutions of Reading: The Social Life of Libraries in the United States,* edited by Thomas Augst and Kenneth Carpenter, 53–71. Amherst: University of Massachusetts Press, 2007.

Griffin, Clifford S. "Religious Benevolence as Social Control." *Mississippi Valley Historical Review* 44 (December 1957): 423–44.

Haberly, Lloyd. "The American Museum from Baker to Barnum." *New-York Historical Society Quarterly* 43 (July 1959): 273–80.

Harris, Michael. "The Purpose of the American Public Library: A Revisionist Interpretation of History." *Library Journal* 98 (September 15, 1973): 2509–14.

Haskell, Thomas L. "Capitalism and the Origins of Humanitarian Sensibility, Part I." *American Historical Review* 90 (April 1985): 339–61.

———. "Capitalism and the Origins of Humanitarian Sensibility, Part II." *American Historical Review* 90 (June 1985): 547–66.

Holley, Edward G. "Academic Libraries in 1876." *College & Research Libraries* 37 (January 1976): 15–47.

Kimball, LeRoy E. "The Old University Building and the Society's Years on Washington Square." *New-York Society Quarterly* 32 (July 1948): 149–219.

Kirschner, Don S. "Ambiguous Legacy: Social Justice and Social Control in the Progressive Era." *Historical Reflections* 2 (Summer 1975): 69–88.

Lewis, David W. "The Reformer as Conservative: Protestant Counter-Subversion in the Early Republic." In *The Development of an American Culture,* edited by Stanley Coben and Lorman Ratner, 64–91. Englewood Cliffs, N.J.: Prentice-Hall, 1970.

Megill, Allan. "'Grand Narrative' and the Discipline of History." In *A New Philosophy of History,* edited by Frank Ankersmit and Hans Kellner, 151–73. London: Reaktion Books, 1995.

Nord, David Paul. "The Authority of Truth: Religion and the John Peter Zenger Case." *Journalism Quarterly* 62 (Summer 1985): 227–35.

———. "The Evangelical Origins of Mass Media in America." *Journalism Monographs* 88 (May 1984): 1–30.

Pawley, Christine. "Beyond Market Models and Resistance: Organizations as a Middle Layer in the History of Reading." *Library Quarterly* 79 (January 2009): 73–93.

Pessen, Edward. "Philip Hone's Set: The Social World of the New York City Elite in the 'Age of Egalitarianism.'" *New-York Historical Society Quarterly* 56 (October 1972): 285–308.

Radway, Janice. "Interpretive Communities and Variable Literacies: The Functions of Romance Reading." *Daedalus* 113 (Summer 1984): 49–73.

Reinhold, Meyer. "The Quest for 'Useful Knowledge' in Eighteenth-Century America." *Proceedings of the American Philosophical Society* 119 (April 1975): 108–32.

Rodgers, Daniel T. "Republicanism: The Career of a Concept." *Journal of American History* 79 (June 1992): 11–38.

Scott, Donald M. "The Popular Lecture and the Creation of a Public in Mid–Nineteenth Century America." *Journal of American History* 66 (March 1980): 791–809.

Sicherman, Barbara. "Ideologies and Practices of Reading." In *A History of the Book in America,* vol. 3, *The Industrial Book, 1840–1880,* edited by Scott E. Jasper, Jeffrey D. Groves, Stephen W. Nissenbaum, and Michael Winship, 279–302. Chapel Hill: University of North Carolina Press, 2007.

———. "Reading and Middle-Class Identity in Victorian America: Cultural Consumption, Conspicuous and Otherwise." In *Reading Acts: U.S. Readers' Interactions with Literature, 1800–1950,* edited by Barbara Ryan and Amy M. Thomas, 137–160. Knoxville: University of Tennessee Press, 2002.

Steiner, Bernard C. "Rev. Thomas Bray and His American Libraries." *American Historical Review* (October 1896): 59–75.

Sterling, David L. "William Duer, John Pintard, and the Panic of 1792." In *Business Enterprise in Early New York,* edited by Joseph R. Frese and Jacob Judd, 99–132. Tarrytown, N.Y.: Sleepy Hollow Press, 1979.

Stevenson, Louise L. "Preparing for Public Life: The Collegiate Students at New York University, 1832–1881." In *The University and the City: From Medieval Origins to the Present,* edited by Thomas Bender, 150–80. New York: Oxford University Press, 1988.

Sullivan, Larry E. "Books, Power, and the Development of Libraries in the New Republic: The Prison and Other Journals of John Pintard of New York." *Journal of Library History* 21 (Spring 1986): 407–24.

Tenenbaum, Susan. "The Progressive Legacy and the Public Corporation: Entrepreneurship and Public Virtue." *Journal of Policy History* 3 (November 1991): 309–30.

Van Slyck, Abigail A. "The Lady and the Library Loafer: Gender and Public Space in Victorian America." *Winterthur Portfolio* 31 (Winter 1996): 221–41.

Waugh, Joan. "'Give This Man Work!': Josephine Shaw Lowell, the Charity Organization Society of New York, and the Depression of 1893." *Social Science History* (Summer 2001): 217–46.

Wiebe, Robert H. "The Social Functions of Public Education." *American Quarterly* 21 (Summer 1969): 147–64.

Wiegand, Wayne. "Introduction: 'On the Social Nature of Reading.'" In *Genreflecting: A Guide to Popular Reading Interests*, 6th ed., edited by Wayne Wiegand, 3–14. Westport, Conn.: Libraries Unlimited, 2007.

———. "'Jew Attack': The Story behind Melvil Dewey's Resignation as New York State Librarian in 1905." *American Jewish History* 83 (September 1985): 359–79.

Wilentz, Sean. "Artisan Republican Festivals and the Rise of Class Consciousness in New York City, 1788–1837." In *Working-Class America: Essays on Labor, Community, and American Society*, edited by Michael H. Frisch and Daniel J. Walkowitz, 37–77. Urbana: University of Illinois Press, 1983.

Williams, Robert V. "The Making of Statistics of National Scope on American Libraries, 1836–1986: Purposes, Problems, and Issues." *Libraries & Culture* (Spring 1991): 464–85.

Wood, Gordon S. "Republicanism and the Political History of Colonial America: Afterword." *Proceedings of the American Antiquarian Society* 102 (April 1992): 205–14.

Wosh, Peter J. "Bibles, Benevolence, and Bureaucracy: The Changing Nature of Nineteenth Century Religious Records." *American Archivist* 52 (Spring 1989): 166–78.

Index